HELP!
Microsoft
Access

HELP!
Microsoft
Access

Miriam Liskin

Ziff-Davis Press
Emeryville, California

Development Editor	Kate Hoffman
Copy Editor	Kate Hoffman
Technical Reviewers	Richard Ozer, Mike Uhlar, and Jay Burnet
Project Coordinator	Kim Haglund
Proofreader	Aidan Wylde
Cover Design	Carrie English
Book Design	Laura Lamar/MAX, San Francisco
Technical Illustration	Cherie Plumlee Computer Graphics & Illustration
Word Processing	Howard Blechman, Cat Haglund, and Allison Levin
Page Layout	Bruce Lundquist
Indexer	Valerie Haynes Perry

This book was produced on a Macintosh IIfx, with the following applications: FrameMaker®, Microsoft® Word, MacLink® *Plus*, Aldus® FreeHand™, Adobe Photoshop™, and Collage Plus™.

Ziff-Davis Press
5903 Christie Avenue
Emeryville, CA 94608

ISBN 1-56276-099-8

Manufactured in the United States of America

♻ The paper used in this book exceeds the EPA requirements for postconsumer recycled paper.
10 9 8 7 6 5 4 3 2 1

CONTENTS AT A GLANCE

TABLE OF CONTENTS

Part 3   Advanced Skills

ACKNOWLEDGMENTS

FIRST, I WILL BE ETERNALLY GRATEFUL TO CINDY HUDSON, PUBLISHER OF Ziff-Davis Press, for twisting my arm and dragging me to the demo that sold me on Access and made me eager to write this book.

My hat goes off to all the folks on the Access team at Microsoft. Microsoft Access was the application that convinced this verbally-oriented, text-based, left-brained, linear-thinking person who secretly believes that one word is worth a thousand pictures to take Windows off the shelf and start using it.

Thanks to the three technical editors who brought very different and equally valuable perspectives to bear on the contents of this book—Richard Ozer, Mike Uhlar, and Jay Burnet.

On the editorial side, my thanks to the editors and proofreaders who worked on this project—Kate Hoffman, Kim Haglund, Aidan Wylde.

Thanks also to the people who helped me with hardware and software struggles engendered by the production of this book—Richard Ozer for upgrading my network and downgrading my video hardware and for listening to me complain about them, and Dan Brodnitz at ZD Press for doing battle in the brave new world of 24-bit color and experimental screen capture programs.

Thanks to Lisa Biow for many informal discussions on database design, referential integrity, GUI user interfaces, and the intricacies of object-oriented, event-driven database programming languages.

Thanks to my long-time friend Cliff Krouse for desert trips and for lending me his wonderful dog.

And to Peter Harrington, a toast to slickrock playgrounds, 7.4 liters, 360-degree panoramic views, and gourmet dinners on warm evenings at "Cafe Rock."

DESPITE THE EFFORT THAT HAS GONE INTO MAKING MICROSOFT ACCESS easy to learn and easy to use, database management is not always an easy subject, and database programs often have a steep learning curve. Some of the blame for this state of affairs stems from the reputation (largely well deserved) acquired by some very popular MS-DOS databases for being difficult to learn and awkward to use. Unfortunately, however, the main reason that database programs are hard to learn is that they are used to solve very complex business problems and to manage massive amounts of data that require a variety of different storage formats—information that would be equally difficult to organize and conceptualize using a manual system. Furthermore, unlike other general-purpose programs such as spreadsheets and word processors, database programs require that you carry out quite a few preliminary steps before you can begin working with the data, and they usually require you to look at your data in ways that do not directly parallel your present manual methods. In these respects, Access is no easier or more difficult to learn than any other powerful and sophisticated database manager.

This book and the disk that accompanies it strive to help you surmount these conceptual barriers and begin doing productive work with Access as quickly as possible. Once you understand the basic database management concepts and decide how to structure your own database application, you will find that the mechanics of using Access to implement your system are very straightforward.

This book is designed for Access users at all levels, and for those who aspire to become Access Basic programmers as well, although Access Basic is covered only briefly.

A Word about Access

Microsoft Access is a relational database management program, which you can use for a variety of database applications, ranging from simple mailing lists or personal contact files to very complex systems such as inventory, accounting, or professional office management databases. Like all database software, Access allows you to define the structures of the tables that will store the information you need to track; design custom data entry forms; enter, edit, and delete data; perform calculations; and view or print reports based on all or selected information from one or more tables.

Access is not a Windows version of a database manager originally written for the character-based MS-DOS environment—it runs only under Windows and was designed from the start for the graphical environment. The Access menus, dialog boxes, and design tools conform closely to the de facto standards adopted by many Windows software developers. If you are familiar with Windows and have used other Windows programs (not necessarily from Microsoft), you will feel right at home in the Access working environment. If Access is your first Windows program, you should realize from the outset that you will be learning about Windows as well as about Access, and you may not realize at first which is which. Although you may find the going a bit tougher than a person who has prior Windows experience, the extra effort will pay off when you buy your *next* Windows program, because what you have learned from your experience with Access will shorten the learning curve for any other Windows software you install.

Users at all levels of expertise can work with Access interactively, by manipulating objects on the screen with the mouse, operating command buttons, choosing items from lists, and selecting options from pull-down menus attached to the main menu bar. This interactive mode offers the immediacy that is reassuring to a beginner—when you issue a command or initiate a task, you get instant feedback—coupled with a flexibility that you will continue to appreciate as you gain proficiency. By selecting objects and commands one by one, you can carry out the activities required to build, update, and maintain a database application in any convenient order. For more experienced users and more mature, stable applications, Access also includes a powerful macro facility, which you can use to automate operations by storing a series of actions (the very same actions you might carry out one by one in the interactive mode) in a macro and then playing back the macro to repeat those actions at a later time. By integrating macros with forms, you can develop a completely automated menu-driven application that could be used by others who know little or nothing about Access itself. None of these activities—including defining and using macros—requires programming, although you might feel that building complex macros does require you to think a bit like a programmer. However, Access also includes a complete programming language called Access Basic, a close cousin of Visual Basic that incorporates commands for manipulating Access tables, queries, forms, and reports.

Although no program can be all things to all users, Access strives to combine ease of use with power and flexibility. Even if you have little experience with Windows (and even if you have no great love for the graphical environment), you will find the Access interactive environment and menu system to be intuitive, well organized, and logically structured. However, ease of *use* and ease of *learning* do not always go hand in hand, and like all powerful programs, Access may be a little intimidating for a novice, simply because there are so many commands and so many options.

Access provides several special tools to help beginners get up and running as quickly and easily as possible. In addition to the standard Windows help system, Access also offers Cue Cards—an adjunct to the help system that prompts you through a number of very common tasks by displaying step-by-step instructions in a series of information windows that remain on the screen while you follow the directions. Access also includes *Wizards*, which help you create a variety of very common form, report, and graph styles. The Wizards display a series of dialog boxes that ask questions and present lists of choices, and based on your answers, generate a form, report, or graph. The Wizards are a boon to the beginner, because they enable you to avoid (or postpone) having to design these documents from scratch. Although they offer only a fraction of the options supported by the Access design tools, the Wizards do not limit the complexity of the documents you can create. The objects they produce are ordinary Access forms, reports, and graphs, which you can open and modify just as you would a document that you created yourself. Thus, the Wizards will prove useful long after you have overcome the initial intimidation you may feel when confronted with a blank design work surface: If one of the layouts and overall styles they can create comes close to satisfying your requirements, beginning with the Wizard and modifying the generated document is often the most efficient way to define a new form, report, or graph.

A Tour of the Chapters

This book is really two books in one—Part 1 is equivalent to an introductory book on Access for people with no prior database experience, and Parts 2 and 3 serve as a comprehensive guide and reference to Access for more experienced users. The disk that comes with the book is also an important and use ful piece of this book/disk resource. Except for the one table and the forms created from scratch in the hands-on examples, it includes all of the tables, queries, forms, reports, macros, and modules mentioned in the examples discussed in the book, and you can use these samples to experiment without risking your own valuable data. If you are working on a database of your own, you might also want to develop this application in parallel.

The first three chapters in Part 1 present a thorough introduction to the basic database management concepts that are a prerequisite to using Access (or any other database program), teach you a practical method for analyzing and planning a database application, and give you a brief guided tour of the Access working environment. Part 1 also presents the fundamentals of using all the Access design tools and teaches you to define all the necessary components of an Access database application—tables, which store the actual data; queries, which are used to select subsets of your data, display data in different orders, perform calculations, and carry out database updates; data entry forms; and reports.

Part 1 concentrates on operations involving just one table at a time (although the examples are drawn from several different tables), and on using the FormWizards and ReportWizards rather than designing forms and reports from scratch.

Part 2 revisits many of the topics introduced in Part 1 in much greater depth, and the material in these chapters will be of interest to nearly all Access users.

Chapter 8 covers a variety of methods for utilizing the relational capabilities Access offers for working with two or more tables together. Chapter 9 presents a more formal, detailed introduction to Access syntax and expressions, and describes methods for using these expressions to carry out calculations. Chapters 10 through 12 cover the form and report design tools in depth. These chapters will teach you how to make extensive modifications to the forms generated by the Access Wizards, and how to build complete forms and reports from scratch if the layouts produced by the Wizards do not fully satisfy your requirements or match your aesthetic preferences. The last three chapters in Part 2 cover reorganizing databases, copying and combining tables, exchanging and sharing data with other programs, and using DDE (Dynamic Data Exchange) and OLE (Object Linking and Embedding) to work with objects created and updated by other programs (such as graphs, pictures, and spreadsheets).

Part 3 covers more specialized topics that may not be of interest to all Access users. In fact, unless you already have considerable experience with other databases, you will probably want to defer the last three chapters until you have been working with Access for a while and know how to carry out all the essential database management tasks interactively.

Chapter 16 describes how to define a password-protected security system to control access to specific database components as well as to the Access program itself, and Chapter 17 covers methods and strategies for sharing data with other Access users on a local area network. Chapter 18 introduces Access macros, and Chapter 19 describes how to integrate macros with forms to add specialized controls, collect selection criteria for a report or data entry session, provide a custom menu bar for a data entry form, and build complete menu-driven applications that shield users from the native Access environment. Chapter 20 presents a brief overview of the two programming languages supported by Access—SQL and Access Basic—and describes how to use these languages for some simple tasks.

How to Use This Book

Like Access itself, this book is ideal for database novices as well as those who need or want to go beyond the most basic tasks, and who are willing to learn some new concepts and a few difficult techniques, but who do not want to become programmers. If Access is your first database program and your application is fairly simple, you may be able to learn most of what you need to know from Part 1. If you already have some experience with other database programs, you will find many of the concepts familiar, and you can concentrate on the material that describes unique aspects of Access and the mechanics of using the Access design tools. More advanced users or programmers may want to skim through Part 1 quickly, but do not succumb to the temptation to skip the introductory chapters entirely—they provide a good introduction to the Access working environment (and, to a certain extent, to the Windows environment), and they include a great many pointers on the best ways to accomplish a given objective in Access. However, this book is really intended for the vast middle ground—people with little or no prior database experience who need to build applications of moderate complexity.

You do not need to have any prior experience with database software in general or with Microsoft Access in particular to understand the material in this book. It does assume, however, that you have a basic familiarity with your PC, know where the special function keys are on your keyboard and how to use them, and know how to use a mouse.

This book also assumes some familiarity with Windows and the terminology used to describe aspects of the graphical user interface. At the very least, you should know how to start up Windows, how to launch Access either from the Program Manager or the File Manager, and how to switch from one running application to another. If Access is your first Windows program, you might want to consult the Microsoft documentation or an introductory book on Windows and spend a little time familiarizing yourself with the working environment and reviewing the basic keyboard and mouse techniques for navigating among the open windows on the desktop, moving and resizing windows, and using the Clipboard to cut and paste objects.

This book uses as a case study a name and address list application for an imaginary nonprofit organization called the Association for a Clean Earth (ACE), a group that concentrates on pollution and other environmental issues. The book follows this case study from the early planning and analysis phases through the development of a complete menu-driven system. The ACE application is typical in its size, scope, and complexity of the database management needs of many small businesses, nonprofit organizations, and departments in larger organizations. The examples (many of which were suggested by the needs of the author's clients) are as realistic as possible, without sacrificing generality.

You will get more out of this book if you read most of it seated at your computer, so that you can try the examples and practice the techniques as they are described. Every chapter includes hands-on examples, and you are strongly urged to take the time to work through most of them, to solidify your understanding of the concepts and to gain confidence working in the Access environment.

As the book progresses, you may feel that some of the examples focus in rather closely on minute details of the ACE system, but try not to lose sight of the forest for the trees. Even if your own database tracks data that bears no resemblance to the names and addresses, contacts, and transactions in the ACE system, you can use the sample database as a model for analogous operations carried out on quite different types of data. The examples were intended to clarify general concepts and to illustrate strategies and methods that are applicable to a broad range of database management needs. If you keep the big picture firmly in mind, you should be able to mix and match these techniques to suit the needs of your own Access database applications.

Because Access is so new, we are all beginners, and exploring a new program to discover its capabilities and tap its power can be exciting and fascinating. If you have used other database programs—either on a PC, a minicomputer, or a mainframe—be receptive to new terminology and new techniques instead of trying to force Access to do things the way you are accustomed to doing them. If you are a programmer, resist the temptation to dive directly into Access Basic, and take the time to explore the interactive environment and the query, form, and report design tools—you will be pleasantly surprised at how much you can accomplish without programming, even if you do end up writing Access Basic programs.

Regardless of how much or how little prior experience you have with computers, the most important assets you can bring to bear are an open mind and a willingness to experiment. If you think you see a different way to accomplish a given objective than the one described in this book, try it: There is often more than one "right" way to carry out a given task, and your way may be as good as or better than the one presented here.

Finally, despite the weighty subject matter and the rather serious tone of this book, try to relax and enjoy the learning process. You might look upon your business application as a game or a puzzle, to which the finished database is the solution. Above all, have some fun with Access!

1

Basic Skills

CHAPTER

1

Introduction to Database Management

A Functional Definition

Definitions of Common Terms

Planning a Database Application

Outlining the System Requirements

Introduction to the ACE Case Study

BEFORE YOU CAN BEGIN TO USE MICROSOFT ACCESS, YOU SHOULD HAVE a clear idea of what a *database manager* (often abbreviated *DBMS* for database management system) is and what it can do for you. The term *database management* is used to describe the full spectrum of operations involved in entering, storing, retrieving, updating, manipulating, and reporting on information. In both your personal and business daily life, you have already encountered numerous record-keeping systems that fit this broad definition, not all of which are computerized. For example, a business bookkeeping system consisting of paper ledger cards and journals is a database management system, as is a medical office management system centered around patient charts or a donor-tracking system maintained on index cards. The computerized analogs—software for accounting, medical office management, and donor-tracking—are also database management systems.

What differentiates Microsoft Access and other general-purpose database software from these programs is the fact that Access gives you complete control over the type, content, and format of the information in your database. A small business might use Access to manage data on customers, vendors, general ledger accounts, orders, payments, cash receipts and disbursements journals, and inventory. A medical office might maintain information on patients, office visits, insurance billing and reimbursements, laboratory tests, and prescriptions. A nonprofit corporation such as the hypothetical Association for a Clean Earth (ACE) used in the examples in this book might track donors and members, manage mailing lists of prospective donors, and record donations and pledges. An individual could use Access to maintain a list of business or personal contacts, keep track of expense records, or catalog book, record, and CD collections. For each of these basic *entities*—a customer, a donor, an office visit, a donation—the database might maintain anywhere from several to hundreds of discrete *items* of information—such as the name, address, telephone number, and last contact date for a donor, or the date, complaint, diagnosis, and follow-up date for a visit to a doctor's office.

This chapter introduces the basic vocabulary and database concepts that will serve as the foundation for all of your work in Microsoft Access. If you have prior experience with other database programs, you will find the concepts familiar, although some of the terminology may be new to you. It also outlines a practical, commonsense method for analyzing your needs and planning a new database application. It would be impossible to overstate the importance of the design process for Access users at all levels, from complete novices to those who have considerable experience with other database software. Spending a little more time up front on the planning stages can save you a great deal of time over the lifetime of the application.

A Functional Definition

If you are new to the world of database management, it is easiest to conceptualize what a database program *is* in terms of what it *does*. Database programs in general, and Microsoft Access in particular, allow you to carry out all of the following operations:

■ Name and describe the individual items of information you want to maintain, grouped according to the entities they describe

■ Enter, search for, edit, and delete data

■ Design custom screen forms for entering, viewing, and editing data

■ Retrieve data based on various search criteria

■ Perform calculations and view or print the results on the screen or store them on disk

■ Select subsets of the data that satisfy various selection criteria

■ Rearrange the data into various orders for screen displays or printed reports

■ Print attractively formatted lists, labels, forms, and reports that include all or selected data, in various orders

As you undoubtedly realize, none of these activities *require* a computer or a database program—long before there were computers, much less PCs, people devised manual systems for maintaining essential business and personal information on paper. Indeed, you may be learning Access for the express purpose of computerizing a paper record-keeping system. As you think about how you will use Access to carry out these fundamental database activities, it might help to visualize the manual analogs. For example, creating a screen form for entering orders is comparable to designing a paper order form that salespeople will use to record orders taken over the phone. Searching for a patient by name or medical record number is analogous to looking in a filing cabinet for the patient's chart. Printing an aging report involves finding all customers with invoices that are not paid in full, calculating the elapsed time since each invoice, and adding the dollar amount into one of several totals based on various predefined aging periods (current, 1 to 30 days, 31 to 60 days, and so on). Of course, using a computer offers significant advantages in speed and accuracy, and in many cases makes it possible, or even easy, to carry out analyses that would otherwise be so complex and time-consuming that you would never attempt them.

You may already have some experience with database management software, especially if you are developing an Access application to replace another computerized record-keeping system: a "canned" package that turned out to be too rigid to meet your growing needs; an outdated program written by a software company that no longer exists; a program that runs only on an obsolete computer; a system designed using a flat-file manager or spreadsheet; or a mainframe or minicomputer application that you are downsizing to run on the PC. If so, you should be familiar with the fundamental database management operations, and you can concentrate on learning the best ways to accomplish them with Access. If Access is your first database program, you can start fresh with no biases or preconceived notions of the way things should be done. In either case, a brief review of some common database terminology will help you avoid confusion, better understand the Access documentation, and communicate clearly with other people involved in the project.

Definitions of Common Terms

If you have never used a database program before, you may find the specialized vocabulary intimidating at first. For the most part, this book avoids using technical terms to describe concepts that can be explained in ordinary colloquial language, but jargon is not all bad, insofar as it allows for communicating succinctly and precisely about database concepts and operations. Understanding the meanings of a few key terms will enable you to better understand the Access documentation and help screens and make sense of what you read about databases in other books and computer industry publications. Furthermore, many specialized database terms have quite different meanings in ordinary English, and some serious misunderstandings can result from confusing the two.

In Microsoft Access, a *database* is the repository of all of the information that pertains to a particular business problem or record-keeping system. Each of the examples cited earlier—the accounting system, the medical office system, and the nonprofit mailing list system—could be set up as a single Access database. You can have as many databases as you wish, and while working with one database, you can access information in other Access databases (as well as data stored in several *foreign*, or *external* formats, such as dBASE, FoxPro, and Paradox files). Thus, a small business might have an accounting database, a prospective customer mailing list database, and a personnel database, which interact only for occasional mailings to both prospective and existing customers.

An Access database consists of one or more *tables*, each of which stores information that shares a common format and in most cases describes a single business entity such as a customer, a patient, or a donation. One individual instance of the type of entity stored in the table—for example, a customer, a patient, an appointment, or a payment—is called a *record*, and each record is made up of discrete items of information called *fields*. Thus, a donor database might have fields for the name, company name, street address, city, state, zip code, and telephone number.

A very simple database might require only one table—for example, a personal contact database might consist of one list of names and addresses—but most require two or more. It is critical to understand from the outset that each table should contain information about just one type of entity. When the items of information that you need to maintain about two entities differ significantly, or you intend to use the information in completely different contexts, you should create separate tables. For example, in a small business accounting database, the items of information required for a customer are quite different from those that describe an inventory item, an order, or a payment. Altogether, a rather small accounting system might comprise between ten and 20 tables, and even a personal contact database might require three or four tables to accommodate names and addresses, appointments, and to-do list items.

Note. The subject of database and table design is covered in more depth in Chapter 3.

The default display format that Access uses to view and edit tables is depicted in Figure 1.1, which shows the main name and address table from the nonprofit case study used throughout this book. The fundamental entity described by this table is a *name* (in most cases, a person, but sometimes a company, family, or couple). This display style, which is called *Datasheet* view, presents the information in the table as a set of rows and columns. Each *row* in the table displays data from one *record* (which describes one person) and each *column* contains data from one *field*. Every field has a name, which you use to identify the field when you design Access forms and queries. By default, Access uses the field names as the column headings in Datasheet view, but as you will see in Chapter 3, you can define an alternative field *caption* to serve as the default label in Datasheet view and in custom data entry screens (you can also use any caption or label you wish to identify a field in a custom screen). In Figure 1.1, you can see the ID Code, Type, Name, Salutation, Company, and Address fields for the first 21 records in the Names table.

If you have used a spreadsheet program such as 1-2-3, Excel, or Quattro Pro, or a database program that uses a similar display format (for example, Paradox), you will quickly feel comfortable working in Datasheet view. If your prior database experience is with Xbase (dBASE, FoxBase+, FoxPro, dBXL, or other compatible programs), you can think of Datasheet view as analogous to the Browse display. However, many database users (including Xbase users) may be more accustomed to seeing data presented in a format in which each row on the screen contains one field and the field names are lined up to the left of the data as prompts. In this format, the screen may accommodate one record, part of a record, or several records, depending on the number of fields in the record and the number of available screen rows (which depends on the current video mode in DOS or the size of the current screen

Figure 1.1

The ACE Names table in Datasheet view

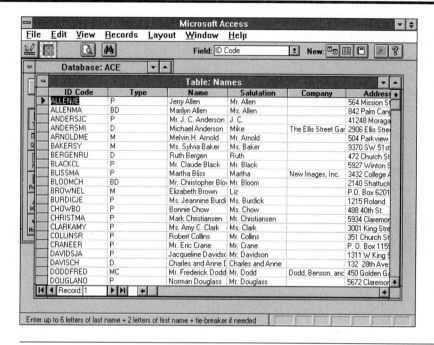

font in Windows). In Access, you must design a data entry form to emulate this display mode, but doing so is very easy (the process is described in Chapter 6). Figure 1.2 shows a simple data entry form of this type from the ACE case study. The record visible on this screen is the first record in the Datasheet display in Figure 1.1.

Although each table should store information about a single functional entity, more often than not you will need to work with more than one type of entity at a time. For example, you might want to see a customer's name and address at the top of a report that lists the customer's orders, or print a patient summary that includes all office visits during the past five years, as well as all prescriptions and treatments. Database managers that allow you to work with two or more tables at once are commonly described as *relational* databases (sometimes abbreviated *RDBMS* for relational database management system), while software that permits access to only one table at a time is usually called a *file manager* or *flat-file database*. Relational database programs, including Microsoft Access, allow you to work with information from two or more tables, linking them on the contents of corresponding fields. In the accounting example, Access would find the orders placed by each customer by searching for records in the order table that have the same name or customer account number.

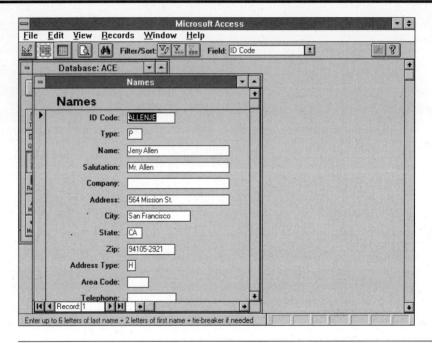

For reasons detailed more fully in Chapter 3, the ability to work with more than one table at a time affords a great deal of flexibility and allows you to structure your tables very efficiently. For example, since the customer name and address is always available in the customer table, you need not waste time and disk space by entering it into each individual order record. However, working with multiple tables simultaneously introduces a measure of complexity into a database application that may seem formidable to a beginner. During the design phase, you must structure the database to support the required relationships between tables. On an ongoing basis, you must be concerned not only with the accuracy of the data in each table, but also with the relationships among tables.

For example, in a donor-tracking application like the ACE case study, you must ensure that for every donation entered into the transaction table, a matching donor exists in the name and address file, and this requirement necessitates a number of additional tests and validation checks. To prevent generating "orphan" transaction records, you must prohibit the addition of a donation for a nonexistent donor, and you must not allow the deletion of any donor who has transactions on file. Furthermore, changing the field or fields that establish the relationship between the donor and transaction tables is dangerous. To avoid dissociating matching donor and transaction records, you must either prohibit changes to the linking fields or ensure that the changes are propagated throughout the set of matching records. The concept of testing or enforcing specific relationships among the tables in a database is referred to in Access as *referential integrity*; you may also encounter the term *relational integrity* in other books and manuals.

In addition to the tables that hold the raw data, an Access database includes a variety of auxiliary *objects*, or components, which store instructions for carrying out the fundamental database operations enumerated earlier in this chapter. These database components include:

- *Queries*, which store instructions for extracting selected data or for performing calculations or table updates

- *Forms*, which describe custom screens used for displaying, entering, and editing data

- *Reports*, which describe the system's output displays and printed documents

- *Macros*, which record sequences of Access commands that you can execute as a batch

- *Modules*, which are programs written in Access Basic

Access stores all of the components of a database—the tables, forms, reports, and so on—in a disk file with a first name that you assign and the extension .MDB. For example, the ACE case study database is stored in a file called ACE.MDB. If you open a database for shared rather than exclusive access, as you would on a network to allow other users to work with it at the same time, Access also creates a matching .LDB file (ACE.LDB for the case study database). Placing all the objects that make up a database in one disk file facilitates backing up and transporting the database (you need not copy the .LDB file, which Access recreates if necessary), and it speeds up disk operations by keeping the number of files in a subdirectory (or subdirectories) to a minimum. At times, you may create tables that you feel should be shared more or less equally among several applications, and that do not seem to fit better in one database than another. Keep in mind, however, that while working with one database, you have full access to tables in any other Access database located anywhere on your hard disk (or on the file server, if you run Access on a network), so placing a table in one database does not limit you to working with that table in only one context.

If you have used other database programs, you may be accustomed to seeing some of the terms defined in this section used quite differently. For example, in the Xbase world, the term *database* is used to describe the type of object that Access calls a *table*, and there is no equivalent for an Access database (although you can use the dBASE IV catalog to maintain a list of the objects used together in an application). Furthermore, Xbase, Paradox, and many other programs store each database and auxiliary component in one or more disk files. In these languages the term *file* is often used interchangeably with *database*. If you have worked with any of these programs, make sure you understand the meanings of the terms defined in this section, *as they are used in Microsoft Access.*

Planning a Database Application

The first steps in computerizing a database application have nothing to do with the computer or with Microsoft Access. Before you begin working with Access, you must outline in as much detail as possible what information the database will maintain and what tasks the application must carry out. Especially if you feel that setting up your application is long overdue, you are undoubtedly eager to sit down at the keyboard and begin building the database immediately, but try your utmost to resist this temptation. The more thoroughly you plan ahead, the less time you will spend later modifying and restructuring the application.

Unless you will be the sole user of the application, some of your co-workers should also be involved in the design process. Anyone in your organization who will later use the application—either entering data, executing queries, or reading the reports—should have a hand in its design. Depending on their positions in your organization, each of these people will bring a different perspective to bear on the design: An executive or manager may have the clearest picture of the analytical reports that the system must produce; the data entry staff probably best understand the work flow and data processing schedule; and the bookkeeper or office manager may have in mind reports or on-screen summaries that would reduce the manual workload of other office staff. Seeking input from all of these sources will provide valuable information about aspects of your organization and its operation that may be unfamiliar to you.

Even if you have used other database software, you will probably find the mechanics of defining the tables far easier than specifying their structures. Designing an Access application does not require advanced knowledge of computers or database theory, and it does not require any knowledge of programming—you can build a rather sophisticated application without writing any Access Basic programs. However, it does involve a degree of abstraction beyond that required to set up a spreadsheet or word-processing document.

The crucial aspect of the design process is deciding how to set up the table structures in order to support the functions the system must carry out, and often, the optimum design does not directly parallel the way the same information is maintained in a comparable manual system. For example, you may think of an order or invoice as a single entity, but in an accounts receivable database, the information printed on an invoice might be derived from four tables: the customer name and address from a customer table; the invoice number, date, shipping method, and dollar totals from an invoice table; the requested items from a line item table; and the product names and prices from an inventory table.

Furthermore, the design phase may turn out to be traumatic for all involved. If you are the owner or manager, you may be forced to reexamine many aspects of your business and rethink operations that you have taken for granted for years. Undoubtedly, you will find some procedures not to your liking, and not all of the problems can be solved easily by computerizing the application. If several staff members are involved in the planning and design of the new system, you may also have to contend with conflicting needs, opinions, and priorities, and with differing interpretations of the same calculations or operations. You may also encounter a good deal of resistance to change among some staff members, who will cling tenaciously to the familiar, even if the new system promises to be far more efficient and easier to use.

The good news is that many people with no prior database experience find that they have a good instinctual "feel" for the process. The ability to think logically and to gather the necessary information in a systematic manner and then organize it coherently is more important than technical expertise. If you have designed successful paper record-keeping systems, you will be able to apply many of the same skills and techniques to building an Access database. Note also that although the planning phase is essential, it need not be overly structured or formal. Whole volumes have been written on database design, and you may want to pursue this subject further if it captures your interest, but in most cases, you need not adhere rigidly to a strict set of design rules, and you need not spend an inordinate amount of time on the process. A relatively informal, commonsense approach to system design is appropriate for most Access databases of moderate size and complexity.

Outlining the System Requirements

The functional definition of database management outlined earlier in this chapter can serve as a convenient framework for a description of your application. You can approach the design process from several different perspectives, but your description of the application will eventually comprise all or most of the following information:

- The types of entities in the system, which will become the tables in the database

- The individual items of information (the fields) that describe each entity

- The appearance of the data entry and display screens, some of which may be modeled on existing paper forms

- The rules that govern data formatting and validation on the data entry and display forms

- The search criteria you will use to find individual records in each table for viewing, updating, printing, or deletion

- The selection criteria that describe the subsets of the data required for reports, displays, and calculations

- The appearance of the printed reports and lists that the system must produce, some of which may be modeled on existing reports and lists

- The different sequences in which records should appear in screen displays and reports

- The calculations or transformations that the system must perform

- The data transfers and batch processing steps, such as posting totals or archiving and deleting obsolete data

You may also gain some insight into the design process from the very basic mechanisms that computers use to process data. Database applications (like many other types of software) receive *input* (either entered through the keyboard or imported from another source), carry out various *processing* functions (calculations and transfers of information) on the input, and produce *output* (screen displays, printed reports, and new data files or tables). When approaching the database design process, many people tend to gravitate toward just one of these phases—some think primarily in terms of the information that should go into the system, some focus on the calculations without first delineating the source of the data, and still others visualize the database solely in terms of the reports it must produce. If several of your co-workers are involved in the design process, you may find that you all have differing (and hopefully complementary) points of view. Whatever your natural inclination, try to give equal attention to the input, processing, and output functions of your application. Categorizing the application components this way often helps clarify the flow of data through the application and ensures that you have not omitted any essential system components.

If the new Access database is replacing an existing manual system, that system is the logical starting point for your description of the application. Even if you already plan extensive revisions, you can begin with an in-depth review of the present manual procedures and then enumerate the additional requirements. If you are designing a replacement for another computer program, you can begin by evaluating this software. In either case, studying the existing system will serve as a convenient focus for your analysis. It will also supply many of the items of information that the new application must maintain and the operations it must carry out, and will suggest additional desirable capabilities. Keep in mind, however, that the new system need not parallel the present one in every detail. The work flow, as well as the information being tracked, may be different—and hopefully better—in the new application, and you may be able to add a number of your "wish list" items to the system. During the planning stages, feel free to list any new features that come to mind, perhaps indicating their priority and if possible, their complexity. You can always postpone implementation of features that turn out to be difficult and eliminate those that prove impossible.

The planning process will necessarily be more difficult if you are building a new application from scratch. For example, you might be bringing in house data processing functions (such as mailing list management or payroll processing) that were previously carried out by an outside service bureau or another department. Your organization may be opening a new office or branching out into a new line of business that demands a new database application. Or you may be designing a brand new application that produces statistics or analytical reports that are far too complex to contemplate producing manually. Without the benefit of an existing model, you must simply begin by describing what you want the system to accomplish. Because your initial conception of the application will be less complete and accurate than when you emulate an existing system, you should be prepared to spend more time and energy both on the initial design and on subsequent revisions during the prototyping stage. Fortunately, Access allows you to restructure your tables without losing data, but repeatedly revising the tables and forms in a database can be time-consuming and frustrating.

You may also gain valuable insights from an examination of commercial programs that handle similar applications, even if you have already decided on the do-it-yourself approach. For example, a nonprofit organization such as the hypothetical Association for a Clean Earth might have decided against purchasing a canned donor management system for various reasons: budget constraints, the limitations or complexities of the available commercial packages, or the flexibility promised by a general-purpose database management program such as Access. However, looking at a few typical donor-tracking systems might suggest additional items of information to include in the database, as well as new reports or statistical analyses.

Studying the Manual System

If your Access application is based on an existing manual system, the best way to begin is to gather a complete set of the paper forms already in use—input forms, transaction or accounting journals, worksheets used to perform calculations or summarize results, documents such as invoices or account statements, and statistical or summary reports. If the new application is replacing another computer program, you can study that program's data entry screens and printed reports just as you would the paper input forms and manually typed reports gathered from a manual system. Your experience (or that of co-workers) running the present system can also be instructive; based on what you like or dislike about its performance and user interface, you can strive to incorporate its virtues into the new application and eliminate its weaknesses.

NOTE. *You may find it convenient to print the data entry screens displayed by your present system so that you can annotate them. You can print an image of most DOS screens by pressing the PrtSc key (Shift+PrtSc on some keyboards). In Windows, pressing PrtSc copies the screen image to the Clipboard, and you can paste this image into a Write or Paintbrush document and then print it.*

The forms that you collect should provide much of the information you need to define the new system's input, processing, and output functions. Together with any co-workers who will be involved with the new application, you can annotate the paper forms to add new items of information, indicate desirable revisions and rearrangements, and cross out items that are no longer required. Studying the existing forms will help ensure that your list of data items is complete, and it will clarify the calculation and data transfer steps. Later in the development process, the input forms (if you use them) can also serve as models for the forms you design for entering and editing data. Matching the data entry screens to existing paper forms can ease the transition to the new system—because it will present a somewhat familiar face—and it facilitates entering data from these forms. For example, if the layout and field entry sequence of an order entry screen approximates the appearance of the paper order form sent in by your customers or filled out by salespeople, entering orders into the database will be easier and faster.

The sample forms that you gather should contain data, and to the extent possible, they should contain *matching* data, to help you trace the flow of information through the system. For example, in the case study system, a blank donor ledger sheet, pledge statement form, and cash receipts journal worksheet are much less useful than a copy of the ledger sheet for a long-standing donor, a cash receipts journal that includes a contribution made by that donor, a thank you letter for that contribution, and a pledge statement sent to the same donor. For brand new reports that have no counterparts in the present system, make a rough sketch of the page layout, including the column headings, data items, formulas for any calculations, and summary statistics. Somewhere on the page, make a note of the *processing sequence* (for example,

"Print in alphabetical order by donor name") and *selection criteria* (for example, "All contributions made in the current month").

In addition to the printed reports that your organization is currently producing, every database should include a class of reports that will be referred to in this book as *complete reference lists*. These reports, which often have no manual analogs, print all the information (all the fields) in all or selected records in one or more tables. Apart from the fact that they do not have direct counterparts in a manual system, it is easy to overlook the need for these reports if you are operating under the pervasive misconception that computerizing a database will eliminate paper from your office. In reality, a printed list may provide faster or easier access to information than looking it up on screen, especially when the computer is otherwise occupied. The lists also serve as a reference to the actual contents of the tables during the testing and debugging stages of system development. For example, if a monthly cash receipts summary in the sample system did not account properly for pledges and pledge payments, you could consult the transaction reference list to determine whether the fault lay in the transaction entry procedures or the pledge computation steps, or whether it was due simply to data entry error.

For each output form (report or screen display), you should list all the following information:

- The data fields that should appear on the report

- The record processing sequence (for example, alphabetical, chronological, or descending numerical)

- The calculations based on fields within a record (for example, a balance computed by subtracting debits from credits)

- Required record groupings and related summary statistics (for example, contribution sums, averages, and counts for each state)

- How often the report is printed

- All possible sets of selection criteria that determine which records should be included on the report (often there are several different criteria for a given printout)

- Any special requests made by colleagues who will also read the report

By studying all the input and output document samples, you should be able to arrive at a preliminary list of all the discrete items of information in your database. If your natural tendency is to focus on the input documents, force yourself to examine the reports as well, because every item that appears in an output document (a report or screen display), that helps to determine the processing sequence or selection criteria, or that contributes to a calculation must be represented in the tables. For each item, try to determine or estimate:

- How many there are at present, as an order of magnitude

- How you expect this number to change in the next two or three years

- How long an individual instance of each functional entity (such as a customer or transaction) is retained in the system

For each of these quantities, an order of magnitude estimate (that is, a number accurate to the nearest power of 10) is sufficient—for example, when you write down the number of customers on file or the number of orders processed per month, the difference between 300 and 500 or between 3,000 and 5,000 is probably not significant, but the difference between 300 and 3,000 is. When your tables are large—10,000 records or more—be prepared to pay special attention to optimizing performance, because the specific methods you choose to carry out certain operations can have a huge impact on how long they take. Note also that the magnitude of numeric data (such as product prices and order totals) is less important than the quantity—in the ACE system, managing thousands of $10 donations requires more time and disk space than handling a few $10,000 donations.

For each individual item of information that your application must maintain, you must decide:

- Which functional entity or entities the item describes

- How big a typical entry is (how many characters or digits are required to store it)

- The standard display format (for example, the punctuation used in a telephone number or Social Security number, or the fact that a state abbreviation must be entered in uppercase)

- The rules governing what constitutes an acceptable entry for the item and whether the item can be left blank (for example, the requirement that an order date must be earlier than the current date or that the zip code must be filled in)

- Whether the value will be entered or generated automatically by the system (for example, the application could generate sequential invoice numbers)

- Whether the original value (entered or calculated) can be changed later

- How often the list of allowable entries in fields such as transaction types (debit, credit, payment, and so on) changes; bear in mind, however, that even if you think certain items such as product codes or sales territories can *never* change, they often do

Enumerating the characteristics of each item in the database in this much detail may seem at first like an onerous chore, but it will save you a great deal of time later on. Access allows you to restructure your tables with little or no loss of data, but the process can be time-consuming if your tables are large. Furthermore, revising the table structures after you have created a great many queries, forms, and reports will necessitate editing each of these objects to conform to the new structures.

Outlining the Work Flow and Schedule

Armed with a set of input forms and output documents, you can proceed to a description of the work flow and processing schedule. If you think visually, you may want to draw an informal flow chart to illustrate the data flow in the application, but if your orientation is primarily verbal, a few sequential lists of processing steps may serve the purpose as well or better. Your goal should be to ensure that you understand the flow of data through the application and the dependencies among the processing and reporting steps. For example, you should have a clear picture of which reports must be printed and which processing steps must be carried out before you "close out" a month, as well as those operations that should not be permitted afterward. The description of the work flow and processing schedule should include all of the following information:

- The sequence in which various types of data are entered and updated

- When and how calculations and transfers of information, such as "posting" and "closing" operations, are performed

- When summary statistics are (or should be) compiled

- When reports are printed

- When and how to archive and purge obsolete data

- How long each operation takes in the present system

- What prior processing steps must be completed before each operation is carried out

- What other processing steps should no longer be permitted after each operation is carried out

Some applications follow a schedule based on the calendar, with weekly, monthly, and/or annual processing cycles; in other cases, the data entry cycle and reporting schedule are determined by an organization's "busy" and "slow" seasons. Whenever possible, you should plan to incorporate more flexibility than you have in your present manual or computerized system. For example, the ACE bookkeeper might request donation reports grouped by type, event, or general ledger account number once a month. If you build in the ability to specify any arbitrary range of dates to select records for this report (this is not difficult to do with an Access query), the accountant could still get the required monthly posting summary, while the fundraising director could use the report to track longer-term trends.

When you outline the processing schedule, be on the lookout for operations that have no obvious manual analogs, which may elude you at first if you do not have much experience with computerized databases. Archiving and purging old data, which in a manual system may be haphazard and unscheduled, often falls into this category. For example, you might not move invoices into archival storage until the filing cabinets in the office fill up, and you might never systematically go through your customer or donor list and discard ledger cards for people who have not placed an order or made a contribution in many years.

Your final outline of the work flow can also serve as the framework for a critical analysis of your present procedures and those you anticipate adding. This analysis can help you evaluate whether computerization will result in true gains in efficiency and productivity. An operation stands to gain the most from computerizing when one or more of the following criteria are satisfied:

- Computerizing allows you to view or print the same information in different orders or print different subsets of the information.

- Carrying out the operation manually requires specialized knowledge or expertise.

- Carrying out the operation manually takes a great deal of time.

- Carrying out the operation manually would be too complex or time-consuming.

- Computerizing the operation results in more timely reports that support management decisions.

Re-evaluating the Field List

After you have completed the initial system description, take some time to re-evaluate the field list (the list of separate items of information in the database) and make sure that each item is really necessary. Comparing the input forms and the system's printed output serves as a reality check to help you avoid a common pitfall—including a great deal of information that is not really required and could be (or is already) maintained just as well or better by hand. A field has a place in your database if it meets one or more of the following criteria:

■ You always need to see the information on screen.

■ The information must appear in at least one report.

■ The information is used in a calculation or statistical summary.

■ The information contributes to the selection criteria that determine which records to include in screen displays, reports, or calculations (for example, you might need to select products by a category code or select orders by salesperson).

■ The information determines the record processing or display sequence (for example, printing labels in zip code order and customer reference lists alphabetically).

■ The information defines a relationship between two or more entities.

There is often no need to include information that you only intend to view or print in more or less the same form in which it is stored in the manual system. Be especially wary of apparent requirements for large amounts of text. Access stores text very efficiently—it uses only enough space for the text you actually enter—so providing for a long text field and then leaving it blank most of the time does not waste disk space. However, entering long text passages can occupy a great deal of data entry time, which will be wasted if you do not in fact need to *manipulate* the information in your application. For example, ACE wants to track contacts with individual donors, members, and prospects, and the fundraising director might be tempted to enter extensive notes on each conversation or phone call into the contacts table. You might also consider entering a description of each donor's interests, activities, and affiliations, to facilitate soliciting contributions for particular causes.

In both cases, the information is probably available already on paper in the form of handwritten notes attached to the donor ledger cards. To determine whether a particular donor has shown a prior interest in or contributed to a particular cause, such as nuclear waste disposal, pulling the ledger card from the file is just as easy as looking up the donor in the database, and you might decide not to take the time to transfer the information into the computer. On the other hand, any information that you need to use in selection criteria—for example, to prepare a list of *all* donors who are interested in nuclear waste disposal—must be in the database at least in abbreviated form. Preparing such a list by hand would necessitate checking each donor's file, a task so tedious that you would probably consider it impossible. In the ACE system, interests are handled using a compromise approach—by entering three keywords that represent a donor's major areas of interest. In addition, a free-form notes field allows for recording other types of detailed information that are deemed essential.

Of course, even if you weigh all the considerations carefully, you may not have all the facts at your disposal that would allow you to make the right judgment in advance. If you err on the side of entering too much information, you will waste disk space and data entry time, and if you err on the side of too little, you will find later that you cannot extract the data subsets you need for reports or screen displays. The best you can do is to try to build into your Access application all the information that may be required to give you the analytical and reporting capabilities you can anticipate at the outset, and to counsel other people who use the application to avoid entering unnecessarily lengthy text passages into the notes fields that you decide to include.

Introduction to the ACE Case Study

This book uses as a case study a mailing list and donor tracking database application written for an imaginary nonprofit organization called The Association for a Clean Earth (ACE for short), which concentrates on pollution and other environmental issues. The group has a mailing list of around 20,000 names, which includes prospects (some derived from lists purchased from other organizations), members (who number about 4,000), donors (people who have made contributions but have not joined ACE), board members, media contacts, sympathetic politicians and lobbyists, and people who signed petitions circulated by ACE. The list is currently maintained by an outside service bureau, which produces occasional reference lists, prints mailing labels for various subsets of the list, and mails the newsletter to all donors, board members, media contacts, politicians, and lobbyists. ACE plans to begin maintaining this list in-house using Microsoft Access.

As you read the description of the Association for a Clean Earth and its needs, imagine that you are a consultant hired to help ACE build its Access database. To obtain a comprehensive picture of the organization and its requirements, you might spend a day or two talking to the executive director, office manager, fund-raising director, bookkeeper, and clerical staff about their needs and expectations for the new system. If possible, you might also watch them work to gain insights into the current procedures.

ACE currently has half a dozen stand-alone personal computers, including 80486-, 80386-, and 80286-based systems. The new Access application will be developed on one of the faster computers (Access requires an 80386 or 80486 microprocessor) and eventually run on a local area network. Some of the information that will become part of the application is currently being maintained by individual staff members, using software less capable than Access or less suited to database management. The smaller name and address lists—the board members, major donors, media contacts, and committee members—are stored in word processor merge files, so that ACE can send personalized letters to these groups. Paper ledger cards are maintained for all donors. The staff is generally computer literate; most staff members feel comfortable with the word processing or spreadsheet software, but they do not use any database programs.

The ACE accounting staff typically handles about 100 to 200 transactions each week, including purchases of small promotional items, pledges and payments on pledges, and outright gifts. The average donation is between $10 and $50, but there are several donors who contribute as much as $10,000 per year. The cash receipts are entered into a spreadsheet, which is used to produce daily and monthly totals. The totals are then entered into a general ledger program that includes fund accounting capabilities. Donations are also posted manually to the donor ledger cards. Thank you notes are sent out no later than two weeks after the receipt of the contribution; ACE uses four or five different standard thank you letters, and chooses the one to send each donor based on the gift amount and the event (if any) that motivated the donation.

ACE conducts at least two major solicitation mailings per year, as well as several smaller mailings to selected donors; these are all carried out by the service bureau that maintains the list. Using the word processor, several staff members send mailings to some or all of the media or political contacts maintained in merge files. The organization would like to consolidate all of its mailing lists, eliminate the duplicate lists, and do more frequent mailings to specific subsets of the list.

The stated goals for the new Access application include the following:

- To bring the mailing list management functions in-house and thereby reduce costs, improve the accuracy of the data, and gain more immediate access to the information

- To increase the frequency and specificity of solicitation letters

- To gain a more accurate and timely picture of contribution trends

- To assess the effectiveness of mailings and other types of solicitations

- To eliminate redundancy and standardize the format used for the various mailing lists

- To reduce the amount of time spent recording, totaling, and posting transactions

- To track the status of pledges and collect a higher percentage of the money pledged

The ACE System Samples

If you imagine that the foregoing description of the fictional Association for a Clean Earth and its needs was garnered from conversations with various staff members, picture also the set of sample documents that you would have collected during the course of your investigations. The samples that describe the manual system presently in use at the Association for a Clean Earth include:

- Mailing labels

- Personalized solicitation letters

- Thank you letters

- A newsletter renewal letter

- A donor ledger card

- Media contact lists

- Political contact lists

- Committee membership rosters

- A page from the cash receipts journal

- A pledge form

By reviewing these documents and comparing them with the notes and lists you made during your conferences with the ACE staff, you might arrive at the following summary of the information to be entered and updated by the new Access application:

- *People on the mailing list*   The name, address and telephone number (which might be either a home or business address), salutation (for personalized letters), source of the original contact, dates of the first and most recent contacts, and some way to mark certain people to exclude them from mail or phone solicitations.

- *Donors*   ACE needs the dollar value and number of contributions year-to-date and overall, several keywords that represent special areas of interest or affiliations, and a free-form text field for more detailed notes.

- *Board members, media contacts, and political contacts*   ACE maintains some of the additional information stored for donors.

- *Contacts*   The contact date, type of contact (mailing, phone call, attendance at an event, etc.), and for some types of contacts, a follow-up date.

- *Financial transactions*   The transaction type, amount, date, payment method (cash, check, etc.), a brief description, and the general ledger account number to which the transaction should be posted. For promotional item purchases, ACE might also need to enter a discount, shipping charge, and sales tax.

- *Committee memberships*   The dates the member joined and left the committee, any officer position held, and space for additional free-form notes.

Calculation and processing functions include:

- Posting transaction totals to the donor records

- Counting the number of donors who satisfy various selection criteria

- Archiving and purging names, contacts, and transactions by date

The reports and printouts include:

- *Mailing labels*   One-across on gummed labels and three-up or four-up on plain paper, printed on a dot-matrix printer. Labels must be printed in either zip code order or alphabetically, and selection criteria might be based on geographical location, category (donor, prospect, media contact, and so on), last contact date, year-to-date or overall contribution totals, and areas of interest.

- *Personalized letters*   Solicitation letters, board meeting notices, committee membership notices, and other letters; printed on letterhead on a laser printer, in either zip code order or alphabetical order. In addition to the selection criteria enumerated for labels, ACE needs to select names for these mailings based on entries in the free-form text field, either by choosing a series of individual names or by entering additional ad hoc criteria.

- *Thank you notes*   Printed on letterhead on a laser printer for all contributions received within a given range of dates.

- *Renewal solicitations*   For all people whose memberships are due to expire within a given range of dates.

- *A complete donor reference list*   All the personal information available, together with all the transactions and contacts that occurred within a specified range of dates.

- *Media contact lists*   In alphabetical order, selected by special interests, with or without a list of recent contacts for each person.

- *Political contact lists*   In alphabetical order, selected by special interests, with or without a list of recent contacts for each person.

- *Committee membership rosters* The names, addresses, and telephone numbers of all current committee members, for one or all committees.

- *A pledge status report* Donors with outstanding pledges, with the pledged amount and all payments made on the pledge.

- *Pledge statements* Printed for all donors with outstanding pledges, to be sent to the donors.

- *Contact summaries* Grouped by contact type or donor, for any specified range of dates.

- *Transaction summaries* Grouped by transaction type, general ledger number, dollar amount range, or donor, for any specified range of dates.

- *Contact follow-up lists* All contacts that require follow-up letters or phone calls during the current week, together with the complete donor information.

- *Annual donation summaries* Necessary for income tax purposes for all donors who have made a contribution during the current year, printed on letterhead on a laser printer.

The table structures used in the case study system are described more fully in Chapter 3, which discusses database design.

Summary

If you have never used a database program or designed a database application, you may find this introduction to the design process a bit overwhelming, especially if you had hoped to just sit down at the keyboard and start entering data. Unfortunately, jumping right in with no preparation—an approach that often works well with spreadsheet or word processing software—can get you in big trouble with databases. Although each generation of database software is easier to use than the last, the kinds of business problems that you can solve with databases, which were complex to begin with, are growing even more complex as PC database programs gain power and speed. Although you may feel stymied at first, spending some time on the planning and design phases will save you considerable time, energy, and frustration later on, because the more planning you do in advance, the less time you will spend revising and restructuring the application as it evolves.

If you have an Access application of your own waiting in the wings, you may want to begin applying the methods outlined in this chapter to this database. If not, give some thought to the ACE system used as a case study—see if you can imagine the present workings of this imaginary nonprofit organization and visualize how the proposed database might help its directors and its office staff to work more efficiently and productively. After a brief detour in Chapter 2 to introduce you to the Access working environment, Chapter 3 describes in considerable detail how to translate your functional requirements into a sound database design.

CHAPTER

2

**Introduction to
Microsoft Access**

*Starting and Quitting
Microsoft Access*

*The Access Program
Window*

The Database Window

*The Access User
Interface*

The Access Help System

THIS CHAPTER INTRODUCES THE MICROSOFT ACCESS WORKING ENVIRON-
ment and user interface, and describes the methods that you will use
to communicate with the software. It describes how to start up and
exit from Access, how to operate the menu system, how to use keyboard and command button shortcuts provided for the most common commands and operations, how to manipulate windows, how to use the help
system, and most important, how to work with databases, which will of course
be the focus of nearly all of your activities in Access.

Access is *not* a new version of a program that originally ran in the character-
based MS-DOS environment—it was designed specifically to run under Windows, and its user interface is modeled entirely on the Windows paradigm. If
you have used other Windows software (not necessarily from Microsoft), many
aspects of the Access working environment should seem familar, including the
appearance of the screen, the menu structure, the help system, and many of the
keyboard commands and mouse techniques used to operate the program. If
Access is your first Windows program, keep in mind that you will be learning
about Windows as well as about Access, and you can take comfort in the knowledge that your experience with Access will shorten the learning curve for your
next Windows program.

This chapter assumes some familiarity with computers and with the basics
of the GUI (graphical user interface) environment. It assumes that you are familiar with your keyboard, including the names, locations, and purposes of
the function keys and cursor movement keys; that you understand how to use
the Shift, Alt, and Ctrl keys to produce key presses such as Ctrl+F4 or Alt+F;
and that you know how to use a mouse and are familiar with terms such as
"point," "click," "double-click," and "drag." Because the Access user interface
is inextricably linked with the Windows interface and shares so many characteristics with Windows itself and with other software designed to run under
Windows, this chapter does briefly review some of the basics. If, however, this
is your first experience with Windows, you may want to consult the Microsoft
documentation or an introductory book on Windows for further information
before you begin working on your Access application.

Regardless of your prior experience with Windows or with other database programs, you will get the most out of this chapter if you read it seated
at the computer. Treat this chapter as a guided tour of the Access working environment, and make the most of this opportunity to experiment with the program without endangering your valuable data—try the examples, and feel
free to spend additional time exploring Access on your own. This chapter assumes that Windows and Access are already installed on your computer, that
you have copied the sample ACE database provided on the disk packaged
with this book into the Access program directory, and that you know how to
start up Windows. If you have not yet installed Access or copied the sample
files, please take a few minutes to do so now, so that you can get the most out
of this hands-on introduction to Access.

Starting and Quitting Microsoft Access

When you install Access, the Setup program automatically creates a Microsoft Access program group with six items in it—program icons for Microsoft Access, Microsoft Access Change Workgroup, Microsoft Access Help, Microsoft ODBC Administrator, and two Notepad text files that contain information which became available after the manuals were printed. This program group, resized so that it is just large enough for the six icons, is shown in Figure 2.1. You can start Access using any of the methods common to all Windows software. From the Program Manager, you can use either of these methods:

- Click on the Microsoft Access program icon and press Enter.

- Double-click on the Microsoft Access program icon.

Figure 2.1

The Microsoft Access program group

From the File Manager:

1. Make sure that the File Manager window displays the directory of the Access program drive. If you need to change drives, click on the appropriate disk drive icon at the top of the File Manager window or use the Select Drive option on the Disk menu.

2. Make sure that the Access program subdirectory is displayed in the File Manager window. If necessary, click on the subdirectory name in the Tree panel or highlight it using the arrow keys.

3. Double-click on the program name MSACCESS.EXE in the directory panel, or highlight the program name and then press Enter.

If you prefer, you can start Access by using the Run command on the File menu in either the Program Manager or File Manager, as follows:

1. Pull down the File menu and choose the Run option.

2. In the Run dialog box, type the command line that starts up Access, including the disk drive and subdirectory, and then click on the OK button

or press Enter. Assuming that Access is installed in a subdirectory named ACCESS on drive C, you would use the following command line:

```
C:\ACCESS\MSACCESS.EXE
```

If you plan to use Access frequently, leaving the Microsoft Access program group open in the Program Manager window will enable you to start Access simply by double-clicking on its program icon. If you use Access in nearly every Windows work session, you can add it to your Startup group so that it starts up automatically at the beginning of every Windows session.

When you are finished with Access, you can exit from the program using any of the methods common to all Windows software:

- Choose the Exit option from the File menu.

- Press Alt+F4.

- Double-click on the close box in the upper-left corner of the Access program window.

- Click once on the close box in the upper-left corner of the Access program window and then select Close from the drop-down menu.

The Access Program Window

When you start up Access for the first time, it displays the Welcome screen illustrated in Figure 2.2, which suggests several ways to begin using or learning about Access. You can close this screen by pressing Enter or by clicking on the Close button in the lower-right corner; if you want to suppress the Welcome screen when you start up Access in the future, click in the check box labeled "Don't display this startup screen again" before you close it.

Nearly all of your work with Access will involve operations on databases, and when no database is open, your options are quite limited. The Access menu bar is dynamic—it changes to display only options and commands relevant to the current environment. In the Startup window, which is displayed after you close the Welcome screen and before you have opened a database, the menu bar contains just two options—File and Help. The Startup window, with the File menu pulled down, is shown in Figure 2.3. "The Access Help System" section later in this chapter describes the Access help system.

As is the case with all Windows software, you can run Access in a window of any size. Most of the illustrations in this book (Figure 2.3 is an exception) show the Access program window maximized—that is, zoomed to fill the entire screen so that no other windows are visible. When you work exclusively or primarily in Access, you will usually want to maximize the window so that you can see as much of your data as possible. If you need to see other running

Figure 2.2
The Access
Welcome screen

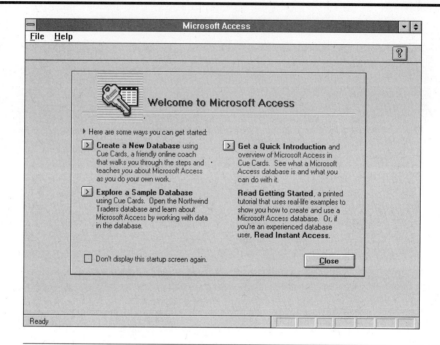

Windows programs as well, you can move and resize the Access window. For example, you might want to monitor another operation running in the background (such as a communications session); view part of a spreadsheet or word processor with which you are exchanging data; or keep part of the Access window visible while you use a word processor to prepare a report based on Access data or write documentation for your Access application.

Many of the basic components of the Access Startup window labeled in Figure 2.3 are common to all Windows software. At the top of the Access window is the standard Windows title bar, with the Control Menu button in the upper-left corner and Minimize and Maximize/Restore buttons in the upper-right corner. You can click on the Control Menu button to pull down the standard Windows Control menu (if you prefer keyboard commands, you can also activate the Control menu by pressing Alt+Spacebar). The Control Menu button also serves as the close box for the window—you can double-click on this button to close the Access program window and thus exit from the program. You can click on the Minimize button to temporarily reduce the Access program window to an icon to "clear the decks" without exiting from Access while you work in another Windows program. The Maximize/Restore button in the upper-right corner of the Access window changes to reflect the current status of the window. When the Access program window is maximized, it

Figure 2.3

The Access Startup window with the File menu pulled down

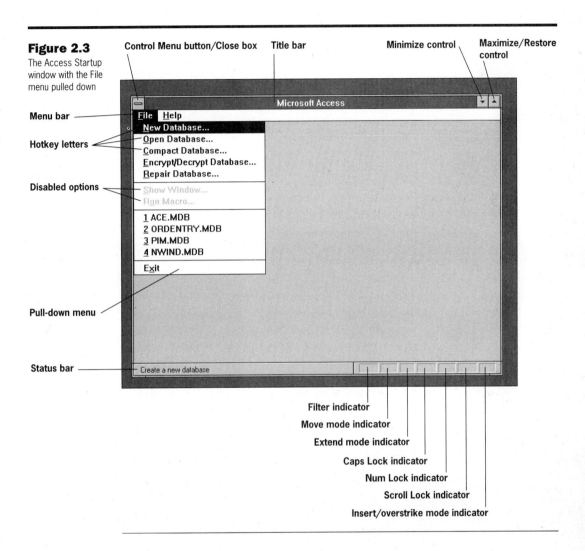

Control Menu button/Close box   Title bar   Minimize control   Maximize/Restore control

Menu bar

Hotkey letters

Disabled options

Pull-down menu

Status bar

Filter indicator
Move mode indicator
Extend mode indicator
Caps Lock indicator
Num Lock indicator
Scroll Lock indicator
Insert/overstrike mode indicator

serves as a Restore button, which returns the window to its former size and position (before you maximized it). Otherwise, as in Figure 2.3, it serves as a Maximize button, and clicking on this button zooms the Access program window to full-screen size.

Below the title bar in the Access window is the menu bar, which consists of a series of options, each of which has an associated pull-down menu of additional commands. Options that lead to dialog boxes rather than immediately carrying out an action are followed by ellipses (three dots), and options that lead to additional menus are followed by a small triangle. In Figure 2.3, you can see that the first five options all lead to additional dialog boxes.

Access uses a check mark symbol, displayed to the left of a menu option, for two different but similar purposes. When a pull-down menu includes two or more mutually exclusive options, Access displays a check mark to the left of the selected option. If a menu option functions as a toggle—that is, it can exist in two states equivalent to on and off—Access displays a check mark to the left of the option when it is turned on. Figure 2.4 shows typical examples of both on the View menu as it appears while you are editing a data entry screen. The first three options are mutually exclusive, and the fact that Form Design is checked means you are working in Form Design view rather than Form view or Datasheet view. The next six options are all toggles; currently, Properties, Ruler, and Grid are turned on and Field List, Palette, and Toolbox are turned off. These two usages of the check mark are differentiated only by the context, but once you become familiar with the menu options, the meaning of each check mark will be reasonably intuitive.

Figure 2.4

An Access menu with toggles and mutually exclusive options

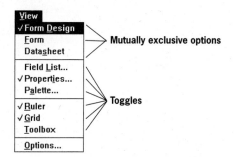

Below the menu bar is the Access tool bar, which displays command buttons that serve as shortcuts for executing certain very commonly used commands. Like the menu bar, the tool bar is dynamic—only command buttons relevant to the current environment, activity, or operation are displayed. In the Startup window, the tool bar contains just one button—the Help button (which has a question mark on its face). This button (described in more detail in the section of this chapter that describes the help system) calls up context-sensitive help about the selected menu option or the task in progress.

At the very bottom of the Access program window is the status bar, which displays additional information about the current working environment. The status bar is divided into two regions. On the left side, Access displays a brief status message or explanation of the currently selected menu option or operation. In Figure 2.3, the status line text "Create a new database" summarizes the purpose of the highlighted menu option, New Database. When you run time-consuming operations, Access displays a thermometer-style indicator in the status bar to inform you of its progress. The right side of the status bar is divided into seven sections that display the current operational mode and the status of the toggle keys on the keyboard, as follows:

Indicator	**Meaning**
FLTR	A *filter* is currently in effect—that is, Access is processing only those records that meet certain selection criteria.
MOV	*Move mode* is active—that is, you are in the process of moving a column in one of the tabular data display modes.
EXT	*Extend mode* is active—that is, you are using the Extend editing keys to select groups of fields or records.
CAPS	Caps Lock is on.
NUM	Num Lock is on.
SCRL	Scroll Lock is on.
OVR	You are editing text in *Overstrike* rather than *Insert* mode— that is, Access replaces existing characters with those you type rather than adding characters to the current line.

The last four indicators, which are displayed when the respective keyboard toggle keys are on, should be familiar to you. Filters are described in Chapter 6, and operations involving the Move and Extend modes are introduced in Chapter 3.

The remainder of the Access window serves as the workspace within which you do all your work with the program. In this region, you can open one or more data display or design windows. You can suppress the tool bar and/or the status bar to gain more working space on the screen through settings in the General Options dialog box accessed by selecting Options from the View menu, which is available whenever a database is open. The general options are described in Chapter 19.

Using the Access Menu Bar

You can use any combination of mouse and keyboard commands (of several different types) to navigate through the menu system and make selections. If most of your prior computer experience is with MS-DOS software, you may be accustomed to using the keyboard; Macintosh and Windows users will usually gravitate toward the mouse. In either case, you will develop your own preferences as you gain more experience with Access, but it is to your advantage to become familiar with all the methods available for issuing commands. For example, when you are designing or modifying a form or report, you will make extensive use of the mouse to manipulate (select, move, re-size, and so on) objects on the form, and if the mouse is already in your hand, using it to operate the menus as well is the most convenient method. In contrast, during an intensive data entry session, you will spend most of your time typing, and using keyboard commands to execute an occasional command is more expedient than reaching for the mouse.

To operate the menu system using the mouse, you can simply "point and click"—position the mouse pointer over the option you want, and click the left mouse button to select it. Thus, you can select any menu bar option and display the associated pull-down menu by clicking on it with the mouse. The pull-down menu remains visible on the screen when you release the mouse button, so you can release the mouse button immediately after clicking on the menu bar option and then click again on the desired pull-down menu option. Alternatively, you can click on a pull-down menu option and continue to hold down the left mouse button as you move the mouse to highlight the desired option. When you release the mouse button, Access executes the highlighted command.

If you prefer to use keyboard commands, you can activate the menu bar by pressing and then releasing either the Alt or F10 key. Once the menu is active, you can point to the option you want by using the Left Arrow and Right Arrow keys to highlight it, and then press Enter to display the associated pull-down menu. When the menu bar is active (you can verify that the menu is active by noting that one of the options is highlighted), you can also choose an option by pressing the underlined letter. Alternatively, you can activate the menu bar and display a pull-down menu by pressing a single Alt-key combination—that is, by holding down the Alt key and pressing the underlined hot-key in the menu bar prompt. For example, you could pull down the File menu by pressing Alt+F. To select an option from a pull-down menu, you can either use the arrow keys to highlight the option and then press Enter, or you can simply press the designated hotkey (the underlined letter in the menu prompt). Note that because the menu is already visible, and the letter you type could not possibly be misconstrued as data, you do not have to hold down the Alt key while you type the letter.

Finally, Access offers Ctrl-key hotkeys for some of the most commonly used commands, such as the editing commands for cutting and pasting text. You can use these hotkeys to execute menu commands with a single keystroke without first activating the menu system or displaying the pull-down menu that contains the options. These hotkeys, when they are available, are identified by the key names displayed in the pull-down menus to the right of the corresponding menu options. For example, Figure 2.5 shows the Edit menu, on which the first five options have hotkey shortcuts. (Unless Access is your first Windows program, this menu should be familiar; all the options except the Relationships option, which is unique to Access, are common to most Windows software.) The keyboard shortcut keys are particularly convenient for cutting and pasting text during an intensive editing session because they enable you to avoid wading repeatedly through the menu system without removing your hands from the keyboard to use the mouse.

Figure 2.5
An Access menu
with Ctrl-key
shortcuts

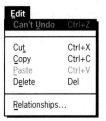

As noted earlier, the Access menu bar is dynamic, and it changes to reflect the current status of the working environment. The number of options in the menu bar and the associated pull-down menus vary, depending on the editing or design environment in which you are working. Access *grays out* pull-down menu options that are currently unavailable (displays them in gray rather than black type, if you are using the default Windows colors). You cannot select a disabled option with the keyboard or the mouse, and if there is a hotkey shortcut, Access ignores it. In Figure 2.3, you can see that the Show Window and Run Macro options in the File menu are currently unavailable (because there are no hidden windows and no macros have been defined yet).

If you want to practice both mouse and keyboard techniques, try using the mouse to choose the Open Database option on the File menu:

1. Click on the File option in the menu bar to pull down the File menu.

2. Click on the Open Database option on the File menu.

3. Click on the Cancel button in the Open Database dialog box to close the dialog box and cancel the command without opening a database.

The equivalent sequence of keyboard commands is as follows:

1. Press Alt+F to pull down the File menu.

2. Press the letter O to select the Open Database option on the File menu.

3. Press the Esc key to close the dialog box and cancel the command without opening a database.

NOTE. *Because there are so many methods for choosing menu commands, this book will in most cases simply tell you which options to choose from which menus, without giving explicit keystroke-by-keystroke instructions for doing so. For example, the instructions for displaying the Open Database dialog box might read, "Choose the Open Database option from the File menu."*

The Startup window File menu includes the following options:

Menu Option	Action
New Database	Creates a new database
Open Database	Opens an existing database
Compact Database	Recopies a database to reduce disk file fragmentation and reclaim unused space
Encrypt/Decrypt Database	Encodes a database to prevent anyone from viewing the contents with disk editors or file repair utilities, or decodes a previously encrypted database
Repair Database	Attempts to repair a damaged or corrupted database
Show Window	Redisplays all hidden windows
Run Macro	Runs a previously defined macro
Exit	Ends your work session and exits from Access

Unless you have just started up Access for the first time, the File menu also includes the names of up to four databases—the last few that you opened in previous work sessions. In Figure 2.3, the names of four databases are visible—ACE.MDB (the case study database supplied with this book), and the three sample databases provided with Access (ORDENTRY.MDB, PIM.MDB, and NWIND.MDB). The database names in the File menu serve as shortcuts for bypassing the standard dialog box used to open a database—you can open any of the listed databases simply by selecting its name from the File menu or typing the corresponding number.

NOTE. *With the File menu pulled down, you can select any of the four listed databases by clicking on the database name, highlighting the name and pressing Enter, or typing the underlined number to the left of the name.*

Opening and Closing a Database

The vast majority of your work with Access will involve operations on databases, and during any given work session, you will almost always have a database open. As noted in the previous section, you can open any of the last four databases you used in earlier work sessions by choosing its name from the File menu. You can open *any* database through the Open Database dialog box invoked by selecting the Open Database option on the File menu. This dialog box, which is patterned on the standard Windows Open File dialog box, is shown in Figure 2.6. Methods for closing a database once it is open are described in the next section.

Figure 2.6

The Open Database dialog box

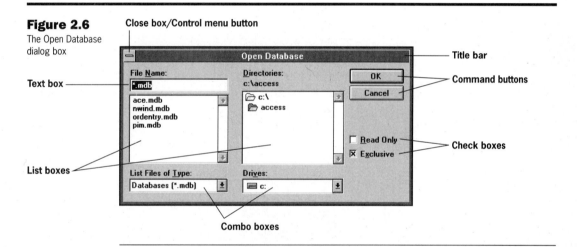

If Access is your first Windows program, take a moment to study the Open Database dialog box and experiment with the various options and *controls*. (In Windows, the term *control* describes any of the numerous mechanisms used to enter data and make selections, including text entry regions, check boxes, radio buttons, command buttons, and list boxes.) If you have used other Windows software, you will recognize the many characteristics that the Open Database dialog box shares with other Windows dialog boxes, as well as the distinctive aspects of the layout and visual appearance that define the unique "look and feel" (the interface display style) of Microsoft Access.

In Windows, a dialog box is a special type of window, which shares some of the characteristics of all windows, but has other properties that support its primary role—collecting all the specific information required to perform a certain task. Like all windows, a dialog box has a title bar and close box, but it does not have Maximize, Minimize, or Restore controls. A dialog box always appears in front of all other open windows, and you can move it (to examine the contents of another window on the desktop) but not resize it.

Once you have opened a dialog box, you must complete the dialog—either by making a selection or canceling the operation that invoked the dialog box—before you can do anything else. When a dialog box is open, the menu bar is inaccessible, and the keyboard and mouse commands that normally allow you to operate the menu or switch windows are temporarily disabled. You can bail out without making a selection (and thus cancel the command or operation in progress) by pressing Esc or by clicking on the Cancel command button present in all dialog boxes. You can exit and place your current selections in effect by using any of the following methods:

- Press a button provided for this purpose, which is usually labeled OK or with a verb that reiterates the purpose of the dialog box (such as Find or Import).

- Double-click on the close box in the upper-left corner of the dialog box.

- Double-click on your selection in a list box (for example, the database name in the Open Database dialog box).

- Press Enter with your selection highlighted.

- Press Ctrl+Enter from anywhere in the dialog box.

You can use any of the standard Windows mouse and keyboard commands to move around in the dialog box and make selections. The control or data entry region that you are currently working with may be described as the *current* or *active* object, or the object that *has the focus*. If you prefer keyboard commands, the safest way to move through the options in turn without actually changing any entries or choosing any options is to use the Tab key to move to the next option and Shift+Tab to move back to the previous option. You can also move directly to any control by using an Alt-key combination—hold down the Alt key and press the underlined letter in the corresponding prompt. For example, in the Open Database dialog box, you can move directly to the Drives combo box by pressing Alt+V. If you are accustomed to pressing the Enter key to move to the next item on a data entry screen, note that in Windows software, this key is not always an innocuous way to exit from a control and move to the next. For example, pressing Enter in a check box toggles the status of this control (checking the box if it is not already checked or unchecking it if it is), and in many list boxes, pressing Enter selects the highlighted item *and* closes the dialog box.

By default, the Open Database dialog box displays databases located in the Access program directory. The General Options dialog box (accessed by choosing Options from the View menu when a database is open) includes an option for specifying a different subdirectory as the default location for databases. This option is explained further in Chapter 19. You can open any database, located anywhere on your hard disk (or on the file server if you are running Access on a network) by typing its path name in the File Name text box. If the database you want to open is in the current working directory, this is often the easiest method. You can also open a database and close the Open Database dialog box by double-clicking on the database name in the scrolling list box, or by highlighting the name then pressing Enter or clicking on the OK button.

Note. You can display the drop-down list associated with a combo box by clicking on the arrow symbol to the right of the text box or by pressing F4 or Alt+Down Arrow.

The Open Database dialog box includes a number of navigation controls intended to help you find and open databases located anywhere on your hard disk without having to remember and type long path names. You can use the Drives combo box to switch to any available disk drive, and the Directories list box to move through the directory tree and choose any subdirectory. As you make your selections from these list boxes, Access updates the database list at the left side of the Open Database dialog box so that it always includes only databases in the currently selected subdirectory. By default, this list includes only files with the standard Access database extension (.MDB), but if you wish, you can edit the *file name skeleton* in the File Name text box to specify any group of files. The List Files of Type combo box offers two file name options—just Access databases (that is, files with the extension .MDB) or All Files (files that match the wildcard pattern *.*). In general, it is inadvisable to deviate from the Access naming conventions, and all the examples in this book use the standard .MDB extension.

The Read Only and Exclusive check boxes specify the editing mode for the database you are opening. By default, Exclusive is checked and Read Only is not. If you check the Read Only check box, Access opens the database for *read-only* access and does not allow you to edit any database component. This option is most useful on a local area network, but you might use it occasionally to avoid accidental and undesirable changes during a work session in which you only intend to view data or execute queries. The Exclusive check box determines whether a database is opened for *exclusive* or *shared* access on a local area network. When you open a database in Exclusive mode, no one else can open it while you have it open; in Shared mode, more than one user can view or edit the database. On a network, you will achieve the fastest performance by checking both Read Only and Exclusive when you open a database (obviously, this may not always be practical).

To practice opening a database, use the Open Database dialog box to open the ACE case study database:

1. Pull down the File menu.

2. Choose the Open Database option to display the Open Database dialog box.

3. Press Tab to move into the File Name list box.

4. Use the Up Arrow and Down Arrow keys to scroll through the list, and note that your current selection is always displayed in the File Name text box.

5. With ACE.MDB highlighted, press Enter or click on the OK button to close the Open Database dialog box and open the ACE database.

To create a new database, choose the New Database option from the File menu. This option invokes a dialog box very similar to the Open Database dialog box, with similar navigation controls that you can use to choose the location for your new database. Note, however, that the list box that displays the names of existing databases is disabled—you *must* enter a name for the new database you are creating. If you type the name of a database that is already present in the current subdirectory, Access displays an alert like the one pictured in Figure 2.7 to ask for permission before overwriting the existing file.

Figure 2.7
Confirming your intention to overwrite an existing database

Access allows you to open only one database at a time, and if you select the Open Database option with a database already open, Access closes this database before it opens the one that you select from the Open Database dialog box. You can close the current database without opening another by using the close box in the Database window (described in the next section) or by using the Close Database option on the File menu (also described in the next section). Note, however, that you may not need to explicitly close a database very often. In particular, you do not have to close the database you are working on before you exit from Access.

If you are already planning to use Access for a specific project, take a moment now to create a new database for your application. However, if you want to continue to explore the Access working environment as you read the rest of this chapter, you might want to reopen the ACE database (which already contains a variety of application components) rather than leaving your new empty database open.

The Database Window

Whenever a database is open, Access displays the Database window, which is shown in Figure 2.8 as it appears after you open the ACE case study database. The Database window serves as a central command post for initiating all the activities associated with databases. By default, the Database window is located in the upper-left corner of the main program window and is sized just large enough to accommodate the three *command buttons* at the top and the six *object buttons* on the left side, but you can move, resize, maximize, or minimize the window according to your needs. For example, if you use very long names for your database components, you might widen the window to accommodate them.

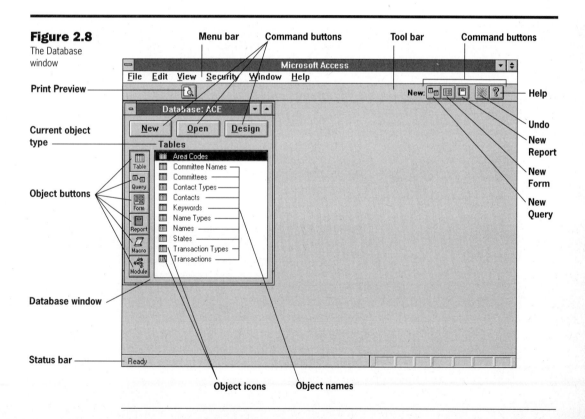

Figure 2.8
The Database window

When a database is open, the Access menu bar expands to include additional options absent from the Startup window menu bar because they are used exclusively for working on a particular database project. The structure of the Access menu bar as it appears in the Database window is diagrammed in Figure 2.9 and in Appendix A. If this is your first exposure to Access, most of the options will be unfamiliar to you, and there is no need to try to memorize them—all the menu commands are described later in this book. For now, simply note the changes in the File menu. When a database is open, the File menu no longer includes the names of the last four databases that you opened, and you must use the Open Database option to open any database. The File menu also includes a Close Database option, which you can use to close the current database without immediately opening another, and offers options for accessing data external to the current database by importing, exporting, or attaching files. The latter options are described in Chapter 15.

Figure 2.9
The structure of the main Access menu bar

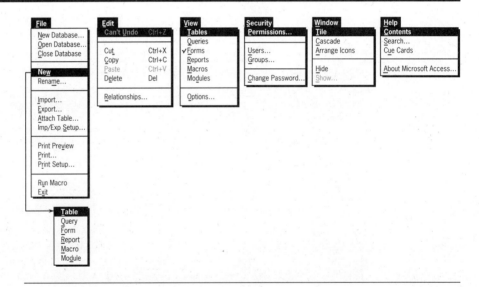

When a database is open, the tool bar includes several buttons not present in the Startup window. These buttons, which are labeled in Figure 2.8, include a Print Preview button, three buttons for creating new queries, forms, and reports, and an Undo button, which reverses your most recent editing command (the symbol on this button depicts an eraser).

As outlined in Chapter 1, an Access database can contain six different types of objects (application components)—tables, queries, forms, reports, macros, and modules. The six *object buttons* at the left side of the Database window provide easy access to these six types of objects, and the command buttons at the top of the window allow you to operate on a particular object of any type. The object buttons are labeled with the names of the objects and the standard Access icons used to represent them. (A complete directory of Access icons can be found in Appendix F.)

One of the object buttons is always selected, and the alphabetical list in the center of the Database window includes only objects of the corresponding type. When you first open a database, the Table button is selected. All of these buttons are *toggle buttons*, and a selected toggle button is displayed in different colors and with shaded borders to suggest that it is depressed, but this rather subtle visual cue may be hard to detect, especially on a black and white monitor. The heading at the top of the object list also indicates the current object type; in Figure 2.8, it is "Tables." To switch to another object type, you can either click on one of the object buttons or you can pull down the View menu and choose the Tables, Queries, Forms, Reports, Macros, or Modules option.

In the center of the Database window, Access displays an alphabetical list of available objects, each accompanied by an icon that represents the object type. In the Database window pictured in Figure 2.8, you can see the names of the ACE tables—Area Codes, Committee Names, Committees, and so on. In this figure, all the table icons are identical, and you might question the need for the icon, but as you will see in later chapters, Access uses different icons to distinguish between objects of slightly different types that fall into the same major class. For example, the icon for a table in another database (made available through the Attach command) is the standard table icon with an arrow superimposed.

If there are too many objects to view at once, Access displays a scroll bar to the right of the object list. You can also use a keyboard shortcut to move quickly to the vicinity of a particular object in a long list (such as the lists in the Database window): Pressing any letter key on the keyboard moves you to the first item in the list that begins with the designated letter. You can resize the Database window to accommodate more objects, but it is likely that you will eventually create a database with more forms or reports than will fit in the Database window, even if you expand it to the full height of the screen.

The three command buttons at the top of the Database window enable you to create, use, or modify any object displayed in the window. You can select a button by clicking on it or by using an Alt-key combination based on the underlined letter (Alt+N, Alt+O, or Alt+D). These buttons are used as follows:

Command Button	Action
New	Creates a new object of the type displayed in the window
Open	Uses the object whose name is highlighted in the window
Design	Opens a Design window to modify the object whose name is highlighted in the window

Access provides several alternatives for creating new objects:

- Make sure the Database window displays objects of the desired type, and click on the New button or press Alt+N.

- Choose the New option from the File menu, and then specify the object type by selecting the Table, Query, Form, Report, Macro, or Module option from a submenu.

- Click on the New Query, New Form, or New Report button in the tool bar.

The precise meaning of the Open option depends on the type of object, but this button always enables you to *use* a previously created object for its intended purpose. Opening a table or a query invokes the default data display and editing environment—the Datasheet window introduced briefly in Chapter 1—and opening a form displays the custom data entry screen described by the form and allows you to enter or edit data through this form. When the Database window displays the list of reports, the Open button is replaced by a Preview button, which carries out a roughly equivalent function—previewing or printing the report. For macros and modules, the button is labeled Run, and selecting it executes the instructions in the macro or module. All of the Open options are described in more detail in the chapters on creating and using objects of each type. You can also open any object by double-clicking on its name in the Database window or by highlighting the name and pressing Enter.

To delete an object, highlight its name in the Database window and press Del or select the Delete option from the Edit menu. Access displays an alert box like the one in Figure 2.10 to request confirmation before deleting the object. Use this option with caution, because *there is no way to recover an object after you have deleted it.* To rename an object, highlight its name in the Database window and select the Rename option on the File menu, which invokes a very simple dialog box that asks for the new name.

Figure 2.10

Confirming your intention to delete a table

The Access User Interface

The Access user interface has much in common with other programs designed specifically for Microsoft Windows, and if you have used other Windows software (not necessarily written by Microsoft), you will quickly feel at home in the Access working environment. Many of the menu options and dialog boxes should also seem familiar, despite the presence of numerous options unique to Access.

Like most Windows programs, Access allows you to open as many windows as you wish, subject of course to practical limits imposed by available memory, the size of your display screen, your willingness to search through the windows to reach the one you want, and your tolerance for screen clutter. You cannot move a window that you open from within Access completely outside the Access program window, although you can position a window so that most of it is "off the edge" of the screen. Figure 2.11 illustrates the appearance of the screen with three windows visible inside the main Access program window—the Database window, an editing window that displays the ACE Names Table in the standard Datasheet format, and a Form Design window opened to edit a data entry screen called Names. As you gain experience and your databases grow in size and complexity, taking the time to arrange your "desktop" carefully can make the difference between productivity and confusion when you work with more than two or three windows at a time.

NOTE. *An individual window opened within the main program window is often called a* document window, *although you may not think of database objects such as tables or data entry screens as documents.*

When at least one window is open, the Window menu includes the types and names of all open windows, listed in the order in which you opened them. In Figure 2.11, which shows the Window menu pulled down, you can see the names of the three open windows, identified as a Database window called ACE, a Table window called Names, and a Form window called Names and Addresses. You can move into any open window by selecting it from the Window menu, and you can cycle through the active windows by pressing Ctrl+F6. In most cases, however, the most convenient method for switching windows is to click the mouse anywhere in the desired window. Even if you generally prefer to use keyboard commands, it is to your advantage to keep at least a small part of each window visible at all times, so that you can use the mouse for switching windows.

You can use the Tile and Cascade options on the Window menu to rearrange your windows into two standard configurations. *Tiling* the windows, as illustrated in Figure 2.12, places them in non-overlapping positions, so that

Figure 2.11

Working with three
open windows

Names table Datasheet window

Database window

Names and
Addresses Form
Design window

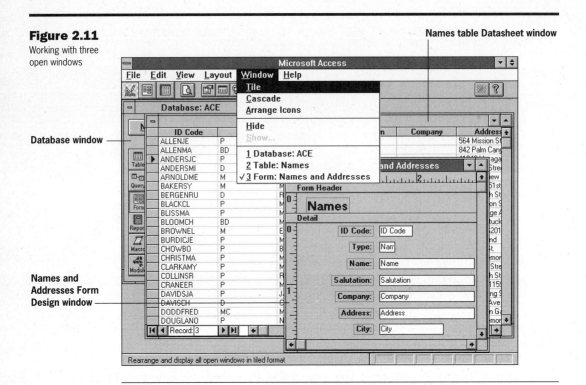

they are approximately the same size and as much as possible of each window
is visible. When you tile four or more windows, Access divides the screen horizontally as well as vertically to allocate the available space in the most useful
way possible, but you will find the Tiled setup most helpful when only two or
three windows are open. *Cascading* the windows, as in Figure 2.13, overlaps
them so that part of each window is visible and the frontmost window occupies the most space. Of course, you can use either of these two standard window configurations as a point of departure for arranging the screen in a
unique way best suited for the task at hand.

You can use all the standard Windows mechanisms—the controls in the
window title bar, the resizing controls in the window borders, the Control
menu options, and any available Ctrl-key shortcuts—to move, resize, close,
minimize, maximize, and restore Access document windows. If you are unfamiliar with Windows, be aware that maximizing document windows is an all-
or-nothing proposition—maximizing one window maximizes all open windows, so you cannot, for example, maximize a table's Datasheet window and
place a smaller form design window on top.

Figure 2.12
Tiling windows

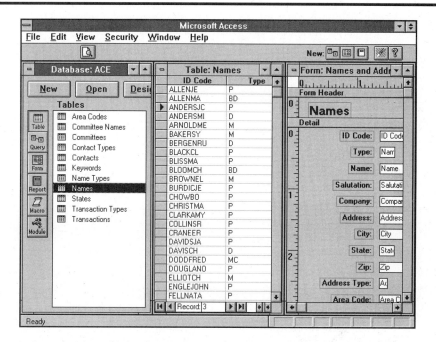

Figure 2.13
Cascading windows

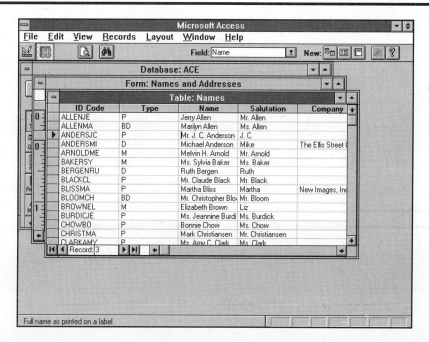

NOTE. *Minimizing or hiding the Database window while you edit data or design forms can help to reduce screen clutter without significantly inconveniencing you. To avoid having to restore the window repeatedly, you can use the buttons on the tool bar or the New option on the File menu to create new objects.*

You can hide the active window (remove it completely from the screen without closing it) by selecting the Hide option on the Window menu. When a window is hidden, it does not appear on the list of window names in the Window menu, and you cannot activate the window by pressing Ctrl+F6. To redisplay a hidden window, you must use the Show option, which appears on the Window menu if the Database window is visible or on the File menu if it is hidden; simply select the window name from the Show Window dialog box, as shown in Figure 2.14, and press Enter or click on the OK button. You need not make it a point to close windows or redisplay hidden windows before you exit from Access; when you run the program again, Access starts up with a clean slate, with no database—and therefore no document windows—open.

Figure 2.14
The Show Window
dialog box

Access Command Keys

You can use any combination of keyboard and mouse commands to manipulate Access document windows and edit text. The mouse techniques, which conform to the standards set by other Windows programs (and many DOS programs that support a mouse), were outlined briefly in the previous section. Table 2.1 lists the most important keyboard commands recognized by Access. The first group, the window manipulation commands, are relevant throughout Access.

The text editing commands are applicable whenever you communicate with Access by typing: when you enter data into a table; type database or object names in dialog boxes such as the Open Database dialog box; edit the description of a bookmark in the help system (described later in this chapter); and many other contexts. If you are not familiar with text editing in Windows, note that most Windows programs use the term *insertion point* for what is usually called a *cursor* in the MS-DOS world—the indicator that marks your current location in the text. The insertion point is commonly displayed as a vertical bar or as an *I-bar* (a vertical bar with small serifs at the top and bottom). There is one crucial difference between DOS and Windows that can trip you up: When you move into a text editing region, Windows programs usually display the entire region selected, and any characters you type *replace* the entire selection. To *edit* the text, you must display an insertion point by pressing F2 or by clicking the mouse anywhere within the text. These commands are described in more detail in Chapter 4, which covers entering and editing data in Access tables.

Table 2.1 **Access Command and Editing Keys**

Key	Action
Window and Object Manipulation Commands	
F1	Opens the Help window and displays context-sensitive help on the current command, menu option, operation, or editing environment
Shift+F1	Activates the question mark pointer for requesting context-sensitive help about any object on the screen
Ctrl+F4	Closes the active window
Alt+F4	Closes the active dialog box or, if no dialog box is open, exits from Access
Ctrl+F6	Cycles to the next open window
F11 or Alt+F1	Moves directly to the Database window from any other open window
F12 or Alt+F2	Opens a Save As dialog box to save the current object under a new name
Shift+F12 or Alt+Shift+F2	Saves the current object and allows you to continue working
Insertion Point Movement Commands	
F2	Switches between editing (with the insertion point visible) and selecting the entire text region
Right Arrow	Moves right one character
Left Arrow	Moves left one character
Up Arrow	Moves up one line or record
Down Arrow	Moves down one line or record
Ctrl+Right Arrow	Moves right one word

Table 2.1   **Access Command and Editing Keys (Continued)**

Key	Action
Insertion Point Movement Commands (Continued)	
Ctrl+Left Arrow	Moves left one word
End	Moves to the end of the line
Ctrl+End	Moves to the end of the field
Home	Moves to the beginning of the line
Ctrl+Home	Moves to the beginning of the field
PgDn	Displays the next screenful of text or records
PgUp	Displays the previous screenful of text or records
Shift+Right Arrow	Selects or unselects the next character
Shift+Left Arrow	Selects or unselects the previous character
Ctrl+Shift+Right Arrow	Selects or unselects the next word
Ctrl+Shift+Left Arrow	Selects or unselects the previous word
Text Editing Commands	
Ctrl+C* or Ctrl+Ins	Copies the selected text to the Clipboard
Ctrl+V* or Shift+Ins	Pastes the contents of the Clipboard into the current text editing environment
Ctrl+X* or Shift+Del or Ctrl+Shift+Del	Deletes (cuts) the selected text and copies it to the Clipboard
Backspace	Deletes the selected text or the character to the left of the insertion point if no text is selected
Del	Deletes the selected text or the character to the right of the insertion point if no text is selected
Ctrl+Z or Alt+BkSp	Deletes text typed since the last movement of the insertion point or undoes the most recent cut, delete, paste, replace, or change to the current record
Esc	Undoes changes to the current field or record

*Note: Ctrl+C, Ctrl+V, and Ctrl+X work only in Windows 3.1.

Properties and Property Sheets

Central to the operational philosophy of Access are the concepts of *objects* and *properties*, which describe the various characteristics of objects. As noted earlier, the term *object* applies to any Access entity that you can select on the screen. Objects come in many sizes and flavors—a database, a field, a form, a report header, a check box, a scroll bar, and a column title are all objects. Each type of object has its own set of properties, which collectively describe all the characteristics of the object that allow it to fulfill its intended purpose. However, some properties apply to many different types of objects. For example, most of the objects that you can put on forms and reports have font, color, size, and position properties.

Access offers a variety of methods for changing properties, some more direct than others. For example, you can resize many objects by using the standard Windows mouse techniques; you can select colors from a *palette* of color samples; you select the font and character size from combo boxes; and you can turn on properties such as boldfacing, underlining, and alignment (justification) by using command buttons in the tool bar. You can also change any property of any object by displaying a *property sheet*, which lists all the properties of the selected object, and entering new values directly in the property sheet. Many properties can *only* be changed through the property sheet, but even when you use this method, Access offers some help—for properties that can take on only a finite number of values, Access provides a combo box that allows you to either type in a value or select one from the drop-down list. Figure 2.15 illustrates a Form Design window labeled to indicate several methods for changing properties of the form as a whole and of individual objects in the form. The property sheet on the right side of the screen describes the text box used to collect the Name field; the combo box used to collect the Display When property is visible in this figure.

You can use any combination of methods to edit properties. Changes that you make on the property sheet are reflected immediately in the object as it appears on the screen, and changes made through other methods are translated to the appropriate values in the property sheet. For example, if you move or resize an object with the mouse, the new position and dimensions appear in the property sheet, and if you enter new values for these properties, the object moves or changes size on the screen. In some cases, one method may have many benefits and few disadvantages. For example, the foreground and background colors for a text box on a data entry form are represented by numbers (in Figure 2.15, the background color property is 16776960). Obviously, selecting the colors from a palette is the method of choice. On the other hand, using the mouse to resize a text box may not always be the best method, although it is certainly the easiest way to establish the approximate size and location. If, however, you need to resize three or four objects to match an existing object, entering the height and width in the property sheets is easier, faster, and much more accurate.

Figure 2.15

Methods for
changing properties

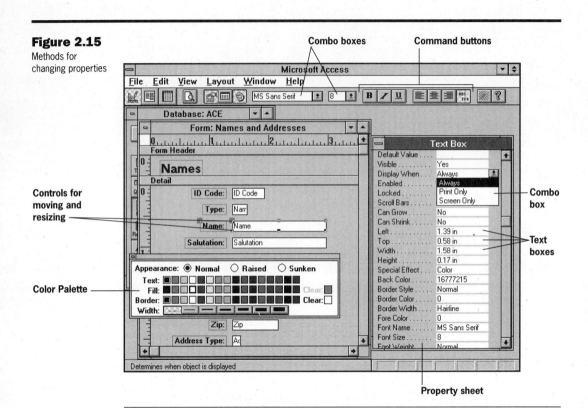

Even if you have encountered these concepts before, the sheer number
of properties can be overwhelming at first. When you begin working with
Access objects, however, you will discover that the meanings of most of the
properties you will need to use immediately—such as the Width, Height, Font
Name, and Font Size properties visible in Figure 2.15—are quite intuitive. In
the chapters that cover the various objects and object design windows, this
book describes most of the properties that are relevant to working in Access
without using the Access Basic programming languages. A complete list of
properties appears in Appendix D.

The Access Help System

Access offers an extensive on-line help system to complement the printed manuals supplied with the software. The Access help facility is based on the standard
Windows help system, which is a separate program that runs in its own window
on the desktop. As noted earlier in this chapter, the Access program group created when you install the program includes a separate icon labeled Access Help,

and you can start up the help system from the Program Manager without first running Access. However, Access automatically closes the Help window when you exit from the program. You can move, resize, maximize, or minimize the Help window as you would any other Windows application window, and Windows automatically reformats the text to conform to the current window size. If you have used other Windows programs, you will find the Access help system familiar. For those who are new to Windows, this section reviews the basics.

You can invoke the help system in several ways, all of which lead into the same network of linked and cross-referenced help screens. To enter the help system at the highest level and search for a particular topic, select the Help option on the main Access menu bar. The associated pull-down menu, which is depicted in Figure 2.16, includes the following options:

Option	Action
Contents	Displays the Table of Contents for the help system
Search	Searches for a specific topic by keyword
Cue Cards	Invokes the Access Cue Cards system
About Microsoft Access	Displays an information screen with the Access copyright notice and a summary of memory and disk space usage

Figure 2.16
The Help menu

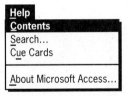

If you have used other Windows software, you will recognize the Contents and Search options, which are part of the standard Windows help system, as well as the About option, which is present in every Windows program (although the specific information displayed in the window invoked by choosing the About option differs). The Cue Cards option activates an adjunct to the help system that displays step-by-step instructions for carrying out the most common Access operations. (Cue Cards are described in detail in "Using Cue Cards," later in this chapter.) If you want information about a particular menu option, command, or function, the easiest way to find it is to choose the Contents option from the Help menu, which displays the Table of Contents screen shown in Figure 2.17.

Figure 2.17

The Help Table of
Contents

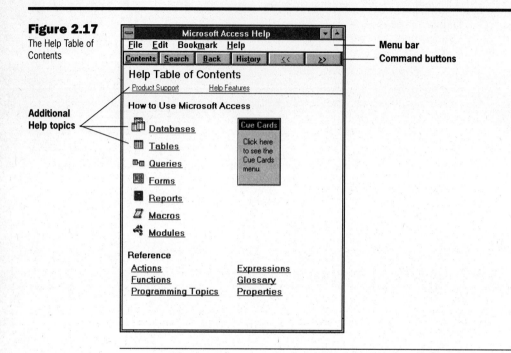

The Help Table of Contents is divided into two major sections. The upper section, like the Database window, is organized around the fundamental Access objects—databases, tables, queries, forms, reports, macros, and modules—and the lower section leads to a series of reference guides, most of which are arranged alphabetically. You will find the object topics most helpful when you need guidance on carrying out a specific operation on a particular type of object. For example, to find out how to create a data entry form for a table, you would start by selecting Forms in the Table of Contents.

In all the help screens, including the Table of Contents, the titles of other help topics are displayed in green letters with a solid underline. Green letters with a broken underline identify topics that do not lead directly to additional help screens; some of these invoke lists of additional help topics, while others lead to a definition of the underlined term. (On a black-and-white display, only the underlines identify these topics.) You can move to any of the cross-referenced topics by clicking anywhere within the topic name. To help you identify these "hot spots," Windows changes the mouse pointer from an arrow to a hand with a pointing finger whenever it is over a topic name or defined term. If you prefer the keyboard, you can press Tab and Shift+Tab to move from one cross-reference topic to another, but using the mouse is much easier and faster.

The Access help system includes an additional cross-referencing tool: Most help screens have a "See Also" list of related topics, which you can view by clicking on the words "See Also" displayed directly below the help topic title. This list may contain references to other help screens, Cue Cards, and the relevant chapters in the printed Access documentation. You can move directly to any one of these topics by clicking on it in the See Also window. Figure 2.18 illustrates the Creating a Table help screen with the See Also list displayed.

Figure 2.18
Displaying the list of related help topics

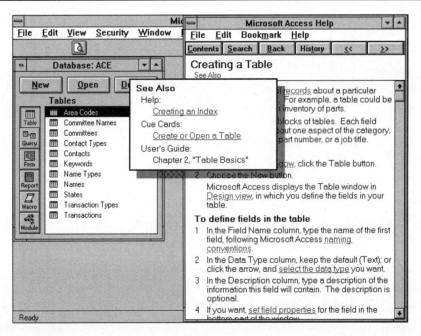

If you are not familiar with the Windows help system, try the following experiments:

1. Select Contents from the Help menu to display the Help Table of Contents.

2. Select Tables from the Table of Contents screen to call up a screenful of topics that describe operations you can perform on tables.

3. Choose the first topic, Creating and Modifying Tables, from this screen to call up the list of topics pictured in Figure 2.19.

Figure 2.19

Help topics related to creating a table

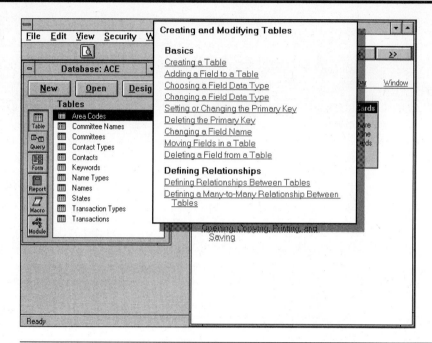

4. Choose Creating a Table from this list to invoke the help screen that describes how to create a table.

5. Click on the word *table* in the first paragraph of the help text to display a definition of the term "table." Figure 2.20 illustrates the appearance of the screen with the definition box displayed.

6. Close the definition box by pressing Esc or by clicking anywhere outside the box.

7. Click on the underlined phrase *See Also* below the help topic to display the list of cross-referenced help topics shown in Figure 2.18.

8. Close the See Also list by pressing Esc or by clicking anywhere outside the list of topics.

9. If you wish, you can continue to explore the help system. When you are ready to exit, close the Help window by pressing Alt+F4 or by choosing the Exit option from the File menu.

You can also obtain *context-sensitive* help—that is, ask for help on the currently selected menu option or the operation in progress—by pressing F1 or

Figure 2.20

Displaying the definition of the term "table"

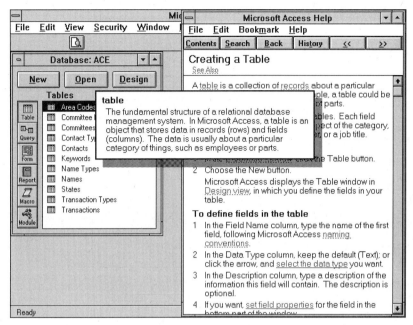

by clicking on the Help button in the tool bar. (The Help button is the one with the question mark icon on its face.) For example, pressing F1 with the File menu pulled down and the Import option highlighted invokes a help screen that describes how to use the Import command. These methods for requesting help are always available, even when a dialog box is active and the main menu bar—and therefore the Help menu—is not accessible. Finally, you can obtain context-sensitive help about a screen region that you cannot enter directly (such as a command button in the tool bar) by pressing Shift+F1. Access responds by displaying a question mark next to the arrow symbol that represents the mouse pointer. To get help about a particular screen object, simply point to the object and click on it.

Keep in mind that the method that you use to enter the help system determines only which topic is displayed first—you can use any combination of the methods described in this section to navigate through the help system and find information on any available subject.

NOTE. *The ability to call up context-sensitive help by pressing Shift+F1 is* not *part of the standard Windows help system and is not available in all Windows programs, although it is present in most Microsoft programs.*

The Help System Menu Bar

Recall that the help system is a separate Windows program with its own menu bar and, below the menu bar, a *button bar* with six command buttons that allow you to navigate through the network of help screens. The menu structure of the help system is diagrammed in Figure 2.21. You can use the Print option on the File menu to print the complete text of the current help topic (not just the text currently visible on the screen), so that you can keep the help text handy for reference while you complete the task you were working on.

Figure 2.21

The structure of the help system menu bar

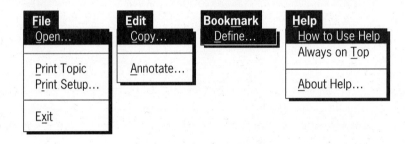

Another method for keeping the Help text available while you continue working is to choose the Always on Top option from the Help menu (that is, the Help menu accessed through the help system menu bar, *not* the Help menu on the main Access menu bar). After you choose this option, the Help window remains in front of *all other Windows application windows*, not just Access document windows. The Always on Top menu option is a toggle; to turn off this feature, simply return to the Help menu and select Always on Top again. (If you are not sure whether the Always on Top option is currently in effect, look for the check mark to the left of this option on the Help menu.)

You can use the Bookmark option to flag help topics so that you can return directly to these topics later in the same work session or in a future Access work session without having to retrace your steps through the help system. To set a bookmark on the current help screen or remove any previously set bookmark, choose the Define option from the Bookmark menu. In response, Access displays the Bookmark Define dialog box, shown in Figure 2.22, which you can use to define a new bookmark or delete an existing one. By default, Access assumes that you want to set a new bookmark, and it proposes the current help topic as the bookmark name, but you can edit the name if you wish. To establish the bookmark and close the dialog box, press Enter or select the OK button. To delete a bookmark, highlight its name in the Bookmark Define dialog box and click on the Delete button or press Alt+D.

Note. To keep the Help system available but not visible during a work session, leave the Help window open, behind the Access program window. You can return to the Help window just as you would switch to any other active Windows program (for example, by pressing Ctrl+Esc to call up the Task Switcher).

Figure 2.22

Defining a bookmark

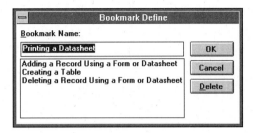

The first nine bookmarks that you define appear on the Bookmark menu numbered 1 through 9 in the order you created them. You can select any of these options to move directly to the corresponding help screen. If you have defined more than nine bookmarks, you must access all but the first nine by choosing the More option added to the bottom of the Bookmark menu. This option brings up the Bookmark dialog box, which enables you to choose *any* bookmark (including the first nine) and display the corresponding help screen.

You can use the Copy option on the Edit menu to copy the text of a help screen (not including any graphics, icons, or controls) to the Clipboard. You might want to do this occasionally to incorporate portions of a help screen into a document you are preparing to describe how to run your application, or to prepare a concise summary of commands or menu options for your own reference.

You cannot edit the text of the Access Help screens, but you can attach additional material to any screen by using the Annotate option on the Edit menu. Choosing this option invokes the dialog box pictured in Figure 2.23, which includes a text editing region, together with command buttons that allow you to save, delete, or edit the annotation, as follows:

Command Button	Action
Save	Saves the annotation and attaches it to the current help screen
Cancel	Exits from the Annotate dialog box without saving your changes
Delete	Deletes the annotation displayed in the dialog box
Copy	Copies the selected text to the Clipboard
Paste	Pastes the contents of the Clipboard into the current annotation

Figure 2.23

Adding annotations
to a Help topic

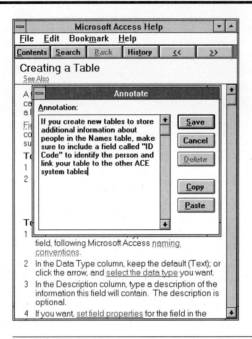

You can use all the standard Windows mouse and keyboard commands to edit the text. When you are satisfied, use the Save button to save your changes and attach the annotation to the current help screen. Henceforth, Access will display a paper clip symbol at the top of the help text to remind you of the presence of the annotation. You can call up the Annotate dialog box to display or edit the text by clicking on the paper clip symbol or by selecting the Annotate option on the Edit menu. To delete an annotation and remove the paper clip marker, click on the Delete button in the Annotate dialog box.

You can use the Copy and Paste buttons to copy material from one annotation to another (or to any other open editing window). The Copy button copies the text to the Clipboard, and the Paste option copies the current contents of the Clipboard into the current annotation. You can use these commands to copy text from one annotation to another, or to transfer material from another Windows application into an annotation. Be careful when you use the Delete command in the Annotate dialog box—the Delete button deletes the entire annotation, *and there is no way to undo the deletion.* To delete only the selected text, press the Del key.

The Help System Command Buttons

The six command buttons below the Help window menu bar serve as navigation shortcuts for moving around in the help system. The buttons are used as follows:

Command Button	Action
Contents	Displays the Help Table of Contents.
Search	Opens the Search dialog box so you can look for a topic by keyword.
Back	Returns to the last help screen displayed.
History	Displays a list of the last 40 help screens displayed, with the most recent one first, so you can easily return to any of these screens.
<<	Displays the previous screen in a series of related help screens. This option is not available when you are viewing the first screen in the series.
>>	Displays the next screen in a series of related help screens. This option is not available when you are viewing the last screen in the series.

The Back, History, >>, and << buttons enable you to move quickly and efficiently along several different paths through the Help system. The Back button is particularly useful for retracing your steps through a series of help screens without having to start over and remember all the options you selected. The History option serves as a convenient shortcut for returning to a particular help topic that you remember reading during the current work session. Once the History window is open, it remains open, together with the Help window, until you close it using any of the standard Windows methods. Unlike bookmarks, the help history list is not retained from one work session to the next.

The Search option enables you to look for help on a specific topic based on keywords associated with the topic. You can access the Search dialog box, shown in Figure 2.24, by selecting the Search button in the Help window or by choosing Search from the Help menu accessed through the main program menu bar. You type the word or phrase that you want to search for in the text box at the top of the Search dialog box. Below this text box is an alphabetical list of *keywords*. As you type, the help system scrolls the list to the keyword that most closely matches your entry; in most cases, you can zero in on the topic of interest by typing just a few letters. At any point (including immediately after opening the Search dialog box if you have absolutely no idea what keyword to type), you can move into the keyword list and browse through the topics. When the desired entry is highlighted in the list box, you can press Enter or select the Show Topics button to display a list of related help topics in the box at the bottom of the Search window. To display the help screen for any of these topics, simply highlight it and select the Go To button. To close the Search dialog box without moving away from the currently displayed help screen, press Esc or use the Close button in the upper-right corner of the dialog box. To try searching for a help topic, use the following steps:

1. Press F1 to invoke the Help system if it is not already open.

2. Press Alt+S or click on the Search command button.

3. Begin typing **formatting** slowly, watching the list of topics as you type. As you type each letter, Access scrolls the list of topics first to "F1 key" (the first entry that begins with F), then to "focus," "For," "Form," and "Format."

4. Double-click on "formatting numbers" in the scrolling list of help topics, or click once and then click on the Show Topics command button. Your screen should look like Figure 2.24.

5. Press Down Arrow until "Formatting a Field" is highlighted or click on this topic, and then click on the Go To button to display the help screen that describes formatting a field.

Figure 2.24

Searching for a help topic by keyword

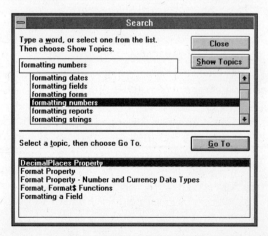

Using Cue Cards

The Access Help system is ideal for looking up the purpose or usage of a particular menu option, reviewing the procedure for carrying out a specific operation that you cannot find in the printed documentation, or requesting help in completing the entries in a dialog box. For the novice who does not know how to begin a complex task or who wants a little more hand-holding, the Access Cue Cards better fit the bill. Cue Cards are an auxiliary help system designed to provide step-by-step instructions for carrying out many common procedures in Access. Cue Cards can prompt you through a lengthy and complex operation such as creating a table or designing a query by asking you at each stage what you want to do next and then displaying one or more screens with specific instructions for accomplishing your stated objective. You can access Cue Cards by selecting the Cue Cards option from the main Access Help menu or by clicking on the large button titled "Cue Cards" in the Help Table of Contents. As noted in the previous section, the See Also list in many of the other help screens also contains cross-referenced Cue Card topics that serve as additional entry points into the Cue Cards system.

Although the Cue Cards appear to be integrated into the Access help system, they are in fact not part of the Windows Help facility and they behave somewhat differently. Unlike the Help window, the Cue Cards screens always appear in front of all other open windows, so they are always visible. Unfortunately, you cannot move or resize the Cue Cards window; its Control menu has just two options—Minimize and Close—and the only control in the upper-right corner of the window is a Minimize control. If the Cue Cards window gets in the way while you are carrying out tasks that occupy most of the screen, such as editing a table or creating a form, your only recourse is to minimize it. To restore the window, click on the Cue Cards icon, which is always located in the lower-right corner of the main Access window. You cannot print the Cue Cards text, but because they are always visible, this is not a serious limitation.

Figure 2.25 illustrates the help screen invoked by requesting Cue Cards. This screen is part of the Access help system, but the Cue Cards screens that Access displays subsequently are not. When you choose a Cue Cards topic, Access closes the Help window and displays instead a Cue Cards window with a list of operations for which instructions are available. Based on the item you select, Access displays a screen with additional information on the selected operation and in most cases offers further choices or asks additional questions. Your responses to these questions determine the path you take through the Cue Cards screens. If you ask for help with a particular task but are not poised to begin that task immediately, Access displays a screen titled "Before You Begin" to notify you of the potential problem. For example, if you request help on table operations before opening a database, Access displays a Cue Card that reminds you, "You don't have a database open" and offers to provide instructions on opening a database (or allows you to continue reading the Cue Cards without first opening a database).

Figure 2.25

The list of Cue Cards topics

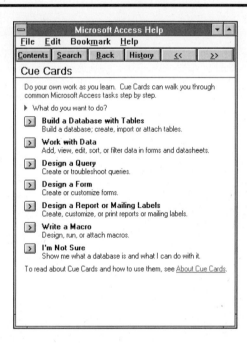

Like the Help window, the Cue Cards window also includes command buttons to help you navigate through the network of available instruction screens. The buttons are used as follows:

Command Button	Action
Menu	Goes directly to the initial Cue Cards screen
Search	Opens the Search dialog box so you can look for a topic by keyword
Back	Returns to the last Cue Cards screen displayed

When there are additional Cue Cards screens on the same topic, a Next button appears in the lower-right corner of the Cue Cards window, and you can use this button to move to the next screen. Figure 2.26 illustrates a typical Cue Cards screen. To reach this screen, use the following series of steps:

1. Choose Cue Cards from the Help menu to display the list of Cue Cards topics.

2. Select the first topic shown in Figure 2.25, Build a Database with Tables.

3. From the list of topics in the Cue Cards window, select Create or open a table.

4. Select the third option, Open an existing table to enter, edit, or view data.

Figure 2.26

A Cue Cards screen

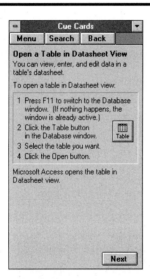

Summary

This chapter introduced the Access user interface and working environment, including the menu system, the help system, and the Database window that will serve as your base of operations for most of your work with Access. If you have used other Windows software, you will find the environment familiar, although you have already seen features unique to Access, some small—like the command buttons in the tool bar—and some large—like the Database window and Cue Cards. For those new to Windows, this chapter was in equal measure an introduction to Windows software in general and to Access in particular. If this is the case, don't worry about trying to distinguish the two—one of the benefits of Windows is the relative uniformity of the user interface across the entire spectrum of applications software, and when you acquire your *next* Windows program, you won't be starting from scratch—much of what you have learned about Access applies to *all* Windows software.

The aim of this chapter was to give you a feel for Access and to introduce the essential user interface concepts that will underlie all of your work with the program. If some of the concepts touched on lightly in this chapter are unfamiliar—if you are not sure of the difference between a form and a report, or you have never recorded a macro or written a module—don't be concerned. All of these subjects are defined and described in detail later in this book. For now, concentrate on learning your way around the Access environment, trying out different arrangements for the windows on the "desktop," and feeling comfortable using both keyboard and mouse commands to operate the menus and manipulate objects. This basic familiarity with the Access user interface will serve you well when you read Chapter 3, which describes how to apply the database design concepts outlined in Chapter 1 to creating the tables required by your application.

3

Designing and Creating a Database

C HAPTER 1 DESCRIBED A BASIC METHOD FOR ANALYZING A DATABASE application and outlining the functional requirements. Armed with the samples, lists, and sketches gathered during the analysis phase, you can proceed to define the structures of the tables that will store the data. You might visualize this step as roughly analogous to designing a set of paper input forms for a manual record-keeping system—you must identify all the data items, give them names, and decide their approximate lengths, although you need not be concerned at this stage with the layout or appearance of the data entry screens. Unless your application is very simple, it is a good idea to sketch out on paper the structures of the tables and the relationships among them before you sit down at the keyboard to create the tables. Even if you have worked with other database programs, a little advance planning on paper will save you time in the long run, because the table structures will require fewer modifications later in the development process.

As noted in Chapter 1, database design is a complex subject that has filled many entire books, but you do not have to know a great deal about theory to build a good application. A few simple principles derived from relational database theory, coupled with a healthy measure of common sense, should guide you toward a sound design. This chapter outlines a practical method for laying out the table structures and illustrates this method with a detailed analysis of the ACE system. If you are already working on an Access application, you can begin to apply these principles to your system, but read the whole chapter before you begin to make sure you have a good grasp of all the terms and concepts. If you are a beginner working on a complex application and the design process seems intimidating, you can take some consolation from the fact that once you have figured out how to structure the tables, creating them is easy.

Laying Out the Database

Based on your lists of functional entities and the individual data items that describe them (which you collected during the system analysis), you can lay out the tables that will make up your Access database and diagram the relationships among them. An Access database can contain up to 32,768 tables, and you can in theory work with up to 254 tables at once. However, a query can only contain 16 tables, and queries (which are described in Chapter 5) are the most powerful and versatile tool that Access provides for viewing data from more than one table at a time. Nevertheless, even this limit is unlikely to prove constraining in the average business application.

If you have little experience with database design, you may have trouble visualizing how each entity in your present system (or your projected new system) corresponds to an Access table. Often, the way you view the components of your manual system hinders your ability to discern all the necessary tables.

For example, as noted in Chapter 1, if you were designing an order-tracking database, you might be accustomed to thinking of an order as a single entity, but in an efficient database design, the information printed on an order or invoice would be drawn from at least four tables: the Customer, Order, Line Item, and Inventory tables. In the ACE system, the most important entities are easier to identify—names (donors, members, prospects, and so on), contacts, financial transactions, and committees.

As you begin laying out the tables, keep in mind the overall goals for the database design:

- To accommodate all the required items of information

- To carry out all the required calculations and processing operations

- To produce all the required reports, lists, and summary displays

- To achieve the best performance possible, given your hardware configuration

- To optimize use of hard-disk space

- To maximize the accuracy, integrity, and consistency of the data

- To provide flexibility for future modifications and enhancements

One good way to organize the database design process is to compile a set of table design worksheets, using a separate sheet of paper for each prospective table. This method enables you to spread out all the worksheets on a table to view the entire system at once or place two similar tables side by side to compare the structures. If you need to start over with one table, you can throw away its worksheet without having to rewrite information about any other tables. To build the worksheets, you can proceed systematically through the sample input and output forms gathered during the analysis phase, together with your additional notes and wish lists, and add fields to the various table structures in any convenient order.

When you actually set up the tables in Access, you must assign each field a name and a data type; if you wish, you can also assign a maximum length (for some field types) and choose a display format. As you read the guidelines presented later in this chapter, you may want to add these details to the table design worksheets. If your application is simple and you have a good grasp of the design, you may be able to write down many of the fields in most of the tables right away, complete with names, lengths, data types, and special formats. If you are less sure of yourself, begin with the tables that you understand best and confine your initial efforts to a bare-bones field list; you can return later to fill in the details and add the more problematic items.

You need not be overly concerned at first about the eventual order of the fields in the tables; when the worksheets are complete, you can go back and number the fields for reference, or you can simply rearrange the fields as you create the tables in Access. Do give some thought to the field order before you set up the tables, because in most contexts, the sequence of the fields in the table structure serves as the default display order. You have complete freedom to rearrange fields in datasheets, forms, and reports, but this process can be tedious in a large table, and placing the fields in approximately the order you use them most often will save you considerable time. Furthermore, the order of the field names in most of the field lists that Access displays matches their sequence in the table structure (a few of the field lists are alphabetical). But don't spend too much time agonizing over the optimum order—you can later move fields around in the structure without losing any data that you have already entered.

The preliminary design worksheets for the main tables in the ACE system are illustrated later in this chapter in the sections that detail the structures of these tables (in Figures 3.3, 3.4, 3.5, and 3.6).

Optimizing the Table Structures

If you are undecided as to where a given item of information belongs, think about which entity it describes most directly. For example, in the manual system in use at the Association for a Clean Earth, the transaction journals include the full name of the person who made the transaction, and the committee rosters include the names, addresses, and telephone numbers of the members. In the Committees or Transactions table, the pertinent item of information is *who the person is*, and these tables need an account number or ID code that identifies the person. However, a name and address describe a *person*, not a transaction or committee, so these fields belong in the Names table.

Because Access allows you to work with multiple tables simultaneously, you can avoid redundancy by eliminating from any table most items of information that you could look up in another. Storing each person's name and address once—in the Names table rather than in each transaction, contact, and committee record—saves disk space and more importantly, prevents inconsistencies. If you included this information in every transaction record, it would be all too easy to enter the same name or address slightly differently or to forget to correct the address in the Names table after entering a new address into a transaction. To print the name and address on a transaction or committee list, you can look it up in the Names table record, using methods described in Chapter 8.

You can also avoid redundancy, improve consistency, and keep your main tables smaller by using short code fields for items that can only assume a finite number of values. For example, in a financial transactions table, you could use a one- or two-character code that identifies the type of transaction—I for invoice, P for payment, D for Debit, C for Credit, A for Adjustment, and so on. For every code field, you can create another table that serves as a lookup table, or reference list of all the possible code values, together with longer text descriptions. These lookup tables play several important roles in a database—you can use them to validate entries in the code fields in the main tables, display lists of allowable code values so you can pick a value rather than typing it, or print the description in addition to or instead of the code itself. The ACE system includes lookup tables for area codes, state abbreviations, committee codes, name type codes, contact and transaction type codes, and keywords.

NOTE. *The term* lookup table *describes the context in which a table is used—the table itself has no special attributes that differentiate it from any other table. For example, the central table in the ACE system—the Names table—functions as a lookup table when you are viewing or printing contact or transaction data.*

In most cases, you do not need fields for any items of information that you could calculate based on other fields in the same table or in other tables. For example, in the ACE system and in most accounting applications, you could compute a person's transaction balance by subtracting the total credits from the total debits, and you could calculate the total debits and total credits based on the matching Transactions table records. However, you may occasionally want to include a few such fields to gain the convenience of having instant access to the totals without opening multiple tables. The structure of the ACE Names table was designed to illustrate both methods; it includes fields for the lifetime total debits and credits, but not for the year-to-date totals, which are computed as needed based on the Transactions table.

An Access table can contain up to 255 fields; if one of the entities in your application requires more than 255 items of information, you can create two or more tables and link them using a query. Access makes efficient use of disk space by storing text in *variable-length* fields that occupy only as much disk space as is required to accommodate your entries. For example, if you enter "Joe Johnson" into a name field, the name takes up only 11 characters of storage space, regardless of the maximum length you specified for the field (the default is 50 characters). One implication of this scheme is that you incur no space or performance penalties for adding fields to a table that are rarely filled in. In the ACE system, you can include in the Names table the fields that are required for everyone on the list (the name and address), as well as the additional information entered for members, donors, board members, and media contacts; in prospect records, which make up 75 percent of the list, you can simply leave these fields blank.

This general rule *does not* apply to multiple sets of identical fields. For example, an ACE member is not likely to serve on more than two committees at once, so you might consider adding two sets of committee fields (the committee ID, date joined, date quit, and so on) to the Names table. However, there are several compelling reasons to create a separate table for the committees. First of all, rules that seem inviolate today are often broken tomorrow. With the committee data stored in the Names table, an ACE member who joined three or four committees would force you to restructure the table and edit every query, form, and report that includes committee data. Furthermore, putting multiple sets of committee fields in the Names table complicates inquiries and reports that focus on the *committee* rather than the *person*, such as the rosters that list all current members of each committee. In general, when the relationship between two types of entities could be described as "one-to-many" (even if the reality is closer to "a few" than "many"), you should create separate tables for the two entities. Thus, because each person might be on several committees, the ACE committee membership data merits its own table.

When you think the table structures are complete, spread out all your worksheets side by side and look them over one last time to make sure that you have not omitted any essential items or included unnecessary fields. Looking at all the table structures together will also help you detect common errors and inconsistencies. In particular, make sure that you have provided a field or fields that enable you to match up corresponding records in the various tables. In the ACE system, the ID Code field serves this purpose for all the main tables. When the same field occurs in more than one table or when two tables contain fields that serve the same general purpose, it is expedient but not necessary to give the fields the same names and data types, (and often, the same lengths and default formats).

Defining the Table Relationships

Implicit in the design process described in the preceding section is defining the relationships among the tables and ensuring that the tables contain the fields necessary to support these relationships. The simplest type of relationship is *one-to-one*—for each record in one table, there is no more than one record in the other.

Creating two tables with a one-to-one relationship is an efficient way to store a large amount of information about a single business entity. You may be forced to use two tables to overcome the limit of 255 fields per table, which might be constraining in a complex personnel or inventory system, but it may be advantageous to do so even when it is not strictly necessary. For example, in the ACE system, you might consider using two tables to store the mailing list data: one that includes just the name and address fields required for everyone on the list, and another for the additional information not required for prospects. You might view the table that stores the supplementary data as an extension or addendum to the name and address table, because you would rarely use it by itself. In contrast, you could use the name and address table alone for operations such as printing mailing labels.

Structuring the database this way results in somewhat faster access in contexts that do not require opening the supplementary table, but it complicates many other operations by forcing you to deal with two related tables rather than one. The ACE system uses one table—the Names table—and demonstrates a variety of techniques for helping you avoid entering data in the fields not required in prospect records. Because Access uses variable-length fields, this strategy does not waste disk space.

Equally common and somewhat more difficult to manage are *one-to-many* relationships, in which a record in one table may have more than one matching record in the other. In the ACE system, the Names table has one-to-many relationships with the Contacts, Transactions, and Committees tables. The table that has the "one" record is often referred to as the *master* or *parent* table, and the table with the "many" records may be called the *transaction*, *detail*, or *child* table. This type of relationship might more accurately be described as "one-to-any number" because it means that there *might* be many records in the child file for a given parent record, not that there *must* be. For example, in the ACE system, a person might belong to one committee, several, or none at all. Also note that from the "point of view" of the child table, the relationship is one-to-one—for each Contacts table record, there is always one and only one matching Names table record. The Access documentation uses the term "many-to-one" to describe this point of view.

Finally, the most complex type of relationship is *many-to-many*—for each record in either table, there may be any number of records in the other. In the ACE system, the Names table has a many-to-many relationship with the reference tables that store the possible values in code fields, such as the States table and the Committee Names table (which stores the list of committee ID codes and descriptions). Consider the logical relationship between people and committees: A person might be on more than one committee, and a committee might have (in fact, usually has) more than one member. When two tables have a many-to-many relationship, there may not be one "point of view" that dominates. For example, in the ACE system, you might just as often want to see a list of names that includes each person's committee memberships as a list of committees that includes the names and addresses of the members.

When two tables have a many-to-many relationship, you must link them by creating a third table, which has a one-to-many relationship with each of the other two. For example, in the ACE system, the Committees table stores the committee membership data that describes the relationship between the Names and Committee Names tables. For every record in the Committees table, there can be many records in each of the other two tables. When you display or print committee membership data, you will often work with all three tables, deriving the fundamental data from the Committees table and additional descriptive information from the other two.

If you plan to use two tables together, you must ensure that there is some field or combination of fields that defines what constitutes matching records. In the ACE system, each of the four main tables has an ID Code field that identifies the person, and each lookup table has a field that matches the code field in the main table. Figure 3.1 diagrams the relationships among the ACE system tables. The one-to-many relationships between the Names table and the Contacts, Committees, and Transactions tables are represented by double-headed arrows, and the many-to-one relationships with the lookup tables are drawn as single-headed arrows. For the sake of simplicity, the many-to-many relationships, usually denoted by double double-headed arrows, are omitted from this diagram.

Note. Chapter 8 introduces a variety of methods for working with multiple tables and preserving the logical relationships between them.

Figure 3.1

The relationships among the ACE tables

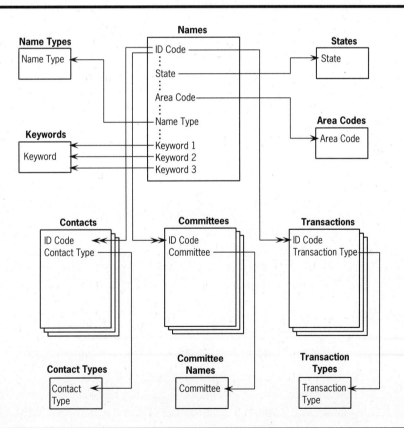

Many applications have two or more levels of one-to-many relationships. For example, in an order-tracking system, the relationships between the customer table and invoice table and between the invoice table and line items table are both one-to-many. The customer and invoice tables are linked by an account number or ID code field, so that you can find the orders placed by a given customer or print the customer's name and address on an invoice. The invoice and line item tables are linked by the invoice number, and the line item table is usually linked to an inventory table in a one-to-one relationship. This model is diagrammed in Figure 3.2. Note that the line item records need not include the customer ID code—the line items are linked to the matching invoice record, which in turn is linked to the customer. However, including the ID code in the line items table would enable you to study customers' ordering patterns based on just two tables—customers and line items—without looking at the order table, which contributes no useful information to the analysis.

Figure 3.2

The table relationships in an order-tracking application

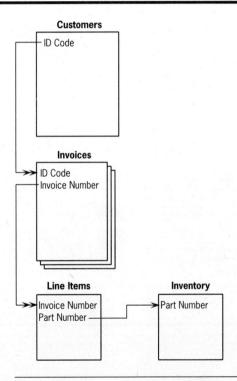

For each pair of related tables, the linking fields must have the same data type, and they should usually have the same length, although Access requires this only for numeric fields. They need not have the same name, but if they do, Access can usually deduce the relationship between the tables, so you do not have to define this relationship explicitly. Of course, this may not be possible; for example, the Names table has three fields for keywords (named Keyword 1, Keyword 2, and Keyword 3), all of which match the Keyword field in the Keywords lookup table. Obviously, you must also enter the same values into the linking field(s) in records that you intend Access to treat as a matching set.

Describing the Fields

Once you have decided which information belongs in each table, you must translate these specifications, which may be rather informal, to a list of fields. In general, each discrete type of information that you may need to deal with separately should be placed in a separate field. To identify all the required fields, you may have to make a concerted effort to avoid being prejudiced by the ways you are accustomed to looking at the information in your manual system.

For example, in a mailing list application you might view an address as a unit, because the component parts—the company name, street address, city, state, and zip code—are invariably printed together on reports, labels, and letters. Access allows you to enter *hard returns* (line breaks) in Text fields, so you could use one field to store a complete address. If you always display and print the address as a unit, using one field is easy and convenient—no special measures are required to handle addresses of different lengths and formats (such as non-U.S. addresses). However, using a single field makes operations on the component parts difficult or impossible without programming—you cannot easily identify records in which the company name is blank; select records by state (for example, to send a mailing to everyone in California three weeks before a local election); or sort a mailing by zip code. In the ACE system, the Names table has one field for the street address (which might include more than one line), and separate fields for the name, company name, city, state, and zip code.

Names can be even more problematic. Based on the foregoing discussion, your first impulse might be to create separate fields for the title (Mr., Ms., Dr., and so on), first name, and last name (and possibly a middle initial). This scheme allows you to construct a salutation based on the title and last name, and it readily handles operations such as searching for people by last name or printing reports in alphabetical order by last name. However, it is not flexible enough to handle the wide variety of names that you will encounter in a typical mailing list. Some names may need a suffix, such as Jr., III, or M.D., instead of or in addition to the prefix title. You might also want to use more formal salutations for some addressees than for others (for example, "Mr. and Mrs. Moore" for a prospect and "Chris" for a board member whom you know personally). Furthermore, a record in a name and address table might not always correspond to one person—it might represent a family, a husband and wife with the same last name, a couple with different last names, three business partners or roommates, or even a job title at a company, such as Public Relations Director (whoever may hold this position at a given time). Finally, in any name and address list, the name is the logical choice for a unique identifier for the record, but a large list will contain many duplicate names.

One very general solution, which is demonstrated in the ACE system, is to use three fields to satisfy all these requirements. A short alphanumeric ID code based on the name serves as the unique record identifier, and separate fields store the name and salutation, entered exactly as you would want to print them on a label or letter. You can base the ID code on either the name or company name so it is easy to remember (or guess), and use one or two tie-breaker digits to distinguish between people with the same name or company name. This strategy is described in more detail later in this chapter in the section that explains the structure of the Names table.

Assigning Index Key Fields

Indexes play a central role in every Access database. An index is an auxiliary database component that stores information from one or more fields in a table, which are called the *keys*, *key fields*, or *index keys*. You can define indexes when you create a table or at any time afterward. Access uses indexes to speed up operations that involve sorting (rearranging) and searching for records (one by one or in groups) based on the key fields. Specific examples of how you can use indexes to expedite or optimize an operation are presented throughout this book, starting with Chapter 5, but keep in mind as you set up your table structures that Access uses indexes for all of the following purposes:

- To speed up the process of displaying records in a sequence other than the order in which they were entered

- To speed up searches for individual records based on unique (or nearly unique) values in the key fields

- To speed up queries that select records based on the contents of the key fields

- To support the relationships between tables

- To prevent the entry of records with duplicate index keys

- To determine the default record display order

You can build as many indexes based on single fields as you wish, and a table can also have up to five indexes based on more than one field. In a complex application, the latter limit may prove constraining, and it may take careful thought to decide which of a dozen or so desirable indexes you should build. In the ACE system, you could use indexes based on the ID Code and Zip fields to print the Names table in alphabetical or zip code order. Another index based on the combination of state, city, and ID code allows you to display or print names grouped by state, within each state by city, and within each city, alphabetically by ID code.

For any index, you can request that Access prohibit duplicate key values. You can use this property to guarantee that the field or combination of fields that you use as the unique record identifier in a table—an ID code, Social Security number, invoice number, medical record number, or check number—is in fact unique in each record. For most indexes, including the zip and state/city/ID code examples cited earlier, this property is obviously inappropriate. The ability to prohibit duplicates based on a particular combination of fields is tied to indexes because without indexes, searching for potential duplicates would not be fast enough to be practical. For example, if Access had to read each record in a 25,000-record table to determine whether the ID code was unique, rather than carrying out a very fast search based on an index, data entry would slow down intolerably.

These general guidelines should suggest at least some of the indexes you will want for each table. Keep in mind also that each index increases the size of the .MDB file, and that creating too many indexes slows data entry, because Access must update each index whenever you add or delete records or edit the index key fields. When your databases are very large, you will have to weigh the trade-off between faster data entry and faster querying and reporting to arrive at the optimum number of indexes for each table. Only experience can tell you where to draw the line, but Access allows you to add or remove indexes at any time. When you set up your first few databases, you need not feel pressured to choose all the right indexes (or for that matter, any indexes) at the outset.

Choosing the Primary Key

For most tables, you should create at least one special index that identifies the *primary key*. The primary key serves two main purposes: It determines the default display order when you view records in Datasheet view or Form view, and it serves as a unique record identifier. Access automatically builds an index based on the primary key, which can consist of one or more fields, and assigns to this index the property that prohibits duplicate key entries. Often, it is immediately apparent which field or fields should make up a table's primary key, because your present record-keeping system may also require a unique identifier for the corresponding entity, such as a Social Security number, order number, ID code, part number, general ledger account, or medical record number.

Note that the primary key might not be the most *convenient* record identifier, and it may play a much smaller role in your Access database than in the system this database replaces. For example, a hospital's patient record-keeping system might use a medical record number as the unique patient identifier, and to maintain compatibility with the existing system or with a larger application running on a mainframe, you may have no choice but to include the medical record number in your patient table. However, no one can force you to search for records based on a unique identifier consisting of a long string of digits that are difficult to type and impossible to remember. Instead, you could build an index for the patient table based on the combination of last name and first name or on an alphanumeric ID code like the one used in the ACE system, and use this key for searches. If several patients had the same names, you could find the one you want by examining other data in the record (including the medical record number). In contexts where a unique identifier is absolutely required, such as posting payments, you could fall back on the medical record number.

If there is no obvious candidate for a primary key, it may be that the table does not really need a unique record identifier. In the ACE system, you might never use the Contacts table in a context that requires retrieving a specific contact record—most of the time, you will view contacts in groups, not individually. Even a combination such as the ID code, contact date, and type of contact is not guaranteed to be unique—a donor could conceivably have multiple contacts of the same type (perhaps phone calls) on the same day.

Relational database theory stipulates that every table *must* have a primary key. You can always create a unique key by adding a *tie-breaker* field to number the records that share the same values in the other components of the key. Access also supports a data type called Counter, which creates a sequential number that is automatically incremented in each new record, and you can use this type of field as the entire primary key (Counter fields are described in more detail later in this chapter). If you object to both of these solutions, Access allows you to break the rules and create a table that has no primary key. However, there are significant advantages to defining one:

- It supports very fast searches for individual records.

- It ensures that by default the record display sequence is based on a meaningful combination of fields, not on the order in which the records were entered.

- It enables you to define default relationships between tables, so that in many situations, you need not specify the links explicitly.

- It enables you to update records (not just view the data) when you work with queries based on more than one table.

If you want to define default relationships between tables that have a one-to-many relationship, such as the ACE Names and Contacts, Transactions, and Committees tables, you *must* define a primary key for the parent table. Indeed, it would make little sense *not* to do so. Without a unique identifier in the parent table, there would be no way for Access (or you, for that matter) to determine which child records belong to a given parent record. The ability to quickly and unequivocally find the matching records in two tables is essential for procedures such as printing multitable reports, calculating transaction totals, or posting transaction amounts to the year-to-date total fields. You must also assign a primary key if you plan to establish relationships in which Access enforces *referential integrity*—that is, prevents you from adding a child record that has no match in the parent table (such as a transaction or contact for a person not yet entered into the Names table) and prohibits the deletion of a parent record that has related child records (for example, a record in the Names table that has matching contact or transaction records).

When you link two tables based on the parent table's primary key, the corresponding field (or fields) in the related table is called a *foreign key*. In most cases, the foreign key is *not* the primary key for the related table. For example, the relationship between the Names and Transaction tables is based on the ID Code field, which is the primary key for the Names table, but which is not unique for each record in the Transactions table. These concepts are explored in more depth in Chapter 8, which introduces a variety of methods for working with multiple tables.

Assigning Names

In Access, a single set of rules governs the allowable names for all objects except databases, including tables, fields, forms, reports, and macros. The name of a database cannot exceed eight characters because Access uses it as the first name of the disk file that houses the database (the extension is .MDB). Most other names in Access can be up to 64 characters long and can contain any combination of letters, digits, spaces, and most punctuation marks; only the symbols used in references to objects in expressions are prohibited—the period (.), exclamation mark (!), and square brackets ([and]). Also note that you cannot use a space or a control character as the first character of a name, but it is generally inadvisable to use control characters at all in Access names. (Control characters, the nonprintable characters with ASCII codes between 0 and 31, are commonly used as commands to control hardware devices such as printers.)

Access uses object names as the default prompts and titles in data entry forms and reports, and naming objects strategically will save you a great deal of time you might otherwise spend editing these names. When Access displays or uses names (for example, in field lists, in the lists of database objects displayed in the Database window, or in field prompts on forms), they appear in the same mixture of uppercase and lowercase that you used when you assigned them. However, references to fields in calculations (such as a computation of a balance as the difference between the total debits and total credits) are *not* case-sensitive—you can type the names in any combination of upper- and lowercase.

The fact that Access supports long names that include spaces enables you to assign very readable names that clearly identify the objects they describe. For example, most people would consider field names such as Zip Code or Area Code clearer and more presentable than ZIPCODE or AREACODE. Because Access nearly always allows you to choose object names from lists rather than typing them, there are few disadvantages to using long names. However, you might consider limiting the length of names that you will use often in calculations, if only to make the expressions that define these calculations shorter and easier to read. In particular, you might want to keep table names short. For example, in the ACE system, the table that stores the mailing list data is called Names, not Names and Addresses.

Using the same name for closely related objects will help you remember the relationships among all the objects in an application. If you use the same field for the same purpose in several tables—such as the ID Code field found in all of the ACE system tables—give the field the same name in each table. This strategy does not lead to ambiguity when you work with multiple related tables, because you can (and often must) include the table name in references to fields in linked tables. Using the same names for corresponding fields in different tables also enables you to use some of the same forms and reports for tables with similar structures. For example, you could define a generic report to print mailing labels from any table, including the ACE Names table, that has fields called Name, Company, Address, City, State, and Zip.

Choosing Data Types

When you define a table, you must specify a *data type* for each field. The data type determines what kind of information Access allows you to enter into the field, the amount of storage space it occupies, the automatic formatting and validation rules applied when you enter data, and the types of operations permitted on the field. Access supports eight data types, listed in Table 3.1 in the order they appear in the combo box you use to specify the data type when you define a table.

A good rule of thumb is to use Text fields, which can accommodate any characters, for data that does not require the special features of any of the other data types. Obviously, fields such as names and addresses should be Text fields, and prices should be Currency or Number fields. If you are not sure which data type to use, think about whether a field requires any of the

---

Table 3.1   **Access Data Types**

Data Type	Contents and Use
Text	Text fields accept all characters that you can generate from the keyboard, including letters, digits, punctuation marks, graphics symbols, foreign language characters, and line- and box-drawing characters. Text fields can be up to 255 characters long and occupy only the space required to store the data you enter.
Memo	Memo fields accept all characters that you can generate from the keyboard, including letters, digits, punctuation marks, graphics symbols, foreign language characters, and line- and box-drawing characters. Memo fields can be up to 32,000 characters long and occupy only the space required to store the data you enter.
Number	Number fields accept only digits and an optional decimal point and/or minus sign. There are five types of Number fields: *Byte* Byte fields accept the positive integers (whole numbers) from 0 to 255, which can be stored in a single byte (character) of disk space. *Integer* Integer fields store whole numbers in the range −32,768 to 32,767 (−32k to 32k), and occupy 2 bytes of storage space. *Long Integer* Integer fields store whole numbers in the range −2,147,483,678 to 2,147,483,647 (−2,000 Mb to 2,000Mb), and occupy 4 bytes of storage space. *Single* Single fields store *single-precision* numeric values in the range −3.4 × 10^38 to 3.4 × 10^38, with up to 7 significant digits. They occupy 4 bytes of storage space.* *Double* Double fields store *double-precision* numeric values in the range −1.797 × 10^308 to 1.797 × 10^308, with up to 15 significant digits, and occupy 8 bytes of storage space.
Date/Time	Date/Time fields represent calendar dates or times and accept only valid date and time entries, entered in a variety of display formats. Date/Time fields always occupy 8 bytes (characters) of storage space.
Currency	Currency fields store double-precision numbers that represent monetary quantities. Access displays currency fields with embedded separators, a decimal point, and a leading or trailing currency symbol. Currency fields always occupy 8 bytes (characters) of storage space.
Counter	Counter fields store Long Integer values that are incremented automatically by Access for each new record you add to a table, so that each record has a unique sequential number in the field. Counter fields always occupy 4 bytes of storage space.
Yes/No	Yes/No fields accept only logical values, which can be expressed as Yes and No, True and False, On and Off, or −1 and 0. Yes/No fields always occupy 1 bit ($^1/_8$ of one byte, or character) of storage space.
OLE Object	OLE object fields store noncharacter data usually created by other software, such as graphics, sound recordings, photographs, video images, or spreadsheets.

---

* In scientific notation, 10^38 means 10 raised to the 38th power, or 1 followed by 38 zeros. Access, and most other software, expresses large numbers using exponential notation, in which 3.4 × 10^38 is written as 3.4E+38.

automatic formatting and validation that Access carries out on data types other than Text or Memo. Also consider whether you need to carry out specialized calculations such as date arithmetic. If you can't decide, Text is usually a safe choice, especially in light of the fact that you will usually be able to change the data type later without losing data you have already entered into the table. (Chapter 14 describes the factors you should take into account when you modify the structure of a table that contains data.)

You should choose one of the numeric data types (Number, Currency, or Counter) for any field that you intend to use in mathematical computations such as addition or multiplication, or in the calculation of statistics such as sums or averages. For whole numbers (numbers with no fractional portion), you can use the Byte, Integer, or Long Integer data types, and for numeric values that must include decimal places, either the Single or Double data types. To conserve storage space, it is best to choose the smallest data type that will accommodate the range of values you anticipate. For example, you could use a Byte field for test scores that always lie between 0 and 100, and Single is adequate for many numeric values encountered in business applications. If you suspect you might need more than seven significant digits, use a Double field instead.

NOTE. *The term* significant *refers to the number of digits used in calculations, regardless of their position relative to the decimal point. Thus, the numbers 1,000,000, 10,000.25, and 100.1111 all have seven significant digits, although they represent quantities of very different magnitudes.*

The Currency data type is a specialized numeric data type equivalent to a Double number. Access automatically formats Currency fields with punctuation based on the International Settings established through the Windows Control Panel. In the United States, Currency fields have a leading dollar sign, commas every three digits, and two decimal places; negative values are enclosed in parentheses. You can customize these settings—for *all* of your Windows programs—through the Control Panel, and you can define custom formats for individual fields within Access. If you find the repeated currency symbols distracting in the Datasheet view and in columnar reports, use the Single or Double data type for monetary values.

The Counter data type is a specialized numeric data type designed for fields, such as invoice numbers or check numbers, that should contain sequential values. You cannot enter a value yourself into a Counter field—in each new record you add, Access automatically updates the Counter fields, entering a value one greater than the number in the previous record. You can also use a Counter field as the primary key for a table if there is no meaningful unique identifier. One potential problem with Counter fields is the fact that Access always begins the numbering sequence with 1.

If you do not need to do arithmetic on a field that consists solely of numeric digits, it may be better to store the data in a text field. Any field that requires embedded punctuation not permitted in Number fields *must* be a Text field. Typical examples include telephone numbers, Social Security numbers, and nine-digit zip codes, all of which include dashes. You must also use the Text data type for any field that might have a leading zero, such as a part number, check number, or five-digit zip code, because in a true number, leading zeroes are meaningless, and Access strips them out. Thus, the zip code 02140 entered into a numeric field would be stored and displayed as 2140 (and mail addressed this way would most likely be returned by the post office). The Text data type is also preferable if you need to specify the maximum length of the field, which is more difficult with Number fields. For example, you might choose the Text data type for an area code to restrict entries in the field to three digits.

In contrast, the Number data types are preferable if you need to sort (rearrange) records based on a field, because Access uses the true numeric values to determine the order. In contrast, Text fields are sorted by alphabetizing, which Access does one character at a time, starting at the beginning of the field, just as you would. Thus, a Text field that contains the characters "100" would fall earlier in the sequence than "21" because 1 alphabetizes before 2, just as any word that starts with the letter A comes before any word that starts with the letter B in alphabetical order, regardless of the second letter. When you store numbers in a Text field, the only way to guarantee correct numerical order is to ensure that all the entries in the field are the same length (by adding leading zeroes if necessary—that is, you would have to enter 21 as 021 and 2 as 002 (assuming that the maximum field width is 3). If this is unacceptable to you (and to others who will also enter data), you must use a Number field instead.

You should nearly always use the Date/Time data type for entering dates or times to take advantage of the special formatting, validation, and *date arithmetic* possible with this data type. Access validates Date/Time fields to prevent you from inadvertently entering impossible dates such as 13/22/93 or 2/29/94 (1994 is not a leap year). It supports all the standard Windows date and time display formats, as well as several others, and it allows you to define custom formats for special requirements such as displaying just the month and year in a format like 2/94 for February 1994.

Regardless of the display format, Access can always arrange records in true chronological order based on a date or time, and it can compare two dates or times to determine which is earlier or later. You can subtract two dates or times to obtain the elapsed time (expressed in days), and you can add or subtract a given number of days from a date to obtain another valid date a specified number of days in the future or past. In contrast, if you were to store a date in a Text field, you would have to rearrange it into year/month/day order to carry out date comparisons or to arrange records in chronological order. As noted earlier, Access alphabetizes Text fields one character at a time, starting with the first character, so "alphabetizing" dates entered into a Text field in the popular MM/DD/YY format would result in placing all the dates in January before any dates in February, regardless of the year.

Yes/No fields were designed to store the answers to yes-or-no questions, and Access accepts only the values "yes," "no," "true," "false," "on," and "off" (in any mixture of upper- and lowercase) in a Yes/No field. If you wish, you can format Yes/No fields to display data as "Yes" or "No," "True" or "False," or "On" or "Off." On data entry forms, you can use check boxes (described in Chapter 6) as an even more graphical representation. Using a Yes/No field makes it much less likely that you will accidentally enter the wrong value than if you used a Text field to store the same information.

Memo fields are useful for storing text passages that are too long to fit within the 255-character limit on text fields. You can store up to 32,000 characters of text in a Memo field, and you can use as many memos as you wish in a table structure. However, you cannot base an index on a Memo field, and performance is somewhat slower. For relatively short notes that would fit comfortably in a Text field, the Text data type is preferable.

The OLE Object data type is used for objects created by other programs that are more complex than the text, dates, or numbers handled by the other Access data types. For example, you might want to add a picture of a person to a name and address database, or embed a spreadsheet created in Microsoft Excel or Quattro Pro for Windows in an estimating database to calculate a numeric value. Handling OLE objects can be complicated and requires some understanding of the objects themselves and the programs used to create them, as well as the mechanisms for mediating the communication between Access and these programs. OLE objects are introduced in Chapter 15.

Assigning Field Widths

As noted earlier in this chapter, Number, Currency, Counter, Date/Time, and Yes/No fields are always fixed in length, and they occupy the same amount of space whether or not you enter any data. For Text fields, Access assumes a maximum length of 50 characters, but you can change this to any number between 1 and 255. Because Text and Memo fields expand dynamically to fill only the space required for the characters you enter, retaining the default length of 50 characters—or even increasing the maximum length—does not waste disk space, but you may want to restrict the field size to conform to the allowable range of values in your application. For example, you might specify a length of 10 for a zip code or 3 for an area code, and you could limit a field provided for notes or comments to 100 characters to restrain the more verbose members of your data entry staff.

It may not be easy to predict in advance the best length for a text field, and in fact, it is not necessary to do so. You can modify the structure of a table later to adjust the field lengths; enlarging a Text field has no effect on data already entered, and if you shorten a field, Access simply truncates the contents to fit. Note, however, that if you have already designed many forms and reports, quite a bit of editing may be required to widen the regions allocated for fields you have lengthened and move adjacent fields to avoid overlapping. Also, if you shorten fields in a large table, you may have to spend considerable time editing the truncated fields afterward to make the truncated entries more presentable.

The ACE System Tables

The sample system used as a case study in this book has four main entities—names, contacts, transactions, and committees—and uses four corresponding tables to store information about these entities. Matching records in all these tables are identified by an ID Code field, which serves as the primary key for the Names table.

The application also includes the small *lookup tables* mentioned earlier in this chapter, which serve as reference lists of all the legitimate values in the various code fields. Each lookup table has two Text fields, one for the code and one for the longer description. In all cases except the Keywords table, the name of the Code field matches that of the corresponding field in the main table; most of the description fields are named Description. As noted earlier, the reference tables are used to validate entries in the code fields to construct lists of allowable entries and to print or display descriptions instead of or in addition to the more cryptic codes. You might want to examine these tables at your leisure; they are introduced in Chapter 8 and used throughout Part II and Part III of this book.

The Names Table

As noted earlier, the central entity in the ACE system—an entry in the mailing list—might be referred to as a "person" or a "name," although a record in the Names table does not necessarily represent just one human being. The Names table stores the basic name and address information that is maintained for every name—prospects, donors, board members, political supporters, media contacts, and others—as well as the more detailed data maintained for all but prospects. Figure 3.3 illustrates a typical table design worksheet for the Names table created by someone who had little prior experience with database design.

The meanings of the fields that make up the address and telephone number should be evident. In accordance with the guidelines presented earlier, the Names table includes separate fields for the full name, entered just as you would print it on a mailing label, and salutation (whatever should follow the word Dear on a personalized letter). Because a name is in fact the most intuitive way to search for a person, the ID Code field is derived from the name—it consists of up to six letters of the last name, the first two letters of the first name, and, if necessary, one or two tie-breaker digits. For example, the first David Smith on the list was assigned the ID code SMITHDA, and the next one SMITHDA01; a third David Smith would be coded SMITHDA02. Beginning the ID code with all or part of the last name also ensures that the default processing order corresponds roughly to alphabetical order. The ID Code field in the ACE system is ten characters long; in a larger table, you could make this field 12 or 15 characters long to avoid generating too many ID codes that would be identical without the tie-breaker. Unless your list is very large, it is not necessary to abide by a rigid set of rules for constructing the ID code, although you may prefer to do so for the sake of consistency. For example, you might include a comma between the portion of the ID code derived from the last name and the beginning of the first name; this scheme would result in the ID code SMITH,DA01 for the second David Smith on the list.

The Name Type field stores a one-character code that identifies the type of record—P for prospect, M for member, D for donor, BD for Board of Directors member, MC for media contact, and so on. The Address Type field stores a similar code used to distinguish between home and work addresses. The Source field contains a short code that identifies the source of the name. In various records, it might refer to the name of an organization from which a mailing list was purchased, the ID code of the person who referred the name, or a code for the event that motivated the person to contact ACE.

The First Contact and Last Contact fields store the dates of ACE's first and last (most recent) contacts with the person. Based on these dates, ACE can periodically purge the Names table to remove people with whom the organization has had no contact for a specified period of time. The Keep Forever field is a Yes/No field used to flag people who should be kept on the list indefinitely, regardless of the last contact date; these people include family and friends, political contacts, and board members. The OK to Send Mail field indicates whether the person should receive mass mailings; ACE can use this field to avoid sending routine solicitations to its major donors, who might resent being badgered for small contributions. The OK to Call field indicates whether a person may be contacted by telephone. The Marker field provides a way to mark certain records that are not easily described by a single expression or global set of selection criteria, so that you can select records individually for special mailings, reports, or calculations.

Figure 3.3

The Names table design worksheet

NAMES TABLE

#	Name	Data type	Length	Format
	~~First Name~~	~~Text~~	~~15~~	
	~~Last Name~~	~~Text~~	~~20~~	
	~~Title~~	~~Text~~	~~10~~	
5	Company	Text	~~50~~ 30	
6	Address	Text	50	
7	City	Text	20	
8	State	Text	2	UPPERCASE
9	Zip	~~Number~~ Text	~~5~~ 10	
12	Telephone	~~Number~~ Text	~~14~~ 8 7	
10	~~Home or work~~ Address type	Text	~~2~~ 1	UPPERCASE
14	First contact	Date		MM/DD/YY
15	Last contact	Date		MM/DD/YY
13	~~Source of referral~~ Source	Text	10	UPPERCASE
16	OK to send mail	yes/no		
17	OK to call	yes/no		
20	Joined	Date		MM/DD/YY
21	Last renewal	Date		MM/DD/YY
28	Notes	Memo		
22	Total debits	Number		
23	Total credits	Number		
	~~YTD debits~~			
	~~YTD credits~~			
	~~Keywords~~	~~Text~~	~~50~~	
24	Last credit	~~Number~~ Date		
18	Keep forever	yes/no		
19	Marker	Text	5	
1	ID code	Text	10	UPPERCASE
~~2~~ 3	Name	Text	30	
4	Salutation	Text	~~75~~ 25	
11	Area code	Text	3	
25	Keyword 1	Text	~~15~~ 10	
26	Keyword 2	Text	~~15~~ 10	
27	Keyword 3	Text	~~15~~ 10	
2	Name type	Text	2	

Notes

Name types:
   M=member
   D=donor
   P=prospect
   BD=Board of Directors
   MC=Media contact
   PC=political contact

Address types:
   H=home
   W=work
   U=unknown

Primary Key: ID Code

ID Code= 6 letters of last name +
   2 letters of first name +
   tie-breaker digits/letters

Indexes: NAME TYPE + ID CODE
   ZIP
   STATE + CITY + ID CODE

The three keyword fields are used to store short codes that ACE uses to categorize people according to their areas of interest. In theory, it would be better to create a separate table for keywords, linked to the Names table by ID Code (much like the Committees table); this strategy would allow you to enter as many keywords as necessary for a given person, and it would facilitate operations such as printing reference lists of all keywords used in the system. However, simple operations carried out much more frequently, such as displaying or printing the keywords associated with a given donor, would be considerably more complicated. In your own applications, if you can reasonably restrict the number of keywords to five or fewer, including them in the record they describe is the most practical, if not theoretically correct, approach. Another way to store keywords, which is the best if you are sure that you only need to use them in record selection criteria, is to create one longer field in which you can enter as many keywords as you wish. Searching for any given keyword within this field is easy, but operations involving single keywords, such as validating your entries by looking them up in a reference table, are much more difficult without programming.

The Total Debits and Total Credits fields accumulate overall lifetime debit and credit totals, and the Last Credit field stores the date of the most recent credit transaction. The field names are intentionally nonspecific to accommodate a variety of transaction types; in your own applications, you might want to use field names such as Total Purchases, Total Payments, Total Donations, and so on. In theory, these totals need not (and should not) be stored in the Names table, because you can calculate them by summing the amounts stored in the Transactions table. In practice, however, storing a few crucial summary statistics on disk affords fast, convenient access to these numbers. If the Transactions table is large, accumulating totals on the fly for a data entry screen would probably seem slow enough to be annoying. If you only need the totals on printed reports, processing speed is less of an issue, and you might opt instead for compiling the totals as needed. The contrast between these two strategies will be illustrated with the year-to-date totals (which are computed on the fly) and overall totals (which are stored in the Names table).

In addition to the primary key, which is based on the ID Code field, the Names table needs indexes based on the Zip field (for printing mailing labels) and on the combination of Name Type and ID Code. The latter index is used for printing reports that group names by type, and it speeds up selections by type (for example, when ACE sends a mailing only to donors or media contacts).

The Contacts Table

The Contacts table stores the information recorded about each contact with a person in the Names table. Typical contacts include mailings, phone calls, attendance at meetings or lectures, and volunteer activities. In an application

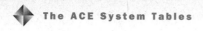
for a professional office (medical, dental, or legal), a contact might be an office visit, a procedure, or a specific type of service performed. Figure 3.4 illustrates the table design worksheet for the Contacts table.

Figure 3.4
The Contacts table
design worksheet

CONTACTS TABLE

#	Name	Data type	Length	Format
1	~~Member name~~ ID Code	Text	10	UPPERCASE
2	Contact type	Text	~~1~~ 2	UPPERCASE
3	Date	Date		MM/DD/YY
6	Follow-up date	Date		MM/DD/YY
~~5~~ 4	Description	Text	~~50~~ 25	
~~4~~ 5	Amount (if any)	Number		

Notes—Contact types: ML=mailing
PH=phone call
NL=newsletter mailing
RN=renewal notice
LE=lecture
BM=board meeting notice
PR=press release

Primary Key: ID Code + Date + Contact type

Indexes: Contact type + Date

The Contact Type field stores a short code that identifies the type of contact, and the Description field stores a longer or more specific description of the individual contact. For example, in a record that describes the annual Christmas card mailing, the Contact Type would be ML (for mailing) and the Description field would contain "Christmas card 1993."

The Date field stores the date of the contact, and Follow-up Date stores an optional date when another action linked to the original contact should take place. If you could always assume a constant interval between the contact date and follow-up date, you would not need the Follow-up Date field, but in the ACE system, this date is not always required, and it is entered manually when necessary. In general, the Contacts table does not store financial transactions, since that is the role of the Transactions table, but it does have an Amount field to record dollar amounts associated with contacts that do not require separate entries in the Transactions table, such as attendance at paid seminars or lectures.

As noted earlier in this chapter, the Contacts table has no intuitively obvious primary key. To display contact records grouped by person, and in chronological order for each person, the primary key is made up of the ID Code, Date, and Contact Type fields. If the table were so large that this combination did not turn out to be unique, you would have two alternatives. One is to add a tie-breaker field to the table structure and to the primary key to differentiate contacts with the same ID code, date, and type. The other is to allow Access to create a primary key for you (as described later in this chapter) by adding a Counter field to the structure. The latter solution is easier, but it would result in basing the default display order on the order in which records were entered into the table rather than on their contents. The Contacts table is also indexed by the combination of Contact Type and Date to produce listings and reports that analyze contact patterns independent of the mailing list.

The Transactions Table

The Transactions table stores information on financial transactions, including purchases, donations, membership dues, pledges, and payments on prior pledges. In an accounting database, the transactions might be purchases, fees for professional services, payments, credits, refunds, and adjustments. Figure 3.5 illustrates the table design worksheet for the Transactions table.

The Transaction Type field stores a short code that identifies the type of transaction. The primary key is based on the Transaction Number field, which contains a unique transaction number. Each record in the Transactions table stores data on one discrete financial transfer. For example, a pledge paid in three installments would have four Transactions table records. In any accounting database, storing both the debit and credit in the same record facilitates some operations, such as calculating the balance or determining whether a pledge was paid in full. However, using a separate record for each transaction affords far more flexibility, because it easily accommodates partial payments and multiple payments, and it enables you to add new transaction types at any time.

Some of the fields in the Transactions table are required only for certain types of transactions. The Tax and Shipping fields apply only to purchases of promotional items such as T-shirts and coffee mugs, and the Discount field is used primarily for purchases but occasionally for events such as conferences or seminars. Rather than adding complexity to the system by storing these quantities in a separate table, the ACE system uses a single table for all the transaction data.

The Payment Form field identifies the form in which a payment was made; typical entries might include VISA, Check, or Cash. In an accounting database, you might also want a field for a credit card number or check number. In the ACE Transactions table, you can use the Reference field for this purpose or for an explanation of the nature or type of transaction. The Posted field is a Yes/No field used to mark a transaction posted after it updates the totals in the

Note. Chapter 18 describes how to use macros to ensure that you can enter only the fields relevant to the current transaction type.

Figure 3.5

The Transactions table design worksheet

TRANSACTIONS TABLE

#	Name	Data type	Length	Format
1	ID Code	Text	10	UPPERCASE
2	Transaction type	Text	~~1~~ 2	UPPERCASE
~~3~~ 4	Date	Date		MM/DD/YY
9	Amount	Number		
10	Payment form	Text	5	~~UPPERCASE~~
11	Reference	Text	50	
13	GL Account ~~number~~	~~Number~~ Text	5	
5	Subtotal	Number		
6	Discount	Number		
7	Tax	Number		
8	Shipping	Number		
12	Posted ~~to GL?~~ to donor	yes/no		
3	Transaction number	Text	5	

Notes—Transaction types: P=purchase
DO=donation
ME=membership dues
PL=pledge
PP=pledge payment
TD=total debits
TC=total credits

Posted= posted to donor total fields yet?

Primary Key: Transaction number

Indexes: ID Code + Date
Transaction type + Date

Names table; this prevents you from accidentally posting a batch of transactions twice. Finally, the GL Account field stores the general ledger account number, so that ACE can produce monthly and annual summary reports that the accountant can use to update the general ledger.

The primary key for the Transactions table is the Transaction Number, and there are two additional indexes that serve the same purposes as the analogous Contacts table indexes—one based on the combination of ID Code and Date, and one based on Transaction Type and Date.

The Committees Table

The Committees table stores information on committee memberships. (The table design worksheet is illustrated in Figure 3.6.) The Committees table requires just a few fields. First and foremost, the ID Code field identifies the person, and the Committee field stores a code that identifies the committee to which the person belongs. The Officer field stores the position, if any, that the person currently holds (for example, Chairperson or Treasurer). The Joined and Quit fields store the dates that the person joined and quit the committee, so that ACE can retain a history of committee memberships as well as identify current members. Finally, the Notes field is a Memo field intended for additional comments, information on previous officer positions, and notes on meeting agendas or action items.

Figure 3.6

The Committees table design worksheet

COMMITTEES TABLE

#	Name	Data type	Length	Format
2	ID Code	Text	10	UPPERCASE
1	Committee ID	Text	10	UPPERCASE
4	Joined	Date		MM/DD/YY
5	Quit	Date		MM/DD/YY
6	Notes	Memo		
3	Officer	Text	12	~~UPPERCASE~~

Notes—Use officer for <u>current</u> officer position, record previous positions in Notes

Primary Key: Committee + ID Code

Index: ID Code + Committee

The primary key for the Committees table is the combination of Committee and ID Code, and an index on the same two fields in the opposite order expedites queries and reports that group the committee records by person rather than by committee.

Creating a Table

To create a new table or modify the structure of an existing table, you use the Table Design view, which is accessed through the Database window. If you want to be able to try all the examples in later chapters, create the ACE Committees table now, using the following steps:

1. If the ACE database is not already open, select the Open Database option on the File menu, and choose ACE.MDB from the list of databases.

2. If the Database window does not already display the list of tables, click on the Table object button or choose Tables from the View menu.

3. Click on the New button, or select New from the File menu and then choose Table from the resulting submenu of object types.

Figure 3.7 shows how the Table Design view window looks after you fill in the specifications for the first field in the Committees table. As in the other Access object design windows, the title bar displays the type of object you are creating and the default name, which for a table object is Table1 (or Table2 if the database already contains a table called Table1). The first time you save the table, Access prompts you for a new name. You might occasionally retain the default name (Table1, Table2, and so on) for experimental tables that are not really part of your database, but you should nearly always assign a more meaningful name. The message region at the left side of the status bar identifies the current mode—Design view—and reminds you of the two most important function keys active in the table design environment—F6 and F1.

Figure 3.7
Defining the first field in the Committees table

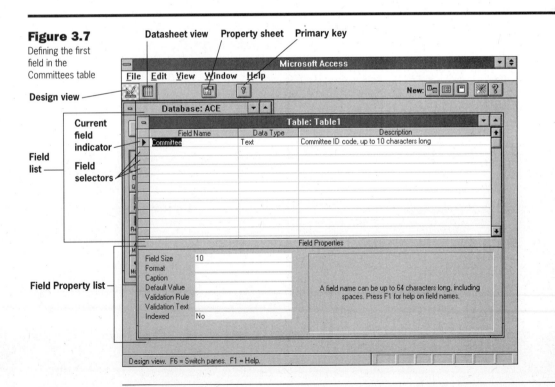

The table design window is divided horizontally into two major regions. In the upper region, you enter the essential characteristics of the fields—their names and data types. In the third column of the table, you can enter an optional description up to 255 characters long that serves to document the usage or purpose of any fields whose names or contents are not self-explanatory. When you enter data into the table, Access displays as much of the description as will fit (about 90 characters) in the left side of the status bar, so you may want to use the beginning of the description for a brief reminder of the purpose of a field or for a list or description of the permissible entries. For example, in Figure 3.7, you can see the description for the Committee field— "Committee ID code, up to 10 characters long." The number of fields that you can see simultaneously depends on the size of the table design window and the current video mode, but you can use the scroll bar at the right side of the window to bring any fields in the structure into view. The buttons immediately to the left of the field names are *field selectors*, and the triangle marks the current field—the one you are defining. You can click on the field selector with the mouse to select the entire row that describes a field (you must select a field before you can move, delete, or copy it).

In the lower portion of the table design window, Access displays the properties of the current field and an information box that displays a brief explanation of the item that currently has the focus and suggests where you can find more help. In Figure 3.7, the Field Name column is selected, so the information box describes the rules governing field names and informs you that you can press F1 for further help on field names. You can use all the standard Windows keyboard and mouse commands to move through the list of fields, enter new ones, and edit previously defined fields.

Obviously, you must enter the field name and description by typing them, but the Data Type entry region is a combo box. If you know the name of the data type you want, you can type it, but you can also display a list of data types by clicking on the arrow symbol in the Data Type column or by pressing Alt+Down Arrow, and then choosing the data type from this list. If you are following along with the examples, use these steps to define the first two fields in the Committees table:

1. If you do not already see an insertion point in the Field Name column of the first row of the field table, move to this column using the arrow keys or by clicking in this column.

2. In the Field Name column, type **Committee**, and press Tab to move to the Data Type column.

3. Click on the arrow symbol to display the list of data types, and then click on Text or press Enter to select Text from the list.

4. Press Tab to move to the Description column, and type **Committee ID code, up to 10 characters long**. Press Tab to move to the Field Name column in the next row.

5. Type **ID Code** and press Tab to move to the Data Type column.

6. In the Data Type column, type **TEXT** (in uppercase), and press Tab to move to the Description column. When you leave the Text column, Access automatically formats your entry so that it appears as "Text" even though you entered "TEXT."

7. Type **ID code for committee member** and press Tab to move to the Field Name column in the third row.

To finish defining the Committee table fields, enter the following field specifications:

Field Name	Data Type	Description
Officer	Text	Current officer position, if any
Joined	Date/Time	
Quit	Date/Time	
Notes	Memo	

You can edit the field list by adding, deleting, or moving fields. To add a field between two others, move to the field that will follow the new one and select the Insert Row option from the Edit menu. To delete the current row, you can use either of the following methods:

- With any column in the row selected, choose the Delete Row option from the Edit menu.

- Select the entire row by clicking on the field selector, and then press Del.

NOTE. *Pressing Del without first selecting a row simply deletes the contents of the current column (the field name, data type, or description), not the field itself.*

To move a field to a new position in the structure, click on the field selector to highlight the field, release the mouse button, and then press the mouse button again and hold it down as you drag the field to its new location. As you move the mouse, Access displays a heavy border line to indicate the new location of the *bottom* of the row that describes the field, but the field specifications remain in the original position until you release the mouse button.

You can assign a primary key based on one or more fields (provided that the order of the fields in the key matches their order in the structure) by selecting the field or fields and then clicking on the Primary Key button in the tool bar or selecting the Set Primary Key option from the Edit menu. To select the components of the key you can use any of the following methods:

- To select one field, make sure that any column in the field's row has the focus or select the row by clicking on the field selector.

- To select two or more consecutive fields, click on the field selector for the first one, and then drag the mouse down to the last field or hold down the Shift key as you click on the field selector for the last field.

- To select nonconsecutive fields, click on the first field selector and then hold down the Ctrl key as you click on additional field selectors.

Access displays a key symbol in the field selector for each field in the primary key. If you are building the Committees table, you can use either of the last two methods to assign the primary key, which consists of the Committee and ID Code fields.

None of these methods allow you to specify a primary key based on two or more fields if the order of the fields in the primary key does not match their order in the table structure, but you can define such a primary key by entering it in the property sheet for the table, as described later in this chapter.

Assigning Field Properties

You assign field properties by making entries in the lower half of the Design view window. To switch between the field list and the property list, you can either press F6 or click anywhere in the desired portion of the window. The property list always displays the properties of the current field (the one that last had the focus in the upper half of the window), and you can scroll through the field list to see the properties of any field. Unfortunately, editing the properties of many of the fields in a table involves switching back and forth repeatedly between the two sections of the Design view window. Some properties are available for all fields, while others apply only to some data types. The properties are used as follows:

Property	Data Types	Meaning
Field Size	Text	Maximum field length
	Number	Type and size of number: Byte, Integer, Long Integer, Single, or Double

Property	Data Types	Meaning
Format	All except OLE Object	Display format, either predefined or custom
Decimals	Number, Currency	Number of decimal places
Caption	All types	Label to use instead of field name in Datasheet view, forms, and reports
Default Value	All except Counter and OLE Object	Value to enter automatically into new records (you can override the default by typing over it)
Validation Rule	All except Counter	Condition that describes what constitutes a valid entry in the field
Validation Text	All except Counter	Error message displayed when entered data does not satisfy the Validation Rule
Indexed	All except Memo and OLE Object	Whether to build an index on the field and what type of index to build

The Default Value, Validation Rule, and Validation Text properties are described in more detail later in Chapter 12, because taking full advantage of these properties requires that you understand how to write Access expressions. However, even a beginner can make use of the other field properties immediately. Before you begin, note that Access uses combo boxes to set many of the properties, so you can either type your entries or select them from a list. This fact might easily escape you because the button you use to display the drop-down list is displayed only when the property has the focus.

Setting the Field Size

The logical place to begin customizing a table structure is to enter the Field Size property for Text fields that should be longer or shorter than the default 50 characters. For Number fields, you cannot specify any arbitrary length; instead, setting the Field Size property involves choosing one of the five number styles enumerated earlier—Byte, Integer, Long Integer, Single, or Double. The Field Size data entry region for Number fields is a combo box, and you can either type your entry or choose it from a drop-down list. Note that the Field Size selections for Number fields describe different types of numbers, with different ranges of acceptable values and storage requirements, *not* simply different display formatting alternatives.

Note. Custom formats are introduced in Chapter 9.

Setting the Default Display Format

The Format property enables you to control the display format, and in some cases, the content of the data entered into a field. For many of the data types, you can choose a predefined format from a combo box, and in most cases, you can also define a custom format. Table 3.2 lists the predefined formats available for Number, Currency, Counter, Date/Time, and Yes/No fields. If you are unfamiliar with the terminology used to describe these formats or if you do not know how your Windows defaults are set, be patient—once you have learned how to enter data into a table (in Chapter 4), you can create a small table with a field of each data type, enter a few records, and experiment with different display formats.

If you choose any of the numeric data types, you can also specify the number of decimal places through the Decimals property. For all the Number formats, the default setting for the Decimals property is Auto; this setting specifies two decimal places for all the types of numbers except integers, which have no decimal places (recall that integers, by definition, are whole numbers). It is entirely up to you to combine the field properties in ways that make sense. For example, Access allows you to display decimal places in an integer or to request more than seven digits for single-precision numbers (although all but the first seven will be dropped).

Remember that many of the Number and Date/Time formats are not specific to Access—they are established for all Windows applications using the International and Date/Time Settings accessed through the Windows Control Panel. If you want to change one of these formats for all of your work in Windows, you should change it in the Control Panel. For example, you can specify whether the short date format includes leading zeroes in the month and day portions, whether years are displayed with two or four digits, and whether the month name is spelled out in full or abbreviated to three letters. To modify any of these formats for Access alone, you must define a custom display format for each Number and Date/Time field, using methods described in Chapter 9.

Access offers three predefined formats for Yes/No fields: You can display their values as Yes and No (the default), True and False, or On and Off. Internally, Yes/No fields are stored as –1 (for Yes) and 0 (for No), but they are displayed this way only if the Format property is blank. When you create a table from within Access, you have to go out of your way to remove the Format property, but when you import data from other applications that support this data type (which is often called *logical* rather than Yes/No), the data is displayed in raw form if you do not modify the table structure to assign one of the three predefined formats.

There are no predefined formats for Text and Memo fields, which were intended to accommodate free-form text that *does not* follow a rigid format. However, you might want to format short Text fields to conform to certain

Table 3.2   Access Display Formats

Format	Description
Number, Currency, and Counter Formats	
General Number	Displays the number exactly as entered
Currency	Displays a currency symbol, separators every three digits, and a decimal point character (for example, $1,253.75); uses a leading minus sign or parentheses for negative values
Fixed	Displays a fixed number of decimal places (for example, 1253.7500)
Standard	Displays separators every three digits, a decimal point, and a fixed number of decimal places (for example, 1,253.75)
Percent	Displays the number multiplied by 100, with a trailing percent sign (%), and with a fixed number of decimal places (for example, 8.75% for .0875)
Scientific	Displays the number in exponential notation (for example, 1.25E+03) for 1,250
Date/Time Formats	
General Date	Displays the date and/or time, with the date in Short Date format and the time in Medium Time format
Long Date	Displays in Windows Long Date format (for example, Tuesday, September 7, 1993)
Medium Date	Displays in Medium Date format (for example, 07-Sep-93)
Short Date	Displays in Windows Short Date format (for example, 9/7/93)
Long Time	Displays in Windows Time format, including hours, minutes, and seconds (for example, 3:24:10 PM)
Medium Time	Displays just hours and minutes (for example, 3:24 PM)
Short Time	Displays hours and minutes using a 24-hour clock (for example, 15:24)
Yes/No Formats	
Yes/No	Displays entries as Yes or No
True/False	Displays entries as True or False
On/Off	Displays entries as On or Off

patterns. You can define custom formats that determine which character positions are mandatory and which are optional, and you can insert punctuation such as the dashes in telephone numbers and Social Security numbers. These and other custom formats are described in Chapter 9. There are two global formatting symbols that are easy to apply and useful in most tables. Entering a less-than sign (<) for the Format property converts any data entered into the field to lowercase, and a greater-than sign (>) converts it to uppercase. You can use these symbols to ensure that fields like an ID code or state abbreviation are always displayed consistently regardless of how they are entered.

Establishing Default Field Captions

The Caption property specifies an alternate field label that becomes the default for all data entry modes, including the Datasheet view and newly created forms. You may want to use a short caption for fields such as Transaction Type or Contact Type ("Type" would be a good choice), which have field names much wider than the data, to avoid having to narrow the columns manually in Datasheet view.

Establishing Default Values

The Default Value property specifies the value that Access enters automatically into new records. For example, you might enter CA in a mailing list table if most of the people on the list reside in California. Establishing a default value can save you quite a bit of typing, and you can always override the default by typing over it or deleting it. You can enter the default value in any of the formats acceptable for the appropriate type, regardless of the display format selected for the field. For example, you could enter a default date as 1/1/93 even if the display format is Long Date.

Defining Indexes

You can use the Indexed property to request an index based on one field and to specify the type of index. If you choose Yes (No Duplicates), Access will not permit you to enter two records with the same value in the index key field. Access automatically assigns this property to the field that you select as the primary key (for single-field primary keys), but the primary key is not necessarily the only field or combination of fields that must be unique in each record in a table. For example, in addition to an alphanumeric ID code like the ID Code field in the ACE Names table, you might have a Social Security number or medical record number that is also unique. If you choose Yes (Duplicates OK) for the Indexed property, Access allows multiple records to share the same key value in the field. Most indexes—the Zip index in the Names table is a good example—must allow duplicates. You can build an index on any type of field except Memo or OLE Object.

Defining Field Properties for the Committees Table

To enter the field properties for the Committees table, use the following steps:

1. In the upper half of the Design view window, make sure that the Committee field is selected (either press Up Arrow until you see the current record indicator in the first record selector or click anywhere in the first row of the table).

2. Press F6 or click in the Field Size text box in the Field Properties region.

3. Type **10** for the Field Size property.

4. Press Down Arrow or Tab to move to the Format property and type **>** to specify uppercase conversion.

5. Press F6 and then press Down Arrow or click in the second row of the field table (the ID Code row).

6. Press F6 or click in the Field Size text box in the Field Properties region.

7. Type **10** for the Field Size property, move down to the Format property, and type **>**.

8. Using the same sequence of steps, select the Officer field and type **12** for the Field Size property.

9. Select the Joined field and move down to the Format property.

10. Press F4 or Alt+Down Arrow or click the arrow at the right side of the data entry region to display the list of date and time formats, and select Short Date from the list. Your screen should look like Figure 3.8 as you choose the format from the drop-down list.

11. Using the same sequence of steps, assign the Short Date format for the Quit field.

Assigning Table Properties

In addition to the properties that describe the individual fields, you can assign properties to the table as a whole by entering them on a table property sheet. To display the property sheet, click on the Properties command button in the tool bar or choose the Table Properties option from the View menu. You can move or resize the Table Properties window at any point so that it does not obscure the part of the Table Design view window you are working on. To remove the property sheet, you can click on the Table Properties button again, select the Table Properties option on the View menu again, or use the close

Figure 3.8

Assigning the
Format property for
a Date/Time field

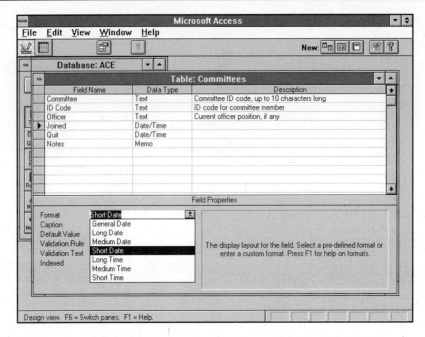

box in the Table Properties window. Figure 3.9 illustrates the property sheet
for the Committees table.

The table properties are very simple and straightforward. The Description property allows you to enter a description of up to 255 characters to further explain the purpose or usage of a table. If you have already assigned a primary key using one of the methods described earlier in this chapter, the name(s) of the component field(s) will appear next to the Primary Key property; if not, you can create the primary key by entering the field name(s) in the property sheet. You *must* use this method to create the primary key if it consists of more than one field and the order of the fields in the key does not match their order in the table structure. For example, if the primary key for the Committees table were based on ID Code and Committee rather than Committee and ID Code, you would have to define it by entering it in the property sheet. You must also use the property sheet to define index keys based on more than one field. In the Primary Key and Index1 through Index5 properties, you enter the field names in the order you want them to appear in the index key, separated by semicolons (;). You can see the specifications for the primary key and the ID Code/Committee index for the Committees table

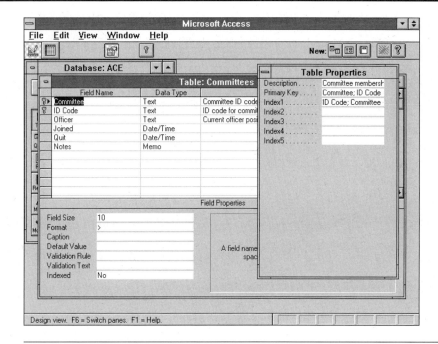

Figure 3.9
Assigning table
properties

in Figure 3.9. To complete your definition of the Committees table, use the following steps:

1. Click on the Properties command button in the tool bar or choose the Table Properties option from the View menu to display the property sheet for the Committees table.

2. Type **Committee Membership History** in the Description property and press Down Arrow.

3. If you have not already assigned the primary key, type **Committee;ID Code** in the Primary Key property and press Down Arrow.

4. Type **ID Code;Committee** in the Index1 property to create an index based on ID Code and Committee.

Saving the Table Structure

To save a new or modified table structure and exit from the Table Design view, you can use any of the standard Windows methods for closing a document window (the easiest ways are double-clicking on the close box in the upper-left corner of the window or pressing Ctrl+F4). Remember that Access displays the table property sheet in its own window; if this window is front-most on the desktop, you must either close it or switch to the Table Design view window before you can close the latter window. You do not have to close the property sheet before you exit from Table Design view; if the property sheet is visible when you close the Design view window, it will reappear the next time you return to Design view to modify the structure of the table.

When you exit from Table Design view after creating a new table or changing the structure of a previously created table, Access displays a dialog box like the one shown in Figure 3.10 to ask whether you want to save your changes. Choose the Yes button to save your changes and exit, No to exit without saving the changes made during the current editing session, or Cancel to return to the Design view window to continue editing. If you have not previously saved the table, Access displays the standard Save As dialog box to collect the table name on the assumption that you probably do not want to retain the default name (Table1, Table2, and so on). If you have not defined a primary key, Access displays the dialog box shown in Figure 3.11 to warn you that your table lacks a primary key and to offer to create one for you. If you choose Yes from this dialog box, Access adds a Counter field called ID to the table structure and makes this field the primary key. The new field becomes the first field in the structure, and all the other fields move down to accommodate it.

Figure 3.10

Saving or canceling changes to a table structure

When you create a new table, exiting and saving your changes takes just a few seconds. If you return to Design view to change the structure of a table that already contains a great deal of data, it may take some time, because Access must recopy all the records to the new format. Some of the factors you should take into account when you restructure a table that contains data are outlined in Chapter 14.

Figure 3.11
Allowing Access to
create the primary
key

Summary

This chapter described a practical method for designing a set of table structures that will support all the functional requirements of your Access application. Translating the samples, documents, and lists you collected during the analysis phase into an efficiently structured, well integrated group of tables can be difficult, especially if your application requires more than two or three tables and you have little or no prior experience with system design. If you feel completely lost, you might concentrate on the most important table or tables in the application, and return later to create the more problematic or less essential tables. If you are impatient to begin using your database application, you may be tempted to skip the paper planning step and begin creating the tables immediately, but try your utmost to resist this temptation. The more time you spend up front refining the design, the less time you will spend changing it later.

Once you have created at least the main tables in your database, you can begin entering some sample data, with the immediate goal of verifying that the table structures are complete and correct. If you found the analysis and design phases frustrating, you will be relieved to discover that working with Access to enter, edit, and view data is easy, intuitive, and straightforward. Chapter 4 describes how to enter and edit records in one table at a time, working in the default Datasheet view, and Chapter 6 introduces the Form Design tool, which enables you to create custom screen forms for viewing and editing tables.

4

Working with Tables in Datasheet View

ONCE YOU HAVE DEFINED THE STRUCTURES OF THE MAIN TABLES IN your application, you can begin entering data and carrying out the other routine maintenance activities required to keep the database accurate and current—searching for records to view or print them, browsing through the data to spot trends, editing records, and deleting records.

In Access, you can carry out all of these activities in a built-in data display and entry form known as the *datasheet*, or *Datasheet view*, which was introduced briefly in Chapter 2. If you prefer, you can also define custom forms for entering data, and there are many advantages to defining forms for the main tables in an application. However, it is best to defer creating the forms until you are sure that your table structures are correct, and in a new application this means waiting until you have entered some sample data and carried out your preliminary testing on this data. The Datasheet view enables you to begin entering data before you are ready to design custom forms (or, if you are new to Access, before you know how to design forms).

In many contexts, the datasheet is also useful throughout the lifetime of an application. Because it displays the maximum amount of data on the screen at once, the datasheet is often the most convenient vehicle for surveying the contents of a table to pick out certain items of interest or to spot trends. For data that appears in tabular form in the manual system, such as invoice line items or financial transactions, Datasheet view may be the most comfortable data entry mode because it most closely resembles the paper system. And, as you will see in Chapter 6, you can gain many of the advantages of working with custom forms while retaining the appearance and behavior of the datasheet.

This chapter describes how to work in Datasheet view and how to customize the layout of the datasheet to suit your preferences and the data entry requirements of a particular table.

Before you begin entering data, give some thought to choosing the records you will use for your initial testing. The sample data should be chosen to help you verify that your database design satisfies the goals outlined in Chapter 3, because no matter how thorough your advance planning is, you will invariably make some mistakes and overlook factors that turn out to be important later on. By putting the application through its paces with small sample tables, you can uncover many potential problems before you have entered (or imported) so much data that changing the table structures necessitates editing a great many records individually afterward (for example, to conform to new field lengths).

The sample data should always be drawn from the real application, *not* from your imagination—when your attention is focused on the system design, you will naturally tend to invent data that conforms to your table structures rather than presenting the full range of challenges that the database will be expected to handle. Using real data will point up missing fields, fields that are too short, and values that you would have sworn were "impossible" when you defined your requirements. When you select the sample data, try to abide by the same guidelines presented in Chapter 1 for gathering samples from the manual system—choose some records that are atypical as well as many that conform to the norms, and enter matching records into the main tables in the application. For example, the sample Names table in the ACE system contains names of all types (prospects, donors, and so on), including some who have a great deal of activity and some with very little, and the data in the sample Contacts, Transactions, and Committees tables is drawn from the same list of people.

The testing phase will also reveal many of the logistical problems you will encounter during the conversion from a manual system or another computer program—you will learn which information will be difficult to find or calculate, and which input documents will serve as the most expedient references when you enter the real data. If you have not yet coded fields such as keywords or assigned ID codes or account numbers, the testing phase will remind you to begin thinking about these issues, and it will give you valuable insights into how these codes should be constructed and how much expertise is required to assign them. For example, if the person who will end up doing most of the data entry does not know enough about your data to assign the keywords, you will have to do so in advance.

Entering the sample data will also enable you to clarify the data entry sequence. You must begin by entering data into the tables that do not depend on any other tables (the Names table in the ACE system) and proceed to the dependent tables (the Contacts, Transactions, and Committees, which should contain only records that match an existing record in the Names table). You will be reminded of which fields should be entered and which can be calculated, and you can outline a data entry sequence that ensures that you enter first all information required for a subsequent calculation or posting step (even if you do not yet know how to perform those calculations).

You should also get a feel for how long the initial data entry will take, so that you can budget this time and decide realistically how much historical data to enter into tables such as the Transactions table. Make allowances, however, for your own unfamiliarity with Access (and perhaps with Windows)—as you gain experience, you will require less time and fewer keystrokes or mouse clicks to accomplish the same objectives.

Working in Datasheet View

You can view, edit, and update any table in Datasheet view. You might regard the datasheet as a specialized type of data entry form—one that Access provides for you as the default form. Figure 4.1 illustrates the ACE Names table datasheet. You may want to open this table now so that you can begin experimenting with the Datasheet view as you read this chapter. To open a table's datasheet, make sure that the Database window displays the list of table names, and then use any of the following methods:

- Highlight the table name in the Database window and press Enter.

- Highlight the table name in the Database window and click on the Open command button.

- Double-click on the table name in the Database window

Figure 4.1

The ACE Names table datasheet

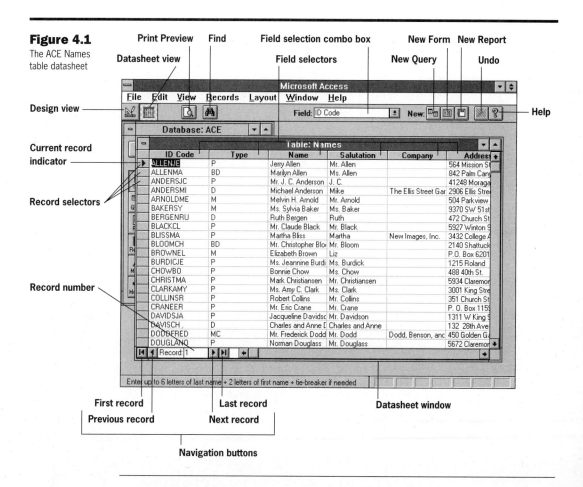

Figure 4.2 diagrams the structure of the Access menu bar in Datasheet view. The meanings of many of the menu options are described later in this chapter.

Figure 4.2

The structure of the Access menu bar in Datasheet view

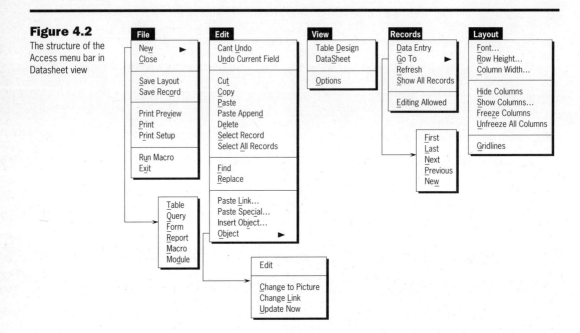

In the datasheet, records are laid out horizontally, with each record on its own row and each field in its own column. Spreadsheet users should feel comfortable immediately in Datasheet view, which closely resembles the standard spreadsheet data layout. If you have used the dBASE or FoxPro BROWSE command to update Xbase databases, you should also feel at home working with the datasheet. You must understand one other specialized term that appears in some of the messages that Access displays in alert boxes and dialog boxes—*dynaset*, which is used to denote the set of records that Access is working with in the current context. A dynaset may consist of all the records in a table—as is the case by default, and in all the examples in this chapter—or a group of records selected based on their contents using a filter or query (described in Chapters 5 and 6).

To the left of each row in the datasheet is a *record selector*—a small button that you can click on to select the whole record (row)—and at the top of each column is a *field selector*, which you can click on to select the field (column). When the mouse pointer is over either type of selector, its shape changes to an arrow, which points to the right for record selectors and down for field selectors (that is, the arrow always points into the record). In the field selectors, Access displays the field names as column titles, in the same mixture of upper- and lowercase you used when you defined the table structure. If you specified an alternate field caption (using the Caption property), the caption appears instead of the field name. For example, in the Names table datasheet, the second field is called Name Type, but the column title in the field selector is Type, the field caption.

If the table has a primary key, records are displayed in primary key order (alphabetical order by ID Code for the ACE Names table); otherwise, they appear in the order they were entered. Although you can see many records at once, you can directly edit just one at a time, and this record may be described as *the current record*, *the selected record*, or *the record that has the focus*. The same terms apply to the field you are currently editing. In Figure 4.1, the ID Code field in the first record has the focus. Access always gives you one or more visual cues (described in more detail later in this section) to identify the current field and record. In the left side of the status bar, Access displays as much as possible of the description for the current field that you entered when you defined the table (approximately 80 characters); if the current field has no description, the status bar displays "Datasheet View." In Figure 4.1, you can see the description for the ID Code field, "Enter up to 6 letters of last name + 2 letters of first name + tie-breaker if needed."

The Datasheet window shares the characteristics of all other Windows document windows—it has a title bar, close box, minimize and maximize/restore controls, and, if there is too much data to fit on the screen at once, horizontal and/or vertical scroll bars. You can move or resize the Datasheet window just as you would any other window. In Access, all window titles include a reminder of the type of object you are viewing or editing, together with the name of the object itself. Thus, the Datasheet window title for the Names table is "Table: Names."

By default, all the columns are the same width—1 inch when the datasheet is printed. In most cases, the width of a column on the screen is *not* 1 inch; for example, in VGA mode on a 13-inch monitor, it is about $1\frac{1}{2}$ inches. The number of fields and records that you can view at once depends on your display hardware and software, the current video mode, and the size of the Datasheet window. In standard VGA mode, with the window in its default size and position (as illustrated in Figure 4.1), you can see six fields from 21 records at a time, but in SuperVGA mode with the Datasheet window maximized, you can see more than twice as much data. You can easily customize the height of the rows, the width of any column, and the character font and size, using commands described later in this chapter.

NOTE. *The height and width of any Access object is expressed in terms of the dimensions of the object on the printed page, not on the screen. The size of the object on the screen depends on the size of your monitor and the current video mode.*

Moving around the Datasheet

You can visualize a table's datasheet as a large chart or worksheet, which is usually too large to fit on the screen all at once. The Datasheet window serves as a view port on this chart, allowing access to a few rows and columns at a time, and you can scroll this view port to examine any portion of the chart you wish. You can use all the standard keyboard commands listed in Table 2.1 to move around the datasheet as you view, edit, and enter data: You can use the arrow keys to move through the table one record or field at a time, and you can also use Tab and Shift+Tab to move horizontally. PgUp takes you to the previous screenful of data, and PgDn takes you to the next; Ctrl+PgUp and Ctrl+PgDn pan the display right and left one screenful of data.

If you prefer to use the mouse, the horizontal scroll bar at the bottom of the Datasheet window and the vertical scroll bar on the right allow you to easily move anywhere in the table. Dragging the scroll box is the fastest way to move to an approximate location in a large table, while the arrows at the ends of the scroll bars are preferable for making fine adjustments in your position.

The Datasheet window also includes several special controls and buttons that serve as additional editing and navigation aids. As noted earlier, a column of *record selectors* appears at the left side of the window. Just as you can move to a field in Table Design view by clicking on the field selector in the desired row, you can move quickly to any record in the datasheet that is visible on the screen by clicking on its record selector. Access displays a marker in the selector next to the current record, which changes as follows to reflect the status of the record:

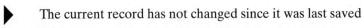 The current record has not changed since it was last saved

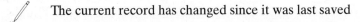 The current record has changed since it was last saved

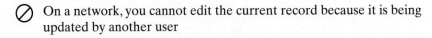 On a network, you cannot edit the current record because it is being updated by another user

You may already have noticed that the horizontal scroll bar at the bottom of the Datasheet window does not occupy the full width of the window. To the left of the scroll bar is a set of VCR-style controls called *navigation buttons* (labeled in Figure 4.1), which you can use to move quickly to the first, last, next, or previous record. You can move to *any* specific record by entering its number in the Record box; to move into this box, either click in it with the mouse or press F5. Note that the record numbers correspond to the display order, *not* to the position that the records physically occupy in the table (the order in which records were entered). Don't try to remember the number associated with a given record from one work session to the next—if you use filters or queries to view records in different orders (using commands outlined in Chapters 5 and 6), a given record may assume many different numbers, based on its varying position in the display sequence. You can, however, use the record numbers as a convenient way to return to a record you were editing a few minutes ago or to move quickly to an approximate position. For example, if you know there are about 5,200 records in a table, you could move to the middle by jumping to record 2,600. (If you are not sure how many records a table contains, use any available method to move to the last record—for example, click on the Last Record control—and check the number displayed in the Record box.) Note, however, that even if you are a confirmed keyboard user, the fastest way to accomplish this move is to use the mouse to drag the scroll box to the middle of the vertical scroll bar.

If you prefer to use menu commands, you will find menu equivalents for the navigation buttons on a submenu invoked by choosing Go To on the Records menu. This submenu, which is depicted in Figure 4.3, includes First, Last, Next, and Previous options, as well as a New option that you can use to begin entering new records.

Figure 4.3

The Go To submenu

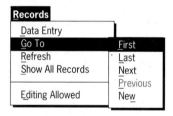

You can move to any field in the current record by choosing its name from a combo box in the toolbar. Figure 4.4 illustrates this combo box with the OK to Send Mail field name highlighted. Remember that in Windows, you can either type an entry in a combo box or select an option from the drop-down list. If your table has many fields and the names are short, you may prefer to click in the text box (rather than on the arrow symbol) and type the field name. If the field you choose is not currently visible, Access scrolls the display in the Database window to bring it into view.

If you want to practice these navigation techniques with the Names table, try the following experiments:

1. Click on the First Record button in the lower-left corner of the Datasheet window to move to the top of the table. Note the current record indicator in the record selector to the left of the ID Code ALLENJE.

2. Press Down Arrow five times to advance to Record 6.

Figure 4.4

Using the Field
Selection combo box

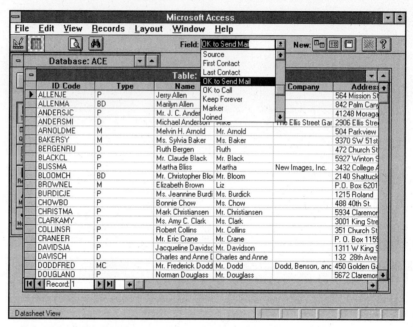

3. Click the right arrow symbol in the horizontal scroll bar at the bottom of the Datasheet window six times, until the City field occupies the leftmost column in the window.

4. Press PgDn to display the next screenful of records. Note that because you did not click in any field in the window after using the scroll bar, the display reverts to the original set of columns (this behavior is common to all Windows document windows).

5. Click on the Maximize button to maximize the Datasheet window

6. Click on the arrow in the Field combo box to drop down the field list, scroll down the list, and select Joined. Note that Access pans the display to the right just far enough to bring the Joined field into view.

7. Pull down the Records menu, select Go To, and select Last from the Go To submenu. Note that Access moves the focus to the last record in the Names table (record 100), but leaves the same column (the Joined field) current.

8. Press Ctrl+PgUp twice to pan the display to the left two screenfuls of fields, and then press Left Arrow twice to return to the first field, ID

Code. Press Left Arrow again and note that moving to the left of the first field takes you to the last field (Notes) in the previous record, as if the datasheet "wrapped around" behind the boundaries of its window.

9. Press Right Arrow to move past the last field and return to the first field in the next record.

10. Press F5 or click in the Record box at the bottom of the window, delete the record number displayed (100), type **1** and press Enter to return to the first record in the Names table.

Entering and Editing Data

By default, Access allows you to move freely around the datasheet and edit data. This property is controlled by the Editing Allowed option on the Records menu, which functions as a *toggle*—choosing this option checks it to allow editing if it is currently unchecked, and removes the check mark to prohibit editing if it is currently checked. The Editing Allowed option is checked by default, so no special actions on your part are required to edit a table. When this option is not checked, Access ignores any keystrokes that would change the contents of a field, and disables all command keys and menu options that are normally used to update data, including the Del key, the Delete option on the Edit menu, the Data Entry option on the Records menu, the New option on the Go To submenu, and the Replace option on the Edit menu (Find is still available). All of these commands are described later in this section. Disabling editing is a convenient way to avoid accidental changes in a work session in which you intend only to view or search for data. As you will see in Chapter 10, data entry forms have a property analogous to the Editing Allowed menu option, which you can use to prohibit editing through a particular form.

When you use the arrow keys to move around the datasheet, these keys take you through the table one field and one record at a time, and Access highlights the field that has the focus. This highlighting tells you that the entire field is *selected*. As in most Windows software, any new data that you type will *replace* the selected text, as you may have discovered inadvertently in the course of your experiments with the Names table. To *edit* the contents of a field, you must deselect the field and switch to Edit mode, either by pressing F2 or by clicking anywhere within the field.

When you are editing a field, Access displays an *insertion point* to indicate where the characters you type will appear, and the Left Arrow and Right Arrow keys move the insertion point within the field rather than taking you to another field. (Recall that *insertion point* is the term used in Windows for the symbol usually referred to as a *cursor* in MS-DOS software.) If you initiate editing by pressing F2, the insertion point appears at the end of the field. If you use the mouse, Access places the insertion point where you clicked; this is the fastest way to get to the precise site you need to edit in a long field. If the data in a field is too long to display within the current column width, Access scrolls the contents to follow as you move the insertion point through the field.

The default typing mode in Access is *Insert mode*—the characters you type are inserted into the data to the left of the insertion point, and the remaining characters move to the right to accommodate the insertion. Access never allows the contents of a field to exceed the maximum length you specified when you defined the table structure, and when you type in insert mode, extra characters do not simply fall "off the end" of the field. To replace characters in a field that is approaching its maximum length, you must first delete the characters you want to remove and then enter the new text. In *Overstrike mode*, the insertion point disappears. Instead, one character in the field is always selected, because each character you type will replace another character—the selected one. You can toggle between Insert and Overstrike mode by pressing the Ins key; if you are not sure which mode is currently active, you can look for an insertion point in the current field or check for the OVR indicator that appears in the lower-right corner of the status bar when you are working in overstrike mode.

Pressing Up Arrow, Down Arrow, or Tab, or using the Left Arrow or Right Arrow keys to move past the first or last character in the current field terminates editing and moves you to another field, which is then selected. You can also terminate editing without leaving the current field by pressing F2, which reselects the entire field. You can select any field on the screen by clicking just to the right of the border line at the left side of the field. Access helps you find this "hot spot" by displaying the mouse pointer as an arrow when it is in this very narrow zone; when the mouse pointer is over any other part of a field, it looks like an I-beam. Remember that whenever you move to another field, Access cancels Edit mode and selects the entire field; to begin editing each new field, you must press F2 or click in the field.

You can use the special shortcut keys listed in Table 4.1 to expedite data entry. The two "ditto" keys—Ctrl+' and Ctrl+"—are particularly useful when you enter data from presorted input materials, since they allow you to enter the same value in a series of records without retyping it, but you can also use these keys when you edit existing records. In all cases, the ditto key copies into the current field the contents of the same field in the record above it in the datasheet.

Saving and Undoing Changes

Access saves data one record at a time—when you move to a new record, it automatically saves all the changes you made to the record that previously had the focus. You can force Access to save the current record at any point

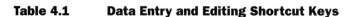
Table 4.1 **Data Entry and Editing Shortcut Keys**

Key	Meaning
Ctrl+;	Enter the current date
Ctrl+:	Enter the current time
Ctrl+Alt+Spacebar	Enter the default field value specified in the table structure
Ctrl+' or Ctrl+"	Enter the value in the same field in the previous record
Ctrl++	Add a new record
Ctrl +−	Delete the current record
Crtl+Enter	Save the current record

without moving to another record by choosing the Save Record option from the File menu or by pressing the equivalent shortcut key, Shift+Enter. Another easy method is to just press Up Arrow and then Down Arrow (or vice versa) to move momentarily to another record and then return to the original to continue editing.

When you begin typing characters in a field (either entering a new value in a blank field or editing existing data), the current record indicator in the record selector changes to a pencil symbol to remind you that you have changed the field. You can undo your changes *before you leave the field* by using any of these methods:

- Press Esc.

- Click on the Undo command button in the tool bar.

- Select the Undo Current Field option on the Edit menu.

These commands undo *all* changes to the current field and restore the original contents. You can use the more specialized Undo Typing and Undo Delete options on the Edit menu to undo the most recent editing changes— that is, all the changes you made since the last insertion point movement commands. These options appear at the top of the Edit menu whenever they are relevant: If your last change involved deleting characters, the first Edit menu option is Undo Delete, and if your last edit added or changed characters, it is Undo Typing. (Before you have changed the current field, the first option on the Edit menu is Can't Undo.) After you choose either Undo Delete or Undo Typing, the first option on the Edit menu becomes Redo Delete or Redo Typing; these commands reverse the Undo action and redo the edit. These specialized commands are most useful when you edit a long text or memo field, and they can save your skin when you move into a field and accidentally type over the contents without looking. For short fields, it is often easier to re-enter the original value (if you remember it) than to use Undo Typing or Undo Delete.

After you move out of a field, you can no longer undo just the edits that you made to that field. If you move to another field in the same record, the second option on the Edit menu changes to Undo Current Record, and you can use this option to undo all the changes you made to the current record. After you move to another record, the first option on the Edit menu changes to Undo Saved Record, and you can use this option to undo the changes to the record you edited most recently. After changing two or more records, there is no way to undo all of your updates.

Data Formatting and Validation

Access allows you to enter data into a field in any format that it recognizes as valid based on the data type. For example, you can enter September 13, 1993 into a date field as 9/13/93, 9-13-1993, Sept 13, 1993, 13-Sep-93, or any other legitimate date format, and you could enter 3:25 in the afternoon as 3:25 PM or 15:25. For Yes/No fields, you can enter the raw values –1 (Yes) and 0 (No), or the more intuitive Yes, No, True, False, On, and Off, in any combination of uppercase and lowercase. As you will see later in this chapter, there are some advantages to using a consistent format—regardless of which format—for a particular field throughout a table, but you are by no means required to do so. Except for Yes/No values, Access stores data exactly the way you enter it, but displays fields in the datasheet as specified by the Format property defined in the table structure (Yes/No fields are stored as –1 and 0). However, Access applies the display format only when you exit a field. For example, the State field in the Names table has the > symbol in the Format property, which specifies uppercase conversion for display purposes. You can enter the two-letter abbreviation for California as "CA," "Ca," or "ca," and when you exit the State field, Access redisplays your entry as "CA."

When you enter data in a text field, the characters you type appear on the screen exactly where you typed them. By default, Number and Date/Time fields are right-justified within the data entry region, and when you enter a value into an empty field, the digits appear at the right side of the field and move to the left as you add digits (unless you are using a form in which you have changed the alignment to left-justified). When you edit a previously entered number or date, each digit you type appears at the position of the insertion point and moves to the left as you enter additional digits.

You can enter a negative number with a leading or trailing minus sign or enclosed in parentheses. If a number has decimal places, you must type the decimal point, but you do not have to type the decimal point if no digits follow. For example, to enter $10.00 into a currency field, simply type 10.

Access always displays the number of decimal places specified through the Decimals property. Other formatting symbols, including the commas and currency symbol, are inserted automatically in the proper positions when you exit the field; if you try to type these characters yourself, Access ignores your keystrokes.

Access does not allow you to enter data in a Counter field. When you add a new record, Access displays Counter fields initially as "(Counter)" and updates their values automatically when you move to another record or choose the Save Record option from the File menu. If you try to change or delete the data in a Counter field, Access displays an error message such as "Control bound to counter column Transaction Number" in the status bar (for a Counter field called Transaction Number) and ignores your entry.

NOTE. *The term* control *in this message derives from the usage of this word by Access (and most other Windows programs) as a generic term for any data entry region on a form (in Access, a datasheet is the simplest type of data entry form).*

If you enter a value that does not pass one of the built-in validation tests applied automatically to fields based on their data type—for example, if you type characters in a Number or Date/Time field, enter a value other than one of those permitted for a Yes/No field, or enter a date such as 13/9/93 (there is no thirteenth month), Access displays an alert box to inform you that "The value you entered isn't appropriate for this field." You can select OK to return to the datasheet and correct your entry (or press Esc to restore the original field value), or you can select Help to display an information screen like the one shown in Figure 4.5 that further explains the problem.

If you enter data that creates a duplicate index key value for any index assigned the No Duplicates property—either the primary key or any other such index—Access displays an alert box that reminds you "Can't have duplicate key; index changes were unsuccessful" and does not allow you to leave the record without correcting the problem. If you aren't sure why your entry is a duplicate, you may have to temporarily substitute a "dummy" value—for example, type XXX in the ID Code field—so that you can leave the record and search for the duplicate.

Adding New Records

In preparation for adding new records to a table, Access displays a blank row at the end of the datasheet with an asterisk (*) in the record selector to distinguish this pseudorecord from the real ones. In this special row, which will become the next new record, Counter fields appear as "(Counter)" and columns for fields with default values (assigned through the Default property when you defined the table) display the default values. As noted earlier in this chapter, the new record row does not appear at the end of the datasheet

Figure 4.5

A help screen that explains an error message

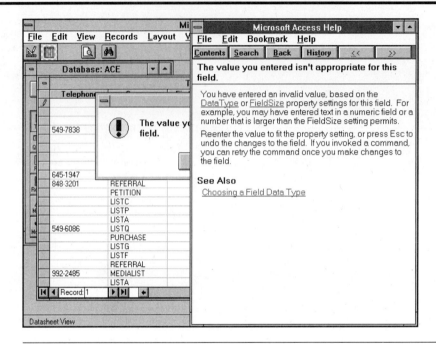

if you have disabled editing by unchecking the Editing Allowed option on the Records menu. Also note that when you open an empty table (one that does not contain any records), Access displays a blank row similar to the new record row except that the symbol in the record selector is the standard current record indicator (a triangle) rather than an asterisk.

To add a new record, simply move into any field in the special blank row and begin to enter data, exactly as you would in an existing record. (The easiest way to move to the end of a table is to click on the Last Record navigation button at the bottom of the Datasheet window.) If you prefer, you can choose the Go To option from the Edit menu and then choose the New option from the resulting submenu or press the equivalent shortcut key, Ctrl++. In a large table, this method is must faster than using the last record button. The minute you begin typing data in a new record, Access replaces the asterisk in the record selector with the pencil indicator and displays a new blank record below the one you are editing. If you choose the Undo Current Record option while entering a new record, Access removes the record from the table and again displays a blank record at the end of the datasheet.

As you add new records to a table, Access displays these records at the end of the datasheet in the order you entered them, although the rest of the records are arranged in primary key order. Often, this is convenient—it allows

you to review or proofread just the new entries by returning to the bottom of the datasheet. The next time you reopen the table after closing it, *all* the records, including those you added most recently, will appear in correct primary key order. If you want to redisplay the entire table with the records you added during the current work session inserted in proper primary key order, you can choose the Show All Records option on the Records menu. This option, which was intended primarily to return to viewing all the records in a table after working with a limited subset described by a filter (described in Chapter 6), is the most expedient way to force Access to redisplay the entire table as if you had just opened it.

If a data entry session will be devoted entirely to adding new records, and you do not need to view or edit records entered previously, you can initiate data entry by selecting the Data Entry option on the Records menu. In this mode, Access displays only the records that you add during the current work session, and it numbers these records in the status bar starting with 1. You can return at any point to viewing and editing all the records in the table by choosing Show All Records from the Records menu.

To enter the sample data into the ACE Committees table, close the Names table to keep the screen uncluttered, and open the Committees table. Note, however, that Access allows you to open multiple tables simultaneously. If you were unsure of any of the committee codes or member ID codes, you might prefer to leave the Names table on the screen (and perhaps open the Committee Names table as well) so you could look up this information. When multiple tables are open, you can move and resize the datasheet windows to keep the information you need in view. For now, keep the working environment simple and just open the Committees table. Because the table is empty, you will see just one blank row with the current record indicator in the record selector and the insertion point in the Committee field. To enter the first two records, use the following steps:

1. Type **FINANCE** and press Tab to move to the ID Code field.

2. Type **ALLENMA** and press Tab to move to the Officer field.

3. Type **Chairman** and press Tab to move to the Joined field.

4. Type **2/3/90** and press Tab twice to skip over the Quit field and move to the Notes field.

5. Type **Ms. Allen was Treasurer of the Finance Committee from 6/90 through 7/91, when she became Chairperson.** Press Tab to move to the Committee field in the next potential new record.

6. Type **lobbying** and press Tab to move to the ID Code field. Note that when you leave the Committee field, Access converts your entry to uppercase.

7. Type **ALLENMA** and press Tab twice to skip over the Officer field and move to the Joined field.

8. Type **June 32, 1991** and press Tab. Access will display an alert box to inform you that "The value you entered isn't appropriate for this field." Choose OK to clear the alert, move the insertion point to the left of the 2, and press Del to delete this digit, leaving the valid date June 3, 1991 in the field. Press Down Arrow to move to the next new record, and then Home to return to the first field. Note that Access redisplays the Joined field in the Short Date format you specified when you created the Committees table.

9. Enter the following committee membership data, experimenting as you see fit with the various entry formats:

Committee	ID Code	Officer	Joined	Quit	Notes
FINANCE	HOWARDJO		1/15/90	2/5/91	
EARTHDAY	HOWARDJO		5/10/91		
NEWS	HOWARDJO		11/10/92		Howard is responsible for compiling events listings for the newsletter. Refer all press contacts to him.
FINANCE	SLATERLO	Treasurer	6/15/92		
FINANCE	THOMPSCH		12/18/91		
NEWS	THOMPSCH		2/6/92		Christine is now the editor of the ACE newsletter.
EARTHDAY	OLSONED		6/18/91	5/20/92	Ed organized the first ACE-sponsored "Run for the Planet" race and fun run, held in San Francisco in 1992.
LOBBYING	OLSONED	Treasurer	5/10/92		
EARTHDAY	FRANKLKA	Chairman	8/1/92		
EARTHDAY	LEEALEX	Treasurer	7/23/90		
LOBBYING	HARRINJU	Chairman	10/20/92		
NEWS	BLOOMCH		3/28/90	3/1/92	
NEWS	BERGENRU	Chairman	8/10/91		
LOBBYING	ROSENBRH		4/1/91	4/5/92	Ralph, not Helen, was the committee member.

Committee	ID Code	Officer	Joined	Quit	Notes
LOBBYING	REEDLUCY		4/18/90	5/1/92	
LOBBYING	LUSUSAN		10/25/90		

At this point, your screen should look like Figure 4.6.

Figure 4.6

The Committees table sample data

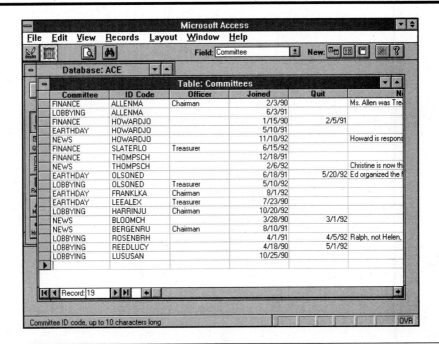

Cutting and Pasting Data

You can use all the standard Windows text editing methods to cut and paste data within a field, to copy data between fields and records, and to copy or delete one or more whole records. If you have little experience with Windows, you may want to experiment with these techniques on the Names table or Committees table as you read this section.

You must begin all cut and paste operations by selecting the text or records that you want to manipulate. Recall that when you first move into a field, the entire field is selected. You can use any of the following methods to select *part* of a field:

■ Click at one end of the desired selection, hold the mouse button down, drag the mouse to the other end, and then release the mouse button.

- Click at one end of the desired selection, release the mouse button, and then hold down the Shift key and click at the other end.

- Press F2 or click within the field, move the insertion point to one end of the desired selection, hold down the Shift key and use the arrow keys to move to the other end of the text, and then release the Shift key.

You can only use these methods to select text *within* a field—there is no way to mark a selection that spans multiple fields, although you can select two or more whole records, using methods described later in this section.

Once you have marked your selection, you can replace, copy, move, or delete it. To replace the selected text, simply type the replacement. To copy the selected text, first use the Copy command on the Edit menu or the equivalent Ctrl+C hot key to transfer the text to the Clipboard. Then move to the location where you want to insert the text (which may be in another field or another record), select the entire field or position the insertion point at the desired position, and then choose the Paste option from the Edit menu or press Ctrl+V. To move the selected text—that is, delete it from its original location and copy it elsewhere—use the Cut command or the Ctrl+X hot key instead of the Copy command or Ctrl+C to move the selected text to the Clipboard.

Note. You will see as you continue to work with Access that you can use the Clipboard to move or copy objects considerably more complicated than part of a field.

NOTE.   *If Access is your first Windows program, note that the Clipboard is a temporary storage area that enables you to transfer data almost anywhere in Windows. To copy or move objects, you must first copy them to the Clipboard, and then insert the contents of the Clipboard at the target location.*

As mentioned earlier, you can select a record by clicking on the record selector or by moving into the record and pressing Shift+Spacebar. You can select a group of adjacent records using methods analogous to those used to select text within a field:

- Click on the record selector for the first or last record in the group, hold the mouse button down, drag the mouse to the other end of the group, and then release the mouse button.

- Click on the record selector for the first or last record in the group, release the mouse button, and then hold down the Shift key and click on the record selector at the other end.

- Move to any field in the first or last record in the group, press Shift+Spacebar, and then hold the Shift key down as you use Up Arrow or Down Arrow to move to the other end of the group.

You can identify the selected records because Access displays them highlighted. Once you have selected one or more records, you can delete them by pressing Del or choosing the Delete option on the Edit menu, and you can copy or cut them to the Clipboard by using the Cut or Copy commands or the equivalent Ctrl+C or Ctrl+X hot keys. You can paste records into the same table, into another table in the same or a different Access database, or even into another application. For example, if you paste a group of records into an Excel spreadsheet, each record becomes a row in the spreadsheet and each field goes into a separate column, creating in effect a spreadsheet that looks exactly like the datasheet. (Exporting data to other programs is covered in more detail in Chapter 14.)

To copy one or more records to another Access table, use the following steps:

1. Copy or cut the records to the Clipboard.

2. Open the target table (you do not have to close the table from which you are copying records).

3. To *add* the records on the Clipboard to the end of the target table, choose Paste Append from the Edit menu (there is no hot key shortcut for this command) or move into the blank row at the end of the table, and then choose the Paste option or press Ctrl+V.

4. To *replace* one or more existing records with the data on the Clipboard, select the record or records you want to replace and choose Paste or press Ctrl+V. The Paste option is only enabled when at least one record is selected; otherwise, you must use Paste Append.

The target table need not have exactly the same structure as the source table, but the fields you transfer must have compatible data types and pass all the validation rules established for the target table. For example, you cannot transfer text into a Number or Date/Time field, and you cannot paste a value longer than the length specified for the target field using the Field Length property. Also, you cannot add records that would result in duplicate values in any index key that you assigned the No Duplicates property, including the primary key. This validation test prevents you from copying records *within* any table that has a primary key, but you might also inadvertently generate duplicate keys when you copy data from one table to another. For example, you could run into problems when you combine two mailing lists that have some names in common (assuming that the primary key is based on the name).

If it detects a key violation during a paste operation, Access displays an alert box to inform you that you "Can't have duplicate key; index changes were unsuccessful." When you click on the OK button in this alert box, Access displays another alert box that asks whether to "Suppress further error messages while pasting?" You can choose Yes to avoid having to acknowledge each error if you are pasting a large group of records, No to continue to receive an error message for each duplicate record, or Cancel to abort the paste operation.

At the end of the paste operation, if any records were copied successfully, Access displays an alert box like the one shown in Figure 4.7 to inform you how many records were copied and give you one last chance to abort the new additions. When you select OK, Access informs you of the disposition of those records that failed any validation test with a message box that reminds you that "Records that couldn't be pasted have been inserted into a new table called 'Paste Errors'." You can open this table as you would any other Access table, fix the problems, copy or cut all the records to the Clipboard, and then return to the target table and retry the paste operation. For example, you could delete genuine duplicates from the Paste Errors table and change the primary key in spurious duplicates to make the primary key fields unique.

Figure 4.7

Confirming or canceling a paste operation

Make sure to erase the Paste Errors table before you retry the paste operation—Access cannot create this table if it is already open and will display the error message "Couldn't lock table 'Paste Errors'; currently in use." If this happens, simply erase the Paste Errors table and try again—the data you cut or copied will still be on the Clipboard.

These simple cut and paste techniques are best suited to copying a few records between tables with similar or identical structures. For copying many records, a query is much faster and affords considerably more flexibility to compensate for different table structures. This more complex subject is covered in greater detail in Chapter 13.

Deleting Records

To delete a record, select it by clicking on its record selector or by pressing Shift+Spacebar, and then press Del or select the Delete option from the Edit menu. You can also use the equivalent shortcut key, Ctrl+–, to delete the current record without first selecting it. In all cases, Access displays an alert box like the one pictured in Figure 4.8 with command buttons that allow you to confirm or cancel the deletion or ask for help. You can delete more than one record at a time by using any of the methods described in the previous section to select a group of adjacent records before you issue the Delete command.

Use these commands with caution—once you have deleted a record, there is no way to recover it.

Figure 4.8
Confirming or
canceling a deletion

To practice deleting records, try the following steps with the Committees table:

1. Click on the record selector for the first Newsletter Committee record (the one with HOWARDJO in the ID Code field).

2. Hold the Shift key down and click on the record selector for the next Newsletter Committee record (the one with THOMPSCH in the ID Code field). Four records should appear highlighted.

3. Press Del to request that Access delete the highlighted records.

4. Choose Cancel from the alert box to abort the deletion.

NOTE. *Although records that you delete disappear immediately from the Datasheet view and are no longer available for editing, reports, or calculations, Access does not immediately erase deleted records from your hard disk. To reclaim the space occupied by deleted records, you must use the Compact Database option on the File menu in the Startup window. This option, which you should not have to run very often, is described in Chapter 13.*

Customizing the Datasheet

Access gives you considerable latitude to customize the appearance and behavior of a table's datasheet, either by using the mouse to directly manipulate various controls on the screen or by using commands on the Layout menu. As noted earlier, you can use methods common to all Windows software to move or resize the Datasheet window itself. Within the window, you can use some of the same techniques to manipulate rows and columns. If you are unfamiliar with the standard Windows direct manipulation techniques, you may find it helpful to observe the shape of the mouse pointer, which changes as you move the mouse around the window to remind you where the "hot spots" are and help you position the mouse correctly before you begin an operation. The various window controls and the shapes the mouse pointer assumes in these regions are indicated in Figure 4.9; all the mouse pointer symbols used in Access are listed in Appendix E.

Figure 4.9

The window manipulation controls and mouse pointer symbols

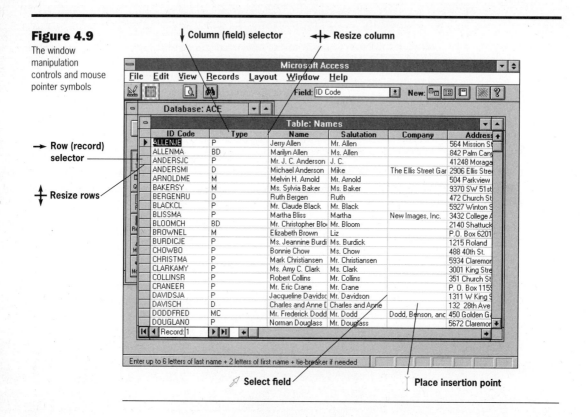

If you want to try the techniques described in this section, take a moment to open the Names table (you can leave the Committees table datasheet open as well if you wish). All of the customization techniques described in this section affect only the appearance of a table's datasheet, *not* the underlying data, so you can feel free to experiment. For example, widening or narrowing a column on the screen has no effect on the Field Size property of the field displayed in the column, and rearranging the order of the columns does not change the sequence of the fields in the table structure.

Changing Column Widths

In nearly all your tables, you will want to widen some columns to accommodate long entries and narrow others to squeeze more data onto the screen. For example, the Name Type field in the Names table is only two characters wide, and the caption that serves as the column title, Type, takes up only four characters. The easiest way to adjust the width of a column is to use the mouse to drag the right column border to a new position, as follows:

1. Move the mouse to the right boundary of the field selector for the desired column. The mouse pointer will change to a vertical line with two horizontal arrows, symbolizing movement of the boundary between columns.

2. Press the left mouse button and hold it down as you move the mouse to drag the column boundary left or right.

3. Release the mouse button when the column is the desired width.

Access does not adjust the data or column title to conform to the new column width until you release the mouse button, so it may take several tries to get the width right.

You can also change the width of the current column by selecting the Column Width option on the Layout menu, which invokes the dialog box shown in Figure 4.10. In this dialog box, the column width is expressed in terms of the average number of characters that will fit in the column, but because most Windows fonts are proportional, this number is only an approximation. You can change the column width by entering a new value in the Column Width box, and you can restore the default width (18.8 characters unless you have changed the font size) by checking the Standard Width box. As a rule, you will get a better sense of how wide a column should be by adjusting it with the mouse and observing how much data is visible, but entering the width directly is the easiest way to set several columns to exactly the same width.

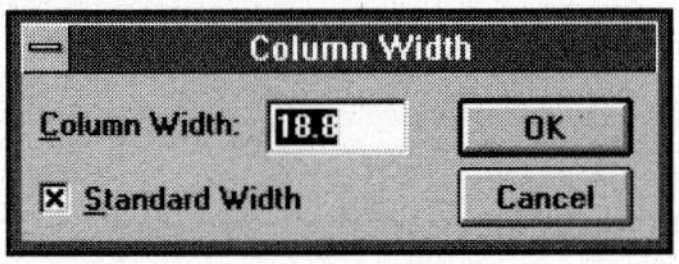

Figure 4.10
The Column Width dialog box

Changing the Row Height

When a table contains Memo or long Text fields, you may want to increase the row height to display more of the contents of these fields. As you will see later in this chapter, you will also have to reset the row height if you switch to a larger or smaller font. To change the height of all the rows in the datasheet (you cannot change the height of an individual row), you can use techniques similar to the ones described in the previous section:

1. Move the mouse to the lower boundary of any record selector. The mouse pointer will change to a horizontal line with two vertical arrows, symbolizing movement of the boundary between rows.

2. Press the left mouse button and hold it down as you move the mouse to drag the row boundary up or down.

3. Release the mouse button when the row is the desired height.

As you drag the lower row boundary up or down, you can use the original grid lines as guides to help you judge the correct height. For example, to establish a row height that accommodates exactly two lines of text, simply drag the row border down until it coincides with the next horizontal boundary line. You can also change the row height by using the Row Height option on the Layout menu, which invokes the dialog box depicted in Figure 4.11. The row height is expressed in points (1 point is $1/72$ inch). You can change the row height by entering a new value in the Row Height box, and you can restore the default height (10.5 points) by checking the Standard Height box. If you are adjusting the row height after changing the font size, using the mouse is easier and faster, but entering the height in the Row Height dialog box is more accurate when you want to establish a new row height that is an exact multiple of the present height.

Figure 4.11
The Row Height
dialog box

When you set the row height greater than the height of the font currently in use, Access word-wraps the data in fields that are too wide to fit within the current column width rather than truncating long entries. Figure 4.12 illustrates the Names table datasheet with the row height set to exactly twice the standard height. You can see that the longer entries in the Name, Company, and Address fields wrap onto the second line, and that the second address line is visible in Christopher Bloom's record. This configuration is especially useful for displaying and entering Memo fields and Text fields intended to hold more than one line of data, such as the Address field in the Names table.

Figure 4.12

Setting the row height to accommodate two lines of text

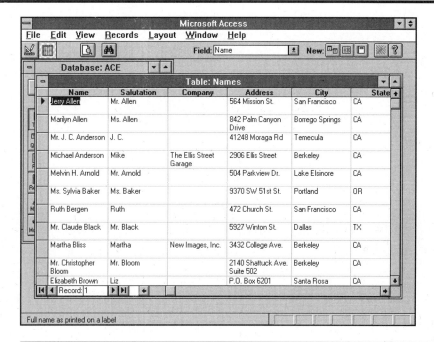

Changing the Font and Font Size

You can change the font and font size for the entire datasheet (but not for individual rows or columns) by choosing the Font option on the Layout menu, which invokes the Font dialog box shown in Figure 4.13. Using the Font, Font Style, and Size combo boxes, you can choose any available font, and any style and size permitted for this font. As you scroll through the list of fonts, the Font Style and Size boxes change to display only the options available for the selected font.

The list of fonts displayed in the Font combo box depends on whether you have enabled TrueType or Adobe Type Manager fonts, but you will always see at least the standard Windows screen and printer fonts. Special symbols to the left of the font names identify the type of font—TT for TrueType, ATM for Adobe Type Manager, and a printer icon for printer fonts (screen fonts have no special symbol). In the Sample region, Access displays a few characters in the selected font, size, and style to help you make your selections, together with a brief description of the font and a reminder about the relationship between screen and printer fonts. For the closest possible match between the screen display and printed output, choose a TrueType or Adobe Type Manager font.

Figure 4.13

The Font dialog box

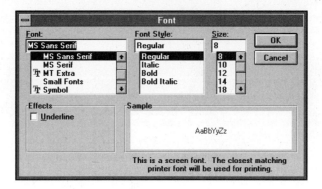

If you plan to change the font, font style, or font size, you should do so *before* you adjust the row height and column widths in the datasheet. Access makes no assumptions about the relationship between the standard datasheet dimensions and the font settings, and it does not automatically adjust the row height or column widths when you change the font attributes. If you establish the font settings first, you can adjust the column widths and row height to conform to the chosen font.

Moving Columns

You can move a column by selecting it and then dragging it to a new position. To select one column, click on the field selector at the top of the column or move into the column and press Ctrl+Spacebar. The column immediately changes color (to white letters on a black background if you are using the default Windows colors) to remind you that it is selected. You can select more than one column by using techniques similar to the ones outlined earlier in this chapter for rows:

- Click on the field selector for the first or last column in the group, hold the mouse button down, drag the mouse to the other end of the group, and then release the mouse button.

- Click on the field selector for the first or last column in the group, release the mouse button, and then hold down the Shift key and click on the selector for the field at the other end.

- Move to any record in the first or last column in the group, press Ctrl+Spacebar, and then hold the Shift key down as you use the Right Arrow or Left Arrow key to move to the other end of the group.

To move the selected column(s), click again in the field selector (or if more than one column is selected, in any of the field selectors) and then use the mouse to drag the column(s) left or right. As you drag, Access displays a heavy vertical line that indicates the new position of the left border of the selected column(s) if you are moving the columns to the left, or the new position of the right border if you are moving the columns to the right. To "drop" the column(s) in the new location, release the mouse button.

If you prefer to use the keyboard, you can select the column(s) you want to move, press Ctrl+F8 to initiate Move mode, and then use the Left Arrow or Right Arrow key to move the selected column(s) to the desired location. To cancel Move mode (whether or not you actually moved any columns), press Esc.

Holding Columns Stationary

You can use the Freeze Columns command on the Layout menu to freeze one or more columns so that they remain stationary on the left side of the datasheet as you pan the display left and right to view other fields. If you choose this option with no columns selected, Access moves the current column (the one that contains the field that has the focus) to the left edge of the window and freezes just that column. If you first select one or more columns, it moves the selected columns to the left and freezes them.

NOTE. *You cannot select noncontiguous columns, so the only way to freeze two or more columns that are not adjacent in the table structure is to move them next to each other before you select them and issue the Freeze Columns command.*

Access displays a slightly heavier vertical grid line to separate the frozen columns from the rest, but otherwise accords them no special treatment—you can move freely into these columns and edit the data, and you can resize but not move them. Note, however, that after panning the display to the right, selecting a frozen column from the Field combo box in the tool bar or pressing Home moves you directly into the column, *leaving the other columns on the screen exactly where they are*, whereas pressing Left Arrow or Ctrl+PgUp pans the display all the way to the left before moving you into the frozen column.

To unfreeze previously frozen columns, choose the Unfreeze All Columns option on the Layout menu. Note that unfreezing columns *does not* return any columns that Access moved before freezing them to their original positions in the datasheet—you must do this yourself.

Hiding Columns

When you use the Datasheet view to update a table with more than a few fields, you often do not need to see all the fields. To expedite working in the datasheet, you can hide the columns that are irrelevant in the current context by selecting them and then choosing the Hide Columns option on the Layout menu.

The Show Columns option on the Layout menu invokes the dialog box shown in Figure 4.14, which serves a dual purpose—it enables you to hide columns as well as to reveal previously hidden columns. (You might interpret the meaning of this command as "Choose the list of columns you want to *show*.") The Show Columns dialog box includes a scrolling list of column titles (*not* field names) with check marks indicating which ones are currently visible. Note that the column names are arranged in alphabetical order, not in the order they occur in the table structure or the order in which they appear in the datasheet.

Figure 4.14
The Show Columns dialog box

To hide a column, highlight its name in the Column list and click on the Hide command button (or press Alt+H). To redisplay a previously hidden column, highlight its name in the Column list and click on the Show command button (or press Alt+S). You can select multiple columns by using any of the standard keyboard and mouse techniques described earlier in this chapter. For example, you can select several consecutive columns by clicking on the name of the first one in the group and then holding the Shift key down as you click on the name of the last, and you can select non-contiguous columns by holding down the Ctrl ley as you click on successive field names. When you are satisfied with the current column list—that is, only the columns you want to be visible are checked—close the Show Columns dialog box by clicking on the Close command button. Using this dialog box is the most efficient way to hide numerous fields that are scattered throughout the datasheet.

Saving the Datasheet Configuration

When you close a datasheet after making any of the changes outlined in this chapter, Access displays an alert box like the one pictured in Figure 4.15 to ask you whether you want to save the current datasheet configuration with the table. For simple tables that require only one basic datasheet layout, you will usually want to save your changes for future work sessions. However, there is no single command that restores the default datasheet layout—you must undo all your changes one by one. Chapter 10 describes how to design a form that describes a customized datasheet, so that you can create as many specialized datasheet configurations as you need for a table.

Figure 4.15

Saving or discarding the datasheet layout

Customizing the Names Table Datasheet

Figure 4.16 illustrates the Names table datasheet with the ID Code and Name fields frozen and the display panned to show the three keyword fields. To reproduce this layout, use the following steps:

1. Open the Names table if it is not already open, and move to the second field in the first record.

2. Use the mouse to adjust the width of the column so it is just wide enough to accommodate the title.

3. Press Tab to move into the Name column, select the Column Width option on the Layout menu, and set the width of the current column to exactly 25 characters.

4. Click on the column selector for the Salutation field, and drag the mouse to the right until the Company column is also selected. Choose the Hide Column option from the Layout menu to hide these two columns.

5. Use the mouse to widen the Address column until you can see the entire address in the second record, "842 Palm Canyon Drive."

6. Use the mouse to narrow the State column until it is just wide enough to accommodate the column title.

7. Select the Show Columns option on the Layout menu, and note that the Company column, which is hidden, is not checked.

8. Scroll down the list of columns until Last Contact is highlighted. Hold the Shift key down and press Down Arrow twice until the Last Contact, Last Credit, and Last Renewal fields are all highlighted.

Figure 4.16

Customizing the Names table datasheet

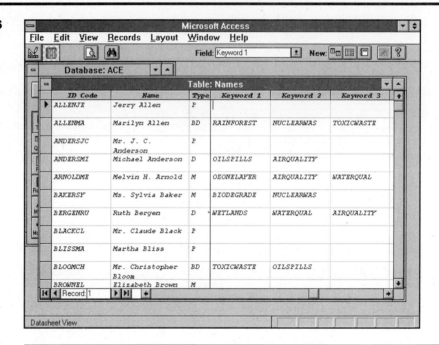

9. Release the Shift key and use the scroll bar in the list box to move down to the bottom of the list. Press and hold the Ctrl key and click on Total Credits, and then on Total Debits. At this point, all five fields you selected will be highlighted (although the first three are no longer visible in the list box).

10. Click on the Hide button or press Alt+H to hide all five selected columns. You may want to scroll back up the list to verify that none of these fields is checked.

11. Click on Close or press Alt+C to close the Show Columns dialog box.

12. Move the mouse to the boundary between any two row selectors and drag the boundary down to the next grid line to set the row height to exactly twice the default. You should see the second address line for at least one of the records (for example, Christopher Bloom or Frederick Dodd).

13. Click on the column selector for the Name column. Press the mouse button again and drag the column to the left until it lies between ID Code and Type.

14. Click on the column selector for the ID Code column, hold the Shift key down, and click on the column selector for the Type column, so that the ID Code, Name, and Type columns are selected. Choose Freeze Columns from the Layout menu to freeze these three columns at the left side of the Datasheet window, and then click anywhere in the window to deselect the columns.

15. Pan the display to the right until you see the three keyword fields. As you go, verify that the first three columns remain frozen at the left side of the datasheet and that the columns you hid are not visible.

16. Select the Font option from the Layout menu and choose the LinePrinter font. Note the message below the Sample box—"This is a printer font. The closest matching Windows font will be used on your screen."

17. Select Italic from the Font Style combo box. Note the new message below the Sample box—"This font style is imitated for the display. The closest matching style will be used for printing."

18. Click on OK to close the Font dialog box.

At this point, your screen should look something like Figure 4.14 (you may see different rows if you scrolled down the screen). Feel free to experiment further, but when you close the datasheet, be sure to choose No in the alert box that asks whether you want to save your changes to the Names table datasheet. If you want to try the examples in the rest of this chapter, you can reopen the Names table immediately.

Searching for Records

The navigation methods described thus far in this chapter serve the purpose admirably when your tables are small and you are familiar with the contents. For tables of more than a few hundred records, tables created by co-workers, and tables that you use relatively infrequently, these methods are inadequate, and you will need to search for records based on their contents. Access offers a versatile search capability that allows you to find an exact or partial match in one field or in all the fields in a table, based either on the true contents of the record or on the data as it is formatted for display.

To initiate a search, choose the Find option from the Edit menu or click on the Find command button on the tool bar (the one with the binoculars symbol on its face). If you want to search just one field, make sure that this field has the focus before you execute the Find command. (You do not have to select the entire column—just make sure that any field in the column is highlighted or contains the insertion point.)

In response to the Find command, Access displays the dialog box pictured in Figure 4.17. To remind you which field has the focus, Access displays its name in the title bar (the column title in the datasheet may be hidden behind the Find dialog box). You enter the *search string*—the value you want to find—in the Find What text box. By default, Access assumes that you want to search only in the current field. To search all fields in the current table, select the All Fields radio button in the Search In region. When you do this, the dialog box title changes from the potentially misleading "Find in field" to "Find."

Figure 4.17

The Find dialog box

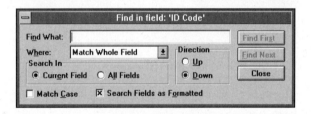

Access also assumes that you want to find an exact match for the search string—that is, the value you enter matches the entire contents of the field or fields you are searching. You can conduct a partial search by choosing Any Part of Field or Start of Field from the Where list box. The Start of Field option is most useful when you cannot remember the full contents of the field or if you suspect it may have been spelled wrong or inconsistently. For example, if you do not remember a donor's ID code, you could enter the first few letters of the last name, which you know must occur at the beginning of the ID Code field. Searching for "Berk" in the City field would find the common misspellings "Berkley" and "Berkely" as well as the correct "Berkeley." Be sure to enter enough characters to avoid finding too many erroneous matches. For example, if you try to find San Francisco by entering "San F," Access will find many other cities besides San Francisco.

If you choose Any Part of Field from the Where list box, Access will find the search string regardless of where it occurs in the field. This option is handy for finding data that you *know* falls somewhere in the middle of the field. For example, if you do not recall a donor's first name, you could search for the last name in the Name field, using the Any Part of Field option. Similarly, if you did not know a person's house number, you could search in the Address field for the street name. Unlike many word processors, Access does not offer an option to search for whole words only, but you can accomplish this by including leading and trailing spaces in the search string. For example, if you want to find John but not Johnson in a name field, enter the search string as " John " so that you are in effect looking for the name, together with the

spaces that precede and follow it. There is also no way to explicitly request
that Access search for the *last* word in a field (this would be particularly convenient for finding last names).

You can use *wildcard* characters in the search string to find groups of
records that have similar values in a field. There are three wildcard symbols,
the first two of which are used exactly as they are in MS-DOS: the asterisk
(*), which stands for any sequence of characters; the question mark (?),
which represents any single character; and the number sign (#), which represents any single digit. For example, searching the Source field for "LIST?"
would retrieve records with the referral sources LISTA, LISTB, LIST1, and
so on, whereas searching for "LIST#" would find LIST1, LIST2, and LIST3,
but not LISTA or LISTB. The wildcards are also useful with date fields—to
find any date in April 1992, you could enter the search string as "4/*/92."

You can further narrow the search criteria to include only a specific set of
characters by entering them into the search string enclosed in square brackets. For example, to search for LISTA or LISTC, you could enter the search
string as "LIST[AC]." You can express a range of consecutive letters or digits
by entering just the first and last, separated by a hyphen. For example, searching for "LIST[A-D]" would find LISTA, LISTB, LISTC, or LISTD. Finally,
you can exclude characters by listing them, preceded by an exclamation point
(!), which you might read as "not." Thus, to search for any referral source that
begins with "LIST" except LISTB, you could enter the search string as
"LIST[!B]."

By default, Access conducts a case-insensitive search—that is, it treats
uppercase and lowercase as identical—but you can request a case-sensitive
search by checking the Match Case check box in the Find dialog box.

The Search Fields as Formatted option determines whether Access
searches based on the way the data is displayed or on the way it is stored. For
example, if you use a custom display format to insert the dash in a telephone
number stored in a Text field, you must include the dash in the search string if
Search Fields as Formatted is checked, and you must *not* include the dash if
this option is not checked. In this example, there is no particular advantage to
conducting the search either way, but for Date/Time and Yes/No fields, which
may contain values entered in several different formats, checking Search
Fields as Formatted and matching the search string to the display format ensures that you will find every matching record. This option can be crucial
when several people enter data into a table—one may enter dates in Short
Date format (for example, 9/2/94), while another prefers Medium Date format (2-Sep-94).

If you initiate the search by selecting the Find First command button,
Access begins searching at the top of the table; if you use the Find Next button, it begins with the current record. When you start with the current record,
you can use the Up and Down radio buttons to choose the search direction.

Selecting Down (the default) causes Access to proceed from the current record toward the end of the table (as if it were moving *down* the datasheet), whereas selecting Up causes Access to search toward the beginning of the table (moving *up* the datasheet). Note that you cannot restrict the search to a group of records by selecting them—if you issue the Find command with a group of records selected, Access cancels the selection before it begins the search. Instead, you must use a query (introduced in Chapter 5) or a filter (described in Chapter 6) to restrict *all* processing, including searches, to a selected group of records.

The Find dialog box remains on the screen until you explicitly close it, which you can do by clicking on the Close button or pressing Esc. When Access finds a record, it highlights the field you were searching, but often you cannot see this field because it is under the dialog box. To verify which record was retrieved, you can look for the current record indicator at the left side of the Datasheet window, or check the record number displayed in the lower-left corner. At any point, you can move the Find dialog box to a more convenient location where it does not obscure the fields you need to see. After Access finds a record, the Find Next command button becomes the default object in the Find dialog box, and you can continue to search for additional matching records by repeatedly pressing Enter. If you want to search a different field, you must close the Find dialog box, move to another column, and choose the Find option again.

You can search again for the last search string entered into the Find dialog box without reopening this dialog box by pressing Shift+F4. Note that regardless of the field you originally searched, Shift+F4 causes Access to look for the search string in the current field.

If Access fails to find a record that matches your search string on the first attempt, it displays the alert box illustrated in Figure 4.18. You can choose OK to acknowledge the error message or Help to display a relevant help screen. If a repeated search initiated by choosing the Find Next option after finding at least one matching record fails, Access displays the alert box shown in Figure 4.19, which asks you whether to continue the search, starting at the beginning of the table (if you set the search direction to Down) or at the end (if the search direction was Up). You might choose Yes if you used the Find Next option to begin the search, thus bypassing records that fall before the current record in the search sequence. If you choose No, the Find dialog box remains visible, and you can either enter new search specifications or close the Find dialog box. When you use the Find command to search for all the records that match a certain pattern (for example, search the Source field for LISTA) rather than to retrieve one specific record, you may want to keep searching until you see the alert box pictured in Figure 4.19 to ensure that you have found all the desired records.

Figure 4.18
The alert box
displayed when a
search fails on the
first attempt

To experiment with various search strategies in the Names table, try the
following steps:

1. Open the Names table if it is not already open and move to the ID Code
   field in the first record.

2. Click on the Find button in the toolbar or select the Find option from the
   Edit menu.

3. Type **DAVISCR** in the Find What box, leave Search In set to Current
   Field, leave Match Case unchecked and Search Fields as Formatted
   checked, select Down as the direction, and click on Find First.

4. Because no record in the Names table has the ID code "DAVISCR,"
   Access displays an alert box to notify you that it has reached the end of
   the table without finding a record. Click on OK to close the alert box,
   change the search string to DAVISCH and click on Find First again. This
   time, Access moves the current record indicator to record 19, the one for
   Charles and Anne Davis.

5. Close the Find dialog box, move to the Name column, and issue the Find
   command again.

6. Type **David** as the search string.

Figure 4.19
The alert box
displayed when a
repeated search fails

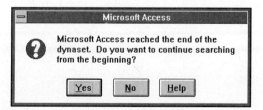

7. Select Any Part of Field from the Where combo box and click on Find First. Access highlights the record for Jacqueline Davidson (you may have to move the Find dialog box to confirm that this is the right record).

8. Select Find Next. Access highlights the record for David Smith (record 84).

9. Select Find Next again. Access highlights the record for another David Smith (record 85).

10. Select Find Next again. This time, Access informs you that there are no more matching records. Select No to discontinue the search, and then close the Find dialog box.

NOTE. *Of all the search methods, the fastest is searching for an exact match on the whole field, and the slowest is searching anywhere in the field. Searching one field is always faster than searching all the fields in a table, and searching for an exact match or at the start of an indexed field is much faster than searching an unindexed field or searching anywhere within any field. Checking the Search Fields as Formatted option slows the search somewhat, but this option may be essential for finding all the matching records.*

Replacing Field Values

The Find commands outlined in the previous section simply locate records based on their contents. You can use the related Replace command to search for one value and replace it with another, not unlike the search and replace operations carried out with a word processing program. You must begin by choosing the Replace command from the Edit menu; there is no equivalent command button in the tool bar. The Replace dialog box is shown in Figure 4.20, with specifications filled in for replacing all occurrences of "PETITION" in the Source field with "SIGNATURE." As in the Find dialog box, you can choose whether to search the current field or all fields and whether the search should be case-sensitive. Instead of the three Where options in the Find dialog box, there is one check box that enables you to specify whether your search string must match the whole field. (Checking the Match Whole Field check box is equivalent to choosing Whole Field in the Find dialog box, and unchecking this box is equivalent to choosing Any Part of Field.)

You can use wildcards in the search string that you enter in the Find What box, but not in the replacement string entered into the Replace With box. For example, to replace "LISTA," "LISTB," and "LISTC" with "LISTABC," you could enter the search string as "LIST[A-C]" and the replacement string as "LISTABC."

You cannot control the direction of the search, but you can fine-tune the replacement process. To step through the table one occurrence at a time, begin by selecting the Find Next command button. As is the case when you

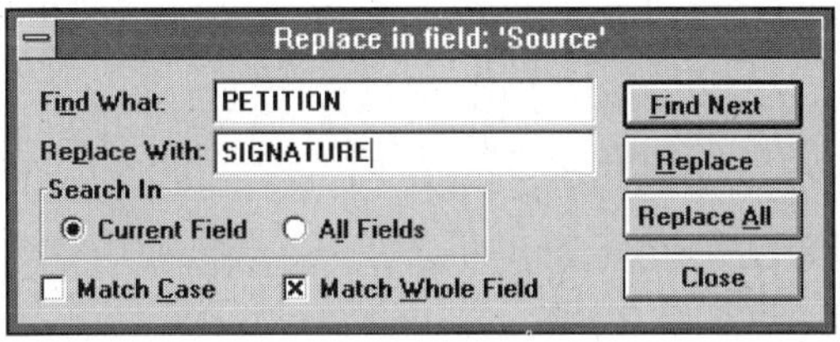

Figure 4.20

The Replace
dialog box

```
┌─────────────────────────────────────────────┐
│ ─    Replace in field: 'Source'              │
├─────────────────────────────────────────────┤
│  Find What:    [PETITION        ]   ┌──────────┐│
│                                     │ Find Next││
│  Replace With: [SIGNATURE|       ]   └──────────┘│
│  ┌Search In──────────────────┐      ┌──────────┐│
│  │ ● Current Field  ○ All Fields│     │ Replace  ││
│                                     └──────────┘│
│                                     ┌──────────┐│
│                                     │Replace All││
│  ☐ Match Case   ☒ Match Whole Field  └──────────┘│
│                                     ┌──────────┐│
│                                     │  Close   ││
│                                     └──────────┘│
└─────────────────────────────────────────────┘
```

search, Access finds the first record that satisfies your search criteria and high-lights the matching data. You can then select the Replace button to replace the highlighted data with the replacement string and search for the next oc-curence, or Find Next to bypass the current record and search for the next match. To discontinue the replace operation at any point, simply close the Re-place dialog box. You can repeat the previous search and replace operation without reopening the Replace dialog box by pressing the same hot key used for searching—Shift+F4.

If the current record does not satisfy the search criteria when you choose the Replace option, Access displays an alert box to warn you that there is "No match to replace in current field." This might happen if you mistakenly pick the Replace command button (instead of Find Next) to initiate the search and replace operation, or if you select this button again after Access has already found and replaced every occurrence of the search string in the table.

At any point during a search, you can choose the Replace All command button to replace all remaining occurrences of the search string without con-firming each one. If you know from the outset that you want to do a global search and replace, you can use this option instead of Find Next to initiate the search. Access always displays an alert box when it reaches the end of the table and offers you the opportunity to begin searching again from the begin-ning. In most cases, this is unnecessary, but you might use it if you suspect you may have inadvertently bypassed a few records while replacing records one at a time. Note, however, that reading through all the records again may take some time in a large table.

After completing a global search and replace operation conducted with the Replace All option, Access displays an alert box like the one in Figure 4.21 to give you one last chance to undo the changes. You can choose OK to continue and save the changes in the table, or Cancel to undo the changes and restore the original field values. Think carefully before you select your re-sponse, because OK is the default choice (the one selected if you press Enter), and this option is potentially very destructive—after you choose OK, you will not have another opportunity to undo the changes you made.

Figure 4.21
Confirming or
canceling a replace
operation

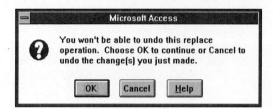

Use the following steps to change the committee code for the Newsletter Committee from "NEWS" to "NEWSLETTER" and change "Chairman" to "Chairperson" in the Officer field:

1. Close the Names table and open the Committees table if it is not already open.

2. Make sure the Committee column in the first record has the focus, and choose the Replace command from the Edit menu.

3. Type **NEWS** in the Find What box and **NEWSLETTER** in the Replace With box.

4. Make sure the Match Whole Field box is checked.

5. Select Find Next to begin the replace operation. Access highlights the first Newsletter Committee record (record 15).

6. Select Replace to replace this field and move to the next occurrence. Access highlights the next Newsletter Committee record (record 16).

7. Continue to select Replace to replace the remaining occurrences of the search string, and then select No when Access asks if you want to continue searching from the beginning of the dynaset.

8. Close the Replace dialog box, press Tab to move into the Officer column, and choose the Replace command again.

9. Type **man** as the search string and **person** as the replacement, uncheck Match Whole Field, and select Replace All to change all occurrences without confirming each one. Because you began the operation at the end of the table, Access immediately informs you that it has reached the end of the dynaset and asks if you want to continue searching from the beginning.

10. Select Yes to continue the search from the beginning of the Committees table. This time, you should see at least one record in which the Officer field reads "Chairperson" when Access informs you that it is at the end

of the dynaset. Select OK in this alert box, and OK again when Access asks you to confirm your changes.

11. Close the Replace dialog box.

Printing a Table

You can use the Print option on the File menu to print all or part of a table, more or less as it appears on the screen in Datasheet view. The resulting printout is relatively crude compared to the effects you can achieve with even the simplest report, but printing the datasheet gives you a fast and easy way to obtain a quick list of some or all of the records in a table.

If you want to print the whole table, you do not have to open it—simply highlight the table name in the Database window, and then choose the Print option from the File menu. Access displays the Print dialog box illustrated in Figure 4.22, which should seem familiar if you have worked with other Windows software. The Print Range selections and printer choices appear in most Windows Print dialog boxes, as does the Setup command button, which leads to another dialog box that enables you to choose a different printer, page size, paper orientation (portrait or landscape), and margins. You can also customize the printer setup before you initiate a particular print job by choosing the Print Setup command on the File menu. This option calls up the same dialog box invoked by the Setup command button in the Print dialog box. If you have only one printer, you may never (or rarely) need to change the Setup options. In fact, to print an entire table, you do not have to change any settings in the Print dialog box—simply select the OK button or press Enter.

Figure 4.22
The Print dialog box

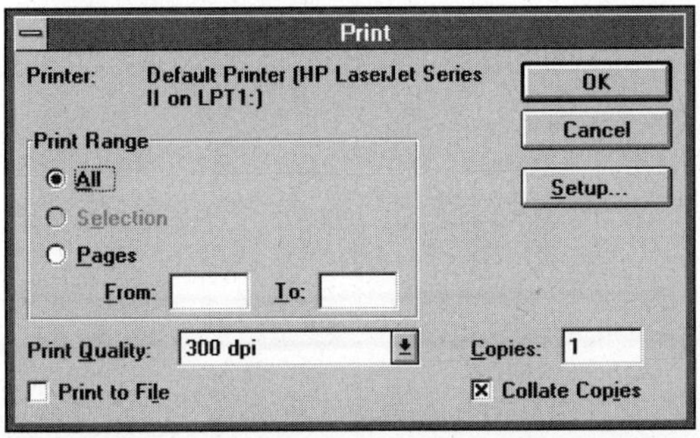

Access prints the table with the same column titles and column widths as in the Datasheet view, so you may not be able to see the full contents of long Text or Memo fields. The number of rows (records) and columns (fields) on each page depends on the font, the page margins, and the paper size and orientation—a page will contain more columns but fewer rows in landscape mode than in portrait mode. Access never splits a column across a page boundary. If each record has too many fields to fit across one printed page, it prints as many continuation pages as necessary to accommodate the additional fields before it goes on to print the next group of records. The print sequence for the Names table, which requires five pages to print all the columns in a given record at the default column width, is diagrammed in Figure 4.23, and the first page of output is illustrated in Figure 4.24.

Figure 4.23

The print sequence for the Names table

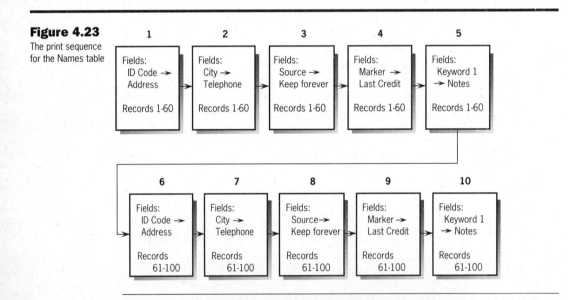

Like most Windows programs, Access makes every attempt to match the printer and screen fonts. If you chose a TrueType or Adobe Type Manager font for the datasheet, the printer font will match the screen font exactly; otherwise, the printer font will be the closest match among the available fonts installed on your system.

In most cases, you will want to make a few modifications to the appearance of the datasheet before you print. In particular, you will often need to adjust column widths and/or the row height to accommodate long Text fields. Because you might want to discard any changes to the datasheet configuration that you made just for printing, it may be preferable to initiate printing from the Datasheet view (using the same Print option on the File menu) rather than from the Database window.

If you feel that the gridlines make the printout too busy, you can turn them off before you print a table by using the Gridlines option on the Layout

Figure 4.24

The first page of the
Names table printout

ID Code	Type	Name	Salutation	Company	Address
ALLENJE	P	Jerry Allen	Mr. Allen		564 Mission St.
ALLENMA	BD	Marilyn Allen	Ms. Allen		842 Palm Canyon Dri
ANDERSJC	P	Mr. J. C. Anderson	J. C.		41248 Moraga Rd
ANDERSMI	D	Michael Anderson	Mike	The Ellis Street Gar	2906 Ellis Street
ARNOLDME	M	Melvin H. Arnold	Mr. Arnold		504 Parkview Dr.
BAKERSY	M	Ms. Sylvia Baker	Ms. Baker		9370 SW 51st St.
BERGENRU	D	Ruth Bergen	Ruth		472 Church St.
BLACKCL	P	Mr. Claude Black	Mr. Black		5927 Winton St.
BLISSMA	P	Martha Bliss	Martha	New Images, Inc.	3432 College Ave.
BLOOMCH	BD	Mr. Christopher Blo	Mr. Bloom		2140 Shattuck Ave.
BROWNEL	M	Elizabeth Brown	Liz		P.O. Box 6201
BURDICJE	P	Ms. Jeannine Burdi	Ms. Burdick		1215 Roland
CHOWBO	P	Bonnie Chow	Ms. Chow		488 40th St.
CHRISTMA	P	Mark Christiansen	Mr. Christiansen		5934 Claremont Ave.
CLARKAMY	P	Ms. Amy C. Clark	Ms. Clark		3001 King Street
COLLINSR	P	Robert Collins	Mr. Collins		351 Church St.
CRANEER	P	Mr. Eric Crane	Mr. Crane		P. O. Box 115924
DAVIDSJA	P	Jacqueline Davidso	Mr. Davidson		1311 W King Street
DAVISCH	D	Charles and Anne D	Charles and Anne		132 28th Ave
DODDFRED	MC	Mr. Frederick Dodd	Mr. Dodd	Dodd, Benson, and	450 Golden Gate Ave.
DOUGLANO	P	Norman Douglass	Mr. Douglass		5672 Claremont Ave.
ELLIOTCH	M	Cheryl Elliot, M.D.	Dr. Elliot		3918 Fruitvale Ave.
ENGLEJOHN	P	John Engle	Mr. Engle		P. O. Box 1112
FELLNATA	P	Ms. Natalie Fell	Ms. Fell		2728 S. University Dr.
FLETCHAR	P	Arnold N. Fletcher	Mr. N. Fletcher		2128 Van Ness Ave
FRANKLKA	M	Karen Franklin	Ms. Franklin		3605 Sacramento
GARCIATO	P	Tony Garcia	Mr. Garcia		2005 Huge Oaks
GOLDMANJA	P	Mr. James Goldman	Mr. Goldman		2110 Van Ness Ave.
GOLDMANRM	P	Roger M. Goldman	Roger		5733 Claremont Ave.
GRAYJON	P	Jonathan Gray	Jonathan		2653 Shattuck
GRAZIAAL	P	Alfredo Graziani	Mr. Graziani		3352 Mission Street
HANCOCED	P	Edward and Marie	Mr. and Ms. Hancoc		8800 Roosevelt Way
HARRINJU	M	Ms. Judy Harrington	Ms. Harrington		239 Nevada Street
HARRISBE	M	Benjamin Harris	Mr. Harris		517 N.W. 19th
HAYESJ	P	J. Hayes			2327 2nd Ave.
HEARNSKL	P	K. L. Hearns	K. L.		4201 Greenwood Ave
HILTONSO	P	Ms. Sonya Hilton	Ms. Hilton		1030 Keeler Ave.
HOWARDJO	M	John Howard, Jr.	Mr. Howard		1460 Calaveras Ave
JACOBSJO	P	Mr. Joseph T. Jaco	Mr. Jacobs		1172 East 90 South
JENKINLO	P	Mr. Louis Jenkins	Mr. Jenkins		702 Roaring Springs
JONESLI	P	Ms. Lillian Jones	Ms. Jones		P. O. Box 12652
JONESMI	P	Michael Jones	Mr. Jones		1570 E. 2nd St.
KATAYAJO	P	Joanna Katayama	Ms. Katayama		561 Mission St.
KESSLERA	P	Andrew Kessler	Mr. Kessler	Best Beans Coffe C	5433 Claremont Ave.
KIMVICTOR	P	Victor Kim	Mr. Kim		1206 Pico Blvd
KINGDAN	P	Daniel King	Dan	Better Homes Realt	1800 Market St.
KOWALSHO	P	Mr. Howard Kowals	Mr. Kowalski		111 SW Gibbs St.
KROUSECL	P	Clifford and Rose K	Cliff and Rose		3022 Luna
LEEALEX	M	Alexander Lee	Mr. Lee		1925 Walnut Ave.
LESSERMA	P	Margaret P. Lesser	Ms. Lesser		383 S. 19th St
LUSUSAN	D	Susan Lu	Ms. Lu		3222 NE 52nd Ave.
MANSONBA	P	Ms. Barbara Manso	Ms. Manson		2600 Van Ness Ave.
MATTHEFR	M	Frank and Ann Matt	Mr. and Mrs. Matthe		8732 Prospect Ave.
MCDANIBU	M	Burton McDaniel	Mr. McDaniel		3106 Bancroft St.
MCGUIRKA	P	Ms. Katherine McG	Ms. McGuire		308 N 300 E
MCKEESU	P	Susan McKee	Ms. McKee		4118 Russell Avenue
MEYERAL	P	Mr. Allan B. Meyer	Mr. Meyer		875 W 500 S
MICHAELPH	P	Philip Michaels	Mr. Michaels		5415 San Jacinto
MILLERJU	P	Julie R. Miller	Ms. Miller	Levinson & Assoc.	1275 4th Street
MILLERWI	P	William Miller	Mr. Miller		805 South Madison

menu in Datasheet view. If you generally prefer to work with gridlines displayed, you can open the table, turn off the gridlines, print the datasheet, and close the table without saving the changes you made to the datasheet. If you do choose Yes from the dialog box that asks "Save changes to table?" Access saves the status of the gridlines along with all the other settings described earlier in this chapter (the font, column widths, and so on). When you print without gridlines, Access still draws a border around the entire table and includes the standard separators between the column names—exactly as the datasheet appears on the screen. If you want to add any further enhancements, such as a page title or page numbers, you must abandon the simple Print option and create a report, as described in Chapter 7.

You can obtain an on-screen preview before you print by choosing the Print Preview option on the File menu or by clicking on the Print Preview command button in the tool bar. Figure 4.25 illustrates the appearance of the Print Preview screen. In Print Preview mode, the Access tool bar contains four command buttons relevant only to the preview operation, together with the Help button; most of the Access menu options are disabled. The navigation buttons in the lower-left corner of the window enable you to move through the print preview page by page.

Figure 4.25
The Print Preview screen

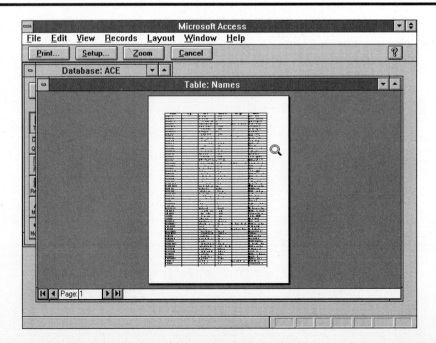

By default, Access shows you the "big picture"—an image of one printed page. When you preview a complex report, this view is convenient for scanning the overall page layout and verifying that the totals and page breaks appear in the right places, but unless you have selected a very large font, you will not be able to read the data. Note that in Preview mode, the mouse pointer is represented by a magnifying glass symbol when it is over the image of the printed page. You can zoom in on any portion of the page and view the text approximately the size it will be printed by clicking in the appropriate region or by using the Zoom command button. Figure 4.26 illustrates this view, which enables you to check the data, as well as the font and other print attributes. When the Preview window is zoomed, you can use the scroll bars or arrow keys to move around and examine any portion of the magnified page.

Figure 4.26
Zooming the Print
Preview screen

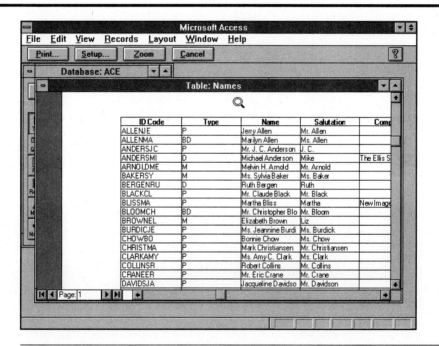

The Print and Setup command buttons invoke the same dialog boxes as the analogous commands on the File menu, which are also available in Print Preview mode. If you decide not to print after all, you can choose Cancel to exit from Print Preview mode and return to the previously active Access environment (the Datasheet or Database window). You must also use the Cancel option to exit from the Print Preview screen after printing records.

To print a portion of a table, you can select the desired records before you issue the Print or Print Preview command, and choose Selection in the Print Range region of the Print dialog box. You can use this technique to print just the new records entered into a table during the current work session or to get a quick hard copy of a group of records adjacent in primary key order. To print a selected range of pages, simply enter the page numbers in the Print Range region of the Print dialog box; this facility is most useful for reprinting pages damaged by a printer jam or for resuming a printout that you interrupted to use the printer for a higher priority task. As noted earlier, you can also select records for printing (and for many other purposes) based on their contents by using a query or a filter, as detailed in Chapters 5 and 6.

To print the ACE Committees table, use the following steps:

1. Open the Committees table if it is not already open, and maximize the Datasheet window.

2. Make the Joined and Quit columns narrower and widen the Notes column to about twice the default width.

3. Set the row height to three times the default height.

4. Select the Gridlines option from the Layout menu to turn off gridlines.

5. Select the Print option from the File menu and select OK to begin printing. The output should look something like Figure 4.27.

6. Close the Committees table without saving the changes you made to the datasheet layout.

Summary

This chapter described how to carry out all the fundamental data entry and update operations required to keep your tables accurate and up to date using a default data entry form known as the datasheet. In the Datasheet view, you can view, edit, or delete existing records, and you can add new records. Because you can specify the default value, display format, and validation rules for a field when you define the table structure, you often do not have to create custom forms simply to ensure accuracy and consistency. For tables with relatively few fields, such as the ACE Committees table, the datasheet may serve admirably as the primary data entry environment throughout the lifetime of an application, especially if you (or other knowlegeable users) are the primary users of the table. In any event, the Datasheet view is more than adequate for entering the sample data that you will use during the initial testing phase of a new application.

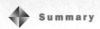

Figure 4.27

The Committees
table printout

Committee	ID Code	Officer	Joined	Quit	Notes
EARTHDAY	FRANKLKA	Chairperson	8/1/92		
EARTHDAY	HOWARDJO		5/10/91		
EARTHDAY	LEEALEX	Treasurer	7/23/90		
EARTHDAY	OLSONED		6/18/91	5/20/92	Ed organized the first ACE-sponsored "Run for the Planet" race and fun run, held in San Francisco in 1992.
FINANCE	ALLENMA	Chairperson	2/3/90		Ms. Allen was Treasurer of the Finance Committee from 6/90 through 7/91, when she became Chairperson
FINANCE	HOWARDJO		1/15/90	2/5/91	
FINANCE	SLATERLO	Treasurer	6/15/92		
FINANCE	THOMPSCH		12/18/91		
LOBBYING	ALLENMA		6/3/91		
LOBBYING	HARRINJU	Chairperson	10/20/92		
LOBBYING	LUSUSAN		10/25/90		
LOBBYING	OLSONED	Treasurer	5/10/92		
LOBBYING	REEDLUCY		4/18/90	5/1/92	
LOBBYING	ROSENBRH		4/1/91	4/5/92	Ralph, not Helen, was the committee member.
NEWS	BERGENRU	Chairperson	8/10/91		

Figure 4.27

The Committees table printout (Continued)

Committee	ID Code	Officer	Joined	Quit	Notes
NEWSLETTER	BLOOMCH		3/28/90	3/1/92	
NEWSLETTER	HOWARDJO		11/10/92		Howard is responsible for compiling events listings for the newsletter. Refer all press contacts to him.
NEWSLETTER	THOMPSCH		2/6/92		Christine is now the Editor of the ACE Newsletter

For larger tables—that is, tables with far too many fields to fit on the screen at once—the datasheet is less convenient. Although you can resize, re-arrange, and hide columns, you can only save one datasheet configuration with the table, and for most tables, there is no single optimum configuration—different users or contexts will demand different screen layouts. Less experienced users may prefer forms that look more like paper forms, and if the data is in fact entered from existing paper forms, any user will be able to work faster and feel more comfortable using screen forms that approximate the appearance of the input forms. Chapter 6 introduces you to designing custom data entry forms, and Chapters 10 and 12 elaborate on this subject.

5

Defining Simple Queries

ONE OF THE KEYS TO TURNING RAW DATA INTO USEFUL INFORMATION is the ability to view data *selectively*—to choose which items of information you want to see in a given context and to arrange these items into a meaningful order. While the simple keyboard and mouse commands described in Chapter 4 suffice for browsing through a small table in Datasheet view, they are tedious and inefficient for tables with more than a few fields and/or more than a few hundred records. The Find command, which serves admirably for retrieving individual records, is of little help in selecting *groups* of records that satisfy certain criteria so that you can view just those records together on the screen. Furthermore, although it is easy enough to customize the datasheet by resizing, moving, and hiding columns, you can only save one configuration, and you will soon grow tired of rearranging the datasheet repeatedly to conform to the varying requirements of different types of inquiries. If your preliminary experiments with the ACE Names table have not already convinced you of these facts, the point will be driven home when you begin working with tables that have thousands of records or with tables created by your co-workers, whose contents are not familiar to you.

You can expedite a variety of data retrieval and display operations by storing the instructions for carrying out each inquiry in an object called a *query*. Queries play several major roles in an Access database application, both passive (in operations that simply read data) and active (in operations that add, delete, or update records). This chapter describes how to create simple *select queries* that store instructions for customizing your view of the data in one table in three crucial ways: selecting which fields and calculated fields to display and where in the datasheet to display them, selecting which records to include, and specifying the order in which to display those records.

The word *instructions* in the foregoing description is crucial to your understanding of Access queries. The query object itself stores only the instructions that you enter using the Query Design tool, *not* the data described by the query. When you run a query, Access displays selected fields and records in the underlying table, not a copy, and if you edit the data, you are updating the table itself. As noted in Chapter 4, the term *dynaset* is used to describe the group of records you are working with in the current context, which may be either an entire table or the data selected by a query. This term should help remind you that because you are looking at the source table itself when you view a query's dynaset, this data is dynamic and always reflects the most current state of the underlying tables. If you have worked with other database programs, you may have seen the term *answer table* used to describe the output of a query. This term is not used in the Access documentation because it connotes working with a copy of the original table, but it may help you visualize the purpose of a query—if a query stores a question you are asking about your data, executing the query gives you the answer.

This chapter concentrates on how to define queries. Keep in mind, however, that you can substitute a query's dynaset (that is, the data selected by a query) for a table in most contexts—you can display the dynaset in Datasheet view, design custom forms to view and update the data, and print the dynaset using the simple commands described in Chapter 4 or by defining custom reports like the ones described in Chapter 7. Note, however, that there is no easy way to print a description of the query design. Chapter 8 describes queries based on more than one table, and Chapters 9 and 13 cover *action queries*, which carry out mass updates on one or more tables.

Defining Simple Select Queries

The Access tool that you use to define queries has an interface patterned on a query design tool called *Query-by-Example* (often abbreviated as *QBE*), which was originally developed for IBM mainframe computers. The name derives from the fact that many implementations of QBE (including the original) make extensive use of *examples*—entries that represent the type of data you want to select or symbolize the relationships between the tables that contribute to the query. The overall layout of the Access query design work surface is similar to other versions of Query-by-Example, and it should seem familiar if you have used other software that includes QBE capabilities, such as dBASE IV or Paradox on a PC, or a mainframe or minicomputer query builder. However, in Access the use of examples is less pervasive—you indicate links between tables by using the mouse to draw lines between the corresponding fields.

To invoke the Query Design tool to begin defining a new query, you can use any of the following methods:

- Make sure that the Database window displays the list of queries (if necessary, click on the Query button in the Database window or choose the Queries option from the View menu), and then click on the New command button or press Alt+N.

- Choose the New option from the File menu, and then choose Query from the submenu of object types.

- Highlight the name of the source table or query in the Database window and click on the New Query command button in the tool bar.

To edit an existing query, make sure that the Database window displays the list of queries and then double-right-click on the name, or highlight the name and either click on the Design button or press Alt+D.

The first step when you design a new query is to identify the source of the data, which can be one or more existing tables or queries. For the sake of simplicity, the term *table* is used exclusively throughout this discussion, but keep in mind that a query can also be based on the result of running another query. When you base one query on another, Access runs the first query and uses the resulting dynaset as the data source for the second query. If you used the method based on the New Query command button to open a new query, Access immediately displays the Query Design window with a list of the fields in the highlighted table or query visible in the upper-left corner. Otherwise, because specifying the data source is central to defining a query, Access immediately displays the Add Table dialog box when you invoke the Query Design tool to begin building a new query. Despite its title, this dialog box, which is shown in Figure 5.1, displays the names of both tables and previously defined queries (and, unfortunately, gives you no way to distinguish between the two). To add a table to the query, you can use any of the following methods:

- Double-click on the name in the Table/Query list.

- Highlight the name in the Table/Query list and press Enter.

- Highlight the name in the Table/Query list and either click on the Add command button or press Alt+A.

Figure 5.1

Adding a table to a query

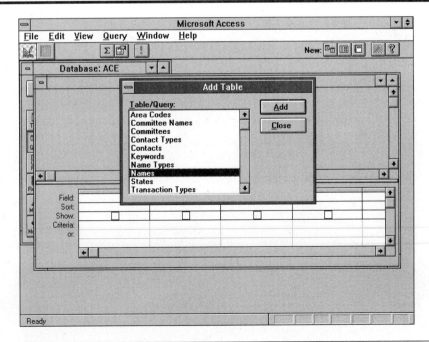

On the assumption that you might want to choose more than one table, Access leaves the Add Table dialog box open until you explicitly close it (either by selecting the Close command button or by using any other available method for closing a Windows dialog box, such as double-clicking on the close box in the upper-left corner). Even when you design a query based on two or more tables, you do not have to select all of the data sources at once—at any point, you can use the Add Table and Remove Table options on the Query menu to add or remove tables. These options, which are very useful when you design multitable queries, are described in Chapter 8; in the meantime, if you inadvertently pick the wrong table or close the Add Table dialog box without choosing a table, simply exit from the Query Design window without saving the query, and start over. If you want to try the examples in this chapter, take a moment to create a new query based on the Names table, using the following steps:

1. Make sure that the Database window displays the list of queries (if necessary, click on the Query button in the Database window or choose the Queries option from the View menu).

2. Click on the New command button or press Alt+N.

3. Highlight Names in the Table/Query list in the Add Table dialog box and press Enter.

4. Click on the Close button to close the Add Table dialog box.

Working in the Query Design Window

Figure 5.2 illustrates the Query Design window as it appears after you have chosen one table (the Names table) and closed the Add Table dialog box. Figure 5.3 diagrams the structure of the Access menu bar in Query Design view (some of the options are described in this chapter, and others are introduced in Part II). The Query Design window shares the fundamental properties of all Windows document windows, with the usual controls for moving, closing, resizing, and scrolling the window. As in all Access object design windows (including the Table Design window described in Chapter 3 and the Form Design and Report Design windows, which are introduced in Chapters 6 and 7), the title bar displays the type of object you are defining—in this case, a select query—and the name of the object itself.

When you begin designing a new query, Access assigns a default name that consists of the word "Query" followed by the next available number—Query1, Query2 (if the database already contains a query called Query1), and so on. The first time you save the query, Access displays a standard Save As dialog box to give you an easy opportunity to rename it. Although you might occasionally retain the default name for an experimental query or one

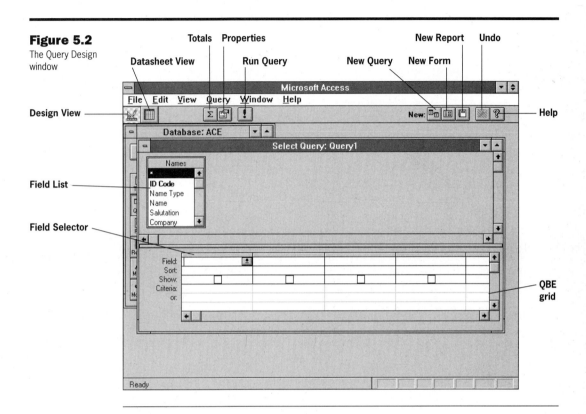

Figure 5.2

The Query Design window

created to carry out a one-time inquiry that will not be used again in the finished application, you should always assign a more meaningful name to any query you intend to retain for repeated use.

The Query Design window is divided horizontally into two major regions, each of which has its own horizontal and vertical scroll bars. As in most implementations of Query-by-Example, the upper region displays information about the sources that contribute data to the query (the input), and the lower region displays information about the output of the query. In the upper portion of the Query Design window, Access displays a field list window for each table or query dynaset that contributes to the query; in Figure 5.2, there is one such field list for the query's only input table, the Names table. You can use the mouse to move and resize a field list as you would a document window, and when you define queries based on more than one table, you can arrange the field lists in any convenient layout. If there are too many to fit on the screen at once, you can use the scroll bars to bring any field list into view.

To remind you which field or fields make up the primary key, Access displays the name(s) (in Figure 5.2, just the ID Code field) in bold type. In a

Figure 5.3

The structure of the
Access menu bar in
Query Design mode

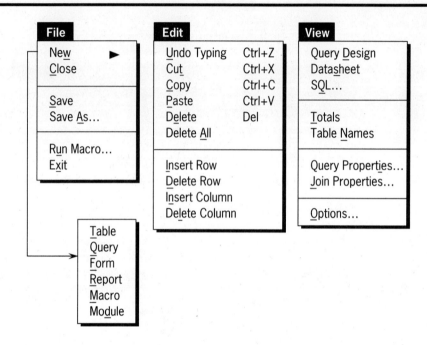

File
New ▶
Close

Save
Save As...

Run Macro...
Exit

Table
Query
Form
Report
Macro
Module

Edit
Undo Typing   Ctrl+Z
Cut   Ctrl+X
Copy   Ctrl+C
Paste   Ctrl+V
Delete   Del
Delete All

Insert Row
Delete Row
Insert Column
Delete Column

View
Query Design
Datasheet
SQL...

Totals
Table Names

Query Properties...
Join Properties...

Options...

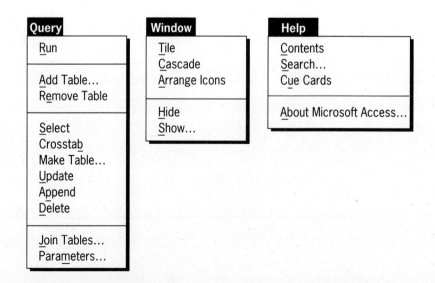

Query
Run

Add Table...
Remove Table

Select
Crosstab
Make Table...
Update
Append
Delete

Join Tables...
Parameters...

Window
Tile
Cascade
Arrange Icons

Hide
Show...

Help
Contents
Search...
Cue Cards

About Microsoft Access...

query based on one table, the primary key plays the same role that it does when you view the table itself—it determines the default display order for the query dynaset if you do not specify a different order (using methods described later in this chapter). In multitable queries, which are introduced in Chapter 8, the primary key is crucial for establishing the linkages between tables that have a one-to-many relationship. The asterisk at the top of the field list is a special symbol that represents *all* the fields in a table, much the way this symbol is used in DOS file names and Access search strings as a wildcard symbol that represents all combinations of characters. Some typical uses for this all-inclusive field symbol are described in the next three sections.

In the lower portion of the Query Design window is a tabular display called the *QBE grid* or *output grid*, in which you enter your description of the query output—the fields and calculated values that you want to see, the sort order (the sequence in which records will be displayed), and the selection criteria that govern which records will be included in the query dynaset. Each column in the output grid represents one data item—a field or calculated field—and you enter instructions based on a given data item in the appropriate row in the item's column. Each row describes one aspect of the output, as follows (all are explained in more detail later in this chapter):

Field	Data item—either a field or calculated field
Sort	Sort order (output display sequence)
Show	Whether to display the data item in the query output
Criteria	Output record selection criteria
Or	Additional output record selection criteria

As in the Table Design view, you can move between the upper and lower portions of the Query Design window by pressing F6 or by clicking anywhere in the desired region. You can adjust the column widths in the output grid by using the mouse to drag the boundary between column selectors left or right, and you can adjust the relative sizes of the upper and lower portions of the window by dragging the heavy horizontal line that separates the two up or down. Until you begin designing more complex queries, you will probably not need more space for the output grid, but you may find it convenient to enlarge the upper portion of the window and expand the field list(s). To configure the Query Design window to display the maximum number of fields from the Names table, you could use the following steps:

1. Maximize the Query Design window. Note that Access leaves the upper portion of the window the same size and adds rows to the QBE grid to fill the extra space.

2. Position the mouse over the dividing line between the two portions of the window (making sure that the mouse pointer changes to a horizontal line with two vertical arrows), press the left mouse button, and drag the boundary about halfway down the lower window.

3. If necessary, adjust the position of the boundary so that the QBE grid contains exactly six rows.

4. Use the mouse to drag the lower border of the Names table field list window down until Source or First Contact is the last field visible.

At this point, your screen should look something like Figure 5.4. Note that you can adjust the column widths in the output grid exactly as in a datasheet. You can also widen as well as lengthen a field list, and if you prefer to use long field names, you might want to do so. However, when you design queries based on more than two or three tables, the advantages of keeping as many tables as possible visible at once usually outweigh the convenience of being able to read the full field names.

Figure 5.4

Displaying the maximum number of fields

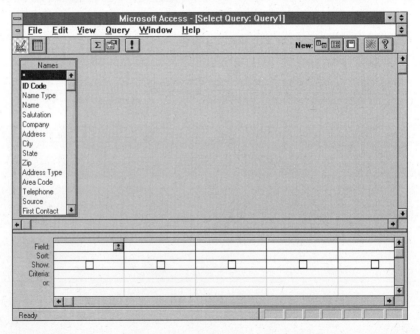

Choosing the Fields

As noted in the introduction to this chapter, one of the main reasons for defining queries is to choose which fields you want to see in a given context. For example, while making telephone calls to ACE members and donors, a staff member might want to see just the name, telephone number, city, state, and possibly donation totals. After you have selected at least one table to contribute data to the query, the next step is to add fields to the output grid. Access provides a variety of methods for choosing the output fields, working either from the field lists in the upper portion of the window or from the output grid itself. To choose fields from the field lists, you can use any of the following methods:

- Double-click on a field name to add the field to the next available column in the output grid.

- Using any of the keyboard or mouse commands described in Chapter 4, highlight one or more field names, use the mouse to drag the highlighted field name(s) down to the output grid, and release the mouse button over any column to "drop" the field(s) there.

- Double-click on the title bar in the field list window to select all the fields, and then use the mouse to drag them to the output grid.

When you use the "drag-and-drop" method to move fields, the shape of the mouse pointer changes as you drag to reflect the selected objects and to guide your manipulation of these objects.

The symbols are as follows:

  One field selected, mouse over the field list or output grid

  More than one field selected, mouse over the field list or output grid

  Mouse over a region where you cannot place fields

Whenever the mouse pointer is over the field list or the output grid, Access displays the pointer as a field icon (a small box with text inside) if one field is selected, or as a stack of field icons if more than one field is selected. When the mouse pointer is over a forbidden area where you cannot place fields (such as the empty space to the right of the field list in the upper portion of the window), it appears as a circle with a slash through it. If you try to drop fields in a forbidden zone, Access simply ignores you. "Dragging-and-dropping" is especially convenient for selecting a group of fields that are contiguous in the field list, while double-clicking on individual field names is the fastest method for choosing fields that are scattered through-out a table structure.

Alternatively, you can select fields from the output grid. Note that each cell in the Field row is a combo box (you can see the button that displays the drop-down list in Figure 5.2 or Figure 5.4). To enter or select a field name, you can use either of the following methods:

- Type a field name in any column in the Field row of the output grid.

- Press F4 or Alt+Down Arrow or click on the button at the right side of the combo box in any column in the Field row to display a field list, and use the keyboard or mouse to scroll through the list and choose a field.

This seeming overabundance of field selection methods is provided partly for convenience and partly out of necessity. If you are working primarily in the lower portion of the Query Design window (entering sorting instructions and selection criteria), you do not have to repeatedly switch back to the upper region each time you want to select another field. On the other hand, you *must* enter the expressions that describe calculated fields by typing them in the Field row—you cannot choose calculated fields from a list. Access therefore allows you to type field names as well.

NOTE. *When you type field names, watch out for one potentially undesirable side effect—if you misspell a field name, Access simply assumes that you are entering a calculated field expression and issues no warning. Problems will then arise when you try to run the query.*

To practice the various field selection methods, choose the fields for the ACE Telephone List query as follows:

1. Double-click on the Name field in the field list in the upper portion of the Query Design window to add this field to the output grid.

2. Position the mouse over the ID Code field, press and hold the left mouse button, drag the field to the output grid, and drop it on top of the Name field. Access inserts a new column for the ID Code field and moves the Name field column to the right.

3. Select both the Area Code and Telephone fields using any method you wish. For example, you can click on Area Code, hold the Shift key down, and click on Telephone. If you want to use only keyboard commands, note that you must press F6 to return to the upper portion of the Query Design window after selecting each field. Drag both fields to the output grid, and release the mouse button with the pointer over the third column.

4. Click three times on the button at the right side of the horizontal scroll bar below the output grid to bring three empty columns into view.

5. Press Right Arrow or click the mouse in the Field row of the first empty column, type **State**, and press Tab to move to the next column.

6. Press F4 or click on the arrow symbol in the Field row to display the list of field names. Choose City from the list and press Tab if necessary to move to the next column.

7. Type **Address** and press Enter. At this point, your screen should look like Figure 5.5.

Figure 5.5

Building the output field list

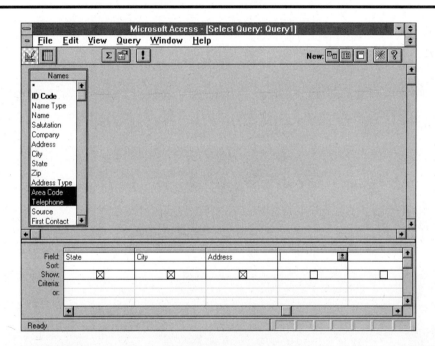

By default, Access checks the box displayed in the Show row for each field that you add to the output grid. If you do not want Access to display a field in the query dynaset, you must uncheck this box. Some reasons for including a field in the QBE grid but not displaying it as part of the output are described later in this chapter in the sections on sorting and specifying selection criteria.

As noted in the previous section, the asterisk symbol at the top of the field list represents all the fields in a table. To include all the fields in a table in the query's dynaset, you can add just the asterisk symbol to the output grid. One advantage of this method is that the asterisk *always* represents all the fields in a table, so you will not have to modify the query if you later change the table structure. To enter sorting instructions or selection criteria based on specific fields, you must also add these fields individually to the output grid and uncheck the Show box so that they do not appear twice in the query's dynaset. (Although it makes no sense to do so, Access allows you to enter sorting instructions or selection criteria in the column occupied by the asterisk symbol.) These methods are described in more detail later in this chapter in the sections on sorting and selecting records.

Editing the Output Grid

You can edit the field list described by the output grid using many of the basic methods outlined in Chapter 4 for customizing the Datasheet view. At the top of each column is a selector analogous to the field selectors in the datasheet, which you can use to select and manipulate columns in the QBE grid. These selectors are narrower than their counterparts in the datasheet because they do not have to accommodate field names, which are entered instead in the Field row of the grid.

You can delete one or more columns by selecting them and then pressing Del or choosing the Delete or Delete Column option from the Edit menu. As a shortcut, you can also delete a single column—the one that has the focus—by choosing the Delete Column option from the Edit menu (without first selecting the entire column). Note, however, that if you choose Delete rather than Delete Column from this menu without first selecting a column, Access deletes the contents of the current cell (for example, the field name), not the whole column. When you delete columns, Access moves the remaining columns to the left to fill in the gap.

You can move columns by selecting and dragging them, and you can insert a column to the left of the column that has the focus by choosing the Insert Column option on the Edit menu. As noted earlier, you can use the drag-and-drop method to insert a field between two others without first clearing an empty column for the field, but you do have to insert a new column if you want to type the field name or create a calculated field between two other columns.

To rearrange the columns in the Telephone List query so that the state and city appear first, and to remove the unneeded Address field, use the following sequence of steps:

1. Click on the column selector for the Address field, and then press Del to delete the column.

2. Click on the column selector for the State field.

3. Hold the Shift key down and click on the column selector for the City field.

4. With the mouse pointer over either of the selectors, press and hold the left mouse button and drag the two columns all the way to the left side of the output grid (to the left of the ID Code field).

5. Click anywhere in the output grid (for example, in the Field row in any column) to deselect the State and City columns. Your screen should look like Figure 5.6.

Figure 5.6

Rearranging the Telephone List query output field list

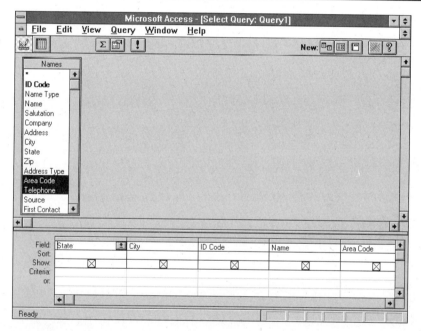

You can assign a new caption for any field in a query by entering it before the field name, followed by a colon. To enter the caption, move into the Field row and either click in the cell or press F2 to display an insertion point. If necessary, move the insertion point to the left of the field name, and type the caption, followed by a colon, and optionally, a space. Note that the caption is used *only* as the column heading in the query's datasheet—it does not change either the field name or the caption in the underlying table structure, and you cannot use it to refer to the field in calculations (you must use the field name).

You might want to retitle a column that displays a field for the same reason you assign captions in the table—to use a shorter name so that you can make a column narrower without obscuring its purpose. You might also prefer to assign a name that more accurately describes the role of a field *in a particular query* than does the field name. For example, in a query that selects donors, you might use "Donor ID" as the caption for the ID Code field or "Donor Name" for the Name field. (Obviously, if you decide you will *always* want to use a different field title, you should modify the table structure and change the field name or caption.) As you will see later in this chapter, you will nearly always want to specify new captions for calculated fields—the default names assigned by Access are usually too long, too cryptic, or both.

Saving the Query Design

To save a new or modified query and exit from the Query Design view, you can use any of the standard methods for closing a Windows document window (for example, double-clicking on the close box in the upper-left corner of the window or pressing Ctrl+F4). To save a query and continue working in Query Design view, you can use the Save Query option on the File menu, which saves the query under its present name, or the Save Query As option (also on the File menu), which allows you to change the name. It is generally a good idea to save a complex query several times before it is complete, in part to reduce the risk of losing all your work if you have a hardware crash or a power failure, and in part to enable you to return to a previous version of the query (by abandoning the current version without saving it) if a round of modifications fails to work as intended.

The first time you save a newly created query, Access displays the standard Save As dialog box, on the assumption that you will want to change the default name (Query1, Query2, and so on). Thereafter, you must use the Save Query As option to change the name. Keep in mind that the Save Query As command creates a *copy* of the query, and if you use it after saving a query under any other name (including Query1), you will have *two* queries in the database. You can take advantage of this fact to create a new query that is very similar to an existing one—simply modify the original query as needed and save the result under a new name.

Every time you close a query after making any changes, Access displays a dialog box like the one shown in Figure 5.7 to ask whether you want to save your changes. You can choose the Yes button to save the query and exit, No to exit without saving the changes you made during the current editing session, or Cancel to return to the Query Design window to continue working on the query. Remember that Access is asking whether you want to save the *query design*—the instructions for extracting data from one or more tables—not the data in the query dynaset (the result of executing the query).

Figure 5.7

Saving or canceling
changes to a query

Executing a Query

You can execute a query from the Query Design window or from the Database window. In most cases, you will run a query several times from the Query Design window as you refine the design, to verify that it performs as expected, and execute the query from the Database window in later work sessions. However, you may at times design a query in which the selection criteria are so highly variable that you would rarely run the query without changing them, and in these cases, you might open the query in Design view, edit the selection criteria, execute the query, and exit without saving your changes. To execute a query from the Query Design view, you can use any of the following methods:

■ Select the Run option from the Query menu.

■ Click on the Run Query button in the tool bar (the button with the exclamation point on its face).

■ Select the Datasheet option from the View menu.

■ Click on the Datasheet command button in the tool bar.

Note that you can use the first two methods to execute *any* kind of query, whereas the last two are available only for select queries; Access disables the Datasheet menu option and the Datasheet command button when you build an action query (action queries are described in Chapters 9 and 13).

To execute a query from the Database window, first make sure that the Database window displays the list of queries (if necessary, click on the Query button in the Database window or choose the Queries option from the View menu), and then use any of the following methods:

■ Double-click on the query name.

■ Highlight the query name and either click on the Open button or press Alt+O.

■ Highlight the query name and press Enter.

When you execute a select query, Access reads the instructions that it stores, carries out the steps required to extract the specified fields and records, and displays this data in Datasheet view. If your tables are small, executing a query takes only a few seconds, but it may take quite a bit longer to process a large table. In most cases, Access will display the first screenful of data almost immediately and continue working in the background to finish extracting the rest. You can begin editing as soon as Access displays data on the screen, and you can move freely around the datasheet. However, if you try to move to a location near the end of the dynaset (for example, by clicking on the Last Record navigation button or by using the vertical scroll bar), you must wait until Access has processed the relevant portion of the table. You can interrupt query execution (for example, if you want to change the query design or return to the Database window to carry out some other task) by pressing Ctrl+Break. Figure 5.8 illustrates the datasheet for the Telephone List query described earlier in this chapter.

Figure 5.8

The Telephone List query datasheet

	State	City	ID Code	Name	Area Code	Telephone
▶	CA	San Francisco	ALLENJE	Jerry Allen		
	CA	Borrego Springs	ALLENMA	Marilyn Allen		
	CA	Temecula	ANDERSJC	Mr. J. C. Anderson		
	CA	Berkeley	ANDERSMI	Michael Anderson	510	549-7838
	CA	Lake Elsinore	ARNOLDME	Melvin H. Arnold		
	OR	Portland	BAKERSY	Ms. Sylvia Baker		
	CA	San Francisco	BERGENRU	Ruth Bergen		
	TX	Dallas	BLACKCL	Mr. Claude Black		
	CA	Berkeley	BLISSMA	Martha Bliss	510	645-1947
	CA	Berkeley	BLOOMCH	Mr. Christopher Blo	510	848-3201
	CA	Santa Rosa	BROWNEL	Elizabeth Brown		
	WA	Bellingham	BURDICJE	Ms. Jeannine Burdi		
	CA	Oakland	CHOWBO	Bonnie Chow		
	CA	Oakland	CHRISTMA	Mark Christiansen		
	CA	Berkeley	CLARKAMY	Ms. Amy C. Clark	510	549-6086
	CA	San Francisco	COLLINSR	Robert Collins		
	TX	San Antonio	CRANEER	Mr. Eric Crane		
	NV	Carson City	DAVIDSJA	Jacqueline Davidsc		
	WA	Seattle	DAVISCH	Charles and Anne D		
	CA	San Francisco	DODDFRED	Mr. Frederick Dodd	415	992-2485
	CA	Oakland	DOUGLANO	Norman Douglass		
	CA	Oakland	ELLIOTCH	Cheryl Elliot, M.D.	510	637-1840
	CA	Berkeley	ENGLEJOHN	John Engle		
	TX	Fort Worth	FELLNATA	Ms. Natalie Fell		
	CA	San Francisco	FLETCHAR	Arnold N. Fletcher		
	CA	San Francisco	FRANKLKA	Karen Franklin		

Microsoft Access - [Select Query: Query1]

File Edit View Records Layout Window Help

Field: State   New:

Record: 1

Two-letter state abbreviation

The result of executing a query is called the *query dynaset*, or, if you display it in Datasheet view, the *query's datasheet*. When you view a query's datasheet, Access behaves for all intents and purposes as if you were viewing a table that consists only of the fields and records described by the query specifications, with the fields arranged in the order you placed them in the output grid. For example, the datasheet in Figure 5.8 looks like a table with six fields—State, City, ID Code, Name, Area Code, and Telephone. However, it is crucial to understand that *the information displayed in the query's datasheet is derived from the underlying tables*. Access does not make a second copy of the selected data—it displays the data from the source tables that is described by the query specifications. Thus, the datasheet in Figure 5.8 displays the State, City, ID Code, Name, Area Code, and Telephone fields from the Names table. If you want to create a separate table that contains a copy of the data described by a select query, you must convert the query to a type of action query called a *make table query*, which is described in Chapter 13.

When you edit a query's datasheet, Access saves your changes one record at a time, just as it does when you edit records in the table's datasheet, and you can use the same undo options to correct mistakes. Because you are working with real data, the basic properties of the fields in the query's datasheet are derived from the underlying table structure. For example, as you can see in Figure 5.8, the status bar displays the descriptions you entered when you created the table, and when you edit data, Access applies any formatting and validation rules defined in the table structure.

You can return to Query Design view from the datasheet by selecting the Query Design option from the View menu or by clicking on the Design tool in the tool bar. Note however that you do not have to return to Query Design view just to save the query. While you are viewing a query's datasheet, the Save and Save As options on the File menu are replaced by Save Query and Save Query As; these prompts should serve to remind you that you are saving the query design, not the data, which does not exist independent of the underlying tables. In general, however, it is advisable to play it safe and save a new or modified query *before* you execute it.

You can use all the commands described in Chapter 4 to customize the appearance of a query's datasheet by changing column widths and freezing, hiding, and moving columns. For example, you might want to adjust some of the column widths in the Telephone List query datasheet to conform to the field widths. Note that moving columns in the datasheet does not change their order in the query itself (you can verify this by returning to the Query Design window), just as rearranging the fields in a table's datasheet has no effect on the order of the fields in the structure. Unfortunately, Access does not save your changes as it does when you customize a table's datasheet, so you must rearrange the datasheet layout each time you execute the query. To save a specific configuration for a query's datasheet, you must design a form based on the query, as described in Chapter 10.

It is worth reiterating that unlike some other programs that use Query-by-Example, Access always displays the actual data from the underlying tables in the query's datasheet, not a copy of this data. Each time you run a query, Access repeats the steps required to extract the data it describes, thus ensuring that the query dynaset is complete and accurate as of the moment you execute the query. When a query is based on a single table and contains no summary statistics, each row in the query's datasheet corresponds to a record in the source table, and you can edit, add, and delete records in the dynaset exactly as you would while working with the table's datasheet. Because you are directly updating the original tables, not a copy, no special measures are required to apply your changes to the source tables. Updating a query dynaset derived from two or more tables is somewhat more complicated, and this subject is covered in Chapter 8. Using queries to compute summary statistics is described in Chapter 9.

You may often find yourself using a select query to quickly scan through large numbers of records, and a query can be an excellent tool for finding records that you need to delete. In most cases, select queries that include just a few fields (such as the Telephone List query) are not well suited to adding records, because all the fields that are not included in the dynaset will be blank in the new records, and filling in this data later, using the default datasheet or a custom form, can be a formidable task. However, in some applications, you may be able to use a select query (perhaps in conjunction with a custom data entry form) to help you fill in only the fields appropriate to a certain type of record. For example, in the ACE system, a query that includes just the Names table fields applicable to prospects would facilitate entering prospect names and addresses without the distraction of the additional fields that are required only for members, donors, and board members. Even more importantly, such a query would improve the accuracy of the database by ensuring that you do not mistakenly enter data into these inappropriate fields.

Defining Calculated Fields

In addition to fields drawn directly from a table, a query can include *calculated fields*—values computed from fields in the table. Strictly speaking, the term *calculated field* is a misnomer, because calculated values are not actually fields. You cannot edit calculated fields, and they are not stored anywhere in the database. *Calculated column* more accurately describes the role that calculations play in a query—they appear in the query's datasheet, but they are not stored in any of the underlying tables. By creating queries that include calculated columns, you can avoid storing in a table information that is easy to compute based on other essential fields. For example, in the ACE system, you could use calculated columns to display a donor's balance (the result of subtracting the Total Credits field from the Total Debits field or vice versa); to determine the length of time ACE has known a member (by subtracting the

First Contact date from the current date or from the Last Contact date); or to combine the area code and telephone number into a single column in a standard format such as (510) 848-3201 or 510/848-3201.

As you learn more about constructing Access expressions (which are explained in more detail in Chapter 9), you will be able to define more sophisticated calculations, but you can begin using calculated fields with just the arithmetic operators that you already know—addition (+), subtraction (–), multiplication (*), and division (/). To create a calculated field, you enter an expression into the Field row in any empty column in the QBE grid. If a field name includes spaces, you must enclose it in square brackets ([]). For example, you could define a calculated field to display donors' balances by using the expression [Total Credits]-[Total Debits]. For field names with no embedded spaces, the brackets are optional, but Access adds them automatically for the sake of consistency when you move to another cell in the output grid. Spaces are not required anywhere within an expression (for example, between field names and operators), and Access sometimes strips out spaces that you enter.

To combine text fields, you can use the + operator or the less familiar *concatenation* operator, which is symbolized by an ampersand (&). Thus, you could combine the area code and telephone into a single calculated field with the expression [Area Code]&"/"&[Telephone], which concatenates (adds together) three text strings—the Area Code field, a constant string consisting of a slash, and the Telephone field.

The fields that you name in a calculated field expression must be drawn from one of the tables that contribute data to the query. Like any other field, a calculated field need not appear in the query's datasheet—you might define a calculated field that defines the sort order or contributes to the selection criteria without actually displaying the calculated value. For example, you might want to select only donors with nonzero balances based on the calculated field described in the previous paragraph. At first, however, including the calculated value as well as all the fields referenced in the expression will make it easier to verify that you have defined the calculation correctly, especially if you are unsure of how to perform a calculation or how to translate a computation into an Access expression.

If you wish, you can specify a name for a calculated field the same way you define the caption for a true field—by entering it before the expression that defines the calculation, followed by a colon. For example, you could assign the name "Balance" to the calculated donor balance field by entering the description of the calculation as Balance:[Total Credits]-[Total Debits]. The name can be any legitimate Access object name, but it cannot duplicate the name of any real field in the table. For example, if you defined a calculated column that combined the Area Code and Telephone fields, you could not use the name Telephone. If you do not provide a name for a calculated

field, Access constructs one that consists of the word "Expr" followed by a sequential number—Expr1 for the first calculated field, Expr2 for the next, and
so on. As is the case with true fields, Access uses calculated field names as the
column titles in the query's datasheet, and unless you are creating a quick-
and-dirty query for occasional use, you will want to assign meaningful names.
Also note that you can refer to one calculated field in the expression that defines another, and using descriptive names will make all your calculated field
expressions more readable.

When you enter a long expression, you may want a little more room to
work than the small box in the QBE grid. You can open up a *Zoom box* that
allows you to see your whole expression by pressing Shift+F2. Figure 5.9 illustrates a Zoom box with the expression that describes the balance calculation
visible. After you finish typing the expression, you can close the Zoom box by
pressing Enter or by using any of the standard Windows methods for closing
a dialog box (such as clicking on the OK button, double-clicking on the close
box, or pressing Ctrl+F4). You may also want to widen columns in the output
grid so you can see more of the expressions they contain while you work with
the query.

Figure 5.9

Using the Zoom box
to enter a calculated
field expression

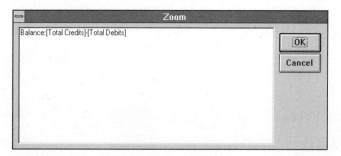

When you view a query's dynaset, calculated fields are indistinguishable
from true fields, with one important exception: Because the data is not stored
anywhere, Access does not allow you to edit calculated fields. (If you begin
typing in a calculated column, Access simply beeps and ignores your keystrokes.) Access updates calculated fields immediately to reflect changes you
make to any of the fields involved in the computations. You can enter sorting
instructions or selection criteria based on a calculated field in the QBE grid
just as you would for a true field, using methods described in the next two sections of this chapter. For example, you might want to select only donors with
nonzero balances or arrange the query output in descending order based on
the balance.

Specifying the Sort Order

By default, Access displays the records in a query's datasheet in primary key order, or, if there is no primary key, in the order the records were entered. Often, this is the order you want; for example, while entering prospect data into the Names table, you would probably want to see records in alphabetical order by ID Code. Often, however, your main reason for defining a query is to sort records into a different order for display purposes.

As you read this section, keep the technical meaning of the term *sort* firmly in mind, because this word is often used in quite a different sense in colloquial speech. In database terminology, sorting means rearranging the sequence of records—either permanently, by rewriting the table on disk in a different order, or temporarily, for display purposes only, as is the case when you sort a query's dynaset. In nontechnical language, the word is often used to mean *select*. For example, a co-worker might say to you, "I want to sort names by state for a mailing," meaning "I want to *select* one state for a mailing." In Access, sorting by state means arranging records in an order that groups all the records with the same value in the State field together. Selecting records by state—so as to display or process only records with a certain value in the State field—is a distinctly different operation, which you can also accomplish with a query, as described in the next section.

The field or fields whose values determine the order of the rows in the query's dynaset are sometimes called *keys* or *sort keys*. The use of the same word—key—for the fields that serve as the basis for indexing and sorting underscores the common purpose of these operations, and in fact, Access uses similar methods internally to carry out these operations. To save time, conserve disk space, and allow you to update a query's dynaset, Access *does not* execute your sorting instructions by recopying all the information in the dynaset into a new order—instead, it builds a list in memory of the key fields in each record, rearranges that list into the specified order, and uses it as a reference for displaying the records in the original table in the right sequence. If you have an index based on one or more of the sort keys, Access uses this index to speed up the process.

You specify the order of the rows in a query's dynaset by entering sorting instructions in the second row of the QBE grid. The sort keys can be fields or calculated fields of any data type except Memo or OLE Object, and you can sort in *ascending* (low to high) or *descending* (high to low) order based on each key field. The interpretation of these terms depends on the data type—they correspond to alphabetical order for Text fields, numerical order for Number, Currency, and Counter fields, and chronological order for Date/Time fields. When you sort on a Yes/No field, the resulting order reflects the raw values stored in the table, –1 for True (or Yes or On) and 0 for False (or No or Off). Thus, all the records with Yes in the sort key field come before records with No in this field. When you sort on a Text field, Access sorts character by character, starting from the left side of the field. It treats uppercase and lowercase letters as equivalent, and numbers and spaces come before A in the sort order. Thus, "12 Main Street" sorts before "123 Main Street" and "LIST1" comes before "LISTA."

To enter sorting instructions in the QBE grid, select either Ascending or Descending from the combo box in the Sort row of the appropriate column. Figure 5.10 illustrates the drop-down list. You can use the third option—(not sorted)—to cancel a previously selected sort order. If you prefer to use keyboard commands, you can type Ascending or Descending (or any abbreviation of these words) in the Sort row. Thus, the fastest and easiest method for specifying the sort order is to type just the letter A or D (Access fills in the rest of the word Ascending or Descending when you move to another cell in the output grid). To cancel a previously established sort order, simply press Del to delete the entry in the Sort row.

Figure 5.10

Choosing the sort order

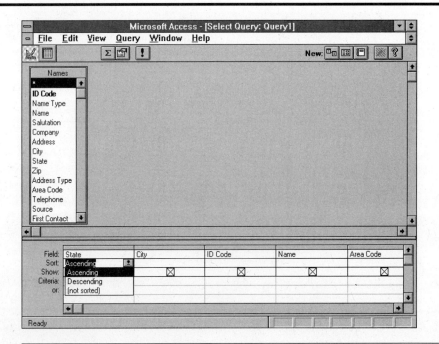

You can only sort on fields that appear in the QBE grid, but you may not always want to see all the sort keys in the query's datasheet. For example, in many of the ACE system queries (including the Telephone List query described in this chapter), the ID Code field is one of the sort keys, so that the query output is arranged in (approximate) alphabetical order. However, you might prefer to omit this field from the query's datasheet and substitute the Name field, which is more complete, readable, and comprehensible to someone who is not intimately familiar with the contents of the Names table. To exclude a field from the dynaset while allowing it to remain in the QBE grid, you can uncheck the check box in the Show row, which determines whether a column appears in the query's dynaset.

NOTE. *When you first test a new query, it is a good idea to leave the check box in the Show row checked for all the sort keys to verify that records are arranged in the right order. You can then uncheck this box for any fields that you do not normally need to see in the query's dynaset.*

At times, you may define a query for the sole purpose of displaying a table in sorted order (another method is described in Chapter 6). The easiest way to define such a query is to add the asterisk symbol displayed at the top of the field list to the output grid, followed by the individual fields that will serve as the sort keys. To exclude these duplicate fields from the output, uncheck the Show check box.

Sorting on Multiple Fields

You can sort on more than one field or calculated field to achieve more complex record groupings. As is the case with indexes, you will probably want multiple sort keys when many records share the same value in the first, or *major*, sort key. For example, if you sort a name and address list by zip code for a mailing, the fact that many people might have the same zip code is unimportant, as long as the labels are printed in proper zip code order. On the other hand, if you were to sort the output of the Telephone List query by state, there would be so many records in each state that you would probably want to see them arranged in some rational sequence within each state—perhaps grouped by area code or city, and then in alphabetical order within each area code or city group. When you define more than one sort key, Access first groups together all the records that share the same value in the first sort key and arranges these groups in the proper order (for example, ascending alphabetical order by state). Within each group of records that share the same value in the first sort key, it arranges records in an order determined by the value of the second sort key, and so on.

When you specify multiple sort keys, the keys can have any mixture of data types, and you can select either ascending or descending order for each. For example, if you added the calculated Balance field to the Telephone List query, you could sort in ascending order by state and in descending order by Balance to place the biggest contributors first within each state group. Within the last group, you cannot predict the order in which Access will display records—it is *not*, as you might have guessed, primary key order—so you should make sure to specify enough sort keys to achieve the desired display order. Thus, to view the Telephone List arranged by state, city, and ID code, you must specify three sort keys, entered using the following steps:

1. If you are still viewing the Telephone List query dynaset, click on the Design button in the tool bar to return to Query Design view.

2. Move to the Sort row in the State column of the QBE grid, and click on the down arrow symbol at the right side of the combo box.

3. Click on Ascending and then press Tab to move into the City column.

4. Type **Ascending** and then press Tab to move into the ID Code column.

5. Type **A** and then press either Left Arrow or Right Arrow to move out of the cell. Note that Access fills in the word Ascending for you.

6. Click on the Run Query command button in the tool bar or select the Run option from the Query menu to execute the query. Your screen should look like Figure 5.11.

7. Click on the Design command button in the tool bar or select the Query Design option from the View menu to return to Query Design view. Choose Save As from the File menu and enter the name **Telephone List by State/City**.

When you specify more than one sort key, Access deduces the order of the keys from their placement in the QBE grid—the major sort key is the one closest to the left side of the output grid, followed by the next one from the left, and so on. In the Telephone List query, and in many other queries as well, the sort order corresponds to the most logical arrangement for the columns in the query's dynaset. At times, however, you will need to deviate from this rule, and the only way to do so is to add two copies of each sort key to the output grid—one placed where you want it to appear in the datasheet and another located where it will assume the correct position in the sort order. To suppress the display of the latter copy of the field, you must uncheck the box in the Show row. For example, to sort the Telephone List query by state, area code, and ID code, you could proceed as follows:

1. Move to the Sort row in the City column of the QBE grid and press Del to erase the sorting instructions entered for this field.

2. Click on Area Code in the field list in the upper portion of the Query Design window, drag this field to the QBE grid, and drop it on top of the City column to insert it between the State and City columns.

Figure 5.11

Sorting by three
fields

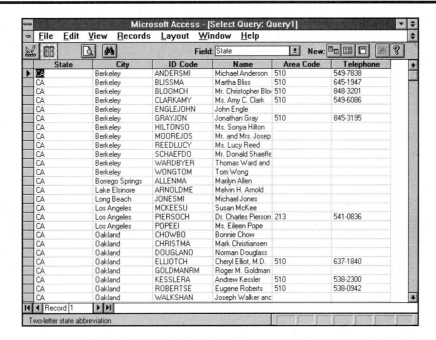

```
━  Microsoft Access - [Select Query: Query1]                     ▼ ┃
▬  File   Edit   View   Records   Layout   Window   Help         ┃
▬▬      ┃     ┃   ┃         Field: State          ┃  New: ▢▣◫▢  ▨ ?
```

State	City	ID Code	Name	Area Code	Telephone	
▶ CA	Berkeley	ANDERSMI	Michael Anderson	510	549-7838	
CA	Berkeley	BLISSMA	Martha Bliss	510	645-1947	
CA	Berkeley	BLOOMCH	Mr. Christopher Blo	510	848-3201	
CA	Berkeley	CLARKAMY	Ms. Amy C. Clark	510	549-6086	
CA	Berkeley	ENGLEJOHN	John Engle			
CA	Berkeley	GRAYJON	Jonathan Gray	510	845-3195	
CA	Berkeley	HILTONSO	Ms. Sonya Hilton			
CA	Berkeley	MOOREJOS	Mr. and Mrs. Josep			
CA	Berkeley	REEDLUCY	Ms. Lucy Reed			
CA	Berkeley	SCHAEFDO	Mr. Donald Shaeffe			
CA	Berkeley	WARDBYER	Thomas Ward and			
CA	Berkeley	WONGTOM	Tom Wong			
CA	Borrego Springs	ALLENMA	Marilyn Allen			
CA	Lake Elsinore	ARNOLDME	Melvin H. Arnold			
CA	Long Beach	JONESMI	Michael Jones			
CA	Los Angeles	MCKEESU	Susan McKee			
CA	Los Angeles	PIERSOCH	Dr. Charles Pierson	213	541-0836	
CA	Los Angeles	POPEEI	Ms. Eileen Pope			
CA	Oakland	CHOWBO	Bonnie Chow			
CA	Oakland	CHRISTMA	Mark Christiansen			
CA	Oakland	DOUGLANO	Norman Douglass			
CA	Oakland	ELLIOTCH	Cheryl Elliot, M.D.	510	637-1840	
CA	Oakland	GOLDMANRM	Roger M. Goldman			
CA	Oakland	KESSLERA	Andrew Kessler	510	538-2300	
CA	Oakland	ROBERTSE	Eugene Roberts	510	538-0942	
CA	Oakland	WALKSHAN	Joseph Walker and			

```
┃◀ ◀ Record: 1    ▶ ▶┃
Two-letter state abbreviation
```

3. In the Sort row for the new Area Code column, type **A** to request an ascending sort, and then press Down Arrow to move into the Show row.

4. Press spacebar to remove the check mark.

5. Click on the Show check box in the ID Code column to remove the check mark and exclude this column from the query output.

6. Click on the Run Query command button in the tool bar or select the Run option from the Query menu to execute the query. Note that within each state, all the records with blank area codes come first, followed by those with legitimate area codes, and that within each area code, records are arranged alphabetically based on the ID Code field even though this field no longer appears in the datasheet.

7. Click on the Design command button in the tool bar or select the Query Design option from the View menu to return to Query Design view. Choose Save As from the File menu and enter the name **Telephone List by State/Area Code**.

Specifying Record Selection Criteria

As important as the ability to select which fields you want to see in a given context is the ability to define record selection criteria. For example, in different contexts the Association for a Clean Earth might want to view quite different subsets of the Names table. A quick review of the functional requirements for the ACE application presented in Chapter 1 will reveal a dozen selections for mailings alone: different solicitation letters are sent to donors and prospects, membership renewal notices are based on the Name Type field (to select members only) and the date of last renewal, press releases go out only to media contacts, and mailings related to special events are sent only to people who live within a reasonable radius of the site. In fact, in most database applications, you will find that you need to work with a subset of the data far more often than with the entire table.

You enter record selection criteria in the rows at the bottom of the QBE grid, starting with the row labeled "Criteria" and continuing onto as many additional rows as necessary. In each row, you can enter record selection criteria based on one or more fields or calculated fields, by entering the various conditions in the appropriate columns. *Each Criteria row describes a complete set of record selection criteria, and the output of the query will include any record that satisfies at least one such set.* Within each row, *all* the criteria must be satisfied to select a record, as if the conditions were combined with "and." The separate criteria rows are combined with "or," and the label for the second Criteria row is intended to remind you of this fact—a query's dynaset will include any record that passes all the tests in the first row *or* all the tests in the second row (or any additional rows below this one). The difference between combining conditions with "and" and "or" is described in more detail later in this chapter, in the section on combining selection criteria.

As is the case with sorting instructions, any field that contributes to the selection criteria must appear in the QBE grid, but you can uncheck the Show check box for any field that you do not need to see in the dynaset. In fact, it is often unnecessary to display fields that define the fundamental selection criteria, especially in queries that select just one value in these fields. For example, if you modified the Telephone List query to select just people in California, you could omit the State field from the output, and the Name Type field would be unnecessary in a query that selects only members. However, a query that selects records based on a range of dates in the Last Renewal fields should probably include the Last Renewal field, so you can see the individual dates. When you first begin experimenting with queries, it is a good idea to include in the output *all* fields that contribute to the selection criteria (and all the sort keys), so that you can verify by inspecting the dynaset that the query selected the right records.

Entering Simple Selection Criteria

The simplest selection criteria specify an exact, or *constant*, value in a field. If the term "constant" is unfamiliar to you, note that this word is used in mathematics and in programming jargon to denote a single arbitrary value of any data type, such as "San Francisco" (a text string), 4/5/93 (a date), 41 (an integer), 12.50 (a Single, Double, or Currency numeric value), or Yes (a Yes/No, or logical, value). To select records in which a particular field matches a constant value, you enter this value in one of the Criteria rows in the field's column in the output grid. For example, you could restrict the Telephone List to people in California by entering CA in the Criteria row of the State column. When Access executes a query, text comparisons are case-insensitive, so you can enter text constants in any mixture of upper- and lowercase. To view only people whose last contact was on April 5, 1992, you could add the Last Contact field to the QBE grid and enter 4/5/92, 5-Apr-92, or April 5, 1992 in this column. To include only records for people who can be contacted by phone, you could add the OK to Call field to the query and enter Yes, True, On, or -1 in this column.

It only makes sense to compare a field to a constant value of the same data type, so Access allows you to enter constants in any format acceptable for the field's data type, using no special punctuation or delimiters. Where your entry might be ambiguous—notably, in Text or Number fields—Access assumes that the data type of your entry matches the data type of the field. For example, if you enter 4/5/92 in the Last Contact column, Access interprets your entry as a date, whereas the same entry in a Text field's column would be read as a character string consisting of six characters (four digits and two slashes). If you enter a value that could not possibly be legitimate, such as "San Francisco" in a date field's column, Access displays an alert box with the rather nonspecific "Syntax error" message.

To ensure consistency and leave no doubt as to the data type of a constant, Access reformats your entry when you leave the cell to conform to its conventions for identifying the data types of constants in expressions—it encloses text strings in double quotes (") and surrounds Date/Time values with number signs (#) as delimiters. (You might view the number sign as a special kind of quotation mark that identifies constant dates just as the more familiar quotation marks identify character strings.) No special symbols are required to recognize numeric values (Currency, Byte, Integer, Long Integer, Single, or Double), which always begin with a numeric digit, minus sign, or decimal point.

To modify the Telephone List query to select people in California, you can use the following steps:

1. Move into the row labeled Criteria in the first column of the output grid (the State column).

2. Type **CA** and press Up Arrow to move up to the Show row. Note that Access adds quotes to your entry.

3. Press Spacebar or click in the check box to uncheck it and exclude the State field from the query dynaset.

4. Execute the query and move to the bottom of the dynaset. You should have 55 records.

Entering More Complex Criteria

The examples in the previous section represent only a small fraction of the wide variety of record selection criteria you can express in Access queries. Access does not restrict you to comparisons between a field and a constant, and it supports many types of comparisons besides determining whether two values are equal. To list just a few of these, you can test whether a field is greater than or less than a given value, not equal to a given value, falls within a certain range, or occurs within a list of values. For example, ACE might want to send a special mailing only to donors whose total credits are between $100 and $1,000, or to members whose last renewal date was more than a year ago, or to new members who joined within the current calendar year. Another very common requirement is selecting not one but several values in the same field. For example, ACE might send a mailing to just members and donors (people with M or D in the Name Type field) or to everyone on the West Coast (California, Oregon, and Washington).

To express these more complex relationships, you use symbols of a general class called *operators*, some of which may be familiar to you if you ever studied algebra, logic, or set theory. You may also see the terms *comparison operators* and *relational operators* for these symbols, which *compare* values or represent the *relationships* between values. Access also recognizes three *logical operators*—And, Or, and Not—which enable you to combine separate conditions into more complex conditions, according to the basic rules of logic. Table 5.1 lists the Access comparison and logical operators.

Despite this rather intimidating terminology, the meanings of most of the comparison operators should be evident from the descriptions. You can use most of these operators with the Text, Date/Time, and numeric data types. Access interprets operators such as <, <=, >, and >= in a manner appropriate to the data type—they refer to alphabetical order (case-insensitive) for Text fields, numerical order for all the numeric data types, and chronological order for Date/Time fields. For example, requesting values greater than or equal to M in a text field (using the >= operator) selects records in which the field begins with M or a letter that follows M in alphabetical order.

To use comparison operators in record selection criteria, you enter an operator symbol followed by a value in the Criteria row in the QBE grid. For example, entering >=#1/1/93# in the Joined column selects people who became

Table 5.1 **Access Comparison and Logical Operators**

Operator	Meaning
Comparison Operators	
=	Equal to
<>	Not equal to
>	Greater than
>=	Greater than or equal to
<	Less than
<=	Less than or equal to
Between...And	Between two values (inclusive)
In	In a list of values
Is Null	Is empty
Like	Matches pattern that includes wildcards
Logical Operators	
And	Both
Or	One or both
Not	Not true
Xor	Exclusive Or (One, but not both)

ACE members on or after January 1, 1993. You might want to add a space between the operator and the value to improve readability, but Access strips out these unnecessary spaces when you move to another cell in the output grid. You can enter the operators represented by words (such as And, Or, and Between) in any mixture of upper- and lowercase; Access converts them automatically to the standard forms listed in Table 5.1. Unlike the operators represented by symbols, these operators *must* be preceded or followed by spaces so that Access can distinguish the operators from other "words" in the condition (such as field names or text constants).

When you use the comparison operators, think carefully about whether the current context demands > or >= (or < or <=). For example, entering >100 in the Total Credits column selects records in which the contents of the Total Credits field is greater than 100, whereas the condition >=100 also includes values exactly equal to 100. The most convenient way to select a range of values is to use the Between operator. For example, you could select people with total credits between $100 and $1,000 by entering Between 100 And 1000 in the Total Credits column.

NOTE.   *The Between operator is* inclusive—*that is, it selects values exactly equal to either range boundary as well as those that fall in between. To exclude one or both boundary values, you must combine two conditions, using methods described later in this section.*

You might think of each entry in a cell in the Criteria row as a kind of equation that states a condition based on a field and another value; only records that satisfy this condition will be included in the query's dynaset. You enter the comparison operator and the value on the right side of the equation explicitly, and Access deduces the field that occupies the left side by the placement of the condition in the QBE grid. For example, entering >=#1/1/93# in the Joined column forms the equation Joined>=1/1/93, a condition that is either true (if the date in the Joined field is January 1, 1993 or later) or false (if the date is earlier than January 1, 1993). Access allows you one shortcut in constructing conditions—you can omit the equals sign when you test a field for equality to a value. (If you prefer, you can include it for consistency; for example, you could enter = "CA" in the State column to select people in California.)

You can use the logical operators to construct conditions that select more than one value in a field. For example, you can select values in the Total Credits field between 100 and 999.99 by entering the condition >=100 And <1000 (using the condition Between 100 And 1000 would include values exactly equal to 100 and 1000). To select people in Oregon and Washington, you could enter "OR" Or "WA" in the State column, and you can select members, donors, and board members by entering "M" Or "D" Or "BD" in the Name Type column. Because the words "and" and "or" are often used differently in colloquial language, be careful to avoid some very common pitfalls when you translate your own requirements or requests from your co-workers into conditions in the QBE grid. For example, you might say out loud, "I want to see members in Oregon *and* Washington," but you must use the Or operator in the condition you enter into the State column. If you wrote the condition as "OR" And "WA", Access would look for records with *both* OR *and* WA in the State field—a condition that does not make sense and can never be fulfilled, because the State field cannot have both of these values at the same time. You can help avoid confusion by remembering that the conditions you write are not applied in some global manner to an entire table, but to *each record* in the table.

You can precede any condition with the Not operator to negate it—that is, to select records that do not satisfy the condition. Often, you can avoid using Not by restating the condition differently; for example, to select everyone whose first contact was not in 1992, you could use either Not Between #1/1/92# And #12/31/92# or <#1/1/92# Or >#12/31/92#. However, most people would find the first version more readable.

The In operator allows you to write an even more concise expression to select any of several discrete values in a field. The In operator must be followed by a list of the acceptable values, enclosed in parentheses. You might read this expression as "a value in the following list." For example, you could select members, donors, and prospects by entering In ("M", "D", "P") in the Name Type column, and you could select people in California, Oregon, and Washington by entering In ("CA", "OR", "WA") in the State column. To select all values except those in a short, finite list, you can add Not to an expression based on the In operator; for example, you can select all name types except media contacts and political contacts with the condition Not In ("MC", "PC").

Note. When you enter a date constant that includes wildcards, do not use the # delimiters. Access requires that any expression that follows the Like operator be enclosed in quotes, but it treats the string as a date in comparisons with date fields.

Access permits the same wildcard symbols in Text and Date/Time comparisons that you can use in the search string you enter in the Find dialog box to locate records one at a time. A value that includes wildcards should be preceded by the Like operator; for example, you can select all first contact dates in March, 1992, by entering Like 3/*/92 in the First Contact column. As a shortcut, you can omit the Like operator, but Access fills it in automatically when you move out of the cell in the output grid. You will find the Like operator particularly useful for selection criteria based on the contents of a Memo field, since the search string will rarely occur at the beginning of the field. For example, you could search for the phrase "board member" in the Notes field by entering the condition Like "*board member*" in the Notes column.

Access allows you to compare a field to the result of evaluating any expression, including the value in another field. For example, you might want to select records from the Names table in which the first and last contact dates are the same or in which the total debits exceed the total credits. To distinguish field names from character string constants, you must enclose them in square brackets ([]). Thus, to select people whose first contact was the only contact—that is, the First Contact field contains the same date as the Last Contact field—you could either add the First Contact field to the QBE grid and enter =[Last Contact] in the criteria row for this field, or add the Last Contact field to the QBE grid and enter =[First Contact] in its criteria row.

Combining Selection Criteria

All of the examples in the previous section selected records based on a single condition entered in one column of the QBE output grid. Access allows you to form more complex selection criteria by combining simple conditions in two different ways: You can select records that satisfy *all* of the conditions, or you can select records that satisfy *any one* of the conditions. Recall that each Criteria row describes a complete set of selection criteria that determines whether a record should be included in the query's dynaset. When you enter conditions in two or more columns in a single Criteria row, Access selects any record that satisfies all of these conditions. In logical terminology, this is equivalent to linking the separate conditions with the And operator. For example, if you enter ="CA" in the State column and ="M" in the Name Type column, the resulting dynaset contains records in which the state is California *and* the Name Type is M.

To select records that satisfy any one of several conditions, you enter the conditions in separate rows of the QBE grid. For example, you could select Names table records in which the state is Oregon *or* Washington by entering ="OR" in the first Criteria row and ="WA" in the second. You can use as many Criteria rows as you need, and if there are too many rows to fit on the screen at once in the default Query Design window configuration, you can enlarge the bottom portion of the Query Design window to devote more space to the output grid, or you can use the vertical scroll bar at the right side of the output grid when you need to view additional rows.

Remember that each Criteria row in the output grid describes a complete, self-sufficient set of conditions that a record must satisfy to be included in the dynaset. Thus, to select members in Oregon and Washington, you must enter ="M" in both criteria rows, as illustrated in Figure 5.12. In this query, the first Criteria row selects records in which the State field is OR and the Name Type field is M, and the second selects records in which the State field is WA and the Name Type field is M. Omitting the condition based on the Name Type field from the second row would result in a query that selects members in Oregon and everyone in Washington, because the second row would have no criteria based on the Name Type field.

If you have used the database commands in spreadsheet programs such as 1-2-3, Excel, or Quattro Pro, this method for entering selection criteria should seem familiar. For many queries, using separate rows is the only way (or the clearest way) to specify independent selection criteria, but you can often express the same conditions using fewer Criteria rows by using the Or operator or the In operator. For example, to select members and donors in California, Oregon, and Washington, you can enter "CA" Or "OR" Or "WA" or In ("CA", "OR", "WA") in the State column and "M" Or "D" in the Name Type column. To enter the equivalent conditions using separate Criteria rows, six rows would be required—one for each possible combination of state and name type.

To experiment with more complex selection criteria in the Telephone List query, try the following:

1. Add the Name Type field to the QBE grid between the ID Code and Name columns by dragging it from the field list and dropping it on top of the Name column.

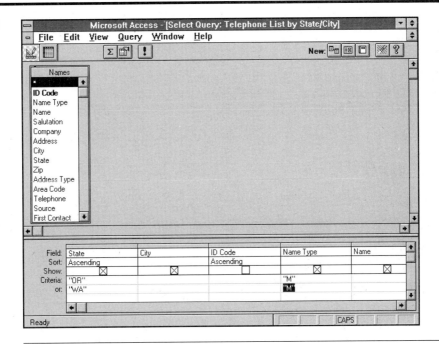

Figure 5.12
Defining complex selection criteria

2. Type **M** in the Criteria row and execute the query. Because you are already selecting records by state, you should see just the 13 members in California.

3. Return to Query Design view and change the entry in the Name Type Criteria row to In (M, D, BD) to select members, donors, and board members.

4. Execute the query again. This time you should see 19 records.

5. Return to Query Design view and move to the calculated Balance column.

6. Enter **>200** to select people with a balance greater than 200 (that is, people whose credits exceed their debits by more than $200).

7. Execute the query again. This time you should see six records.

Handling Null Values

In many queries, especially those with selection criteria based on a Number or Currency field, you must take into account a very important fact that may not be intuitively obvious unless you are a statistician: A field that has no value entered into it is considered to have a special value known as *null*. If this concept is new to you, note that a null value in a Number field is quite different from the legitimate numeric value zero. This distinction, which is rare among PC database programs, makes certain queries a bit more complicated, but it is crucial to statistical calculations (many of which you can carry out using queries) that should ignore null values rather than treating them as zeroes. In particular, you might want to count only the non-null entries in a field, and you will nearly always want to exclude nulls from averages.

A null value is equivalent to "Not available" or "No value," and Access assumes no relationship between a null and any other numeric or date/time value—it is not equal to, less than, or greater than any other value. Thus, records in which the Total Credits field is null will not be included in the output of a query that selects records with 0 in this field or one that selects values less than any constant value. Similarly, a query that selects people with last contact dates earlier than a particular date will not retrieve records in which the Last Contact field is null.

If you need to write an expression that describes null or non-null values, you can use the special Is operator with the Null keyword: The expression Is Null selects just null values in a field of any data type, and Is Not Null selects only non-null values. For example, you could use the condition Is Null to search for records in which a field such as Address, City, State, or Zip (none of which should ever be empty) was inadvertently left blank. Note that most of the conditions you write will automatically exclude null values, so you will rarely need to use the expression Is Not Null.

Defining Parameter Queries

Often, the selection criteria for an inquiry are always based on the same field or fields, but the actual value you want to select varies. For example, ACE might want to view or print the Telephone List for one state or for a particular state and city—but not always the same state and city. You can avoid having to repeatedly edit a query to change the value entered in the Criteria row by creating a *parameter query* that prompts you to enter the values you want to select each time you run the query. Parameter queries are especially valuable in an application that will also be used by co-workers who have less experience than you do with Access and who might not know how to edit a query to modify the selection criteria.

When you run a parameter query, Access displays a dialog box to prompt you for each field that you identify as a *parameter*, or variable input. To define the prompts that you want Access to display in these dialog boxes, you enter them in a Criteria row enclosed in square brackets. The prompt can be up to 40 characters long—approximately the width of the text box in the dialog box that Access displays to ask you to enter the parameter values. It should usually include a reference to the field, but the Access documentation recommends that you do not use the field name alone as a prompt. For example, you might use [Enter a state abbreviation:] or [Which state do you want?] in the State column, and a similar prompt in the City column. Figure 5.13 illustrates the dialog box that Access displays to prompt you for the state when you run a parameter query based on the Telephone List.

Figure 5.13

Running a parameter query

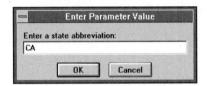

In addition to the parameters, a parameter query can include static selection criteria based on any other fields in the output grid. For example, if you entered "M" in the Name Type column, the parameter query just described would select only members in the state you entered in response to the parameter prompt. You can also combine parameters with other criteria based on the same column. For example, you could use the condition >=1/1/92 And <=[Enter ending First Contact date:] to use a constant value for the earliest date in a range but prompt for the upper range boundary.

You can use the Between and Like operators to prompt for more complicated selection criteria. You must enter a prompt for each separate value that you need to collect. For example, you could prompt for a range of dates in the Last Contact field with a parameter entry such as Between [Earliest last contact date] And [Latest last contact date]. Access treats each item enclosed in square brackets as an independent parameter, and it displays a separate dialog box for each parameter—in this example, one for the earliest last contact date and another for the latest (as well as additional dialog boxes for any other parameters specified in other columns).

If you might need to include wildcard symbols in the value you enter for any parameter, you can enter a parameter expression preceded by the Like operator. For example, you could prompt for a partial value in the Name field with an entry such as Like [Enter all or part of the name]. Obviously, the person who runs the query must understand how to use the Access wildcard symbols. You cannot prompt for a list of values, but you can include a parameter prompt in the list of values that follow the In operator. For example, you could use the parameter prompt In ("CA", [Enter a state other than California:]) to create a query that selects CA and one other state.

If the rules for constructing the parameter expression seem confusing, think of each expression enclosed in brackets as a substitution item. When you run a parameter query, Access prompts you for each item in turn and substitutes the values you enter for the parameter prompts in the QBE grid. Thus, the expression Between [Earliest last contact date] And [Latest last contact date] might become Between 1/1/92 And 12/31/92—a legitimate expression for specifying selection criteria based on the Last Contact field.

To convert the Telephone List by State/City query into a parameter query, use the following steps:

1. Move into the Criteria row for the Balance column and press Del to delete the condition you entered previously.

2. Make sure that the entry in the Name Type Criteria row is In ("M", "D", "BD") to select members, donors, and board members.

3. Make sure that the State, City, and ID Code columns all include sorting instructions requesting an ascending sort, and that the Show box for the ID Code column is not checked.

4. In the Criteria row for the State column, enter **[Enter a state abbreviation:]**.

5. Add the Last Contact field to the QBE grid after the Balance column.

6. In the Criteria row for the new column, enter **Between [Earliest last contact date] And [Latest last contact date]**.

7. Execute the query and enter **CA** for the state, **1/1/92** for the earliest last contact date, and **4/30/92** for the latest last contact date. The dynaset should include ten records.

8. Use the Save As option on the File menu to save the query under the name Telephone List by State/City (Parameter).

Summary

This chapter described how to define simple select queries based on one table (or on another query) that enable you to view all or selected fields and calculated fields from all or selected records, and to sort the query output into any order. The fact that Access gives you such precise control over the contents of a query's dynaset allows you to work with your tables far more efficiently by viewing only the information relevant to the current context. This power will be multiplied when you learn how to design queries based on more than one table, using techniques described in Chapter 8. Keep in mind as you experiment with simple queries that their utility is not limited to viewing and updating data on the screen. Access always allows you to use tables and query dynasets interchangeably, and a great deal of your work with the program will involve the use of queries. In particular, you will often want to design custom forms based on queries to view or update specific data subsets, and many (if not most) of your reports will print or display selected data derived from one or more tables by running a query.

   This chapter emphasized the methods used to *define* queries that extract exactly the data you need from a single source table or query. To a certain extent, you can customize the *appearance* of a query's datasheet, using the same methods described in Chapter 4 for configuring a table's datasheet. However, you cannot save the configuration with the query. To overcome this rather significant limitation, you must define a custom form that looks like the datasheet. Chapter 6 describes how to design this type of form (as well as several other types), and how to use a similar tool—filters—to specify sorting instructions and selection criteria for data viewed through a custom form.

6

Defining and Using Simple Data Entry Forms

Using the FormWizards

Using a Form to Enter and Edit Data

Using Filters to Sort and Select Records

Editing a Form

SO FAR, YOU HAVE DONE ALL OF YOUR WORK WITH ACCESS TABLES AND queries using the default Datasheet view. The fact that Access provides a convenient screen for viewing and updating data allows you to begin working with a new table immediately without first taking the time to design a custom screen. Furthermore, as noted in Chapter 1, even if you intend to use forms in the finished application, it is often prudent to defer their creation until you have entered some sample data and run the system through its paces to make sure that your table structures are correct and complete. If this testing reveals errors in your initial database design (as it usually does), you will not have to redesign forms created to match the original structures. For small tables with few fields, the default datasheet may be the ideal data entry environment even in the finished application, and in a very simple database, you may never need additional forms.

In most database applications, however, forms play a crucial role in the data entry and update process, and Access provides a sophisticated design tool that you can use to create a wide variety of custom screen forms. Regardless of your prior database experience, there are many advantages to designing custom forms. As noted in Chapter 2, one of the most common form styles presents one record at a time on the screen, and for entering and editing records, this narrow view is often preferable to the datasheet (which is better suited to surveying the contents of a table or query dynaset and spotting trends). Typically, you can fit all or most of the fields in a table on one or two screens, and you can arrange the fields in any convenient order on these screens. You can allocate as much space as you need for Memo fields or long text fields, group related items together, draw lines and boxes to identify logical field groups, and include descriptive prompts and informative text to guide you (or other users) through the data entry process. If you have an artistic bent, you can dress up your forms with a wide variety of fonts, type styles, boxes, colors, and shading.

By matching the layout of your screen to the paper input forms from which you will enter the data, you can speed up data entry and facilitate proofreading. Even if you do not use paper input forms, designing different screen forms for different purposes or for different users ensures that only the information relevant to the task at hand appears on the screen, presented in a format that is clear, appropriate, and helpful. For example, you might design at least two data entry screens for the ACE Names table—one that includes *all* the fields and one, intended for entering and updating prospects, that includes just the name and address fields. By using the prospect form to enter prospect names and addresses, you can avoid being distracted by fields that are irrelevant to prospects and, more importantly, ensure that you do not inadvertently fill in some of these fields.

Even if you prefer to update some tables in Datasheet view, there is one very significant advantage to creating a custom form. By using a form rather than the default datasheet, you gain the ability to use *filters* to define record selection criteria and sorting instructions. As you might guess from this description, a filter is much like a query, but defining a filter is more immediate (you can do so without leaving the data entry form) and less permanent (you need not save filters that you do not plan to use again).

You can design data entry forms from scratch, but Access provides a tool called *FormWizards* that you can use to build several types of forms very quickly and easily by choosing options from a series of dialog boxes. This chapter describes how to use the FormWizards to create two basic types of data entry forms for updating single tables, and how to modify the resulting forms to make them more useful and intuitive. Chapter 8 describes how to use the FormWizards to design multitable forms, and Chapter 10 describes in more detail some of the ways that you can customize the appearance and content of Access forms (as well as reports). Chapter 12 explains how to use many of the same *controls* in your forms that Access (and other Windows programs) use to collect information—check boxes, radio buttons, list boxes and combo boxes, and so on—and you can include pictures and other graphics in a form. Chapter 12 also describes how to build forms from scratch, but even when you become a form design expert, you may never abandon the Wizards.

Using the FormWizards

The easiest and fastest way to create a new form is to use one of the Access FormWizards to lay out the form, and then modify the result if necessary. More often than not, you will want to rearrange at least a few of the fields, but allowing Access to build the first version of the form can save you a considerable amount of work and, even more important if you are a novice user, reduce the intimidation that you may feel when confronted with a blank form design work surface and an unfamiliar set of tools.

To begin designing a new form, you can use any of the following methods:

- Make sure that the Database window displays the list of forms (if necessary, click on the Form button in the Database window or choose the Form option from the View menu) and then click on the New command button or press Alt+N.

- Choose the New option from the File menu, and then choose Form from the submenu of object types.

- Highlight a table or query name in the Database window and click on the New Form command button in the tool bar (the second of the three new object buttons).

To edit an existing form, make sure that the Database window displays the list of forms, and then highlight the name and either click on the Design button, press Alt+D, or double-click the right mouse button.

When you use any of these methods to begin designing a new form, Access displays the New Form dialog box shown in Figure 6.1, which enables you to either invoke a FormWizard or start from scratch with a blank form. In either case, the first step is to use the combo box at the top of this dialog box to choose the table or query that you want to update using the form. If you choose a table, Access automatically opens the table when you later open the form. If you choose a query, Access executes the query each time you open the form and displays only the records selected by the query in the order specified by any sorting instructions in the query. In the drop-down list associated with the Select A Table/Query combo box, there is no way to distinguish between tables and queries, so you may want to make a note of the correct table or query name before you choose the New Form option. If you do not choose a table or query, or if you type the name instead of selecting it from the drop-down list and misspell it, Access displays an alert box to remind you that "You must select an existing table or query to use a Form-Wizard or ReportWizard."

Figure 6.1

Choosing the data source and method for creating a new form

Note also that Blank Form is the default button in the New Form dialog. If you want to use the FormWizards, be careful *not* to press Enter after typing or selecting the table or query name; instead, press Tab to move to the Form-Wizards button and then press Enter, click on the FormWizards button, or press Alt+W. (If you inadvertently choose the Blank Form option, just close the Form Design window without saving the blank form and start over.)

Choosing the Form Style

When you choose the FormWizards option, Access displays the dialog box shown in Figure 6.2, which prompts you to choose a FormWizard based on the overall form style that you want to create. The left side of this dialog box presents graphical representations of the various styles (unfortunately, with no indication of the correspondence between the diagrams and the names of the styles listed on the right). Note that this dialog box includes *all* the types of objects that you can create using Access Wizards, including both forms and reports. The four form styles, which are labeled in Figure 6.2, produce the following results:

Single-column	A form style with the fields lined up in a single vertical column, with field names to the left as prompts.
Tabular	A form style with the fields arranged in columns, somewhat like the datasheet, with the field names at the top of the form as column titles.
Graph	A graph created by Microsoft Graph.
Main/Subform	A multitable form based on two tables that have a one-to-many relationship, with the fields from the parent table at the top of the form in single-column style and the related records in the child table displayed below in a datasheet.

Figure 6.2
Choosing the overall form style

Single-column

Tabular

Main/subform

Graph

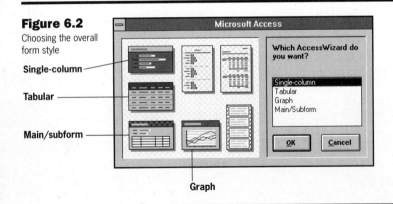

This chapter describes how to build single-column and tabular forms. The main/subform form style is covered in Chapter 8, which discusses working with multiple tables, and graph forms are covered in Chapter 15.

The tabular form style is most useful for forms that display just a few fields, such as the Committees table form illustrated in Figure 6.3; if you have to scroll back and forth to bring different groups of fields into view, this form style shares the disadvantages of the datasheet. The single-column style is preferable for tables with too many fields to fit comfortably in the datasheet or a tabular form. For forms that include fewer than about 15 fields, you may be able to use the single-column form created by the FormWizard with no modifications. An example of the default single-column layout, based on the Committees table, is shown in Figure 6.4. When you design a form for a table with more fields, such as the Names table, you will probably want to rearrange the form to place several short fields side-by-side or group fields into blocks so as to fit more information on the screen at once.

Figure 6.3

A tabular form

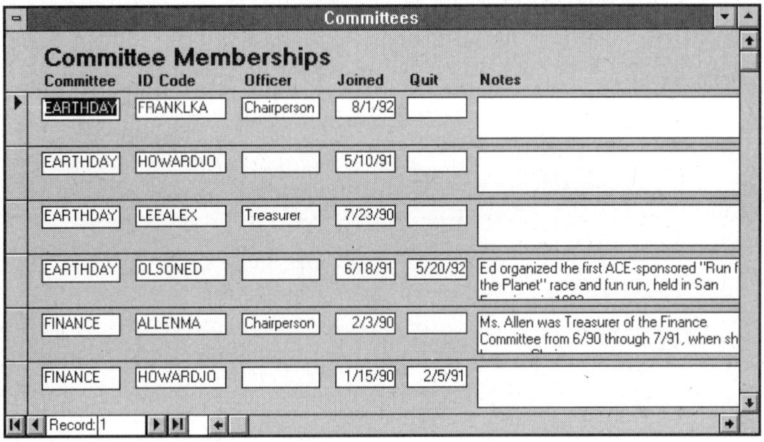

Figure 6.4

A single-column form

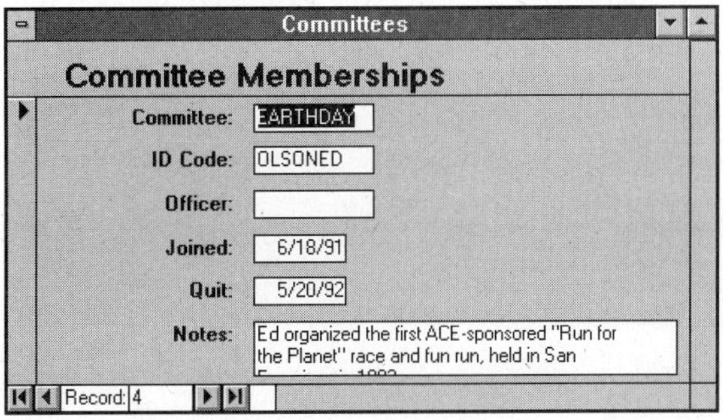

Choosing the Fields

After you choose the form style, Access displays a dialog box like the one shown in Figure 6.5, which enables you to choose which fields you want to include in the form. On the left side of this dialog box is a small picture that symbolizes the overall form style selected in the previous step with the heading areas (the header that appears at the top of the form and the field labels) represented by thick black blocks, and the fields themselves by thinner lines. The image in Figure 6.5 corresponds to the single-column form style, and the dotted line in the middle of the form is a "page break" included to remind you that the form will display more than one record at a time if space permits.

Figure 6.5

Choosing the fields
to include on a form

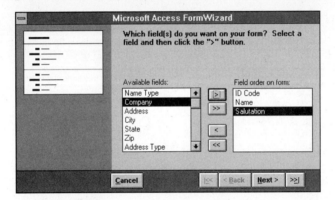

You can use the two scrolling lists in the right portion of the dialog box to build and edit the list of fields that you want to include in the form. The Available Fields list on the left includes all the fields that you have not already selected, in the order they occur in the table structure, and the Field Order on Form list on the right displays the fields you have chosen to include on the form. Figure 6.5 shows how the two lists would look after three fields from the Names table—ID Code, Name, and Salutation—have been selected. Between the two lists are four command buttons, which you can use to move fields between the two lists, either one at a time or all at once. The buttons are used as follows:

> Moves the highlighted field to the Form list

>> Moves all fields to the Form list

< Removes the highlighted field from the Form list

<< Removes all fields from the Form list

To choose a field and move it from the Available Fields list to the Form list, you can either double-click on the field name or highlight the field name in the Available Fields list and then click on the > button. To remove a field from the Form list and move it back to the Available Fields list, double-click on the name in the Form list, or highlight the field name in the Form list and then click on the < button. Be careful *not* to press Enter after highlighting a field name—in the FormWizard dialog boxes, pressing Enter closes the field selection dialog box and advances you to the next step in the form creation sequence. After you choose a field from either list, Access automatically highlights the next field, so you can add or remove several fields in turn without moving the mouse by simply clicking repeatedly on the < or > button.

Access places the fields in the Form list—and in the resulting form—in the order you select them from the Available Fields list, and once you have selected a field, there is no direct way to move it up or down to a new position in the Form list. To move a field, you must use a method based on the fact that Access adds each new field to the form list immediately *after* the highlighted field: Remove the field from the Form list, highlight the remaining field that should precede it, and then add the field back to the Form list.

The command buttons at the bottom of the Field Selection dialog box (and all subsequent dialog boxes) enable you to move forward or backward in the FormWizard sequence. You can choose Next > at any point to go on to the next step or < Back to return to the previous step to edit your prior selections. The |<< button returns you directly to the first step (choosing the fields), and the >>| button jumps to the last step (displaying the form or editing it using the Form Design tool) if you know you do not need to override the default selections in any of the remaining dialog boxes. At any point, you can use the Cancel button or press Esc to abort the form design process and return to the Database window.

Choosing the Overall Look of the Form

After choosing the fields you want on the form, you can press Enter or click on the Next > command button to move to the next dialog box, shown in Figure 6.6, which prompts you to choose the overall look of the form. If you are unfamiliar with the five options, you can use the arrow keys or the mouse to move through the radio buttons and watch the image displayed on the left side of the form change to reflect the currently selected form style. The Committees table forms in Figures 6.3 and 6.4 illustrate the standard look. Figure 6.7 shows what the form in Figure 6.4 would look like with the boxed, chiseled, embossed, and shadowed looks. If this is your first experience with the Access form design process, note that the standard look, while visually the least exciting, produces a form that is easiest to modify. If you intend to move the fields around in the form, you may want to stick with this form look for a while; the other choices, which yield data entry areas comprised of several boxes and lines as well as the text box and its label, are considerably more difficult to rearrange.

Figure 6.6

Choosing the look of
a form

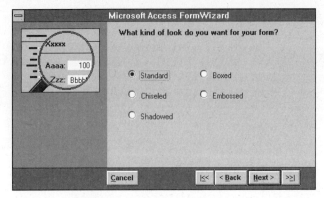

Titling and Saving the Form

The last FormWizard dialog box, which is illustrated in Figure 6.8, prompts you to enter a title for the form; the title is displayed as a header at the top of the data entry window when you use the form to enter data. In the Committees table forms in Figures 6.3 and 6.4, the title is "Committee Memberships," and in the forms in Figure 6.7 it is "Committees." Do not confuse the title with the name of the form, which you enter later, when you save the form for the first time. By default, Access proposes the name of the table or query on which the form is based as the title, and if your table and query names are reasonably descriptive, you will often end up retaining this title (as was done in the forms in Figure 6.7). However, you might want to choose a more specific title for a form used for a specialized purpose or to update a particular subset of the data. For example, in the Names table form described later in this chapter, which is used to update prospect names and addresses, the title is "Prospects."

After you enter the title, you can click on the Open command button to open the form in Form view and begin updating data, or click on the Design button to move to the Form Design window to modify the form. Figure 6.9 illustrates the Prospects form with a record from the Names table displayed.

Even if you know that some modifications will be required, you might want to open the form first and page through a few records to check for unforeseen problems, such as data entry regions too short to accommodate their contents. For example, looking at a few records in the Prospects form will show you that the ID Code text box is too short for many of the ID codes, the Zip text box is too small for the ten-digit zip codes, and the Address box displays only the first line of the two-line addresses. (The first two of these problems are visible in Figure 6.9.)

Figure 6.7

Boxed, chiseled,
embossed, and
shadowed forms

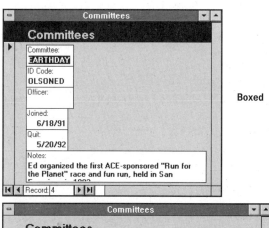

Boxed

Chiseled

Embossed

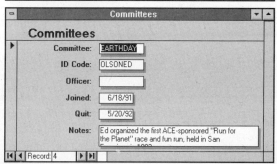

Shadowed

Figure 6.8

Entering the form title

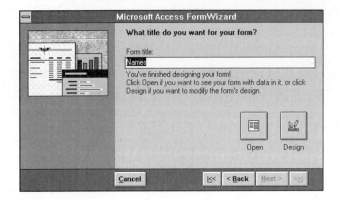

Figure 6.9

Using the Prospects form to view records

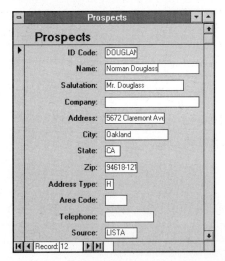

You use exactly the same methods to save a form that you use for any other Access object. You can save the form at any time by using the Save or Save As options on the File menu. If you have not yet saved the form when you close it for the first time, Access displays the dialog box illustrated in Figure 6.10 to ask whether you want to save the form. If you choose Yes, Access displays the standard Save As dialog box to prompt you to enter a new name. For many forms, including the Prospects form described later in this chapter, the same word or phrase used as the form title serves equally well as its name, and matching the name and title will help you remember the name and purpose of the form.

Figure 6.10

Saving a new form

Creating the Committee Memberships Form

To create a simple data entry form for the Committees table, use the following steps:

1. Make sure that the Database window displays the list of forms (if necessary, click on the Form button in the Database window or choose the Forms option from the View menu), and then click on the New command button or press Alt+N.

2. Click on the arrow symbol at the right side of the Table/Query combo box to display the list of table and query names, and choose Committees from the list (remember *not* to press Enter after you highlight or click on the table name).

3. Click on the FormWizards button or press Alt+W.

4. In the form style selection dialog box, click on OK to retain the default style (single-column).

5. In the field selection dialog box, click on the >> button to select all the fields in the Committees table. All the field names will move from the Available Fields list to the Form list.

6. Click on the Next button or press Alt+N to go on to the next step.

7. In the form look selection dialog box, click on the Next button or press Alt+N to retain the default form style (standard) and move to the next step.

8. In the final dialog box, press F2 or click in the text box to display an insertion point, and edit the form title so it reads **Committee Memberships**.

9. Click on the Open command button to open the new form in Form view. Your screen should look like Figure 6.11. Use the navigation buttons to scan through a few records.

10. Select the Save option from the File menu and enter the name **Committees** for the form.

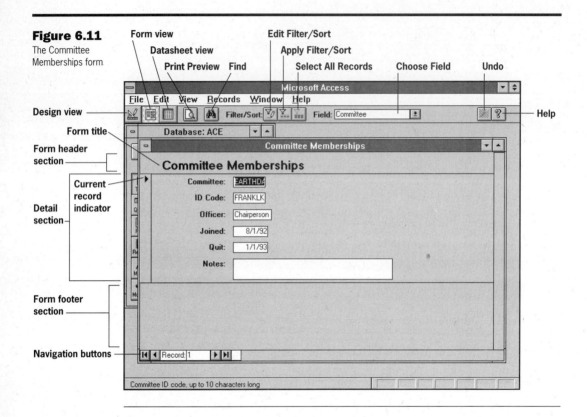

Figure 6.11

The Committee Memberships form

Using a Form to Enter and Edit Data

Apart from the appearance of the screen, updating a table using a custom form has much in common with working in Datasheet view. Like the datasheet, the forms built by the Access FormWizards use the field names (or captions for fields that have them) as labels to identify the fields. In a single-column form, the labels are displayed to the left of the data entry regions, followed by colons; the labels are right-justified, so the colons line up in a column. In a tabular form (such as the Committees table form shown in Figure 6.3), Access places the labels in the form header to serve as column titles. Most fields are displayed and collected in data entry regions called *text boxes* (even if they happen to collect numeric or Date/Time fields) that by default are one line deep, and Memo fields are collected in text boxes approximately two lines deep. Yes/No fields are displayed as check boxes. Note that all of these aspects of the form's appearance are consequences of the decisions made by the FormWizards—you need not adhere to the same display style in the forms you create from scratch.

As in the datasheet, Access bases the lengths of the data entry regions on the field lengths, and in most forms, at least a few of the text boxes will be too short for a typical record. This is especially likely for code fields, such as the ID Code, State, and Source fields in the ACE Names table, which are entered in all uppercase, because in the proportional Windows fonts, uppercase characters take up more space than the average mixture of upper- and lowercase that Access uses to estimate the widths of the text boxes. You will often want to increase the depth as well as the width of the text boxes used to collect Memo fields and Text fields that commonly occupy two or more lines (such as the Address field in the Names table). You might also want to move the prompts for the check boxes used to collect Yes/No fields to the right of the check boxes to conform to the standard Windows convention. As you will see later in this chapter, modifying the form to make these changes is very easy.

Access displays the name of the form in the Form Window title bar. The form title appears *inside the window*, in a section of the form called the form header. If you consider the title to be redundant (in a form whose title matches its name), you can easily delete the title—and if you wish, the entire form header section—in the Form Design window, as described later in this chapter. The Form view window has all the same controls as the Datasheet view window, including the scroll bars and the navigation buttons in the lower-left corner, and the Edit and Records menus include the same editing and navigation commands. The current record indicator is displayed in the left window border; in a single-column form that displays one record (or part of a record) at a time, this marker is useful primarily in its role as a status indicator—as in the datasheet, it changes to a pencil symbol when you have changed the current record and to a circle with a line through it when another user on your network is editing the record. In a tabular form such as the Committees table form in Figure 6.3, the current record indicator also reminds you which record has the focus. If you based the form on a table or on a query with no sorting instructions, Access displays records in primary key order; otherwise, the order is determined by the sorting instructions in the query.

You can use all the keyboard and mouse commands described in Chapter 4 to move around the form and enter or edit data. When you are mostly viewing and editing records, you will probably find the mouse more convenient than the keyboard for operating the navigation controls, but during an intensive data *entry* session, you may prefer not to move your hands off the keyboard. Remember that the best keys to use for moving between fields are Tab (to move forward) and Shift+Tab (to move backward). When you work with a single-column form, PgUp and PgDn take you to the previous and next records, respectively. As in the datasheet, Access saves data one record at a time—when you move past the last field, Access saves the current record and displays the next one. You can use the Find command to search for records, and you can use the Replace command to replace data. All the standard methods for adding new records are available—you can move past the last record in the table, press Ctrl++, choose the Data Entry option on the Records menu, or choose the Data Go To option on the Records menu and then select New from the resulting submenu. As in the datasheet, Access immediately fills in all default values and Counter field values. To delete a record, click in the record selector on the left side of the form (or choose Select Record from the Edit menu), and then press Del or select Delete from the Edit menu.

In keeping with the fundamental role of a form—namely, to provide a display alternative to the datasheet—you can switch to the datasheet at any point by clicking on the Datasheet command button in the tool bar or by choosing the Datasheet option from the View menu. To return to the form, click on the Form View button or choose Form from the View menu. You can switch to the Form Design window to modify the form by clicking on the Design button at the left side of the tool bar or by choosing Form Design from the View menu. The ability to alternate at will between Form view and Datasheet view gives you the flexibility to choose the display mode that best suits your needs at any moment. In a typical data entry session, you might prefer the datasheet for searching for records or scanning through a table to spot trends, but the Form view is usually more convenient for entering new records or doing extensive editing. If you created a form primarily to gain access to the filter commands described in the next section, you might prefer the Datasheet view.

When you print a form from the Datasheet view—even if you initiated data entry by opening a form—the printout looks just like the datasheet, as described in Chapter 4. When you print from the Form view window or by choosing the Print option from the File menu with a form name highlighted in the Database window, the printout resembles the appearance of the form on the screen. Access prints the form title just once at the very beginning of the listing, and it fits as much data on each page as possible, splitting a record (and at times, a Memo field or long Text field) across a page boundary if necessary. The default forms generated by the FormWizards have no delimiters between records, but you can easily edit these forms to add a dividing line or a special symbol after the last field in the form. Figure 6.12 illustrates the printout of the tabular Committee Memberships form, and Figure 6.13 illustrates the first page of the printout of the single-column Committee Memberships form. Printing a page or two of data using a custom form is the fastest way to generate a quick hard copy of one or more individual records. If you frequently need to print data in the same layout as a data entry form, you can use the Save As Report option on the File menu to create a report that looks just like the form, and then edit this report using methods described in

Chapter 7, to customize it for printing. Unfortunately, there is no way to print the form specifications (a description of the form layout and the controls it contains).

Figure 6.12

The printout of a tabular form

Committee Memberships

Committee	ID Code	Officer	Joined	Quit	Notes
EARTHDAY	FRANKLKA	Chairperson	8/1/92		
EARTHDAY	HOWARDJO		5/10/91		
EARTHDAY	LEEALEX	Treasurer	7/23/90		
EARTHDAY	OLSONED		6/18/91	5/20/92	Ed organized the first ACE-sponsored "Run for the Planet" race and fun run, held in San Francisco in
FINANCE	ALLENMA	Chairperson	2/3/90		Ms. Allen was Treasurer of the Finance Committee from 6/90 through 7/91, when she became Chairperson
FINANCE	HOWARDJO		1/15/90	2/5/91	
FINANCE	SLATERLO	Treasurer	6/15/92		
FINANCE	THOMPSCH		12/18/91		
LOBBYING	ALLENMA		6/3/91		
LOBBYING	HARRINJU	Chairperson	10/20/92		
LOBBYING	LUSUSAN		10/25/90		
LOBBYING	OLSONED	Treasurer	5/10/92		
LOBBYING	REEDLUCY		4/18/90	5/1/92	
LOBBYING	ROSENBRH		4/1/91	4/5/92	Ralph, not Helen, was the committee member.
NEWS	BERGENRU	Chairperson	8/10/91		
NEWSLETT	BLOOMCH		3/28/90	3/1/92	
NEWSLETT	HOWARDJO		11/10/92		Howard is responsible for compiling events listings for the newsletter. Refer all press contacts to him.
NEWSLETT	THOMPSCH		2/6/92		Christine is now the Editor of the ACE Newsletter

Figure 6.13

The printout of a single-column form

Committee Memberships

Committee:	EARTHDAY
ID Code:	FRANKLKA
Officer:	Chairperson
Joined:	8/1/92
Quit:	
Notes:	

Committee:	EARTHDAY
ID Code:	HOWARDJO
Officer:	
Joined:	5/10/91
Quit:	
Notes:	

Committee:	EARTHDAY
ID Code:	LEEALEX
Officer:	Treasurer
Joined:	7/23/90
Quit:	
Notes:	

Committee:	EARTHDAY
ID Code:	OLSONED
Officer:	
Joined:	6/18/91
Quit:	5/20/92
Notes:	Ed organized the first ACE-sponsored "Run for the Planet" race and fun run, held in San Francisco in

Committee:	FINANCE
ID Code:	ALLENMA
Officer:	Chairperson
Joined:	2/3/90
Quit:	
Notes:	Ms. Allen was Treasurer of the Finance Committee from 6/90 through 7/91, when she became Chairperson

Using Filters to Sort and Select Records

One of the main advantages of using forms, even if the layout of the Datasheet view suits your data entry needs and personal preferences, is the ability to define and apply *filters* to customize the record display sequence and selection criteria. Although the Form view and Datasheet view are in many ways interchangeable—in fact, you might view the datasheet as a specialized type of form—Access allows you to use filters when you work with a form, but not in the table's raw datasheet. This seemingly arbitrary limitation is largely mitigated by the fact that you can always switch to the Datasheet view after opening a form, and you can use filters in any data entry session initiated by opening a form. To work in an environment exactly equivalent to the table's datasheet, you can define a form that includes all the fields in the table, open the form, and switch immediately to Datasheet view. Chapter 10 describes how to make a simple modification so that the form appears initially in Datasheet view rather than Form view.

Whenever a form is open, the tool bar contains three command buttons for working with filters; these buttons are labeled in Figure 6.11. The symbols on the buttons suggest the purpose and usage of a filter, which you might visualize as a funnel with a special kind of filter paper inside. When you "pour" a table into the filter, only the records described by your selection criteria pass through, and they emerge in the order specified by your sorting instructions. The symbol on the Apply Filter/Sort button represents the selection process by showing one of the records below the funnel enabled and the other two dimmed, and the symbol on the Show All Records button depicts the funnel dimmed and all three records below it enabled. If your form is based on a query rather than a table, the sorting instructions in the filter override those in the query, and the selection criteria specified by the filter are superimposed on those in the query, so that only records that satisfy both sets of conditions are displayed.

To define a filter, click on the Edit Filter/Sort button in the tool bar or choose the Edit Filter/Sort option from the Records menu. Access filters share many of the characteristics of queries, and in keeping with this similarity, the design tool that you use to build filters looks much like the Query Design tool. Figure 6.14 illustrates the Filter window as it appears when invoked from the Committee Memberships form pictured in Figure 6.3. The filter in this figure specifies sorting by ID Code and Committee (the primary key is based on Committee and ID Code) and selects only current committee members (records in which the Quit field is null).

The most notable differences between the Query Design and Filter Design windows are due to the fact that a filter governs only record selection criteria and sorting instructions—the form controls which fields from which tables are available. Thus, you cannot add or remove tables as you can in the

Figure 6.14

Defining a filter

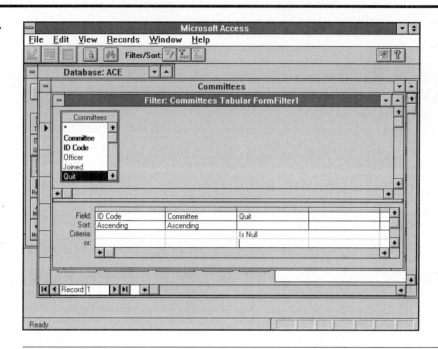

Query Design window, you do not use the output grid to customize the field list, and there is no Show row in the output grid. The only fields you need to add to the output grid in the lower half of the Filter Design window are those that contribute to the selection criteria or specify the sort order. Note that the field list in the upper portion of the Filter Design window includes all the fields in the underlying table (or query), even if the form does not, so you can use any fields you wish in the selection criteria or sorting instructions. As noted in Chapter 5, there is often no need to include in a form the fields that are fundamental to the selection criteria. For example, the Prospects form described later in this chapter does not include the Name Type field, because this form is intended to update records that all have the same name type.

To place a filter in effect, you can click on the Apply Filter/Sort command button in the tool bar or select the Apply Filter/Sort option from the Records menu. If you wish, you can close the Filter window first, but if you plan to change the filter specifications several times during a work session, you might prefer to leave it open. If the form window is larger than the Filter Design window, you might want to rearrange the windows on the screen so that at least a small portion of the Filter Design window remains visible while you are working in the form. You can then easily switch between viewing data in the form window and editing the filter by clicking in the appropriate window.

Whenever a filter is in effect, Access displays the FLTR indicator in the status bar to remind you that you are not viewing all the records in the original table or query. To cancel the current filter and return to viewing the entire table (or, if your form is based on a query, all the records selected by the query), click on the Show All Records button or select the equivalent Show All Records option from the Records menu. Note that you can easily alternate between applying the filter and viewing all the records by clicking on the Apply Filter/Sort and Show All Records buttons—Access remembers the most recent filter specifications even if you close the Filter Design window.

The advantage to using a filter rather than a query is immediacy—you can modify the filter at any point to change the selection criteria or sort order without closing or modifying the form. The advantage of a query is convenience—you can return to exactly the same sort order and selection criteria in a later work session without having to redefine them. In general, you should use queries for data configurations that you use frequently or repeatedly, and filters for ad hoc inquiries that demand unique record selection criteria or sorting instructions. You can combine the two to obtain a very detailed picture of a particular data subset. For example, one good way to edit prospect records in the Names table is to define a query that selects prospects (based on the Name Type field) and sorts the list by state, city, and ID code, and then use filters to refine the selection criteria during a given work session.

The sample ACE database includes a form called Prospects, which was designed using the FormWizards. The data source for this form is a query, also named Prospects, which selects records in the Names Table in which the Name Type field is P. To experiment with the Prospects form, use the following steps:

1. Close the Committee Memberships form if it is still open.

2. Make sure that the Database window displays the list of forms, highlight the Prospects form, and press Enter or click on the Open command button to open the form. Access runs the Prospects query and displays the first record in the dynaset (the record for Martha Bliss) in Form view.

3. Click on the Datasheet button in the tool bar or select Datasheet from the View menu to switch to Datasheet view. Note that records are displayed in primary key order (alphabetical order by ID code) because the Prospects query contains no sorting instructions.

4. Maximize the datasheet window.

5. Click on the Last Record navigation button and note that there are 69 records in the dynaset.

6. Click on the Edit Filter/Sort button to invoke the Filter Design window.

7. Drag the State field to the output grid and enter **CA** in the Criteria row to select only the prospects in California.

8. Click on the Apply Filter/Sort button to return to the datasheet, scroll down to the bottom of the dynaset, and observe that there are now 35 records, all of which have CA in the State column.

9. Click on the Edit Filter/Sort button to return to the Filter Design window.

10. Change the entry in the Criteria row to **In ("OR", "WA")**.

11. Drag the First Contact field to the output grid and enter **Descending** in the Sort row to arrange the records in reverse chronological order based on the first contact date.

12. Return to the datasheet, and note that the dynaset contains nine records, all of which have OR or WA in the State column.

13. Scroll to the right to bring the First Contact field into view, and note that the rows are arranged in descending order based on this date.

14. Return to the Filter Design window and type **> 1/1/91** in the Criteria row of the First Contact column.

15. Return to the datasheet and note that the dynaset now contains four records, still arranged in descending order by first contact date.

As noted earlier in this section, filters and queries have a great deal in common, and you can use them interchangeably in several ways. Access allows you to work with only one filter at a time and provides no direct way to save a filter per se. However, you can preserve a filter in the database by using the Save As Query option on the File menu to save the filter as a standard Access query. This option is available only while you are working in the Filter Design window, not while you are viewing the form. A query that you create using the Save As Query option has no built-in connection to the form you were using when you defined it, and you can use it exactly as you would any other query. Like all queries, it does contain a reference to the original data source, which might be either a table or another query; if it is a query, Access runs the first query and uses the resulting dynaset as the data source.

While using a form to view or update data, you can use the Load from Query option on the File menu to invoke a filter previously saved as a query, *or any other select query based on the same table or query as the current form.* Like the Save as Query option, Load from Query is available only from the Filter Design window, not in Form view. When you load a query, Access displays the sorting instructions and selection criteria from the query in the Filter Design window. You can apply the filter as is by immediately clicking on the Apply Filter/Sort button, or you can use it as a point of departure for creating a more complex filter.

Editing a Form

As noted earlier in this chapter, the Access FormWizards do a good job but rarely produce a form that you would consider perfect. A little bit of experimentation with a newly created form will usually reveal at least a few minor problems, some attributable to the Wizards—such as text boxes that are too small to accommodate their contents—and others to you—for example, fields that you placed in less than ideal positions in the data entry sequence. You might also want to change a few basic properties of the overall form layout, such as centering the form title or deleting it entirely, or moving check box prompts to the standard location to the right of the check boxes.

Often, a few modifications to one of the standard layouts yields a far more useful and attractive form. For example, in the tabular form pictured in Figure 6.3, moving the Officer field below the ID Code and the Quit date below the Joined date would enable you to widen the Notes field without devoting more total space to each record. The Prospects form shown in Figure 6.15 was created by revising the default single-column layout as follows:

- The ID Code, Name, Salutation, Company, Address, City, State, Zip, and Address Type fields were widened.

Figure 6.15
The modified Prospects form

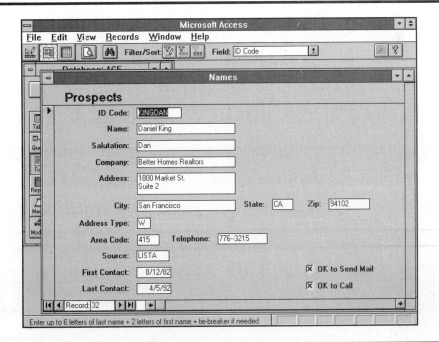

- The height of the Address field was increased to accommodate two lines of text.

- The State and Zip fields were moved to the right of the City field.

- The prompts for the State and Zip fields were left-justified.

- The Telephone field was moved to the right of the Area Code field.

- The OK to Send Mail and OK to Call fields were moved to the right of the First Contact and Last Contact fields.

- The check boxes were moved to the left of the prompts, the colons were removed from the prompts, and the check boxes were aligned vertically with the Zip text box prompt.

The commands that you can use to make these modifications are all described in the remainder of this chapter.

To move to the Form Design window to modify a form created by a Form-Wizard, you can use any of the following methods:

- When you use a FormWizard to create a new form, choose the Design button rather than the Open button in the last dialog box displayed by the Wizard.

- Make sure that the Database window displays the list of forms (if necessary, click on the Form button in the Database window or choose the Forms option from the View menu), highlight the desired form, and then click on the Design command button, press Alt+D, or double-click the right mouse button.

- With a form displayed on the screen, either in Form view or Datasheet view, click on the Design command button in the tool bar or choose the Form Design option from the View menu.

Figure 6.16 illustrates the Form Design window with the single-column Prospects form created by the Access FormWizard on the work surface. In this figure, the Form Design window is maximized, and unless you are working with a very small form or editing two forms simultaneously, you will usually want to maximize the window to view as many objects and tools as possible. If you want to experiment with this form, you can use the Form-Wizards to reproduce it, or you can open the form named Prospects Initial Design in the sample ACE database. Figure 6.17 diagrams the Form Design menu bar; some of the options are described later in this section, and the rest are covered in Chapters 10 and 12.

Figure 6.16

The Form Design window

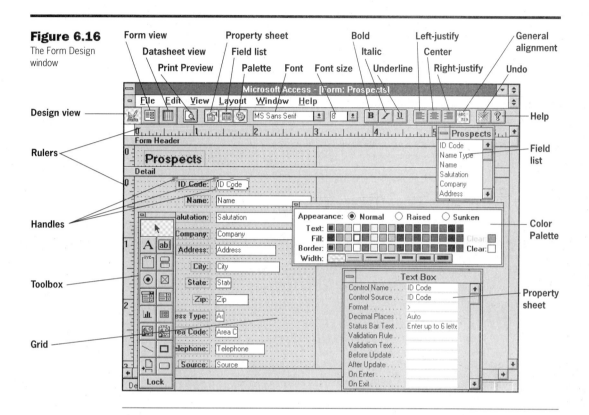

If you adjust the size of the Form Design view window, Access uses the new window size when you later open the form in Form view. You can also match the size of the window to the dimensions of the form by choosing the Size to Fit Form option from the Window menu in Form view; this is often the easiest way to resize the window after you make extensive modifications to the form.

You should recognize the basic components of the form in Figure 6.16, including the title and the text boxes used to collect the fields, from your experience with the Committee Memberships form created earlier in this chapter. It is worth reiterating an important aspect of the way Access treats forms—the form itself and every component of the form is an *object*, and every object has properties that you can inspect and modify independently. You have already had a brief introduction to the concept of objects when you created the Committees table. The table as a whole is an object with certain properties (the description, primary key, and five multifield index keys), and each field in the table is also an object with its own properties (the data type, field size, format, caption, and so on). A form is considerably more complex than a table, and it

Figure 6.17

The Access menu bar in the Form Design window

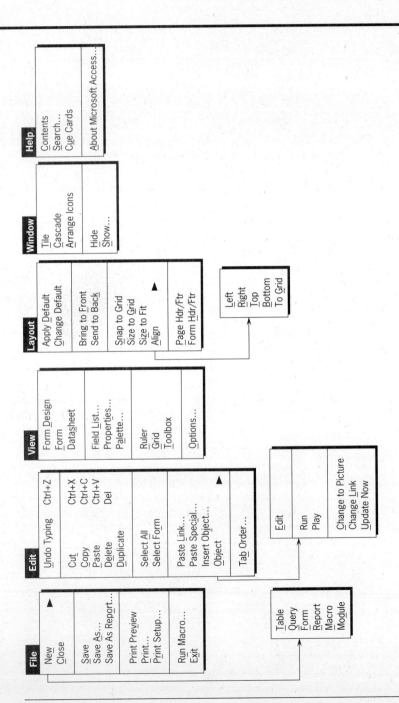

can contain more types of objects, and in most cases, more individual objects. However, the same basic principle applies: An Access object may be made up of other objects, and the behavior and appearance of each object is described by its properties.

Although you may perceive a form such as the one in Figure 6.16 as consisting primarily of *fields*, Access uses the more general term *control* to refer to all the types of objects that you can include in a form, not all of which carry out functions directly related to collecting data. For example, you might use command buttons in a form to serve as specialized navigation controls, to trigger the display of related subforms, or to carry out actions such as displaying a graph or performing a statistical calculation. The term *control* derives from the fact that certain objects, such as check boxes, radio buttons, and command buttons behave like specialized knobs, levers, or push buttons—they allow you to carry out actions or enter data without typing. These more complex objects are covered in Chapter 13; for now, you can devote your attention to the simple objects that make up the forms created by the Access FormWizards—text boxes (which collect most data fields of all data types, not just Text fields), text objects (such as the title in the form header), and check boxes (which are used to collect Yes/No fields).

Keep in mind that Access objects come in many sizes and degrees of complexity, and a given object may be comprised of other objects. Just as a form is itself an object that contains other objects, many of the objects in a form are also made up of more than one object. In particular, the text boxes and check boxes that make up the forms generated by the FormWizards consist of two objects—a label and a data entry region. Access allows you to treat the two components as a single object or manipulate them separately. To avoid confusion, this book usually uses the term *control* for the whole object and *object* for the individual components.

In a text box control, the name displayed within the text box object is the field name. In the forms created by the Access Wizards, the text in the label objects matches the field names, but you can edit the labels if you wish without affecting the data entry regions. Be careful not to edit the field name displayed in the text box object when you intend to change the label—entering a new field name in the text box changes the data displayed in the text box (or yields an error message if your entry does not match the name of a field in the table or query you are updating with the form). If you wish, you can delete the label object without removing the associated field from the form. For example, in the Prospects form, if you move the State field next to the City field, you might remove the label for the State field and change the City field label to "City/State."

Access provides two types of assistance to help you place and align objects on a form: horizontal and vertical rulers displayed along the upper and left edges of the form, and an alignment grid that consists of a network of small dots at evenly spaced intervals. Both the rulers and the grid are visible in Figure 6.16. The rulers are useful for judging the overall size, placement, and alignment of objects, while the grid allows for much finer control. As noted in Chapter 4, the units of measure used in the rulers (by default, inches) refer to the space an object will occupy when you print a form, *not* the apparent size of the object on the screen, which depends on the size of your monitor and the current video mode. By default, the rulers are displayed and the grid is not, but you can use the Ruler and Grid options on the View menu to turn either one on or off.

To allow for very precise control over the size and placement of small, closely spaced objects, Access allows you to adjust the horizontal and vertical grid spacing, either of which can range from 2 to 64 dots per ruler inch. However, Access displays the grid only when both settings are no finer than 16 dots per inch. The default grid spacing in forms created by the FormWizards is 64 dots horizontally by 64 dots vertically, so even if you check the Grid option on the View menu, you will not be able to see the grid. You can use the grid to align objects even if the grid is invisible because the spacing is too fine, but if you are new to Windows, you will probably find it reassuring to see the dots. Chapter 10 describes how to set the grid spacing for a particular form by editing the form's property sheet; the methods described in this chapter for aligning objects do not depend on the grid.

The Form Design window includes a variety of specialized tools and controls that you can use to customize the appearance of a form, all of which are visible in Figure 6.16. The tool bar includes combo boxes for selecting the font and font size, as well as command buttons that control overall text attributes (boldfacing, italics, and underlining) and alignment (justification). The View menu includes options for toggling the display of the four specialized windows—the toolbox, field list, color palette, and property sheet—and there are equivalent command buttons in the tool bar for all but the toolbox. You can create new controls of 16 different types by selecting them from the toolbox, associate a specific field with a control by selecting it from the field list, and customize colors and border styles by making selections from the color palette. You can also change these and many other characteristics of an object by making entries in the object's property sheet. All of these techniques are described in Chapters 10 and 12.

The Form Sections

Any Access form—including both data entry forms and reports (which are described in Chapter 7)—can have any or all of five standard *sections*. At the heart of every form is the detail section, which appears once for each record when you use the form to display or print data and usually contains most of the fields. In addition, a form can have a header, which is always displayed at the top of the screen, and a footer, which is always present at the bottom; when you print a form, these sections are printed just once, at the top of the first page and at the end of the last, respectively. A form can also have a page header and/or footer, which are not displayed on the screen but appear on each page when you print the form. Figure 6.18 shows a version of the Prospects form that has all five sections. (The expressions in the page header, page footer, and form footer sections print the current date, page number, and total number of records, respectively). As you might surmise, the page header and footer are more useful in reports than in forms, but you can include these sections in any form if you wish. The screen forms built by the FormWizards have a form header section, which contains the title, an empty form footer section, and no page header or page footer.

Figure 6.18

A form with form header, page footer, detail, page footer, and form footer sections

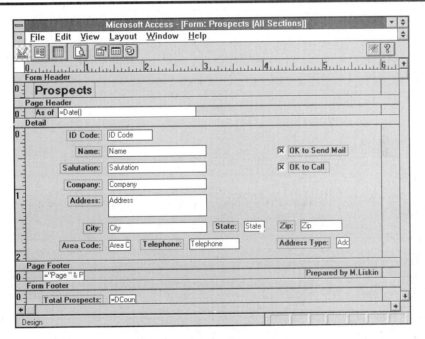

The vertical line at the six-inch mark on the horizontal ruler in the Prospects form in Figure 6.18 indicates the width of the form. If you do not maximize the Form view window, Access sizes the window just large enough to display this line near the right-hand border. In forms created by the FormWizards, the width is based on the size of the longest field (Name or Company in the Prospects form).

You can change the size of any form section by dragging one of its boundaries with the mouse. You can adjust the size of the form header or form footer section by dragging the lower boundary up or down, and you can change the height of the detail section by dragging the lower boundary of the detail section. To change the width of the form, drag the vertical boundary line left or right (working from any of the form sections).

NOTE. *If you are not sure which line represents the section boundary, watch the shape of the mouse pointer as you move around the form; it changes to a horizontal line with vertical arrows when the mouse is positioned over the "hot spot" used to resize a section.*

You can remove an empty report section by dragging the lower boundary up until it meets either the top of the window (for the form header section) or the lower boundary of the section above, but if you attempt to use this method to remove a form section that contains any objects (such as the form title), the section boundary reappears just below the lowest control in the section when you release the mouse button. You can eliminate both the form header and form footer at the same time by choosing the Form Hdr/Ftr command on the Layout menu. This command functions as a toggle—when the menu option is checked, the form includes both header and footer sections; when it is not, the form has neither. The Page Hdr/Ftr option serves the same purpose for the page header and page footer sections. If either of the relevant form sections contains any objects when you try to uncheck the Form Hdr/Ftr or Page Hdr/Ftr option, Access displays the dialog box pictured in Figure 6.19 to warn you that removing these form sections will destroy the objects they contain. Of course, you can later restore either or both sections, but there is no way to retrieve the prior contents. To create a form that has a header but not a footer (or vice versa), make sure the Form Hdr/Ftr or Page Hdr/Ftr option is checked, and shrink the unwanted section on the form until it disappears.

Figure 6.19

Removing a header
or footer section
that contains objects

Selecting Objects

Most of the modifications that you make to the forms created by the Access
FormWizards will involve moving, resizing, or editing individual *controls*,
and even a diehard keyboard user will find the mouse to be the best tool for
carrying out these manipulations. Before you can move, resize, or modify an
object, you must *select* it. It is usually easiest to do this with the mouse, by
clicking anywhere within the object's boundaries. You can also press Tab or
Shift-Tab to cycle through all the objects in a form section in turn, and this
method may be more convenient for selecting very small objects or objects
hidden behind other objects. To select a report section, such as the form
header or detail section (which you might want to do to gain access to its
property sheet), click anywhere in the section *except* within a control. You
can verify that a section is selected because the section identifier band at the
top changes color. Note that selecting an object—or all the objects—in a section does *not* select the section itself. To select the form as a whole, you must
click outside any other object. If the form does not occupy the entire Form
Design window, you can simply click to the right of the vertical line that
marks the right-hand boundary. When the form is as wide as the window, you
can either click in the box to the left of the horizontal ruler, or you can
choose the Select Form option on the Edit menu.

When you select an object, Access displays *handles* in its borders. As the
name suggests, you can "grab" the handles with the mouse and pull them in
various directions to move or resize the object. Figure 6.20 illustrates the
Committee Memberships form with the Committee and Notes fields selected;
the labels in this figure indicate the purposes of the various handles and the
shapes of the mouse pointer when it is over each type of handle. (Selecting
more than one object at a time is described shortly.) In a control made up of
two component objects, such as a text box, the handles appear in the object in
which you clicked. To create Figure 6.20, the mouse was clicked in the label
object in the Committee control, and in the text box portion of the Notes control. If you inadvertently click in the wrong object, simply click again in the
desired object.

The number of handles Access displays in an object depends on its size.
All objects have handles in the four corners, and very small objects, such as
check boxes, have only these handles, which enable you to perform any resizing operation. Most text boxes and labels also have handles in the top and
bottom borders, which you can use to change the height of the object. Access
also displays handles in the right and left borders of an object if it is more
than one line deep (the Notes field text box includes these handles, and the
Committee field label does not). If you are new to Windows, you may feel
that finding the right spot to grab in a small object requires some very fine

Figure 6.20

Selected objects, their handles, and their corresponding mouse pointer shapes

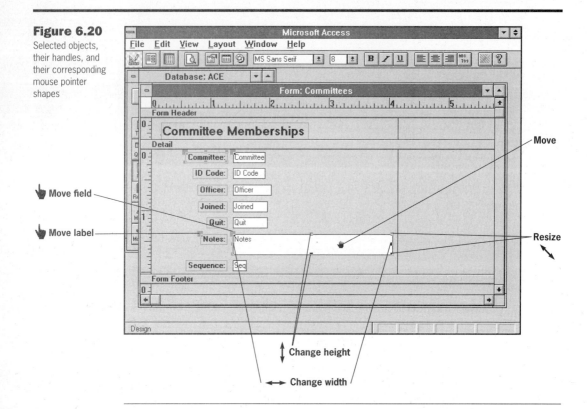

eye-mouse coordination. Watching the mouse pointer change shape as you move over the object is the best way to identify the "hot spots."

It is often convenient to be able to select more than one object at a time. For example, you might want to move several objects that form a logical group while retaining their relative positions, or change the font, font size, or alignment of several text boxes or labels. Access offers a variety of methods for selecting multiple objects. You can select *all* the objects in a form by using the Select All option on the Edit menu. This option is particularly convenient for changing the font used for all or nearly all the objects in a form (Chapter 10 describes how to change fonts).

To select a group of objects that lie within a rectangular region on the form, start with the mouse pointer at one of the corners of this imaginary rectangle, press and hold the left mouse button, drag the mouse to the diagonally opposite corner to delineate the group of objects, and release the mouse button. The rectangle need not lie entirely outside the group, but it must either enclose or overlap every object. For example, to select the Committee, ID Code, and Officer text boxes on the Committee Memberships form, you could begin with the mouse anywhere to the left of the Committee label and end up anywhere to the right of the Officer text box. When you release the mouse button, Access displays handles in *all* the objects in the selected group. As you drag the group of objects, the rectangle that surrounds them follows the mouse, and Access displays indicators in the rulers to mark the borders of the rectangle.

You can select *any* group of objects, regardless of their location on the form, by selecting one and then holding the Shift key down as you click on additional objects. While you hold the Shift key down, clicking on a selected object deselects it. These methods are particularly convenient for selecting just the labels or just the text boxes in a group of controls, so that you can align them after moving or resizing some of the objects, fine-tune the spacing between them, or change their visual attributes.

Moving and Resizing Objects

To move a control as a whole (keeping the same spacing between the label and the text box), you position the mouse over any part of the control *except* one of the handles, press the left mouse button, drag the control to its new position, and release the mouse button. When the mouse is in the right position to move an object, the mouse pointer looks like an open hand, and you might visualize the move operation as analogous to placing your hand over a piece of paper on your desk and pushing it around. As you drag a control around the form, its outline follows the mouse; unfortunately, this outline gives you no indication of the relative sizes and positions of the individual objects that make up controls such as text boxes. Access also displays horizontal and vertical markers in both rulers that indicate the current positions of the object borders to help you judge the object's size or placement. When you make gross rearrangements in a form such as moving a field, don't worry about lining up the objects precisely—it is easier to adjust the spacing afterwards using the Align commands on the Layout menu. These commands are described later in this chapter. Note also that you can select a control and begin moving it without letting up the mouse button—simply position the mouse over the object, press and hold the left mouse button (you will see the handles appear and the pointer change to the open hand shape), and begin moving the control.

If you want to move just one of the two objects that make up a control such as a text box or check box, you must use the large *move handles* in the upper-left corners of the objects. When you position the mouse over either of these handles, the mouse pointer looks like a hand with a pointing finger to symbolize the finer degree of control that you have, compared to moving the control as a whole (which you do with the pointer that looks like an open hand). To resize either object independently, make sure that the sizing handles are visible in the object you want to resize (if they are not, click in the object), and drag one of the handles. You will find it easiest to change the height of an object without affecting its width by using the handles in the upper and lower borders, and to widen or narrow an object without affecting its height by using the handles in the left and right sides.

To limit the movement of an object to one axis (either horizontal or vertical), press the Shift key before you select the object, and continue to hold it down as you move the selected object with the move handle in the upper-left corner. The direction you move the object determines the axis along which movement is permitted—if you first move the object up or down, you will *only* be able to move it up or down, and if you first move it left or right, you will *only* be able to move it left or right. This technique enables you to easily adjust the horizontal placement of an object (for example, to make room for widening another object) without disrupting its horizontal alignment with adjacent objects.

To move two or more objects as a group, select all of them, and then position the mouse over any of the objects, press the mouse button, and drag the group to a new location on the form. Watch the mouse pointer carefully before you click and begin dragging—clicking anywhere except inside one of the selected objects (for example, in the small space between objects) deselects the entire group. This behavior may be frustrating when you encounter it by mistake, but you can also use it to your advantage—if you realize you have selected the wrong objects, simply click elsewhere on the form to deselect the group and then start over.

You can cancel any move or resizing operation by pressing the Esc key and holding it down as you release the mouse button. If you change your mind *after* releasing the mouse button, you can use the Undo Move or Undo Sizing option which appears on the Edit menu after you have completed a move or sizing operation. If you prefer, you can press the equivalent shortcut key, Ctrl+Z.

Moving objects with the mouse is fast, immediate, and intuitive, but this method does not lend itself to aligning objects precisely. One way to realign a group of objects after you have rearranged a form originally built by the Form-Wizards is to use the alignment commands on the Layout menu (Chapter 10 describes another method based on the grid). To align two or more objects, select all of them and then choose the Align command on the Layout menu. Access displays a submenu of alignment choices, which are used as follows:

Option	Meaning
Left	Aligns the left edges of the selected objects with the leftmost object in the group
Right	Aligns the right edges of the selected objects with the rightmost object in the group

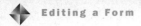

Top	Aligns the upper edges of the selected objects with the upper-most object in the group
Bottom	Aligns the lower edges of the selected objects with the lowest object in the group
To Grid	Aligns the upper-left corner of each selected object with the nearest grid point

If you want Access to adjust the positions of both objects in a control such as a text box, make sure to select both objects by clicking in each one (you will see handles in both objects).

Editing Text and Label Objects

To edit a text object (such as the form title) or the label object associated with a control such as a text box or check box, you must first display an insertion point within the label. If the object is already selected, you can simply click *again* anywhere within the label. If not, click twice (do *not* double-click—pause momentarily between clicks) in the label, once to select it, and again to display the insertion point. You can then move the insertion point to the desired location and add or delete characters as you wish. After you finish editing, you can press Enter to remove the insertion point, restore the handles, and reselect the label or text object as a whole, or you can click anywhere else on the form to deselect the object and go on to your next task.

When you edit a text or label object, Access expands the object if you add text, but it does not shrink the object if you delete characters. (If there is no visible border around the object, its size does not matter; if the object does have a border, you must resize it after you edit the text.) In the forms built by the Access FormWizards, all the labels are right-justified, and they expand to the left as you add characters, leaving the colons lined up equidistant from the adjacent text boxes.

Customizing the Committee Memberships Form

To practice the techniques described in the preceding sections, you can rearrange the Committee Memberships form so that it looks approximately like Figure 6.21. Do not be overly concerned with the precise alignment of the controls that you move and resize—the next section describes some easy methods for correcting the alignment. If you are familiar with Windows software, you might want to see if you can match Figure 6.21 without specific instructions. If you need some guidance, use the following sequence of steps:

1. If the Prospects form is currently open, close it.

Figure 6.21

The modified
Committee
Memberships form

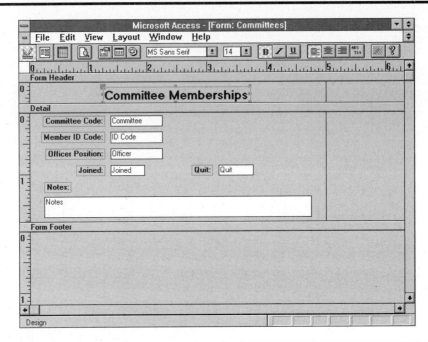

2. Make sure that the Database window displays the list of forms, and open the Committee Memberships form in Design view by highlighting its name (Committees) and clicking on the Design button or pressing Alt+D.

3. Maximize the Form Design window.

4. If the rulers are not already visible, pull down the View menu and select Rulers.

5. Drag the vertical line that represents the right-hand form border to the right to line up with the 5-inch mark in the ruler at the top of the window.

6. Click in the text box object in the Committee control and use the handle in the lower-right corner to widen the text box until its right border lines up with the 2¼-inch mark in the ruler.

7. Repeat these steps to widen both the ID Code and Officer text boxes to match the new width of the Committee field.

8. Click twice in the ID Code label to display an insertion point, move the insertion point to the far left of the label, and type **Member** (followed by a space), so that the label reads Member ID Code:.

9. Edit the label for the Committee control so it reads **Committee Code:**.

10. Edit the label for the Officer control so it reads **Officer Position:**.

11. Click in the Quit control and drag it to a new position next to the Joined control, so that the left border is about $2^3/_4$ inches from the left edge of the form.

12. Click in the Notes control and use the move handle in the upper-left corner of the label (not the text box) to move it to a position about $1/_4$ inch from the left edge of the form and about $1^1/_8$ inches from the top.

13. Click in the Notes text box and use the move handle in the upper-left corner to move it to the left so its left border lines up with the left border of the label.

14. Click again in the text box and use the resizing handle in the right border to stretch it to about $4^3/_4$ inches in the ruler.

15. Click in the form title (the text box in the form header section), and using the ruler as a guide, move it to the right until it is approximately centered. Your screen should look like Figure 6.21.

16. Click on the Form button in the tool bar to switch to Form view.

17. Click on the Restore button to restore the window to its former size, and adjust the size of the window to match the size of the form.

18. Use the navigation buttons to examine several Committees table records.

19. Click on the Design button in the tool bar to return to Form Design view.

20. Click in the Joined text box.

21. Press and hold the Shift key and click in the Quit text box and then in its label. You should see handles in both text boxes and in the Quit label. Release the Shift key.

22. Pull down the Layout menu and choose Align, and then select Top from the submenu of alignment choices. If you want to see a more dramatic demonstration of the alignment commands, you might try moving the Quit field so it is noticeably lower than the Joined field before you correct the alignment.

23. When you are satisfied with the appearance of the Committees form, use the Save option on the File menu to save the revised form.

Changing the Tab Order

When you enter data using a single-column form designed by the FormWizards, pressing the Tab key moves you through the fields in the only possible sequence—from top to bottom. In a form with several fields on the same row, Access moves through the screen from top to bottom, and within each row, from left to right. (If two controls are not aligned at precisely the same height—for example, if you placed the Quit field in the Committees form slightly below the Joined field—Access would still move across the horizontal set of controls before proceeding to the next one that lies entirely below the group.) When you rearrange a form generated by the FormWizards, Access preserves the original tab order.

By and large, the default tab order is fine for simple forms, including the current version of the Committee Memberships form, but in a more complex form, you might want to group objects into columns and change the tab order so that the Tab key moves you down one column and then up to the top of the next. To edit the tab order, choose the Tab Order option from the Edit menu. Access displays the dialog box shown in Figure 6.22 (the list of objects in Figure 6.22 is derived from the single-column Prospects form). You must work with one form section at a time; you select the section by choosing one of the three radio buttons in the upper-left corner of the dialog box (there are no buttons for the page header or page footer sections). In the Prospects form, it only makes sense to change the tab order of the objects in the detail section. If the form has no header and footer sections, the corresponding radio buttons are disabled.

Figure 6.22

The Tab Order dialog box

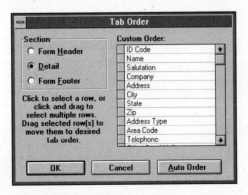

You customize the tab order by using the object selectors to rearrange the objects in the Custom Order list on the right side of the Tab Order dialog box. You can use all the techniques described in Chapter 4 to manipulate the list items. For example, to move an object, click on the selector, release the mouse button, and then click again and drag the object to its new position. To move a group of adjacent objects, select them by clicking on the first object and then holding down the Shift key while you click on the last. You can then drag the entire group to a new position in the list. You can restore the default order at any point by clicking on the Auto Order command button or by pressing Alt+A. Remember that changing the tab order *does not* move the objects themselves—it simply determines the order in which the Tab key moves you through the objects when you use the form to enter data. In most cases, you will already have rearranged the fields on the form before you reset the tab order.

Summary

This chapter described how to use the Access FormWizards to create two types of simple forms (single-column and tabular) for viewing and updating data derived from one table or query. By using custom forms, you can make great strides toward creating a data entry environment that is more helpful, friendly, and aesthetically pleasing, and more closely tailored to the preferences of the users and to the requirements of the specific task at hand. Forms also confer another significant advantage—they grant access to filters, which you can use in place of or in addition to queries to customize the sort order and record selection criteria in effect during a given data entry session.

The FormWizards are ideal for beginners, because they prompt you through the process of describing the basic form layout with a series of dialog boxes. Chapter 13 describes how to build forms from scratch, but even when you know how to do so, you may find that using the FormWizards to expedite the construction of many forms and then modifying the resulting forms can save you considerable time.

This chapter concentrated on the basic structure and layout of an Access form, and on how to use forms to update tables. If you are impatient to begin improving on the aesthetics, Chapter 10 describes how to customize the font, font size, color, and other visual attributes of the objects in your forms. This chapter also emphasized the use of forms for viewing and updating data on the screen, touching only briefly on the fact that you can also use a form to print data in the same layout. Printing a form is convenient when you occasionally want a hard copy of the data you are viewing on the screen. For more complex page layouts used *only* to display or print data (not to update the underlying tables), you can define reports; this topic is introduced in Chapter 7.

CHAPTER

7

**Defining Simple
Reports**

*The Structure of an
Access Report*

Using the ReportWizards

*Previewing and Printing
a Report*

Modifying a Report

YOU HAVE ALREADY SEEN HOW TO PRINT THE DATASHEET OF A TABLE or query in exactly the same form that Access displays the data on the screen. By combining various techniques described in Chapters 4 and 5, you can exercise very precise control over the contents of this listing, and to some extent, customize its appearance. You can use a query or a filter to specify record selection criteria and sorting instructions, and you can rearrange the datasheet by adjusting column widths and positions or by hiding columns you do not need to see. Because printing a datasheet is fast, immediate, and requires very little preparation, this is often the best way to produce a quick hard copy of a specific subset of your data, to document a series of ad hoc inquiries, or to print the results of performing a few calculations.

For reports that have a more complex structure or those that demand a more attractive layout, Access provides a Report Design tool very similar to the Form Design tool described in Chapter 6. You can use this tool to produce a wide variety of printed output, including columnar reports with subtotals and other summary statistics, reports that fill in or emulate preprinted forms (such as insurance or personnel forms), mailing labels, personalized letters, and many others. This chapter introduces the Report Design tool and describes how to use the Access ReportWizards to easily and quickly produce several very common report layouts.

When you design simple forms like the ones described in Chapter 6, intended primarily for entering and updating records (rather than viewing or summarizing data), you will naturally tend to focus on the detail section, which contains most or all of the controls used to collect the data. In contrast, even a very basic report will have a title, page header and/or page footer, and often, record groupings with their own headers and footers as well. Unless you are the only person who will read the report, you will have to devote some time and energy to aesthetic considerations such as page layout, font style and size, and how best to use attributes such as boldfacing and underlining for emphasis.

Furthermore, even for plain vanilla reports such as in-house accounting summaries, you will be forced to spend more time fine-tuning the page layout. When you view data on the screen using a large form, you can scroll the display window in any direction to view different portions. Obviously, a form is most useful when all the information you need to see at once fits on the screen at the same time, but as any spreadsheet user can attest, this is not always possible. In contrast, when you design a report, you must take into account the dimensions of the physical pages on which the report will be printed and take measures to ensure that the page breaks occur in reasonable places.

If you are new to Windows, note that in Access, as in most software designed for graphical environments, the differences between data entry forms and reports are much fewer and less significant than in software originally written for character-based environments. In the early days of DOS, the capabilities of most printers far exceeded the resolution possible with the video cards and display screens in common use, and the software allowed you to print reports that you could not possibly reproduce on the screen. In Access, the main differences between forms and reports are the fact that forms are used to *enter* and *edit* data, whereas reports only allow you to view or print information and the fact that a report can include groups with subtotals and summary statistics. Otherwise, reports and forms are nearly interchangeable— you can define forms that display data without allowing updates, you can print a form, you can save a form as a report, and you can view a report on the screen. In keeping with these parallels, the Report Design tool has a great deal in common with the Form Design tool introduced in Chapter 6.

In a typical application, however, you will need many reports that do not resemble screen forms and have a considerably more complex structure or page layout. The Access ReportWizards, and to a lesser extent the Report Design tool itself, operate under somewhat different assumptions than the corresponding form design tools, as befits the different contexts in which forms and reports are typically used. Keep in mind as you read this chapter, which concentrates on reports that you can produce with the ReportWizards, that none of these assumptions is carved in stone—you can change most characteristics of the forms and reports created by the Wizards, and you can produce nearly any effects you wish on forms and reports that you design from scratch.

This chapter concentrates on using the ReportWizards to design several very common types of reports—single-column reports that resemble the single-column forms described in Chapter 6, columnar layouts with groups and totals, and mailing labels—and on making minor modifications to the resulting reports. Chapter 10 describes how to further customize the appearance and behavior of both reports and forms, and Chapter 11 describes how to construct more complex reports, either from scratch or by extensively modifying reports generated by the ReportWizards.

The Structure of an Access Report

Like forms, Access reports are made up of *sections*. There are seven types of sections, which are defined by their positions in the printing sequence. Reports can have the five sections described in Chapter 6, as well as two others not permitted in forms. In a report (but not in a form), you can group records based on the contents of a particular field (or, as you will see in Chapter 9, an expression)—that is, print each set of records that have the same value in the group field together, and bracket each group with a header and/or footer section.

The seven basic report sections are as follows, listed in the order they usually fall in the printing sequence:

Section	Purpose
Report header	Printed once at the beginning of the report; may be used to print a cover page, descriptive header, or narrative introduction
Page header	Printed once at the top of each page; may include the report title, date, page number, and column headers
Group header	Printed once at the beginning of cach group; usually includes the contents of the field or expression that defines the group (the value that all the records in the group have in common)
Detail	Printed once for each record in the underlying dynaset; may include fields, calculated values, and explanatory text
Group footer	Printed once at the end of each group; usually includes totals or other summary statistics for the group
Page footer	Printed once at the bottom of each page; may include the date, page number, a key to abbreviations used in the report, or a document name or version number
Report footer	Printed once, at the end of the report; may be used to print a concluding statement, grand totals, or overall summary statistics

Figure 7.1 illustrates the first and last pages of a simple report based on the ACE Names table that has all seven types of sections. Access permits up to ten levels of groups in a report, and the report in Figure 7.1 has two: It lists people grouped by state and within each state by city, with debit and credit subtotals for each city and each state, and grand totals at the end of the report. Even if you have not worked with Access before, the purposes of the seven report sections should be reasonably clear from this sample; reports produced by many other computer programs (and manually prepared reports) share the same basic structure.

The report in Figure 7.1 includes all the possible types of sections, in part to illustrate their positions and purposes and in part because all of these sections are often required in columnar reports with groups and summary statistics. Regardless of the overall report style, all of the sections are optional. As

Figure 7.1
A columnar report
with all seven
basic report
sections

Left margin

Top margin
Report header
Page header
State group header
City group header

Detail

City group footer

Page footer
Bottom margin

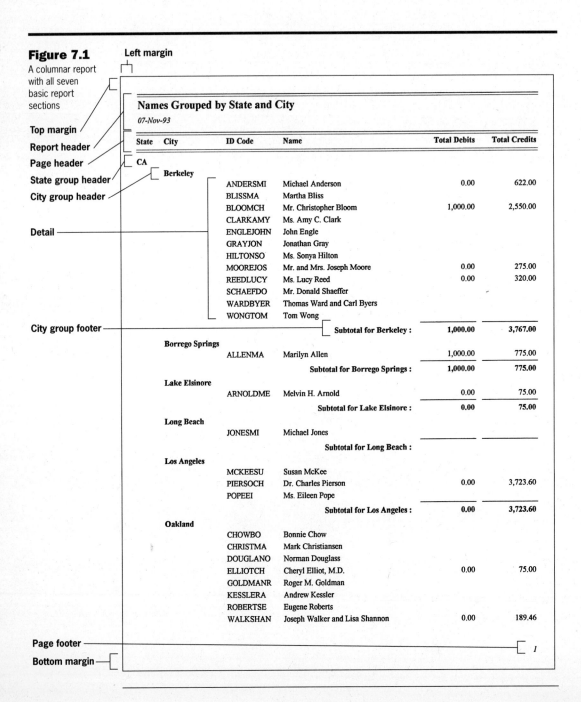

Names Grouped by State and City
07-Nov-93

State	City	ID Code	Name	Total Debits	Total Credits
CA					
	Berkeley				
		ANDERSMI	Michael Anderson	0.00	622.00
		BLISSMA	Martha Bliss		
		BLOOMCH	Mr. Christopher Bloom	1,000.00	2,550.00
		CLARKAMY	Ms. Amy C. Clark		
		ENGLEJOHN	John Engle		
		GRAYJON	Jonathan Gray		
		HILTONSO	Ms. Sonya Hilton		
		MOOREJOS	Mr. and Mrs. Joseph Moore	0.00	275.00
		REEDLUCY	Ms. Lucy Reed	0.00	320.00
		SCHAEFDO	Mr. Donald Shaeffer		
		WARDBYER	Thomas Ward and Carl Byers		
		WONGTOM	Tom Wong		
			Subtotal for Berkeley :	**1,000.00**	**3,767.00**
	Borrego Springs				
		ALLENMA	Marilyn Allen	1,000.00	775.00
			Subtotal for Borrego Springs :	**1,000.00**	**775.00**
	Lake Elsinore				
		ARNOLDME	Melvin H. Arnold	0.00	75.00
			Subtotal for Lake Elsinore :	**0.00**	**75.00**
	Long Beach				
		JONESMI	Michael Jones		
			Subtotal for Long Beach :		
	Los Angeles				
		MCKEESU	Susan McKee		
		PIERSOCH	Dr. Charles Pierson	0.00	3,723.60
		POPEEI	Ms. Eileen Pope		
			Subtotal for Los Angeles :	**0.00**	**3,723.60**
	Oakland				
		CHOWBO	Bonnie Chow		
		CHRISTMA	Mark Christiansen		
		DOUGLANO	Norman Douglass		
		ELLIOTCH	Cheryl Elliot, M.D.	0.00	75.00
		GOLDMANR	Roger M. Goldman		
		KESSLERA	Andrew Kessler		
		ROBERTSE	Eugene Roberts		
		WALKSHAN	Joseph Walker and Lisa Shannon	0.00	189.46

1

Figure 7.1

A columnar report
with all seven
basic report
sections
(Continued)

State	City	ID Code	Name	Total Debits	Total Credits
			Subtotal for TX :	1,000.00	1,540.50
UT					
	Moab				
		MCGUIRKA	Ms. Katherine McGuire		
			Subtotal for Moab :		
	Ogden				
		SMITHDA01	David Smith		
			Subtotal for Ogden :		
	Provo				
		MEYERAL	Mr. Allan B. Meyer		
			Subtotal for Provo :		
	Salt Lake City				
		JACOBSJO	Mr. Joseph T. Jacobs		
		SMITHAJ	Andrea J. Smith	0.00	14.00
			Subtotal for Salt Lake City :	0.00	14.00
			Subtotal for UT :	0.00	14.00
WA					
	Bellingham				
		BURDICJE	Ms. Jeannine Burdick		
			Subtotal for Bellingham :		
	Olympia				
		ROSENBRH	Ralph and Helen Rosenberg	0.00	50.00
			Subtotal for Olympia :	0.00	50.00
	Seattle				
		DAVISCH	Charles and Anne Davis	0.00	547.00
		HANCOCED	Edward and Marie Hancock		
		HEARNSKL	K. L. Hearns		
		SMITHRO	Robert A. Smith		
			Subtotal for Seattle :	0.00	547.00
			Subtotal for WA :	0.00	597.00
			Grand Total :	3,500.00	14,800.44

State group footer ⎯

Report footer ⎯

5

is the case with forms, you can remove the report header, report footer, page header, or page footer if these sections are not required. Many columnar reports have no groups, and in reports that do, you may not need separate header or footer sections for every group; for example, in a report with no group summary statistics, the group footers are generally unnecessary. You can even omit the detail section to produce a report that prints *only* group and overall summary statistics without any detail information from the records that make up each group. Some of these variations are described in this chapter, while others, which require editing report properties, are covered in Chapters 10 and 11.

Although it makes sense to think about the report sections as occupying particular positions in the print processing sequence, you need not define the sections in this order when you build a report from scratch or edit a report generated by the ReportWizards. In fact, the most efficient way to fine-tune the report layout is to work from the inside out, beginning with the detail section, which contains the data derived from individual records in the source table or query. After you are satisfied with the size and placement of the objects in the detail section, you can adjust the positions of the corresponding items in other sections to match—move the column titles in the page header section to align with the columns below, place the summary statistics in the group footer and report footer sections under the matching columns, and so on.

The data printed on an Access report can be derived from one or more tables or queries. As explained in Chapter 5, a query is nearly always equivalent to a table, and you can substitute a query for a table in most contexts. If you base a report on a query, Access executes the query each time you run the report, so the report always contains the most up-to-date information, based on the contents of the underlying tables. If the query includes record selection criteria, only the records that satisfy these criteria, *as of the moment you begin the report*, are included. If you base a report on a parameter query, Access runs the query as usual, prompts you to enter values for all the parameters, and includes on the report only the records that match these values.

Using the ReportWizards

The easiest and fastest way to define a new report is to use one of the Access ReportWizards to create the basic layout and then use the Report Design tool to modify the resulting report if necessary. As is the case with screen forms, allowing a Wizard to build the first version of a report can save you a considerable amount of work, even if the report will require extensive rearrangements or enhancements. The ReportWizards work much like the Form Wizards described in Chapter 6, and you can use all the same methods to navigate through the sequence of dialog boxes and make selections. Of course, many of the individual dialog boxes are different, due in some cases to fundamental differences between reports and forms, and in others to differing assumptions that Access makes about the typical uses of forms and reports.

To begin creating a new report, you can use any of the following methods:

- Make sure that the Database window displays the list of reports (if necessary, click on the Report button in the Database window or choose the Report option from the View menu) and then click on the New command button or press Alt+N.

- Choose the New option from the File menu and then choose Report from the submenu of object types.

- Highlight the source table or query in the Database window, and click on the New Report button in the tool bar (the last of the three new object buttons).

To call up the Report Design tool to edit an existing report, make sure that the Database window displays the list of reports and then highlight the name and either click on the Design command button, press Alt+D, or double-click the right mouse button.

Regardless of how you initiate the report design process, Access displays the New Report dialog box pictured in Figure 7.2 (which is virtually identical to the New Form dialog box described in Chapter 6) to allow you to choose the table or query that will supply the data for the report and decide whether to use the ReportWizards or start from scratch with a blank report. Most of the examples used to illustrate the report definition sequence are based on the Names table, and you should choose this table if you are following along. Later in this chapter, a more complete hands-on exercise demonstrates how to create a simple report based on the Committees table.

Figure 7.2

Choosing the data source and method for creating a new report

As noted in Chapter 6, the list of table and query names accessed through the Select A Table/Query combo box gives you no way to differentiate tables from queries, so you may want to make a note of the correct table or query

name before you choose the New Report option. If you do not choose a table or query, or if you type the name instead of selecting it from the drop-down list and you misspell the name, Access displays an alert box to remind you that "You must select an existing table or query to use a FormWizard or ReportWizard." Recall also that if you want to use the ReportWizards, you should *not* press Enter after you type or select the table or query name, because Blank Report is the default button in the New Report dialog box. (If you inadvertently choose the Blank Report option, just close the Report Design window without saving the new report and start over.)

Choosing the Report Style

When you choose the ReportWizards option from the initial dialog box, Access displays the dialog box shown in Figure 7.3, which prompts you to choose a ReportWizard based on the overall report style you want to create. The left side of this dialog box displays graphical representations of the various form and report styles (with no indication of which is which). You should recognize the four form styles from Chapter 6; the report styles, which are labeled in Figure 7.3, produce the following results:

Single-column   A report in which the fields are lined up in a single vertical column, with the field names to the left as prompts

Groups/Totals   A columnar report with up to three groups, which includes group subtotals and grand totals for all the numeric fields

Mailing Label   A report that prints labels or other types of forms in which records may repeat both horizontally and vertically on the page

Figure 7.3
Choosing the overall report style

The single-column report style, which closely resembles the single-column data entry forms created by the FormWizards, is ideal for tables that have too many fields to fit on one page in a columnar format, especially for tables that have more than a few long Text or Memo fields. Figure 7.4 illustrates the first page of a single-column report based on the Committees table. You can also use this report style as the point of departure for creating reports that fill in the data on preprinted forms such as insurance forms or tax returns, or for more complex reports that include all the lines, boxes, and text required to *replace* one of these paper forms. A single-column report is also easily converted to a multitable report based on two or more tables that have a one-to-many relationship (Access provides a FormWizard for creating multitable forms, but not a comparable ReportWizard). Chapter 11 describes how to add one or more tabular lists of contacts, transactions, or committees to a single-column report that includes the name and address fields of ACE members.

The groups/totals style is a tabular layout best suited to columnar listings that require only a few lines for each record (often, only one line). The report in Figure 7.1 is a typical example of this report style. The ReportWizard places all the fields you select on one line, but you can easily rearrange the fields onto two or more rows, using techniques already familiar to you from your experience with the Form Design tool. Of course, if you use the methods described in Chapter 10 to add new objects to a report created by the Report-Wizards, you can place them anywhere you wish. The ReportWizard generates group header sections for up to three groups that you define, and if there are numeric fields on the report, it generates group footer sections with subtotals for all the numeric fields. You might also want to compute additional statistics such as counts or averages, and print some or all of these statistics in the group header sections instead of the group footers. Chapter 9 describes how to define statistical calculations in a report.

Mailing label reports, as suggested by the name, can be used to print name and address labels one or more across, on either gummed labels, laser printer label sheets, or as Cheshire labels printed on plain paper, which are later sliced up and affixed to your mail pieces by a service bureau. Figure 7.5 shows two-across mailing labels printed in zip code order from the ACE Names table. You can also use this report style to produce many other types of labels, such as inventory stock labels, file folder labels, and name tags. What might not be so obvious is the fact that you can use mailing label reports to print data on index cards or Rolodex cards, as well as two- or three-column reference lists printed on plain paper rather than on mailing label stock.

Figure 7.4
A single-column
report

Committee Memberships
07-Nov-93

Committee: EARTHDAY
ID Code: HOWARDJO
Officer:
Joined: 5/10/91
Quit:
Notes:

Committee: EARTHDAY
ID Code: LEEALEX
Officer: Treasurer
Joined: 7/23/90
Quit:
Notes:

Committee: EARTHDAY
ID Code: OLSONED
Officer:
Joined: 6/18/91
Quit: 5/20/92
Notes: Ed organized the first ACE-sponsored "Run for the
Planet" race and fun run, held in San Francisco in
1992.

Committee: EARTHDAY
ID Code: FRANKLKA
Officer: Chairperson
Joined: 8/1/92
Quit:
Notes:

1

Figure 7.5

A mailing label report

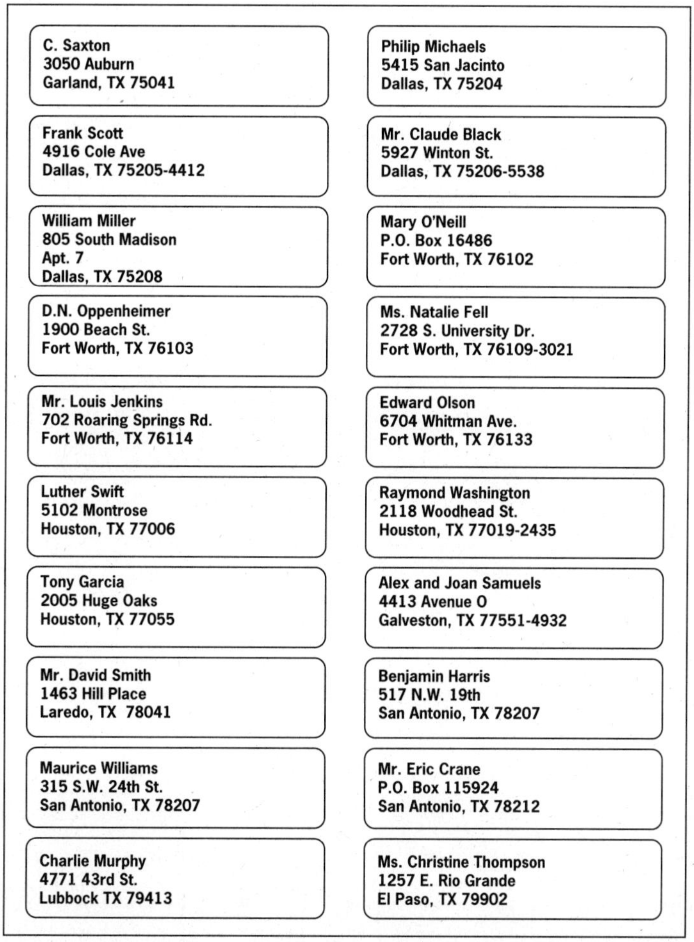

C. Saxton 3050 Auburn Garland, TX 75041	Philip Michaels 5415 San Jacinto Dallas, TX 75204
Frank Scott 4916 Cole Ave Dallas, TX 75205-4412	Mr. Claude Black 5927 Winton St. Dallas, TX 75206-5538
William Miller 805 South Madison Apt. 7 Dallas, TX 75208	Mary O'Neill P.O. Box 16486 Fort Worth, TX 76102
D.N. Oppenheimer 1900 Beach St. Fort Worth, TX 76103	Ms. Natalie Fell 2728 S. University Dr. Fort Worth, TX 76109-3021
Mr. Louis Jenkins 702 Roaring Springs Rd. Fort Worth, TX 76114	Edward Olson 6704 Whitman Ave. Fort Worth, TX 76133
Luther Swift 5102 Montrose Houston, TX 77006	Raymond Washington 2118 Woodhead St. Houston, TX 77019-2435
Tony Garcia 2005 Huge Oaks Houston, TX 77055	Alex and Joan Samuels 4413 Avenue O Galveston, TX 77551-4932
Mr. David Smith 1463 Hill Place Laredo, TX 78041	Benjamin Harris 517 N.W. 19th San Antonio, TX 78207
Maurice Williams 315 S.W. 24th St. San Antonio, TX 78207	Mr. Eric Crane P.O. Box 115924 San Antonio, TX 78212
Charlie Murphy 4771 43rd St. Lubbock TX 79413	Ms. Christine Thompson 1257 E. Rio Grande El Paso, TX 79902

Designing Single-Column and Groups/Totals Reports

The sequence of dialog boxes displayed by the ReportWizards when you choose single-column or groups/totals is very similar (with the obvious exception of the screens you use to define the report groups). The mailing label sequence, which is quite different, is described later in "Using the Mailing Label ReportWizard."

Choosing the Fields

After you choose the report style, Access displays a dialog box like the one shown in Figure 7.6 to allow you to choose the fields you want to include on the report. On the left side of this dialog box is a small picture of the overall report style selected in the previous step with the heading areas (both the Report header and the field labels) represented by thick black blocks, and the fields themselves by thinner lines. The image in Figure 7.6 corresponds to the single-column report style. The dotted line in the middle of the report is a record separator included to remind you that Access will print more than one record per page if space permits; this line is absent from the graphical representation of a groups/totals report, which always includes many records on each page. The actual report generated by the single-column ReportWizard does not include a separating line between records, but you can easily add one using methods described in Chapter 10, and for reports that include more than a few fields from each record, it is often desirable to do so.

Figure 7.6

Choosing the fields to include on a report

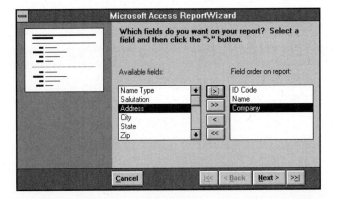

You can use the two scrolling lists in the field selection dialog box to build and edit the list of fields that you want to include in the report, exactly as in the analogous step in the form design process. The Available Fields list on the left includes all the fields in the underlying table or query that you have not already selected (in the same order in which they occur in the table structure or query dynaset), and the Field Order on Report list includes the fields you have chosen to appear on the report. In Figure 7.6, three fields from the Names table—ID Code, Name, and Company—have been selected. You can use the four command buttons between the lists to move fields one at a time or all at once in either direction, as follows:

>   Moves the highlighted field to the Report list

>>   Moves all fields to the Report list

<   Removes the highlighted field from the Report list

<<   Removes all fields from the Report list

Defining Report Groups

The next step, if you chose the groups/totals report style in the first ReportWizards dialog box, is using the dialog box pictured in Figure 7.7 to define up to three report groups. In the diagram on the left side of this dialog box, a thick black line represents the group header in the position it will occupy on the finished report (above and to the left of the records in the group). Figure 7.7 shows the specifications for the two groups in the report pictured in Figure 7.1, which are based on the State and City fields. If you do not need groups, simply move to the next step without choosing any fields from the Available Fields list.

Figure 7.7

Defining the report groups

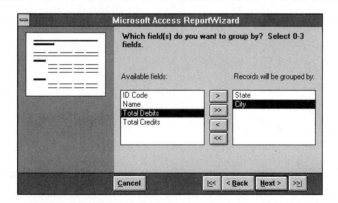

You can only base a group on a field that appears in the report, so the Available Fields list in the group dialog box includes only the fields you selected in the previous step in the order you chose them. This restriction makes sense when you consider the fact that the ReportWizard places the fields that define the groups in the group header section to identify the groups.

Note that you may want to define groups simply to obtain the group headers and breaks between groups generated by the ReportWizards, even if a report does not include any numeric fields and therefore does not require group summary statistics. Later in this chapter, you will create a Committees Membership Roster with no summary statistics at all, in which Committees table records are grouped by committee. You might also want to add statistics such as the number of records in each group or the maximum or minimum value in a date field, none of which depend on numeric fields. Chapter 11 describes how to compute these and other summary statistics.

If you requested at least one group, Access displays a second dialog box to collect more specific information on how to define each group. This dialog box is shown in Figure 7.8 for a report with groups based on the State and City fields, such as the report in Figure 7.1. If you have more than one group field, you must select a grouping method for each one, which you can do by highlighting each field in the Available Fields list in turn and then selecting the grouping method from the list on the right.

Figure 7.8

Selecting the grouping method for each group field

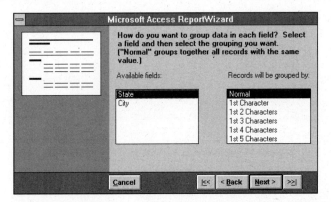

The choices displayed in the scrolling list of grouping methods depend on the data type of the group field currently highlighted in the Available Fields list. For all data types, the default choice, which Access uses if you do not make another selection, is Normal, which creates a separate group for each distinct value in the group field. Thus, choosing Normal for the State and City fields results in a report with a group for each state, and within each state, a group for each city, as shown in Figure 7.1.

The additional choices in the grouping methods list box depend on the data type of the group field. For Text fields, as you can see in Figure 7.8, you can also elect to base the groups on the first character or the first two, three, four, or five characters of the field. For example, Figure 7.9 illustrates an alphabetical reference list in which the groups are based on the first character of the ID Code, and the resulting group header sections print the single letters that identify the groups. Another common application for grouping on a partial field value is printing mailing summary reports that count the number of labels printed in each two- or three-digit zip code group. (A method for printing these counts on summary labels is described in Chapter 11.)

Figure 7.9

Grouping on the first
letter of a Text field

Alphabetical Telephone List

07-Nov-93

ID Code	Name	City	State	Area Code	Telephone
A					
ALLENJE	Jerry Allen	San Francisco	CA		
ALLENMA	Marilyn Allen	Borrego Springs	CA		
ANDERSJC	Mr. J. C. Anderson	Temecula	CA		
ANDERSMI	Michael Anderson	Berkeley	CA	510	549--7838
ARNOLDME	Melvin H. Arnold	Lake Elsinore	CA		
B					
BAKERSY	Ms. Sylvia Baker	Portland	OR		
BERGENRU	Ruth Bergen	San Francisco	CA		
BLACKCL	Mr. Claude Black	Dallas	TX		
BLISSMA	Martha Bliss	Berkeley	CA	510	645--1947
BLOOMCH	Mr. Christopher Bloom	Berkeley	CA	510	848--3201
BROWNEL	Elizabeth Brown	Santa Rosa	CA		
BURDICJE	Ms. Jeannine Burdick	Bellingham	WA		
C					
CHOWBO	Bonnie Chow	Oakland	CA		
CHRISTMA	Mark Christiansen	Oakland	CA		
CLARKAMY	Ms. Amy C. Clark	Berkeley	CA	510	549--6086
COLLINSR	Robert Collins	San Francisco	CA		
CRANEER	Mr. Eric Crane	San Antonio	TX		
D					
DAVIDSJA	Jacqueline Davidson	Carson City	NV		
DAVISCH	Charles and Anne Davis	Seattle	WA		
DODDFRED	Mr. Frederick Dodd	San Francisco	CA	415	992--2485
DOUGLANO	Norman Douglass	Oakland	CA		
E					
ELLIOTCH	Cheryl Elliot, M.D.	Oakland	CA	510	637--1840
ENGLEJOHN	John Engle	Berkeley	CA		
F					
FELLNATA	Ms. Natalie Fell	Fort Worth	TX		
FLETCHAR	Arnold N. Fletcher	San Francisco	CA		
FRANKLKA	Karen Franklin	San Francisco	CA		
G					
GARCIATO	Tony Garcia	Houston	TX		
GOLDMANJA	Mr. James Goldman	San Francisco	CA		
GOLDMANR	Roger M. Goldman	Oakland	CA		
GRAYJON	Jonathan Gray	Berkeley	CA	510	845--3195
GRAZIAAL	Alfredo Graziani	San Francisco	CA		
H					
HANCOCED	Edward and Marie Hancock	Seattle	WA	206	781--9853
HARRINJU	Ms. Judy Harrington	San Francisco	CA		
HARRISBE	Benjamin Harris	San Antonio	TX		

1

The additional grouping methods for Date/Time fields are Year, Quarter, Month, Week, Day, Hour, and Minute. The first five of these are particularly useful for accounting reports and financial projections, which often require subtotals based on calendar intervals. For example, Figure 7.10 shows a donation summary based on the ACE Transactions table with monthly totals obtained by selecting Date as the group field and Month as the grouping method. Note that Access automatically sorts records based on the entire field, so that reports such as the one in Figure 7.10 are printed in overall chronological order and each group represents *one month in one year*. In contrast, if the sort order matched the grouping method, Access would sort the data in Figure 7.10 by month alone, and all the donations in January of any year would be grouped together, followed by all the donations in February, and so on.

For all of the numeric data types, the choices are based on ranges of values specified as intervals of 10, 50, 100, 500, 1,000, 5,000, 10,000, 50,000, 100,000, or 500,000. If these intervals do not suit your needs, note that you can use *any* interval in a report that you create from scratch, and you can edit a report generated by the ReportWizards to modify the interval. Figure 7.11 illustrates a donation summary that groups contributions in $50 increments.

NOTE. *In any report with groups, Access omits the group header and footer sections for any group that contains no detail records. Thus, the 150–199, 200–249, 300–349, 350–399, 400–449, and 450–499 groups are mising from the report in Figure 7.11.*

Choosing the Sort Order

For both single-column and groups/total layouts, the next dialog box, shown in Figure 7.12 for a groups/totals report, prompts you to choose the sort order. In a single-column report or in a groups/totals report with no groups, the sort keys you select determine the overall order for all the records printed on the report.

In a report with groups, Access automatically sorts the source dynaset by all the group fields, in an order that matches the hierarchy of the groups, to guarantee that all the records in each group are adjacent in the processing sequence. For example, in a report grouped by state and city, Access sorts first by the State field and within each state by the City field to ensure that all the records in each state are grouped together, and within each state, all the records in each city are grouped together. The group fields are therefore absent from the Available Fields list in the sort dialog box, and a brief reminder under the diagram on the left side of the dialog box explains why: "The report will already be sorted by the grouping fields you've selected." The sort keys you select determine the order of the records *within the smallest group* (in this example, the order of the records in each city).

Figure 7.10

Grouping by month
based on a
Date/Time field

Donations by Month

07-Nov-93

Date	Type	ID Code	Amount	Pmt Form	Reference
January 1992					
1/22/92	DO	DAVISCH	50.00	Check	Check #467
			50.00		
February 1992					
2/21/92	DO	ALLENMA	250.00	Check	Check #381
			250.00		
March 1992					
3/22/92	DO	FELLNATA	50.00	Check	Check #862
			50.00		
April 1992					
4/8/92	DO	ANDERSMI	100.00	Check	Check #1005
			100.00		
May 1992					
5/12/92	DO	PIERSOCH	500.00	Check	Check #318
5/19/92	DO	SWIFTLU	35.00	Check	Check #3750
			535.00		
		Grand Total :	985.00		

1

Figure 7.11
Grouping by $50
intervals based on a
Number field

Donations by Amount
07-Nov-93

Amount	ID Code	Date	Payment Form	Reference
Donations from 0 to 49				
35.00	SWIFTLU	5/19/92	Check	Check #3750
Donations from 50 to 99				
50.00	DAVISCH	1/22/92	Check	Check #467
50.00	FELLNATA	3/22/92	Check	Check #862
Donations from 100 to 149				
100.00	ANDERSMI	4/8/92	Check	Check #1005
Donations from 250 to 299				
250.00	ALLENMA	2/21/92	Check	Check #381
Donations from 500 to 549				
500.00	PIERSOCH	5/12/92	Check	Check #318

1

Figure 7.12

Choosing the sort order

You can choose up to three sort keys, all of which must be among the fields printed on the report. Thus, in the report in Figure 7.1, you cannot sort the records in each city by ID Code, but you can omit this field from the detail section of the report and print only the Name field. Both of these limitations apply only to sorting instructions specified through the ReportWizards, and you can overcome them by editing the resulting report. For example, to sort by ID code but print the Name field in its place, add both fields to the report, and then edit the form created by the ReportWizards and delete the ID Code field from the detail section. You can also edit or add to the sorting instructions for the report using a dialog box displayed from the Report Design view. When you specify sorting instructions using this method (which is described in Chapter 11), Access does not limit you to three sort keys.

When you define a report based on a query that also includes sorting instructions, the grouping and sorting specifications you enter in the report (either through the ReportWizards dialog boxes or by editing the report) override any sorting instructions present in the query. This precedence gives you the flexibility to use the same query for many reports, printed in various orders and with different record groups. Whether to base a report on a query or simply enter the sorting instructions in the report is a matter of discretion for a report that prints all the records in a table. If you already have a query that includes the appropriate sorting instructions, you can use it; if not, there is no need to define one—simply enter the sorting instructions in the report. If you need a query to establish selection criteria (such as the query that selects only donation transactions for the reports in Figures 7.10 and 7.11), you can enter the sorting instructions either in the query or in the report.

Choosing the Overall Look of the Report

The next dialog box, which is shown in Figure 7.13, prompts you to select the overall look of the report; this step should seem familiar from your experience with the FormWizards. Most of the report examples presented thus far in this chapter, including the one in Figures 7.1 and 7.4, use the Executive look. Figures 7.14 and 7.15 illustrate the Presentation and Ledger looks with reports that include the same data as Figure 7.4. As is the case with forms, you will find the two report styles that have the fewest lines and boxes—Executive and Presentation—far easier to modify than the Ledger style, and if you can foresee the need for extensive modifications to a report created by the ReportWizards, you may want to stick with these choices at first.

Figure 7.13

Choosing the look of a report

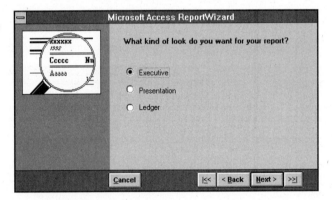

Titling and Saving the Report

Finally, Access displays the dialog box shown in Figure 7.16 to prompt you for the report title, which is printed in the report header section at the very beginning of the report. In the Committees table reports in Figures 7.4, 7.14, and 7.15, the title is "Committee Memberships." Do not confuse the title with the *name* of the report, which you enter later, when you save it for the first time. By default, Access proposes the name of the table or query on which the report is based—"Names" in Figure 7.16—as its title. Usually, you will want to enter a more specific title, because most database applications include more than one report based on each table.

One aspect of the report design that you will often want to change is the location of the report title, which the ReportWizards place in the report header, not the page header. By default, single-column and mailing label reports do not have a page header section, and this section on a groups/totals report contains only the column titles. If you prefer to repeat the report title on each page, you can edit the report created by the ReportWizard to add a page

Figure 7.14

The Presentation
report look

Committee Memberships
07-Nov-93

    <u>**Committee:**</u> EARTHDAY
     <u>**ID Code:**</u> HOWARDJO
      <u>**Officer:**</u>
       <u>**Joined:**</u>   5/10/91
        <u>**Quit:**</u>
       <u>**Notes:**</u>

    <u>**Committee:**</u> EARTHDAY
     <u>**ID Code:**</u> LEEALEX
      <u>**Officer:**</u> Treasurer
       <u>**Joined:**</u>   7/23/90
        <u>**Quit:**</u>
       <u>**Notes:**</u>

    <u>**Committee:**</u> EARTHDAY
     <u>**ID Code:**</u> OLSONED
      <u>**Officer:**</u>
       <u>**Joined:**</u>   6/18/91
        <u>**Quit:**</u>   5/20/92
       <u>**Notes:**</u> Ed organized the first ACE-sponsored "Run for
               the Planet" race and fun run, held in San
               Francisco in 1992.

    <u>**Committee:**</u> EARTHDAY
     <u>**ID Code:**</u> FRANKLKA
      <u>**Officer:**</u> Chairperson
       <u>**Joined:**</u>   8/1/92
        <u>**Quit:**</u>
       <u>**Notes:**</u>

1

Figure 7.15

The Ledger report look

Committee Memberships

07-Nov-93

Committee:	EARTHDAY
ID Code:	HOWARDJO
Officer:	
Joined:	5/10/91
Quit:	
Notes:	
Committee:	EARTHDAY
ID Code:	LEEALEX
Officer:	Treasurer
Joined:	7/23/90
Quit:	
Notes:	
Committee:	EARTHDAY
ID Code:	OLSONED
Officer:	
Joined:	6/18/91
Quit:	5/20/92
Notes:	Ed organized the first ACE-sponsored "Run for the Planet" race and fun run, held in San Francisco in
Committee:	EARTHDAY
ID Code:	FRANKLKA
Officer:	Chairperson
Joined:	8/1/92
Quit:	1/1/93
Notes:	
Committee:	FINANCE
ID Code:	THOMPSCH
Officer:	
Joined:	12/18/91
Quit:	
Notes:	
Committee:	FINANCE
ID Code:	ALLENMA
Officer:	Chairperson
Joined:	2/3/90
Quit:	
Notes:	Ms. Allen was Treasurer of the Finance Committee from 6/90 through 7/91, when she became
Committee:	FINANCE
ID Code:	HOWARDJO
Officer:	Treasurer
Joined:	1/15/90
Quit:	2/5/91
Notes:	

1

Figure 7.16

Entering the report title

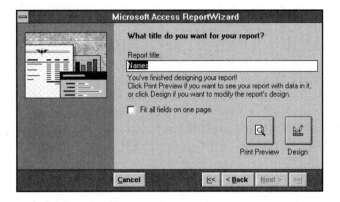

header section if necessary and move the report title into this section. The specific methods for manipulating report sections and moving objects are described later in this chapter in the section entitled "Modifying a Report."

After you enter the report title, you can use the Print Preview command button to see how the report will look when printed, or you can use the Design button to move to the Report Design view to immediately begin modifying the report. In most cases, it is a good idea to preview a few pages to check for unforeseen problems, even if you already have some modifications in mind.

When you design a groups/totals report, the title entry dialog box also contains one seemingly unrelated item—a check box labeled "Fit all fields on one page," which specifies how to handle reports with too many columns to fit on one page using the standard column widths. If you leave this option unchecked, Access handles the report the same way it prints the datasheet—as described in Chapter 4, it prints multiple pages for each group of records, so that you can lay the pages side by side to see all the fields in a given record on one line. Checking this box causes Access to narrow the columns enough to fit all the fields on one page. In calculating the new column widths, Access gives priority to numeric and Date/Time fields, which are meaningless when truncated, and subtracts space from Text columns instead. This option is most useful when the report is not much wider than the page, especially if most of the columns contain Text fields. In a report with too many fields, the result will be many columns whose contents (and titles) are indecipherable. If you want to see a graphic demonstration of when *not* to use this option, try checking it for a report that contains all the fields in the Names table.

You use exactly the same methods to save a report that you use to save any other Access object. You can save the report at any time by using the Save or Save As options on the File menu. If you have not yet saved the report when you close it for the first time (by pressing Ctrl+F4 or double-clicking on the close box), Access displays the dialog box shown in Figure 7.17 to ask whether you want to save it. If you choose Yes, Access displays the standard Save As dialog box to prompt you to enter a new name. For many reports, including most of the examples in this section, the report title or an abbreviated form of the report title serves well as the report name, and matching the name and title will help you remember the name and purpose of the report.

Figure 7.17

Saving a new report

Creating the Committee Membership Roster

To create a simple committee membership roster based on the Committees table, use the following steps:

1. Make sure that the Database window displays the list of reports (if necessary, click on the Report button in the Database window or choose the Reports option from the View menu) and then click on the New command button or press Alt+N.

2. Click on the arrow symbol at the right side of the Table/Query combo box to display the list of table and query names, and choose Committees from the list (remember *not* to press Enter after you highlight or click on the table name).

3. Click on the ReportWizards button or press Alt+W.

4. In the report style selection dialog box, choose Groups/Totals.

5. In the field selection dialog box, click on the >> button to select all the fields in the Committees table, and then click on the Next button or press Alt+N to go on to the next step.

6. In the group field selection dialog box, make sure that the Committee field is highlighted (it is the default because it is the first field in the list), and click on the > button to select this field. Click on the Next button or press Alt+N to go on to the next step.

7. Make sure that Normal is highlighted in the grouping methods list (it is the default), and click on the Next button or press Alt+N to move to the next step.

8. In the sort specifications dialog box, make sure that the ID Code field is highlighted (it is the default because it is the first field in the list), and click on the > button to select this field. Note that Committee, which you selected as the group field in step 6, is not available as a sort key—Access automatically sorts first by the group field (in this case, Committee), and then by any additional sort keys you select (in this case, ID Code). Click on the Next button or press Alt+N to go on to the next step.

9. In the report look dialog box, click on the Next button or press Alt+N to retain the default report style (Executive), and go on to the next step.

10. In the title dialog box, press F2 or click in the text box to display an insertion point, and edit the report title so it reads Committee Membership Roster.

11. Click on the Print Preview command button to preview the report. Your screen should look like Figure 7.18.

12. Select the Save option from the File menu and enter **Committee Membership Roster** when Access prompts you for the report name.

Figure 7.18

Previewing the Committee Membership Roster

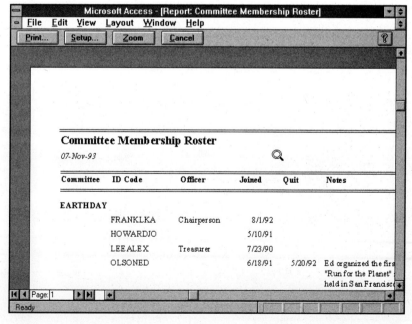

Committee	ID Code	Officer	Joined	Quit	Notes
EARTHDAY					
	FRANKLKA	Chairperson	8/1/92		
	HOWARDJO		5/10/91		
	LEEALEX	Treasurer	7/23/90		
	OLSONED		6/18/91	5/20/92	Ed organized the firs "Run for the Planet" held in San Francisc

Using the Mailing Label ReportWizard

If you choose the Mailing Label report style from the first ReportWizards dialog box, the subsequent sequence of dialog boxes is quite different from the steps used to define single-column and groups/totals reports, although a few of the dialog boxes are similar.

One major difference manifests itself in the very first dialog box, the one in which you choose the fields that you want on the report. In a single-column or groups/totals report, Access takes complete control of the page layout—all you need to do is pick the fields. In contrast, the ReportWizard that creates mailing labels treats a label as a series of lines made up of fields, punctuation marks, and text, and it allows you to specify the contents of each line by using the dialog box shown in Figure 7.19. As in the analogous dialog box displayed by the other two ReportWizards, the Available Fields list contains all the fields in the source table or query. Instead of a simple list of selected fields, however, the box on the right marked "Label Appearance" displays a representation of the finished label. The label shown in Figure 7.19 has four lines; the first three print the Name, Company, and Address, respectively, and the fourth prints the City, State, and Zip fields in the standard form (with a comma and space following the City field and two spaces between the State and Zip fields).

Figure 7.19

Defining the label contents

In addition to the Available Fields list, the dialog box includes a number of special buttons, each with a symbol on its face that indicates its purpose. Each field or symbol you select is added to the label line that you are currently building. You might visualize this dialog box as a kind of typewriter with a limited number of keys, which you press one at a time to produce the corresponding symbols on the label. You can use any of the methods described earlier in this chapter to choose fields from the Available Fields list:

clicking on the field name and then on the > button or double-clicking on the
field name. The best way to add a space or punctuation mark to the label is to
click on the corresponding button (you can use the keyboard to make your selections, but the process is too cumbersome to be practical).

As you select each item, Access adds it to the current label line in the
Label Appearance box. You can pan the display to view all of a long label line
by clicking on the two buttons labeled with arrows below the Label Appearance box. Spaces are represented in this diagram as vertically centered dots
to distinguish them from periods. Be careful to explicitly include all the
spaces you need between items placed on the same line of the label (by clicking on the Space button). By default, the mailing label ReportWizard places
the items you select one after the other, with no intervening spaces.

Because you might place more than one item on each line of the label,
you must indicate the end of each line by clicking on the button with the ↵
symbol on its face, which represents the Enter key. You cannot add a hard return to the end of the current label line by pressing the Enter key on your
keyboard—pressing Enter moves you to the next ReportWizard dialog box.
If you make this mistake, simply press the <Back button in this dialog box to
return to the field selection screen.

You can combine these techniques as follows to construct the mailing
label shown in Figure 7.19:

1. Highlight the Name field and click on the > button.

2. Click on the Enter button to advance to the next label line.

3. Highlight the Company field and click on the > button.

4. Click on the Enter button to advance to the next label line.

5. Highlight the Address field and click on the > button.

6. Click on the Enter button to advance to the next label line.

7. Highlight the City field and click on the > button.

8. Click on the Comma button.

9. Click on the Space button.

10. Click on the State field and then click on the > button.

11. Click twice on the Space button.

12. Click on the Zip field and then click on the > button.

13. Click on the Enter button to advance to the next label line.

You can add free-form text to a label by entering it in the text box below the Available Fields list and then clicking on the button labeled Text-> to move the text onto the current label line. You can use this option to create a label line that consists entirely of an arbitrary text string, such as "Merry Christmas" or "Thank you for your order" or a special code that identifies a mailing. You can also combine text and fields on the same line. For example, you could precede a contact name with "Attention:" or "Attn:" or print a code that identifies the mailing. Figure 7.20 illustrates both of these uses of text on a label.

Figure 7.20

A mailing label that includes text

. By default, Access allows each label line to grow or shrink as necessary to accommodate the data and avoid blank lines. For example, if the Address field includes multiple lines, all of these lines appear on the label. If the Company field is blank, Access suppresses the blank line that would result from printing it on the label and prints the Address field on the line immediately following the Name field. To deliberately leave blank lines on a label, you can click on the Enter button once for each hard return you want, just as you would press Enter repeatedly if you were typing the label on a typewriter.

In the next dialog box in the mailing label design sequence, you choose the sort order, using a dialog box that looks just like the one displayed by the other two ReportWizards. There is one small difference—the mailing label ReportWizard allows you to sort on *any* field in the underlying table or query, not just on a field that appears on the label. Although the mailing label ReportWizard does not display the group dialog box, a mailing label report can include groups. For example, in a mailing label report sorted by zip code, you might want to group by the first two or three digits of the zip code or add a group footer section that prints a summary label at the end of each group. Chapter 11 describes how to edit the mailing label report and add the group specifications and the statistics in the group footer section.

There is no dialog box comparable to the one that allows you to choose the overall look of a single-column or groups/totals report. All mailing labels generated by the ReportWizards use 8-point Arial type (presumably to help you squeeze more text onto a small label), but you can edit the resulting report to change the font or font size, using methods outlined in Chapter 10.

After you specify the sort order, Access displays the dialog box pictured in Figure 7.21, which allows you to select the label dimensions and overall page layout. If you use Avery labels, the easiest way to choose an option from the rather long list is to search for the Avery label code number in the first column. The second column of the list contains the dimensions of one label, and the third column displays the number of labels across the page. If you choose the Metric radio button in the upper-right corner of the dialog box, the Avery code numbers change to those in common use in Europe, and the dimensions in the second column are expressed in millimeters rather than inches.

Figure 7.21

Choosing the label dimensions and page layout

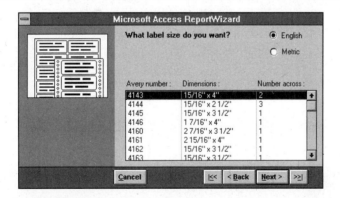

The last dialog box in the mailing label ReportWizard sequence simply allows you to preview the labels on the screen or move immediately to the Report Design view to modify the report. This dialog box resembles the comparable one displayed by the single-column and groups/totals Report-Wizard except that it does not prompt you for a report title. If you wish, you can modify the report to add a page title.

As is the case with all other reports, you can save a mailing label report at any time by using the Save or Save As options on the File menu. If you have not yet saved the report when you close it for the first time (by pressing Ctrl+F4 or double-clicking on the close box), Access displays the dialog box shown in Figure 7.17 to ask whether you want to save it, and if you choose Yes, it displays the standard Save As dialog box to prompt you for the report name.

Previewing and Printing a Report

When you use any of the ReportWizards to design a new report, it is usually a good idea to preview the report and inspect at least a few pages of data, even if you already plan to edit and modify the report. When you preview a simple datasheet, looking at the first page or two may suffice to check the contents and page layout. In contrast, a complex report has more potential problem sites, and you may need to examine the display in the Print Preview window more closely to find all of them. Previewing the report is the best way to check for unforeseen problems such as inappropriate page breaks, data regions too narrow for the contents, or incorrectly justified column titles. (The ReportWizards left-justify the titles over columns that contain Date/Time and numeric fields, but most people would prefer to right-justify titles over these fields.) If a groups/totals report is just a little too wide for the page, you might be able to make all the fields fit by resetting the left and right margins, making some columns narrower, and moving fields closer together. In the reports presented as examples earlier in this chapter, all of these problems were corrected by editing the report in the Report Design window.

Access offers two slightly different preview modes for reports—Sample Preview and Print Preview. Both accurately reproduce the visual appearance of the report, so you can check the page layout, margins, column widths, font, font size, and print enhancements. The Print Preview includes all the data in the underlying dynaset (the table or query that supplies the data on the report). In contrast, the Sample Preview includes only a small sample set of records. Because sorting or executing a query can take quite a bit of time if your tables are large, Access provides the Sample Preview as a way to avoid these lengthy procedures if all you want to do is check the page layout of a report. The records in the Sample Preview are real, but they may not appear in exactly the right order. The Sample Preview includes the groups you requested, but not every individual group (for example, in a report with groups based on the State field, only a few states will be represented), each group will contain only a few records, and the group statistics will not be correct. While the Print Preview will take longer if your tables are large, you may need to use it at times to verify the correct performance of a report that includes complex calculations.

The Sample Preview option is accessible only from the Report Design view through the Sample Preview option on the File menu. To move to the Print Preview screen, you can use any of the following methods:

- In the last ReportWizards dialog box, use the Print Preview command button.

- In the Database window, use the Preview command button.

- In the Database window, highlight the name of the report and press Enter.

- In the Database window, double-click on the report name.

- In the Database window or Report Design window, choose the Print Preview option from the File menu.

- In the Database window or Report Design window, click on the Print Preview button in the tool bar.

NOTE. *The Print Preview button in the last ReportWizards dialog box leads to the full Print Preview mode, not to the more limited Sample Preview. When you design a brand new report based on a large table, you might prefer to choose Report Design instead of Print Preview and then invoke the Sample Preview window from the File menu in the Report Design view.*

The Sample Preview and Print Preview windows themselves are indistinguishable. If you forget which option you chose while you are previewing a report, pull down the File menu and look for the check mark that appears next to either the Print Preview or Sample Preview option. In every respect, the Print Preview window looks and works just as it does when you preview the printed appearance of a table or query dynaset, and you can use the navigation controls in the Print Preview window as described in Chapter 4 to view any portion of the report.

If you exit from the Print Preview screen by using the Cancel command button on the tool bar, Access returns you to the environment from which you started—either the Database window or the Report Design window. If you arrived at the Print Preview screen from the last ReportWizards dialog box after creating a new report, Access leaves you in the Report Design window. If this seems strange, keep in mind that the ReportWizards create a report much the way that you would (in fact, Access briefly displays the Report Design window before switching to Print Preview mode). If you do not want to modify the report, simply save it and return to the Database window. If you exit from the preview screen by closing the Print Preview window (for example, by pressing Ctrl+F4 or clicking on the close box), Access returns you to the Database window.

You can initiate printing from many different places in Access:

- From the Sample Preview or Print Preview screen, click on the Print command button in the tool bar or press P (the hotkey shortcut).

- From either preview window, the Database window, or the Report Design window, choose the Print option from the File menu.

- From the Print Setup dialog box, click on the OK command button.

When you print from the Print Preview or Sample Preview screen, the data on the printed report matches the data displayed in the preview window. If you use the Sample Preview to save time while you refine a report layout, make sure that you exit from the Sample Preview screen and initiate printing from another location in Access to ensure that the printout includes all of the data.

When you use any of the methods just enumerated to initiate printing, Access displays the Print dialog box illustrated in Figure 7.22, which allows you to customize a few global aspects of the printout. You should recognize this dialog box from Chapter 4, if not from prior experience with other Windows programs. At the top of the dialog box, Access displays the currently selected printer; if you need to switch to another printer, you must do so through the Print Setup dialog box, which you can reach by clicking on the Setup button. You can choose to print any range of pages by using the radio buttons and page range text boxes in the Print Range region of the Print dialog box. The Selection radio button, which you can use to print just the selected rows of a datasheet, is disabled because there is no comparable method for manually selecting a portion of a report. Note that you do not have to select the Pages radio button before entering the starting and ending page numbers in the From and To text boxes—entering values in these text boxes automatically selects the Pages radio button.

Figure 7.22

The Print dialog box

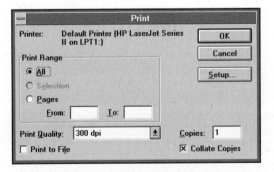

You can use the Print Quality combo box to select the overall resolution for the report. The choices that appear in the drop-down list depend on your printer, but they are always listed with the highest resolution first. In general, the higher the quality, the slower the printing speed. If speed is of the essence, you may want to choose a lower print quality, but some reports, especially those with embedded graphics or many print enhancements, may demand the highest available resolution. Access uses the Windows Print Manager (unless you disabled it through the Windows Control Panel), which allows you to print in the background while you continue to work on other tasks in Access or another Windows program, so choosing a high resolution usually does not seriously inconvenience you.

You can print multiple copies of a report by entering the desired number of copies in the Copies text box. If you leave the Collate Copies check box checked (as it is by default), Access prints each complete copy of the report before starting the next; if you uncheck this check box, it prints each page the requested number of times before going on to the next page.

The Print to File option allows you to route the report output to a text file on disk instead of to the printer. The resulting file includes all the commands and formatting instructions that would normally be sent to the printer, and you can print it later by copying it to the printer. When you choose this option, Access displays a simple dialog box to collect the name of the output file. You can later use the MS-DOS COPY command (executed from a DOS window or from outside of Windows) to print the file. Because the file includes printer control codes, the file name must be followed by the /B option to ensure that DOS treats the file as *binary*, rather than as a pure text file. For example, to print a file called NAMES.RPT, you would use the following COPY command:

```
COPY NAMES.RPT/B PRN:
```

When you select the OK option in the Print dialog box, Access sends the output to a temporary file on disk, which is then processed by the Windows Print Manager. As it feeds the output to the Print Manager, Access displays the status window pictured in Figure 7.23 to inform you of its progress. Once Access has finished processing the file, you can go on to other database tasks while the Print Manager sends the report to the printer. At any point after you initiate printing, including the period while Access is sending the output to the Print Manager, you can switch to another Windows application. Working in another program will slow printing somewhat, but it does allow you to make productive use of your computer while Access is processing the report.

Figure 7.23
The print status window

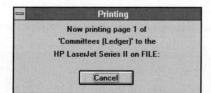

If your databases are very large, you should be aware that the size of the temporary file that stores the report output is limited to 128Mb (or, more realistically, the amount of free space on your hard disk). In the unlikely event that this limit proves constraining, you can print a very long report in several sections. One way to do this is to base the report on a query, and modify the selection criteria in the query to select various segments of the data in turn. For example, to print a report in alphabetical order by ID code in sections, you could define a query that selects a range of ID codes and print, say, the ID codes between A and L, and then the ID codes between M and Z. To avoid having to repeatedly modify the query, you could define a parameter query that prompts you to enter a range of ID codes.

Customizing the Print Setup

You can use the Print Setup dialog box to choose the printer you want to use for a particular report run or to customize several aspects of the page layout. Recall that you can reach this dialog box by using the Setup button in the Print dialog box or by choosing the Print Setup option on the File menu. The exact choices that appear in the drop-down lists associated with the Size and Source combo boxes in the Paper region depend on your printer, but the other options are always the same. As is the case when you print a datasheet, you can choose either portrait (upright) or landscape (sideways) orientation, and you can reset the left, right, top, and bottom margins as you see fit. However, the interaction between the margins established in the Print Setup dialog box and the dimensions defined in the report itself is somewhat more complex.

Access always adjusts the number of lines printed on each page based on the page length and the top and bottom margins, and it always respects the left and right margins entered in the Print Setup dialog box. If you also include blank space above the text in the page header section and below the text in the page footer section, this space is *added* to the page margins. (In most cases, you should avoid this practice and use the Print Setup dialog box to control the top and bottom margins.)

Determining the width of the printable region on the page is a bit more complicated. The width is a property of the report itself, and it does not change automatically if you switch to landscape mode or choose a wider paper size. (In contrast, a datasheet has no predetermined width, and Access prints as many columns as it can fit on the page.) The left margin specifies how much blank space appears to the left of the report area, and the report width and the right margin interact to determine how far the data extends to the right. If the report is too wide, Access breaks each group of records onto multiple pages.

The Print Setup dialog box allows you to customize several other aspects of the print layout and record processing sequence that are not intrinsic to the report. To access these special options, which are available only when you print a form or report (not when you print a datasheet or a query), select the More button in the Print Setup dialog box. Access responds by expanding the Print Setup dialog box, as illustrated in Figure 7.24, to accommodate additional options displayed below the margin settings.

Figure 7.24

The expanded Print Setup dialog box

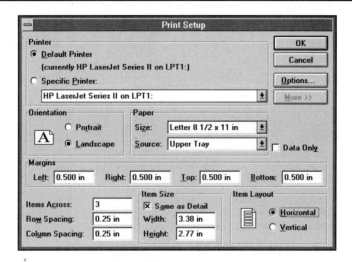

You can use the Items Across and Item Layout options to print records in repeating groups both across and down the page. You might be interested to learn that this is the method that Access uses to print mailing labels (and other forms designed with the Mailing Label Wizard) two or more across, but you can use it for other types of forms as well (a mailing label is, after all, no different from any other type of report). When you print records two or more across, the Column Spacing entry specifies the spacing between columns. In any report, you can specify the additional space between records by entering it in the Row Spacing text box; this option is grouped together with Items Across and Column Spacing because it is often used in conjunction with these options to control the spacing on reports that print multiple records per page. Figure 7.25 illustrates a simple name and address list printed three across in landscape mode, with the margins set so that exactly six records fit on a page. The settings used to achieve this result are visible in Figure 7.24: Items Across was set to 3, Row Spacing to .25 inches, and Column Spacing to .25 inches.

The Item Layout option in the lower-right corner of the Print Setup dialog box interacts with the Items Across setting to control the record printing sequence. If you select the Horizontal radio button (the default), Access prints successive records across the page before moving down to the next

Figure 7.25

Printing records three across

Name and Address List
07-Nov-93

ID Code: ALLENJE	**ID Code:** ALLENMA	**ID Code:** ANDERSIC
Name: Jerry Allen	**Name:** Marilyn Allen	**Name:** Mr. J. C. Anderson
Salutation: Mr. Allen	**Salutation:** Ms. Allen	**Salutation:** J. C.
Address: 564 Mission St.	**Address:** 842 Palm Canyon Drive	**Address:** 41248 Moraga Rd
City: San Francisco	**City:** Borrego Springs	**City:** Temecula
State: CA	**State:** CA	**State:** CA
Zip: 94105-292	**Zip:** 92004	**Zip:** 92390
Area Code:	**Area Code:**	**Area Code:**
Telephone:	**Telephone:**	**Telephone:**
OK to Send Mail: Yes	**OK to Send Mail:** No	**OK to Send Mail:** Yes
OK to Call: Yes	**OK to Call:** Yes	**OK to Call:** No
ID Code: ANDERSMI	**ID Code:** ARNOLDME	**ID Code:** BERGENRU
Name: Michael Anderson	**Name:** Melvin H. Arnold	**Name:** Ruth Bergen
Salutation: Mike	**Salutation:** Mr. Arnold	**Salutation:** Ruth
Address: 2906 Ellis Street	**Address:** 504 Parkview Dr.	**Address:** 472 Church St.
City: Berkeley	**City:** Lake Elsinore	**City:** San Francisco
State: CA	**State:** CA	**State:** CA
Zip: 94702	**Zip:** 92330	**Zip:** 94114
Area Code: 510	**Area Code:**	**Area Code:**
Telephone: 549-7838	**Telephone:**	**Telephone:**
OK to Send Mail: Yes	**OK to Send Mail:** Yes	**OK to Send Mail:** No
OK to Call: Yes	**OK to Call:** Yes	**OK to Call:** Yes

group of lines. The page reproduced in Figure 7.25 was printed this way. If you select the Vertical radio button, Access moves down each column before proceeding across to the next column. This format, which is sometimes referred to as *snaking columns*, is often preferable for mailing labels and for name and address reference lists such as membership or telephone directories. These two different print orders are illustrated in Figure 7.26, which indicates the positions that the first six records in the name and address list would occupy in both cases. As is the case with forms, there is unfortunately no way to print the report design specifications.

Figure 7.26
The horizontal and vertical item layouts

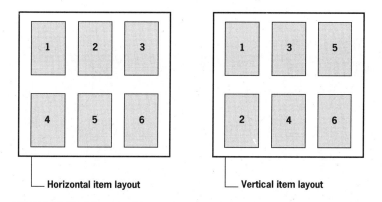

Horizontal item layout   Vertical item layout

The options in the Item Size region control the size of the print area allocated for each record in the detail section. If you leave the Same As detail check box checked (as it is by default), the dimensions of the detail section match those saved with the report. If you uncheck this box, you can enter new dimensions in the Width and Height text boxes underneath. You can use these options to directly control the exact size of each detail record. Note however that it is your responsibility to ensure that the size you enter is large enough to accommodate all the data. To restore the default dimensions, simply check Same as Detail again.

If you displayed the Print Setup dialog box from either preview window, Access redisplays the preview image with all the new settings in effect when you exit by using the OK command button. Working from the Print Preview window, you can very easily fine-tune the report layout (for example, by trying out different margin settings) without wasting time or paper by repeatedly printing the report. If you made any changes in the Print Setup dialog box, Access prompts you to save your changes when you eventually close the report. If you elect to save your changes, Access saves the new setup specifications with the report, so you can print the report again using the same page layout without returning to the Print Setup screen.

Modifying a Report

As noted earlier in this chapter, you will usually want to modify the reports produced by the Access FormWizards. For example, in the Committee Membership Roster created earlier in this chapter, you might want to widen the Committee and ID Code fields, right-justify the column headers for the Joined and Quit fields over the columns of dates, and move the report title from the report header section into the page header section. You might also want to make more substantive changes or additions to the report, such as printing membership counts in the Committee footer and report footer sections or adding calculated fields to the detail section. For example, Chapter 9 describes how to calculate the length of time a person has served on each committee and print the average membership duration in the Committee group footer.

To invoke the Report Design tool to modify a form created by a Report-Wizard or to design a new report from scratch, you can use either of the following methods:

- After using the ReportWizards to create a new report, choose Design rather than Print Preview in the last dialog box.

- Make sure that the Database window displays the list of reports (if necessary, click on the Report button in the Database window or choose the Reports option from the View menu), and then double-right-click on the report name or highlight the report, and then click on the Design command button in the tool bar or press Alt+D.

Figure 7.27 illustrates the Report Design window with the Committee Membership Roster report visible on the work surface and the window maximized to display as much of the layout as possible. Figure 7.28 diagrams the Report Design menu bar; some of the options are described later in this section, and the rest are covered in Chapters 10 and 12. As you can see, the Report Design view has much in common with the Form Design view described in Chapter 6, and you can use the same basic techniques described in Chapter 6 to modify the report layout.

The Committee Membership Roster report has all seven types of sections permitted in an Access report. The report header section, which is printed once at the very beginning of the report, contains two thin horizontal lines, the report title, and an expression that prints the current date below the title, using a built-in Access function that evaluates to the current date and time. (Access functions in general, and the Now function in particular, are described in Chapter 9.) The page header section contains the column titles, enclosed between two sets of thin lines.

Figure 7.27

The Report Design
view

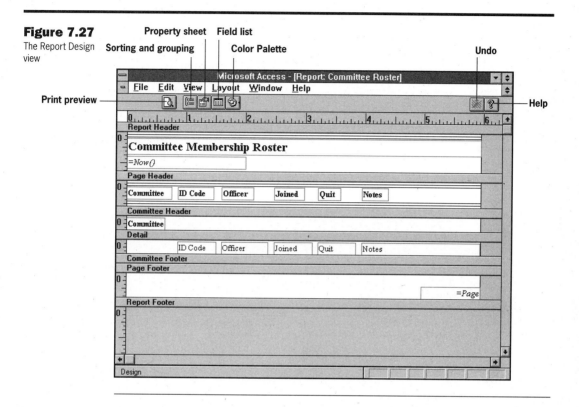

The Committee Membership Roster has one group, based on the Committee field, which is printed in the group header section to identify the
records in each group. You might want to add a word or phrase to the Committee header to further explain the Committee field—perhaps "Committee
ID Code:" before the Committee field or "Committee" after it. Alternatively,
you might want to look up the committee name in the Committee Names
table and print the name instead of or in addition to the committee code.
Chapter 8, which covers multitable reports, describes how to do this, and
Chapter 10 describes how to add text to any report section. Because there are
no numeric fields, the Committee group footer and report footer sections,
which normally contain subtotals, are empty. The page footer section contains
a single object, a reference to a report property that prints the page number.
Chapter 10 describes how to print page numbers in more complex formats,
such as "Page 1" or " - page 1 -".

Most of the Committees table fields are in the detail section. One fact that
may not be obvious is that the ReportWizards usually treat long Text fields
and Memo fields (such as the Notes field) differently than the FormWizards

Figure 7.28
The Access menu
bar in the Report
Design view

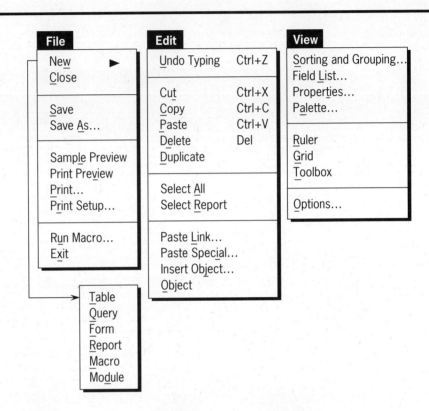

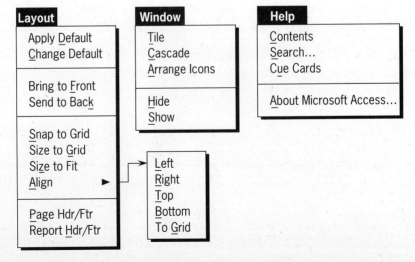

and allow these fields to expand onto as many lines as necessary to accommodate all of the text. On a form, Access restricts *all* fields to fixed-size boxes. There are two reasons for this difference. Keeping the size of each record constant is more important in a data entry screen, where consistency will help you enter and edit data faster and more efficiently. Furthermore, because you can easily scroll through the full contents of any field, viewing a long field in a small box is not much of an inconvenience. In most columnar reports, it makes little difference how much space each record occupies or how many records fit on a page; if this is not the case, you can limit the size of any field using a property described in Chapter 10. There is one exception to this general rule: If you choose the ledger look, the ReportWizards truncate Text and Memo fields to fit within two lines (Figure 7.15 illustrates this behavior).

Note that none of these characteristics of the Committee Membership Roster (including the treatment of the Notes field) is intrinsic to the Access Report Design tool—they are all derived from the assumptions made by the ReportWizards. You could create a similar layout—or any variation of this basic layout style—from scratch, and you can modify any aspects of the report that you don't like, including the ones noted here.

Working in the Report Design View

You can use all the simple techniques introduced in Chapter 6 to select and manipulate objects in the Report Design view. As in the Form Design view, you can use the Page Hdr/Ftr and Report Hdr/Ftr options on the Layout menu to add or remove these pairs of report sections; Access issues the usual warning if you try to delete any sections that still contain objects. You can use the same methods to change the size of any report section (dragging one of its boundaries with the mouse) or to change the width of the report (dragging the vertical boundary line that marks the right margin to the left or right).

The Form Design and Report Design environment are governed by the same customization options (accessed by choosing Options from the View menu), so if you turned on the rulers or grid for forms, these alignment guides will also be displayed in the Report Design window. As is the case with forms, the grid spacing in reports created by the ReportWizards is too fine for Access to display the grid, but Chapter 10 describes how to modify this setting so you can see the grid. The Report Design tool provides the same tools and controls as the Form Design tool (the property sheet, tool box, field list, and palette), accessed through the same tool bar command buttons and View menu options. There is one additional command button in the tool bar, which is marked Sorting and Grouping in Figure 7.27. Chapter 11 describes how to use this option to specify the groups and sorting instructions in a report that you create from scratch, or to modify the groups and sort order selected through the ReportWizards dialog boxes.

In keeping with the close parallel between forms and reports, the Access manuals and help screens refer to the objects in reports as *controls*, although you cannot manipulate them as you do when you edit data using a custom form. Some of the controls lend themselves equally well to displaying and printing data. For example, if you use the Save as Report option briefly introduced in Chapter 6 to create a report that looks just like a data entry form, Access prints check boxes exactly as it displays them on the screen, and this format is equally intuitive to most people when they read the report (although of course you cannot check or uncheck the box). Some controls—such as list boxes, combo boxes, and command buttons—are less applicable to printing. When you use the Save as Report option in Form Design view to create a report derived from a form, you may want to remove command buttons and substitute text boxes for list boxes and combo boxes.

In a single-column report such as the one in Figure 7.4, the label printed to the left of each field is part of the text box control that prints the field, as in the single-column forms described in Chapter 6. In a groups/totals report like the Committee Membership Roster, the column titles in the page header section are independent *label objects* not connected to the corresponding fields in the detail section. Although you should be aware of this difference, it does not limit your ability to manipulate a field and its label together or separately in either type of layout—you can move or resize a field and its label separately, and you can select and move independent objects together.

Modifying the Committee Membership Roster

To review the basic techniques for moving and resizing objects, try making a few simple modifications to the Committee Membership Roster. Figure 7.27 shows the report produced by the ReportWizard, and Figure 7.29 illustrates the end result. The steps are as follows:

1. Make sure that the Database window displays the list of reports and open the Committee Membership Roster report in Design view by highlighting its name and clicking on the Design button or pressing Alt+D.

2. Maximize the Report Design window.

3. If the rulers are not already visible, pull down the View menu and select Rulers.

4. Click in the Committee field text box in the Committee group header section and use the handle in the lower-right corner to widen it to 1¼ inches (since the field is located at the left edge of the report, the right side should line up with the 1¼-inch mark in the horizontal ruler).

Figure 7.29

The modified
Committee
Membership Roster

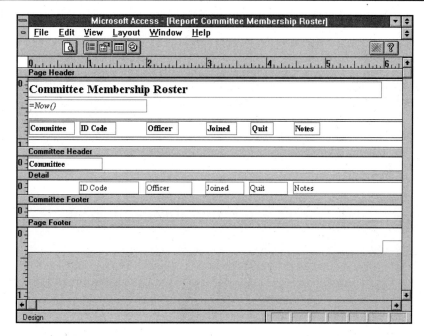

5. Drag the vertical line that represents the right-hand report border to the right to line up with the 7-inch mark in the ruler at the top of the window. This position is "off the edge" of the screen (on a standard VGA monitor), but Access allows you to move or drag any object to any position in the ruler. The easiest way to adjust the position precisely is to drag past it to bring the desired portion of the ruler into view and then move the border back to the left.

6. Click in the Joined field, and then hold the Shift key down and click in turn in the Quit field, the Notes field, and each of the corresponding text objects in the page header section.

7. Release the Shift key, position the mouse over any of the selected objects, press and hold the left mouse button, and drag the selected objects to the right so that the left edge of the Joined field is at the 3-inch mark in the ruler.

8. Click anywhere outside the selected objects to deselect them, and then click in the Notes field text box to select it. Widen this object so that it extends almost to the right border of the report (at about $6^7/8$ inches in the ruler).

9. Select the Officer field text box and the matching text object in the page header section, and move both objects to the right, so the left edges align with the 2-inch mark in the ruler.

10. Select the first horizontal rule in the report header section. (Some fine mouse control may be necessary to find the right place to click. If you are having trouble, select any object in the report header section and press Tab to cycle through the objects until the right one is selected.) Grab the handle at the right side of the line and widen the line to 6 $7/8$ inches. Repeat this process for each of the lines. Chapter 10 describes an easier way to re-size several objects to the same dimensions, so don't worry if you end up with a slightly jagged line or if the lines are not exactly the same length.

11. Move the page number in the page footer section to the right, so it lines up with the new right edge of the report.

12. Use the horizontal scroll bar to bring the whole ID Code field into view and widen this field until the right edge lines up with the 1 $7/8$-inch mark in the ruler.

13. Drag the boundary between the Committee footer and page footer sections down to open up the Committee footer section. Adjust the height to about $1/4$ inch.

14. Select one of the horizontal lines below the column titles in the page header section and press Ctrl+C to copy it to the Clipboard.

15. Click in the Committee footer section and press Ctrl+V to paste in the contents of the Clipboard. Move the line, which should still be selected, down to the middle of the Committee footer section.

16. Drag down the boundary between the page header and Committee group header sections to enlarge the page header section to about 1 $1/8$ inches.

17. Select all the objects in the page header section. The easiest way to do this is to place the mouse below the Committee text object (and below the lines), press and hold the left mouse button, and drag the mouse up and to the right, releasing it in the top right area of the report section. Make sure that you see handles in all the objects in the page header section, and move all these objects down almost all the way to the bottom of the section.

18. Select all the objects in the report header section, and use the mouse to drag the selected objects down to the page header section. Adjust the spacing of the objects if you are not immediately satisfied with the appearance of the new page header section.

19. Pull down the Layout menu and select Report Hdr/Ftr to remove these sections, which are now both empty. Your screen should look like Figure 7.29.

20. Choose Print Setup from the File menu and set the left and right margins to .5 inches so that the whole report fits on one page (with 7 inches of data and 1-inch margins, the report is 9 inches wide, slightly too wide to fit on 8½-by-11-inch paper). Click on the OK button to close the Print Setup dialog box and return to the Report Design view.

21. Select the Sample Preview option from the File menu to preview the layout of the report. Note that only about ten records are displayed.

22. Click on the Cancel command button in the tool bar to return to Report Design view, and click on the Print Preview button in the tool bar or select the Print Preview option from the File menu to preview the layout of the report, including all the data.

23. Click on the Setup command button to display the Print Setup screen again and switch to Landscape mode so that the report occupies two pages. Verify that the report title now prints on the top of each page (you moved it into the page header section).

24. Click on the Print command button to display the Print Setup dialog box, and make sure that the All radio button is selected in the Print Range area. If you have a printer available, click on OK to print the report. (If you do not have a laser printer, you might want to switch back to Portrait orientation first.)

25. Double-click on the close box or press Ctrl+F4 to close the Print Preview window. When Access displays the dialog box that asks whether you want to save the changes to the report, select Yes.

Summary

In the early stages of the development of an application, most of your attention may be focused on entering and editing data, but you probably do not need to be convinced of the crucial role that printed reports will play in the finished application. Despite the myth of the paperless office, it is often faster and easier to find the information you need in a given situation by referring to a printed list rather than by looking it up on-screen, especially if you are not seated at your keyboard when the demand arises. Printed reports are also the principal vehicle you will use to share your raw data, as well as calculations and summary statistics derived from this data, with other people (both co-workers and people outside your organization). Many of these people will know little or nothing about computerized databases in general nor about

Access in particular, and some will not know or care how you produced the reports.

This chapter described how to use the Access ReportWizards to define three simple types of reports—single-column reports that resemble the single-column forms described in Chapter 6, tabular reports that may contain record groups and group totals, and mailing labels. Even this brief introduction should give you a taste of the wide range of printed formats that you can produce using the Access Report Design tool. All of the reports in this chapter were based on data derived from a single table or query. Chapter 8 describes how to construct more complex reports based on two or more source tables. If you are working on a database application of your own, you might want to review the report samples and wish list items collected during the system planning and analysis phase and think about how you might go about designing Access reports to produce some of the required printouts.

As is the case with forms, the easiest and fastest way to produce a given report often involves using the ReportWizards to produce the basic layout and then modifying the resulting report as necessary. Of course, for reports that do not resemble one of the three simple layouts that the Wizards can produce, you will have to start from scratch, and Chapter 12 describes how to do this. Like Chapter 6, Chapter 7 concentrated on the basic structure, layout, and content of an Access report. When you design reports intended primarily for other users or reports that must emulate or replace preprinted forms, you must devote more attention to aesthetic considerations. Chapter 10 describes how to add lines and boxes to a report and how to customize the font, font size, and other visual attributes of the data and text.

As noted in Chapter 6, Access forms and reports have much in common and in many contexts are interchangeable—you can print a form and you can view a report on the screen. Obviously, you must use a form in any situation that demands (or permits) updating data. For producing an occasional hard copy of the data displayed on the screen, you can simply print the form. If you end up using this printout frequently, you can save the form as a report, modify the report if necessary, and use it independent of the original data entry form. For listings with groups and summary statistics, and for output that is nearly always printed, you can design reports and use the Print Preview option to view the results on the screen on those occasions when a hard copy is not required.

Working with Multiple Tables

Performing Calculations

Customizing Reports and Forms

Designing Reports

Designing Forms

Reorganizing Databases

Importing, Exporting, and Attaching Tables

Working with External Objects

2

Intermediate Skills

8

Working with Multiple Tables

THUS FAR, ALL OF YOUR WORK WITH ACCESS HAS INVOLVED VIEWING OR updating one table at a time, although you have had at least a brief introduction to most of the tables in the ACE case study. However, the database design principles outlined in Chapter 3 emphasized the importance of creating a separate table for each discrete functional entity in an application. If you adhere to these principles when you set up your own Access database, as did the fictional staff members who designed the ACE application, you will find that you often need to access information from several tables simultaneously. Access allows you to define queries based on up to 16 tables and to work with data drawn from 254 tables at once overall—limits that are unlikely to prove constraining in the average business or personal application.

At times, you may want to open several tables without formally linking them. For example, you might want to use one table as a reference guide while you enter or update records in another. No special preparations are required to use several tables together for this purpose—simply open one table in Datasheet view or Form view, return to the Database window (by clicking on an exposed portion of the window with the mouse or by choosing its name from the Window menu), and open another datasheet or form. The key to making the most of this technique is to arrange the various windows on the desktop so that you can see the portions of each that you need in the current context. Unless you have a very large monitor, some overlap is usually inevitable, but try to make sure that at least a small portion of each window is visible on the screen at all times so that you can easily switch windows by clicking the mouse in some exposed portion of the desired window.

Figures 8.1 and 8.2 illustrate two typical configurations. In Figure 8.1, the Contacts, Contact Types, and Names tables are open in Datasheet view, so that when you are entering contacts, you can see a list of all the legitimate contact type codes and view any information on file about the person whose contact record you are entering or editing. The first three columns in the Names table datasheet are frozen to keep the ID Code, Name Type, and Name fields visible at all times, and in this figure, the display was panned to the right to bring the debit and credit total fields into view.

Figure 8.2 illustrates a window configuration suitable for using the form designed in Chapter 6 to update the Committees table with the Names and Committee Names tables open in Datasheet view for reference. In this setup, the Names table datasheet lies mostly behind the other windows, and when you move into this window to find a name, it will cover most of the Committees table form. To keep a particular Names table record visible when you return to the Committee Memberships form, you would have to make sure it is displayed in the lower part of the datasheet, which is not behind the form window. When more than one datasheet or form is open, you can move freely among the windows and you can enter or edit records as well as view them. For example, if you could not find the person for whom you were entering a

Figure 8.1

Viewing three
datasheets at once

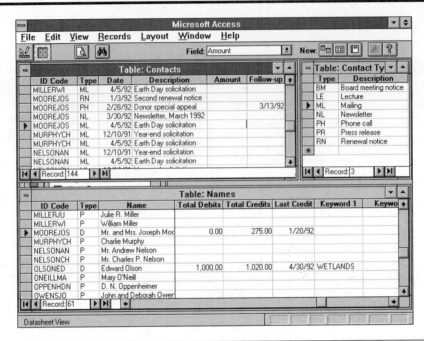

contact or committee membership, you could simply add a new record to the Names table.

In these two examples, opening several tables simultaneously offers a measure of convenience, and it helps you to maintain the integrity and accuracy of the data. For example, seeing the list of contact types or committee names encourages you to enter correct data in the Contact Type or Committee field by making it easy to find the code you want. However, these methods depend on your understanding of the table relationships and on your willingness to adhere to the business rules based on these relationships. If you were updating the Contacts table using the setup in Figure 8.1, nothing would prevent you from adding a record to the Contacts table with an ID code that did not match any existing record in the Names table. Opening several tables in this way is most appropriate for users who are knowledgeable about Access, are familar with their data, and are conscientious and meticulous about preserving the table relationships. In most cases, however, you will want Access to do more of the work of enforcing the proper relationships behind the scenes.

You can formalize the linkages between tables by defining default relationships, which Access stores in the database and uses in a variety of contexts to determine how to link tables. You can also link tables any way you

Figure 8.2

Viewing two datasheets and a form

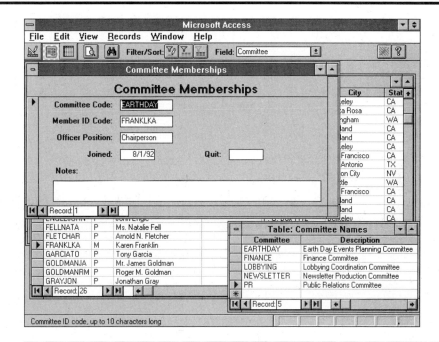

see fit in a query, and then use the query to view or print data (in Datasheet view, through a form, or through a report) rather than opening the tables separately. Queries are a very powerful tool for working with multiple tables, especially for viewing or printing data. You can use queries to update tables that have a one-to-one relationship, and with some limitations, to update tables that have a one-to-many relationship. Access also provides a FormWizard that builds a form in which selected fields from the parent table are displayed at the top of the screen and multiple related records from the child table appear in a datasheet below. The forms created by this FormWizard are easy to use and easy to modify (to incorporate data from more than two tables), and they closely parallel many of the paper forms used to record the same data.

This chapter describes how to use all of these methods for working with related tables, which you can use separately or in combination in your own applications. Additional techniques for computing statistics, "looking up" specific values in a related table, and building more complex multitable forms and reports (from scratch and by modifying the forms produced by the Wizards) are described in the following four chapters.

Defining Default Relationships

In most business databases, the main tables have certain relationships that are integral to the structure of the application. For example, the Names table is central to the ACE application, and this table has one-to-many relationships with each of the other main tables—the Contacts, Transactions, and Committees tables. In different contexts, you may use any of these tables alone or in various combinations, and your "point of view" may focus either on the parent or the child table. In all cases, however, the fundamental relationships between the tables are the same—for each record in the Names table, there may be any number of matching records (or none) in the other three tables, and in all cases, the matching records are identified by the same contents in the ID Code field, which is common to all the tables.

Access allows you to formally define the relationship between any two tables and save this information in the database. Defining the relationships between the main tables in an application offers two significant advantages. First, it allows Access to deduce how to link the tables when you design multi-table queries, forms, and reports, so you often do not have to define any linkages explicitly. Second, it allows you to request that Access help you maintain *referential integrity* by enforcing the relationships between tables. In the world of relational databases, the concept of referential integrity, also known as *relational integrity*, encompasses a variety of rules for adding, changing, and deleting records in linked tables. The relationship between the tables may be one-to-one or one-to-many, but one table is always regarded as the *primary* or independent table, and the other as the *related* or dependent table. In a one-to-many relationship, the primary table is the parent table (the table with one record); in a one-to-one relationship, it is the table that can exist independently of the other.

Access can enforce referential integrity in two ways: It prohibits you from deleting a record in the primary table if matching records exist in the related table, and from adding or editing a record in the related table so that it no longer matches any existing record in the primary table. Some other databases provide additional capabilities, such as *cascading* deletions or updates (that is, deleting all the child records if you delete the parent, or changing the contents of the linking field in the child records to reflect changes you make in the parent record). In Access, these operations must be carried out with SQL commands or by writing Access Basic programs. A few simple examples are presented in Chapter 20.

Defining relationships does not constrain you to working with the tables only in certain configurations or prohibit you from linking the tables in other ways if you wish, so you have little to lose by doing so. Predefining the table relationships is convenient for all Access users, and it is especially valuable when you set up a database that will also be used by less knowledgeable co-workers who may not understand the mechanics of linking tables. The enforcement option affords an additional measure of security, but you do give up a measure of flexibility if you enable it, and you may not always want to pay this price.

To define default relationships, make sure that the Database window is frontmost on your Access desktop, and choose the Relationships option from the Edit menu. You do not have to first display the list of tables—the Relationships option is available whenever the Database window has the focus. You define the table relationships in the dialog box pictured in Figure 8.3; this example illustrates the specifications for the relationship between the Names table and Transactions table.

Figure 8.3

Defining the relationship between two tables

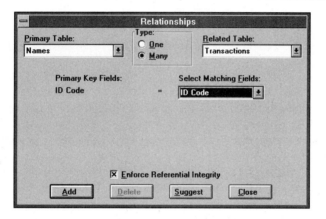

You select the tables whose relationship you are defining by using the two combo boxes at the top of the Relationships dialog box, and you use the Type radio buttons to specify whether the relationship is one-to-one or one-to-many *from the point of view of the primary table.* Before you begin, give some thought to which table is the primary table and which one is the related table. In a one-to-one relationship that you are defining solely to specify the default linkage between two tables, it makes no difference which is the primary table and which is the related table. In a one-to-many relationship, the primary table is the table with the one record, and the related table is the one with the many matching records. If you want Access to enforce referential integrity based on a one-to-one or one-to-many relationship between two tables, the primary table must be the one that can exist independently of the other. In all relationships between the main tables in the ACE database, the Names table is the primary table, because it is legitimate to enter a record into this table that has no match in any of the other tables, whereas you cannot have a Contacts, Transactions, or Committees table record that has no match in the Names table.

If you choose the Relationships option from the Edit menu with the list of tables displayed in the Database window, the name of the highlighted table will appear in the Primary Table combo box; otherwise, the data entry region is blank. In any event, you can choose any table you wish from either combo box. Below the Primary Table combo box, Access displays the field or fields that make up the primary key for the selected table. To the right of each component of the primary table's primary key is a combo box that enables you to select the matching field in the related table. When you define a one-to-many relationship, the drop-down list associated with this combo box includes all the fields in the related table of the same data type as the corresponding component of the primary key in the primary table. If the relationship is one-to-one, the list includes only the primary key field from the related table. This limitation makes sense in light of the fact that only the existence of such an index can guarantee that there is only one matching record in the related table for each record in the primary table. (If there could be more than one matching record, the relationship would be one-to-many, not one-to-one.) The field or fields in the related table that correspond to the primary key in the parent table are called the *foreign key*.

Every relationship you define must be based on the complete primary key of the primary table. Thus, to define a default relationship between the Names table and Name Types table based on the Name Type field, you must choose the Name Types table as primary and define a one-to-many relationship rather than choosing the Names table as primary and defining a one-to-one relationship (because the ID code field is not present in the Name Types table). This may seem like a fine distinction if you are accustomed to looking at your tables from different points of view in different contexts. From the point of view of the Name Types table, its relationship with the Names table is one-to-many, whereas from the point of view of the Names table, the relationship is one-to-one—for each record in the Names table, there is just one matching record in the Name Types table. With this particular pair of tables, you will nearly always work from the point of view of the Names table and look up the one matching record in the Name Types table. However, defining the default relationship as one-to-one would not fully describe the linkage—if either of two related tables might have more than one match in the other, you must take this fact into account and define the relationship as one-to-many.

The matching fields in the primary and related tables need not have the same names, but they must be the same data type. For any numeric data type, they must also be the same size; you cannot, for example, match an Integer field in one table with a Double field in the other. There is one apparent exception to this rule: You can define a linkage based on a Counter field and a Long Integer field, because internally, these two data types are stored the same way. If the matching fields do have the same names, you can use the Suggest button at the bottom of the Relationships dialog box as a shortcut to find them. If

Access cannot find any fields in the related table with the same names as the primary key fields in the primary table, it displays an alert box to inform you that "There are no matching fields to suggest." If it can find a match for some but not all the components of the primary key, it fills them in but does not allow you to save the relationship until you have identified the others.

Enforcing Referential Integrity

To turn on the enforcement option for the relationship you are defining, check the Enforce Referential Integrity check box at the bottom of the Relationships dialog box. You can enable the Enforce Referential Integrity option for both one-to-one and one-to-many relationships. This option causes Access to protect the relationship between the two tables in the following ways:

■ It prohibits you from adding a record to the related table in which the foreign key does not match an existing record in the primary table.

■ It prohibits you from changing a record in the related table so that the foreign key no longer matches an existing record in the primary table.

■ It prohibits you from deleting a record from the primary table if there are matching records in the related table.

One of the advantages of using this option is that Access enforces referential integrity *in all contexts*—when you update either table in Datasheet view or in Form view, when you update the dynaset of a query based on one or both of the tables, and when you use an action query to carry out mass updates (action queries are described in Chapters 9 and 13). In fact, if you check Enforce Referential Integrity for a relationship between two tables in which any of the existing records violate the referential integrity rules, Access displays an alert box like the one in Figure 8.4 when you attempt to save the relationship. If you violate the first or second of the three rules cited earlier while updating a table, Access displays the alert box shown in Figure 8.5 and refuses to accept the record. If you violate the third rule, it displays the alert box shown in Figure 8.6 and does not delete the record.

Figure 8.4
A warning that existing data violates referential integrity

Figure 8.5
A warning that you are violating referential integrity by adding or changing a record

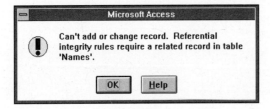

Figure 8.6
A warning that you are violating referential integrity by deleting a record

The Enforce Referential Integrity option gives you one easy way to preserve the relationship between two tables in an Access database, which might otherwise be damaged by spelling or typographical errors in the linking fields entered by well-meaning users who do not understand the relationships and interactions among the tables, or by users who deliberately circumvent the rules when it seems expedient. Of course, you might not need or want such rigid control, especially if you are the sole user and would violate the rules only with good reason. Note also that if much of the data that your application will maintain originated outside of Access (perhaps using another PC database or spreadsheet, or an entirely different application running on another type of computer), it is best to defer enabling the Enforce Referential Integrity option until you have imported all the data and checked for mismatches (using methods described later in this chapter in the section on creating outer joins).

As noted briefly in the introduction to this chapter, several types of referential integrity rules supported by some other database management programs are *not* available in Access. For example, you might want the ability to *cascade* changes and deletions so that updates to the primary tables are propagated throughout the related tables. In Access, there is no single command for deleting a parent record together with all related child records or to change the contents of the linking field in the parent record and all the child records. Editing all the records individually is tedious at best, and any child table records that you overlook will in effect disappear from the database after you edit the linking field in the parent table. The Enforce Referential

Integrity option will further complicate the operation by preventing you from editing the parent record while related child records exist, and from editing the child records until there is a new parent record with a matching value in the linking field. Thus, to change a person's ID Code in all the main ACE system tables, you must add a new record to the Names table with the new ID code, change the ID code in all the matching contact, transaction, and committee membership records individually, and then delete the original Names table record. There is also no way to add records to two tables in tandem— that is, automatically enter a parent record if you add a child record that does not already have a matching record in the parent table. Chapter 20 describes how to use Access Basic to overcome some of these limitations.

Saving and Deleting Relationships

To save a relationship in the database, click on the Add command button at the bottom of the Relationships dialog box or press Alt+A. This button is enabled only when you define a new relationship or modify a previously defined relationship. You must select the Add option for each relationship you define in a given work session.

To edit or delete a previously defined relationship, simply choose the two tables from the Primary Table and Related Table combo boxes. Access will display the linking fields from the two tables, disable the Add button, and enable the Delete button. If you click on the Delete button, Access cancels the relationship (it does not delete either table from the database). If you change the relationship by choosing a different matching field for any component of the primary key, Access enables the Add button again. Note that if you change the primary key for a table, you must redefine any relationships based on the key. Also, Access will not allow you to delete a table from a database if it is involved in any predefined relationship—you must first delete the relationships.

When you are finished editing relationships, you can close the Relationships dialog box by clicking on the Close command button, using the hotkey shortcut (Alt+C) or by using any of the other standard methods for closing a Windows dialog box.

NOTE.   *There is no way to display or print a list of all the relationships defined for a database, so you might want to make a list (on paper or using a text editor) if your database is complex enough that you might not easily remember all the relationships. One way to graphically display all the table relationships and primary keys is to define a query that includes all the main tables. Access will draw lines to indicate the table linkages, as shown in Figure 8.7. You can then press PrtSc to capture the image to the Clipboard, and print it using Paintbrush or Write. Unfortunately, you cannot distinguish one-to-one from one-to-many relationships.*

Figure 8.7

A query that illustrates the default relationships in the ACE system

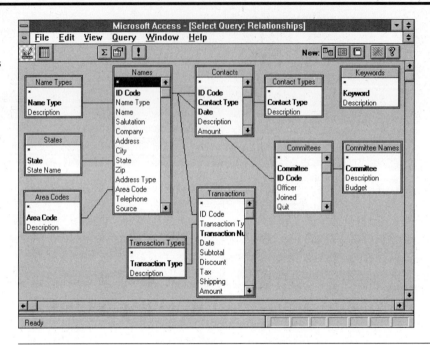

The Relationships in the ACE System

Table 8.1 lists the default relationships required in the ACE database on the sample disk packaged with this book. As you can see, there are relationships between all the major tables, as well as relationships between the main tables and the reference tables that store the legitimate values in the code fields in the main tables. All the relationships are one-to-many, and the Enforce Referential Integrity option is enabled for all except the relationship between the Names table and Area Codes table (because enforcing referential integrity would prevent you from leaving the Area Code field in the Names table blank). Note that no default relationship is defined between the Keywords and Names tables, because the Keywords table is used to look up matching values for three different fields in the Names table (Keyword 1, Keyword 2, and Keyword 3).

To add the Committees table relationships, use the following steps:

1. Make sure that the Database window is frontmost on the desktop, and choose the Relationships option from the Edit menu to display the Relationships dialog box.

2. Select the Names table from the Primary Table combo box.

3. Select the Committees table from the Related Table combo box.

Table 8.1   The Default Relationships in the ACE System

Primary Table	Related Table	Type	Fields	Enforce
Names	Contacts	One-to-many	ID Code	Yes
Names	Transactions	One-to-many	ID Code	Yes
Names	Committees	One-to-many	ID Code	Yes
Area Codes	Names	One-to-many	Area Code	No
Name Types	Names	One-to-many	Name Type	Yes
States	Names	One-to-many	State	Yes
Contact Types	Contacts	One-to-many	Contact Type	Yes
Transaction Types	Transactions	One-to-many	Transaction Type	Yes
Committee Names	Committees	One-to-many	Committee	Yes

4. Make sure that the Many radio button is selected in the Type region between the two combo boxes.

5. Click on the Suggest combo box, and note that Access displays the name of the ID Code field in the Select Matching Fields combo box.

6. Check the Enforce Referential Integrity check box.

7. Click on the Add command button to save the relationship.

8. Select the Committee Names table from the Primary Table combo box, leave the Committees table selected in the Related Table combo box, and leave the Many radio button selected in the Type region.

9. Select the Committee field from the Select Matching Fields combo box.

10. Check the Enforce Referential Integrity check box.

11. Click on the Add command button to save the relationship.

12. Close the Relationships dialog box.

Defining Multitable Queries

One of the most powerful and flexible methods for working with multiple tables is by defining queries. The Query Design tool, which was introduced in Chapter 5, allows you to define queries based on up to 16 tables with up to

255 fields or expressions in the output grid. Regardless of whether you have predefined default relationships between the source tables, you can establish any linkages that make sense in a particular query.

As outlined in Chapter 5, the first step in creating any query is to choose at least one table as a data source. If you wish, you can choose all the required tables at once, when Access displays the Add Table dialog box for the first time. To add more tables later, you can use the Add Table option on the Query menu to redisplay the Add Table dialog box. Figure 8.8 illustrates the Query Design window as it would look after adding three tables—the Names, Contacts, and Contact Types tables—to a new query and closing the Add Table dialog box.

Figure 8.8

Adding three tables to a query

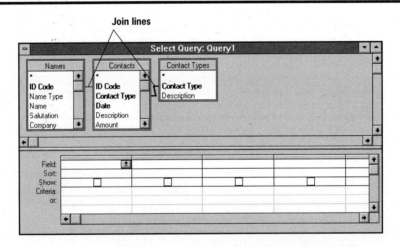

Access displays the field lists from up to five tables side by side in the upper portion of the Query Design window, and it begins a new row if you add a sixth table. You can move or resize any of the field lists as you see fit. As you will see later in this chapter, a few strategic rearrangements can help to clarify the relationships in a complex query. You can use the Tab and Shift+Tab keys to move among the field lists, but it is usually easier to move directly to a particular field list by clicking in the desired list with the mouse. To remove a table from the query, use either method to select the corresponding field list (making sure that any field in the list is highlighted), and then press Del or choose the Remove Table option on the Query menu.

You can add fields from any of the source tables to the output grid, refer to any field in the expression that defines a calculated column, and base selection criteria and sorting instructions on fields from any of the source tables. If you choose field names from the combo boxes in the output grid, you will see that Access includes a reference to the table in each field name so that you can distinguish between identically named fields from different tables. Figure 8.9 illustrates the drop-down list for the query shown in Figure 8.8.

Figure 8.9

Choosing fields in a multitable query

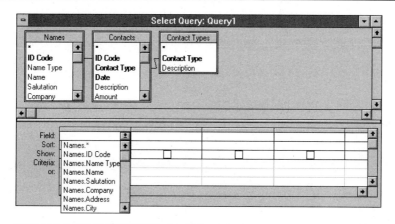

You need not include the linking fields in the output grid. For example, you might link the Contacts and Names tables based on the ID Code field but display the Name field from the Names table instead of the ID Code field. As in a single-table query, you can simply uncheck the Show box for any fields that you do not want to include in the query dynaset. Often, you will add a table to a query simply to define the selection criteria. For example, you might use a query based on the Names and Transactions tables to print mailing labels in which all the fields are derived from the Names table. However, the selection criteria might depend only on the Transactions table (this query is described in more detail later in this chapter, in the section "Defining Multitable Reports").

Joining Tables in a Query

When you create a query based on more than one table, you must establish linkages called *joins* between the tables to define what constitutes a pair of matching records. Like the default relationships described earlier in this chapter, the joins in a multitable query are based on the presence of identical data in the common fields, which must be of the same data type. Unlike the default relationships, table links in a query can be based on any field or combination of fields—they need not be based on the primary key of either table or on index key fields (although the query will execute faster if they are).

In the Query Design window, the linkages are represented by *join lines* connecting the corresponding fields. In the query in Figure 8.8, the linkage between the Contacts and Contact Types tables is based on the Contact Type field, and the linkage between the Contacts and Names tables is based on the ID Code field. When it executes this query, Access finds matching pairs of records in the Contacts and Contact Types tables by searching for the same value in the Contact Type field, and it identifies matching records in the Contacts and Names tables by examining the contents of the ID Code field. Using a query based on these three tables in place of the Contacts table enables you to display the description stored in the Contact Types table in addition to or instead of the Contact Type field, and to display the full name stored in the Names table in addition to or instead of the ID Code.

If you defined default relationships between any pair of tables in the query, Access automatically joins the tables based on these relationships and draws the join lines for you. If you did not define default relationships, you must join the tables by using the mouse to identify each pair of corresponding fields, as follows:

1. Position the mouse pointer over the linking field in one field list. The mouse pointer changes to the standard Access field icon.

2. Press and hold the left mouse button and drag the mouse over to the other field list.

3. Release the mouse button when the field icon is positioned over the linking field.

There is no equivalent keyboard method—you must use the mouse to define table joins.

NOTE. *You cannot use the Join Tables option on the Query menu to join tables; if you choose this option, Access displays an alert box that informs you "To join two tables, use your mouse and drag a column from one table to another."*

Because you can define linkages based on more than one field, Access does not automatically delete one join line when you create another. If you want to *replace* one linkage (for example, one deduced from a predefined default relationship) with a linkage based on different fields, you must delete the original join line yourself. To delete a linkage between two tables, select the join line by clicking on it and then press Del or choose the Delete option from the Edit menu. If you are not adept at using the mouse, you may have trouble finding the right place to click to select the join line, and Access does not help you by changing the shape of the mouse pointer (as it does in many other contexts). However, you can confirm that the join line is selected because Access displays it as a heavier line. In Figure 8.8, the join line between the Contacts and Contact Types field lists is selected.

In a simple query, arriving at the optimum arrangement for the field lists in the upper portion of the Query Design window is often a simple matter of strategically choosing the order in which you add the tables to the query. For example, if you chose the Contacts table first, then the Names table, and finally the Contact Types table, the join line that connects the Contacts and Contact Types tables would pass behind the Names table, making it harder to discern the relationships between the tables. In a complex query, you may want to resize some of the field lists and rearrange them more extensively. Figure 8.10 illustrates a typical layout for a query based on seven tables. Note that refining the layout of the field list can be tedious and time-consuming, and if you are the only person who will modify the query, the benefits may not be worth the trouble.

Figure 8.10

Rearranging the field lists in the Query Design window

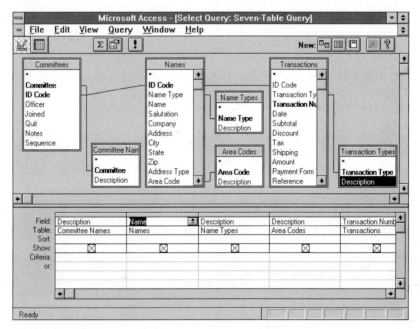

Identifying the Source Tables

By default, Access gives you no indication of which table is the source for a given column in the output grid. In simple queries in which the source tables have only the linking fields in common, this may not be a problem. On the other hand, in the query pictured in Figure 8.8, you could easily confuse the Description fields from the Contacts and Contact Types tables, which store very different information. There is an easy solution to this problem—select the Table Names option on the View menu to display the Table row in the output grid. The Table row is visible in Figure 8.11, which illustrates a simple query based on the same three tables shown in Figure 8.8. Figure 8.12 illustrates the result of running the query (with the Datasheet window maximized and several of the column widths adjusted).

Figure 8.11

A simple query based on three tables

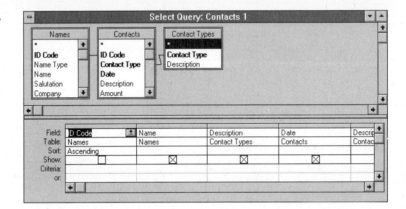

Figure 8.12

The result of running a three-table query

Name	Contact Types.Description	Date	Contacts.Description	Amount
Jerry Allen	Mailing	12/10/91	Year-end solicitation	
Jerry Allen	Mailing	4/5/92	Earth Day solicitation	
Marilyn Allen	Newsletter	3/30/92	Newsletter, March 1992	
Marilyn Allen	Board meeting notice	3/15/92	Board meeting notice	
Mr. J. C. Anderson	Mailing	12/10/91	Year-end solicitation	
Mr. J. C. Anderson	Mailing	4/5/92	Earth Day solicitation	
Michael Anderson	Phone call	2/28/92	Donor special appeal	
Michael Anderson	Newsletter	3/30/92	Newsletter, March 1992	
Michael Anderson	Mailing	4/5/92	Earth Day solicitation	
Michael Anderson	Lecture	4/22/92	Earth Day lecture	15.00
Melvin H. Arnold	Newsletter	3/30/92	Newsletter, March 1992	
Melvin H. Arnold	Mailing	4/5/92	Earth Day solicitation	
Ms. Sylvia Baker	Newsletter	3/30/92	Newsletter, March 1992	
Ms. Sylvia Baker	Mailing	4/5/92	Earth Day solicitation	
Ruth Bergen	Renewal notice	3/1/92	First renewal notice	
Ruth Bergen	Mailing	4/5/92	Earth Day solicitation	
Ruth Bergen	Phone call	2/28/92	Donor special appeal	
Ruth Bergen	Newsletter	3/30/92	Newsletter, March 1992	
Ruth Bergen	Lecture	4/22/92	Earth Day lecture	15.00
Mr. Claude Black	Mailing	4/5/92	Earth Day solicitation	
Mr. Claude Black	Mailing	12/10/91	Year-end solicitation	
Martha Bliss	Mailing	4/5/92	Earth Day solicitation	
Martha Bliss	Mailing	12/10/91	Year-end solicitation	
Mr. Christopher Bloom	Newsletter	3/30/92	Newsletter, March 1992	
Mr. Christopher Bloom	Lecture	4/22/92	Earth Day lecture	15.00
Mr. Christopher Bloom	Board meeting notice	3/15/92	Board meeting notice	20.00

Record: 1

Full name as printed on a label

When two fields in the output grid have the same name, Access includes a reference to the table name in the column title displayed in the field selector in the datasheet; you can see the titles "Contact Types.Description" and "Contacts.Description" in Figure 8.12. In a query created for your own use, you may not mind these titles, but if you plan to print the query output for someone who might not understand that "Contacts.Description" means "the Description field from the Contacts table," you can simply assign new names for one or both of these columns.

When you drag a field to the output grid or choose it from a combo box in the Field row, Access can identify the source table even if you do not display the Table row in the output grid. When you type a field name that is present in more than one source table in an expression, Access has no way of knowing which table you mean, and it displays an alert box with the error message "Ambiguous field reference" followed by the name of the offending field when you run the query. In the query in Figure 8.12, it is obvious why you would have to identify the source of a field named "Description," which stores entirely different data in the Contacts and Contact Types tables. However, you must also name the source table when you refer to the linking fields in an expression, even though the contents are always the same, and it usually makes no difference which table you choose. To identify the source table, you can use the same notation Access uses in the field lists and in the query dynaset—the name of the table, followed by a period (.) and then by the field name. If either name contains spaces, you must enclose it in brackets; otherwise the brackets are optional. For example, you would write the name of the ID Code field from the Names table as [Names].[ID Code].

Creating a Three-Table Query

To define a query that displays the Committees table data, together with the name of the committee and the name of the committee member, use the following steps:

1. Make sure that the Database window displays the list of queries (if necessary, click on the Query button or choose Queries from the View menu), and click on the New command button or press Alt+N.

2. Choose all three tables—the Names table, the Committees table, and the Committee Names table—from the list in the Add Table dialog box, and then close the dialog box. If you defined the default relationships described earlier in this chapter, Access will join the tables for you, and you will see join lines between the Committee fields in the Committee Names and Committees tables, and between the ID Code fields in the Committees and Names tables. If these joins exist, skip to step 5.

3. If the Committees and Names tables are not already joined, position the mouse over the ID Code field in the Committees table, press and hold the left mouse button, drag the mouse over the ID Code field in the Names table, and release the mouse button.

4. If the Committee Names and Committees tables are not already joined, position the mouse over the Committee field in the Committee Names table, press and hold the left mouse button, drag the mouse over the Committee field in the Committees table, and release the mouse button.

5. Double-click on the title bar in the Committees field list to select all the fields. Position the mouse over any of the highlighted fields, press and hold the left mouse button, and drag all the fields to the output grid.

6. Drag the Name field from the Names table to the output grid, and drop the field on top of the Officer field to insert it between the ID Code and Officer fields.

7. Press F2 or click in the Field row in the Name column, move the insertion point to the left of the field name, and type **Member Name:** to add a new column title for this field.

8. Drag the Description field from the Committee Names table to the output grid, and drop the field on top of the ID Code field to insert it between the Committee and ID Code fields.

9. Press F2 or click in the Field row in the Description column, move the insertion point to the left of the field name, and type **Committee Name:** to add a new column title for this field.

10. Choose the Table Names option from the View menu to add the Table row, which displays the names of the source table for each column, to the QBE grid. Your screen should look like Figure 8.13.

11. Choose the Save As option from the File menu, and enter the name **Committees with Names** for the query.

12. Click on the Run Query command button in the tool bar or choose Run from the Query menu to display the query dynaset in Datasheet view. Your screen should resemble Figure 8.14. Verify that the committee names match the committee codes and that the member names match the ID codes.

13. Click on the Design command button in the tool bar or choose Query Design from the View menu to return to the Query Design window.

Figure 8.13

A query that displays committee and committee member names

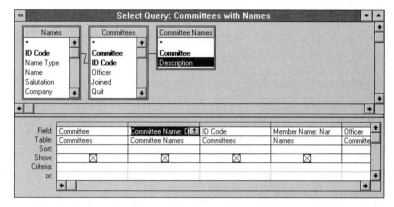

Figure 8.14

The Committees with Names query datasheet

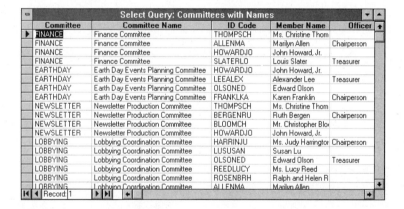

14. Click in the Show boxes in the Committee and ID Code columns to suppress display of these columns in the query datasheet, and run the query again to view the results. If you wish, you can maximize the datasheet window and adjust the column widths to conform better to the data.

15. Close the datasheet window.

Table Join Mechanisms

Understanding the mechanisms that Access uses to join tables and produce the query dynaset is crucial to using multitable queries effectively. Unfortunately, these mechanisms may not seem intuitive (or even reasonable) at first, and even after you have gained considerable experience, the table joins may not reflect your mental picture of the data you intended to extract when you designed the query. For example, in the Committees with Names query defined in the previous section, you might view the Committees table as central and the Names and Committee Names tables as reference tables. You might visualize the table relationships in this query as one-to-one linkages intended to support lookups; for each record in the Committees table, you want to find one matching record in the Names table (based on the ID Code field) and one matching record in the Committee Names table (based on the Committees table).

To understand the way that Access executes a query, you must abandon this teleological viewpoint. The query dynaset can potentially include one row for each pair of records in the source tables. The joins in the query limit this output to pairs of *matching* records. By default, Access treats every join in a query as an *equi-join*, which results in selecting *every pair of matching records between the two joined tables, and no others*. You might visualize this process for the Committees and Names query as follows: Access finds every pair of matching records in the Committees table and Names table based on the ID code, and then finds every pair of matching records between the resulting dynaset and the Committee Names table. Actually, you cannot predict the order in which Access will join the tables, but it makes no difference—the result would be the same if it first joined the Committees and Committee Names tables and then joined the Names table to the result. Because there is only one record in the Names table and one record in the Committee Names table for each Committees table record, the final dynaset contains exactly the desired data.

It is entirely up to you to define joins that make sense based on the contents of the tables in a multitable query. If you join two tables based on fields that do not contain common data (for example, the ID Code and Committee fields), the query dynaset will be empty. If you do not define any joins, the dynaset will contain one row for each pair of records in the two tables. For example, if you create a query based on the Committees and Names tables and do not join the tables, the dynaset will contain 1,800 rows—the result of pairing each of the 18 Committees table records with each of 100 Names table records. Adding the Committee Names table to the query without joining it to the Committees table will yield a dynaset with 9,000 rows, because each of the 1,800 rows in the original dynaset will be paired with each of the five Committee Names table records. Creating a multitable query with no joins is permitted because it sometimes makes sense to do so (to find every possible combination of records in two tables). If your tables are large, defining such a query by mistake (by neglecting to specify a join) can be costly in terms of time and disk space.

By definition, an equi-join selects all possible pairs of matching records between two tables *and only those records*. In the Committees and Names query, if any Committees table record does not have a match in the Committee Names or Names table, it will not be represented in the query dynaset. Depending on your purpose in creating the query, this may or may not be what you want. For example, if you intended to use the Committees and Names query to print a new version of the Committee Membership Roster, the default equi-join gives you exactly the output required for the report. Considered from the point of view of the Committees table, there should never be a record with no match in either of the other two tables. If there were mismatches, however, this query would give you no clue to their existence, and in the real world, tables often contain this kind of "bad" data, especially during the testing stages of application development or in tables imported from external sources.

Furthermore, when two tables have a one-to-many relationship, you may in some contexts want to include every record in the parent table in the output of a query, regardless of whether there is a matching record in the child table. For example, in the ACE system, you might want to print a report that includes the name and address of every person, together with a list of transactions for those people who have transactions or committee memberships for the people who have served on committees. By default, joining the Names table and Transactions table will yield a dynaset with one row for each pair of matching records, and people with no transactions will not be represented. To solve this problem, you must use an *outer join*.

Using Outer Joins

To display all the records in one table, regardless of whether there is a match in another, you must change the default equi-join to an *outer join*, which by definition includes at least one row for each record in one of the joined tables. If there are matching records in the other table, the dynaset will include one row for each pair. Deciding whether to treat a linkage between tables as an equi-join or as an outer join depends on the logic of the application—on business rules rather than database integrity rules—and it is up to you to specify which type of join you want. To edit the join properties, double-click on the join line or click once on the join line and then choose the Join Properties option from the View menu (this menu option is enabled only when the join line is selected). Because it may be hard to position the mouse precisely over this fine line, you may prefer to use the latter method, which allows you to verify when the join line is selected.

The Join Properties dialog box, which is shown in Figure 8.15 for a join that links the Names and Transactions tables, always offers three options. The first describes the default equi-join, and the other two describe the two possible outer joins. You can select an option by clicking on the associated radio button or by pressing an Alt-key combination based on the underlined number. When you close the Join Properties dialog box after choosing either of the outer join options, Access redisplays the join line that connects the two tables as an arrow pointing away from the table in which you elected to display all the records. Creating an outer join usually implies that the two tables have a one-to-many relationship and that you want to see every record in the parent table, regardless of whether there are matching child records. At times, you may use an outer join in situations that do not conform to this profile. For example, you could use an outer join that displays all the records in the Transactions table to find "orphan" transaction records with no matches in the Names table (presumably, so you can correct them).

Figure 8.15

The Join Properties dialog box

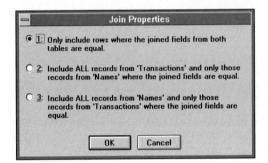

Figure 8.16 illustrates a query based on an outer join between the Names and Transactions table, and Figure 8.17 shows the resulting dynaset. In the rows that represent records in the Names table with no matches in the Transactions table, all the columns derived from the Transactions table are null. Figure 8.17 includes three names that have no transactions—J.C. Anderson, Claude Black, and Martha Bliss. When there is more than one matching transaction record for a name record, the dynaset includes one row for each pair of matching records (just as in an equi-join). In Figure 8.17, you can see four rows for Marilyn Allen's four transactions, and two for Michael Anderson's two transactions.

You can use the Unique Values Only option to create a query dynaset in which each row is unique (that is, Access eliminates any duplicate values). To enable this option, which is disabled by default, choose the Query Properties option from the View menu or click on the Properties command button in the tool bar to display the Query Properties dialog box, and check the Unique Values Only check box. This option, which also applies to queries based on a single table, is particularly useful in multitable queries intended to select records in the parent table that have one or more matches in the child table. For example, you might define a query based on the Names and Transactions tables that

Figure 8.16
An outer join

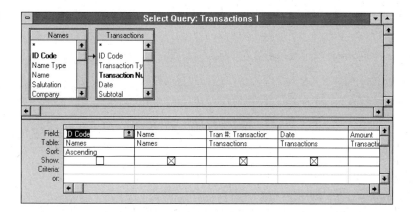

Figure 8.17
The Names and Transactions query dynaset

Select Query: Transactions 1

Name	Tran #	Date	Amount	Pmt Form	Reference
Jerry Allen	14971	1/28/92	25.92	Check	Recycle T-shirts, Check #48
Marilyn Allen	14932	12/28/91	1,000.00	Check	Pledge
Marilyn Allen	14933	12/28/91	250.00	Check	Pledge payment #1, Check #1283
Marilyn Allen	14979	2/21/92	250.00	Check	Check #381
Marilyn Allen	15000	4/25/92	250.00	Check	Pledge payment #2, Check #1479
Mr. J. C. Anderson					
Michael Anderson	14990	4/8/92	100.00	Check	Check #1005
Michael Anderson	14935	12/31/91	522.00		Total credits as of 12/31/91
Melvin H. Arnold	14936	12/31/91	75.00		Total credits as of 12/31/91
Ms. Sylvia Baker	14992	4/10/92	25.00	Check	Check #2301
Ruth Bergen	14988	3/25/92	25.00	Check	Check #528
Ruth Bergen	14937	12/31/91	2,452.00		Total credits as of 12/31/91
Ruth Bergen	14972	1/28/92	14.46	VISA	Save the Wetlands T-shirt, 4591-2S
Mr. Claude Black					
Martha Bliss					
Mr. Christopher Bloom	14984	3/7/92	1,000.00		Pledge
Mr. Christopher Bloom	14985	3/7/92	250.00	Check	Check #793
Mr. Christopher Bloom	14938	12/31/91	2,250.00		Total credits as of 12/31/91

Record: 1

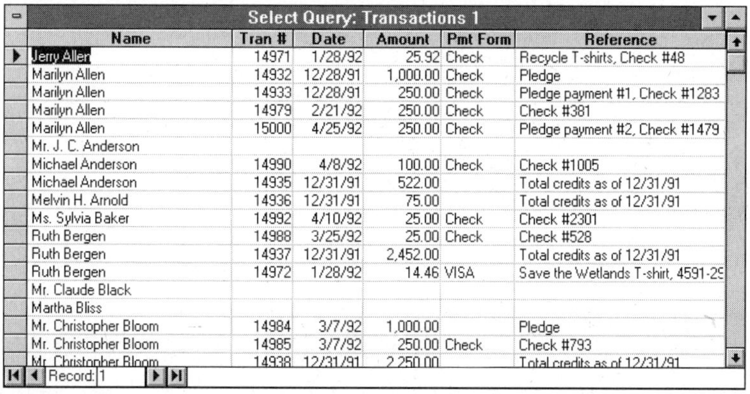

selects everyone who has made a donation within a certain range of dates, and use this query as the data source for a mailing label report. To avoid printing multiple labels for a person who made two or more donations within the specified time period, you can check the Unique Values Only option.

To convert the Committees with Names query created earlier in this chapter to an outer join, use the following steps:

1. Make sure that the Database window displays the list of queries (if necessary, click on the Query button or choose Queries from the View menu), and open the Committees with Names query in Design view.

2. Double-click on the join line between the Committees and Names tables in the upper portion of the Query Design window to display the Join Properties dialog box.

3. Click on the second radio button or press Alt+2 to select the outer join option that includes all records from the Names table.

4. Close the Join Properties dialog box, and note that the join line between the Names and Committees tables is displayed as an arrow that points toward the Committees table.

5. Double-click on the join line between the Committees and Committee Names tables in the upper portion of the Query Design window to display the Join Properties dialog box.

6. Click on the third radio button or press Alt+3 to select the outer join option that includes all records from the Committees table.

7. Close the Join Properties dialog box, and note that the join line between the Committees and Committee Names tables is displayed as an arrow that points toward the Committee Names table.

8. Execute the query and note that Access displays all the records in the Names table, regardless of whether there are matching Committees table records.

9. Close the query without saving your changes.

Using Self-Joins

One of the most efficient mechanisms for cross-referencing records in the same table is to use a *self-join*—a query that links two copies of the same table. Just as an equi-join enables you to find all the records in one table that match each record in another, you can use a self-join to find the set of records that match another record *in the same table*. For example, you might want to produce a list of committee members that includes both the name of the member and the name of the committee chairperson. To do this, you must define a query that matches up each record in the Committees table with the other record in this table that has the same value in the Committee field and has "Chairperson" in the Officer field. Figure 8.18 illustrates a very simple query that displays this data.

To create a self-join, simply choose the same table twice from the Add Table dialog box when you define the query. To distinguish the two copies of the table, Access creates an *alias*, or alternate name, for the second copy by adding a numeric suffix. In Figure 8.18, you can see that the second of the two Committees table field lists is titled Committees_1; the member data is

Figure 8.18

A query based on a self-join

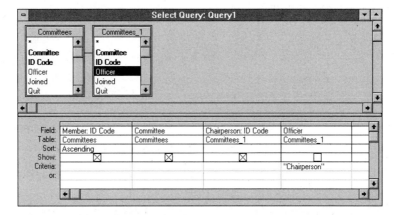

derived from the Committees field list, and the chairperson data is derived from the Committees_1 field list. As in any other query, you can link the two tables by any common field or fields that make sense in the context of the inquiry you are carrying out. In the Committees table self-join, the join is based on the Committee field, and the selection criteria are based on the Officer field from the Committees_1 field list to limit the output to pairs of records in which the Committees_1 record represents a committee chairperson. Note that the output grid includes two copies of the ID Code field—one from the Committees field list, which identifies the committee member, and the other from the Committees_1 field list, which identifies the chairperson. Figure 8.19 shows the output of the query.

Figure 8.19

The self-join dynaset

Member	Committee	Chairperson
ALLENMA	LOBBYING	HARRINJU
ALLENMA	FINANCE	ALLENMA
BERGENRU	NEWSLETTER	BERGENRU
BLOOMCH	NEWSLETTER	BERGENRU
FRANKLKA	EARTHDAY	FRANKLKA
HARRINJU	LOBBYING	HARRINJU
HOWARDJO	NEWSLETTER	BERGENRU
HOWARDJO	EARTHDAY	FRANKLKA
HOWARDJO	FINANCE	ALLENMA
LEEALEX	EARTHDAY	FRANKLKA
LUSUSAN	LOBBYING	HARRINJU
OLSONED	LOBBYING	HARRINJU
OLSONED	EARTHDAY	FRANKLKA
REEDLUCY	LOBBYING	HARRINJU
ROSENBRH	LOBBYING	HARRINJU
SLATERLO	FINANCE	ALLENMA
THOMPSCH	NEWSLETTER	BERGENRU
THOMPSCH	FINANCE	ALLENMA

You can make the query more useful by adding the full names of the member and chairperson, as well as the committee names. To include both member names, you must add two copies of the Names table to the query, one joined to the Committees field list (to display the member's name) and the other to the Committees_1 field list (to display the chairperson's name). Figure 8.20 illustrates the final version of the Committee Members and Chairpersons query, and Figure 8.21 illustrates the output. If you wanted to include only current committee members, you could enter the condition Is Null in the Criteria row for the Quit column.

Figure 8.20

The Committee Members and Chairpersons query

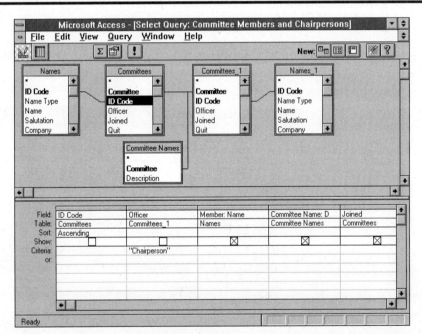

Updating Query Dynasets

As you begin to design more complex queries, you will find that Access does not always allow you to update all (or in some cases, any) of the data in the resulting dynaset. Although you may be dealing with a variety of seemingly very different queries, there is one global rule that determines whether you can update the data displayed in a query dynaset: *Access allows you to update fields that are derived unambiguously from one record in a source table.* This condition is fulfilled for many select queries based on one table, but not every query based on one table results in an updateable dynaset—as you will see in Chapter 9, when you use a query to calculate summary statistics, each row in

Figure 8.21

The output of the Committee Members and Chairpersons query

Member	Committee Name	Joined	Quit	Chairperson	Notes
Marilyn Allen	Lobbying Coordination Committ	6/3/91		Ms. Judy Harrington	
Marilyn Allen	Finance Committee	2/3/90		Marilyn Allen	Ms. Allen was Treasurer
Ruth Bergen	Newsletter Production Committ	8/10/91		Ruth Bergen	
Mr. Christopher Bloom	Newsletter Production Committ	3/28/90	3/1/92	Ruth Bergen	
Karen Franklin	Earth Day Events Planning Co	8/1/92		Karen Franklin	
Ms. Judy Harrington	Lobbying Coordination Committ	10/20/92		Ms. Judy Harrington	
John Howard, Jr.	Newsletter Production Committ	11/10/92		Ruth Bergen	Howard is responsible fo
John Howard, Jr.	Earth Day Events Planning Co	5/10/91		Karen Franklin	
John Howard, Jr.	Finance Committee	1/15/90	2/5/91	Marilyn Allen	
Alexander Lee	Earth Day Events Planning Co	7/23/90		Karen Franklin	
Susan Lu	Lobbying Coordination Committ	10/25/90		Ms. Judy Harrington	
Edward Olson	Lobbying Coordination Committ	5/10/92		Ms. Judy Harrington	
Edward Olson	Earth Day Events Planning Co	6/18/91	5/20/92	Karen Franklin	Ed organized the first AC
Ms. Lucy Reed	Lobbying Coordination Committ	4/18/90	5/1/92	Ms. Judy Harrington	
Ralph and Helen Rosenberg	Lobbying Coordination Committ	4/1/91	4/5/92	Ms. Judy Harrington	Ralph, not Helen, was th
Louis Slater	Finance Committee	6/15/92		Marilyn Allen	
Ms. Christine Thompson	Newsletter Production Committ	2/6/92		Ruth Bergen	Christine is now the edito
Ms. Christine Thompson	Finance Committee	12/18/91		Marilyn Allen	

Record: 1

the dynaset contains aggregated data derived from a group of records in the source table, and Access does not allow you to edit any of the rows.

In a query based on two tables that have a one-to-one relationship, you can update fields derived from either table, and Access applies the changes to the appropriate record in the source table. If you delete a row, Access deletes the source records from both tables. Access allows you to add a "record" to the query dynaset only if the table linkage is based on fields for which there are indexes that do not permit duplicate values. (Often, but not necessarily, the tables are linked by their primary keys.) When you attempt to add a record to such a dynaset, Access tries to add a record to each of the two source tables. If the linking field is included in the query dynaset, Access adds a record to both source tables and fills in the value you entered into the linking field in one table in the corresponding field in the other. If you did not include the linking field in the output grid, there is no way to fill in this field, but Access does not allow an index key field for which duplicates are prohibited to be null. Instead, it displays an alert box warning you that you "Can't have null value in index" and refuses to accept the new record.

If you link two tables that have a one-to-many relationship with an equi-join, you can update fields in the child table because each row in the query dynaset represents one row in the child table. You cannot update the parent table if the output grid includes any fields from the child table. If all the fields in the dynaset come from the parent table, and the child table is required only to specify the sorting instructions or selection criteria, you can update rows in the dynaset. In a query that includes two or more one-to-many linkages, you can only update the child file at the lowest level. For example, in a query based on a customer table, an invoice table, and a line item table, the relationships between the customer and invoice tables and between the invoice and line item tables are both one-to-many, and you could update only the fields derived from the line item table.

The reason for this restriction is that a given value from the parent table may be displayed many times in the dynaset (once for each matching child record), but there is in fact only one copy in the parent table. If you did not understand this fact, you might try to change the contents of one of the parent fields thinking that you were updating only data pertaining to one child record, when in fact you would be changing a single record in the parent table. For example, in a query based on the Names and Transactions table, you might see a row with the name Jerry Allen and recognize that the transaction in fact belonged to Marilyn Allen. If you attempted to correct this problem by changing "Jerry Allen" to "Marilyn Allen" in the Name column, you would in fact be changing the Name field in Jerry Allen's Names table record to Marilyn Allen. To prevent errors due to this very common misunderstanding, Access prohibits the update.

At times, however, changing the data in the parent table is exactly what you need to do. For example, while editing transaction records using the same Names and Transactions table query, you might notice that you had misspelled Marilyn Allen's name. If Access allowed you to edit the Name field, you could correct the error once and the new data would appear immediately in all the rows representing Marilyn Allen's transactions. To overcome this limitation, you must define a form based on the query and change the form property that specifies which tables Access allows you to update. The method for doing this is described in Chapter 10.

When you work with a query dynaset based on an equi-join, you can add records, which Access places in the child table. If you delete a row, Access deletes the corresponding record from the child table, leaving the parent record intact. In both cases, the reason is the same—each row in the dynaset represents one record in the child table.

When you link two tables that have a one-to-many relationship with an outer join, Access may impose additional restrictions. A query dynaset resulting from an outer join that includes all the records in the child table, regardless of whether there are matching records in the parent table, behaves just like an equi-join. You can update the child table fields but not the parent table fields, and you can add or delete records from the child table because (as in an equi-join), each row in the dynaset represents a record in one table—the child table.

If the query dynaset includes all the records in the parent table, regardless of whether there are matching records in the child table, Access does not allow you to update any fields from either table. As outlined earlier in this section, you cannot update the parent table in a query dynaset that includes fields from the child table. The additional prohibition on updating the child table fields is due to the fact that if there is no matching record in the child file for a given parent record, the child columns will be blank in rows that represent this parent record. However, you cannot distinguish these columns visually from fields in legitimate child file records that happen to be blank, and if you entered data in these columns, Access would have no place to store it. Rather than make the decision row by row or risk confusing you by allowing you to edit some rows but not others, Access prohibits all updates in this type of query. You cannot add or delete rows in the dynaset of an outer join, because Access cannot determine which table to update.

In a multitable query that is updateable—such as an equi-join between two tables—Access enforces referential integrity *in the query dynaset* by refusing to allow you to enter a value in the linking field that would disrupt the link between a pair of records. Thus, in a query based on the Names and Transactions tables that displays the ID Code column from the Transactions table, you cannot enter a new transaction record in which the ID code does not match an existing record in the Names table. Also, you cannot change the ID Code field in an existing transaction record to a value that does not match a Names table record, although you can change the ID Code field to another legitimate ID code. These referential integrity tests are carried out even if you did not check the Enforce Referential Integrity option for a default relationship between the two tables, or for that matter, even if you did not define a default relationship. Any attempt to change data in a way that would disrupt the linkage established in the query results in an alert box like the one shown in Figure 8.22.

Figure 8.22

A warning that you are violating referential integrity in a query dynaset

In a dynaset resulting from an outer join that selects every record from the child table regardless of whether there is a match in the parent table, Access allows you to enter any value you wish in the linking field, because by definition, this type of outer join permits mismatches between the two tables.

NOTE. *You can circumvent all of these restrictions by abandoning the default Datasheet view and designing forms to update multiple tables. Some of the methods for doing so are described in the next section of this chapter, and some are presented in Chapter 10.*

Defining Multitable Forms

One way to create a form based on two or more tables is to define a query that selects the required data from the tables and then use the query as the data source for a new form. For example, Figure 8.23 illustrates a simple form called Contacts with Names based on a query of the same name, which selects all the fields in the Contacts table, together with the Name field from the matching Names table record and the Description field from the matching Contact Types table record. This form was created by making a few simple modifications to a single-column layout generated by the FormWizards—moving the Name field adjacent to the ID Code field, and placing the Description field next to the Contact Type field.

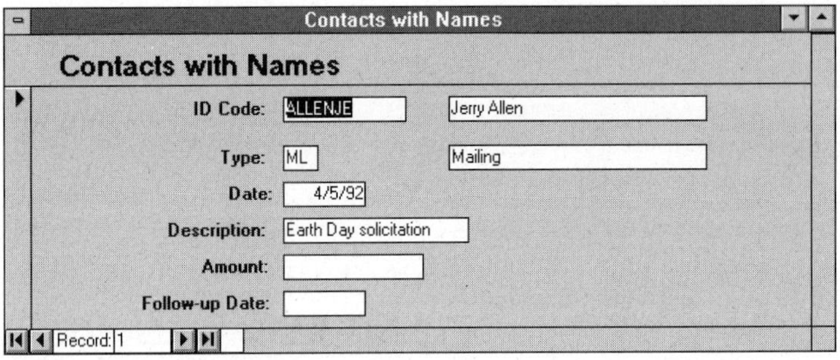

Figure 8.23

A simple form based on a multitable query

When you use a form based on a query, the same rules govern which fields and records you can update as when you work in the default Datasheet view. For example, in the Contacts with Names form, you can update only the Contacts table fields. This should make sense when you consider that the datasheet is really just an alternative form style, not a fundamentally different data entry mode.

Forms like the one in Figure 8.23 are ideal for updating one table while displaying matching fields from other tables that serve as lookup or reference tables. You might create a similar form for the Names table that displays data from several lookup tables—the Name Types, Area Codes, States, and Keywords tables. For updating tables that have a one-to-many relationship, however, you will often want forms that more closely reflect your intuitive view of the data. For example, in the ACE system, you might want a form that resembles the manual ledger sheets maintained for donors, in which the Names table fields appear at the top of the form and the related Transactions table records are listed below in a tabular format. You would use this form as you would the analogous paper form—by searching first for the Names table record and then moving at will between the two sections of the form to update information in either or both tables.

Because the requirement for this form style is so common, Access provides a FormWizard to define it. In the first FormWizards dialog box, this form style is called *Main/Subform* because Access creates it by building two separate forms: a single-column layout for the parent table and a form that displays records in Datasheet view for the child table. Access then inserts the datasheet form into the single-column form as a *subform*. You can create forms that include one or more embedded subforms yourself or add a subform to a form originally created by the FormWizards, using methods described in Chapter 12. Figure 8.24 illustrates this form style with a form that updates the Names and Contacts tables.

Figure 8.24

A main/subform
data entry form

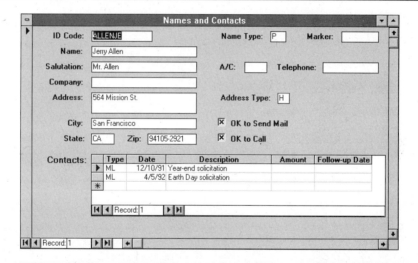

To create a main/subform form, choose the parent table or query from the New Form dialog box (the first dialog box displayed when you initiate the design process), and then choose Main/Subform from the first FormWizards dialog box. The FormWizard next displays the dialog box pictured in Figure 8.25 to allow you to choose the table or query that you want to update in the subform. Above the familar Tables/Queries list, Access displays a reminder of the name of the source table or query for the main form (in Figure 8.25, this is the Names table).

Next, the FormWizard displays two field selection dialog boxes, first for the main form source table and then for the subform source table. In both of these dialog boxes, the diagram on the left side depicts the basic layout of this form style, and an arrow points to the portion of the form for which you are

Figure 8.25

Choosing the table or query for the subform

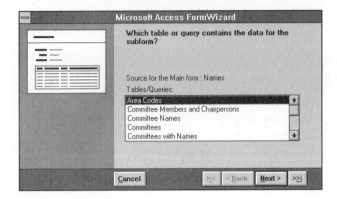

currently choosing fields. If you want to display more than a few fields from the parent table, some modifications to the form generated by the FormWizard will be necessary to ensure that all the parent table data and a reasonable number of child records are visible at the same time. You may prefer to choose just a few fields in the FormWizards dialog box and then add the rest when you edit the resulting form later.

Figure 8.26 shows the dialog box displayed for the Contacts table subform illustrated in Figure 8.24. In most cases, you will add all or nearly all of the fields in the child table to the subform. It is usually *not* necessary to include the field or fields that define the relationship between the two tables in the subform, which displays only the records in the child table that match the current record in the parent table. This strategy is illustrated in the form in Figure 8.24, in which the subform includes all the Contacts table fields except the ID Code field (and in Figure 8.26, which shows the field list for the subform). The easiest way to establish the field list is to click on the >> button to add all the fields to the Fields on Subform list, and then remove the unneeded fields (in Figure 8.26, just the ID Code field was removed). Note, however, that if you do not want the order of the columns in the subform datasheet to match the order of the fields in the underlying table structure, you will have to choose the fields one by one.

The FormWizard that creates the main/subform layout displays exactly the same dialog box as the other FormWizards to enable you to choose the overall look of the form and to enter the form title. When you exit from the last FormWizards dialog box, Access displays the alert box shown in Figure 8.27 to remind you that you must save the subform before it can complete the form (Access cannot insert the subform into the main form until it has been saved on disk). When you click on OK to acknowledge this message, Access displays the standard Save As dialog box to prompt you for a name

Figure 8.26
Choosing the fields
in the subform

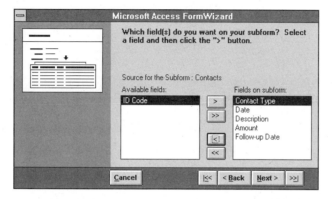

for the subform. At this point, you have not yet saved the main form, which still retains the default name assigned to new forms (Form1, Form2, and so on). You can save the main form whenever you wish by using any of the standard methods used to save forms (for example, by using the Save option on the File menu).

Note that the main/subform FormWizard does not ask you how to link the parent and child tables, because in most cases, Access can deduce the relationship without additional input from you. If you have predefined a default relationship between the source tables (or queries), Access links the tables based on the same fields that define this relationship. If you did not define a default relationship, Access looks for fields in the child table with the same names as the primary key fields in the parent table. Thus, when generating the form shown in Figure 8.24, Access could link the Names and Contacts tables based on the ID Code field (the primary key in the Names table) even without the default relationship described earlier in this chapter. In the rare instances that Access cannot automatically create the link, you must do so by editing the properties of the subform object on the main form (Chapter 10 describes how to access the object property sheets in Form Design view).

Figure 8.27
Saving the subform

Using a Main/Subform Form

When you use a main/subform form to view data, the subform appears in a window of its own, which is enclosed completely within the main form. Access displays one record from the parent table in the main portion of the form, and all the matching records from the child table in the subform. If there are too many child records to fit in the space allotted to the subform, it displays a vertical scroll bar on the right side of the subform window. The subform looks and behaves much like the standard Datasheet view, except that you cannot move or resize it in Form view (you must modify it in Form Design view, using methods described in the next section). Each window has its own set of navigation controls and its own current record indicator. When you use the navigation controls or the equivalent menu options to move around in the parent table, Access automatically updates the subform datasheet to display only the matching records. When you use the navigation controls or the equivalent menu options to move through the records in the subform, Access interprets the First Record and Last Record commands relative to the group of records that match the current record in the parent table.

You can use all the standard keyboard, mouse, and menu commands to edit, add, or delete records in either table. When you add a record to the child table in the subform, Access automatically fills in the values of the linking fields based on the current parent record, even if these fields are not displayed in the subform. In both tables, Access saves your changes whenever you leave the current record. When you move into the subform after changing the parent record, Access saves the parent record first, and the only way to undo the changes to the parent record is to return to the main portion of the form and use the Undo Saved Record option on the Edit menu. If you find these details confusing, watch the shape of the current record indicators in the main form and subform as you move around the screen.

When you are editing records, the easiest way to move directly to any control in the main form or subform is to use the mouse, but during an intensive data entry session, you may prefer keyboard commands, which do not require you to take your hands off the keyboard. When you advance past the last field in the main form (by pressing Tab or Down Arrow), Access moves into the subform datasheet. The first time you enter the subform for a particular parent record, Access highlights the first field of the first record; subsequently, Access returns you to the field that had the focus the last time you were working in the subform. You can move from the subform back to the last object in the main form (the one that precedes the subform object in the tab order) by pressing Ctrl+Shift+Tab, and you can move to the first field in the main form by pressing Ctrl+Shift+Home. If there are objects in the main form after the subform object in the tab order, you can move from the subform to the first object that follows the subform by pressing Ctrl+Tab; in a form that has no objects after the subform (such as the form shown in Figure 8.24), this command moves you to the next record in the main form.

When you use a main/subform form to update tables, Access treats the parent table—the one displayed in the main form—as the primary table. In a sense, the records in the subform are just "along for the ride." You can define filters based on the parent table or query but not on the child table displayed in the subform—when you choose the Filter/Sort option, Access displays the field list for the parent table in the Filter Design window, even if you were in the subform window when you issued the command. This limitation can be frustrating if each parent record has more than a few dozen matching records in the child file, but it is partially mitigated by the fact that you can use the Find command to search for records in either table, and you can use the scroll bar in the subform to move quickly to any point in the datasheet. If the record selection criteria you want to impose on the child file are relatively constant, a more general solution to the problem is to use a query as the data source for the subform. You can gain an additional measure of flexibility by defining a parameter query. For example, you could define a parameter query based on the Contacts table that prompts you to enter a range of contact dates and/or a list of contact types and substitute this query for the Contacts table in forms like the one in Figure 8.24. Note, however, that Access reruns the query and prompts you for all the parameters each time you move to a new record in the Names table.

When you use a main/subform form created by the FormWizards, you can switch to Datasheet view for the table in the main form, but you cannot switch to Form view from the subform. Unlike the rules that govern the use of filters, these properties arise from assumptions made by the FormWizards, not from intrinsic properties of the forms themselves. You can modify the main form and/or subform to specify which views are permitted for each and which view is the default (the view displayed when you first open the form), just as you can for any other form, using methods described in Chapter 10. If you modify the subform to allow access to Datasheet view, you can use the Subform Datasheet option on the View menu to alternate between Form view and Datasheet view. This option is disabled when the Datasheet view is prohibited for the subform; it is also temporarily disabled whenever a field in the main portion of the form has the focus.

Modifying the Subform

As you should already know from your experience with the other Form-Wizards, you will often want to modify a form created by an Access Wizard. The modifications typically required in the main form are the same as those you might make in any single-column form—changing field widths and re-arranging the fields. The changes you will want to make in the subform are similar to the datasheet customizations described in Chapter 4—primarily, changing column widths to conform to their contents and freezing columns at the left side of the datasheet if there are too many fields to fit on the screen at once. Many of the changes you will make in a table's raw datasheet are unnecessary in a subform; because you have already chosen the fields that will appear in the datasheet and their order, you will rarely have to move, add, remove, or hide columns.

A few modifications are motivated by the assumptions made by all the Access FormWizards, including the one that creates main/subform forms. In particular, the column titles in the datasheet, like all field labels in forms generated by the FormWizards, include trailing colons, which in the datasheet are unsightly and unnecessary. These colons were removed in the subform pictured in Figure 8.24.

Before you can create a main/subform layout from scratch or modify one built by the FormWizards, you have to understand the basic structure of this type of form and the interaction between the main form and the subform. Remember that the subform is an independent form that is stored separately from the main form in the database and appears in the list of forms displayed in the Database window. You can open and use the subform independently, and you can insert the same subform into more than one main form (which you may have created from scratch or with the FormWizards). In the main form, the subform is treated as a single control, which is on equal footing with all the other controls in the form, and which you can move or resize like any other object.

Figure 8.28 illustrates the form pictured in Figure 8.24 in Form Design view. As is the case with all the other types of controls, Access displays the data source for a subform object—the name of the subform—in the upper-left corner of the object. You can move the subform anywhere on the main form and you can resize it just as you would any other object—by selecting it and manipulating the handles in its borders. Unfortunately, Access does not display any of the details of the datasheet layout that you might want to use as guides for adjusting the size of the subform object. To view or change the subform layout, you must open the subform in Design view. You can open a subform from the Database window, just as you would any other form, but in most cases, it is more convenient to edit the subform from within the main form. To open the subform in Design view, make sure that the subform object is not currently selected (that is, no handles are visible in its borders and there is no insertion point inside), and double-click anywhere within the object borders.

Although the subform is displayed in Datasheet view when you use the form, Access displays it as a single-column form in Design view. If this seems surprising, remember that the Form view and Datasheet view are two alternative display modes for the same form. Both the main form and the subform generated by the Access FormWizard are single-column forms, but the default display mode for the subform (which is established through a property

Figure 8.28

The Names and
Contacts form in
Design view

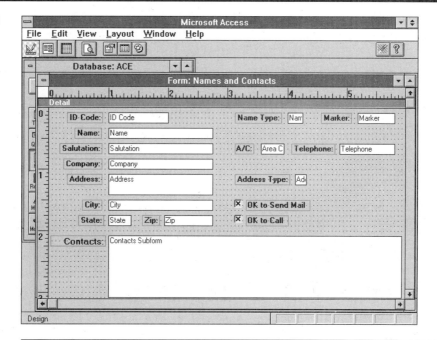

described in Chapter 10) is Datasheet view. Figure 8.29 illustrates the Contacts subform in Design view. If you remove a field in this view, it will disappear from the datasheet, and if you add a field, using methods described in Chapter 10, it will appear in the datasheet. Note, however, that the order of the columns in the datasheet is determined by the tab order of the controls in the form, *not* by their arrangement on the screen. When you add a new field to the form, it will be last in the tab order (and therefore in the datasheet), regardless of its placement on the form. To move the column to its proper position, you must use the Tab Order option on the Edit menu (described in Chapter 6) to revise the tab order.

If you edit the field labels in the form (for example, to remove the colons), the changes are reflected in the column headings in the Datasheet view. Other modifications, such as changing the font, font size, or display attributes of the labels, affect only the way the subform looks in Form view (if Form view is permitted), not the appearance of the datasheet. Note also that the size of the datasheet itself is determined by the size of the subform object in the main form, not by the size of the Form Design view window.

To customize aspects of the subform relevant only in Datasheet view (such as column widths and row height), you must make the changes in Datasheet view. You can use any of the standard methods to switch to Datasheet

Figure 8.29

Displaying the
subform in
Design view

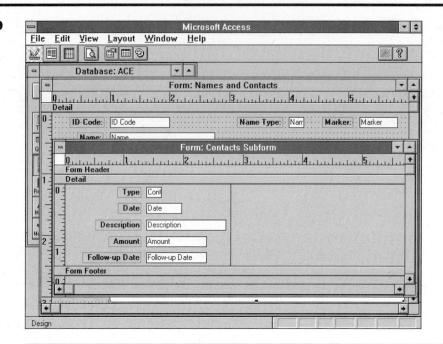

view—either click on the Datasheet command button in the tool bar or choose
Datasheet from the View menu. Note that the resulting display is *not* a special
"datasheet design view"—it is the standard Datasheet view for the table or
query on which the subform is based, and it displays live data from the underlying dynaset. If you edit records, the changes are saved on disk as always.
However, you will rarely want to change or add records in this view, especially
in light of the fact that the linking fields, which are usually absent from the subform, are required to enable you to identify records in the child table.

Fine-tuning the appearance of the subform datasheet is complicated by
the fact that you cannot see the columns in the subform object when you edit
the main form, and it is difficult to judge the appropriate column widths in
the datasheet without seeing the size of the subform object. Because you
must edit the datasheet in Datasheet view, not Form Design view, the tools
that are so helpful in Form Design view (such as the rulers and grid) are not
available. One good strategy for configuring the subform datasheet is to move
the Datasheet window so that you can also see the subform object in the
main form and resize it to match the size of the subform object. Figure 8.30
illustrates this window setup for the Contacts subform.

Figure 8.30

Editing a subform
datasheet while
viewing the
main form

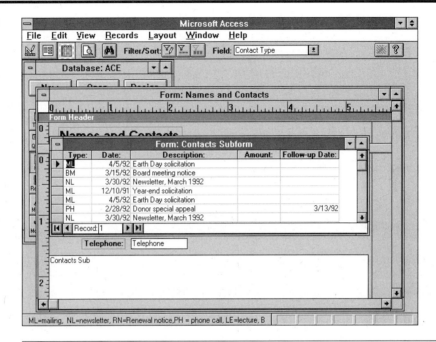

NOTE. *The subform datasheet will include a vertical scroll bar when there are too many child records to fit on the screen at the same time; be sure to leave room for the scroll bar when you lay out the datasheet window.*

Any changes you make to the appearance of the datasheet are saved with the subform, and you must save the subform before you can redisplay the composite form and see your modifications. If you close the subform window, Access prompts you as usual to save the form, but you can save the subform without closing the window by using the Save option on the File menu. After you save the subform, you must force Access to reload the subform into the main form. If the main form is still open, click anywhere in the subform object (make sure you see an insertion point inside the object), and then press Enter. Access does not display any confirmation after reloading the form, so you may want to switch momentarily to Form view to verify the effects of your changes. If the main form is not already open when you modify the subform, this step is unnecessary—Access reloads the subform every time you open the main form in Design view.

Creating a Form to Update the Names and Committees Tables

To update committee membership data, you might want a form similar to the one shown in Figure 8.24, which displays several fields from the Names table in the main portion of the form and the matching Committees table records in the subform. To make the committee membership datasheet more informative, you could base it on a query that includes the Description field from the Committee Names table rather than on the Committees table alone. First, create the query as follows:

1. Make sure that the Database window displays the list of queries (if necessary, click on the Query button or choose Queries from the View menu), and click on the New command button or press Alt+N.

2. Choose the Committees table and the Committee Names table from the list in the Add Table dialog box, and then close the dialog box. If you defined the default relationships described earlier in this chapter, Access will join the tables for you.

3. If you do not see a join line between the Committee fields in the two tables, position the mouse over the Committee field in the Committee Names table, press and hold the left mouse button, drag the mouse over the Committee field in the Committees table, and release the mouse button.

4. Double-click on the title bar in the Committees field list to select all the fields, and drag all the fields to the output grid.

5. Drag the Description field from the Committee Names table to the output grid, and drop the field on top of the ID Code field to insert it between the Committee and ID Code fields.

6. Press F2 or click in the Field row in the Description column, move the insertion point to the left of the field name, and type **Committee Name:** to add a new column title for this field.

7. Click on the Run Query command button in the tool bar or choose Run from the Query menu to display the query dynaset in Datasheet view. Verify that the committee names match the committee codes.

8. Close the query and enter **Committees with Committee Names** when Access prompts you for a new name.

   To create the data entry form, use the following steps:

1. Make sure that the Database window displays the list of forms (if necessary, click on the Form button or choose Forms from the View menu), and click on the New command button or press Alt+N.

2. In the New Form dialog box, select Names from the Select A Table/Query combo box, and then click on the FormWizards button or press Alt+W.

3. Choose Main/Subform from the first FormWizards dialog box.

4. In the dialog box that prompts you to select the data source for the subform, choose Committees with Committee Names.

5. In the field selection dialog box for the main form, choose the ID Code, Name, Company, Address, City, State, Zip, Area Code, and Telephone fields.

6. In the field selection dialog box for the subform, click on the » button to move all the fields to the Fields on Subform list. Highlight the ID Code field in this list, and click on the < button to remove this field from the Subform list.

7. Choose the Standard look for the form.

8. Type the form title, **Names and Committee Memberships**, in the last FormWizards dialog box, and then click on the Open command button to display the form with data.

9. Click on the OK button in the alert box that reminds you that Access must save the subform, and enter **Committee Memberships Subform** when Access prompts you for the subform name.

10. The form built by the main/subform FormWizard should look like Figure 8.31. Click on the Design command button in the tool bar to display the main form in Design view. Use the Form Hdr/Ftr option on the Layout menu to remove the form header and form footer sections. Resize and re-arrange the objects in the main form, including the subform object, so that the form looks approximately like Figure 8.32. Note that you must scroll the display to the right to resize the subform object, which is wider than the screen. Remember also to scroll the display down and move the lower form boundary up to approximately $1/8$ inch below the lower border of the subform object.

11. Click on the Form View button to display the new version of the form, and use the navigation controls to move to the next Names table record, which has committee membership data. The form should look like Figure 8.33. Click on the Design button in the tool bar to return to Form Design view.

12. Double-click in the subform object to open the subform in Form Design view.

13. Edit each of the labels to remove the colons that follow the field names.

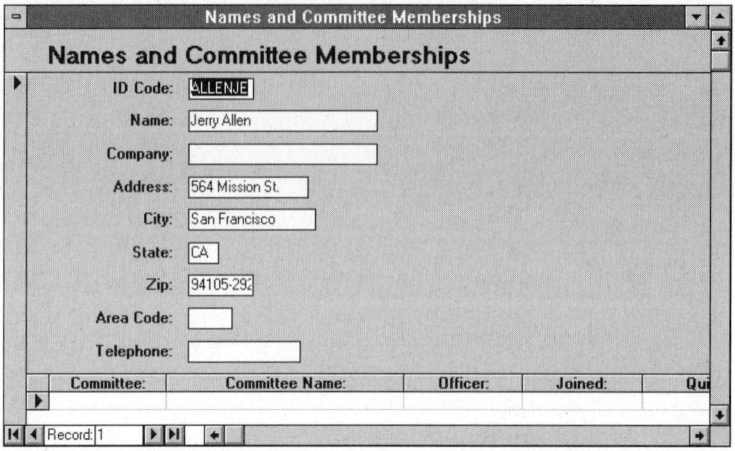

Figure 8.31

The first version of the Names and Committee Memberships form

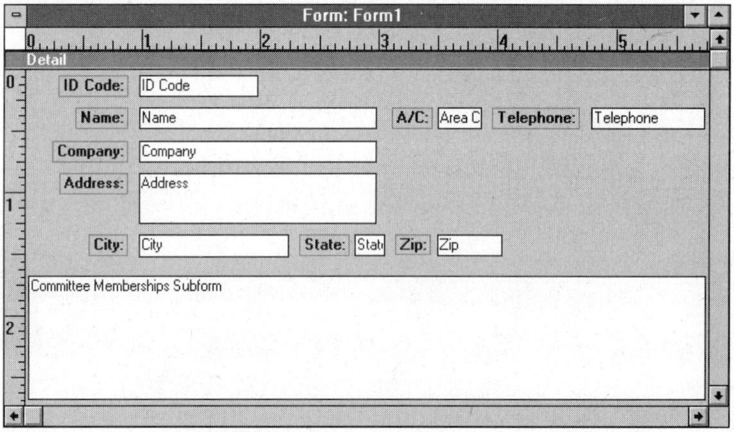

Figure 8.32

Modifying the main form

14. Click on the Datasheet button in the tool bar to display the subform in Datasheet view. Move and resize the window so that the subform object in the main form is also visible, and adjust the column widths to approximately match Figure 8.34. Select the Committee column and select the Freeze Columns option on the Layout menu.

15. Save the subform, click in the subform object on the main form, and press Enter to reload the subform.

Figure 8.33

The modified Names and Committee Memberships form

Figure 8.34

Modifying the subform

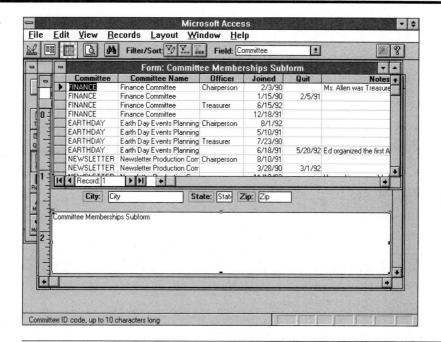

16. Click on the Form View button in the tool bar, and page through a few records in the Names table. Find a person who has committee membership data, and experiment with the navigation controls in the subform.

17. Save the form under the name **Names and Committee Memberships**.

Defining Multitable Reports

Many of the considerations outlined in the previous sections on designing multitable forms also apply to multitable reports. However, there is one significant difference: Reports are not used to update tables, so there is no penalty for using a query as the data source. As noted earlier in this chapter, starting with a query also enables you to base the selection criteria on a table that does not even appear in the output. For example, to print mailing labels for ACE members who have made donations during a certain period of time, you could base the mailing label report on a query that links the Names and Transactions tables. All the selection criteria in this query would be based on fields derived from the Transactions table, although the name and address fields printed on the labels all come from the Names table. Parameter queries are ideally suited to reports like these, because each report run may require that you select different values in the fields on which the selection criteria are based. For example, each mailing label run might be derived from transactions entered during a different range of dates.

This approach is ideal for reports that you visualize as being based primarily on one table, with one or more fields looked up in other tables that serve as reference lists. Typically, these reports are columnar layouts, and you can often create them using the groups/totals ReportWizard. This type of report has much in common with a datasheet, although at times you may need more than one printed line per record to accommodate all the required fields. Figure 8.35 illustrates one page of a report similar to the Monthly Donation Summary report illustrated in Figure 7.10, except that it includes all types of transactions, not just donations. The data source for the report is the query pictured in Figure 8.36, which is based on the Names, Transactions, and Transaction Types tables. The Transactions table is linked to the Names table by ID Code and to the Transaction Types table by Transaction Type. The report includes the Name field from the Names table as well as the ID Code field from the Transactions table, and the Description field from the Transaction Types table instead of the Transaction Type field. Note that the query includes all the fields from the Transactions table (not all of which are printed on the report in Figure 8.35), so that you can use the same query for other reports as well.

There is no Access ReportWizard analogous to the FormWizard that creates a main/subform data entry screen, but you can design similar forms yourself by adding a subreport to any other type of report, including one created by a ReportWizard. (Chapter 12 describes how to build reports from scratch that include one or more subreports.) One shortcut for creating this type of report is to use the main/subform FormWizard to create a similar form, edit the form, and then use the Save As Report option to save the form as a report. You can then edit the report as necessary. Figure 8.37 illustrates a report based on the form pictured in Figure 8.24. Although the portions of the report

Figure 8.35

A report that
includes data from
three tables

Transactions by Month
30-Nov-93

Date	Description	Name	Amount	Pmt Form	Reference
December 1991					
12/28/91	Pledge payment	Marilyn Allen	250.00	Check	Pledge payment #1, Check #12
12/28/91	Pledge	Marilyn Allen	1,000.00	Check	Pledge
12/31/91	Total credits	Michael Anderson	522.00		Total credits as of 12/31/91
12/31/91	Total credits	Melvin H. Arnold	75.00		Total credits as of 12/31/91
12/31/91	Total credits	Ruth Bergen	2,452.00		Total credits as of 12/31/91
12/31/91	Total credits	Mr. Christopher Bloom	2,250.00		Total credits as of 12/31/91
12/31/91	Total credits	Elizabeth Brown	25.00		Total credits as of 12/31/91
12/31/91	Total credits	Charles and Anne Davis	450.00		Total credits as of 12/31/91
12/31/91	Total credits	Cheryl Elliot, M.D.	50.00		Total credits as of 12/31/91
12/31/91	Total credits	Ms. Natalie Fell	125.00		Total credits as of 12/31/91
12/31/91	Total credits	Karen Franklin	100.00		Total credits as of 12/31/91
12/31/91	Total credits	Ms. Judy Harrington	50.00		Total credits as of 12/31/91
12/31/91	Total credits	Benjamin Harris	100.00		Total credits as of 12/31/91
12/31/91	Total credits	John Howard, Jr.	50.00		Total credits as of 12/31/91
12/31/91	Total credits	Alexander Lee	100.00		Total credits as of 12/31/91
12/31/91	Total credits	Susan Lu	525.00		Total credits as of 12/31/91
12/31/91	Total credits	Frank and Ann Matthews	125.00		Total credits as of 12/31/91
12/31/91	Total credits	Burton McDaniel	75.00		Total credits as of 12/31/91
12/31/91	Total credits	Mr. and Mrs. Joseph Moore	250.00		Total credits as of 12/31/91
12/31/91	Total credits	Edward Olson	545.00		Total credits as of 12/31/91
12/31/91	Total debits	Dr. Charles Pierson	1,500.00		Total debits as of 12/31/91
12/31/91	Total credits	Dr. Charles Pierson	3,200.00		Total credits as of 12/31/91
12/31/91	Total credits	Ms. Lucy Reed	320.00		Total credits as of 12/31/91
12/31/91	Total credits	Ralph and Helen Rosenberg	50.00		Total credits as of 12/31/91
12/31/91	Total credits	Louis Slater	75.00		Total credits as of 12/31/91
12/31/91	Total credits	Alice Snowden-Weiss	75.00		Total credits as of 12/31/91
12/31/91	Total credits	Luther Swift	175.00		Total credits as of 12/31/91
12/31/91	Total credits	Bert Thomas	25.00		Total credits as of 12/31/91
12/31/91	Total credits	Ms. Christine Thompson	150.00		Total credits as of 12/31/91
12/31/91	Total credits	Joseph Walker and Lisa Shanno	175.00		Total credits as of 12/31/91
12/31/91	Total credits	Mr. and Mrs. Earl Williams	50.00		Total credits as of 12/31/91
			14,914.00		
January 1992					
1/28/92	Purchase	Jerry Allen	25.92	Check	Recycle T-shirts, Check #48
1/28/92	Purchase	Ruth Bergen	14.46	VISA	Save the Wetlands T-shirt, 459
1/12/92	Membership	Charles and Anne Davis	25.00	Check	Check #452
1/22/92	Donation	Charles and Anne Davis	50.00	Check	Check #467

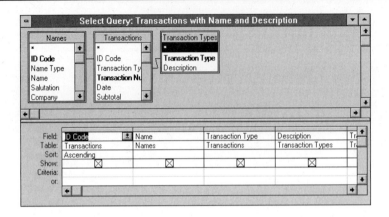

Figure 8.36

The source query for the Monthly Transaction Summary report

derived from the main form may require very few modifications, the same is usually not true of the subform. In particular, you may want to turn off the gridlines, resize the subform object, and change the property that controls whether the subform object and the entire detail section can shrink based on the amount of space they actually occupy. (When it creates the report, Access maintains a fixed size for the detail section, and it allows the subform to grow to accommodate all the child table records, but not to shrink.)

The following modifications were required to turn the report created by the Save as Report option into the page layout in Figure 8.37:

- The page header and footer sections were added.

- The background color was changed from gray to white.

- A dividing line was added at the bottom of the detail section.

- A copy of the Contacts Subform called Contacts Subreport was substituted for the original subform object.

- The subform object was resized.

- The gridlines were turned off for the subform datasheet.

- The subform object properties were changed to allow the subform to shrink as well as expand.

- The detail section properties were changed to allow the section to shrink based on the amount of data printed for each Names table record.

You already know how to make some of these changes; the others are described in Chapter 10.

Figure 8.37

A report created
from a form

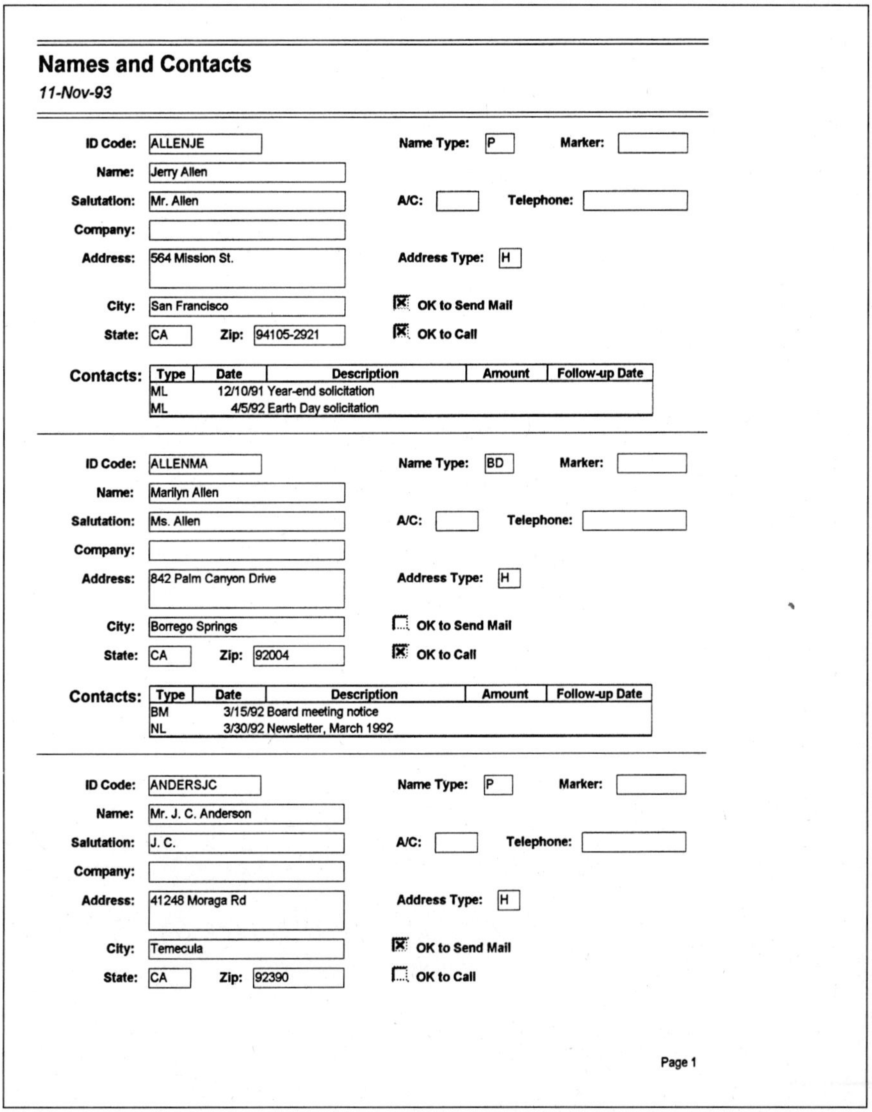

Names and Contacts
11-Nov-93

ID Code: ALLENJE	**Name Type:** P **Marker:**
Name: Jerry Allen	
Salutation: Mr. Allen	**A/C:** **Telephone:**
Company:	
Address: 564 Mission St.	**Address Type:** H
City: San Francisco	☒ **OK to Send Mail**
State: CA **Zip:** 94105-2921	☒ **OK to Call**

Contacts:

Type	Date	Description	Amount	Follow-up Date
ML	12/10/91	Year-end solicitation		
ML	4/5/92	Earth Day solicitation		

ID Code: ALLENMA	**Name Type:** BD **Marker:**
Name: Marilyn Allen	
Salutation: Ms. Allen	**A/C:** **Telephone:**
Company:	
Address: 842 Palm Canyon Drive	**Address Type:** H
City: Borrego Springs	☐ **OK to Send Mail**
State: CA **Zip:** 92004	☒ **OK to Call**

Contacts:

Type	Date	Description	Amount	Follow-up Date
BM	3/15/92	Board meeting notice		
NL	3/30/92	Newsletter, March 1992		

ID Code: ANDERSJC	**Name Type:** P **Marker:**
Name: Mr. J. C. Anderson	
Salutation: J. C.	**A/C:** **Telephone:**
Company:	
Address: 41248 Moraga Rd	**Address Type:** H
City: Temecula	☒ **OK to Send Mail**
State: CA **Zip:** 92390	☐ **OK to Call**

Page 1

When you embark on extensive modifications to the subform, keep in mind that it is a subform, not a subreport. You can also embed one report in another, as a subreport. Remember also that there is only one copy of the subform, which is stored as an independent object in the database, although it may be linked to two or more other forms and reports. In most cases, it is impractical to use the same subform in a data entry form and in a report, because the two environments usually demand different display attributes. If you create a report from a form simply because it is so convenient to use the main/subform FormWizard, you can modify the subform to suit the requirements of the report. If you want to also use the original form for data entry, you will usually want to make a copy of the subform, modify the copy, and substitute the copy for the original subform in the report (as was done to create the form in Figure 8.37). Chapter 10 describes how to change the data source for any control on a report or form, including a subform.

Another logical way to structure a multitable report based on two tables that have a one-to-many relationship is to start with a groups/totals layout that prints the desired fields from the child table and expand the group header section to accommodate the data from the parent table. This report structure parallels the one-to-many relationship between the tables. If the report group is based on the same field that defines the relationship between the tables, the group header is printed once for each discrete value in this field—that is, once for each record in the parent table—and the child records are printed in the detail section. You can use the ReportWizards to produce the basic layout. The most expedient way to set up the report is to use as the data source a query that includes all the fields you want on the report but choose only the child table fields in the field selection dialog box displayed by the ReportWizard. You can then modify the report to expand the group header section and add the data from the parent table. Figure 8.38 illustrates the first page of a report based on the Names and Transactions tables using this strategy.

Often, a groups/totals report based on two tables is sorted on the field that links the two tables (the ID Code field in the report in Figure 8.38). If you use this strategy to print a report based on a query that links two tables with an outer join rather than an equi-join, the query output grid should include the linking field from the parent table, not the child table. This is essential to ensure that the rows in the query dynaset that represent parent records with no matches in the child table appear in the correct order. For example, in a query based on an outer join between the Names and Transactions table, if you chose the ID Code field from the Transactions table rather than the Names table and sorted the output by ID Code, all the rows that represent Names table records with no matching transactions would sort first, grouped together at the top of the dynaset, because the ID Code field in these records would be empty (like all the other columns derived from the Transactions table).

Figure 8.38

A groups/totals report based on a multitable query

Transactions by Name

11-Nov-93

ALLENJE   Jerry Allen   **Telephone:**
564 Mission St.
San Francisco   CA   94105-2921

Type	Tran #	Date	Amount	Pmt Form	Reference
Purchase	14971	1/28/92	25.92	Check	Recycle T-shirts, Check #48
			25.92		

ALLENMA   Marilyn Allen   **Telephone:**
842 Palm Canyon Drive
Borrego Springs   CA   92004

Type	Tran #	Date	Amount	Pmt Form	Reference
Pledge payment	14933	12/28/91	250.00	Check	Pledge payment #1, Check #1283
Pledge	14932	12/28/91	1,000.00	Check	Pledge
Donation	14979	2/21/92	250.00	Check	Check #381
Pledge payment	15000	4/25/92	250.00	Check	Pledge payment #2, Check #1479
			1,750.00		

ANDERSMI   Michael Anderson   **Telephone:**   510   549-7838
The Ellis Street Garage
2906 Ellis Street
Berkeley   CA   94702

Type	Tran #	Date	Amount	Pmt Form	Reference
Total credits	14935	12/31/91	522.00		Total credits as of 12/31/91
Donation	14990	4/8/92	100.00	Check	Check #1005
			622.00		

ARNOLDME   Melvin H. Arnold   **Telephone:**
504 Parkview Dr.
Lake Elsinore   CA   92330

Type	Tran #	Date	Amount	Pmt Form	Reference
Total credits	14936	12/31/91	75.00		Total credits as of 12/31/91
			75.00		

1

Although the report in Figure 8.38 is quite simple, it can serve as a model for a variety of other reports that look quite different but share the same underlying data setup. For example, the report in Figure 8.38 contains exactly the same data as an account statement, and converting this report to a statement would require very few modifications (foremost among them would be the addition of a page break after each ID code group). To produce a statement (or, in an order-tracking database, an invoice), you could use a very similar query, with selection criteria based on the transaction date (and perhaps the transaction type).

Creating the Committee Memberships Report

To practice the report techniques outlined in this section, build a report that lists ACE committee memberships. This report will be based on an equi-join, so it will include only people who have served on at least one committee. First, create the query as follows:

1. Make sure that the Database window displays the list of queries (if necessary, click on the Query button or choose Queries from the View menu), and click on the New command button or press Alt+N.

2. Choose the Committees table and the Names table from the list in the Add Table dialog box, and then close the dialog box. If you defined the default relationships described earlier in this chapter, Access will join the tables for you based on the ID Code field.

3. If you do not see a join line between the ID Code fields in the two tables, position the mouse over the ID Code field in the Committees table, press and hold the left mouse button, drag the mouse over the ID Code field in the Names table, and release the mouse button.

4. Double-click on the title bar in the Committees field list to select all the fields, and drag all the fields to the output grid.

5. Add the Name, Company, Address, City, State, Zip, Area Code, and Telephone fields from the Names table to the output grid.

6. Close the query and enter **Committees and Names** when Access prompts you for the name.

Use the Access ReportWizards to build a groups/totals report based on the Committees and Names query as follows:

1. Make sure that the Database window displays the list of reports (if necessary, click on the Report button or choose Reports from the View menu), and click on the New command button or press Alt+N.

2. In the New Report dialog box, select Committees and Names from the Select A Table/Query combo box, and then click on the ReportWizards button or press Alt+W.

3. Choose Groups/Totals from the first ReportWizards dialog box.

4. In the field selection dialog box, choose the ID Code, Committee, Officer, Joined, Quit, and Notes fields (in that order).

5. Choose ID Code in the group selection dialog box, and retain the default grouping method (Normal) for the ID Code group.

6. In the sort order dialog box, choose Joined to sort the committee membership records for each person in chronological order.

7. Choose the Presentation look for the report.

8. Enter the title **Committee Memberships** in the last ReportWizards dialog box, and then click on the Print Preview command button to display the report. Your screen should look like Figure 8.39.

9. Save the report under the name **Committee Memberships**.

Figure 8.39

The first version of the Committee Memberships report

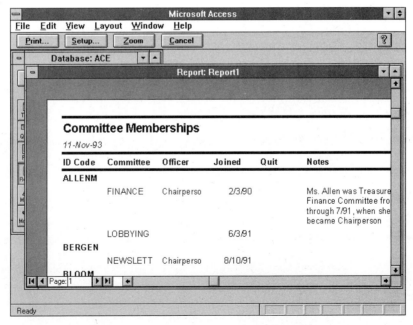

10. Open the report in Design view and examine the form created by the ReportWizard.

Chapter 10 describes how to add the name and address to the ID Code header section in the Committee Memberships report and how to add the full committee name to the detail section. You could use the same techniques to modify the Committee Membership Roster report created in Chapter 7 so that it includes the name and address of each member as well as the ID Code. Chapter 11 describes how to build more complex reports that include all the contact, transaction, and committee membership data for each person in the Names table.

Summary

This chapter outlined some basic strategies for working with more than one table at a time. A solid understanding of these techniques is essential for building real-world database applications, nearly all of which require more than one table. If you adhere to the design guidelines presented in Chapter 3 and create a table for each distinct entity in your application, you will find that even a simple application has more than one main table, as well as numerous small reference tables (like the Name Types and Committee Names tables in the ACE system), and more often than not, you will need to see information from more than one of these tables at a time. Conversely, if you feel confident that you can extract the information you need from three or four tables, you will be less likely to compromise on these design principles.

You can greatly simplify the mechanics of working with multiple tables by defining default relationships, stored in the database, to describe the linkages between the tables in a database. Defining the default relationships enables Access to deduce the right way to link two tables in a query and how to link a main form and subform in a composite data entry form based on a one-to-many relationship. For Access users at all levels, ranging from beginners to programmers, this convenience alone should be a compelling reason to define default relationships.

Whether to also enable the Enforce Referential Integrity option is a matter of discretion. If less experienced users will be entering data, this option helps preserve the proper relationships among the tables, but more advanced users may not want to be constrained by the referential integrity rules. If you decide not to use this option, remember that the responsibility for maintaining referential integrity lies entirely with you; you will have to ensure that identical values are entered into the linking fields in related tables, that you do not delete a parent record and leave "orphaned" records in the related child tables, and that any changes you make to the linking fields are propagated through all the matching records in all the affected tables. If you want more control rather than less, you can use techniques based on macros and modules (described in Chapters 18, 19, and 20) to add, change, or delete sets of records in two or more related tables.

This chapter emphasized the use of queries to link tables, and defining queries is the easiest and most flexible method available in Access for displaying or printing data from two or more tables. Chapter 9 illustrates some techniques for performing calculations based on data in two or more tables, again relying heavily on the Query Design tool. Remember as you read the rest of this book that a query can substitute for a table in nearly any context—it can serve as the data source for a form, a report, or anotmher query. Many of the queries used as illustrations in this book include only the fields required to illustrate a particular principle. In your own applications, you may prefer to include enough fields from all the source tables that a given query can serve several different purposes.

As noted briefly in this chapter, displaying or printing data from multiple tables is easy, while *updating* information in the dynaset of a multitable query is subject to some additional restrictions. In the default Datasheet view, these limitations were designed to protect data from unintentional damage by users who do not fully understand the table relationships. In custom forms, you can modify these restrictions or remove them entirely if you wish, using techniques described in Chapters 10 and 12.

9

Performing
Calculations

Building Expressions

*Compiling Summary
Statistics*

Updating Tables

Y OU HAVE ALREADY HAD A VERY BRIEF EXPOSURE TO PERFORMING
calculations in Access in Chapter 5, which described how to add calculated columns to a query. In a real application, you will need to
carry out more complex calculations on values of many different
data types—Text, Date/Time, and Yes/No, as well as the various numeric data
types—and in order to do so you must learn how to construct the expressions
that define them. As you design increasingly sophisticated queries, you will
also need to write more complex expressions to define the selection criteria.
This chapter presents an in-depth survey of all of the components that you
can use in Access expressions, including operators, identifiers, and functions,
and describes how to build expressions to manipulate values of all data types.

This chapter also introduces several techniques for calculating summary
statistics comparable to those printed in the group footer and report footer
sections of a groups/totals report. As you may already suspect, the easiest way
to carry out all of these calculations is by defining a query. Using a type of
query known as a *totals query*, you can compute a variety of statistics, including sums, counts, averages, and standard deviations, based on all or selected
records in a table or for multiple groups of records. The Query Design tool
also supports an easy mechanism for generating *crosstabs*, or *cross-tabulations*,
which compute the value of a single summary statistic for each possible combination of two different variables.

Finally, this chapter describes how to define *update queries*, which—unlike
select, totals, and crosstab queries—permanently update the contents of fields
in one or more tables. You can use update queries to carry out mass updates
on all or selected records, provided that you know how to write the expressions that describe the desired changes.

The examples in this chapter are all based on queries, because using a
query is the easiest and fastest way to test a variety of expressions in a very
flexible, responsive environment. In a real application, query datasheets are
just one of many vehicles that you will use to display the results of calculations. Chapter 10 describes how to add calculated values, including summary
statistics, to Access reports and forms, and many additional examples are presented throughout the remainder of this book.

Building Expressions

In a typical Access database application, you will need to perform far more
complex calculations than the simple arithmetic used in the queries described
in Chapter 5, and to do so you must learn to write the *expressions* that describe these calculations. As noted briefly in Chapter 5, an expression may be
made up of *constants*, *operators*, *object identifiers* (such as field names), and
functions, all combined according to the rules of Access syntax. (Don't worry
if any of these terms are unfamiliar to you—they are all defined and described

in more detail in this chapter.) Expressions can range in complexity from the short and simple [Total Credits]–[Total Debits] used to compute a donor's balance to considerably longer, more complex expressions involving many fields and functions.

To many people, the terms "calculation" and "expression" have mathematical connotations, but keep in mind as you study this chapter that arithmetic calculations represent just a small subset of the ways you can manipulate data stored in Access tables. For example, you can subtract two dates or times to obtain the elapsed time, and you can concatenate (add together) text strings such as a first name and last name or city, state, and zip code. If it seems strange to apply the term *calculation* to operations performed on Date/Time or Text fields, it might help to think of the terms *operation*, *manipulation*, and *transformation* as synonyms, which might be used interchangeably with *calculation*.

An expression can incorporate elements of different data types, subject to the rules that govern the use of Access operators and functions, but regardless of the number and complexity of its component parts, *an expression always evaluates to a single value of a particular data type*. For example, adding or subtracting two numbers produces another number. However, adding a number to a date or time yields a Date/Time value, and subtracting two dates or times yields a numeric value (the number of days between the two dates). You can use an expression wherever a single value of the output data type is permitted—to define the default value for a field in a table, to describe a validation condition, to define the contents of a column in a query, to display a calculated value on a data entry form or print it on a report, to name just a few.

Chapter 5 also introduced another type of expression that you might not recognize as such if you have not studied logic or programming—*logical expressions*, which evaluate to the logical values Yes (True) or No (False). (The terms "True" and "False" are more commonly used in logic, mathematics, and programming jargon, but may be less intuitive than "Yes" and "No" to nonprogrammers.) You can think of logical expressions as *conditions*, because they are used to describe *the conditions under which data should be selected or accepted*. For example, in a query, entering >=#1/1/93# in the column that represents the Joined field in the ACE Names table forms a condition that selects records in which the date in the Joined field is on or after January 1, 1993. Note that >=#1/1/93# does not represent a complete logical expression, which normally consists of two values separated by an operator—for example, Joined>=#1/1/93#. In the QBE grid (and in several other contexts in Access covered later in this chapter), the field name on the left side of the operator is implied, rather than stated explicitly, by your placement of the condition in the Joined column in the QBE grid. When Access executes the query, it evaluates this expression for each record in the underlying table and includes in the query dynaset only records in which it evaluates to True (Yes).

Your experience with queries should stand you in good stead when you begin experimenting with expressions, because the easiest and fastest way to try out the results of evaluating a variety of expressions is to use them to define calculated columns in a query. Try to choose a fairly small table (that is, one with few records) that includes fields with a variety of data types. The ACE Names table is a good example: Because it has only 100 records, any query you define should execute very quickly, and the table includes most of the Access data types. If you want to use this technique to test the expressions used as examples in this chapter, you might want to take a moment now to create a query based on the ACE Names table or on a similar table from your own database.

Identifying Data Types and Objects

To evaluate an expression, Access must be able to determine the data type of each component, as well as the type of object that each *identifier*, or name, represents. For example, if you were to enter Date in an expression on a form, Access would have to determine whether this identifier referred to a field named Date, a table named Date, a control named Date, a form named Date, or a constant text string four characters long.

Access always knows the data type of any field, because it is stored in the table structure. As noted in Chapter 5, Access can often determine the data type of a literal (constant) value from the context in which it is used. For example, when you enter a single value in the Criteria row in the QBE grid, Access assumes that the data type matches that of the field or expression in the column. When the data type of a Text constant is not obvious from the context, you must enclose it within single or double quotes (' or "). The pound sign (#) serves the same purpose for Date/Time values. No special delimiters are required for Yes/No values or for any of the numeric data types—Access always interprets the single words Yes, No, True, False, On, and Off as logical constants (you must use quotes around these words when you use them as Text constants), and it treats any value that begins with a digit, decimal point, plus sign (+), or minus sign (−) as a number.

The same considerations apply to determining what type of object an identifier represents. For example, the identifier Names might refer to a field, a table, a query, a report, a form, a macro, or a module. You already know that in a query, field names are identified by enclosing them in square brackets (which are optional if the field name does not include any embedded spaces). In fact, fields are just one of many types of Access objects, and the square brackets are used throughout Access as a delimiter for object identifiers. You may recall from Chapters 6 and 7 that every object in an Access form or report has a name; you must use this name, enclosed in square brackets if it contains spaces, to refer to the object in an expression in the same form.

To refer to a field in another form or report—for example, to refer to a field in a subform in the expression that defines the value of a calculated value in the main form—you must include both the form name and the object name, as well as an identifier that differentiates between forms and reports. To separate the components of complex object identifiers, you use exclamation points (!) and periods (.). For example, to refer to an object named Address on an independent form (not a subform) called Prospects, you would use the expression

```
Forms![Prospects]![Address]
```

If the Address object were located on a report rather than a form, the equivalent expression would be

```
Reports![Prospects]![Address]
```

Finally, you can refer to object properties in an expression by writing the name of the object and the name of the property, separated by a period. For example, [Name].FontName refers to the Font Name property of an object called Name. When you refer to an object in a subform, it is treated as a *property* of the subform. Thus, you would refer to an object called Total on a subform named Transactions as

```
[Transactions].Form![Total]
```

This rather intimidating notation is described further in Chapters 10, 11, and 12, and the use of properties in expressions is explored in more detail in Part III in the chapters on macros and Access Basic programming.

Using Operators

Chapter 5 briefly introduced the familiar arithmetic operators, as well as the relational (comparison) and logical operators used to write logical expressions (conditions). Table 9.1 presents a more complete list of all the Access operators, the allowable data types for the *operands* (the values on both sides of the operator), and the operations they perform.

Table 9.1   Access Operators

Calculation Operators

Symbol	Data Types	Meaning
+	All numeric	Addition
	Text, Memo	Text string concatenation
	Date/Time	Adds number of days to a date or time
−	All numeric	Subtraction
	Date/Time–numeric	Subtracts number of days from a date or time
	Date/Time–Date/Time	Calculates elapsed time in days between two dates or times
*	All numeric	Multiplication
/	All numeric	Division
\	Integer, Counter	Integer division (integer portion of the result of dividing one integer by another)
^	All numeric	Exponentiation (raising a number to a power)
Mod	All numeric	Modulus (remainder resulting from dividing one number by another)
&	Text, Memo	Text string concatenation

Comparison Operators (All apply to all data types except OLE Object)

Operator	Meaning
=	Equal to
<>	Not equal to
>	Greater than
>=	Greater than or equal to
<	Less than
<=	Less than or equal to
Between...And	Between two values (inclusive)
In	In a list of values
Is Null	Is null (has no value)
Like	Matches pattern that can include wildcards

Table 9.1   **Access Operators (Continued)**

Logical Operators

Operator	Meaning
And	Both
Or	One or both
Not	Not
Xor	One, but not both
Eqv	Logically equivalent (both True or both False)
Imp	Logical implication

The addition (+), subtraction (–), multiplication (*), and division (/) operators behave as you would expect from your experience with doing arithmetic on paper or using a calculator. If you have little experience with mathematics or programming, the other mathematical operators may be unfamiliar. The exponentiation operator raises the number that precedes it to a power specified by the number that follows it (that is, multiplies the number by itself the specified number of times). For example, the expression 3^4 evaluates to 3 raised to the 4th power (3*3*3*3, or 81). You may be more accustomed to seeing exponentiation written using superscript notation—for example, 3^4. Although it is technically possible to reproduce this notation on the screen in a graphical environment like Windows, entering it would be far less convenient than using the ^ operator, and in a small font, an expression like 3^4 could easily be misread as the number 34.

The \ operator carries out *integer division*, which yields the integer portion (the result of dropping any fractional part) of the result of dividing one integer by another. If either operand is not an integer, Access rounds it off to the nearest integer before carrying out the division. For example, to evaluate the expression 164.25\6.8, Access rounds off 164.25 to 164, rounds off 6.8 to 7, divides 164 by 7, and drops the fractional portion of the result (23.429) to yield 23. The Mod operator (which is represented by the % symbol in some other programming languages) yields the *remainder* that results from an integer division. For example, 164 Mod 7 is 3 (if you were forbidden to use fractions, you would say that 164/7 is 23, leaving a remainder of 3). You can use the \ and Mod operators to convert between different units of measure. For example, to convert days to weeks and days, you could use the \ operator to compute the number of weeks, and the Mod operator to calculate the number of additional days: 164 days is 23 weeks (164\7) and 3 days (164 Mod 7).

One very common operation that has no real analog in manual information management systems is text *concatenation*, which is symbolized in Access by the & operator (in some contexts, the + operator is also permitted, but for the sake of consistency, it is not recommended). Concatenating text strings "adds" them together so that the beginning of the second string immediately follows the end of the first with no intervening spaces. The ability to so easily combine text strings allows you to structure your tables efficiently, placing each discrete item of information in a separate field, without sacrificing the ability to use them together when necessary. For example, in the reports produced by the mailing label ReportWizard, Access uses the & operator to combine items that you place on the same line of the label into a single expression. If you edit the Name and Address Labels report in the ACE database (which was created using the ReportWizard), you will see that the city/state/zip line was constructed by combining five text strings (three fields and two constant text strings), using the following expression

```
[City]&", "&[State]&"  "&[Zip]
```

Unlike some other programs, Access is very lenient about combining text strings with values of other data types. For example, you can concatenate a constant text string that stores a prompt message with a Date/Time or numeric field in expressions such as

```
"Last Contact Date"&[Last Contact]
```

or

```
"Balance is "&[Total Credits]-[Total Debits]
```

In forms and reports, expressions like these are rarely necessary—it is easier to display the balance in a text box with an attached label (like the text boxes in a single-column report layout). However, you might use this technique to print a number or date on the same line as a Text field on a mailing label. For example, to print the last renewal date on the Name line, you could use the expression

```
[Name]&"      "&[Last Renewal]
```

Note. Although you can use the + operator to concatenate two text strings, you *must* use & to combine values of different data types.

You can carry out simple date arithmetic calculations by using the same + and − operators you rely upon to add and subtract numbers. Access allows you to add a number to a date or subtract a number from a date to yield a date a specified number of days in the future or past. For example, in a query based on the Transactions or Contacts table, the expression [Date]+14 evaluates to the calendar date 14 days after the date stored in the Date field. You might also use this expression in a macro that fills in the default value for the

FollowUp field in a form used to update the Contacts table, so that the follow-up date is automatically set to two weeks from the contact date (using techniques described in Chapter 18). On an invoice for a customer with payment terms of net 30 days, you could use a similar expression based on the invoice date to print the due date. If you subtract two dates, the result is a number that represents the number of days between the two dates. Exactly the same operations are permitted with Date/Time values that represent times or dates and times.

To make good use of Access' date/time arithmetic capabilities, you must understand that Date/Time values are stored internally as numbers in which the integer portion represents the date and the fractional portion the time. When you subtract Date/Time values that include times (or that only represent times, as in a scheduling or time-keeping application), you may obtain results like 10.25 (ten days and six hours) or 0.33333333 (eight hours). You can use the Format function (which is described later in this chapter) to display the results of such calculations in a more presentable and useful format. You can also use the DateAdd and DateDiff functions to carry out date calculations and display the results in any convenient units (for example, months, weeks, or hours).

Using Functions

A *function* is a named operator that allows you to perform more complex calculations and data manipulations than the simple operators listed in Table 9.1. *Every function accepts specific types of input and returns as output a single value of a specific data type.* To take a simple example drawn from mathematics, the Sqr (square root) function takes a number or any expression that evaluates to a number as input and returns as output the square root of this number (a number which, when multiplied by itself, yields the original number). You can visualize a function as a kind of "black box"—a machine that accepts a specific type of raw materials as input, processes this input, and cranks out a particular product as output. Functions enable you to perform complex calculations and data transformations that would otherwise be difficult or impossible, or which you simply do not know how to carry out manually (although you may have learned a manual method for extracting square roots in school).

To include an Access function in an expression, you write the function name, followed by the inputs to the function enclosed in parentheses. Function inputs are sometimes called *arguments* (a term derived from mathematical terminology). You can write the function name in any mixture of upper- and lowercase; the examples in this book conform to the conventions used in the Access manuals—every function name begins with a capital letter and consists primarily of lowercase letters, except that in function names composed of two or more words or abbreviations (for example, DateAdd and DateDiff, which are described in this section), additional letters are capitalized to improve readability. Access permits a space between the function name and the left parenthesis that follows (many other programming languages do not), but your expressions will be less ambiguous if you omit this optional space.

Remember that *a function evaluates to a single value of a particular data type, and you can use a function reference anywhere that Access permits a value of this data type.* For example, you could use the square root of 36 in an expression by writing the function reference Sqr(36), and you could compute the square root of the Total Credits field with the expression Sqr([Total Credits]). Although the latter calculation makes little sense in the ACE application, the expression Sqr([Total Credits]) is syntactically correct—the input to the Sqr function can be any numeric value. However, attempting to extract the square root of a Text or Date/Time value will yield an error message (for example, in a query, Access displays "#Error" in the output column).

When a function requires more than one input, you must list the inputs in a specific order, separated by commas, within the parentheses that follow the function name. For example, the Pmt function, which calculates the periodic payment on an amortized loan, takes five inputs: the periodic interest rate, the total number of payment periods, the loan amount, the value of the loan at the end of the loan term, and a number that specifies when the payment is due (0 if the payment is due at the end of each period or 1 if it is due at the beginning). To calculate the monthly payment on a $12,000 loan amortized over five years (60 months) at 9 percent annual interest (.75 percent or .0075 per month), you would use the expression Pmt(.0075,60,12000,0,1).

Not every function requires that you provide explicit input and, in fact, some functions do not permit any. For example, the Date function (written as Date( )) evaluates to the current date, the Time function (written as Time( )) yields the current time, and the Now function (written as Now( )) evaluates to the current date and time. All of these functions obtain their input by reading the system clock and therefore require no input from you. Although in some contexts Access allows you to omit the parentheses, in most cases they are required, and it is good practice to *always* include them to unambiguously identify every function reference, especially if you have fields with the same names (for example, the ACE Contacts and Transactions tables have fields named Date). Thus, in a query based on the Transactions table, you could compute the age of a transaction in days with the expression Date( )–[Date].

Although Access offers a number of mathematical and trigonometric functions, most business applications do not require very complex math. More often, you will use functions for manipulating text strings, performing date and time calculations, or formatting other computed results to render them more useful or more presentable. Three functions are particularly handy for manipulating dates and times: DatePart, which evaluates to one portion of a date or time; DateAdd, which returns the result of adding a given interval to a date or time; and DateDiff, which returns the result of subtracting two dates or times, expressed in terms of a particular time interval. One of the inputs to all of these functions is a character string that represents the time interval, using the following abbreviations:

Abbreviation	Time Interval
yyyy	Year(s)
q	Quarter(s)
m	Month(s)
y	Day of the year (1 for January 1, 2 for January 2, and so on)
d	Day(s)
w	Day of the week (1 for Sunday, 2 for Monday, and so on)
ww	Week(s)
h	Hour(s) (based on a 24-hour clock)
n	Minute(s)
s	Second(s)

You can use the DateAdd function to add a given interval to a Date/Time value or, despite the connotations of the name, subtract an interval from a date or time. For example, determining the date exactly three months after or six months prior to a given date is not easy using simple date arithmetic, because the calculation must take into account the fact that not all months are equal in length. The DateAdd function takes three inputs: the text string that represents the interval, the number of intervals you want to add or subtract (negative numbers represent subtraction), and the date. For example, you could compute the calendar date two months prior to the date stored in the Last Contact field in the Names table with the expression

```
DateAdd("m",-2,[Last Contact])
```

The DateDiff function accepts as input an interval and two Date/Time values, and returns as output the result of subtracting the first date or time from the second, expressed in terms of the specified interval. For example, to calculate the number of weeks since the last contact, you could use the expression

```
DateDiff("ww",[Last Contact],Date())
```

If the order of the dates in this expression seems backward, it might help to think of this function as calculating the distance between the two dates on a time line, in which earlier dates are to the left of later dates, or as the elapsed time *from* the first date *to* the second.

The DatePart function takes two inputs—an interval and a date—and returns as output the specified portion of the date. For example, the expression DatePart("w",[Date]) evaluates to the day of the week (1 for Sunday, 2 for Monday, and so one) on which the date stored in the Date field falls, and DatePart("m",[Date]) yields the month (also expressed as a number). Access also offers a group of more specific functions that serve similar purposes—the Day, Weekday, Month, Year, Hour, Minute, and Second extract the specified portion of a Date/Time value. For example, the expression Hour([Appointment Time]) yields the hour portion of the time stored in a field called Appointment Time (15 for an appointment at 3:30 p.m.).

The IIf function enables you to make simple decisions by testing a condition and choosing one of two different values as output, depending on the outcome. This function, whose name means *immediate if*, takes three inputs: the condition to be tested, the value you want the function to return if the condition evaluates to Yes (True), and the value you want the function to return if the condition evaluates to No (False). (If you have used spreadsheet programs, note that the Access IIf function is identical to the @IF function in Lotus 1-2-3 and the IF function in Excel.) You might use this function to print two different messages on an invoice or statement, depending on the amount due. For example, if the invoice amount is stored in a field called [Invoice Amount] and the prepayment (if any) is stored in a field called [Prepayment], you could use the following expression to label the net amount:

```
IIf([Invoice Amount]>[Prepayment],"Amount due",
"No payment due")
```

In this expression, the condition compares the invoice and payment amounts. If the invoice amount exceeds the amount paid, the condition evaluates to True, and the output of the function is the first message, "Amount due." Otherwise, it evaluates to the second message, "No payment due."

If you are really interested in only one of the two values, you can use an empty string—a text string of length 0, expressed as "" (a pair of quotes with no text in between)—to represent the other. For example, to print the message "Overdue" if more than 30 days have elapsed since an invoice date and print nothing if the invoice is not overdue, you could use the expression

```
IIf(Date()-[Date]>30,"Overdue","")
```

As you can see from this last example, you can use one function as input to another. This ability to *nest* functions (place one function reference inside another) is not exceptional—the input to a function can be any expression that evaluates to a value of the required data type, including a constant, a field name, the result of evaluating another function, or in fact any other expression. To take another simple example, you could modify the previous example to test for an invoice more than one month old (rather than 30 days old) by using the DateDiff function, as in the expression

```
IIf(DateDiff("m",[Date],Date())>=1,"Overdue","")
```

These examples barely begin to scratch the surface of what you can accomplish with functions. Access offers a wide array of functions, which are listed in the Access documentation, in the Help system and in Appendix C of this book. Some of the functions are useful only to programmers, but many will prove valuable in the interactive environment. If you have used functions in other languages or programs—for example, if you have used spreadsheets—you will find many Access functions familiar and will quickly add many new functions to your repertoire. If the concept is new to you, you may be overwhelmed by the sheer number of functions. Don't try to memorize too many at once—periodically browsing through one of the aforementioned function references will bring functions to your attention that you overlooked previously because you had no need for them. Many additional examples and usage suggestions for Access functions are presented throughout the remainder of this book.

Adhering to the Rules of Precedence

When Access evaluates a complex expression, it does not simply proceed from left to right. Instead, it performs the indicated operations in an order governed by the rules of *precedence*. To ensure that your expressions produce the results you intended, you must understand these rules. When it evaluates an expression, Access processes the components in the following order:

1. Function evaluation

2. Arithmetic operators:

    1. Exponentiation

    2. Negation

    3. Multiplication and division from left to right

    4. Integer division

    5. Mod calculations

    6. Addition and subtraction from left to right

3. String concatenation

4. Comparison operators from left to right

5. Logical operators:

    1. Not

    2. And

    3. Or

    4. Xor

    5. Eqv

    6. Imp

To adhere to this order of precedence, Access may have to scan through a complex expression several times. If you have never encountered the concept of precedence before, you may not be prepared for the fact that the result of evaluating an expression according to these rules is often *different* from the value obtained by simply proceeding from left to right. For example, suppose you wanted to calculate the profit margin on an inventory item by subtracting your cost (stored in a field named Cost) from the selling price (stored in a field named Price) and dividing the result by the selling price. For an item that costs you $3 and sells for $4, the profit margin is .25 (25 percent). If you wrote the expression as [Price]–[Cost]/[Price], Access would perform the division *before* the subtraction—that is, it would divide the cost by the price and subtract the result (.75) from the price, to yield 3.25 (or 325%).

Problems like this are particularly insidious because the erroneous expression is often syntactically correct and yields a legitimate result (as in this example), so Access does not display any warning or error message. If you do not carefully examine the query or report in which you used such expressions, you might not notice the problem for some time. However, this example should point up the necessity for the rules of precedence—in a different context, you might in fact need to perform the division first, and Access must provide a way to differentiate between all the possible orders of evaluation, which in a complex expression may number considerably more than two.

You can override the default rules of precedence by using parentheses in an expression. Access always begins within the innermost set of parentheses and works its way outward, treating the result of evaluating each expression enclosed in parentheses as a single value. Thus, the correct way to write the expression that defines the profit margin is ([Price]–[Cost])/[Price]. You can nest parentheses (include one expression in parentheses entirely within another) as deeply as necessary to specify the correct order of evaluation. This fact has a beneficial side effect—if you forget the rules of precedence, you can simply add extra parentheses to force Access to evaluate an expression in the order you intended.

Formatting Calculated Values

If you have tried any of the examples presented thus far in this chapter or experimented with calculated columns in your own queries, you are undoubtedly already dissatisfied with the default display formats used for calculated numeric and Date/Time data. For example, all numbers except integers are displayed in General Number format, whereas you would almost always prefer a display format with a fixed number of decimal places so that all the values in a column of numbers line up. You can solve some of these problems by using the Format function, which allows you to specify the display format for both fields (to override the display format stored in the table structure) and calculated values.

The Format function takes two inputs: the expression that yields the value you want to format, and a literal text string (enclosed in single or double quotes) that describes the display format. If you want to use one of the standard formats available for fields (that is, one of the valid entries for the Format property in the table structure), you can simply refer to it by name. For example, to display a donor's balance in a query dynaset using the Currency format (with a currency symbol, two decimal places, separators every three digits, and negative numbers enclosed in parentheses), you could specify the contents of the column in the QBE grid as

```
Balance:Format([Total Credits]-[Total Debits],"Currency")
```

If you need to review the available format choices, they are listed in Table 3.1.

If none of the predefined formats suits your needs, you can define a custom display format by combining the symbols and abbreviations listed in Table 9.2. You might think of a custom format string as a kind of template, or pattern, that Access applies to the data. Each component of the format string represents either one character position in a numeric or Text value or one component in a Date/Time value. For example, to display numeric values up to $9,999,999.99 with a leading dollar sign, embedded comma separators, and two decimal places, and always at least one digit to the left of the decimal point, you could use the format string $#,###,##0.00. The format string 0.0000% displays a calculated ratio as a percent with four decimal places.

NOTE. *In all format strings, you can add a –, +, $, (,), or space by typing it explicitly. All other special symbols (including the backslash) must be enclosed in quotes or preceded by a backslash (\).*

Table 9.2   The Format String Symbols

Symbol	Meaning
Numeric Values	
Empty string	No formatting
0	Display a digit if present or a zero if not, including all leading and trailing zeroes
#	Display a digit if present and drop all leading and trailing zeroes
. (period)	Insert decimal point
%	Multiply the value by 100 and add a % sign in the specified position
, (comma)	Insert a comma if there is a digit on both sides
E–, E+, e–, or e+	Display in exponential notation. E– and e– display a minus sign before negative exponents; E+ and e+ display a plus or minus sign before all exponents.
*	Use the following character as a fill character to fill any empty space in the display format
Date Values	
: (colon)	Insert a colon between hours and minutes or between minutes and seconds
/	Insert a slash between day and month or month and year
d	Display the day as a number between 1 and 31
dd	Display the day as a number between 1 and 31 with a leading 0 for numbers less than 10
ddd	Display the day name as a three-letter abbreviation
dddd	Display the day name spelled out in full
ddddd	Display full date in Windows Short Date format (usually m/d/yy)
dddddd	Display full date in Windows Long Date format with day and month names spelled out in full
w	Display the day of the week as a number between 1 and 7
ww	Display the week of the year as a number between 1 and 52
m	Display the month as a number between 1 and 12
mm	Display the month as a number between 1 and 12 with a leading 0 for numbers less than 10

Table 9.2 **The Format String Symbols (Continued)**

Symbol	Meaning
mmm	Display the month name as a three-letter abbreviation
mmmm	Display the month name spelled out in full
q	Display the quarter of the year as a number between 1 and 4
y	Display the day of the year as a number between 1 and 366
yy	Display the year as a two-digit number
yyyy	Display the year as a four-digit number
h	Display the hour as a number between 0 and 23
hh	Display the hour as a number between 0 and 23 with a leading 0 for numbers less than 10
n	Display the minutes as a number between 0 and 59
nn	Display the minutes as a number between 0 and 59 with a leading 0 for numbers less than 10
s	Display the seconds as a number between 0 and 59
ss	Display the seconds as a number between 0 and 59 with a leading 0 for numbers less than 10
ttttt	Display full time in Windows Time format (usually h:mm:ss)
AM/PM	Display time using 12-hour clock, followed by AM or PM
am/pm	Display time using 12-hour clock, followed by am or pm
A/P	Display time using 12-hour clock, followed by A or P
a/p	Display time using 12-hour clock, followed by a or p
AMPM	Display contents of the 1159 or 2359 string in the WIN.INI file using 12-hour clock
c	Display the date portion in ddddd format and the time in ttttt format

Text String Values

@	Display a character if present or a space otherwise, filling in characters from right to left by default
&	Display a character if present, filling in characters from right to left by default

Table 9.2	The Format String Symbols (Continued)
Symbol	**Meaning**
<	Convert to lowercase
>	Convert to uppercase
!	Fill in characters from left to right instead of right to left

The Format function is especially useful for displaying dates and times, in part because the standard formats are less likely to satisfy all of your requirements. Also, as is the case with computed numeric values, you *must* use this function to format calculated dates and times. By combining the symbols in Table 9.2, you can easily construct custom Date/Time formats. For example, the format string mm/yy displays just the month and year, and the format string d-mmmm-yyyy defines a format similar to the Medium Date format (which would be described as d-mmm-yy) but with the month name spelled out in full and a four-digit year. If you want to make sure that all the dates in a column line up, you can use the format string mm/dd/yy, which adds leading zeroes to day and month numbers less than ten, instead of short date format. To display an appointment time as just the day name and the time (for example, Tuesday 2:30 pm), you could use the string dddd h:mm am/pm.

Remember that to include any literal characters not listed in Table 9.2 in a format string, you must enclose them in quotation marks. Thus, to display a date in a format similar to Long Date but without the day of the week, you must enclose the comma and space in quotes in the format string, which could be written mmmm d", "yyyy. Because there are double quotes within the format string, the entire format string must be enclosed in single quotes when you use it as input to the Format function, as follows:

```
Format([Last Contact], 'mmmm d", "yyyy')
```

Access provides a few custom format symbols for text strings. The > and < symbols, which were introduced briefly in Chapter 3, display a text string in all uppercase or all lowercase letters, respectively. To specify a more detailed display format, you can build a custom format string in which each character position is represented by a @ or & symbol. If you use @, Access adds a space for every blank character position, so the resulting string always has the same length; if you use the & symbol, the string is only as long as the number of characters you actually enter. You can use custom formats to automatically insert the punctuation in telephone numbers and Social Security numbers. For example, using the format string @@@-@@@@ to describe the display format for a telephone number would enable you to enter it as seven digits without typing the dash.

The simple examples presented thus far define a single format that Access applies to all possible values for the field or query column it describes. If you need more flexibility, you can include up to four different parts in a numeric format string, separated by semicolons, which Access uses as follows:

One section   Applies to all values.

Two sections   The first applies to positive and zero values.

                  The second applies to negative values.

Three sections   The first applies to positive values.

                  The second applies to negative values.

                  The third applies to zero values.

Four sections   The first applies to positive values.

                  The second applies to negative values.

                  The third applies to zero values.

                  The fourth applies to null values.

One very common application for these complex format strings is defining different display formats for positive, negative, and zero values. For example, to display negative values enclosed in parentheses rather than with a leading minus sign, you could use the format string

```
#,###,##0.00;(#,###,##0.00)
```

If you omit any section, Access assumes that it is the same as the first section. To omit a section *between* two others, you must include a semicolon as a placeholder for each of the missing sections. For example, you could use the following format string to display positive and negative values in a style similar to the built-in Standard format but display 0 as "Zero" and null values as "N/A":

```
#,###,##0.00;;"Zero";"N/A"
```

A custom text format string can include two parts, the first of which is applied to non-null values and the second to null values.

NOTE.   *You cannot include any of the built-in formats (such as Currency or Short Date) in a format string with more than one section; instead, you must construct the equivalent format using the symbols in Table 9.2 (for example, m/d/yy for Short Date).*

The custom format strings described in this section are not limited to use in the Format function—you can enter the same strings (*not* enclosed in quotes) for the Format property in a table structure, and as you will see in Chapter 10, for the corresponding property for a field or calculated field on a form or report. In these contexts, but unfortunately *not* in the Format function, you can add a color name (Black, Blue, Green, Cyan, Red, Magenta, Yellow, or White), enclosed in square brackets, to any component of the format string. For example, you could modify the format string in the previous example as follows to display positive values in black, negative values in red, and zero and null values in blue:

```
#,###,##0.00;#,###,##0.00[Red];"Zero"[Blue];"N/A"[Blue]
```

Think carefully about whether you want to use formats to insert punctuation into a field (for example, the @@@-@@@@ format for a telephone number), because Access does not store the punctuation with the data. Thus, a telephone number field entered with this format contains just the seven digits you actually typed, and you must use the Format function to insert the dash every time you display or print it. Unless the format is essential for preventing invalid entries into the table, it is usually more inconvenient than helpful.

Compiling Summary Statistics

All of the expressions presented thus far in this chapter carry out calculations based on one record in a table or one row in a query dynaset. If you use an expression to define a calculated column in a query, Access performs the calculation for each row in the query dynaset. In a form, the same expression displays the results of the calculation for each record displayed using the form. Access also offers several methods for compiling summary statistics based on some or all of the records in a table or query dynaset. For example, you can calculate sums and averages of any numeric value for an entire dynaset, for a group of records described by selection criteria that you specify, or for each group of records in a report that includes record grouping instructions. All of these methods make use of the Access *aggregate operators* and the corresponding *aggregate functions* to compute the statistics.

Note. Do not confuse the Min and Max operators, which find the lowest and highest values in a field, with the First and Last operators, which find the values in the first and last records in the dynaset (or group), based on the order specified by any sorting instructions in the query.

If you only need to see the summary statistics (not the individual detail records that contribute to the totals), the easiest and most powerful method is to define a *totals query*. You can then view the statistics in the standard Datasheet view, or define a form or report based on the query to present them in a more attractive format. To create a totals query, select the Totals option from the View menu in Query Design view, or click on the Totals command button in the tool bar (the one with the Σ symbol on its face). If you have never seen this symbol before, note that it is the Greek letter sigma, which is commonly used in mathematics to represent sums. Access adds a new row to the output grid labeled Total, in which you describe the statistics you want to calculate by entering the aggregate operators listed in Table 9.3. The cells in the Totals row are combo boxes, and you can use the standard Windows methods to enter the aggregate operators: You can type them, select them from a drop-down list, or if the operator begins with a unique letter, type the first letter and move out of the cell (this method will not work for the very commonly used Sum operator because the StDev operator also begins with the letter S).

Table 9.3   **Using Aggregate Operators in Summary Statistics**

Aggregate Operator	Meaning	Data Types
Sum	Sum (total)	All numeric, Date/Time, Yes/No
Avg	Average (mean)	All numeric, Date/Time, Yes/No
Min	Minimum (smallest)	All numeric, Date/Time, Yes/No, Text
Max	Maximum (largest)	All numeric, Date/Time, Yes/No, Text
Count	Number of non-null values	All data types
StDev	Standard deviation	All numeric, Date/Time, Yes/No
Var	Variance	All numeric, Date/Time, Yes/No
First	Value from first row	All data types
Last	Value from last row	All data types

To compute statistics based on all the records in a table, you must build an output grid that has an aggregate operator in every column. Figure 9.1 illustrates a query based on the Names table that was designed to calculate the sum of the total debits, sum and average of the total credits, the total number of records, and the earliest and latest first contact dates. Figure 9.2 shows the result of running the query. As you can see in this figure, Access assigns column titles that combine the names of the aggregate operators and the fields on which the statistics are based. These names—SumOfTotal Debits, MinOfFirst Contact, and so on—are usually much wider than the columns would otherwise need to be to accommodate the computed statistics, and they are obscure and confusing to less experienced users. You can assign new titles as you would for any other calculated columns—by entering them before the field names in the Field row in the QBE grid. Figure 9.3 illustrates a new version of the query pictured in Figure 9.2 with more readable column titles.

Figure 9.1

A query that computes summary statistics based on an entire table

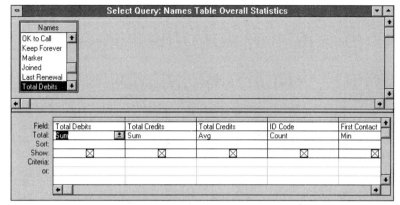

Figure 9.2

The output of the Names Table Overall Statistics query

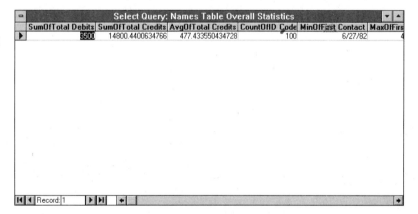

There is a very important difference between the dynaset of a query that includes only summary statistics (or indeed *any* summary statistics) and the dynasets of select queries like the ones described in Chapters 5 and 8. In a select query dynaset, every row is derived from one record in one of the underlying source tables (or queries). In the query in Figure 9.2 (and in Figure 9.4), the numbers in the single row in the dynaset are aggregate statistics derived from many (possibly all) of the records in the source table. Because each row in the dynaset does not represent a single record in an underlying table, you cannot edit any of the data displayed in a totals query dynaset.

Figure 9.3

Assigning more
readable column
titles for the
statistics

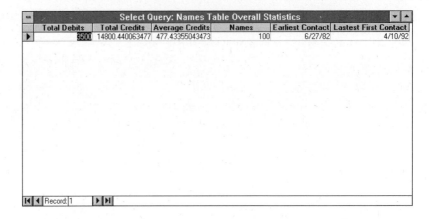

Figure 9.4

Calculating statistics
based on different
numbers of records

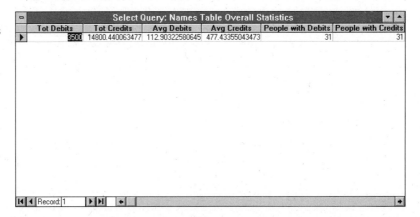

You may recall from Chapter 5 that Access differentiates between null and zero values in numeric fields. All of the Access aggregate operators implicitly exclude null values (but not zero values), and this distinction is crucial to correctly computing statistics such as averages and counts. For example, there are 100 records in the Names table. However, the computation of the average credits is based on the 31 records that have non-null values in the Total Credits field. Thus, the Average Credits column in the query represents *the average value for people who have credits*—the sum of the Total Credits field in the 31 records in which this field is not null divided by 31. This is nearly always the way you would want to calculate an average—if you were to divide the sum by 100 (the total number of records in the table), the average would reflect 69 records that are in fact irrelevant and would thus be much smaller than the true average. The difference is likely to be even more dramatic in a real application, when you will often need to compute statistics based on very small subsets of a large table.

If Access did not automatically exclude null values, you would have to write explicit selection criteria to do so, and often, this would force you to use multiple queries to produce summary statistics that Access can in fact calculate in a single query. Figure 9.4 illustrates a new version of the query in Figure 9.1 that includes a column for the average debits, as well as two new columns that count the number of records in which there are Total Debits and Total Credits entries. In the original query, the record count column was based on the ID Code field and thus displayed the number of records with non-null values in this field (that is, all the records in the Names table because the ID Code field is the primary key and cannot be null). By applying the same aggregate operator to several other fields in a table, you can determine how many records have non-null values in various fields. In the Names table, the same number of people have debits and credits (although either or both of these fields may be zero), so the two counts in Figure 9.4 are the same, but in another table, this might not be the case. For the same reason, the number of records that contribute to the averages in their respective columns might also be different.

You have also undoubtedly noticed that Access displays the results of performing mathematical calculations in General Number format. There are two problems with this format—it usually displays more decimal places than you would consider meaningful, and often two similar columns have different numbers of decimal places. The extra decimal places usually result from calculations that involve division (such as the computation of an average), but round-off errors (very small errors in the way that Single and Double numbers are stored) may produce the same results in simple sums, such as the Total Credits column in Figures 9.2 and 9.4. If you intend to display or print the query dynaset using a form or report, the easiest way to correct this problem is to specify a new display format for the text boxes that display the statistics on the form.

To format the statistics displayed in the query's Datasheet view, you must use the Format function, but doing so is not quite as straightforward as you might hope. You cannot use as input to the Format function the field name in the Field row of the output grid—the input must be the *result* of carrying out the statistical calculation. You must therefore abandon the aggregate operators entered in the Totals row of the output grid and substitute expressions based on the corresponding aggregate *functions*. These functions, which have the same names as the aggregate operators, each take one input— the expression on which you want to base the calculation. For example, the expression Sum([Total Credits]) computes the sum of the Total Credits field, and Avg([Total Debits]) computes the average of the Total Debits. Thus, you could calculate the average credits and display the result in Currency format by entering the following expression in the Field row of the output grid:

```
Avg Credits:Format(Avg([Total Credits]),"Currency")
```

When you define the summary calculation within the expression in the Field row, you must enter Expression in the Totals row. If the Totals row contains an aggregate operator when you run the query (which might easily happen if you edit a previously defined column to add the formatting instructions), Access displays an alert box like the one in Figure 9.5. This rather cryptic error message derives from the fact that internally, Access generates an expression based on an aggregate *function* for each aggregate *operator* in the query. Including both in the same column results in nesting aggregate functions, which is not permitted.

Figure 9.5

The error message displayed when you use an aggregate operator and an aggregate function together

You can also use aggregate functions to circumvent another limitation of totals queries—namely, the fact that you cannot base summary statistics directly on calculated columns. For example, you cannot compute the sum or average of the donor balances in the Names table by entering the expression that computes the balance in the Field row of the QBE grid and then entering Sum or Avg in the Total row. Instead, you must use an expression like the following in the Field row:

```
Balance:Sum([Total Debits]-[Total Credits])
```

To define a simple totals query based on the Transactions table, use the following steps:

1. Make sure that the Database window displays the list of queries, and click on the New command button or press Alt+N.

2. Choose the Transactions table from the Add Table dialog box, and then close this dialog box.

3. Select Totals from the View menu or click on the Totals button in the tool bar to add the Total row to the output grid.

4. Add two copies of the Amount and Date fields to the output grid.

5. In the Totals row, choose Sum in the first column, Avg in the second column, Min in the third column, and Max in the fourth column.

6. Edit the entry in the Field row for the first column to add the column title **Total Amount:** before the Amount field name.

7. Edit the entry in the Field row for the second column to add the column title **Average Amount:** before the Amount field name.

8. Edit the entry in the Field row for the third column to add the column title **Earliest Date:** before the Date field name.

9. Edit the entry in the Field row for the fourth column to add the column title **Latest Date:** before the Date field name.

10. Save the query under the name **Transaction Statistics**.

11. Execute the query. Your screen should look like Figure 9.6.

Figure 9.6

Running the Transaction Statistics query

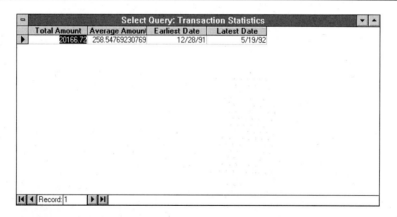

Computing Group Statistics

The queries in the previous section computed statistics based on all the records in the source table. Access also allows you to group records in a query and compute the same summary statistics *for each group*. Processing a query with groups is much like printing a groups/totals report, which also groups records based on one or more expressions and calculates summary statistics for each group. Each row in the dynaset of a totals query that includes groups is analogous to a group footer section in a groups/totals report, but unlike the report, the query dynaset does not include a "detail section." If you need to see the records in each group in addition to the summary statistics, you should in fact define a groups/totals report; Chapter 11 describes how to add statistics other than sums to the groups/totals reports generated by the ReportWizards.

You may have noticed that when you add a new column to a totals query, Access displays "Group By" in the Totals row. This entry (which you can also type directly or choose from the drop-down list), identifies the columns that define the groups. By default, Access checks the Show box for each column with Group By in the Totals row. You can uncheck this box if you wish, but it makes little sense to do so. Figure 9.7 illustrates a new query created by adding the State field to the query pictured in Figure 9.4 and removing one of the two columns that count records, and Figure 9.8 shows the result of running this query, with some of the column widths adjusted to match the data and the column headings. As in a report, you can define more than one record group. Figure 9.9 illustrates the result of adding the City field to the output grid as well, so that the query groups records by state and city, and each row in the dynaset represents one unique combination of state and city.

Figure 9.7

Defining a totals query with groups

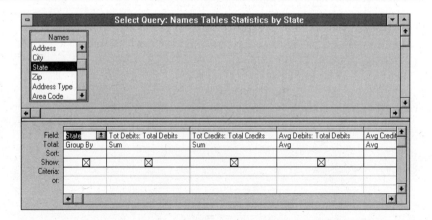

Access does not limit you to grouping records by individual fields—you can also base a group on the value of any expression. (As you will see in Chapter 11, the same is true of groups in reports.) For example, you could group records in the ACE Transactions or Contacts table by year by basing the groups on the expression DatePart("yyyy", [Date]).

Figure 9.8

The output of the Names Table Statistics by State query

State	Tot Debits	Tot Credits	Avg Debits	Avg Credits	People	Earliest Contact	Lastest First Contact
CA	2000	11898.94006	100	594.94700317	20	6/27/82	7/25/91
NV	0	75	0	37.5	2	1/20/84	8/2/90
OR	500	675	250	337.5	2	9/30/86	4/10/92
TX	1000	1540.5	250	385.125	4	8/12/82	11/28/91
UT	0	14	0	14	1	11/26/84	7/10/91
WA	0	597	0	298.5	2	1/1/80	8/22/91

Select Query: Names Table Statistics by State — Record: 1

Figure 9.9

A query with two groups

State	City	Tot Debits	Tot Credits	Avg Debits	Avg Credits	People	Earliest Contact	Lastest F
CA	Berkeley	1000	3767	250	941.75	4	9/30/82	
CA	Borrego Springs	1000	775	1000	775	1	8/12/82	
CA	Lake Elsinore	0	75	0	75	1	6/23/86	
CA	Long Beach					0	4/14/83	
CA	Los Angeles	0	3723.6001	0	3723.600098	1	10/8/82	1
CA	Oakland	0	264.460007	0	132.2300034	2	6/27/82	
CA	San Diego	0	75	0	75	1	9/14/84	
CA	San Francisco	0	2868.87996	0	478.1466599	6	8/12/82	
CA	San Jose	0	50	0	50	1	11/19/87	
CA	San Leandro					0		
CA	Santa Monica					0	12/7/83	
CA	Santa Rosa	0	50	0	50	1	2/24/83	
CA	Santee	0	150	0	150	1	1/27/86	
CA	Temecula					0	6/28/90	
CA	Venice	0	100	0	100	1	6/13/85	
NV	Carson City					0	1/1/88	
NV	Fernley					0	5/5/87	
NV	Las Vegas	0	25	0	25	1	2/10/90	

Select Query: Names Tables Statistics by State and City — Record: 1

In any totals query with groups, Access automatically sorts the output in ascending order by each of the grouping fields, starting with the one closest to the left side of the output grid and proceeding toward the right. You can override the default sort order by entering Descending in the Sort row. Note, however, that if you enter explicit sorting instructions in any column in the output grid, you must do so for every group column, not just the ones you want in descending order.

To add group specifications to the Transaction Statistics query, try the following steps:

1. If the Transaction Statistics query is not still open, open it in Design view.

2. Drag the Transaction Type field to the output grid, and drop it on top of the Total Amount column so it becomes the first column in the output grid. Edit the entry in the Field row to add the column title **Type:**. Note that Access automatically enters Group By in the Total row.

3. Execute the query and note that the dynaset includes seven rows, one for each transaction type, sorted in ascending order by transaction type.

4. Return to Query Design view.

5. Click in the second column in the output grid to select it, and press the Ins key to insert a new column to the left of this column.

6. Click in the Field row of the new column and enter the following expression:

```
Year:DatePart("yyyy",[Date])
```

7. Press Down Arrow to move down into the Total row, and type **Group By** (or just **G**) to change the Expression operator to Group By.

8. Run the query again and note that the output contains one row for each year within each transaction type (only two transaction types—PL, which represents pledges, and PP, which represents pledge payments—have entries in both 1991 and 1992). Your screen should look like Figure 9.10.

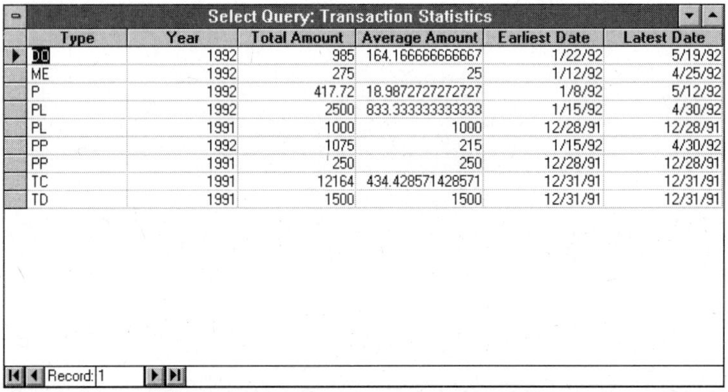

Figure 9.10

Grouping transactions by type and year

Type	Year	Total Amount	Average Amount	Earliest Date	Latest Date
DO	1992	985	164.166666666667	1/22/92	5/19/92
ME	1992	275	25	1/12/92	4/25/92
P	1992	417.72	18.9872727272727	1/8/92	5/12/92
PL	1992	2500	833.333333333333	1/15/92	4/30/92
PL	1991	1000	1000	12/28/91	12/28/91
PP	1992	1075	215	1/15/92	4/30/92
PP	1991	250	250	12/28/91	12/28/91
TC	1991	12164	434.428571428571	12/31/91	12/31/91
TD	1991	1500	1500	12/31/91	12/31/91

Defining Selection Criteria in Totals Queries

You can include selection criteria of two types in a totals query: criteria that describe which records in the underlying table should contribute to the summary statistics and criteria that describe which groups should be included in the query dynaset. This distinction may not be apparent at first, because often the selection criteria are based on the fields that define the groups, and when this is the case, the two types of criteria are equivalent. For example, in the query in Figure 9.8, you might want to select records—and thereby groups— by state. You could limit the query output to people on the West Coast by entering In ("CA","OR","WA") in the criteria row in the State column in the QBE grid. When you select just one value in a group field—for example, limit the Names Table Statistics by State or Names Table Statistics by State and City query to records in California—you may not need to see the State column in the output, and you can uncheck the Show box for this column.

To define selection criteria based on other fields in the source table to specify which records contribute to the statistics, you must add these fields to the output grid, enter Where in the Total rows, and enter the selection criteria as usual in the Criteria rows. You might think of the Where operator as meaning, "I want to include only records *where* the following criteria are satisfied" (the word itself derives from its usage in the SQL SELECT statement, which Access uses internally to execute queries). Figure 9.11 illustrates a query that groups records by state but includes in the statistics only the records that represent members, donors, and board members, based on the contents of the Name Type field.

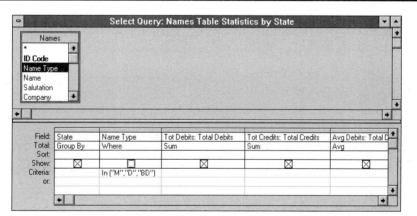

Figure 9.11

A totals query with selection criteria based on the source table

The selection criteria entered in a column with Where in the Totals row are applied to individual records in the source table, and the selected records may have many different values in the fields on which the criteria are based, so it makes little sense to display these fields in the query dynaset. When you enter Where in the Total row, Access therefore automatically unchecks the Show box for the column; if you try to check it again, Access displays the alert box pictured in Figure 9.12 to remind you why this is forbidden. As in a select query, the criteria you enter in the Criteria rows for fields with the Where operator in the Total row apply to the entire record, not to one field. Thus, you cannot define a query in which different selection criteria describe the records that contribute to each summary statistic.

Figure 9.12

The alert box displayed if you try to include source table fields in the query output

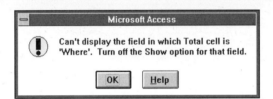

If the selection criteria that you define are not satisfied by any record in a group, Access eliminates the entire group from the query dynaset—that is, every row in the dynaset represents at least one record in the source table. For example, when you run the query in Figure 9.11, the output includes only five rows rather than six, because there are no members, donors, or board members in Utah. The selection criteria in a totals query can be as complex and diverse as those in a select query, and they can be based on any combination of fields in the source tables, including the group fields and any others.

You can also define selection criteria based on the group statistics themselves by entering them in the Criteria rows of the columns that represent summary statistics. For example, to include only groups made up of at least four people, you could enter >=4 in the People with Credits or People with Debits column, and to include only groups with at least $1,000 in credits, you could enter >=1000 in the Total Credits column. Selection criteria based on the groups are implemented *after* Access executes the instructions in the query, to exclude groups that do not pass all the specified tests. In contrast, selection criteria entered in a column with Where in the Total row are applied *during* query execution, to determine which records in the source table contribute to the query output. You can combine both types of criteria in the same query if you wish.

Note that Access interprets *any* entries in the Criteria rows of columns that contain aggregate operators as selection criteria that apply to the groups. If you also want to specify record selection criteria based on one of the fields that contribute to the summary statistics, you must add a second copy of the field to the output grid, enter Where in the Total row for this second copy, and enter the record selection criteria in this column. Make sure you understand the difference between these two types of criteria. If you enter >=1000 in the Totals Credits column with the Sum operator in the Total row, the query dynaset includes only rows that represent groups in which the sum of the Total Credits field is 1,000 or greater. In contrast, if you entered the same condition in a Total Credits column with the Where operator in the Total row, only records in which the Total Credits field is 1,000 or greater would contribute to the overall sums and other statistics.

To add selection criteria to the Transaction Statistics query, use the following steps:

1. If it is not still open, open the query in Design view.

2. Add the Date field to the output grid.

3. Enter **Where** in the Total row for the Date column, and enter **Like */*/92** in the Criteria row to select dates in 1992.

4. Return to the second column and edit the contents of the Field row so it reads **Month:DatePart("m",[Date])**.

5. Choose Ascending in the Sort row for the Type column.

6. Choose Descending in the Sort row for the Month column.

7. Execute the query again and note that the dynaset has one row for each combination of transaction type and month, and that within each transaction type, the rows are arranged in descending order by month. If necessary, adjust the column widths so that you can see all the columns. Your screen should look like Figure 9.13.

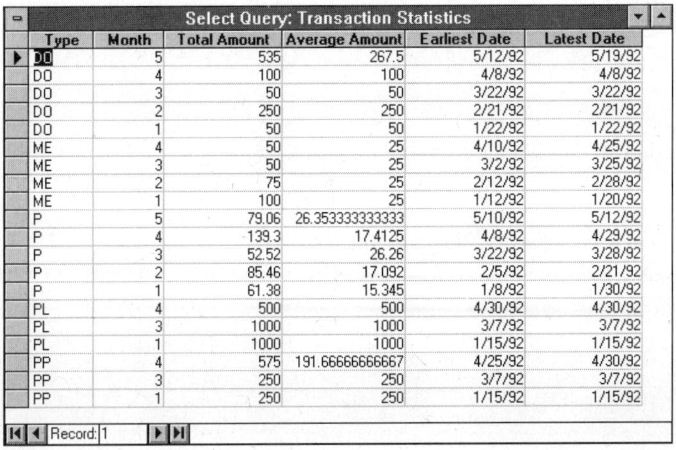

Figure 9.13

Transaction statistics grouped by type and month

Type	Month	Total Amount	Average Amount	Earliest Date	Latest Date
DO	5	535	267.5	5/12/92	5/19/92
DO	4	100	100	4/8/92	4/8/92
DO	3	50	50	3/22/92	3/22/92
DO	2	250	250	2/21/92	2/21/92
DO	1	50	50	1/22/92	1/22/92
ME	4	50	25	4/10/92	4/25/92
ME	3	50	25	3/2/92	3/25/92
ME	2	75	25	2/12/92	2/28/92
ME	1	100	25	1/12/92	1/20/92
P	5	79.06	26.353333333333	5/10/92	5/12/92
P	4	139.3	17.4125	4/8/92	4/29/92
P	3	52.52	26.26	3/22/92	3/28/92
P	2	85.46	17.092	2/5/92	2/21/92
P	1	61.38	15.345	1/8/92	1/30/92
PL	4	500	500	4/30/92	4/30/92
PL	3	1000	1000	3/7/92	3/7/92
PL	1	1000	1000	1/15/92	1/15/92
PP	4	575	191.66666666667	4/25/92	4/30/92
PP	3	250	250	3/7/92	3/7/92
PP	1	250	250	1/15/92	1/15/92

Record: 1

8. Return to Query Design view and enter **>=100** in the Total Amount column to select only groups with a transaction total of $100 or more.

9. Execute the query again and note that the dynaset now contains only 11 rows—one for each combination of transaction type and month in which the contents of the Total Amount column is 100 or greater.

10. Save the query and close it.

Like a select query, a totals query can be based on more than one table. For example, you could design a query to display transaction totals derived from the Transactions table together with selected fields from the matching record in the Names table. Figure 9.14 illustrates a query based on the Names and Transactions tables that displays year-to-date debit and credit totals, together with the total number of transactions for each person. In this query (which is in the ACE sample database packaged with this book), the ID Code and Name columns have Group By in the Totals row. Of course, these fields do not define two distinct groups, but every column *displayed* in the dynaset of a totals query must either be a group field or a summary field (although the QBE grid can also include fields present solely to define selection criteria). The third column, titled Transactions, is a summary column based on the Transaction Number field, in which the Total row contains the Count operator to count the number of non-null values in the Transaction Number field in each ID Code group.

Figure 9.14

Computing totals based on two tables

ID Code	Name	Transactions	YTD Debits	YTD Credits
ALLENJE	Jerry Allen	1	0	25.92
ALLENMA	Marilyn Allen	2	0	500
ANDERSMI	Michael Anderson	1	0	100
BAKERSY	Ms. Sylvia Baker	1	0	25
BERGENRU	Ruth Bergen	2	0	39.46
BLOOMCH	Mr. Christopher Bloom	2	1000	250
BROWNEL	Elizabeth Brown	1	0	25
COLLINSR	Robert Collins	1	0	14.46
DAVISCH	Charles and Anne Davis	3	0	97
DOUGLANO	Norman Douglass	1	0	21.6
ELLIOTCH	Cheryl Elliot, M.D.	1	0	25
FELLNATA	Ms. Natalie Fell	1	0	50
HARRINJU	Ms. Judy Harrington	2	0	52.42
HARRISBE	Benjamin Harris	1	0	13.5
HAYESJ	J. Hayes	1	0	28.92
KATAYAJO	Joanna Katayama	1	0	12.46
KINGDAN	Daniel King	1	0	12.46
LUSUSAN	Susan Lu	2	500	125
MANSONBA	Ms. Barbara Manson	1	0	10.96
MATTHEFR	Frank and Ann Matthews	1	0	25
MICHAELPH	Philip Michaels	1	0	13.5
MOOREJOS	Mr. and Mrs. Joseph Moore	1	0	25

Select Query: Names and YTD Totals

Record: 1

The calculation of the total debits and credits is more complicated. To distinguish between debits (pledges) and credits (all other transactions), you must examine the Transaction Type field. To accumulate total debits, you can use the Sum aggregate function to sum the result of evaluating the expression

```
IIf([Transaction Type]="PL",Amount,0)
```

In each record in the source table, this expression evaluates to the value of the Amount field if the condition is True (that is, if the transaction type is PL for "pledge") and to 0 otherwise. When you sum the resulting numeric values, only pledge transactions contribute to the total, because the expression evaluates to 0 for all other transaction types. Thus, the complete expression in the Field row of the output grid is

```
YTD Debits:Sum(IIf([Transaction Type]="PL",Amount,0))
```

To compute the total credits, you must reverse the two alternative values specified as inputs to the IIf function, so that the expression evaluates to 0 if the transaction type *is* a pledge and to the contents of the Amount field otherwise. The complete expression is

```
YTD Credits:Sum(IIf([Transaction Type]="PL",0,Amount))
```

In both cases, Expression was entered in the Total row to inform Access that the computation of the summary statistic is included in the expression in the Field row.

Defining Crosstab Queries

The examples in the last few sections illustrated a variety of techniques for computing summary statistics based on one or more tables. Access provides a special shortcut for creating one very common type of statistical chart called a *crosstab* (this term is short for *cross-tabulation*). A crosstab is a table that displays the value of one expression for every possible combination of two different variables, one of which provides the row titles and the other the column titles. Figure 9.15 illustrates a crosstab based on the Name Type and State fields in the Names table. In this query, each row represents one state, each column represents one name type, and each cell in the table displays the number of records with a given combination of name type and state. This arrangement was chosen because in a larger mailing list, there are likely to be many more states than name types, but you could just as easily have used the states as the column titles and the name types as the row titles—in both cases, the table would include every possible combination of name type and state.

Figure 9.15

A crosstab query based on name type and state

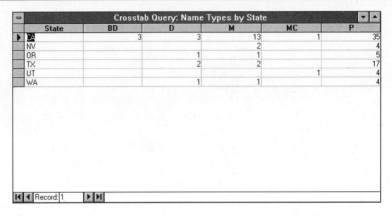

To define a crosstab query, you begin by selecting the Crosstab option from the Query menu. Access adds two rows to the output grid, one labeled Total and one labeled Crosstab. You must add three columns to the output grid to define the essential components of the crosstab: one that identifies the rows, one that identifies the columns, and one that identifies the value that appears in the individual cells in the crosstab. The latter is always a summary statistic—a count, sum, average, and so on—and this is the reason that Access automatically provides a Total row. The order of the three columns in the output grid is immaterial—you identify the role of each column by your entry in the Crosstab row. Like the Total row, the Crosstab row is a combo box, and you can either type your entry or choose it from a drop-down list with four choices: Row Heading, Column Heading, Value, and (not shown). Figure 9.16 illustrates the Name Types by State query in Design view.

Figure 9.16

Defining a crosstab query

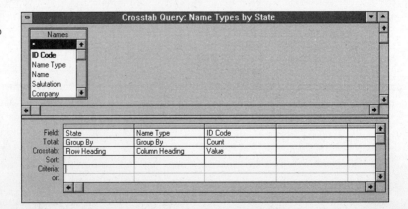

You must enter Group By (the default) in the Total row for the columns in the QBE grid that identify the row and column headings in the crosstab. In the column that identifies the value displayed in the table, you can enter any of the available statistics in the Total row; in Figure 9.16, you can see the Count operator in the ID Code column.

Access automatically sorts the rows in a crosstab query dynaset in ascending order based on the field that supplies the row headings, and it arranges the columns in ascending order based on the field that supplies the column headings. You can override the default sort order by entering Descending in the Sort row for either or both of these fields.

If you enter selection criteria in the Criteria rows for the Row Heading or Column Heading fields, these criteria govern which complete rows or columns are included in the crosstab. For example, to display only members, donors, and board members in California, Oregon, and Washington, you could enter In ("CA","OR","WA") in the Criteria row for the State column and In ("M","D","BD") in the Criteria row for the Name Type column.

To define record selection criteria that govern which records in the source table contribute to the crosstab, you can include additional columns in the output grid. As in the totals queries described earlier in this chapter, you must enter Where in the Total row for these columns and enter your selection criteria in the Criteria rows. A crosstab query with no selection criteria contains one row for every possible value of the field that supplies the row headings and one column for every possible value of the field that supplies the column headings, based on the data in the source table. If you include record selection criteria based on other fields in the source table, Access includes in the output only rows and columns with at least one non-null value. Thus, if you added the Total Credits column to the query in Figure 9.13 and entered >=500 in the Criteria row to select people with at least $500 in total credits, the query dynaset would include four rows (representing California, Oregon, Texas, and Washington) and two columns (representing board members and donors), because no one in Nevada or Utah had $500 in credits, nor did any prospects or media contacts.

You can exert more stringent control over the contents and sequence of the columns in a crosstab by specifying fixed column headings. For example, you might want to arrange the columns in a sequence other than ascending or descending order, or ensure that certain columns are always present even if all the rows are null (due to the current contents of the source table or the current selection criteria). Specifying fixed column headings will also improve query execution speed, and if your tables are large, the difference in performance may be significant. Note that this choice is appropriate only if the allowable values in the field that provides the column headings change very infrequently. For example, if ACE were to add a new name type, it would not be reflected in a name type/state crosstab query with fixed column headings unless you remember to edit the query and add a new column. Note also that there is no comparable option to specify fixed row headings, and this limitation may dictate which variable you choose for the row and column headings.

To enter the fixed column headings, choose the Query Properties option from the View menu, or click on the Properties command button in the tool bar to display the Query Properties dialog box, which is pictured in Figure 9.17 with new column headings for the query in Figure 9.15 filled in. You must check the Fixed Column Headings check box to gain access to the text box below, in which you enter the column headings in the order you want them to appear in the query output. You can separate the values with semicolons or commas (as in Figure 9.17), or you can enter each one on a new line (to move to a new line without closing the dialog box, press Ctrl+Enter). With the fixed column headings in Figure 9.17, the resulting crosstab always includes columns for members, donors, and board members, even if you add selection criteria that exclude California, where all the ACE board members reside.

Figure 9.17

Specifying fixed column headings

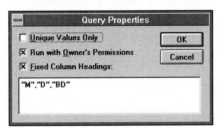

Unfortunately, you cannot use this method to customize the *appearance* of the column headings, which must exactly match the contents of the corresponding field in the source table. This restriction is due to the fact that Access compares the field contents to the specified column headings to determine which column (if any) a given record belongs in. If you enter a column title that does not match any value in the corresponding field in the source table, all the rows in this column will be blank in the query dynaset. Note that it is very easy to do this unintentionally—by misspelling or mistyping one of the legitimate values—so it is a good idea to scan the query output for columns that should never be completely blank. If you prefer to display more descriptive row or column titles, you can create a reference table (like the Names Types or States tables in the ACE system), and use the longer description fields from these tables in the crosstab. To create a version of the query in Figure 9.15 that displays the name type descriptions and state names, use the following steps:

1. Make sure that the Database window displays the list of queries, and click on the New command button or press Alt+N.

2. Choose the Names, Name Types, and States tables from the Add Table dialog box, and then close this dialog box.

3. Because there are default relationships between the Names, Name Types, and States tables, Access should automatically join the tables based on the Name Type and State fields.

4. If you do not see the join line between the Names and Name Types tables, drag the Name Type field in the Names table field list onto the Name Type field in the Name Types table field list.

5. If you do not see the join line between the Names and States tables, drag the State field in the Names table field list onto the State field in the States table field list.

6. Add the State Name field from the States table, the Description field from the Name Types table, and the ID Code field from the Names table to the output grid.

7. Edit the entry in the Field row of the State Name column to change the column title to **State**.

8. Choose the Crosstab option from the Query menu.

9. Choose the Row Headings option from the Crosstab combo box in the State column, and press Tab to move to the next column in the output grid.

10. To choose the Description column as the Column Headings identifier, type **C** in the Crosstab row. Press Tab to move to the next column in the output grid.

11. Using any method you wish, select Value for the Crosstab entry in the ID Code column.

12. In the Total row of the ID Code column, choose Count.

13. Save the query under the name **State/Name Type Crosstab**. Your screen should look something like Figure 9.18. (In this figure, the Query Design window is somewhat larger than the default size, and the upper portion of the window was enlarged to accommodate enough of the Names table field list to show both join lines.)

Figure 9.18

Creating the
State/Name Type
Crosstab query

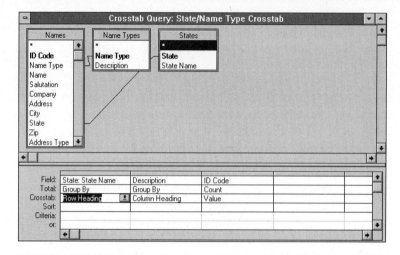

14. Execute the query and verify that it contains six rows (one for each state) and five columns (one for each name type). The name type descriptions should appear in the column selectors as column titles, and the state names should be displayed in the first column of the query dynaset. Return to Query Design view.

15. Choose the Query Properties option from the View menu.

16. Check the Fixed Column Headings check box and enter the following list of column titles in the box below: **Prospect,Member,Donor**. Close the Query Properties dialog box. (If you redisplay the Query Properties dialog box, you will see that Access has added quotation marks around the three column titles.) Note that you might ideally prefer the headings Prospects, Members, and Donors, but you must match the headings to the contents of the Description field in the Name Types table, which are all singular, not plural.

17. Run the query again and note that there are only three columns, which appear in the order you listed them in the Query Properties dialog box. Your screen should look like Figure 9.19.

18. Save the query again and close it.

Figure 9.19

The output of the State/Name Type Crosstab query

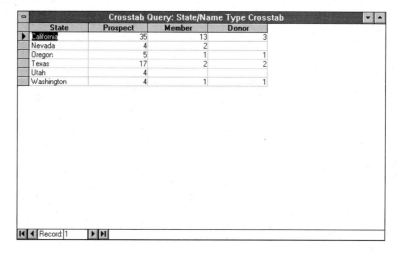

State	Prospect	Member	Donor
California	35	13	3
Nevada	4	2	
Oregon	5	1	1
Texas	17	2	2
Utah	4		
Washington	4	1	1

Record: 1

Updating Tables

All of the techniques described thus far for performing calculations simply displayed or printed the results without affecting the underlying tables. At times, you will also need to update tables en masse, and you can do so with a type of *action query* called an *update query* (other types of action queries, which append, delete, and copy records, are described in Chapter 14). Unlike select, totals, and crosstab queries, action queries carry out permanent—and at times, irreversible—updates on the source tables.

You can use an update query to zero out fields that store year-to-date or month-to-date statistics at the end of the respective accounting periods, to enter a calculated value in all or selected records in a table, or to "plug in" a value in a large group of newly entered or imported records. For example, if ACE imported a mailing list of records from a specific geographical area that did not include an area code field, you could use an update query to fill in the area code in the new records. You will also use update queries to fill in the values of new fields that you add to a table after you have already entered a large amount of data. For example, you might decide to add a Balance field to the Names table instead of calculating the balance on the fly when it is needed, and you could use an update query to fill in the balance for all existing records.

If you decide to include in a table fields that can be calculated based on the contents of other fields in the record (such fields are never necessary but often convenient), you can improve the accuracy of the data by using a query to fill in these fields. For example, in the forms you use to enter data into the Transactions table in the ACE system, you could omit the Amount field and use a query (which is described in this section) to calculate it afterward.

Of course, queries cannot solve all the logistical problems you may encounter. Consider, for example, the steps you would have to take to update a mailing list when a geographical region is split into two area codes. In the densely populated urban areas where this is likely to happen, it is not always possible to define the new area code region by a simple range of zip codes (or even two or three zip code ranges). Entering the new area code in the relevant portion of the list might require an update query with record selection criteria based on the city, zip code, or both, and invariably this procedure will miss enough records that you will have to go over this list manually afterward. Nevertheless, carrying out the bulk of the work with a query can save you a substantial amount of time.

Access uses a variation of the standard query icon—one that includes an exclamation point to the right of the two linked datasheet symbols—to identify update queries (and all other action queries) in the Database window. To create an update query, open a new query and choose the Update option from the Query menu. An update query does not display any data—Access leaves the query specifications visible in Query Design view while it carries out the table updates. You should add to the output grid only the fields that will be updated by the query and fields that contribute to the record selection criteria. For example, you could use an update query to fill in the Amount field in new Transactions table records. This field, which is included in the table structure simply for convenience, is computed by subtracting the discount from the subtotal and adding the tax and shipping charges. To carry out this update for all the records in the Transactions table, you need only add the Amount field to the output grid. To update only recently entered records, you might add the Date or Transaction number to the output grid and define selection criteria based on these fields to identify new records. Figure 9.20 illustrates a query that updates the Amount field in records added after January 1, 1993.

After adding each field you need to update to the output grid, you enter the expression that defines the new value in the Update To row that appears directly below the Field row. There is no Show or Sort row in the QBE grid, because an update query does not display data. Your entries in the Update To row can be very simple—for example, a constant text string such as "510" (an area code) or an expression such as Date( ) (to enter the current date into a Date/Time field)—or quite complex, as may be required to perform some mathematical calculations.

Figure 9.20

Defining an update query

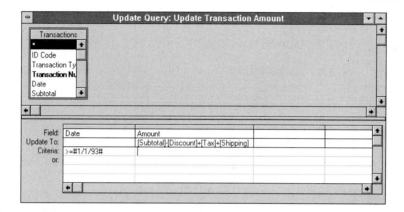

Many mathematical calculations are complicated by the fact that Access always ignores null values. This default assumption, which greatly simplifies compiling statistics, can be inconvenient when you carry out simple arithmetic calculations in which you would prefer to treat null values as equivalent to 0. For example, the query in Figure 9.20 updates the Amount field in the Transactions table using the expression

```
[Subtotal]-[Discount]+[Tax]+[Shipping]
```

When you execute this query, Access updates only records in which none of these fields is null—if the Discount, Tax, or Shipping field is null rather than 0, it bypasses the record.

You can sometimes prevent problems like this by using default values and/or validation conditions in the source table to discourage or prohibit the entry of null data in the first place. For example, in the ACE Transactions table, the Default Value property for all of the numeric fields is 0, and the Validation Rule property is the condition Is Not Null. By assigning the default values, you can ensure that all numeric fields have non-null values without having to enter them explicitly in every record. However, this approach is unsuitable for the Total Debits and Total Credits fields in the Names Table, because it would complicate computing statistics based on these fields (which can legitimately be null in all records except those that represent members and donors).

If you suspect that there may be null values in a table, you must use expressions based on the IIf function to treat them as 0, as in the following, which computes a donor's balance:

```
IIf([Total Credits] Is Null,0.00,[Total Credits])-
IIf([Total Debits] Is Null,0.00,[Total Debits])
```

To avoid this complexity, the Names table never contains a null value in only the Total Credits or Total Debits field. If one of these fields has a non-zero value, the other contains a zero. Obviously, a rather simple expression can grow quite a bit in length and complexity if many of its components might be null. For example, if you assume that the Subtotal field in the Transactions table is never null but the Shipping, Discount, or Tax might be, you could write the following expression to compute the amount:

```
[Subtotal]-IIf([Discount] Is Null,0.00,[Discount])+
IIf([Tax] Is Null,0.00,[Tax])+
IIf([Shipping] Is Null,0.00,[Shipping])
```

As in any other query, you can place additional columns in the output grid to specify record selection criteria. For example, to update only records in California, you could add the State field to the output grid and enter "CA" in the Criteria row. To update only transactions entered after November 1, 1993, you could add the Date field from the Transactions table to the output grid and enter the condition >=#11/1/93# in the Criteria row. You can also enter selection criteria based on the field you are updating. For example, you could use the condition Is Null Or =0 to update only transaction records in which the Amount field is empty or zero.

When you execute an update query, Access reads through the source tables and displays an alert box like the one in Figure 9.21 to inform you how many records will be affected and give you one last chance to bail out without performing the update. If you select OK, Access proceeds to update the tables, and there is no way to undo the changes, short of defining another update query that reverses the effects of the first (which is not always easy or even possible). You may want to make a backup copy of an important table (or the entire database) before you execute a potentially destructive update query that you have never tested on live data. If the source tables are large, both the preprocessing phase and the actual update may take some time, and Access displays a percentage indicator in the left portion of the status bar to inform you of its progress.

Figure 9.21

Confirming or canceling an update query

The message in the alert box pictured in Figure 9.21 tells you how many records the query will update, and you may be able to use this number to verify that your selection criteria describe the right group of records. Another valuable technique for previewing the effects of an update query is to first define a roughly equivalent select query—one that displays the results of performing the proposed calculation for the same group of records—and scan the resulting dynaset for potential problems. For example, Figure 9.22 illustrates the data displayed by a select query intended to preview the effects of a query that updates the Amount field in the Transactions table. The New Amount column is computed using the same formula that you would enter into the Update To row of the Amount column in the update query, and all the fields that contribute to the calculation are included to help you spot problems. Note that the computed values in the New Amount column are displayed in General Number format. However, when you run the equivalent update query, the predefined format for the Amount field (Standard format) ensures that they are always displayed with embedded commas and two decimal places.

Figure 9.22

Previewing the effects of an update query

ID Code	Transaction Number	Subtotal	Discount	Tax	Shipping	New Amount
ALLENMA	14932	1,000.00	0.00	0.00	0.00	1000
ALLENMA	14933	250.00	0.00	0.00	0.00	250
MATTHEFR	14934	125.00	0.00	0.00	0.00	125
ANDERSMI	14935	522.00	0.00	0.00	0.00	522
ARNOLDME	14936	75.00	0.00	0.00	0.00	75
BERGENRU	14937	2,452.00	0.00	0.00	0.00	2452
BLOOMCH	14938	2,250.00	0.00	0.00	0.00	2250
BROWNEL	14939	25.00	0.00	0.00	0.00	25
PIERSOCH	14940	1,500.00	0.00	0.00	0.00	1500
ELLIOTCH	14941	50.00	0.00	0.00	0.00	50
MCDANIBU	14942	75.00	0.00	0.00	0.00	75
LUSUSAN	14943	525.00	0.00	0.00	0.00	525
LEEALEX	14944	100.00	0.00	0.00	0.00	100
HOWARDJO	14945	50.00	0.00	0.00	0.00	50
HARRISBE	14946	100.00	0.00	0.00	0.00	100
HARRINJU	14947	50.00	0.00	0.00	0.00	50
FELLNATA	14948	125.00	0.00	0.00	0.00	125
DAVISCH	14949	450.00	0.00	0.00	0.00	450

Record: 1

Once you have confirmed that the query processes the right records and correctly performs all the calculations, you can delete the unneeded columns and convert the select query to an update query. The easiest way to avoid retyping any lengthy expressions you used to describe calculations is to use the standard cut and paste commands to copy each expression in the Field row to the Clipboard and paste it into the Update To row in the update query. You can then replace the expressions in the Field row with the names of the fields you need to update.

You can define an update query based on more than one table. For example, as noted in Chapter 3, if you do decide to include summary fields such as

Total Debits and Total Credits in a parent table like the ACE Names table, you should structure the table that provides the source data for these fields so that you can easily reconstruct the totals if they are damaged by a system crash or data entry error. For this reason, the ACE Transactions table includes records that establish the total debits and total credits as of the startup date for the application (with Transaction Types TD and TC, respectively). Figure 9.23 illustrates a query based on the Transactions and Names tables that updates the totals in the Total Debits and Total Credits fields in the Names table based on the transactions. In this figure, the second column was widened enough so that you can see the entire expression in the Update To column; the expression in the Total Credits column is identical except of course for the field name. The selection criteria in the Posted column ensure that the query processes only transactions in which the Posted field is No, and the query changes the Posted field in the Transactions table to Yes to prevent posting the same transaction twice.

Figure 9.23

A query that updates one table based on data in another

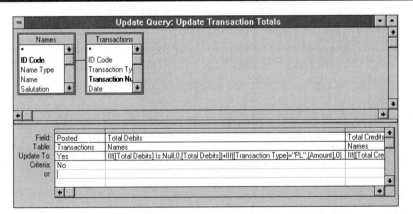

Remember that a multitable query processes *each pair of matching records* in the linked tables. The expression that you enter in the Update To row for the Total Debits and Total Credits columns must describe the update that you want to carry out *for each such pair of records*. If it seems strange to update a field using an expression that refers to the same field, consider how Access executes the query: It first evaluates the expression in the Update To row and then plugs this value into the field specified in the Field row.

To treat null values as equivalent to zero, you must use an expression based on the IIf function similar to the ones outlined earlier in this section. If you did not have to account for null values, the expressions in the Update Transaction Totals query in Figure 9.23 could be considerably simpler. The other complication in this query is the fact that pledge transactions should update the Total Debits field, while all other transactions should be added to the Total Credits field. To make this distinction, the expressions that describe the value to be added to the Total Debits and Total Credits fields are also based on the IIf function, which in this case tests the value of the Transaction Type field to determine whether the transaction is a pledge.

Summary

This chapter introduced a variety of methods for carrying out calculations, some passive (which only display or print the results) and some active (update queries, which store the computed values in a table). This chapter emphasized the use of queries, in part because defining a query is the fastest, most flexible tool for trying out a variety of expressions and calculations, and in part because queries will continue to serve as one of the main tools you will use in your ongoing work with Access to perform calculations, although you will often want to use reports and forms to present the results in a more attractive format than the simple query datasheet. As you will see in the next few chapters, you can use many of the same expressions used in the queries in this chapter in the forms and reports that you design.

This chapter presented a somewhat formal summary of the elements of Access expressions—constants, identifiers, operators, and functions—and the rules of syntax that govern how you may combine these elements to form expressions. If you have worked with other database programs or with spreadsheets—which rely more heavily than databases on constructing expressions—you should find many of the concepts and some of the operators and functions familiar, and you can concentrate on remembering the specifics of Access syntax. If you are a relative newcomer to computers, you may feel somewhat overwhelmed. Try to solidify your understanding of the concepts presented in the first half of this chapter by designing some simple queries based on the ACE system tables or on the tables in your own Access database before you try to memorize a great many details.

Note also that some of the operators and functions may seem intimidating simply because you do not understand and have no need for the data manipulations and transformations they carry out. For example, if you are not a scientist or engineer, you may have no need for the exponentiation operator (^) or for format strings that specify exponential notation, and if you are not a financial analyst you may never use the Pmt (payment) or NPV (net present value) functions. As you gain confidence, you may want to periodically look through the function references in Appendix C and in the Access documentation—functions that seemed impossibly arcane and complex at first may attract your attention later when you have more experience using functions in Access expressions.

10

Customizing Reports and Forms

Understanding Properties

Working in Design View

Adding Objects to a Form

Setting Overall Form and Report Properties

HAPTERS 6, 7, AND 8 DESCRIBED HOW TO USE THE ACCESS FORMWIZARDS and ReportWizards to create new documents, and how to modify the resulting forms to better suit your needs. These chapters concentrated on aspects of the forms and reports closely related to their *contents*—the data displayed or printed using the form—and in the early stages of application development, this should indeed be your focus. Access also offers a variety of options for customizing the *appearance* of forms and reports. Once you are satisfied that a form or report performs as it should, you can turn your attention to esthetic considerations, which are especially important in an application that is also used by colleagues and co-workers who know less than you do about Access.

As you may have gathered from prior experience with other Windows software, it is easy to get carried away and waste considerable time tinkering with the visual attributes of the objects on a form, and if you are not a graphic designer, the results are often garish and distracting. Nevertheless, some attention to the esthetics of a form or report can vastly improve its usefulness. By using graphic devices such as lines, boxes, color, different fonts, and attributes such as boldfacing and underlining, you can group related items on a form or report, distinguish between similar items, emphasize the most important data, and facilitate finding specific information on a crowded screen or printed page.

This chapter describes a variety of methods for customizing the appearance and behavior of both forms and reports. Some of these techniques are applicable only to forms or only to reports, but many serve equally well for both, and in these instances the word *document* is used as a generic term that encompasses both forms and reports. You may find it strange to call a data entry form a document—which in colloquial usage connotes printed material—but this word is used by many Windows programs to refer to any form, report, or graphic image that you can create and modify.

To carry out the modifications described in this chapter, it is essential that you understand the concept of *properties*, which fully describe the appearance and behavior of all Access objects. This chapter outlines methods for customizing objects that involve editing properties directly, and explains how the direct manipulation techniques introduced in Chapter 6 affect the corresponding object properties.

The examples in this chapter are based on the Committee Memberships form designed in Chapter 6 and the Committee Memberships report defined in Chapter 8. You will gain a great deal by working through all the examples in this chapter using these forms. If you are also building your own Access application, take the time to practice these techniques further by customizing the reports and forms in your own database—you will find that operations that seem convoluted and cumbersome when you first read about them become second nature after a few hours of hands-on practice.

Understanding Properties

An understanding of *properties* is central to all of your work with Access, especially the process of designing and modifying reports and forms. As you already know, *the appearance and behavior of every Access object is described by its properties*, and when you modify any object, you are directly or indirectly changing its properties. You have already seen several examples of the properties that describe Access objects of various types. When you create a table, using methods outlined in Chapter 3, you can define properties for the table as a whole (the Description, Primary Key, and Index1 through Index5 properties) and for the individual fields in the table (the Field Size, Format, Decimal Places, Caption, Default Value, Validation Rule, Validation Text, and Indexed properties). In Chapters 8 and 9, you were introduced to query properties, and in the discussion of multitable queries, to join properties.

As you can see from these examples, the properties themselves and the methods that you use to customize them can be quite different for the various types of objects. Obviously, the same is true of the properties of forms, reports, the sections that make up these documents, and the controls that they contain, although some properties—such as position, size, color, and font— are common to many types of objects. When you work in Form Design or Report Design view, the property sheet changes dynamically to display only properties relevant to the selected object: If the form as a whole is selected, the property sheet displays the properties of the form or report; if one section is selected, it displays the properties of that section; and if one object is selected, it displays the properties of the object. For controls composed of more than one object, such as a text box with an associated label, the property sheet is different for the text box and the label.

In preparation for working with property sheets, you might want to briefly review the methods for displaying the property sheet and for selecting various parts of a document. You can display the property sheet by clicking on the Property Sheet command button in the tool bar, by selecting the Properties option on the View menu, or by double-clicking anywhere on the form. To select the document as a whole, you can click in the small box to the left of the horizontal ruler or to the right of the right form border; if you click to the left of this border, you will select the section in which you clicked, not the document itself. You can also select the whole document by choosing the Select Form or Select Report option from the Edit menu. To select a section, click anywhere in the section except inside one of the objects in the section. Once you have selected a section, you can press the Tab or Shift+Tab key repeatedly to cycle through the sections in turn; you can use the same method to cycle through the controls *within* a section. With the property sheet displayed, this gives you an easy way to review the properties of all the sections or all the objects (and to find small, obscure objects that are otherwise hard to select, such as thin lines). When more than one object is selected (for example, if you select several controls in the detail section), Access blanks out the property sheet.

You can *always* modify the properties of any Access object by making entries in a property sheet. For some properties of some objects, additional methods are available—including the direct manipulation techniques described in Chapters 6 and 7—but whichever method you use, the net effect is the same. Direct manipulation is by far the most efficient method for changing some properties, while others lend themselves better to entering values in the property sheet; for still other properties, both methods offer advantages in different contexts. For example, direct manipulation with the mouse is usually the easiest way to change the size and position of an object, especially in combination with the alignment grid (described later in this chapter) and the Align commands on the Layout menu. However, if you are working in the property sheet of a particular control and making numerous changes, it is easy enough to enter new values for the Height, Width, Left, and Top properties to make a slight adjustment in the size or line up the object with its neighbors.

In any case, all of the changes you make using direct manipulation techniques are immediately reflected in the relevant property sheet, whether or not the property sheet is currently displayed on the screen. Unless you are already quite familiar with the concept of properties (from your experience with other software), you might want to leave the property sheet visible at all times while you edit your first few Access forms and reports to solidify your understanding of how the changes you make in Design view affect the properties of the objects in the document.

Working in Design View

When you modify a report or form, be it a document that you created from scratch or one originally generated by one of the Access Wizards, you can use a variety of techniques to add new controls and modify the appearance and behavior of existing controls. Chapters 6 and 7 described some of the ways that you can modify a form or report by directly manipulating objects in Form Design or Report Design view—that is, moving, resizing, or copying objects. Access also provides several specialized tools for customizing documents, some of which were briefly mentioned earlier: the alignment grid, the command buttons and combo boxes in the tool bar, the color palette, the toolbox, the field list, the property sheet, and for reports (but not forms), the Sorting and Grouping dialog box. Figure 10.1 illustrates the Committee Memberships report created in Chapter 8 with all of these special tools visible on the work surface, arranged so that they overlap as little as possible. In this chapter, you will learn how to add the members' full names and addresses to this report.

Figure 10.1

The Access design tools

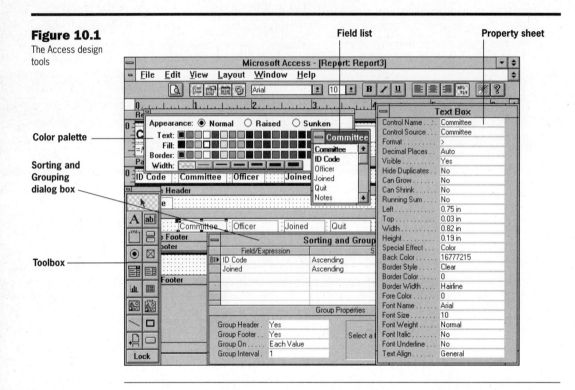

Obviously, you will usually prefer to work in a less cluttered environment than the screen pictured in Figure 10.1. If you are working in Super VGA mode on a large monitor, you may be able to leave all of the tools in full view on the screen without obscuring much of the document itself, but in most cases you will have to be more selective. You can display or remove any of these special tools from the work surface by using options on the View menu and, for all the tools except the toolbox, command buttons in the tool bar. Note that like the corresponding View menu options, the buttons in the tool bar function as toggles, and their appearance simulates push-button toggle switches—when you press a command button to display the associated tool, the button appears depressed below the plane of the screen, and when you press the button again to remove the tool from the screen, the button "pops up" again.

When you experiment with the special tools in Report Design and Form Design view, keep in mind that you can resize the windows in which Access displays the property sheet, field list, and sorting and grouping instructions; in each case, Access displays a vertical scroll bar whenever there are more entries than will fit within the window. Because the toolbox and color palette windows must always be large enough to accommodate all of the special buttons they contain, you cannot resize either of these windows. One of the best ways to get a tool or window out of the way temporarily when you know you will be using it again in the current work session is to push it mostly "off the edge" of the screen. As long as some part of the title bar remains visible, you can easily grab the window with the mouse and bring it back to the middle of the screen. This technique is particularly useful for the property sheet, which is large enough to get in the way but useful enough that you will want to refer to it repeatedly as you fine-tune the appearance of a document. Figure 10.2 illustrates the Committee Memberships report in Design view with the toolbox, color palette, and property sheet all pushed most of the way off the screen.

Figure 10.2
Moving tools partly
off the screen

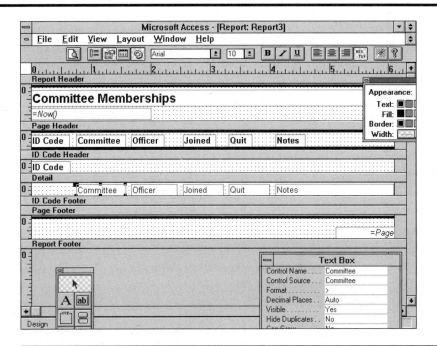

The examples in this chapter are based on the Committee Memberships form defined in Chapter 6 and the Committee Memberships report defined in Chapter 8. If you plan to try the examples in this chapter, take a moment now to open the Committee Memberships form and familiarize yourself with the various property sheets:

1. Open the Committee Memberships form in Form Design view, and maximize the Form Design window.

2. If the property sheet is not already visible, display it by selecting the Properties option from the View menu, clicking on the Property Sheet command button in the tool bar, or double-clicking anywhere on the form.

3. If necessary, move the property sheet to the right side of the screen, leaving the vertical scroll bar in the Form Design window and at least some of the form background visible to the right of the property sheet, and adjust its size so that it is almost the full height of the screen.

4. Click in the form header section. Note that the property sheet now displays the properties of the form header section.

5. Press Tab several times to cycle through the form sections, and note that the property sheet always displays the properties of the currently selected section.

6. Choose the Select Form option from the Edit menu to redisplay the property sheet for the form as a whole.

Using the Alignment Grid

As noted in Chapters 6 and 7, you can display an alignment grid in Report Design and Form Design view to help you resize and line up objects. The grid spacing is controlled by two properties of the document as a whole, which are named Grid X (for the horizontal, or X-axis) and Grid Y (for the vertical, or Y-axis). The spacing of the grid dots can range from 1 to 64 dots per inch, both vertically and horizontally (that is, the Grid X and Grid Y properties can each take on any value between 1 and 64), but the grid is visible only when the spacing is no finer than 16 dots per inch in both dimensions. In the forms created by the Wizards, the grid is set to 64 by 64 dots. If you want to see the grid, you can edit the property sheet for the document and reset the Grid X and Grid Y properties. Typical settings range from 10 to 16 dots per inch.

Although you can use the grid to line up controls visually, the grid can also play a more active role. Checking the Snap to Grid option on the Layout menu ensures that when you move or resize an object, Access *snaps*, or aligns, the object to the grid after you release the left mouse button. When you move an object, Access adjusts its position if necessary so that the upper-left corner is superimposed on a grid dot, and when you resize an object, Access adjusts the size so that whichever borders you moved line up with the nearest gridline. When you work with the the Snap to Grid option turned on, you can move and resize objects very quickly without disrupting their alignment, and your forms will not suffer if you lack dexterity with the mouse.

When you define new documents from scratch, the Snap to Grid option may provide all the help you need in placing and sizing controls. However, when you modify a form created by an Access Wizard, you will find your efforts hampered by the fact that after you change the grid spacing to make the grid visible, few if any of the controls added by the Wizard will line up with the grid. You can correct the alignment of existing objects by using either the Align to Grid command (invoked by selecting Align from the Layout menu and then choosing To Grid from the submenu of alignment options) or the Size to Grid option on the Layout menu. In both cases, you must begin by selecting the objects you want to align. Both the Align to Grid and Size to Grid options move each selected object so that its upper-left corner aligns with the nearest grid dot. The Size to Grid option also adjusts the size of each object so that all of its borders are superimposed on grid lines.

What may be less intuitively obvious is that you can use the Snap to Grid, Align to Grid, and Size to Grid options even when the grid is too fine to see. At the finest setting (64 by 64 dots) these options are of little help, but they can be quite useful with the grid set to intermediate values around 20 by 20 dots (a very useful grid density in a crowded form with many small objects) where they offer the same assistance as they do with the coarser grid settings.

Use the grid options to prepare for editing the Committee Memberships report as follows:

1. Click in the top row of the property sheet, and then press Down Arrow to move down through the properties until you get to the Grid X property. Note that many of the property sheet entries are combo boxes that enable you to select options from a drop-down list instead of typing them.

2. Enter **16** for the Grid X property and press Down Arrow to move down to the Grid Y property.

3. Enter **16** for the Grid Y property and press Enter.

4. Choose the Select All option on the Edit menu. Note that Access blanks out the property sheet because multiple objects, which all have different properties, are selected.

5. Pull down the Layout menu, and if the Snap to Grid option is not already checked, select this option.

6. Choose the Size to Grid option from the Layout menu.

7. Click in the background portion of the detail section of the form to deselect all the selected objects.

8. If all the text boxes and labels except the Notes text box are not the same height (the Size to Grid option sometimes adjusts the size of an object to

conform to the "wrong" grid line), adjust them so that they are all three grid dots (0.19 inches) high.

9. Click in the Committee text box in the detail section to select just this object. Your screen should look like Figure 10.3.

Figure 10.3

Displaying the alignment grid and the property sheet

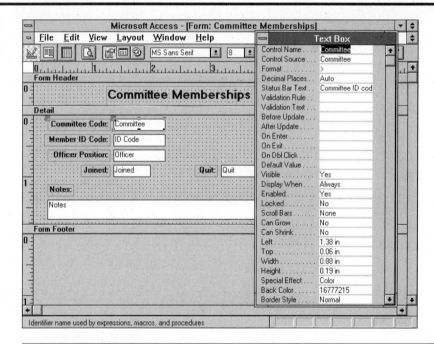

Modifying Colors

You can use the color palette to customize the colors, border and line thicknesses, and overall visual attributes of objects on forms and reports. You can use colors in a form to highlight important areas, to emphasize the similarity between certain controls, or simply to make a form more pleasing to the eye and therefore easier to work with in a long data entry session. Obviously, unless you have a color printer you should be sparing in your use of colors other than shades of gray in reports that you intend to print more often than you will view them on the screen.

The color palette, which is visible earlier in Figure 10.1, contains a set of radio buttons for customizing the overall appearance of a control; three rows of color buttons for selecting the text, fill (background), and border colors; two check boxes that specify attributes of the background and border; and seven toggle buttons for selecting the thickness of lines and borders. Not all of these properties are applicable to every control, and those that are not available for the currently selected object remain visible but are disabled. For example, only the fill colors are enabled when a form or report section is selected, because the background color is the only meaningful property for a document section. By far the easiest way to make selections in the color palette is to use the mouse, but if you wish you can use the Tab and Shift+Tab keys to move from one group of controls to the next or previous group, and the Left Arrow and Right Arrow keys to move from one option to the next within each group.

For every object that displays text (including text objects, check boxes, text boxes, and the labels associated with text boxes), you can choose all three colors—the text color, fill color, and border color. The check boxes to the right of the fill and border color selections determine whether these colors are solid or transparent (clear). Checking the Clear box essentially renders the background or border colors invisible and allows the color of the object below (or the document background) to show through. By default, both check boxes are checked for text boxes and their associated labels; if you uncheck them, you will see that the background color is white, the border is black, and the border width is the thinnest of the seven choices. The Clear check box for the fill color is disabled for all controls except label objects, but you can emulate its effect by choosing a fill color that matches the background color assigned to the form section that contains the object. For all bordered objects (including text boxes and label objects), you can customize the border width by selecting one of the seven buttons at the bottom of the color palette.

You can use the Appearance radio buttons to create two different three-dimensional looks. The Raised option adds light shadows on the left and upper sides of an object, and dark shadows on the right and lower sides to create the illusion that the object is raised above the plane of the screen. The Sunken option reverses these shadows to make the object appear to be sunken below the plane of the screen. These attributes are used automatically by Access to make command buttons resemble three-dimensional buttons, which appear raised by default and depressed after they are selected, but you can also use them to good effect to display data in text boxes. Figure 10.4 shows a very simple form that illustrates both the Raised and Sunken effects in several typical color combinations. Note also that in the forms generated by the FormWizards, check boxes have the Sunken attribute; if you prefer a two-dimensional check box, you can select the Normal radio button in the color palette or set the Special Effect property to Color.

As is the case with all object properties, you can establish the colors, border characteristics, and overall appearance of any object by making entries in the property sheet. Figure 10.5 illustrates the Committee Memberships form in Form Design view with the color palette and property sheet visible, and the palette labeled with the names of the corresponding properties. A glance at

Figure 10.4

Using the Raised and Sunken attributes for text boxes

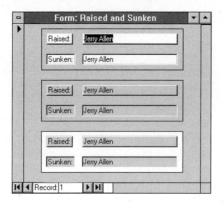

the numbers that represent the colors (for example, 16777215 for the white background color of the selected object) should convince you that it is far easier to use the palette to choose colors. Note, however, that entering the numeric values in the property sheet is the only way to select colors other than the 16 choices in the color palette, although considerable experimentation may be required to achieve the desired effects.

Many of the other properties are easy to customize by making entries in the property sheet, especially in light of the fact that most of them can be selected from combo boxes. For example, you can choose Normal or Clear for the Back Style and Border Style properties, which correspond to the two check boxes in the color palette, and you can select the thickness of any line, rectangle, or border by choosing one of the seven options in the Border Width combo box—Hairline, 1pt, 2pt, 3pt, 4pt, 5pt, and 6pt (like font sizes, border thicknesses are expressed in points). The Special Effect property offers three choices—Color, Raised, and Sunken—which correspond to the three Appearance radio buttons. Choosing Color, which corresponds to the Normal button, cancels either of the other two special effects, perhaps because all objects have colors, even if they are the default colors and therefore constitute the "normal" selection.

To experiment with colors in the Committee Memberships form, use the following steps:

1. If the color palette is not visible, select the Palette option from the View menu or click on the Color Palette command button in the tool bar.

2. Move the palette to the lower-left corner of the screen into the unoccupied region in the form footer.

Figure 10.5

The properties customized using the color palette

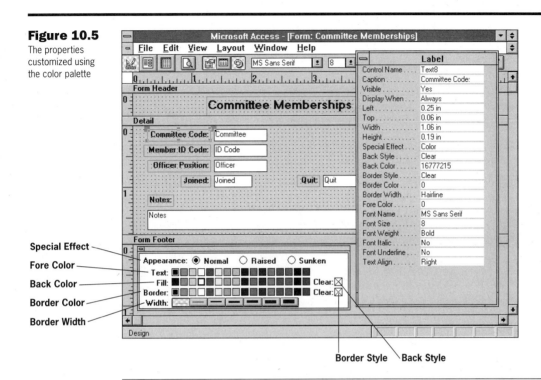

3. Click in the form header section. Note that only the fill colors are enabled and that the third color box (light gray) is selected; the Back Color property displays the code that corresponds to this color (12632256).

4. Click on the dark blue color box in the palette (the second from the right). Note that the Back Color property changes to 8388608.

5. Drag the lower boundary of the form header section down slightly, so that a small part of the form background is visible below the text object. Note that the Snap to Grid option applies to resizing form sections as well as objects, and the lower form boundary snaps to the nearest grid line when you release the mouse button.

6. Click in the text object in the form header to select it. Choose the same dark blue as the section background for the text color, white for the fill color, and light gray for the border color. Uncheck both the Fill and Border check boxes to make these colors visible. Click on the third button in the Width row to widen the border.

7. Click on the Form View command button in the tool bar, or select Form from the View menu to view the effects of your color selections.

8. Click on the Design View command button in the tool bar, or select Form Design from the View menu to return to Form Design view.

9. Remove the color palette from the screen (by unchecking the Palette option on the View menu, clicking on the Color Palette command button in the tool bar, or using any of the standard Windows methods for closing a window).

Changing Text Properties

You can customize the font and other attributes of any object that displays text by editing the Font Name, Font Size, Font Weight, Font Italic, Font Underline, and Text Align properties in the property sheet, all of which are combo boxes. You can also use controls in the tool bar as shortcuts for selecting some of the most common attributes, and where they are available, these controls offer a significant advantage—they enable you to apply the same attribute to more than one object at a time, simply by selecting all the desired objects and then operating the control. In contrast, the property sheet offers more choices for some of the properties, but it only allows you to work with one object at a time. Figure 10.6 illustrates the correspondence between the command buttons and the text properties.

The Font Name and Font Size combo boxes in the tool bar and the property sheet display exactly the same lists of fonts and font sizes, and you can use them interchangeably. The actual values that appear in the drop-down lists depend on the fonts installed through Windows—you may find screen fonts, printer fonts, TrueType fonts, and/or Adobe Type Manager fonts. All the font sizes are expressed in points, and the actual values listed in the Font Size combo box depend on the currently selected font, because not all fonts are available in every size. For this reason, it is best to choose the font first if possible. The fastest way to resize labels to match their contents after changing the font size is to select one or more label objects and then choose the Size to Fit option on the Layout menu.

NOTE. *In most Windows software, the size of a font and the thickness of lines and boxes are expressed in* points, *a unit of measure that originated with typesetting. Because nearly all Windows fonts are proportional, the size reflects the height, not the width, of a character or line. One point represents about $1/72$ inch.*

The Font Weight property governs the thickness of the characters. The drop-down list attached to the combo box in the property sheet offers nine choices—Thin, Extra Light, Light, Normal, Medium, Semi-bold, Bold, Extra

Figure 10.6

The controls used to customize text properties

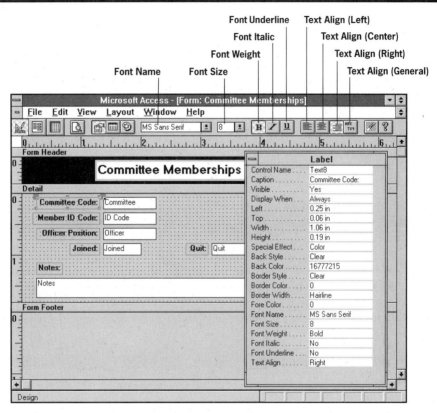

Bold, and Heavy—but you will only be able to distinguish all of these visually in very large fonts. In the default forms and reports generated by the Access Wizards, the Font Weight property is set to Normal for text boxes, and to Bold for text box labels and the label objects used for titles and column headings. You can toggle between Bold and Normal by pressing the command button labeled "B" in the tool bar, but you must use the property sheet to select the other seven choices. There are only two choices for the Font Italic and Font Underline properties—Yes and No—and you can use the corresponding command buttons in the tool bar as shortcuts for toggling these attributes on or off.

The Text Align property governs the alignment of text or data within the region allocated for the object on the document. The Left, Center, and Right options should be familiar to you from your experience with word processors or other software. The General alignment option left-justifies text and right-justifies numeric and Date/Time values. In the single-column forms and reports generated by the Access Wizards, all the text boxes are assigned General alignment (to accommodate any data type), and the labels are assigned Right alignment to display them in a column right-justified to the left of the text boxes. In most cases, this arrangement should prove satisfactory.

In tabular forms and groups/totals reports, the text objects that serve as the column titles are also given General alignment, and this is often *not* desirable. First of all, the width of a label object is based on the length of the label text, which usually does not match the width of the text box that displays the corresponding field. Second, because the labels are text strings, they are all displayed left-justified. The result, for a simple tabular form based on the Committees table, is illustrated in Figure 10.7. The labels that serve as the headings for the Joined and Quit fields would look better if they were right-justified over the data (the same would be true of the titles for any numeric fields, of which there are none in this form). Correcting this problem requires two steps: First, you must either match the widths of the label objects that display the titles to the corresponding text boxes or move the labels so they align with the right edges of the text boxes; then set the Text Align property for each label to Right.

Figure 10.7

The text boxes and text objects created by the tabular FormWizard

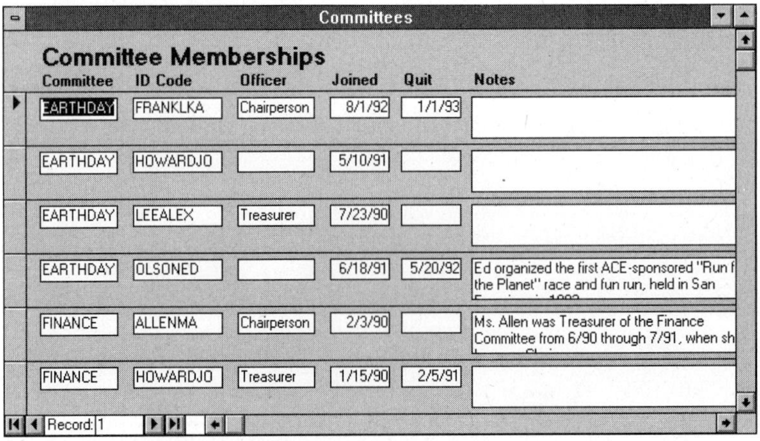

You can also use the Text Align options to center a title (displayed in a label object) on the page or within any other arbitrary width—make the label object as wide as the region within which you want to center it, and then choose Center for the Text Align property to center the caption within the object width.

To customize the text attributes so that the Committee Memberships form resembles Figure 10.8, try the following steps:

1. Click on the label for the Notes text box (not the data entry region). Using the combo box in the tool bar, select 10 for the font size.

2. Widen the label object slightly to accommodate the larger type, and click on the Left alignment button in the tool bar to line up the label text with the text box below.

3. Select the text object in the form header section. Select Yes from the combo box used to enter the Font Underline property in the property sheet, and note that the corresponding command button in the tool bar now appears depressed. Click on this button to turn off underlining, and note that the previous setting (No) reappears in the property sheet.

4. Select all the text boxes (not the labels) by holding down the Shift key as you click in each object in turn.

5. Using the Font Name combo box in the tool bar, select Courier (if this font is available) or a similar font. (You cannot use the corresponding combo box in the property sheet because multiple objects are selected.)

6. Choose 10 from the Font Size combo box in the tool bar.

7. Click on the Form View command button in the tool bar or select Form from the View menu to display the form, and use the navigation controls to display a few records. Note that "Chairperson" no longer fits in the Officer text box.

8. Return to the Form Design view and widen the Committee, ID Code, and Officer text boxes about $1/4$ inch. Widen the Joined and Quit text boxes about $1/8$ inch.

Figure 10.8
The modified Committee Memberships form

9. Select the Joined and Quit text boxes, and click on the Left Alignment button in the tool bar to left-justify these date fields so that the Joined date lines up with the three Text fields above it.

10. Preview the appearance of the form once more. Your screen should look like Figure 10.8.

11. Save and close the Committee Memberships form.

Adding Objects to a Form

To add new controls to a form or report, you use the field list and toolbox, either together or separately; the most efficient method depends on the type of control and the data source. Access recognizes three general types of controls:

- *Bound* controls, which display or collect data from a table or query dynaset

- *Unbound* controls, which display lines, rectangles, or text not derived from a table or query dynaset

- *Calculated* controls, which display the result of evaluating an expression (which may or may not depend on any table or query dynaset)

When you add a control to a document using just the toolbox, Access creates an unbound control, so this method is ideal for controls that have no inherent connection to the source table or query—such as label objects, lines, rectangles, and text boxes that display the current date or time. To add a calculated control to a form, you must begin with an unbound control and then enter the expression that defines the calculation (as described later in this section). If you inadvertently create an unbound text box or check box, you can bind the control to a field after the fact, and if you choose the wrong field, you can change the field to which the control is bound without deleting and recreating the control from scratch. However, there are significant advantages to using the field list for any object that you know in advance will be derived from the source table or query. When you add a control to a document using just the field list, Access creates a bound text box. By combining these methods—using both the toolbox and field list—you can create an object of any type and bind it to the desired source field in a single step.

Creating Unbound Controls

The toolbox contains 16 buttons, which you can use to create unbound controls of all the types that Access supports. Figure 10.9 illustrates the toolbox with the purposes of the buttons indicated. You can add any type of control to a document by using the following steps:

1. Click on the appropriate object button in the toolbox. The shape of the mouse pointer changes to a symbol that matches the icon on the face of the selected toolbox button with a crosshair to the left.

2. Position the crosshair where you want the upper-left corner of the control on the form.

3. Add the control to the document:

   ■ To create a control of the default size, click again.

   ■ To create a control of any arbitrary size, press and hold the left mouse button and drag the outline of the control to the desired size.

Figure 10.9

The toolbox

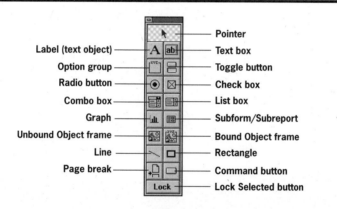

Label (text object)	Pointer
Option group	Text box
Radio button	Toggle button
Combo box	Check box
Graph	List box
Unbound Object frame	Subform/Subreport
Line	Bound Object frame
Page break	Rectangle
Lock	Command button
	Lock Selected button

What happens next depends on the type of object you are creating. When you create a label object, Access immediately displays an insertion point within the object frame so you can begin typing the text. If you did not specify the size of the text object, the frame expands as you type to accommodate your entry; if you did, you must resize the object later if necessary. You can use the Size to Fit option on the Layout menu to resize any object frame to match the contents; this option is particularly useful for independent label objects and the labels associated with other controls, such as text boxes and check boxes.

When you use this method to create a labeled control (such as a check box or text box), note that the position of the crosshair indicates the location of the upper-left corner of the control itself, not the associated label. The default spacing between the two objects that make up labeled controls depends on the type of control, based on conventions that are fairly standard in Windows software. For example, Access places a text box label to the left of the text box, whereas a check box label is displayed to the right of the check box. However, the placement of the label is governed by properties described later in this chapter, which you can modify if the defaults do not suit your needs or preferences. For example, as noted in Chapter 6, the FormWizard that creates single-column forms places check box labels to the left of the check boxes, so that all the data entry regions on the form (most of which are text boxes) line up.

If you are new to Windows and find it hard to judge the right location for an object, don't waste too much time agonizing over the placement—Access leaves the newly created object selected, so you can easily move or resize it after you release the mouse button. If you change your mind about which type of control you want to create after selecting one of the buttons in the toolbox, simply click on another button, or click on the large button at the top of the toolbox with the arrow symbol on its face to return to using the mouse as a passive pointer.

Note that the object button you selected in the toolbox remains depressed while you are placing the control on the document; when you release the mouse button, Access automatically deselects the object button and reselects the pointer arrow button at the top of the toolbox. As is the case with the toggle buttons in the tool bar, Access displays the currently selected button so that it appears depressed and in slightly different colors (although this distinction may be hard to see on some monitors).

NOTE. *If you plan to add several controls of the same type to a form, you can avoid having to repeatedly reselect the same object button by clicking on the Lock button at the bottom of the toolbox. When the Lock button is selected, every object button you click on remains selected until you choose another. To cancel this mode, simply click on the Lock button again.*

Creating Bound Controls

The easiest way to add a bound control to a document is to choose the data source from the field list, which you can display by clicking on the Field List button in the tool bar or by selecting Field List from the View menu. By default, Access creates a text box, and if this is the control type you want, no additional measures are necessary. You can add one or more text boxes at a time by using the following steps:

1. Select one or more fields in the field list.

2. If you selected one field, you do not have to release the mouse button after clicking on the field. If you selected more than one field, position the mouse pointer over any of the selected fields, and press and hold down the left mouse button. The shape of the mouse pointer changes to

the standard icon for a field (if one field is selected) or to a stack of fields (if more than one field is selected).

3. Position the mouse pointer where you want the upper-left corner of the first text box (not the associated label) on the form.

4. Release the mouse button.

When you use this method, Access creates one or more text boxes in the default size. You cannot adjust the size of the text boxes as you can when you create an object using only the toolbox, but it is easy enough to do so afterward. Remember to position the field icon where you want the upper-left corner of the first (or only) text box, not the attached label. If you selected more than one field, Access places the text boxes one below the other, lined up in a vertical column.

You can use a similar method that also makes use of the toolbox to create a single bound object of any type (including a text box):

1. Click on the appropriate object button in the toolbox. The shape of the mouse pointer changes to a symbol that matches the icon on the face of the selected toolbox command button with a crosshair to the left.

2. Position the mouse pointer over the desired field in the field list, and press and hold down the left mouse button.

3. Position the crosshair where you want the upper-left corner of the control on the form.

4. Release the mouse button to create a control of the default size, or hold the left mouse button down and drag the outline of the control to the desired size.

Be careful not to release the mouse button after you select the source field name in the field list—if you do, Access creates an unbound control, as if you had never selected a field from the field list.

You can *bind* an unbound control to a field in the source table or change the field bound to the control by specifying the *control source*. You can do this by typing a field name within the object frame on the work surface (simply select the object and then click again inside the object frame to display an insertion point), but it is often easier to edit the Control Source property in the property sheet. The data entry region for this property is a combo box, and you can either type the field name directly or choose it from a drop-down list that includes the same field names as the field list. Note that there is no entry in the property sheet for the object type, and there is no easy way to convert an object of one type to another (for example, to turn a check box into a text box or vice versa). To change the type of control used to display or collect a particular field, you must delete the original control and replace it with another of the desired type.

Apart from convenience, choosing the data source from the field list rather than entering it later offers one important advantage—a control that you create using the field list *inherits*, or acquires, some of the properties of the underlying field. All bound objects on both forms and reports inherit the Format property specified in the table structure, and numeric fields inherit the Decimal Places property as well. In forms, bound controls also inherit the Description, which supplies the value for the Status Bar Text property (the text displayed in the status bar when the control has the focus), Default Value, Validation Rule, and Validation Text (the error message displayed when entered data does not satisfy the validation rule) properties. These properties are irrelevant in reports, which do not collect data. You may have noticed this inheritance in the ACE Committees table forms created using the FormWizards. For example, when you use any of these forms to update records, the status bar displays the same messages as when you update the Committees table in Datasheet view. Note that the inherited properties serve only as default values for the corresponding entries in a control's property sheet—you can override the defaults for a particular form or report by editing the property sheet.

Creating Calculated Controls

Note. The name of a calculated control cannot be the same as the name of any field or calculated field in the source table or query.

To add a calculated control to a form or report, you must begin with an unbound control—for example, a text box—and then set the Control Source property to the expression that defines the calculation. As noted earlier, you can type the control source directly in the object frame on the work surface, or you can enter it in the property sheet. In both cases, you must precede the expression with an equals sign (=) to distinguish it from a field name. The expression can be as simple or as complex as you wish—the calculations you can carry out are limited only by your ability to construct valid Access expressions to describe them.

Defining Control Names and Captions

When you add a control to a form, Access assigns a name constructed by combining a word that describes the type of object—Text, Line, Box, Field, Button, PageBreak, or Embedded—plus a sequential number—1 for the first object (of any type) that you place on the form, 2 for the next, and so on. For example, if you add an unbound text box to a form that already includes seven objects, Access assigns the name Field8 to the text box and the name Text9 to the label. You may have noticed that in the documents created by the Access Wizards, the names of objects match the names of the source fields (or calculated fields). If you want to adhere to this convention, which makes for very readable and intuitive object names, you must enter the new names yourself for the objects that you add to any form (including one originally generated by a Wizard)—there is no property or option that you can set to request that Access assign object names based on the source fields. In most cases, you can retain the default names for label objects, but you will usually want to assign more meaningful names to any controls that you might want to refer to elsewhere in a document.

Remember that the Control Name property specifies a name used internally by Access to refer to an object. For objects that display text rather than data—independent label objects and the labels associated with labeled controls—be sure you understand the difference between the Control Name property and the Caption property, which specifies the text displayed in the document. To change the text displayed on the screen, you must edit the Caption property, not the Control Name property. For controls that display or collect data, be careful not to confuse the Control Name property with the Control Source property, which identifies the source of the data displayed or collected by the control. In the documents generated by the Wizards, these two properties are assigned the same value, but they are used quite differently. When you type directly in the object frame on the work surface, you are in effect editing the Control Source property for a text box and the Caption property for a label object, *not* the name of the object. When you add a new unbound control to a document, you will see a graphic reminder of this distinction—Access displays "Unbound" within the object frame on the form to remind you that the control is not yet associated with any field in the source table or query.

To make matters even more confusing, when you add any labeled object (such as a text box) to a form, Access matches the Caption property of the label to the Control Name property for the control. For example, if Access assigns the name Field10 to a new text box object, the Caption property of the associated label is Field10, and the Control Name property is Text11. However, if you change the Control Name property for the text box, Access *does not* automatically change the label's Caption property to match.

Adding Objects to the Committee Memberships Report

Recall that the Committee Memberships report defined in Chapter 8 did not include the name and address fields derived from the Names table. To add these fields to the ID Code header section of the report, as shown in Figure 10.10, use the following steps:

1. Open the Committee Memberships report in Design view (you do not have to close the Committee Memberships form first), and maximize the Report Design window.

Figure 10.10

Adding the name
and address fields
to the Committee
Memberships report

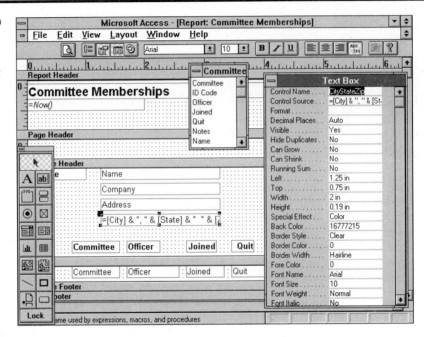

2. If the property sheet is not visible on the work surface, display it by selecting the Properties option from the View menu or clicking on the Property Sheet command button in the tool bar.

3. If necessary, move the property sheet to the right side of the screen, leaving the vertical scroll bar and at least some of the report background visible to the right of the property sheet, and adjust its size so that it does not
   obscure the horizontal ruler at the top of the Report Design window.

4. Set the Grid X and Grid Y properties to 16 dots per inch. If the grid is
   not visible, check the Grid option on the View menu.

5. Choose the Select All option from the Edit menu, and then select Size to
   Grid from the layout menu to resize and align all the objects in the report
   to the grid.

6. Make sure that the Snap to Grid option on the Layout menu is checked.

7. Drag the lower boundary of the ID Code header section down until this
   section is about 1 1/2 inches high.

8. If the field list is not visible on the work surface, select the Field List option from the View menu, or click on the Field List command button in

the tool bar. Position the field list to the left of the property sheet, and adjust its size so that six or seven field names are visible.

9. In the field list, select the Name, Company, and Address fields (the easiest way to do this is to click on the Name field, and then hold the Shift key down and click on the Address field).

10. Press and hold the left mouse button and drag the selected fields into the ID Code header section. Release the mouse button with the stacked fields icon directly to the right of the ID Code text box, at about the 1½-inch mark in the horizontal ruler.

11. Select all three labels by clicking in the Name label and then holding down the Shift key as you click in each of the other two labels. Press the Del key to delete the selected labels.

12. Select all three text boxes and adjust the position of the group so that they are lined up with the 1¼-inch mark in the horizontal ruler.

13. Adjust the width of all three text boxes (one at a time) to exactly 2 inches.

14. If the toolbox is not visible on the work surface, select the Toolbox option from the View menu. Position the toolbox in the lower-left corner of the Report Design window.

15. To create an unbound text box, click on the Text Box button in the tool box, position the crosshair over the grid dot below the Address text box, press the left mouse button and drag the text box to match the size of the three text boxes above it.

16. Delete the label to the left of the new text box.

17. Click in the text box and type the expression that displays the City, State, and Zip fields combined into a single text string

    `=[City]&", "&[State]&"  "&[Zip]`

    Press Enter and observe that your expression appears in the Control Source property in the object property sheet.

18. Click in the data entry region next to the Control Name property, delete the default name, and type the name **CityStateZip**.

19. Widen the ID Code text box to 1 inch.

20. Delete the ID Code label in the page header section (*not* the text box that displays the ID code in the ID Code header section) and both of the lines in this section.

21. Select all the remaining objects in the page header section, and move them into the ID Code header section below the member name and address. Your screen should look something like Figure 10.10 (in this figure, the CityStateZip text box is selected to display the property sheet for this object).

22. Shrink the page header section to nothing.

23. Select Print Preview from the File menu or click on the Print Preview command button in the tool bar to preview the appearance of the report. With the Preview window zoomed, your screen should look like Figure 10.11.

Figure 10.11

Previewing the modified Committee Memberships report

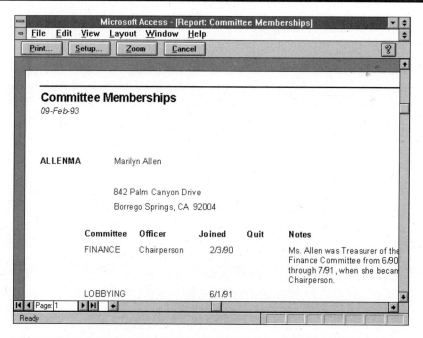

Duplicating Objects

Chapter 6 described how to copy any portion of a form or report by using the Clipboard: Simply select the desired objects, use the Copy command on the Edit menu (or the equivalent hotkey, Ctrl+C) to copy these objects to the Clipboard, and then use the Paste command on the Edit menu (or the equivalent hotkey, Ctrl+V) to paste the contents of the Clipboard back onto the form. When you use this method, Access places the copy in the upper-left corner of the current form or report section, leaving the new objects selected so you can easily move them to a new location. This method is particularly convenient for copying several objects *of different types* (such as a text box, an adjacent rectangle that forms a shadow, and a surrounding border) as a group while preserving the relationships among them.

The Duplicate option on the Edit menu serves as an alternative method for replicating one or more existing objects. To use this method, select the desired objects and then choose the Duplicate option from the Edit menu. Using the Duplicate command is the easiest way to add several equally spaced (horizontally or vertically) controls to a form in rapid succession. The first time you use this command, Access superimposes the copy on the original, slightly offset to the right and down, and leaves the new object(s) selected. If you move the new objects and repeat the Duplicate command, Access places each subsequent copy so it has the same position relative to the last copy that this copy had to the original. Thus, if you move the first copy $1/8$ inch below the first, with the left edges aligned, Access will place the next copy $1/8$ inch below the second, aligned on the left.

When you use the Duplicate command, Access assigns a new name to each control, but copies the control source and caption (for labeled controls); obviously, you will want to edit these properties to make each control unique.

Working with Text in Forms and Reports

As the control names suggest, text boxes are the primary tool you will use to display or print text stored in Access tables, and label objects give you the means to display or print free-form text not directly or indirectly derived from a table. You have already seen some examples of how to use labels—they serve as the report titles and column titles in the documents created by the Wizards. You might also want to include longer text passages to provide instructions on how to use a form, to print footnotes that explain the abbreviations or special symbols in a report, to list the legitimate entries in a field, or to display more detailed information about a field than you can fit in the status bar. You could use a lengthy text passage to print a report introduction or cover page, or even to print the full text of a personalized letter.

Note. If you need to scroll through the text, you must use a text box whose Control Source property is set to an expression or constant text string rather than a label, as demonstrated in the personalized letters in Chapter 11.

Recall that when you use the toolbox to create a new label object, you can either use the mouse to predefine the size or you can simply begin typing and allow Access to expand the object frame to accommodate your entry. If you predefine the size of the text object, Access word-wraps the text you enter to fit within the specified width and adds new lines as necessary. Of course, after you finish entering the text, you can resize the frame, and in most cases, you will end up alternately adjusting the size of the frame and editing the contents to fit your message within the available space on the document. You must ensure that all of your text fits in the frame—you cannot add scroll bars to a label object in a form as you can in a text box used to display the contents of a field. Note also that if you change the font, font size, font weight, or other text attributes, you will usually have to resize the object. Figure 10.12 illustrates a screen with a long label that explains the purposes of the Committee Code and Member ID Code text boxes.

Figure 10.12
Using a text object
to display information

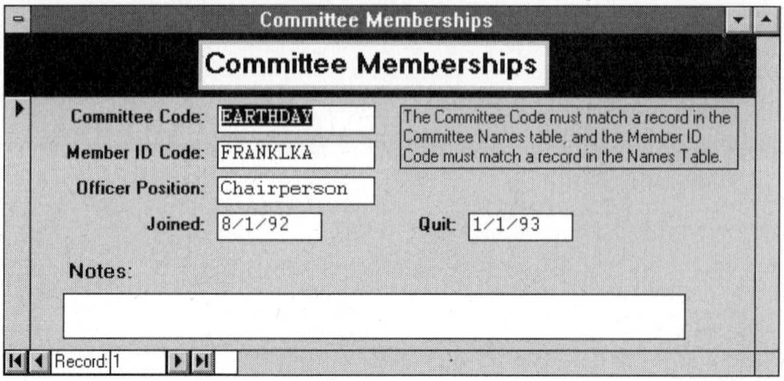

As you enter or edit the text in a label object, you can add a hard return to begin a new line at any point by pressing Shift+Enter. If you add a brand new label to a document and add a hard return while allowing Access to expand the object frame to accommodate your entry, Access sets the width of the frame to match this line (of course, you can resize it later if necessary).

You already know how to add text boxes to a form or report, and how to modify many of the characteristics of these controls. By default, text boxes are labeled, but it is easy to delete the label if you do not need it to identify the data displayed or collected in the text box. If you change your mind after deleting the label object originally associated with a text box (or any other labeled control), you can re-create it by adding a label object to the document. However, even if you place this object next to the text box, Access does not assume any connection between the two—it treats the new label as an independent control. To associate the label with an existing control, you must select the label object and use the Cut option on the Edit menu (or press Ctrl+X) to delete it from the form and copy it to the Clipboard. Then select the control with which you want to associate the label, and select the Paste option from the Edit menu (or press Ctrl+V). Regardless of where you typed the label on the work surface, Access moves it so that it assumes the position normally occupied by a label for the associated control; you can then move or resize it just as you would the original label.

Most of the other difficulties you will have with text in forms have to do with displaying and printing long Text and Memo fields, and both the problems and the solutions are somewhat different for forms and reports. In a

form, you will usually want each of the objects (including text boxes) to occupy a fixed amount of space, but without limiting your ability to view or edit the full contents of a long Text or Memo field. If you display the field in a text box that accommodates only one line of text, you must use the Left Arrow and Right Arrow keys to move through the text, and this technique is obviously unwieldy for fields that contain more than a few dozen words. If the text box is deep enough to accommodate more than one line, Access word-wraps the text to fit within the frame.

Note. Access displays scroll bars in a text box only when the control has the focus.

You can add a vertical scroll bar (but not a horizontal scroll bar) to facilitate using the mouse to scroll through a long Text or Memo field by setting the Scroll Bars property to Vertical. Figure 10.13 illustrates the result of adding a vertical scroll bar to the text box used to collect the Notes field.

Figure 10.13

Adding a vertical scroll bar to a text box

Committee Memberships
Committee Memberships

Committee Code: EARTHDAY	The Committee Code must match a record in the Committee Names table, and the Member ID Code must match a record in the Names Table.
Member ID Code: OLSONED	
Officer Position:	
Joined: 6/18/91	**Quit:** 5/20/92

Notes:

Ed organized the first ACE-sponsored "Run for the Planet" race and fun run, held in San Francisco in

Record: 4

In a report, you do not have the option to scroll through a lengthy text passage to view all of the contents, but Access allows you to decide whether or not to print all of the text. By default, Access treats text boxes on a report as fixed in size and truncates text that will not fit within the allotted space. However, in a report, which is usually not limited to a fixed number of pages, you will often want to allow text objects—and therefore, the report sections that contain these objects—to grow or shrink depending on the amount of data they contain. This behavior is controlled by the Can Grow and Can Shrink properties, which apply to individual objects and to report sections; both properties can take on the values Yes or No. In most cases, you will want to set Can Grow to Yes for Text fields that might require more than one line—such as the Address field in the ACE Names table—and for Memo fields, which might vary considerably in length. Most of the Access ReportWizards set Can Grow to Yes for Memo fields (unless you choose Ledger for the overall report look).

If you set the Can Grow property to Yes for any control in a report section, Access automatically sets the Can Grow property to Yes for the section as a whole. (If you change this property back to No for all the controls in the section, Access *does not* automatically reset this property for the section as a whole, although the net effect is the same.) Note that this is *not* always what you want. For example, in a mailing label report, you might set Can Grow to Yes for the Address field, but this property must be set to No for the detail section as a whole to ensure that each record fits within the physical boundaries of a mailing label. On a mailing label, you must set the Can Grow property to Yes for the Address field only if you can guarantee that even the longest address will fit on a label.

You can use the Can Shrink property to suppress the blank lines that would otherwise result from empty fields (such as the blank line between the name and address in Figure 10.11 due to the empty Company field). To ensure even spacing between those lines that are present, you must eliminate the blank space *between* the text objects, which you cannot suppress. To make these modifications in the Committee Memberships form, use the following steps:

1. Select the Company text box and set the Can Shrink property to Yes either by typing **Yes** or by choosing this option from the combo box.

2. Select the Address text box, and set both the Can Grow and Can Shrink properties to Yes.

3. Move the Company, Address, and CityStateZip text boxes up so that the top border of each object is superimposed on the lower border of the one above.

4. Move the text objects that print the committee headings up closer to the name and address block. Your screen should look like Figure 10.14 (in this figure, the Address field is selected to display the property sheet).

5. Preview the report and confirm that each address block is exactly large enough to accommodate the contents and contains no blank lines.

Drawing Lines and Rectangles

You can use lines and rectangles (boxes) to emphasize important parts of the form, to dress up an otherwise plain report or form, or to group related items together on the screen or printed page. You have already seen numerous examples in the forms and reports generated by the Access Wizards. In particular, if you choose the Executive or Presentation look for a report, Access uses lines of various thicknesses to set off the report header, page header, and group header sections.

Figure 10.14

Setting the Can
Grow and Can
Shrink properties

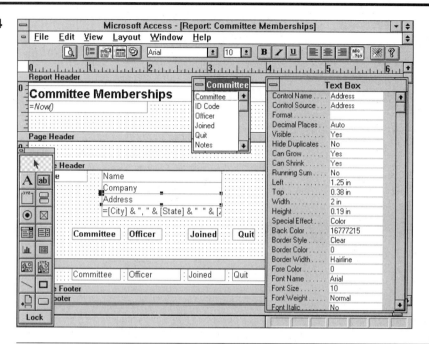

You can combine lines and rectangles with bordered field objects to create more complex effects in a form or report. For example, if you choose Boxed for the overall look of a form, the FormWizards move the labels directly above the associated text boxes and surround the label and the text box with a rectangle just barely larger. Figure 10.15 illustrates the Committees (Boxed) form from the sample ACE database in Design view with the Committee data entry region "exploded" to show the component parts. Several other properties contribute to the overall look in this form style: the color of the label is bright blue rather than black, the Font Weight property is Normal rather than the usual Bold for the label, and the Font Weight property is Bold rather than Normal for the text box. The Border Style property was set to Clear for both the text box and the label to make these borders invisible; instead, a rectangle object surrounds the text box and its label.

The Shadowed form look created by the FormWizards is also created with rectangles—for each field, there is a dark gray rectangle exactly the same size, positioned slightly below and to the right of the text box to create the dropped shadow.

Drawing a line or rectangle is easy:

1. Click on the Line or Rectangle button in the toolbox.

Figure 10.15

Creating the Boxed form look

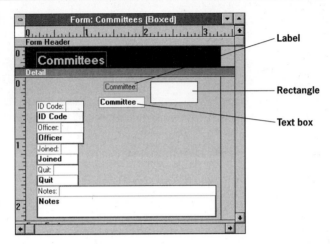

2. Position the mouse pointer crosshair over the location where you want one end (for a line) or one corner (for a rectangle).

3. Press and hold the left mouse button, drag the mouse to the other end (for a line) or opposite corner (for a rectangle) of the new object, and release the mouse button.

When you place any new object on a document, Access lays it over any other objects that it overlaps. Thus, if you draw a rectangle around one or more existing objects, it initially covers these objects completely. If you are using the rectangle as a frame, you can check the Clear box next to the Fill color samples in the color palette to make the background transparent and reveal the objects below. When you draw a solid colored rectangle, such as the ones used to create the dropped shadows in Shadowed forms, you cannot make the background transparent. Instead, you must use the Bring to Front or Send to Back option on the Layout menu to change the "stacking order" of the objects in the form. You can either select the original objects and choose Bring to Front, or select the rectangle and choose Send to Back; the latter method is easier if the newly created rectangle covers the existing objects completely.

If you want to draw a vertical or horizontal line, you can use the alignment grid as a guide, but as implied by the symbol on the face of the Line button in the toolbox, Access also allows you to draw diagonal lines. You can move or resize lines and rectangles just as you can any other objects, and you can customize the line width of either object by clicking on one of the Width buttons in the color palette or editing the Border Width property in the property sheet.

Note. The Can Grow and Can Shrink properties do not apply to rectangles, so you should not surround a text box that can grow with a rectangle. (This is the reason that the Can Grow property is set to No for all text boxes in Ledger reports, which include rectangles.) Instead, set the Border Style property to Normal for the text box.

Note that you cannot stretch a line to convert it to a rectangle, which is an entirely different type of object—if you pull the handle in the middle of a line, Access moves the midpoint of the line in the indicated direction, thus creating a diagonal line.

To add lines to the Committee Memberships report to match the Print Preview window shown in Figure 10.16, use the following steps:

1. Make sure that the property sheet, toolbox, and color palette are visible in the Report Design window. You can close the field list if it is currently displayed.

2. Move the property sheet down so that most of it is off the bottom of the screen and most of the ID Code header section is visible.

3. Click on the Line button in the toolbox. Position the crosshair on the grid dot just below the lower-left corner of the Committee text object, press the left mouse button, drag the line all the way to the right edge of the report, and release the mouse button.

4. Drag the lower boundary of the ID Code header section up until it is just below the new line.

5. Open up the ID Code footer section until it is about ¼ inch deep.

Figure 10.16

Adding lines to a report

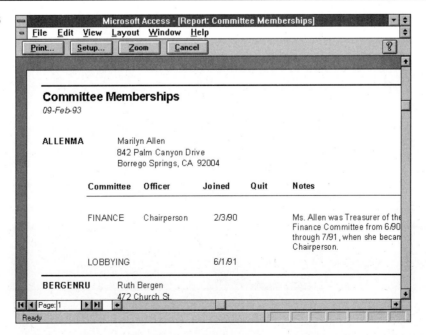

6. If necessary, move the toolbox and property sheet so that neither window covers up any of the ID Code footer section.

7. Using the same method as in step 3, draw a line the full width of the report in the middle of the ID Code footer section.

8. Click on the third button in the Width section of the color palette to make the new line thicker.

9. Preview the report. Your screen should look like Figure 10.16.

Adding Page Breaks

You can add a page break to a form or a report by using the Page Break tool in the toolbox. In a form, a page break allows you to use the PgUp and PgDn keys to move rapidly between "pages" (screens) when you use the form to update data. Page breaks work best in a form that displays several different categories of information, each on its own screen. For example, you could create a two-page form for updating the Names table with the name and address fields required for all records on the first page and the additional fields that are not filled in for prospects on the second. Chapter 18 describes how to use command buttons to switch between form pages, but you can always use the PgUp and PgDn keys to move from one page to another.

In a report, you can use page breaks to force Access to begin a new page *within* a report section even if additional space remains on the current page. For example, in a single-column or similar layout for a table that has too many fields to fit on one page, you could use a page break to specify exactly where the break should occur. To force a page break at the beginning or end of a section, you can set the Force New Page property for the report section to Before Section (to start a new page before printing the section), After Section (to start a new page after printing the section), or Before & After (to force page breaks both before and after the section).

To create a page break, click on the Page Break button in the toolbox and then click on the form at the vertical position where you want the page break. You cannot control the horizontal position or length of the page break symbol, which—unlike its counterpart in most word processing programs—does not extend all the way across the screen. Access always displays the page break as a short dotted line at the left edge of the form design window, regardless of where you clicked in the form, and it ignores any attempt to resize this symbol it or move it to the right.

Changing Default Object Properties

You have just learned how to change the default properties for individual objects of various types. You can change the defaults themselves for all the controls of a particular type on a particular form or report by editing the default property sheet for the control. To display this property sheet, make sure that both the toolbox and the property sheet are visible, and click on the appropriate button in the toolbox. Access displays a default property sheet for the selected type of control, which you can verify by the presence of the word "Default" in the title bar. Instead of proceeding to choose a field from the field list, simply edit any of the listed properties in the default property sheet. The current settings in the default property sheet always determine the properties of new objects that you add to a document. As is the case when you customize the properties of a single object, you can choose colors and border characteristics from the color palette, but you must enter other properties that you might normally change using direct manipulation techniques (such as the Width and Height properties) by typing them in the property sheet.

The default property sheets are similar but not identical to the standard property sheets that describe individual objects of the corresponding types. Obviously, the default property sheet does not have the Control Name, Control Source, or Caption properties, but there are more significant differences that you might easily overlook at first glance. For example, the default property sheet for text boxes, which is illustrated in Figure 10.17, has properties that govern the relationship between the text box and the associated label object.

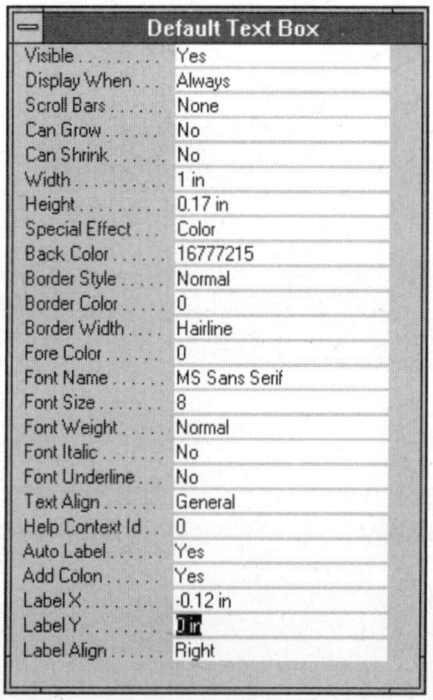

Figure 10.17

The default property sheet for text boxes

Default Text Box	
Visible	Yes
Display When	Always
Scroll Bars	None
Can Grow	No
Can Shrink	No
Width	1 in
Height	0.17 in
Special Effect	Color
Back Color	16777215
Border Style	Normal
Border Color	0
Border Width	Hairline
Fore Color	0
Font Name	MS Sans Serif
Font Size	8
Font Weight	Normal
Font Italic	No
Font Underline	No
Text Align	General
Help Context Id	0
Auto Label	Yes
Add Colon	Yes
Label X	-0.12 in
Label Y	0 in
Label Align	Right

The Auto Label property determines whether Access automatically adds a label to each new text box. When you set up forms such as mailing labels or columnar reports from scratch, you can set Auto Label to No to suppress the labels (in a columnar format, the column titles are separate label objects in the page header section or a group header section). The Add Colon property determines whether there is a trailing colon at the end of the label caption, and the Label Align property specifies the alignment of the caption within the text object frame. You would probably want to set Add Colon to No when you set up a form intended primarily for use in Datasheet view, where the labels are displayed as column titles in the field selectors at the top of the window.

The Label X and Label Y properties specify the position of the label relative to the text box object, expressed in inches measured along the respective axes. Negative values indicate placement to the left on the X-axis or below on the Y-axis. The defaults are –0.12 for Label X (so the label appears 0.12 inch to the left of the text box) and 0 for Label Y (so the label is at the same height as the text box). To create the Boxed form look shown in Figure 10.15, the Form-Wizard sets the Label X property to 0 to line up the label horizontally with the text box, and sets Label Y to –0.15 to position the label just above the text box.

If you have already customized many of the properties of a particular object, you can use it as a model to establish the default properties for all objects of the same type. To use this method, select the object and then choose the Change Default option from the Layout menu. In many cases, you will want to make additional changes in the default object property sheet to set properties that are not applicable to individual objects (such as the Auto Label or Add Colon properties for text boxes), but you can nevertheless save considerable time and avoid duplicated effort by deriving the default properties from an existing object.

Recall that the default properties are applied only to new objects that you place on the document. However, you can assign the current default properties to existing objects by selecting them and then choosing Apply Default from the Layout menu. You can use this technique to modify multiple objects in a form generated by one of the Access Wizards. For example, you could change the colors, border style, or label position of all the text boxes in a form. However, even if you set Auto Colon to No, the Apply Default option does not remove the colons from existing labels—Access respects this property only when you add a new text box to a document. Thus, you cannot use this technique to remove the colons from the labels in the subforms generated by the Main/Subform Form-Wizard, which displays the child records in Datasheet view.

NOTE. *You can only change the default properties of one type of object at a time. If you use a combination of objects to create a certain visual effect (like the boxed and shadowed form styles), you cannot describe the entire group using default properties. The easiest way to replicate a group of objects is to use the cut and paste methods described earlier in this chapter.*

Setting Overall Form and Report Properties

The Form and Report properties, which are established through the property sheets illustrated in Figures 10.18 and 10.19, govern the overall properties and behavior of a document as a whole. Several of the properties are common to both forms and reports, while others apply only to one type of document. You are already familiar with the Grid X and Grid Y properties, which enable you to customize the alignment grid spacing.

Figure 10.18

The report
property sheet

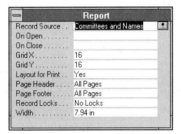

Report	
Record Source . .	Committees and Names
On Open	
On Close	
Grid X	16
Grid Y	16
Layout for Print . .	Yes
Page Header	All Pages
Page Footer	All Pages
Record Locks . . .	No Locks
Width	7.94 in

Figure 10.19

The form
property sheet

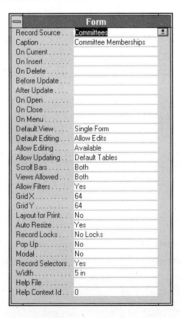

Form	
Record Source . .	Committees
Caption	Committee Memberships
On Current	
On Insert	
On Delete	
Before Update . . .	
After Update	
On Open	
On Close	
On Menu	
Default View	Single Form
Default Editing . . .	Allow Edits
Allow Editing	Available
Allow Updating . .	Default Tables
Scroll Bars	Both
Views Allowed . . .	Both
Allow Filters	Yes
Grid X	64
Grid Y	64
Layout for Print . .	No
Auto Resize	Yes
Record Locks . . .	No Locks
Pop Up	No
Modal	No
Record Selectors .	Yes
Width	5 in
Help File	
Help Context Id . .	0

The Record Source property listed at the top of both property sheets identifies the source table or query for a form or report. If you need to change the data source after you have created a document, you can do so by editing this entry in the property sheet. (You *must* use this method to identify the record source if you bypassed the Select a Table/Query combo box in the New Form or New Report dialog box and moved directly to a blank document.) For example, you might want to use a report originally designed for a particular table to print a subset of the data (selected by using a query) or use the same generic mailing label report for several similarly structured name and address tables. Often, you will change the data source from a table to a query in reports or forms designed early in the application development cycle before you were prepared to deal with any unnecessary complexities. For example, in the ACE system, you might decide to add fields from the Names table to a report originally based only on the Transactions table by defining a query that links the two tables and then using this query as the record source for the report. You can type the table or query name directly in the property sheet, or you can choose it from a drop-down list that includes all available tables and queries. (You may want to widen the property sheet temporarily if it is not wide enough to distinguish between similarly named queries.)

The Layout for Print property determines whether Access uses screen or printer fonts in the document. If you set Layout for Print to Yes, the font name lists associated with the combo boxes in the tool bar and in the property sheet will include only printer fonts. By default, this property is set to Yes for reports and to No for forms, but you might also want to select Yes for forms that you intend to display and print interchangeably. If you have already chosen screen fonts for objects on the screen, Access will substitute the closest available printer font when you print the form. Note, however, that if you have TrueType or Adobe Type Manager fonts, choosing these fonts will ensure that the appearance of a document on the screen always matches the way it will look when printed, regardless of the value of the Layout for Print property; this property simply safeguards against choosing inappropriate fonts.

Setting Overall Form Properties

As you can see by comparing Figures 10.18 and 10.19, forms have far more properties than reports. You can use the overall form properties to solve some of the problems noted in Chapters 6 and 8. For example, as noted in Chapter 6, even if you prefer the layout of the datasheet, you may need to design forms so that you can save more than one customized data sheet layout for a table or to gain access to the Filter/Sort options, which are not available in the default Datasheet view. By default, Access displays all forms in Form view, although you can switch to Datasheet view at any time, but you can use the Default View property to specify which view you want to use as the default for a particular form. You can choose Single Form to display one record at a time, Continuous Forms to display as many records as will fit on the screen at once (as in the tabular form pictured in Figure 6.3), or Datasheet. If you examine the main form and subform created by the main/subform FormWizard, you will see that the Default View property is set to Single Form for the main form and to Datasheet for the subform. Remember that the Default View property only governs which view appears when you first open a form—it does not prevent you from switching to Form view or Datasheet view. To restrict the form to just one display style, you can use the Views Allowed property, which you can set to Form, Datasheet, or Both (by default, this property is set to Both). You can take advantage of these properties to build forms that store several different datasheet configurations for the same table. Simply design a form for each custom datasheet layout, adjust the appearance in Datasheet view, and set the Default View property to Datasheet. You can set the Views Allowed property either to Datasheet or Both, depending on whether you ever need to use the form in Form View. In a form that will be used only in Datasheet view, you need not be concerned with the layout of the fields in the form.

You can use the Default Editing, Allow Editing, and Allow Updating properties to control whether a form can be used to update or add records to a table. The Allow Editing property, which you can set to Available or Unavailable, controls the status of the Allow Editing option on the Records menu, which is disabled if you choose Unavailable. The Default Editing property can take on three values, which have the following effects:

Allow Edits	Allows you to add, edit, and delete records
Read Only	Forbids all updates
Data Entry	Allows you to add new records but not view existing records

Note that setting Default Editing to Read Only is not a foolproof way to prevent editing—it simply prohibits editing by default, when you first open the form. You can still choose the Allow Editing option on the Records menu if you want to edit data. To prohibit editing entirely, you can set Default Editing to Read Only and set Allow Editing to Unavailable. Similarly, the Data Entry option does not prevent you from viewing the entire source table or query dynaset—you can still use the Show All Records option on the Records menu to exit from data entry mode and see previously entered records.

The Allow Filters property governs access to the Filter/Sort options. If you choose No, Access disables the three Filter/Sort command buttons in the tool bar and the corresponding options on the Records menu.

You may recall from Chapter 8 that by default Access does not allow you to update fields derived from the parent table when you update a query dynaset based on tables with a one-to-many relationship. You can override this default by resetting the Allow Updating property, which is normally set to Default Tables, to Any Tables. (However, you will still not be allowed to update the dynasets of totals queries, in which each row might represent more than one record in the underlying source tables.) You can also set this property to No Tables to prohibit all table updates and thus render the form read only. When you do this, Access displays the message "Form is read only" in the status bar if you try to edit any field, and it disables *all* the menu options that would enable you to add or delete records.

The form properties also give you a degree of control over the navigation aids displayed when you use the form. The Scroll Bars property determines whether Access displays horizontal and/or vertical scroll bars in the form window. Unlike the corresponding property for text boxes, the form property offers four choices—Neither, Horizontal Only, Vertical Only, and Both. You might want to turn off the scroll bars in a form with page breaks to gain complete control over which group of fields is displayed at any given moment; however, if you ever intend to use a form in Datasheet view, you will probably want to retain both scroll bars. The Record Selectors property determines whether Access displays the standard navigation controls in the lower-left corner of the form window border. This option has no effect on the menu bar—even when you set Record Selectors to No to suppress the navigation controls, you can still move around in the table by using the options on the submenu invoked by choosing Go To from the Records menu. Unless you plan to provide your own custom navigation controls (usually in the form of command buttons, using techniques outlined in Chapter 18), you will usually want to retain the standard navigation controls.

The Auto Resize property, which is Yes by default, requests that Access resize the form window large enough to accommodate a whole record (if possible). If Auto Resize is set to No, the form is displayed the same size it was the last time you saved it. Note that the Auto Resize option governs only how a form behaves when you open it from the Database window (or from another form)—if you move to Form view from Design view, Access does not resize the window. The easiest way to resize the window after you modify a form is to use the Size to Fit Form option in the Window menu.

Setting Section Properties

You can use the section property sheets to customize the behavior of individual sections of a form or report. As noted briefly earlier in this chapter, you can set the Can Grow and Can Shrink properties for a report section to determine

whether it can vary in size depending on its contents. You may also want to set
the Visible property for a section to No to suppress the section in a particular
print run. For example, in a report with groups, you might at times suppress the
detail section and print only the group header followed immediately by the
group footer (which contains group summary statistics). The other section
properties that you will find useful immediately are those that control various
aspects of pagination.

You can use the Page Header and Page Footer properties (which are
available only for reports, not forms) to specify when to print the page header
and page footer sections. By default, both properties are set to All Pages, and
Access prints the header and footer on all pages of the report, including the
report header and report footer sections. You can choose Not with Rpt Hdr,
Not with Rpt Ftr, or Not with Rpt Hdr/Ftr to suppress the page header or
page footer section on either or both of these sections. For example, you
might want to omit both the page header and footer from the report header
section if you use this section to print a cover page, and you might suppress
the page footer (which typically contains a page number) in the report footer
section if you use this section for overall summary statistics that you distribute separately, without the detail pages of the report. Note, however, that
Access always keeps track of the current page number even if you do not
print it—regardless of whether you print the page header or footer in a one-
page report header section, the next page of the report will be numbered 2,
not 1. You can circumvent this limitation with a macro, using a technique outlined in Chapter 18.

As noted earlier, you can force a page break at the beginning or end of
any report section (or both) by resetting the Force New Page property for the
section. The Keep Together property, which you can set for any section of a
report or form except the page header or page footer, determines whether
Access attempts to print the entire section together on one page. When you
set this property to Yes, Access begins a new page before it prints the section
if not enough lines remain on the page for the whole section. For example, in
a report like the new version of the Committee Membership report created in
this chapter, you might set Keep Together to Yes for the ID Code header section so that a member name and address are never split across a page break.
Setting this property to Yes for the detail section would ensure that all of a
person's committee memberships are printed on the same page. If the section
is too long to fit on one page (for example, if the memo fields are very long or
if there are a great many detail records), Access ignores the Keep Together
property and splits the section across a page boundary.

Finishing the Committee Memberships Report

To produce the final version of the Committee Memberships report, begin by converting the report header section to a cover sheet and customizing the overall form properties and the properties of the individual report sections:

1. Make sure that the toolbox, color palette, and property sheet are visible on the screen (you may have to move these tools around to gain access to various portions of the report as you carry out the steps in this section).

2. Choose Select Report from the Edit menu to display the overall property sheet for the report.

3. Enter **8** for the Width property to widen the report.

4. Select Not with Rpt Hdr for the Page Footer property to suppress the page number on the report header page.

5. Expand the page header section to ½ inch deep.

6. Click anywhere in the report header section to display the property sheet for this section.

7. Change the Height property to 7 to expand the report header section, and set the Force New Page property to After Section to force a page break and print the section as a separate cover sheet.

8. Delete the heavy line above the report title, and move the text object that prints the report title down so that the upper border lines up with the 4½-inch mark in the vertical ruler.

9. Using the combo box in the tool bar, select 24-point type for the report title.

10. Resize the text object (make it narrower and deeper) so that the text wraps onto two lines.

11. Click on the Center alignment button in the tool bar to center both lines of text within the frame.

12. In the property sheet, select 2 pt. for the Border Width property. Note that the corresponding button is selected in the color palette. Set the Border Style to Normal rather than Clear, and note that the Clear box to the right of the Border color samples in the palette is no longer checked.

13. Using the Rectangle tool in the toolbox, draw a rectangle around the report title object slightly larger than the text object (one or two grid dots should separate the rectangle from the object border). Click on the third

Width button in the palette to match the width of the rectangle to the text object border. Select Send to Back from the Layout menu to move the rectangle behind the text object.

14. Click the mouse outside the rectangle and drag it to enclose both the rectangle and the report title object. Move both objects to the right so they are centered on the page (not on the screen).

15. Move the calculated control that prints the date to about ¹/₂ inch below the report title, and widen it to match the width of the surrounding rectangle.

16. In the object property sheet, edit the Control Source property sheet to read

```
"=As of " & Format(Now(),"Long Date")
```

Delete the previously established setting for the Format property, which is no longer needed. Set the Font Italic property to No, and set the Text Align property to Center. Your screen should look something like Figure 10.20.

17. Set the Keep Together property to Yes for the ID Code header section.

Figure 10.20

The cover page for the Committee Memberships report

18. Move the calculated control that prints the page number in the page footer to the far right edge of the report.

19. Click in the text box on the work surface to display an insertion point, and edit the expression to read **"Page " & Page** (the word "Page" followed by the value of the Page property, which matches the current page number). Click on the Font Italic button in the tool bar to turn off italic for the page number.

20. Preview or print the report and confirm that Access begins a new page after printing the report header section and that the date and page number are printed in the correct formats.

The remaining modifications involve adding a count of the number of committees to the ID Code footer section and adding the committee name to the detail section, so that the report resembles Figure 10.21. The steps are as follows:

1. Move the Committee text box to the far left edge of the detail band, shrink it to about 1/4 inch wide, and set the Visible property to No to render this field invisible. You cannot delete this control, because it is required to find the matching record in the Committee Names table (as outlined in step 4).

2. Move the Officer, Joined, Quit, and Notes fields as far as possible to the right.

3. Using the toolbox, add an unbound text object to the detail band to the right of the Committee text box, at the 1/2-inch mark in the horizontal ruler, and widen this object to fill all the available space. Delete the attached label object.

4. Click in the text box object and enter an expression based on the DLookUp function that looks up a match for the Committee object in the Committee Names table and returns the full committee name. The DLookUp function takes three inputs, all of which are text strings. The first specifies the value you want to return (in this case, the Description field from the Committee Names table), the second specifies the source of the data (in this case, the name of the source table), and the third specifies the condition that describes how to find the right record in the source table. The expression is as follows:

```
=DLookUp("[Description]", "Committee Names",
"[Committee] = Form.[Committee]")
```

The condition in this expression searches for a value in the Committee field that matches the value of the Committee object in the current form.

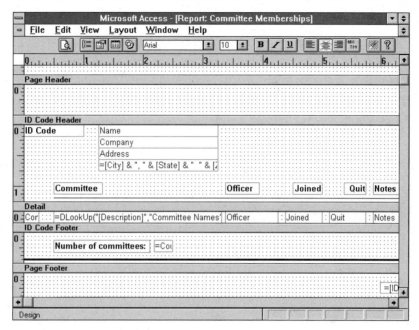

Figure 10.21

The final version of the Committee Memberships report

---

5. Move the text objects that display the column titles in the ID Code header band to line up with the matching text boxes in the Detail band, placing the Joined and Quit labels so that they align with the right side of the corresponding text boxes. Select Right alignment for both of these text objects.

6. Move the line under these text objects to the left to line up with the new position of the Committee label, and widen this line almost to the right edge of the report.

7. Widen the heavier line in the ID Code footer section so it too extends almost to the right edge of the report.

8. Expand the ID Code footer section to about ½ inch deep.

9. Move the line down to the bottom of the section.

10. Add an unbound text box above the line. Type **Number of committees:** in the Caption property for the label. Widen the label object to match the length of the caption and position the label directly under the text box that prints the name of the committee.

11. In the text box, type the expression **=Count([Committee])** to compute the number of committee membership records. Because this aggregate function appears in a group footer section, Access automatically applies the calculation to the records in the group, not the entire dynaset on which the report is based. At this point, your screen should look something like Figure 10.21. (All the tools were removed from the work surface in this figure to reveal as much of the report design as possible.)

12. Preview or print the report, and then save it. Figure 10.22 illustrates the first page of data.

Summary

This chapter introduced a variety of specific techniques for customizing forms and reports—those that you created from scratch as well as documents originally generated by the FormWizards and ReportWizards. If the number of details seems overwhelming, concentrate for now on those attributes and properties for which you can find immediate use in your own forms. Strive to understand the crucial concept that is fundamental to working with Access forms and reports—the fact that the appearance and behavior of all Access objects, from the largest (a form or report) to the smallest (a label object) are described by their properties. If this concept is new to you, consider leaving the property sheet visible at all times as you work in Form Design and Report Design view; this should cement the relationship between the various methods used to customize properties (direct manipulation with the mouse, the color palette, and so on) and the properties themselves, and also will remind your of the properties available for the various types of objects.

Like Chapters 6 and 7, this chapter concentrated on the mechanics of modifying existing reports and forms. Chapters 11 and 12 describe how to build new reports and forms from scratch without using the Wizards, but more importantly, they outline strategies for building a variety of reports and forms typical of those required in the average Access database application. Make sure you feel reasonably confident using the techniques described in this chapter before you begin constructing these more sophisticated documents.

Figure 10.22

The first page of data printed by the Committee Memberships report

ALLENMA	Marilyn Allen 842 Palm Canyon Drive Borrego Springs, CA 92004				
Committee		**Officer**	**Joined**	**Quit**	**Notes**
Finance Committee		Chairperson	2/3/90		Ms. Allen was Treasurer of the Finance Committee from 6/90 through 7/91, when she became Chairperson
Lobbying Coordination Committee			6/3/91		
Number of committees:	2				

BERGENRU	Ruth Bergen 472 Church St. San Francisco, CA 94114				
Committee		**Officer**	**Joined**	**Quit**	**Notes**
Newsletter Production Committee		Chairperson	8/10/91		
Number of committees:	1				

BLOOMCH	Mr. Christopher Bloom 2140 Shattuck Ave. Suite 502 Berkeley, CA 94704				
Committee		**Officer**	**Joined**	**Quit**	**Notes**
Newsletter Production Committee			3/28/90	3/1/92	
Number of committees:	1				

FRANKLKA	Karen Franklin 3605 Sacramento San Francisco, CA 94118				
Committee		**Officer**	**Joined**	**Quit**	**Notes**
Earth Day Events Planning Committee		Chairperson	8/1/92		
Number of committees:	1				

Page 2

11

Designing Reports

YOU ALREADY KNOW HOW TO USE THE ACCESS REPORTWIZARDS TO produce several very common types of reports—single-column layouts, columnar layouts with groups and/or totals, and mailing labels—and how to modify the resulting reports to enhance their appearance and customize them to your detailed requirements. If one of these basic layouts comes close to meeting your needs, allowing the ReportWizards to generate a report initially and then editing the result in Report Design view is often the most efficient way to produce the desired layout. If not, you will be forced to build a report from scratch, starting with a blank form. You might also want to forgo the convenience of using the ReportWizards if you do not like the default stylistic conventions adopted by the Wizards—the font, font size, use of lines and borders, and so on.

This chapter describes how to create a report from scratch by adding sections and objects to a blank report. You already have enough experience working in Report Design view that you should feel comfortable with the mechanics of building the report. If you find the blank report intimidating, the best way to surmount this barrier is to start by placing the most important objects—the text boxes that print the fields in the detail section—on the work surface. Don't waste too much time agonizing over the position, size, and visual attributes of these objects—you can customize all of these properties later and add the more problematic items, such as calculated values, later. If your preferences differ significantly from the Access defaults, you can avoid having to customize a great many object properties individually by using methods described in this chapter to define default object properties, either for a particular report or for all future reports you add to your database.

This chapter also rounds out the discussions in Chapters 7, 8, and 10 with a detailed explanation of the mechanisms for defining and modifying the sorting and grouping instructions, and for building composite reports with one or more subreports. These techniques are illustrated with a variety of reports that might be considered prototypical layouts. If you are building an Access database of your own, try to visualize how you might use these generic report types in your application, and how you might mix and match the report components described in this chapter to produce additional report styles and layouts.

Defining a Report from Scratch

To define a new report from scratch, begin by using any of the standard methods to initiate the report design process:

- Make sure that the Database window displays the list of reports, and then click on the New command button or press Alt+N.

- Whenever the Database window is visible, choose New from the File menu and then choose Report from the submenu of new object types.

- Highlight a table or query name in the Database window, and then click on the New Report command button in the tool bar (the third of the three new object buttons).

As described in Chapter 7, Access responds by displaying the New Report dialog box shown in Figure 7.2. If you wish, you can choose the source table or query for the report by making a selection from the combo box at the top of the New Report dialog box, but when you define a report from scratch, you can specify the data source later by entering the name of a table or query in the Record Source entry on the report property sheet. (In contrast, when you use a Wizard to define a form or report, Access displays an error message and refuses to close the New Report dialog box until you have chosen the data source). To exit from the New Report dialog box, select Blank Report, either by clicking on the Blank Report command button, by pressing Alt+B, or by pressing Enter (Blank Report is the default option in this dialog box).

The ability to begin defining a report without choosing a data source gives you the flexibility to create reports that do not depend on any table—such as preprinted input forms (on which you will later enter data by hand), return address labels (which contain only text), or composite reports made up of several independent subreports. Until you have chosen the data source, both the Field List toggle button in the tool bar and the corresponding option on the View menu are disabled, so you cannot display the field list. However, you can edit other aspects of the layout and add controls that do not depend on tables.

Figure 11.1 illustrates a blank report in Report Design view, with the property sheet visible on the work surface to show the default report properties. By default, Access displays only the three most commonly used report sections—the page header, page footer, and detail section. The blank report is 5 inches wide, the detail section is 1 inch high, and the page header and footer sections are each 1/4 inch high. The grid spacing is 10 dots per inch horizontally by 12 dots per inch vertically, although the grid will be visible only if the Grid option on the View menu was checked the last time you worked in Report Design view.

When you create a report from scratch, exactly the same tools, command buttons, and menu options are available in Report Design view as when you edit a report generated by the ReportWizards, and you can use all of the methods described in Chapter 10 to add or remove sections, add controls, and customize the appearance of the report. Although you may at first find the blank Report Design screen intimidating, designing a report from scratch is far less tedious than you might expect—and often less tedious than making extensive modifications to a report generated by the ReportWizards. You can

Figure 11.1

A blank report

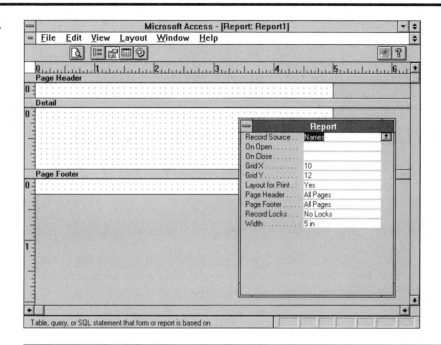

save a great deal of time by customizing the default property sheets for text boxes, labels, and other controls that you commonly use in reports *before* you add any controls to the report, so that you do not have to change numerous properties of a great many objects individually afterward. In most cases, you should choose a moderately coarse grid density (between 10 and 16 dots per inch both vertically and horizontally), display the grid, and enable the Snap to Grid option to facilitate placing, moving, and resizing objects. If you need to make fine adjustments to some controls to fine-tune the report appearance, you can change the grid settings later.

Customizing the Report Design Environment

You can customize several aspects of the default form and report design environment by selecting Options from the View menu and then choosing Form & Report Design from the scrolling list of option categories. Figure 11.2 illustrates the Options dialog box with the default settings for the Report and Form Design view options visible in the Items list. Note that you do not have to call up the Options dialog box from Form Design view or Report Design view to customize the Form & Report Design options—you can choose Options from the View menu whenever a database is open to edit the options in any available category. As suggested by the description, the Form & Report Design options affect both Form Design and Report Design views—you cannot choose different settings for forms and reports. The options are used as follows:

Form Template	Specifies the template for forms not created using the FormWizards.
Report Template	Specifies the template for reports not created using the ReportWizards.
Objects Snap to Grid	Determines whether the Snap to Grid option on the Layout menu is initially enabled.
Show Grid	Determines whether the Grid option on the View menu is initially enabled.
Selection Behavior	Determines which objects Access selects when you drag the mouse around them. If you choose Fully Enclosed, only objects that are completely surrounded are selected; if you retain the default choice, Partially Enclosed, all objects that are partially enclosed are selected.
Show Ruler	Determines whether the rulers are initially displayed.

The Form Template and Report Template options specify the names of a form and report that you want Access to use as *templates* for forms and reports *not* created using the Wizards. The default templates are both named

Figure 11.2

Customizing the Form & Report options

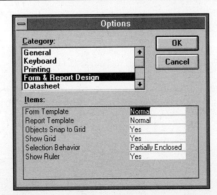

Normal. The template governs many detailed characteristics of a form or report, including all of the following:

- Which sections are initially displayed

- The width of the form or report and the height of each section

- The default properties of all objects (the report or form as a whole, the individual sections, and all types of controls)

You can use any report as a template, including one that you created for use in a database application, but it is preferable to create a special report that serves *only* as a template. This strategy ensures that you do not inadvertently alter the default settings used for future reports by editing the report that serves as the template. To create a special template report, simply open a blank report, establish all the desired property settings, and save the report. You need not add any controls to the report to customize the default control properties—with the toolbox, property sheet, and color palette visible on the work surface, simply click on the appropriate button in the toolbox to display the default property sheet, and edit the properties as you see fit by using the color palette and the controls in the tool bar, or by making entries directly in the property sheet. Figure 11.3 illustrates a report template that incorporates the following changes from the built-in defaults:

- The grid spacing was set to 16 dots per inch both vertically and horizontally.

- The Report Hdr/Ftr option was selected (in the default template, Page Hdr/Ftr is already selected).

- The section heights were set to $1/2$ inch for the report header and page header sections, 1 inch (the default) for the detail section, $1/4$ inch (the default) for the page footer, and 1 inch for the report footer.

- The width of the report was set to 7 inches.

- The font size was set to 10 points.

- The Auto Label property for the default text box was set to No.

Remember that even if the form or report template includes objects, Access does not copy these objects to new reports created with this template in effect—the template describes only the *properties* of a report and the objects you place on the report, not its contents.

Note that all of the options established through the Options dialog box, including the form and report templates, are global settings that apply to all of your work with Access—they are not local to the database that was open when you selected them. There is no built-in provision for customizing the

Figure 11.3

Defining a template report

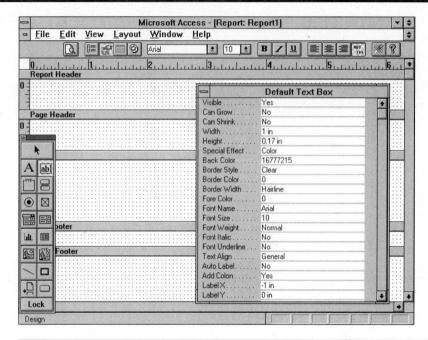

settings for just one database. However, Access looks for the form or report named as the template in the current database, and if it cannot find the template, it reverts to the built-in defaults referred to as the Normal template. To use different form or report templates, simply create a unique form or report template in every database and *assign the template the same name in each database* (names like Report Template or Form Template are good choices). Unfortunately, using the same template in all your Access databases requires more work, because you must copy or export the template form or report to each new database you create (using commands described in Chapter 14). In either case, remember to enter the template names in the Form Template and Report Template settings in the Options dialog box.

Customizing the Sorting and Grouping Instructions

All of the reports described thus far that included groups or summary statistics were generated by the groups/totals ReportWizard. When you design a report from scratch, you must obviously define the sorting and grouping instructions yourself, but you may also need to modify the groups or change the sort order in a report originally created using the groups/totals ReportWizard. Access allows up to ten groups and/or sort levels in the data source for a report. If the report is based on a query, this limit applies to groups and sorting instructions specified in the query as well as to those defined in the Sorting and Grouping dialog box. As in a query, you cannot sort or group on Memo or OLE Object fields. To add to or change the grouping and sorting instructions, you must display the Sorting and Grouping dialog box, either by clicking on the Sorting and Grouping command button in the tool bar or by selecting the Sorting and Grouping option from the View menu. Figure 11.4 illustrates the Names by State and City report (originally described in Chapter 7) in Report Design view, with the Sorting and Grouping dialog box visible on the screen.

Figure 11.4

The Sorting and Grouping dialog box

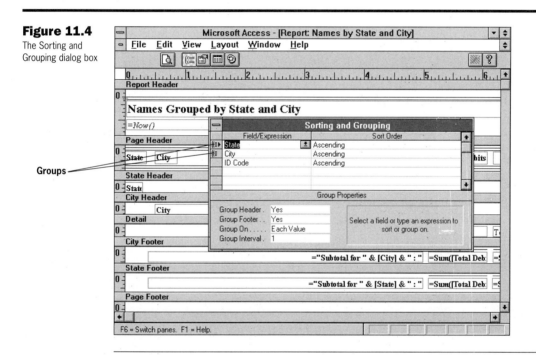

Like the Table Design view window, the Sorting and Grouping dialog box is divided into two major regions. The upper portion of the window displays the fields on which the sorting and grouping instructions are based, and the lower portion describes the properties of the groups. As in Table Design view, you can move between the upper and lower regions by pressing F6 or by clicking anywhere in either region. By default, the Sorting and Grouping dialog box displays only five full rows, but you can enlarge the window if you need to see more. You can change the relative widths of the Field/Expression and

Sort order columns by using the mouse to drag the boundary between the two column selectors either to the left or to the right.

You use the Sorting and Grouping dialog box to define both report groups and sorting instructions. You can sort without defining any groups, but the converse is not true: If you want groups, you *must* sort the source table or query to ensure that all the records in each group are in fact adjacent in the report processing sequence. For example, if you did not sort the Names by State and City report by state, Access would begin a new group each time the State field changed, and there would be more than one group for each state. You must therefore fill in sorting instructions for each field or expression you enter in the Field/Expression column; when you add a new row, Access enters the default sort order (ascending) automatically. To identify the groups, Access displays the standard grouping icon (a series of lines that represent records with brackets delineating the groups) in the row selectors for the rows that represent groups. In Figure 11.4, you can see that the Names by State and City report has groups based on State and City, but not on ID Code, which serves only as a sort key.

To define sorting instructions, you list the sort keys from major to minor order (from the largest groups to the smallest) in the Sorting and Grouping dialog box. Just as in a query, the sort keys can be fields or expressions, and you can choose ascending or descending order for each sort key. All of the entries in the upper half of the Sorting and Grouping dialog box are combo boxes, so you can make your selections by typing them or by selecting them from drop-down lists. As in Query Design view, the easiest way to select the sort order is to type A or D in the Sort Order column. Note that the Field/Expression combo box includes all the fields in the source table or query—and only those fields. When you design a query that will serve as the data source for a report, remember to include in the output grid any fields that you intend to sort or group on, even if they will not appear on the report.

If you want to base sorting or grouping instructions on an expression, you must type the expression in the Field/Expression column, preceded by an equals sign, as you do when you define a calculated control on a report or form. For example, to sort the records in each city in descending order by the balance (the difference between the credits and debits), you could enter =[Total Credits]–[Total Debits] in the Field/Expression column, and choose Descending from the Sort Order combo box. If your field names are long or you sort on complex expressions, you may want to make the Field/Expression column (and perhaps the Sorting and Grouping dialog box as a whole) wider.

You can use the standard methods based on the selector buttons to the left of the rows to edit the list of sorting and grouping instructions. To move a row, click on the selector to highlight the whole row, and then drag the row to a new position. If you move a row that represents a group, Access immediately rearranges the group header and footer sections on the report to conform to

Figure 11.6

Sorting in descending order by date

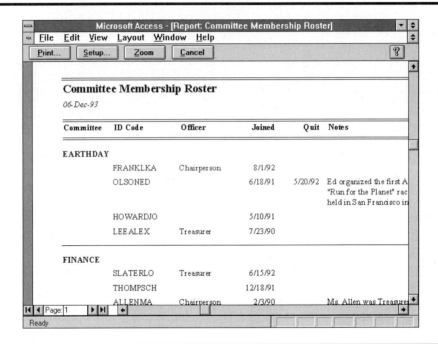

Defining the Group Properties

You customize the four properties that describe each group in the property sheet in the lower half of the Sorting and Grouping dialog box, much the way you enter field properties in the lower portion of the Table Design window. In Figure 11.4, the properties of the State group are visible. The Group Header and Group Footer properties, which you can set to Yes or No, determine whether the respective sections are present in the report. Note that setting either of these properties to No is *not* equivalent to reducing the height of the section to zero—setting the Group Header or Group Footer property to No removes the corresponding section completely, so that not even the identifying band appears on the Report Design work surface. In a report with four or five groups, deleting unneeded header or footer sections can save considerable space on a crowded screen.

In the reports generated by the groups/totals ReportWizard, both Group Header and Group Footer properties are set to Yes for every group. The group header sections print the fields that define the groups, and if there are no totals in the group footer section (because you did not include any numeric fields on the report), this section is present but empty in Report Design view. As noted in Chapter 10, you will often want to modify the group header sections to display additional descriptive information. In other cases, you might prefer to conserve space on the printed page by deleting the group header sections for relatively small groups like the city groups in the Names by State and City report.

Figure 11.7 illustrates a version of this report in which the City field is printed as one of the columns in the detail section, rather than as a separate group header, and the records in each group are arranged in descending order by total credits. To avoid printing the group field (in this case, the city) over and over, you can suppress all but the first occurrence of the field in a series of records that share the same value by setting the Hide Duplicates property to Yes. Note that this report layout is practical only if there is enough room in the detail section for the group field. This is always the case in the layouts created by the groups/totals ReportWizard, in which Access does not place other fields below the text boxes that print the group fields in the group header sections. However, if you later decide you need more columns in the report, you might prefer to move the fields in the detail section to the left under the headers to gain space for additional fields or calculated controls. To reproduce the report in Figure 11.7, use the following steps:

1. Open the Names by State and City report in Report Design view.

2. Move the City text box from the city header section into the detail section, placing it slightly higher than the other text boxes. Select the City and ID Code text boxes, select Align from the Layout menu, and then choose Bottom from the submenu of alignment options.

3. If the property sheet is not already visible, click on the Property Sheet button or choose the equivalent option from the View menu to display it.

4. Set the Hide Duplicates property to Yes for the City text box.

5. Delete the label object above the State text box from the page header section.

6. Move the label object that identifies the City field to the left to align with the City text box in the detail section. To align the objects, hold the Shift key down and click in the City text box so that both the label and the text box are selected, select Align from the Layout menu, and then choose Left from the submenu of alignment options.

7. Click on the Sorting and Grouping button or choose the equivalent option on the View menu to display the Sorting and Grouping dialog box.

8. Press Down Arrow to highlight the City row, and note that the Group Header and Group Footer properties are both set to Yes.

9. Press F6 to move down to the property sheet in the lower portion of the dialog box, and type **No** for the Group Header property. Notice that the

Figure 11.7

A report with a
group that has no
group header

Names Grouped by State and City

09-Dec-93

City	ID Code	Name	Total Debits	Total Credits
CA				
Berkeley	BLOOMCH	Mr. Christopher Bloom	1,000.00	2,550.00
	ANDERSMI	Michael Anderson	0.00	622.00
	REEDLUCY	Ms. Lucy Reed	0.00	320.00
	MOOREJOS	Mr. and Mrs. Joseph Moore	0.00	275.00
	CLARKAMY	Ms. Amy C. Clark		
	ENGLEJOHN	John Engle		
	GRAYJON	Jonathan Gray		
	SCHAEFDO	Mr. Donald Shaeffer		
	HILTONSO	Ms. Sonya Hilton		
	WARDBYER	Thomas Ward and Carl Byers		
	LISKIN	Miriam Liskin		
	WONGTOM	Tom Wong		
	BLISSMA			
		Subtotal for Berkeley :	**1,000.00**	**3,767.00**
Borrego Springs	ALLENMA	Marilyn Allen	1,000.00	775.00
		Subtotal for Borrego Springs :	**1,000.00**	**775.00**
Lake Elsinore	ARNOLDME	Melvin H. Arnold	0.00	75.00
		Subtotal for Lake Elsinore :	**0.00**	**75.00**
Long Beach	JONESMI	Michael Jones		
		Subtotal for Long Beach :		
Los Angeles	PIERSOCH	Dr. Charles Pierson	0.00	3,723.60
	MCKEESU	Susan McKee		
	POPEEI	Ms. Eileen Pope		
		Subtotal for Los Angeles :	**0.00**	**3,723.60**
Oakland	WALKSHAN	Joseph Walker and Lisa Shannon	0.00	189.46
	ELLIOTCH	Cheryl Elliot, M.D.	0.00	75.00
	KESSLERA	Andrew Kessler		
	DOUGLANO	Norman Douglass		
	CHRISTMA	Mark Christiansen		
	ROBERTSE	Eugene Roberts		
	CHOWBO	Bonnie Chow		
	GOLDMANR	Roger M. Goldman		
		Subtotal for Oakland :	**0.00**	**264.46**
San Diego	MCDANIBU	Burton McDaniel	0.00	75.00
	HAYESJ	J. Hayes		-1.00
		Subtotal for San Diego :	**0.00**	**74.00**
San Francisco	BERGENRU	Ruth Bergen	0.00	2,491.46

1

City group header section disappears from the report. (If the section had still contained any objects, Access would have asked for confirmation before deleting it.)

10. Click in the row selector for the ID Code field, press Del, and select OK in the alert box that asks you to confirm your intention to delete the row.

11. In the same row, type **Total Credits** in the Field/Expression column (or select this field from the drop-down list), and select Descending in the Sort Order column. Your screen should look like Figure 11.8.

12. Preview or print the report and confirm that it resembles Figure 11.7.

13. Save the report under the name Names by State and City 2, and close the report.

Figure 11.8

The revised Names by State and City report

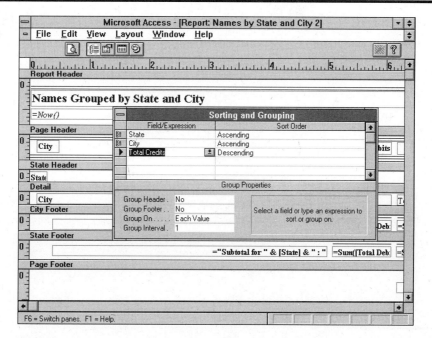

Defining the Grouping Method

You use the Group On and Group Interval properties to define the grouping method—that is, to specify whether the groups are based on the whole field or expression entered in the Field/Expression column of the Sorting and Grouping dialog box or on a part of this value. These two properties serve the same purpose as the choices you make in the grouping methods dialog box displayed by the groups/totals ReportWizard, although you have considerably more flexibility in specifying the interval. The default choice for the Group On property is Each Value, which corresponds to the Normal choice in the ReportWizard dialog box and which creates a group for each distinct value in the group field or expression. The other permissible entries for the Group On property depend on the data type of the group field or expression, and the easiest way to choose one is to select it from the drop-down list associated with the Group On combo box. You must enter the Group Interval property, which is always a number, by typing it.

The groups/totals ReportWizard adds a calculated control to each group header section to display an expression that matches the grouping method. For example, in the Donations by Month report described in Chapter 7 and shown in Figure 7.10, the group header sections identify the months, and in the Donations by Amount report pictured in Figure 7.11, the group header sections print the range of donation amounts in the groups. When you build a report from scratch or add new groups to an existing report, you must construct the expressions printed in the group header and group footer sections to describe the groups, and this is sometimes a far from trivial task.

For Text expressions, the only choices for the Group On property are Each Value (the default) and Prefix Characters, which bases the groups on one or more characters, taken from the beginning of the group field. The number of characters is specified by the value you enter for the Group Interval property. For example, in the Alphabetical Telephone list pictured in Figure 7.9, the groups are based on the first character of the ID Code field. Figure 11.9 illustrates this report in Report Design view, with the Sorting and Grouping dialog box visible and the ID Code group row selected. Note the expression in the group header section, which uses the Left function to extract the first character of the ID Code field. The Left function takes two inputs—an expression that evaluates to a text string, and a number that specifies the number of characters you want to extract from the left side of this string—and it returns as output the resulting shorter text string. Thus, the expression Left([ID Code], 1) evaluates to the first character of the ID Code field.

For Date/Time fields, the choices for the Group On property are Year, Quarter, Month, Week, Day, Hour, and Minute (exactly the same choices offered by the groups/totals ReportWizard). You can further customize the size of the groups by choosing an interval other than 1 (an option not offered by the ReportWizard). Figure 11.10 illustrates a version of the Donations by Month report (which was created using the groups/totals ReportWizard and then modified) in which each group represents two months, and Figure 11.11 illustrates the report in Report Design view. To create the groups, the Group On property was set to Month and the Interval property to 2.

Figure 11.9

Grouping by the first character of a Text field

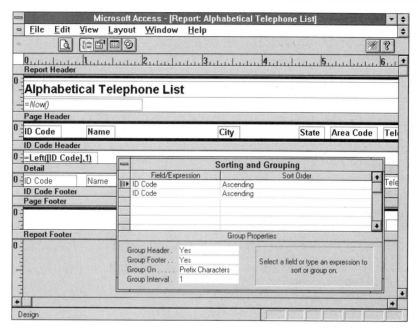

In this example, defining the groups is easy, but the expression that constructs the group header, which is visible in Figure 11.11, is rather complex. The first part is identical to the expression generated by the ReportWizard in a report grouped by month:

```
Format([Date],"mmmm yyyy")
```

This expression uses the Format function to display the month and year portions of the Date field, with the month name spelled out in full (for example, January 1993). To describe a date range that spans two months, you must concatenate this expression with a simple text string (" to ") and another expression that represents the last month in the range. You may recall that you can use the DateAdd function to add a given number of time intervals to a Date/Time field. Thus, the expression DateAdd("m",1,[Date]) represents the end of the two-month range. This expression (visible in Figure 11.11) can serve as input to the Format function, which converts the computed date to the proper format:

```
Format(DateAdd("m",1,[Date]),"mmmm yyyy").
```

For numeric data types, you can group on any interval by choosing Interval for the Group On property and entering the interval in the Group Interval

Figure 11.10

A report with groups based on two-month intervals

Donations by Month
09-Dec-93

Date	Type	ID Code	Amount	Pmt Form	Reference
January 1992 to February 1992					
1/22/92	DO	DAVISCH	50.00	Check	Check #467
2/21/92	DO	ALLENMA	250.00	Check	Check #381
			300.00		
March 1992 to April 1992					
3/22/92	DO	FELLNATA	50.00	Check	Check #862
4/8/92	DO	ANDERSMI	100.00	Check	Check #1005
			150.00		
May 1992 to June 1992					
5/12/92	DO	PIERSOCH	500.00	Check	Check #318
5/19/92	DO	SWIFTLU	35.00	Check	Check #3750
			535.00		
		Grand Total :	985.00		

1

property. You may recall that the groups/totals ReportWizard allows only a specific list of predefined intervals (10, 50, 100, 500, 1,000, 5,000, 10,000, 50,000, 100,000, and 500,000). When you define or modify a group in the Sorting and Grouping dialog box, you can enter any number you wish.

As is the case with Date/Time groups, writing an expression that describes the range of values in the group header section is usually far more difficult than defining the group. Figure 11.12 illustrates the Donations by Amount report shown in Figure 7.11, which was created by the ReportWizard

Figure 11.11

Defining the two-
month groups

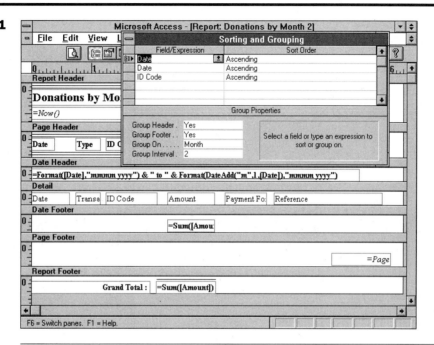

and has groups based on an interval of 50 in the Amount field. The expression
that defines the beginning of the range—([Amount]\50)*50—uses integer division (symbolized by the backslash) to find the number of $50 intervals in the
amount. For example, if the Amount field in the current record contains
75.00, [Amount]\50 evaluates to 1. Multiplying this value (the number of intervals) by 50 (the value of the interval) yields the beginning of the range (in this
case, 50). The end of the range should be 1 less than the result of adding 50 to
the starting value (for example, the end of the range that begins with $50 ends
with $99, not $100). To compute the end of the range, you must add the interval (in this case, 50) to the value of the Amount field, use integer division to
divide the result by 50, multiply the result of this division by the interval, and
then subtract 1, using the expression (([Amount]+50)\50)*50–1. For example,
if the value of the Amount field is 75.00, adding 50 yields 125, and 125\50 evaluates to 2; multiplying 2 by 50 yields 100, and subtracting 1 yields 99.

In both of the expressions that define the range boundaries, the parentheses are necessary to override the default precedence of multiplication over integer division. For example, if you omitted the parentheses from the expression
that defines the beginning of the range, Access would multiply 50 by 50 and
then use integer division to divide the Amount field by the result, rather than
performing the integer division first and multiplying the result by 50. Note also

Figure 11.12

A report with groups based on $50 intervals

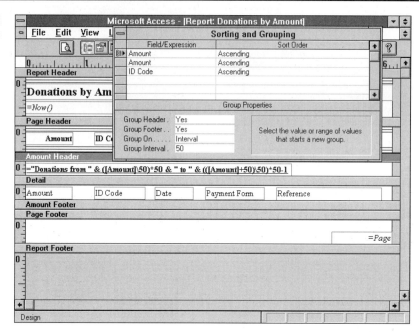

that strictly speaking, the group headings are not accurate—in fact, the group headed "Donations from 50 to 99" also includes transactions between $99.00 and $99.99. To correct the heading and add dollar signs, you could use the following expression:

```
"Donations from $" & ([Amount]\50)*50 & ".00 to $" &
((([Amount]+50)\50)*50-.01
```

In this expression, including the dollar signs and the pennies in the text strings is easier than using the Format function to display the calculated values in Currency format.

Because Yes/No values are stored as numbers, you can select Interval for the Group On property, but it makes little sense to do so, since there can only be two possible values (–1 for Yes and 0 for No) in the field.

As illustrated by all of the preceding examples, when you choose a value other than Each Value for the Group On property, you must also sort by the same field to ensure that all the records in each group are adjacent in the processing sequence. Thus, the Donations by Amount report is grouped by $50 intervals in the Amount field, sorted by Amount, and sorted within the Amount groups by ID Code.

Computing Summary Statistics

Chapter 9 described how to use aggregate operators such as Sum, Avg, and Count and the identically named aggregate functions in a totals query to compute overall statistics for an entire query dynaset or for groups of rows that share the same value in one or more fields. You can also use aggregate functions in a report with groups to carry out the same types of calculations. You have already seen numerous examples of the use of one of the aggregate functions—the Sum function, which is used in groups/totals reports generated by the ReportWizards to compute group subtotals and overall totals for all the numeric fields in the detail section. All of the aggregate functions are listed in Table 11.1. As noted in Chapter 9, all of the aggregate functions exclude null values, and this default assumption is nearly always what you want when you carry out mathematical calculations. When you use the Count function to count the number of records in a group, be sure to choose a field that can never be blank (such as one of the components of the primary key for the underlying table).

When you use the aggregate functions in a report, Access interprets the range of records that contribute to the statistics relative to the placement of the calculation: In a group header or footer section, statistics reflect the

Table 11.1 **Aggregate Functions**

Function	Result
Sum	The sum
Avg	The average (arithmetic mean)
Count	The number of records
First	The value in the first record
Last	The value in the last record
Max	The maximum value
Min	The minimum value
StDev	The standard deviation in a population sample
StDevP	The standard deviation in a population
Var	The variance in a population sample
VarP	The variance in a population

records in the group, and in the report header or footer, they reflect all the records in the source dynaset. Figure 11.13 illustrates a version of the Names Grouped by State and City report that includes the number of people in each city and state and the average credit total for each state. The counts in the group summary sections are computed by the expression Count[ID Code], which counts Names table records with non-null values of the ID Code field (that is, all the records in the group, because the ID Code field can never be null), and the average credits in the state footer section is computed by the expression Avg([Total Credits]). The fact that Access can deduce the appropriate range of records to include in the summary statistics means that you can use the cut and paste techniques described in Chapter 10 to very quickly replicate the summary calculations defined in one group footer section in other group footers or in the report footer section.

The placement of the state count merits special attention. Unlike many other database programs, Access does not limit you to placing statistics *after* the detail records they summarize. Normally, when a group header section is printed, Access has not yet processed the data that makes up the detail section that follows, but if you include summary statistics in any header section, Access makes multiple passes through the source dynaset and calculates any required statistics in advance. Another typical application for this powerful capability is computing percentages of a total. In the report in Figure 11.13, you could calculate the percentage that each city represents of the state total by creating a calculated control in the city header or footer section whose value is defined by an expression that divides the city total by the state total. For example, if the controls that compute these sums are named City Credits and State Credits, you would use the expression [City Credits]/[State Credits] and select Percent for the Format property to print the result as a percentage with two decimal places. A more complex example is presented later in this chapter, in the section on using subreports to construct composite reports.

Access also provides an easy way to carry out one other very common type of calculation—computing a running sum. For example, Figure 11.14 illustrates a transaction summary intended to serve as a computerized analog of a manual ledger sheet or transaction journal. In this report, transactions are grouped by ID Code and sorted within each group by date, so that transactions are printed in chronological order for each person. The number printed in the Amount column is calculated using an expression that prints pledges as negative numbers and all other transaction types as positive:

```
=IIf([Transaction Type]="PL",-[Amount],[Amount])
```

To compute the running sum in the Balance column, you define a control using *exactly the same expression* and set the Running Sum property to Yes. If the report includes groups, Access automatically resets the sum to zero at the beginning of each group. There is no comparable property that would enable

Figure 11.13

A report with sums, counts, and averages

City	ID Code	Name	Total Debits	Total Credits
		Subtotal for CA :	2,000.00	11,898.94
		Average Credits:		216.34
NV (Names: 6)				
Carson City	DAVIDSJA	Jacqueline Davidson	0.00	0.00
	Names: 1	Subtotal for Carson City :	0.00	0.00
Fernley	PLUMMERN	Nick Plummer	0.00	0.00
	Names: 1	Subtotal for Fernley :	0.00	0.00
Las Vegas	THOMASBE	Bert Thomas	0.00	25.00
	NELSONCH	Mr. Charles P. Nelson	0.00	0.00
	Names: 2	Subtotal for Las Vegas :	0.00	25.00
Reno	JONESLI	Ms. Lillian Jones	0.00	0.00
	Names: 1	Subtotal for Reno :	0.00	0.00
Sparks	WILLIAEA	Mr. and Mrs. Earl Williams	0.00	50.00
	Names: 1	Subtotal for Sparks :	0.00	50.00
		Subtotal for NV :	0.00	75.00
		Average Credits:		12.50
OR (Names: 7)				
Eugene	SCHULTAN	Andrew Schultz	0.00	0.00
	Names: 1	Subtotal for Eugene :	0.00	0.00
Portland	LUSUSAN	Susan Lu	500.00	650.00
	BAKERSY	Ms. Sylvia Baker	0.00	25.00
	ROBBINCY	Ms. Cynthia Robbins	0.00	0.00
	WILLIAAR	Mr. Arnold G. Williams	0.00	0.00
	KOWALSH	Mr. Howard Kowalski	0.00	0.00
	ZUCKEREL	Elizabeth and Michael Zuckerm	0.00	0.00
	Names: 6	Subtotal for Portland :	500.00	675.00
		Subtotal for OR :	500.00	675.00
		Average Credits:		96.43
TX (Names: 21)				
Dallas	BLACKCL	Mr. Claude Black	0.00	0.00
	MILLERWI	William Miller	0.00	0.00
	MICHAELP	Philip Michaels	0.00	0.00
	SCOTTFR	Frank Scott	0.00	0.00

3

you to calculate a running *count*, but you can do this easily by defining a calculated control with the constant value 1 and assigning Yes to the Running Sum property for this control.

Figure 11.14

A report that prints a running sum

Transaction Summary Report

Thursday, December 9, 1993

Date	Tran #	Transaction	Amount	Reference	Balance
ALLENJE	**Jerry Allen**				
1/28/92	14971	Purchase	25.92	Recycle T-shirts, Check #48	25.92
ALLENMA	**Marilyn Allen**				
12/28/91	14932	Pledge	-1,000.00	Pledge	-1,000.00
12/28/91	14933	Pledge payment	250.00	Pledge payment #1, Check #1283	-750.00
2/21/92	14979	Donation	250.00	Check #381	-500.00
4/25/92	15000	Pledge payment	250.00	Pledge payment #2, Check #1479	-250.00
ANDERSMI	**Michael Anderson**				
12/31/91	14935	Total credits	522.00	Total credits as of 12/31/91	522.00
4/8/92	14990	Donation	100.00	Check #1005	622.00
ARNOLDME	**Melvin H. Arnold**				
12/31/91	14936	Total credits	75.00	Total credits as of 12/31/91	75.00
BAKERSY	**Ms. Sylvia Baker**				
4/10/92	14992	Membership	25.00	Check #2301	25.00
BERGENRU	**Ruth Bergen**				
12/31/91	14937	Total credits	2,452.00	Total credits as of 12/31/91	2,452.00
1/28/92	14972	Purchase	14.46	Save the Wetlands T-shirt, 4591-298	2,466.46
3/25/92	14988	Membership	25.00	Check #528	2,491.46
BLOOMCH	**Mr. Christopher Bloom**				
12/31/91	14938	Total credits	2,250.00	Total credits as of 12/31/91	2,250.00
3/7/92	14984	Pledge	-1,000.00	Pledge	1,250.00
3/7/92	14985	Pledge payment	250.00	Check #793	1,500.00
BROWNEL	**Elizabeth Brown**				
12/31/91	14939	Total credits	25.00	Total credits as of 12/31/91	25.00
2/28/92	14982	Membership	25.00	Check #978	50.00
COLLINSR	**Robert Collins**				
2/12/92	14976	Purchase	14.46	Rain Forest T-shirt, Check #601	14.46
DAVISCH	**Charles and Anne Davis**				
12/31/91	14949	Total credits	450.00	Total credits as of 12/31/91	450.00
1/12/92	14964	Membership	25.00	Check #452	475.00

Page 1

Other Applications for Report Groups

As you gain experience with grouping and sorting, you will discover additional applications for report groups that might not be obvious at first when you use them to print subtotals in columnar reports. For example, you can use groups to print zip code bundling labels in a mailing label report. The report form shown in Figure 11.15 has a group based on the first two characters of the Zip field; a sample of the output is shown in Figure 11.16. The bundling labels, which include the zip code prefix and the number of labels in the group, are printed in the group footer section. The expression that prints the zip code prefix uses the Left function described earlier in this section to extract the leftmost two characters of the Zip field: Left([Zip],2). The expression that computes the count is based on the Count function: Count([Zip]). For large mailings, you could add another group *within* the two-digit zip code group based on the first *three* digits of the zip code.

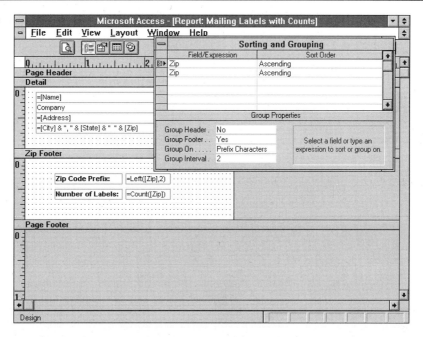

Figure 11.15

Defining groups in a mailing label report

To ensure that the bundling label does not disrupt the alignment of the text on subsequent labels, you must set the height of the zip group footer section to exactly match the height of the detail section. If you use the mailing label ReportWizard to create the report and then modify it to add the Zip group, note that Access sets the height of the detail section to 0.06 inches less

Figure 11.16

A mailing label report with zip code bundling labels

than the label height you chose in the last ReportWizard dialog box, and sets the row spacing in the Print Setup dialog box to 0.06 inches. Thus, for labels with a nominal height of 1 inch, it sets the height of the detail section to 0.94 inches. This strategy guarantees that there is always at least a small amount of space between labels, but it will not work in a label report with a group footer section. To achieve exactly the right spacing for the group footer labels, you must change the row spacing to 0 and set the height of both the detail section and the Zip group footer section to exactly match the label height (1 inch in the example in Figure 11.15).

Printing Personalized Letters

There is no Access ReportWizard for defining mail-merge forms such as personalized letters, but you can create many simple letters by designing reports from scratch. Figure 11.17 illustrates a typical short letter, in this case a thank you note that acknowledges a donation. The data source for this report is a parameter query called Names and Donations by Date, which includes all the fields in the Transactions table, together with the name and address fields from the Names table. The query prompts you to enter a range of transaction dates and also includes fixed selection criteria based on the Transaction Type field to select only donations (records in which the transaction type is "DO").

Figure 11.17

A thank you letter

The Association for a Clean Earth

501 Capp Street
San Francisco, CA 94110
(415) 864-0051

December 9, 1993

Charles and Anne Davis
132 28th Ave
Seattle, WA 98122-6218

Dear Charles and Anne,

    On behalf of the staff and Board of Directors of the Association for a Clean Earth, I would like to thank you for your recent contribution. We understand how hard it is to give during these uncertain economic times, and we appreciate your support.

    As you know, we rely heavily on donations from people like you in our ongoing efforts to preserve our planet and create a safe and healthy environment for future generations.

Sincerely,

Jean Gordon, Executive Director
The Association for a Clean Earth

Note. Chapter 15 describes how to incorporate a more elaborate logo created using a graphics program or by scanning a printed copy into an Access report.

Figure 11.18 illustrates the Thank You Letters report in Report Design view. The report form has only one section—the detail section—which includes the ACE name and return address (so that the report can be printed on plain paper instead of preprinted letterhead), the inside address, the body of the letter, and the closing signature. To print on preprinted letterhead, you could simply adjust the top margin (in the Print Setup dialog box) so that the first object on the report prints below the organization name and address. If you have to print on hand-fed sheets of letterhead, you must change the Paper Source setting in the Print Setup dialog box from the default (Upper Tray on a laser printer or Tractor on a dot-matrix printer) to Manual Feed, so that the Print Manager pauses between pages to allow you to insert a new sheet of paper.

The fields that make up the inside address block are arranged just as they would be printed on a mailing label, with the Can Grow property set to Yes for any fields that might occupy more than one line (the Address field in the ACE system) and the Can Shrink property set to Yes for any fields that might be blank (the Company field in this example). The opening salutation line is formed by an expression that concatenates three text strings—the constant string "Dear " (including the trailing space), the Salutation field, and a second constant string that prints the comma. The body of the letter consists of one long label object that contains two fixed paragraphs of text. The closing signature lines could have been included in this label, but using a separate object affords a measure of convenience—you can more easily edit the text of the letter to create a new report without changing the signature lines. To ensure that each letter begins on a new page, the Force New Page property is set to After Section for the detail section.

Ideally, you might also want a report such as the Thank You Letters report to print a matching envelope for each letter. If you have used word processing programs with mail-merge capabilities, you may be accustomed to printing an envelope as the last "page" of a document that produces letters. However, this approach is usually not practical in Access if you have a laser printer, because you must print envelopes in landscape rather than portrait orientation. If you define a separate report for printing envelopes, you can simply select the orientation in the Print Setup dialog box, but you cannot switch from portrait to landscape orientation and back in the middle of a report. You cannot solve this problem by using an embedded subreport to print the envelope, because Access ignores the print setup specifications defined with the subreport and uses the settings established in the main report.

The most expedient solution to this problem is to use a separate report form to print the recipients' addresses on mailing labels or on envelopes. By using the same query as the data source for the reports that print the letters and the labels or envelopes, you can at least ensure that the two reports produce matching output, although you must take care while stuffing the envelopes to

Figure 11.18

The Thank You
Letters report

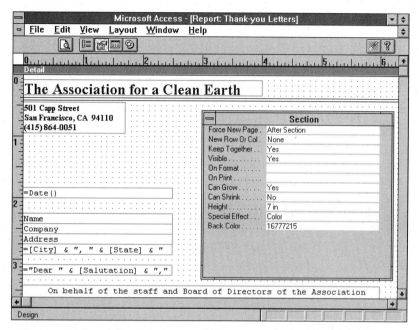

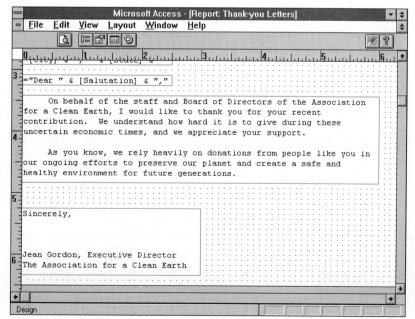

keep the two forms in sync. Figure 11.19 illustrates a simple report for printing envelopes, including the ACE name and return address. If you are printing the envelopes on a laser printer, remember to customize the settings in the Print Setup dialog box to select the correct envelope size, orientation (landscape), and paper source (Manual Feed or Envelope Feed), as shown in Figure 11.20.

Figure 11.19

A report for printing envelopes

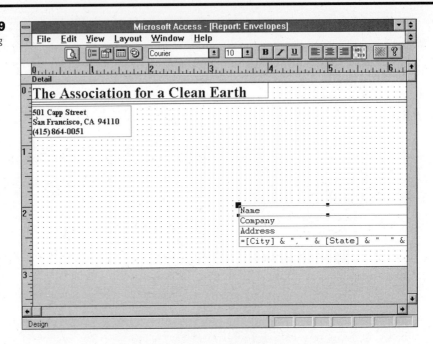

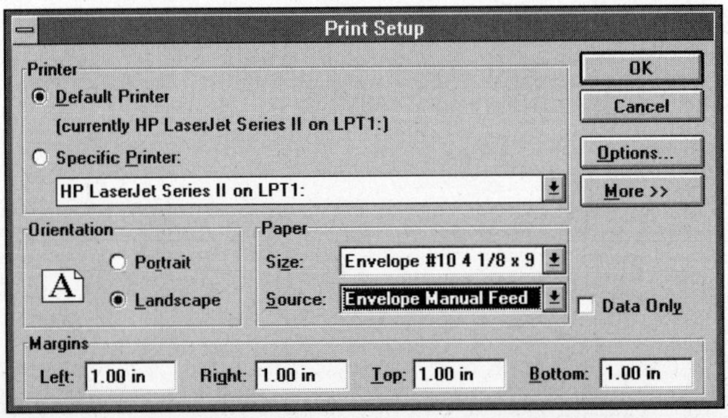

Figure 11.20

The Print Setup options for printing envelopes on a laser printer

The simple thank you letter in Figure 11.17 is easy to design and print, but unfortunately it is a good example of the type of letter that many businesses and nonprofit organizations *do not* want to send to their clients, customers, or donors. This letter is personalized only in the sense that it contains the recipient's name and address and a salutation based on the name, but the text of the letter is exactly the same for every donation. To vary the text of the letter based on information in the source table or query, you must merge fields with the fixed portions of the text by writing expressions that concatenate the text with the data fields. Figure 11.21 illustrates a report that produces a more personalized thank you note with the date and amount of the donation printed within the body of the letter. In this report, the first paragraph is a single expression that combines several constant text strings with expressions based on the Amount and Date fields. The expressions that print the Amount and Date fields should seem familiar—both use the Format function to convert the raw data to more suitable display formats. Note that you cannot write an *expression* to define the caption displayed in a label object—instead, you must use a text box with no attached label.

Figure 11.21

A report that prints personalized letters

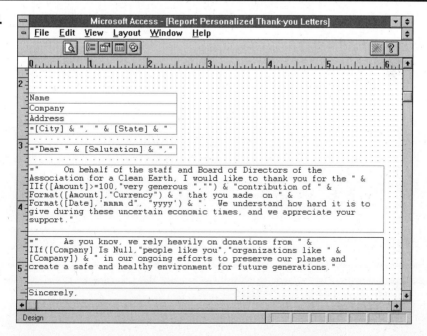

To further customize the text of the letter, you can use the IIf function to change the wording according to the result of evaluating expressions based on fields in the source table or query. For example, the first paragraph of the letter in Figure 11.21 contains the following expression:

```
IIf([Amount]>=100, "very generous ", "")
```

This expression evaluates to the phrase "very generous " (including the trailing space) if the Amount field is greater than or equal to $100.00, or to an empty string (a text string of length 0) otherwise. Thus, the first sentence reads, in part, "thank you for the contribution" for donations less than $100, and "thank you for the very generous contribution" for donations of $100 or more. A similar expression in the second paragraph prints the phrase "people like you" if the company name is null (empty) or a phrase that includes the company name if it is present. When you design complex letters like these, you may want to display more than one or two letters in Print Preview mode to make sure that all the possible combinations of data produce grammatically correct results.

When you use any of these techniques to vary the text of a letter, make sure that you set the Can Grow property for the text boxes that print the expressions to Yes, so that they can expand to accommodate long field insertions and variable wording. There is one potentially serious limitation: The maximum length for a text expression (a text string that results from evaluating an expression) is 255 characters, so you cannot construct a very long paragraph. This limitation *does not* apply to label objects, and you can in most cases edit the letter strategically so that the paragraphs with variable contents are relatively short, and the longer fixed portions are printed using label objects. A nontechnical word of caution may also be in order: Be careful not to go overboard with the personalizations in the letter—using a person's name four or five times in a one-page letter is a dead giveaway that the letter was produced by a computer.

Some other limitations are not so easily overcome. For example, you cannot format individual words or phrases within a text string (for example, to underline or boldface them). If this type of detailed formatting is essential or if you need to print very complex mail-merge forms, you may find it easier to export the data and use a word processing program such as Microsoft Word or Ami Pro to print the letters. Chapter 14 outlines some techniques for exchanging data with other software, and Chapter 20 describes how to call a word processor from Access to print forms such as personalized letters one at a time.

Using Subreports

As noted in Chapter 8, there is no ReportWizard analogous to the main/sub-form FormWizard, although most applications demand this type of layout at least as often in reports as in data entry forms. If you are determined to use the Wizards, you can build a form using the main/subform FormWizard and use the Save as Report option in Form Design view to save the form as a report. However, this method is far from ideal, because you will usually have to modify the subform extensively to better suit the requirements of a printed document. Instead, you can incorporate one report into another as a subreport.

This approach gives you the flexibility to create many different types of composite reports, including layouts with more than one subreport. For example, Figure 11.22 illustrates one page of a report that serves as a prototype for what you might call a "complete reference list"—a report that is centered around the main entity in the application and includes all the matching records from all the related tables. In the ACE system, this report is the computerized analog of the manual ledger cards—it includes all the information on file about one person.

Most database applications should include at least one report of this type; if there is more than one major entity, you may need more than one such report. For example, in an order-tracking database application, you might print a vendor reference list that includes all of your purchases from each vendor as well as a customer reference list that includes all orders and payments made by your customers. In the report in Figure 11.20, the fields from the Names table are printed at the top of the page (together with some fields derived from the various reference tables using the DLookUp function), with the contacts and transactions in columnar subreports below. Although this report style is quite common, Access does not limit you to this combination of layout styles for the main report and subreports—the subreports could also be single-column or tabular layouts. Later in this section, you will add a third subreport, which prints the committee membership data, to this report.

To create a report that includes subreports, you must first build the main report and the subreport(s), using any combination of methods you wish—for each of the component reports, you can use one of the ReportWizards, create the report from scratch, or begin with one of the ReportWizards and modify the generated report. Before you begin, you should understand how Access links a subreport to the main report. Figure 11.23 illustrates the ACE Member Reference List in Report Design view with the Contacts subreport selected and its property sheet visible so that you can see the three properties that define the linkage—Source Object, Link Child Fields, and Link Master Fields.

The Source Object property identifies the subreport by name; because the embedded object can be either a form or a report, Access adds the prefix Report or Form to distinguish between the two. Thus, the source object for

Figure 11.22

A report with two subreports

Member Reference List
28-Dec-93

ALLENMA　　　　　　　　Board member

Marilyn Allen　　　　　　Source:　PURCHASE　　First Contact:　8/12/82　　Total Debits:　1,000.00
(Ms. Allen)　　　　　　　　　　　　　　　　　　　Last Contact:　3/30/92　　Total Credits:　775.00
　　　　　　　　　　　　　　　　　　　　　　　　　　　　　　　　　　　　　Last Credit:　4/25/92

842 Palm Canyon Drive　　Address Type:　Home
Borrego Springs, CA 92004
　　　　　　　　　　　　　　☐ OK to Send Mail　　　Joined:　9/30/87
Telephone:　　　　　　　　☒ OK to Call　　　Last Renewal:　10/1/91

Keywords:　RAINFOREST　　Notes:
　　　　　　NUCLEARWAS
　　　　　　TOXICWASTE

Contact Type		Date	Description	Amount	Follow-Up
BM	Board meeting notice	3/15/92	Board meeting notice		
NL	Newsletter	3/30/92	Newsletter, March 1992		

Transaction Type		Date	Tran #	Description	Amount	Pmt Form	G/L Acct
DO	Donation	2/21/92	14979	Check #381	250.00	Check	31040
PP	Pledge payment	4/25/92	15000	Pledge payment #2, Check #14	250.00	Check	31030
TC	Total credits	12/31/92	15088	Total credits as of 12/31/92	500.00		
TC	Total credits	12/31/92	15053	Total credits as of 12/31/92	500.00		
TC	Total credits	12/31/92	15018	Total credits as of 12/31/92	500.00		

Figure 11.23

Linking the main report and subreports

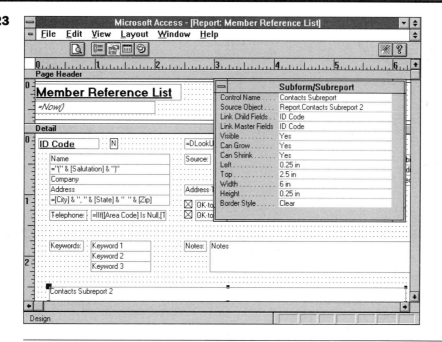

the Contacts Subform object is listed as "Report.Contacts Subreport 2" in the property sheet. (The prefix is displayed in the subreport object itself only when you click again inside the object frame to display an insertion point.)

The Link Child Fields and Link Master Fields properties specify the fields that define the linkage between the source tables or queries for the subreport and main report. These tables or queries for the two reports can have either a one-to-one or one-to-many relationship, but the data source for the main report always controls the report processing sequence—Access reads through this dynaset in sequence and for each record (or row in a query dynaset), prints all the matching records in the source table or query for the subform. Thus, the data source for the main report is always called the *master* and the subreport data source is the *child*, even if the subreport data source is the parent table in a one-to-many relationship. If this seems confusing, remember that *in the context of the report*, the table printed in the main report is the independent one, in which every record is printed whether or not there are any matching records in the data source for the subreport.

The legitimate entries in the Link Child Fields and Link Master Fields properties are described by rules similar to those that govern the default table relationships stored in the database. You can enter one or more field names, separated by semicolons if there is more than one field. The linking fields need not have the same names, but there must be the same number of fields and they must have the same data types (except that, as is the case with table relationships, you can match a Counter field with an Integer field). You cannot link the reports based on an expression. If you need to use an expression in either linking property, the data source for either or both reports must be a query that includes a calculated column defined by the desired expression. You can then enter the name of this column in the Link Child Fields and/or Link Master Fields property.

NOTE. *You do not have to print the linking fields, either in the main report or the subreport, although it is a good idea to do so during the testing stages. For example, in the Member Reference List, both subreports are linked to the main report by the ID Code field, but this field is printed only in the main report (and it could be omitted from the main report as well if you prefer to identify people only by name).*

In many cases, you will not have to enter the Link Child Fields and Link Master Fields properties, because Access can deduce the linking fields. If you stored a default relationship between the two source tables or queries in the database, Access links the reports by the same fields that define this relationship. If there is no default relationship stored in the database, Access looks for fields in the data source for the subreport that match the primary key of the table printed in the main report. If there are no matching fields or if the main report is based on a query rather than on a table (and therefore has no primary key), Access cannot determine how to link the reports, and you must enter the linking fields in the Link Child Fields and Link Master Fields properties yourself.

Correctly defining the linkage is essential to ensure that Access prints the right data in the subreport, which should contain only records in which the linking fields match their counterparts in the main form. If some records in the data source for the main report might not have any matching records in the subreport's data source, you may want to set the Can Shrink property to Yes for the subreport object so that it occupies no space on the printed page, especially if there are objects on the main report below the subreport. You should also make sure that all the fixed text (such as the report header and column titles) and summary statistics associated with the subreport are printed in the subreport, rather than in the main report, so that they are omitted if the subreport is empty.

Because pagination is controlled entirely in the main report, Access does not print the page header and footer defined in the subreport, so you cannot place the column titles and summary statistics in these sections. In the subreports in Figure 11.22, which are used *only* as subreports (they are never printed independently), these objects are located in the report header and report footer sections. If the subreport includes groups, Access prints the group header and footer sections, so if you prefer, you can define groups based on the linking fields and print the summary statistics in the group header or footer. This is the best strategy if you also want to print the subreport as an independent report, but often, the differing page formatting requirements for independent reports and subreports make it unrealistic to do so. Of course, you can also define additional groups to further subdivide the records in the subreport. For example, you could define a group in the contacts subreport based on the contact type or the date to print groups *within* the subreport.

Adding a Subreport to a Main Report

Once you understand the relationship between the data sources for the main report and subreport, placing the subreport object on the main report is very easy. One method involves using the mouse to drag the subreport from the Database window onto the main report, as follows:

1. Make sure that the main report is open and the Report Design window is not maximized, so that you have easy access to the Database window.

2. Select the Database window and make sure that it displays the list of reports.

3. Position the mouse over the name of the subreport, press and hold the left mouse button, drag the subreport onto the main report, and release the mouse button.

4. Select the Report Design window, maximize it if you wish, and move and resize the subreport object as necessary.

If you prefer to work entirely from within the Report Design window, you can use the same method that you use to add any other type of object to a report:

1. Make sure that the toolbox is visible on the screen.

2. Click on the subreport button in the toolbox.

3. Position the crosshair symbol in the mouse pointer where you want the upper-left corner of the subreport.

4. Define the size of the subreport using one of the following methods:

   - To create a subreport of the standard size, click the left mouse button.

   - To place the subreport on the main report and resize it, press and hold the left mouse button, drag the mouse pointer to the location of the lower-right corner of the subreport, and release the mouse button.

Whichever method you use, don't worry too much about the exact size and location of the subreport—you will undoubtedly end up moving and resizing it more than once before you are satisfied with the report layout. By default, Access creates a label for the subreport and places the label object above the subreport, lined up with the left border. When you use the drag-and-drop method to create the subreport object, Access assigns it a name that matches the subreport itself and uses the same name as the caption for the associated label. When you use the toolbox method, Access creates an unbound subreport with an arbitrary name such as Embedded29, and you must identify the subreport by entering its name in the Control Source entry in the report property sheet. This data entry region is a combo box, so you can type the report name if you know it or select it from a drop-down list like the one shown in Figure 11.24. Note that this list includes the names of all the forms as well as the reports in your database, because a report can contain a subform or a subreport. Once you have identified the source object, Access fills in the linking fields if possible, based on the criteria outlined earlier in this section.

It is a good idea to keep the property sheet visible while you create the subreport object (or display it afterwards), so that you can verify whether Access was able to deduce the linking fields, and enter or edit them yourself if necessary. You may also want to change the Control Name property—to

Figure 11.24
Choosing the subform or subreport

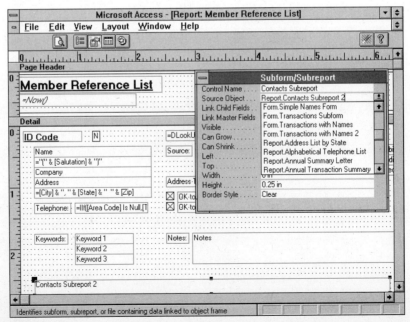

shorten a long name assigned by Access (which matches the control name to the subreport name) or to assign a more meaningful name if you began with an unbound subreport. The name will prove important if you need to refer to the subreport elsewhere—for example, to display fields from the subreport or use them in calculations on the main report. Otherwise, you may not care much about the object name. Often, you will want to move the associated label and change the caption or delete the label object entirely. As noted earlier, you will usually want to set the Can Shrink property to Yes for a columnar subreport to eliminate the unsightly gap that would otherwise appear on the printed page if there are no records in the subreport's data source that match the current record in the main report. By default, Access sets the Can Grow property to Yes for a subreport, but leaves Can Shrink set to No. Because Access will expand the subreport as necessary when it prints the report, you can reduce the height of the subreport object to $1/4$ inch or less to facilitate editing the report in Report Design view.

As described in Chapter 10, you can call up the subreport in Report Design view by double-clicking on the subreport object. Often, you will end up modifying both the main and subreports several times to achieve a pleasing layout, and leaving both reports open in Report Design view is the most efficient way to do this. Remember that you must save the subreport (although you do not have to close it) and reload it into the main report before you can preview the report. To reload the subreport, select the subreport object, click again inside the object border to display an insertion point, and press Enter.

To practice these techniques by adding the committee membership data to the Member Reference List, begin by defining the subreport pictured in Report Design view in Figure 11.25, using the following steps:

1. Make sure that the Database window displays the list of reports, and click on the New command button or press Alt+N.

2. In the New Report dialog box, choose the Committees with Committee Names query as the data source.

3. Click on Blank Report or press Enter to open a blank report.

4. Maximize the Report Design window.

5. If the property sheet is not visible, click on the Property Sheet button in the tool bar, or select the Property Sheet option from the View menu. Move the property sheet to the lower-right side of the screen.

6. Set the Grid X and Grid Y properties to 16 to set the grid spacing to 16 dots per inch both horizontally and vertically. If the grid is not already visible, select the Grid option on the View menu to display it. If the Snap to Grid option on the Layout menu is not already checked, check it.

Figure 11.25

The Committees Subreport

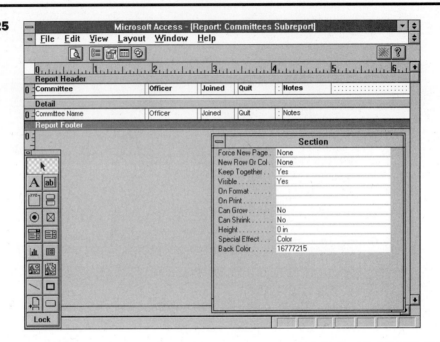

7. Set the Width property to 7 inches.

8. Using the Page Hdr/Ftr and Report Hdr/Ftr options on the Layout menu, remove the page header and footer sections and add the report header and footer sections to the layout.

9. If the field list is not visible, click on the Field List button in the tool bar, or select the Field List option from the View menu. Move the field list to the upper-right side of the screen.

10. If the toolbox is not visible, select the Toolbox option from the View menu. Move the toolbox to the lower-left corner of the screen.

11. Click on the text box button in the tool box to display the property sheet for the default text box. Set the Auto Label property to No.

12. Drag the Committee Name, Officer, Joined, Quit, and Notes fields from the field list to the detail section, placing all the fields in one row. Adjust the field widths to approximately match Figure 11.25. (The Notes field text box should extend almost to the right border of the report.) Set the Can Grow property to Yes for the Notes field.

13. Click on the Lock button in the toolbox, and then click on the label object button. Create label objects in the report header section to identify the columns in the detail section.

14. Click again on the Lock button (to turn off the lock option), and then click on the arrow symbol at the top of the toolbox.

15. If necessary, resize the label objects that identify the Joined and Quit fields to match the text boxes below. Right-justify both labels, either by using the button in the tool bar or by setting the Text Align property in the property sheet to Right.

16. Select all the text objects in the report header section, and click on the Bold button in the tool bar.

17. Click on the line button in the toolbox and draw a horizontal line that coincides with the lower borders of the label objects in the report header section and that extends the full width of the report.

18. In the property sheet for the line object, select 1 point for the Border Width property.

19. Adjust the height of the detail section to match the height of the text boxes it contains, and reduce the height of the report footer section to zero. Your screen should look something like Figure 11.25.

20. Use the Save As option on the File menu to save the report under the name **Committees Subreport**, leaving the report open in Report Design view.

To add the Committees Subreport to the Member Reference List, so that the finished report resembles Figure 11.26, use the following steps:

1. If the Member Reference List is not already open in Report Design view, return to the Database window and open it.

2. Expand the height of the detail section to about $4\frac{1}{2}$ inches.

3. Move the line object below the transactions subreport down almost all the way to the bottom of the detail section.

4. Click on the subreport button in the toolbox, and then click anywhere below the transactions subreport to place a new subreport object on the report.

5. Move the toolbox out of the way or remove it entirely from the screen.

6. Select the label for the new subreport and press Del to delete it.

Figure 11.26

The printed Member
Reference List

Member Reference List
28-Dec-93

ALLENMA   Board member

Marilyn Allen   Source: PURCHASE   First Contact: 8/12/82   Total Debits: 1,000.00
(Ms. Allen)   Last Contact: 3/30/92   Total Credits: 775.00
                                                                                Last Credit: 4/25/92

842 Palm Canyon Drive   Address Type: Home
Borrego Springs, CA 92004
                            ☐ OK to Send Mail   Joined: 9/30/87
Telephone: ☒ OK to Call   Last Renewal: 10/1/91

Keywords: RAINFOREST   Notes:
            NUCLEARWAS
            TOXICWASTE

Contact Type		Date	Description	Amount	Follow-Up
BM	Board meeting notice	3/15/92	Board meeting notice		
NL	Newsletter	3/30/92	Newsletter, March 1992		

Transaction Type		Date	Tran #	Description	Amount	Pmt Form	G/L Acct
DO	Donation	2/21/92	14979	Check #381	250.00	Check	31040
PP	Pledge payment	4/25/92	15000	Pledge payment #2, Check #14	250.00	Check	31030
TC	Total credits	12/31/92	15088	Total credits as of 12/31/92	500.00		
TC	Total credits	12/31/92	15053	Total credits as of 12/31/92	500.00		
TC	Total credits	12/31/92	15018	Total credits as of 12/31/92	500.00		

Committee	Officer	Joined	Quit	Notes
Finance Committee	Chairperson	2/3/90		Ms. Allen was Treasurer of the Finance Committee from 6/90 through 7/91, when she became Chairperson.
Lobbying Coordination Committee		6/3/91		

Page 1

7. Adjust the width of the new subreport object to 7 inches and the height to ¹/₄ inch. If necessary, move the subreport so that it is ¹/₄ inch below the transactions subreport and its left border lines up with the other two subreports.

8. In the subreport property sheet, change the Control Name property to **Committees Subreport**.

9. Display the drop-down list of forms and reports in the Source Object combo box, and choose Report.Committees Subreport from the list.

10. Enter **ID Code** for both the Link Child Fields and Link Master Fields properties.

11. Set the Can Shrink property to Yes.

12. Move the line object to ¹/₄ inch below the new subreport, and adjust the size of the detail section again so its border is just below the line. With the Committees Subreport object selected, your screen should look like Figure 11.27.

13. Preview the report and then save it under the name Member Reference List 2. The report should look like Figure 11.26.

Figure 11.27

The Member Reference List in Report Design view

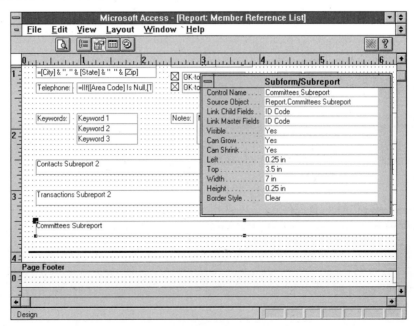

In all of the examples presented thus far, the subreports have a columnar layout similar to those produced by the groups/totals ReportWizard, but you are by no means restricted to this report design. Figure 11.28 illustrates a committee membership report in which the main and subreports are both modified single-form layouts. Figure 11.29 illustrates a layout that places the subreport to the right of the fields in the parent table. This placement does not prevent the subreport from expanding and contracting as necessary to accommodate the number of records it contains. Note that as in any other layout that prints several objects next to each other on the same line, you cannot easily suppress blank lines due to an empty Name or Company field. Even if you set the Can Shrink property to Yes for these fields, Access prints them (resulting in a blank line), because there is data to the right on the same line.

You can also use subreports to produce composite documents composed of two or more independent reports, which may have entirely different data sources and have no fields in common (and therefore no linkages). Figures 11.30 and 11.31 illustrate two typical examples: a report that prints several different kinds of summary statistics, and one that prints a comprehensive list of the codes stored in the various reference tables in the ACE database. (Using techniques described in Chapter 15, you can also include graphs in reports like these.) Creating composite layouts like these is very straightforward: After designing the separate reports that will become the subreports, open a new blank report without choosing any table or query as the data source, and add as many subreports as you wish to the detail section. You can then add report header, report footer, page header, and/or page footer sections to the main report as necessary. For example, the Overall Summary Statistics report in Figure 11.30, which is shown in Report Design view in Figure 11.32, includes a report header section (which prints the report title and date) and a page footer section (which prints the page number). The Code Reference List, the first page of which is shown in Figure 11.31, has page header and footer sections, but no report header or report footer.

Both of the subreports in Figure 11.30 make use of the technique described earlier in this chapter for computing percentages of totals. In both cases, the data sources for the reports are queries that compile the raw statistics—the sums and counts. The percentages are calculated within the report, by using a calculated control whose value is obtained by dividing the relevant number in the detail band by the corresponding total. For example, the percentage to the right of the Number column in the Transaction Summary Statistics by State report is the result of dividing Number (the number of transactions of a given type in a given state) by Type Total (the calculated control that prints the sum in the group footer section).

Figure 11.28
A modified single-column subreport

Committee Membership List
28-Dec-93

ALLENMA   Board member

Marilyn Allen   Source: PURCHASE   First Contact: 8/12/82   Total Debits: 1,000.00
(Ms. Allen)   Last Contact: 3/30/92   Total Credits: 775.00
                                                                          Last Credit: 4/25/92

842 Palm Canyon Drive   Address Type: Home
Borrego Springs, CA 92004 ☐ OK to Send Mail   Joined: 9/30/87
Telephone: ☒ OK to Call   Last Renewal: 10/1/91

Keywords: RAINFOREST   Notes:
            NUCLEARWAS
            TOXICWASTE

Committee Memberships:

Committee: FINANCE   Finance Committee   Chairperson
Joined: 2/3/90
Quit:
Notes: Ms. Allen was Treasurer of the Finance Committee from 6/90 through 7/91, when she
            became Chairperson.

Committee: LOBBYING   Lobbying Coordination Committee
Joined: 6/3/91
Quit:
Notes:

Figure 11.29

Placing a subreport next to objects in the main report

Names and Contacts
09-Dec-93

ALLENJE

Jerry Allen

564 Mission St.
San Francisco, CA 94105-2921

Contacts:

	Contact Type	Date	Description	Amount	Follow-up
ML	Mailing	4/5/92	Earth Day solicitation		
ML	Mailing	12/10/91	Year-end solicitation		

ALLENMA

Marilyn Allen

842 Palm Canyon Drive
Borrego Springs, CA 92004

Contacts:

	Contact Type	Date	Description	Amount	Follow-up
NL	Newsletter	3/30/92	Newsletter, March 1992		
BM	Board meeting notice	3/15/92	Board meeting notice		

ANDERSJC

Mr. J. C. Anderson

41248 Moraga Rd
Temecula, CA 92390

Contacts:

	Contact Type	Date	Description	Amount	Follow-up
ML	Mailing	4/5/92	Earth Day solicitation		
ML	Mailing	12/10/91	Year-end solicitation		

ANDERSMI

Michael Anderson
The Ellis Street Garage
2906 Ellis Street
Berkeley, CA 94702

Contacts:

	Contact Type	Date	Description	Amount	Follow-up
PH	Phone call	2/28/92	Donor special appeal		3/13/92
NL	Newsletter	3/30/92	Newsletter, March 1992		
ML	Mailing	4/5/92	Earth Day solicitation		
LE	Lecture	4/22/92	Earth Day lecture	15.00	5/1/92

ARNOLDME

Melvin H. Arnold

504 Parkview Dr.
Lake Elsinore, CA 92330

Contacts:

	Contact Type	Date	Description	Amount	Follow-up
NL	Newsletter	3/30/92	Newsletter, March 1992		
ML	Mailing	4/5/92	Earth Day solicitation		

BAKERSY

Ms. Sylvia Baker

9370 SW 51st St.
Portland, OR 97219

Contacts:

	Contact Type	Date	Description	Amount	Follow-up
NL	Newsletter	3/30/92	Newsletter, March 1992		
ML	Mailing	4/5/92	Earth Day solicitation		

Page 1

Figure 11.30

A composite report that prints several types of summary statistics

Association for a Clean Earth

Summary Statistics

December 9, 1993

Name Types by State

State	Prospects	%	Members	%	Donors	%
California	35	51%	13	68%	3	43%
Nevada	4	6%	2	11%	0	0%
Oregon	5	7%	1	5%	1	14%
Texas	17	25%	2	11%	2	29%
Utah	4	6%	0	0%	0	0%
Washington	4	6%	1	5%	1	14%
Totals:	**69**		**19**		**7**	

Transaction Summary Statistics by State

Description	Number	%	Total	%	Average
Donation					
California	3	50%	850.00	86%	283.33
Texas	2	33%	85.00	9%	42.50
Washington	1	17%	50.00	5%	50.00
Total:	6		985.00		375.83
Membership					
California	7	64%	175.00	64%	25.00
Oregon	1	9%	25.00	9%	25.00
Texas	2	18%	50.00	18%	25.00
Washington	1	9%	25.00	9%	25.00
Total:	11		275.00		100.00
Pledge					
California	2	50%	2,000.00	57%	1,000.00

Figure 11.30

A composite report that prints several types of summary statistics (Continued)

Oregon	1	25%	500.00	14%	500.00
Texas	1	25%	1,000.00	29%	1,000.00
Total:	**4**		**3,500.00**		**2,500.00**
Pledge payment					
California	3	50%	750.00	57%	250.00
Oregon	1	17%	125.00	9%	125.00
Texas	2	33%	450.00	34%	225.00
Total:	**6**		**1,325.00**		**600.00**
Purchase					
California	11	50%	206.72	51%	18.79
Nevada	1	5%	11.50	3%	11.50
Oregon	2	9%	68.50	17%	34.25
Texas	6	27%	79.00	20%	13.17
Utah	1	5%	14.00	3%	14.00
Washington	1	5%	22.00	5%	22.00
Total:	**22**		**401.72**		**113.71**
Grand Totals:	**49**		**6,486.72**		

Figure 11.31

A composite report that prints a complete code reference list

Code Reference List

December 9, 1993

Name Types

BD	Board member
D	Donor
M	Member
MC	Media contact
P	Prospect

Contact Types

BM	Board meeting notice
LE	Lecture
ML	Mailing
NL	Newsletter
PH	Phone call
PR	Press release
RN	Renewal notice

Transaction Types

DO	Donation
ME	Membership
P	Purchase
PL	Pledge
PP	Pledge payment
TC	Total credits
TD	Total debits

Page 1

Figure 11.32

The Overall
Summary Statistics
report in Report
Design view

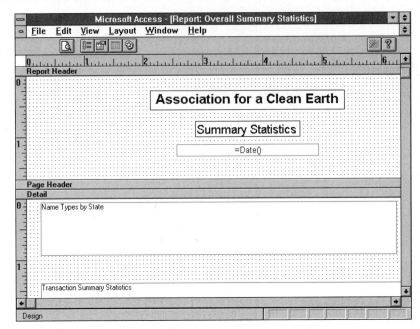

Printing Summary Statistics in the Main Report

In the examples presented thus far, all the summary statistics calculated in a subreport were printed in the report footer section of the subreport. Because Access automatically restricts the subreport to records that match the current record in the source table or query for the main report, the summary statistics also reflect just this group of records. Although you must compute the summary statistics in the subreport, you can print them in the main report if you prefer to place them elsewhere on the page. To prevent Access from printing the summary statistics in the subreport, you can set the Visible property to No for the report section that contains them (typically, the report footer section) or for the controls themselves if you do not want to omit the report footer section entirely.

In the main report, you must refer to an object in the subreport by using an expression that combines the name of the subreport object (*not* the name of the independent report form that you embedded in the main report to create the subreport), the type of form, and the name of the object itself. This notation can be somewhat confusing, and you will find it easier to construct the required expressions if you assign the subreport object a short, simple name (such as Transactions rather than Transactions Subreport) and give the controls in the subreport meaningful names (for example, Tran Count or Tran Sum for transaction summary statistics) rather than retaining the default names assigned by Access (Field10, Field45, and so on). To refer to a control named Tran Count, which is located in a subreport object called Transactions, you could use either of the following expressions:

```
Transactions.Report![Tran Count]
```

or

```
Transactions.Report.[Tran Count]
```

If the subreport object name includes embedded spaces, you must enclose it in square brackets, as in the following:

```
[Transactions Subreport].Report![Tran Count]
```

This method works fine if the subreport is never empty; when it is (because there are no records in the data source for the subreport that match the current record printed in the main report), Access cannot evaluate any expression that refers to controls in the subreport, and it prints "#Error" on the report.

The only way to solve this problem is to write an expression in the main report that computes the desired statistics independent of the subreport. The advantage of this method is that you can also use it *without* printing a subreport, to include on a report the types of summary statistics that you might calculate using a subreport, but without printing any detail records. You can compute all the standard summary statistics by using *domain aggregate functions*, which calculate statistics over a specified *domain*, or group of records. The domain aggregate functions have their names constructed by prefacing names of the corresponding functions that compute summary statistics in queries and reports with the prefix "D." For example, the DSum function computes a sum, and DCount calculates a count.

The domain aggregate functions all take three inputs: the expression you want to compute, the name of the table or query that will supply the data, and a description of which records to include in the totals (that is, a description of the domain). All three inputs must be specified as text strings enclosed in quotation marks. For example, you could use the following expression to compute the number of transactions for the current record in the main report:

```
DCount("[Transaction Number]", "Transactions",
    "[ID Code]=Report![ID Code]")
```

In this expression, the first input specifies the field to count, the second the name of the data source (the Transactions table), and the third selects records in this data source in which the ID Code matches the contents of the control named ID Code on the current report.

Hybrid Reports

Not every report falls neatly into one of the categories described thus far—single-column, groups/totals, mailing labels, letters, envelopes, and so on. These categories serve as a convenient framework for identifying some very common types of reports, but many others could only be described as hybrid formats that share some of the attributes of several different report layouts. When you set out to design a new report or emulate one of the forms in your manual system, keep in mind that you are free to build a report by placing any objects you wish in any of the report sections. Figure 11.33 illustrates a report that combines some of the attributes of the personalized letters described earlier in this chapter with a columnar subreport. This report prints a year-end statement of each donor's financial transactions to serve as a summary of the tax-deductible contributions made during the year. The name and address block and the narrative sections of the report are printed using the same techniques you would use in a personalized letter, and the transaction summary is a subreport.

The data source for the main report is a query called Names, Addresses, and YTD Totals, which is very similar to the Names and YTD Totals query described in Chapter 9 except that the output grid includes the address fields

Figure 11.33

A simple composite report

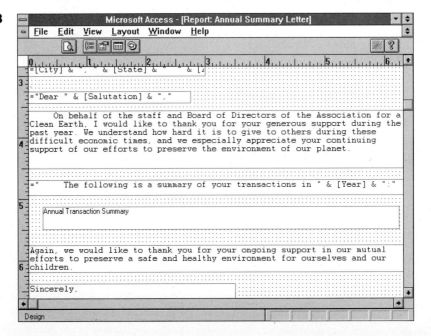

from the Names table. The data source for the subreport is the Annual Transaction Summary query pictured in Figure 11.34, which is based on the Names,
Transactions, and Transaction Types tables. The output grid includes all the
fields in the Transactions table, together with the Description field from the
Transaction Types table and the name and address fields from the Names
table (the name and address fields are not required in the subreport but were
included to make the query more generally useful in the ACE system). The selection criteria are based on the calculated column called Year (the second
column from the left in Figure 11.34), which uses the Year function to extract
the year portion of the transaction date. The expression entered in the Criteria row selects records in which this year matches the year portion of the current date (expressed via the Date function). The embedded subreport is a
very simple columnar layout which lists the basic facts about each transaction, together with a transaction count and dollar total. Note that this report
uses an expression based on the IIf function (as described in Chapter 9) to
treat pledges as negative numbers and all other transaction types as positive
numbers. Figure 11.35 illustrates the output.

Figure 11.34

The Annual
Transaction
Summary query

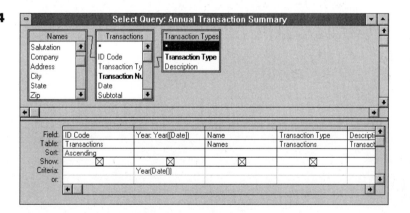

Summary

This chapter introduced the basic techniques that you can use to create a report from scratch, starting with a blank form, and described how to make fundamental changes in the structure and layout of reports originally created
using the Access ReportWizards. These methods were illustrated with a variety of prototypical reports that you *cannot* produce using only the Wizards.
Chapter 12 presents a similar discussion of techniques applicable to data
entry forms.

Figure 11.35

The printed annual transaction summary letter

The Association for a Clean Earth

501 Capp Street
San Francisco, CA 94110
(415) 864-0051

December 29, 1992

Edward Olson
6704 Whitman Ave.
Fort Worth, TX 76133

Dear Mr. Olson,

    On behalf of the staff and Board of Directors of the
Association for a Clean Earth, I would like to thank you for
your generous support during the past year. We understand how
hard it is to give to others during these difficult economic
times, and we especially appreciate your continuing support of
our efforts to preserve the environment of our planet.

    The following is a summary of your transactions in 1992:

Transaction Type	Date	Tran #	Description	Amount	Pmt Form
Pledge payment	1/15/92	14968	Pledge payment #1, Check #37	250.00	Check
Pledge	1/15/92	14967	Pledge	-1,000.00	
Membership	1/15/92	14966	Check #3702	25.00	Check
Pledge payment	4/30/92	15006	Pledge payment #2, Check #39	200.00	Check
Number of Transactions:		**4**		**-525.00**	

Again, we would like to thank you for your ongoing support in
our mutual efforts to preserve a safe and healthy environment
for ourselves and our children.

Sincerely,

Jean Gordon, Executive Director
The Association for a Clean Earth

If you have little prior experience with database software, you may find the blank report somewhat intimidating, but in fact, most of the barriers to defining new reports from scratch are psychological rather than technical. Once you feel comfortable working without the reassuring framework of a report generated by the ReportWizards, you will find that building a report from scratch is often just as fast (and at times, faster) than making extensive enhancements and rearrangements to a report defined by one of the Wizards. On the other hand, if you generally like the overall appearance and layout of the reports produced by the Wizards, you may continue to use them as a point of departure even after you feel comfortable designing your own reports.

The reports described in this chapter are specific to the ACE case study application, but their overall structure and layout are typical of the kinds of printouts required in many Access databases. If you are working on an application of your own, you may want to take some time to cement your understanding of all the concepts presented in Chapters 7, 8, 10, and 11 by designing some of the reports. Otherwise, you might practice your report design skills by building some of the other reports listed in the outline in Chapter 1 of the functional requirements of the ACE system.

12

Designing Forms

YOU ALREADY KNOW HOW TO USE THE ACCESS FORMWIZARDS TO
produce several very common types of reports—single-column layouts, tabular forms that display more than one record at a time,
and main/subform layouts—and how to modify the resulting forms
to enhance their appearance and customize them to your detailed requirements. If one of these basic layouts comes close to meeting your needs, allowing the FormWizards to generate a form initially and then editing the result
in Form Design view is often the most efficient way to produce the desired
layout. Even in a relatively complex application, you will find that this strategy will enable you to produce most of the forms you need. At times, however, you may be forced to build a form from scratch, or you may choose to
do so if you do not like the default stylistic conventions adopted by the Wizards. This chapter describes how to create a form from scratch by adding objects to a blank form.

Given your prior experience with both the Report Design view and Form
Design view, you should feel comfortable with the mechanics of building a
basic form. This chapter describes how to use the more complex controls—
check boxes, option buttons, toggle buttons, option groups, list boxes, and
combo boxes—none of which are present in any of the forms generated by
the FormWizards. These controls will help you to build forms that are easier
to use, require less typing, and better protect the accuracy and integrity of the
data in your tables. However, this plethora of controls introduces a large measure of complexity to both the technical and nontechnical sides of the form
design process. Although you will quickly master the mechanics of defining
these controls, if you have little experience with Windows, you may find it difficult to decide when and how to use each one. This chapter presents some
usage suggestions, but the most valuable source of guidance is the user interface of Access itself, and any other Windows software you use. By studying
the dialog boxes and data entry screens displayed by these programs, you can
gain valuable insight into the advantages of using the various controls in different contexts.

Of course, in databases that you build for your own use, you should feel
free to design screens that precisely suit your own preferences, but there are
compelling arguments in favor of conforming to the Windows standards, even
if you do not particularly care for the graphical user interface (GUI) environment. One of the virtues of Windows is the consistency of the user interface
across the broad spectrum of applications software, which makes it easier to
learn new programs that otherwise have very little in common with the Windows software you have used before. If your data entry screens adhere to the
generally accepted Windows interface standards, other users who are familiar
with Windows will find it easier to learn how to work with your database application as well.

If you are new to Windows and to Access, you may at first concentrate on
making your screens easy to *learn*; you should also strive to make them easy

to *use* on an ongoing basis. Striking the right balance can be a touchy proposition—a screen with a great many "gadgets" (check boxes, list boxes, and so on) may seem less intimidating to a person who is unfamiliar with the contents of your tables, but for a more experienced user, typing short code fields is faster than searching for the right entry in a long list. This particular problem is readily solved by replacing list boxes with combo boxes, which allow you to type your entry or choose it from a drop-down list, but not all of your design conflicts will be this easy to resolve. If possible, try also to make your screens equally easy to operate with the mouse and the keyboard. Some users will have a consistent preference for one method or the other, but many people end up using different data entry and editing techniques in different situations. For example, using the mouse is the easiest way to operate the navigation controls and jump from one field to another on a crowded screen when you edit existing records, but when you enter many new records in succession, having to take your hands off the keyboard to use the mouse will just slow you down.

On the technical side, this chapter addresses several topics that were bypassed earlier, although they apply to table design as well as form design—defining default values for fields and specifying validation rules. These subjects were deferred until you learned enough about constructing expressions to describe default values and validation rules of real-world complexity. Finally, this chapter presents additional techniques for using subforms to build more complex forms than the ones described in Chapters 6, 8, and 10. As in Chapter 11, the examples in this chapter are intended to illustrate prototypical form layouts, which you can mix and match as you see fit in your own Access applications.

Designing Forms from Scratch

As is the case with reports, you can create many of the forms required in an Access application by using the FormWizards, and if one of these layouts comes close to satisfying your requirements, you can save a great deal of time by allowing one of the Wizards to generate the form and then modifying the result as necessary. The main motivations for starting from scratch are largely the same as those cited for reports in Chapter 11—to produce form layouts that are not supported by any of the FormWizards and to use stylistic conventions that differ significantly from those adopted by the FormWizards. To create a new form from scratch, begin by using any of the standard methods to initiate the form design process:

- Make sure that the Database window displays the list of forms, and then click on the New command button or press Alt+N.

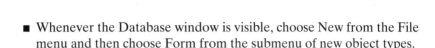

- Whenever the Database window is visible, choose New from the File menu and then choose Form from the submenu of new object types.

- Highlight a table or query name in the Database window, and click on the New Form command button in the tool bar (the third of the three new object buttons).

As described in Chapter 6, Access responds by displaying the New Form dialog box shown in Figure 6.1. If you wish, you can choose the source table or query for the form by making a selection from the combo box at the top of the New Form dialog box, but when you define a form from scratch, you can specify the data source later. (In contrast, when you use a Wizard to define a form or report, Access displays an error message and refuses to close the New Form dialog box until you have chosen the data source.) To exit from the New Form dialog box, select Blank Form, either by clicking on the Blank Form command button, by pressing Alt+B, or by pressing Enter (Blank Form is the default option in this dialog box).

As is the case with reports, if you did not choose a table or query in the New Form dialog box, you can specify the data source by entering its name in the Record Source property entry in the property sheet for the form. Note, however, that the main reason you enter Report Design view without specifying a data source is to build a report made up entirely of unrelated subreports, whereas you will rarely design forms of this type—forms are nearly always used to enter and edit data in one or more tables. In the later stages of application development, you may use forms to collect temporary variables that are not stored in any table—for example, to solicit selection criteria on the fly before printing a report or executing a query—but many nonprogrammers will never try these relatively advanced uses of forms.

Figure 12.1 illustrates a blank form in Form Design view, with the property sheet visible on the work surface to show the default form properties. As you can see if you compare this figure with Figure 11.1, a form has more properties than a report. Unlike reports, forms often require only one section—the detail section—and this is the only section present in the blank form. The default size of the detail section is the same as on a blank report—1 inch high by 5 inches wide, and the grid density is set to 10 dots per inch horizontally by 12 dots per inch vertically.

You may recall from the section entitled "Customizing the Report Design Environment" in Chapter 11 that the grid spacing is one of the default settings established for both the Form Design and Report Design views through the Form & Report Design options accessed by choosing Options from the View menu. If you altered the Form & Report Design options while working with reports, you will find the same settings in effect in Form Design view, and you may need to rethink some of your choices after you have had more experience working with forms. You can define a template form using

Figure 12.1

A blank form

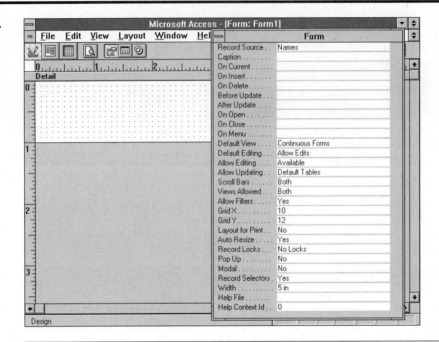

the same method described for template reports in Chapter 11, and the best way to define different options for new forms and reports is to define a template form and a template report that reflect your preferences, and enter their names in the Options dialog box.

Customizing Default Values and Validation Rules

Once you have created a blank form, you can use all of the methods described in Chapter 10 to add controls and customize the appearance of the form. As noted in Chapter 11, you can save a great deal of time by customizing the default property sheets in advance for the types of controls that you know you will be using in the form, so that you do not have to individually change numerous properties of a great many objects afterward. Chapter 10 concentrated on properties that are common to both forms and reports—those that affect the appearance and format of the data. When you design data entry forms, you must also be concerned with properties that are relevant only to the data entry process. Once you have created the basic form layout (whether you began with one of the FormWizards or built a custom form from scratch), you can turn your attention to aspects of the design that make the form easier to use and that encourage (or force) the users to enter more accurate and complete data. These issues merit some consideration even in simple forms that you design for your own use, and they can be vital in forms used by less knowledgeable co-workers and staff members.

As you have undoubtedly noticed, several of the properties of controls (such as text boxes) created using the field list are derived from the analogous properties stored in the table structure—the control name from the field name; the Status Bar Text property from the field description; and the Format, Decimal Places, Default Value, Validation Rule, and Validation Text properties from the identically named properties in the table. You can override these entries *for a particular form* by entering new values in the object's property sheet.

NOTE.   *If you create an unbound control using just the toolbox and later enter the field name in the Control Source property, Access binds the control to the field but does not retrieve the aforementioned properties from the table structure.*

The original discussion of these field properties presented in Chapter 3 was relatively abbreviated, but now that you know more about defining custom display formats and writing Access expressions, you can make much better use of all of them. Data formatting, which is important in both forms and reports, was described in Chapter 9. The next two sections of this chapter cover the Default Value, Validation Rule, and Validation Text properties in more detail. Keep in mind that you can use the same expressions to define field properties stored in the table as you can for the corresponding form object properties. After you read Chapter 13, which describes how to change the structure of a table that contains data, you may want to return to some of your tables to specify default values and validation rules.

Specifying Default Values

The Default Value property specifies a value that Access enters automatically into new records that you add to a table. (Remember that the default value is *not* entered into existing records, even when you edit a record in which the field is blank.) If you store a default value in the table structure, Access uses it in Datasheet view and as the initial setting for the Default Value property in every form you create, provided that you use the field list to add the field to the form. If you edit the Default Value property for a text box in a particular form, the value you enter overrides the one stored in the table structure *when you enter data using that form.*

When you update a table in Datasheet view or Form view, Access fills in the default value immediately whenever you add a new record, so there is never any doubt what the default value is. If you want to override the default value in a particular record, you can simply delete it or type over it. Establishing a default value can save considerable time in the course of a lengthy data entry session (especially for longer fields), and it reduces the likelihood that typographical or spelling errors will introduce inconsistencies—if not inaccuracies—into the database. The only potential problem is that you may fail to notice the default value if the field is off in the corner of a crowded form, especially if the field should be blank in the record you are entering.

You can use any expression to define the Default Value property for a field in a table or for a control on a form. Often, the default value is a simple constant. For example, the default value for the State field in the Names table is "CA," because most new contacts are in ACE's home state of California. The default value for all the numeric fields in the Transactions table is 0.00, so that these fields can never be null. Using 0 as a default value is the easiest way to avoid some of the problems described in Chapter 9 that arise from null values, without having to explicitly enter 0 into every numeric field when you add records or include tests for null values in every query that you design.

Now that you understand more about constructing Access expressions, you can define more complex, flexible, and useful default values. For example, you could use the expression Date( ) (the result of evaluating the Date function, which yields the current date) as the default value for the Date field in a table such as the ACE Contacts or Transactions table, or the First Contact field in the Names table. Similarly, you could use the Time function to enter the current time into a Date/Time field formatted to display times, or you could use the more general Now function for *any* Date/Time field. To enter a date or time that differs from the current date or time by a fixed interval, you can use a simple expression like Date( )+14 or Date( )–7 or a more complex expression based on the DateAdd function, such as DateAdd("m", 2, Date()), which describes a date two months in the future, or DateAdd("h", -1, Now()), which computes a time one hour before the current time. In any event, the complexity of the default value is limited only by your ability to construct an expression that accurately describes your requirements. Remember that when you enter an expression rather than a constant in the Default Value property for a field in a table or a control on a form, you must preface the expression with an equals sign (=).

You might hope to base the default value for one field on the value of another field in the same table or on the same form. For example, in the Contacts table, you might want to enter a date that is two weeks after the contact date into the Follow-up Date field. However, you *cannot* accomplish this simply by entering the expression [Date]+14 as the default value for the Follow-up Date field, because Access calculates and fills in all the default values (as well as the values of Counter fields) at the instant you add each new record, and at that point, you have not yet entered a value into the Date field. To change the contents of a field dynamically, based on the value entered in another field in the same table, you must use a macro, as described in Chapter 18.

As noted briefly in Chapter 10, you may at times want to define a default value for a field in a form that does not allow you to enter or change the field. For example, in a form intended to enter only prospect records into the Names table (such as the Prospects form defined in Chapter 6), you could assign "P" as the default value for the Name Type field, which has no default stored in the table structure. The field must be present on the form, but you can render it invisible by setting the Visible property to No. The easiest way to display the field but prohibit editing is to set the Locked property to Yes for the control that collects the field. You might also consider setting the Enabled property to No to disable the control, but this method has two disadvantages. First, Access does not display the label object associated with a disabled control, so you must replace it with an independent label object. Also, Access "grays out" disabled controls (as it does disabled menu options), so the data may be hard to read when you use the form.

To define the default value for the Date field in the Committees table, use the following steps:

1. Make sure that the Database window displays the list of tables, and open the Committees table in Table Design view.

2. Press Down Arrow three times or click in the Field Name column for the Joined field, and then press F6 or click in the Default Value entry in the lower half of the Table Design window.

3. Type **=Date()** to specify the current date as the default value for the Joined field.

4. Close the Table Design window and select OK when Access displays an alert box to ask whether you want to "Save changes to Table 'Committees'?"

Validating Data

You may recall from Chapter 4 that even without explicitly defined rules, Access performs several types of automatic validation, mostly based on the data type of the field you are updating. For example, you cannot enter an invalid date such as 11/31/93 (November does not have 31 days) or time 11:75:00 (there are only 60 minutes in an hour) into a Date/Time field, and the only permissible entries in a Yes/No field are Yes, No, True, False, On, and Off. Violating any of these rules invokes an alert box with an error message like the one in Figure 12.2, which simply informs you that you have entered inappropriate data without elaborating on the precise nature of the problem. Access checks the data against its built-in validation rules the instant you try to move out of a field, so you cannot temporarily leave a bad value in the field and return to correct it later. Although this behavior can be inconvenient at times, it makes sense when you consider that validation rules based on the data type can be evaluated solely in the context of the current field—they do not depend on any other fields or records.

Figure 12.2

The error message displayed when a field fails a built-in validation test

In a table that has a primary key or any indexes that do not permit duplicate key values, Access tests new or edited records to ensure that none of the key field values duplicate any other existing record. Access also validates records based on any default table relationships stored in the database for which you checked the Enforce Referential Integrity option (as described in Chapter 8). Both of these types of validation rules are applied when you attempt to save the new or changed record, either by moving to another record or by choosing the Save Record option on the File menu. Unlike validations based on the data type, these tests may depend on more than one field in the current record (an index key may be based on two or more fields), and they must also take into account the relationship of the current record to other records in the same or another table. The validations that encompass the record as a whole are therefore carried out when you declare all your edits to the current record complete by attempting to save it.

You can define additional conditions that individual fields must satisfy by entering them in the Validation Rule property in the table structure. Like a default value, a validation rule that you store in the table applies in Datasheet view and supplies the initial value for the corresponding property for controls used to collect the field in forms, provided that you use the field list to add the control to the form. If you want to use a different validation rule in a particular form, you can enter it in the Validation Rule property for the control that collects the field. In both cases, the expression that defines the validation rule must be a logical expression—one that evaluates to Yes or No (True or False), such as the expressions that you might use to define selection criteria in a query.

The simplest validation tests compare the contents of a field to a constant value. For example, you could prohibit the entry of a date later than the current date in a Date/Time field with the condition <=Date(), and you could limit entries in a numeric field to values over 100 with the condition >=100.

The easiest way to test for a range of values is to use the Between operator in a condition like Between 1/1/93 And 12/31/93. You can use the In operator to test for a small number of possibilities. For example, you could validate the Address Type field in the Names table with the condition In ("H","W","U").

NOTE. *If there are more than a few allowable values, it is better to create a reference table and define a default relationship than to list the values explicitly in a validation rule, especially if you anticipate editing the list of permissible values. If you "hard-code" the field values in the table (or in forms used to update the field), you will have to search for and change all of these validation rules if you add or delete a code rather than simply making the update in one place in the reference table.*

If you want to prohibit leaving a field blank (null), you can use the condition Is Not Null, which applies to fields of any data type. In the ACE system, this condition is used to validate the Address and City fields in the Names table, the Date fields in the Contacts and Transactions table, and the Subtotal and Amount fields in the Transactions table. Remember that if you do not want to allow null values, *you must write a condition that explicitly excludes nulls*, because Access does not evaluate the validation rules if you leave a field blank. Thus, the complete condition used to validate the Address Type field in the Names table is as follows:

```
In ("H","W","U") And Is Not Null
```

However, you do not have to test for null values in a field on which one of the default relationships defined for a table is based—when Access fails to find a match in the related table, it will reject the null field value. For example, in the ACE system, the Names table is linked to the States table based on the State field, and because the States table has no record in which the State field is blank, Access will not allow you to leave the State field blank in the Names table.

Some validations are considerably more complex, and many are difficult or impossible without programming. For example, consider the criteria that determine what constitutes a valid United States zip code—it must either be exactly five digits long or it must consist of five digits, a dash, and four more digits. Postal codes from other countries have different—and often equally complicated—rules. For example, a Canadian postal code is exactly seven characters long and must conform to the following pattern: letter, digit, letter, space, digit, letter, digit (for example, M8Z 2S5). Testing for all of these possible patterns generally requires programming. If you only have to validate U.S. zip codes, a reasonable compromise might be to carry out a few simple tests based on the length of the zip code and the presence of the dash, which you can do with the following expression:

```
Len([Zip])=5 Or (Len([Zip])=10 And Mid([Zip],6,1)="-")
```

The first part of the condition, which uses the Len function to measure the length of the Zip field, evaluates to True (Yes) if the field is 5 characters long. The second part of the condition consists of two conditions linked with And, so both must be true in a valid zip code:

```
(Len([Zip])=10 And Mid([Zip],6,1)="-")
```

The first of these two conditions tests the length of the Zip field, and the second uses the Mid function (Mid stands for "Midstring") to test for the dash. The Mid function, which extracts characters from the middle of a text string to yield another text string, takes three inputs: the original text string, a numeric expression that represents the starting position of the desired extract, and another numeric expression that describes its length. Thus, the expression Mid([Zip],6,1) evaluates to the portion of the Zip field that begins with the sixth character and is one character long, which must be a dash in a ten-digit zip code. Note that the parentheses that enclose these two conditions are present only to make the complete expression that describes the validation rule more readable. The default precedence of And over Or would result in evaluating the full condition exactly the same way—that is, it would evaluate to True if either the length of the Zip field was 5 or if the length was 10 and the sixth character was a dash.

To ensure that the Zip field cannot be left blank, you must add the condition Is Not Null, as follows:

```
Is Not Null And (Len([Zip])=5 Or (Len([Zip])=10 And
Mid([Zip],6,1)="-"))
```

In this case, the parentheses around the length tests *are* necessary. Without them, Access would combine the conditions Is Not Null and Len([Zip])=5, and separately combine the conditions (Len([Zip])=10 and Mid([Zip],6,1)="-"), rather than testing Is Not Null as a separate condition and then combining the outcome with the result of evaluating the other conditions.

Unlike default values, validation rules can be based on other fields in the same table, because they are evaluated one by one *as you leave each field*, rather than all at once for every field in the record. For example, to ensure that the last contact date is never earlier than the first contact date, the validation rule for the First Contact field in the Names table is <=[Last Contact] and the validation rule for the Last Contact field is >=[First Contact]. In your own databases, you might also want to add a test based on the current date, as in the following condition (used to validate the First Contact field):

```
<=[Last Contact] And <=Date()
```

To exclude blank dates, you would have to add the standard test for null values:

```
Is Not Null And <=[Last Contact] And <=Date()
```

Not every validation test based on several fields in a table is as straightforward as the last few examples, and sometimes validating a *combination* of fields is possible only in a form. For example, in the Names table, you might want to allow either the Name or Company field, but not both, to be blank. However, you cannot simply use conditions like the following for the Name and Company fields:

```
Is Not Null Or [Company] Is Not Null
```

and

```
Is Not Null Or [Name] Is Not Null
```

The problem is that Access evaluates the validation rule for the Name field the instant you leave the field, at which point the Company field is likely to still be blank even if you intend to fill it in. Validations like this must be carried out using a data entry form that calls a macro to carry out the validation when you save the record, using techniques described in Chapter 18.

At times, you may want to validate a field with a lookup in another table that does *not* depend on a default relationship, either because you cannot define one or because you do not want Access to enforce referential integrity. For example, in the ACE system, because the Keywords table is used to validate three different fields in the Names table—Keyword 1, Keyword 2, and Keyword 3—you cannot define a default relationship between the two tables. In another example, you cannot enforce referential integrity between the Names table and the Area Codes table, because doing so would prevent you from leaving the Area Code field in the Names table blank.

In these situations, you can use the DLookUp function to carry out the validation. Recall that this function performs a lookup in another table and returns a specific value from that table. If the lookup fails to find a matching record, the DLookUp function evaluates to a null string, and you can test for this outcome in a validation rule, using a condition like the following:

```
DLookUp("[Description]","Keywords","[Keyword]=[Keyword 1]")
Is Not Null
```

In this example, the DLookUp function searches for a record in the Keywords table in which the Keyword field matches the Keyword 1 field in the current table (the Names table). The return value (the result of evaluating the function) is the Description field from the Keywords table, but returning the Keyword field would work just as well because it too would be null if the DLookUp function failed to find a matching record. The return value itself is unimportant—you need only determine whether it is null.

If you enter data in a field that does not satisfy the condition in the Validation Rule property, Access displays the alert box pictured in Figure 12.3 when you attempt to leave the field. You can use the Validation Text property to define a custom error message to replace the generic one in Figure 12.3. For example, you could use the message "Address cannot be blank" for the Address field in the Names table, or the message "Last Contact must be after First Contact" for the Last Contact field. Access adjusts the size of the alert box to accommodate a longer message (up to 255 characters), such as the Validation Text for the Zip field, which summarizes all the tests the Zip field must pass—"Zip Code must be 5 digits or 10 digits with a dash after the first five digits." Unless you will be the sole user of a database and you are sure you will remember all the data validation rules, it is a good idea to use the Validation Text property to customize the error message for every field you validate with the Validation Rule property.

Figure 12.3

The default alert box displayed when you enter invalid data

To define validation rules and error messages in the Committee Memberships form defined in Chapter 6 and customized in Chapter 10, use the following steps:

1. Open the Committee Memberships form in Form Design view.

2. If the property sheet is not visible, display it by clicking on the Property Sheet button in the tool bar or by selecting Property Sheet from the View menu.

3. Click in the Officer text box (not the associated label), and note that the Status Bar Text property matches the field description stored in the table structure: "Current officer position, if any."

4. Click in the Validation Rule property, and then type **In ("Chairperson", "Secretary", "Treasurer")** and press Enter.

5. In the Validation Text property, type **Officer position must be "Chairperson", "Secretary", or "Treasurer"**. (If you prefer, you can use the cut and paste commands to copy the validation rule and then edit the text instead of typing it from scratch.)

6. Click in the Joined text box, and then type **<=[Quit] And Is Not Null** in the Validation Rule property.

7. In the Validation Text property, type **Joined must be an earlier date than Quit**.

8. In the Default Value property, type **=Date()**.

9. Click in the Quit text box, and then type **>=[Joined] And Is Not Null** in the Validation Rule property.

10. In the Validation Text property, type **Date quit must be later than date joined**.

11. Click on the Form View button in the tool bar or select Form from the View menu.

12. In the Committee text box, type **XX** and press PgDn to attempt to save the record and move to the next record. Access displays the alert box shown in Figure 12.4 to inform you that you have violated the referential integrity rules defined in the database.

Figure 12.4

The error message displayed when you violate referential integrity

13. Select OK and then press Esc to abort your entry in the Committee field.

14. In the Quit field for the first record, type **1/1/92** and press Tab. Access displays an alert box that displays the validation text for the field, as shown in Figure 12.5.

15. Select OK and then press Esc to abort your entry in the Quit field.

16. Click on the Datasheet View button in the tool bar or select Datasheet from the View menu. Scroll down to the bottom of the datasheet, and observe that the special row that represents a new record has the current date (the default value) displayed in the Joined column.

17. Close the window and select Yes when Access displays an alert box to ask whether you want to "Save changes to Form 'Committee Memberships'?"

Figure 12.5

The custom error message defined by the Validation Text property

Using Controls in Forms

In the data entry forms you have worked with thus far, most of the fields were collected in text boxes (with a few check boxes for Yes/No fields). Access also provides all the other standard controls used in Windows (and other graphical environments) to enter data, including radio buttons, toggle buttons, list boxes, and combo boxes. Obviously, you will continue to use text boxes to collect Text, Date/Time, and numeric fields that must be able to accept any value, but the more complex controls are useful for more specialized purposes. In the sections that follow, the controls are grouped according to the most common ways that they are used in Windows data entry screens and dialog boxes. As you read about these controls, think about how you might use them in your own Access forms. Note also that you can use all of these controls in reports—and you can print forms that include them—but the ones that are designed specifically to facilitate data entry are used far more commonly in forms.

Collecting Yes/No Fields

Access provides several types of specialized controls intended primarily for collecting Yes/No fields, one of which—check boxes—should already be familiar to you from the forms generated by the FormWizards. You can also use *option buttons* (which are more often called *radio buttons*) and *toggle buttons*, as well as text boxes. Several examples of each of these controls are visible in the form pictured in Figure 12.6, which illustrates several different display styles for each of these controls; Figure 12.7 shows the same form in Form Design view. Unlike most of the forms in the ACE system, this one was *not* intended to be a realistic example of a data entry form—it contains several different controls that collect the same fields, and serves primarily to introduce a variety of methods for using these controls to collect Yes/No fields.

Figure 12.6

Using check boxes, option buttons, toggle buttons, and option groups

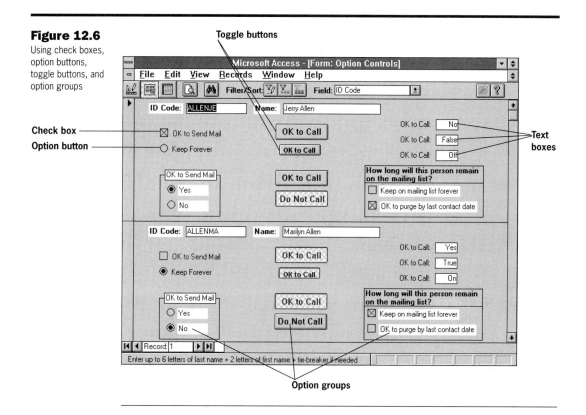

You can also use check boxes, option buttons, and toggle buttons to display and collect numeric data, a fact that should not be surprising in light of the fact that Access stores and manipulates Yes/No fields as numbers (–1 for Yes and 0 for No). For example, if you use a check box for a numeric field, Access displays the box checked if the field contains any nonzero value, unchecked if it contains zero, and grayed out when the field is empty (null). In rare cases, you might use check boxes this way simply to distinguish between zero and nonzero values, but they are not very useful for entering numeric data, because checking the box automatically enters –1 into the underlying field, and unchecking the box changes its value to 0. Single check boxes are most often used for Yes/No data. The next section describes how to create option groups made up of one or more check boxes, option buttons, or toggle buttons to collect two or more different numeric values.

For collecting Yes/No fields in a table, option buttons and toggle buttons serve as alternative visual metaphors that are functionally equivalent to check boxes. Below the ID Code text box in the form in Figure 12.6 is a check box that collects the OK to Send Mail field and an option button that collects

Figure 12.7

Defining check boxes, option buttons, toggle buttons, and option groups

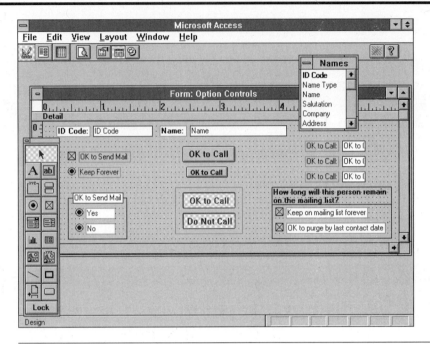

the Keep Forever field. Under the Name field text box there are two toggle buttons of different sizes that both collect the OK to Call field. You can create these objects by using the toolbox alone or in combination with the field list, following the basic methods outlined in Chapter 10. If you like the look of option buttons, feel free to use them instead of check boxes, but you should be aware that most Windows and Macintosh software uses option buttons only in groups, in which each button represents one of several mutually exclusive alternatives for the same field. Using option buttons this way is described later in this chapter, in the section entitled "Using Option Groups."

Option buttons look and work much like check boxes. Access displays a dark dot inside the circle to the left of an option button prompt when the value of the underlying field is Yes; when the field value is No, the circle appears empty. Toggle buttons are used more often to set environmental options and execute commands than to collect data, and you already have considerable experience operating these controls—the command buttons in the tool bar are all toggle buttons. Like a push-button toggle switch, a toggle button can exist in two states (on and off), and the visual representation of this control simulates the simple switches found on stereos, appliances, and other electronic equipment—the button appears raised when it is off (unselected) and sunken when it is on (selected). Because it can be hard to distinguish between the raised and sunken attributes for a small button, Access also changes the color of the button when it is depressed.

Access does not allow you to resize a check box or option button (although you can adjust the size of the attached label as you would for any other labeled control), but you can create a toggle button of any size. By default, Access creates square buttons (like the ones in the tool bar) $\frac{1}{2}$ inch on each side with faces that are blank in preparation for adding a picture or symbol. If you want to display a picture on a button, you must create the image in advance (using a drawing program such as Paintbrush), store it in a disk file, and enter the name of this file in the Picture property. This procedure is described in more detail in Chapter 15, which covers working with graphic images created outside of Access. When you use a toggle button to execute a command or establish an environment setting, placing a picture on its face to symbolize its purpose is ideal. While you might occasionally use a picture on a button used to collect data—for example, the image of a telephone on the OK to Call button—a caption is usually more appropriate.

You can enter a caption on a toggle button using either of the two methods described earlier for label objects—by entering the text in the Caption property or by clicking inside the button object on the form and typing the caption. The toggle button just below the Name field in Figure 12.6 was resized to accommodate the caption, which in this case matches the field name. To maintain consistency with the appearance of all Windows command buttons, Access by default uses the System font for button labels and displays the label boldfaced (you can change either of these assumptions by editing the property sheet for the default toggle button). The System font is available in only one size (10 point), and changing the Font Style property has no effect on its appearance. To create a small button, like the second of the two OK to Call buttons in Figure 12.6, you can switch to the similar Arial font (or any other font you prefer) and choose a smaller font size so that you can fit the caption on the button face. In any font except System, you do not have to set the Font Style to Bold, but you will usually want to do so.

Although controls like check boxes are intuitive and easy to use (especially for those who prefer the mouse to the keyboard), do not overlook the fact that you can use the familiar text box to display and collect Yes/No data. Using text boxes is ideal for forms that are used more often for displaying or printing data rather than for entering or editing, and for situations in which you might frequently want to switch to Datasheet view. Figure 12.8 illustrates the Option Controls form in Datasheet view; the check boxes (and option buttons, none of which are visible in this figure) look peculiar in this context, and fields collected with toggle buttons are displayed as they are stored internally—as numbers.

The default format for text boxes used to collect Yes/No fields displays the values as "Yes" or "No," but you can set the Format property to True/ False or On/Off if you prefer. Examples of all three choices are visible on the

Note. You cannot display both a picture and a caption on a toggle button.

Figure 12.8
Check boxes and
toggle buttons in
Datasheet view

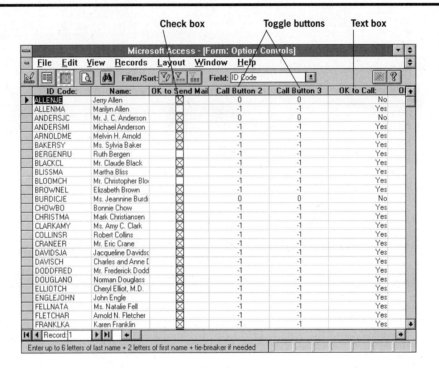

upper-right side of the form in Figure 12.6. Note that some customization of the default text box is usually necessary when you use this control for Yes/No fields. The default text box is wider (at 1 inch) than you will need for any of the standard display formats, and the default label is usually too small and too far from the text box itself.

All of the examples in this section illustrated ways to display and collect *fields* in a table. You can also use check boxes, option buttons, and toggle buttons to display the result of evaluating a logical expression. For example, you could create a check box with the label "Balance Due" and define the control source as the expression [Total Debits]>[Total Credits], which evaluates to True (Yes) when the debits exceed the credits and to False (No) otherwise.

Using Option Groups

The preceding section described how to use single check boxes, option buttons, and toggle buttons to display and collect Yes/No data. You can also place these controls in groups of two or more in which each object represents a different possible value for a single field. In this context, option buttons are used far more frequently than the other two types of controls in Windows and other GUI environments, although you might want to use check boxes in a form that you print frequently to emulate the appearance of an existing preprinted form. You are probably more familiar with the term *radio buttons* to describe a group of option buttons, which behave like the pushbuttons on an old-fashioned car radio—only one button at a time can be pushed in (selected), and pressing one button deselects the previously selected one. If you deviate from this convention and use check boxes or toggle buttons in an option group, make sure that the prompts on the screen clearly indicate their purpose to help other users of the form understand that the group represents just one field. The bottom half of the screen in Figure 12.6 contains examples of all three types of option groups—two option buttons that collect the OK to Send Mail field, two toggle buttons that collect the OK to Call field, and two check boxes that collect the Keep Forever field.

To further confuse the issue, Access itself uses option buttons both singly and in groups, with no clear indication (apart from the context) of which is which. For example, the set of buttons on the far left side of the tool bar function as a group—they represent mutually exclusive views (Design, Form, and Datasheet views in Figure 12.6), and only one at a time can be selected. In contrast, the buttons that represent the various tools (the property sheet, field list, and color palette) and those used to select type attributes (bold, underlined, and italic) are independent toggle buttons, any or all of which might be selected at any given moment.

There is one significant limitation on the use of option groups in Access: They can only be used to collect numeric values, not text strings. All of the option groups in Figure 12.6 collect Yes/No fields, which are stored internally as numbers, but option groups are far more commonly used to represent three or more alternative field values. If you plan to enter data only through custom forms, where you will never see the raw contents of a field, you can simply use a Byte or Integer field instead of a Text field for items such as the address type in the Names table and then display and collect the values with an option group. For example, in the hypothetical numeric Address Type field, you could use 1 to represent "Home," 2 to represent "Work," and 3 for "Unknown." This strategy is less convenient if you frequently work in Datasheet view, where the numeric values are unsightly and far less intuitive than the one-character codes used in the Names table (H, W, and U). Chapter 18 describes a method for using macros to overcome this limitation.

The crucial fact to keep in mind when you use option groups is that the option group object itself—represented visually in Form Design or Report Design view by the frame that surrounds the individual check boxes, option buttons, or toggle buttons—is bound to the underlying field. The individual objects within the frame have no direct connection to this field, although they represent the different possible values that the field can assume.

You can create an option group by using the toolbox either alone or in combination with the field list. If you use the field list, Access enters the selected field name in the Control Source property for the group; if you use the toolbox alone, you must enter the field name yourself in the Control Source property for the option group. By default, Access draws a square frame on the form 1 inch on each side to represent the option group, with a label (identical to the field name if you use the field list to create the option group) superimposed on the upper border. In the first option group in Figure 12.6, this label was enlarged slightly, and in the third group, it was moved and resized to accommodate a much longer prompt; in the second of the three option groups, the label was removed entirely. In most cases, you will also need to resize the frame to conform to the number and size of the controls you place inside.

To create the individual check boxes, option buttons, or toggle buttons inside the group frame, which are unbound controls, you use the toolbox alone. You can then edit the Caption property for the labels so that they describe the options they represent (and, if you wish, the default control names assigned by Access). Remember that you have considerable latitude in writing the label text; for example, in Figure 12.6, the check box labels in the option group that collects the Keep Forever field are quite a bit longer and more descriptive than the field names.

To establish the correspondence between the controls and the underlying field values, you enter the values in the Option Value property for the controls. When you use the form to edit an existing record, Access selects the object whose Option Value property matches the contents of the field, and when you select one of the controls, it stores the value of the Option Value property in the field. When you create an option group, Access assigns a value to each control as you add it to the group, starting with 1 for the first object, 2 for the second, and so on. However, you can edit the Option Value property to assign any integer values, which need not be sequential. For example, in the option groups in Figure 12.6, the Option Value property is –1 for the control that represents Yes and 0 for the control that represents No. Access does not display an error message if you accidentally assign the same value to more than one control in a group, so if you use the Duplicate command to copy an object, you must remember to change the Option Value property in the copies.

You can move an existing control into a group, but you cannot do so by using the mouse to drag it inside the group frame. Instead, you must use the cut and paste commands to remove the object from the form and then add it back. If you simply drag an existing object into the frame, it will retain all of its original properties, including the Control Source property, and will remain an independent control that happens to be superimposed on the option group. Also note that when you use the cut and paste method to add an existing control to a group, Access sets the Option Value property to –1, so you must edit this property to assign the correct value afterwards.

Access treats an option group as a unit in Form Design view. You can select the entire group—the option group object and the controls it contains—by clicking on the frame. You might want to do this to move the group as a whole while retaining the relative positions of all the component objects. To move just one of the objects within the frame, click instead in this object. If you do not want to display the frame in Form view or Report view, you can set the Border Style property to Clear (or check the corresponding check box in the color palette); in Figure 12.6, the second of the three option groups (the one that contains two toggle buttons) has no frame. In most cases, however, you will want to retain the frame to reinforce the idea that the controls within represent alternative values for one field, not independent data items.

To practice using option groups, begin by adding a field to the Committees table to store a code that represents the committee member's willingness to be publicly associated with the committee:

1. Make sure that the Database window displays the list of tables.

2. Highlight the name of the Committees table, and click on Design or press Alt+D to open the table in Design view.

3. Enter the name of the new field, **Public Exposure**, in the Field Name column of the first blank row (directly below the Notes field), and press Tab to move to the Data Type column.

4. Type **Number** or select this option from the drop-down list of data types, and press Tab to move to the Description column.

5. Type the allowable values for the Public Exposure field: **1=Do not publish name, 2=Publish in member directory, 3=List as press contact**.

6. Press F6 to edit the field properties and type **Byte**, or select this option from the drop-down list of field sizes.

7. Press Ctrl+F4 to close the Table Design window, and choose Yes in the alert box that Access displays to ask whether you want to save your changes.

Next, edit the Committee Memberships form to add an option group to display and update the new field, using the following steps:

1. Open the Committee Memberships form in Form Design view, and maximize the window.

2. Expand the height of the detail section to $2^3/_4$ inches, and move the Notes field text box and the attached label down to the bottom of the detail section.

3. Make sure the property sheet, toolbox, color palette, and field list are visible on the work surface, and make sure that none of these tools covers the region on the left side of the form between the Joined and Notes fields.

4. Click on the Option Group button in the toolbox, and then drag the Public Exposure field from the field list onto the form, placing it between the Joined and Notes fields.

5. In the property sheet for the option group, verify that the name of the Public Exposure field appears in the Control Source property. Delete the list of field values displayed in the Status Bar Text property.

6. Move and resize the frame so that it is as high as possible, with the left side at the $\frac{1}{4}$-inch mark in the horizontal ruler and the right side at the $2\frac{1}{2}$-inch mark.

7. Click on the Option Button button in the toolbox. In the property sheet for the default option button, change the Label X property to 0.75 to move the label to the right of the option button, and change the Label Align property to Left.

8. Add three unbound option buttons in a vertical column inside the group frame. Note that the three buttons are assigned successive numeric values, starting with 1, in the Option Value property.

9. Click in the label object attached to the first option button, click again to display an insertion point, delete the default caption, and type **Do not publish name**.

10. Click in the label object attached to the second option button, click in the Caption property entry in the property sheet, delete the default caption, and type **Publish in member directory**.

11. Using either method, enter the caption for the third button, **List as press contact**.

12. Click in the label for the option group, click in the Clear check box next to the fill color samples in the palette, and then click on the light gray color sample to match the background color to the form.

13. Move and resize the objects in the frame if necessary, so that all the option buttons and all the labels are lined up. Your screen should resemble Figure 12.9.

14. Click on the Restore button to restore the window to its former size.

15. Switch to Form view to display the first record in the Committees table, and click in the third radio button to select "List as press contact."

Figure 12.9

Adding an option group to the Committee Memberships form

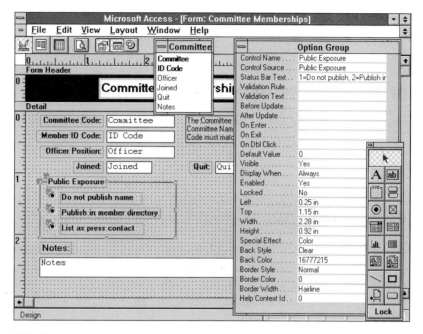

16. Move to the next record, and click in the first radio button to select "Do not publish name."

17. Switch to Datasheet view, and note that the entry in the Public Exposure field is 3 in the first record and 1 in the second.

18. Close the form and save it.

Using List Boxes and Combo Boxes

The option groups described in the previous section are just one of several controls that enable you to choose a field value from a list rather than typing it yourself. You can also create two types of list controls—list boxes and combo boxes. Figure 12.10 illustrates both pages of a two-page data entry form for the Names table that includes a list box (to collect the Address Type field) and several combo boxes, with the drop-down list for the Name Type combo box visible on the screen. Either type of list can have one or more columns; in the form in Figure 12.10, the State combo box has one column, and the others all have two to display both the code and the longer description.

When you use a form to enter data, Access highlights the row in a list box that matches the value in the underlying field, and it displays the raw field

Figure 12.10

Using list boxes
and combo boxes
in a form

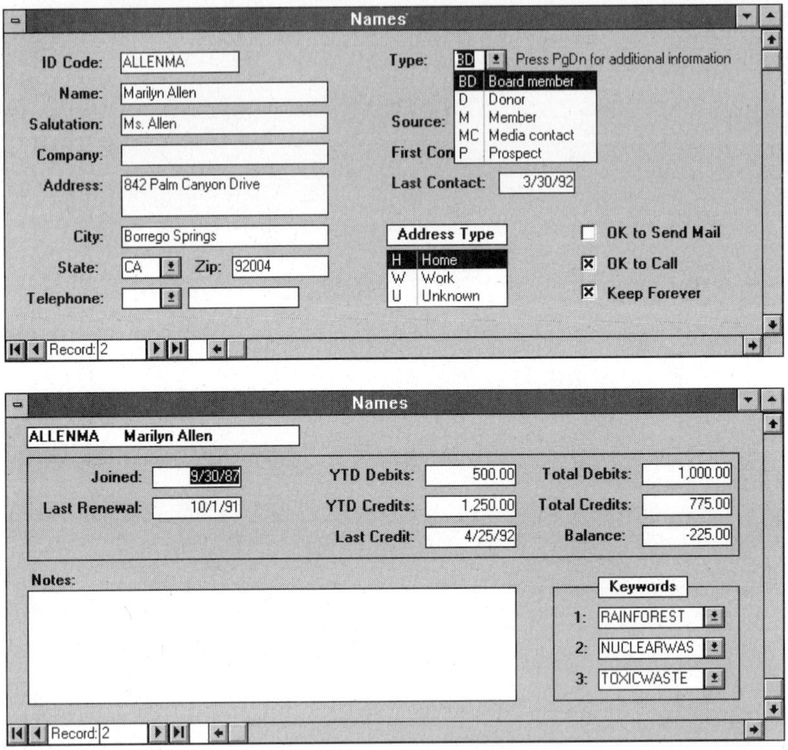

value in the text entry region associated with a combo box. In Datasheet
view, it is impractical to display all the items in a list box, and Access displays
both types of list as combo boxes. In a new record, when the field collected
using a list box is empty, no row is highlighted. You can use the Tab key to
move past a list box without selecting a value, but once you have chosen one,
you cannot blank out the field using the form (of course, you can do so in
Datasheet view). Note also that clicking the mouse anywhere in a list selects
a value—if you are not sure you want to do this, you must use the keyboard
to move past the list control or click elsewhere on the form with the mouse.

Like option groups, list boxes are best suited to relatively short lists displayed on relatively uncrowded screens, while combo boxes, which take up
only a little more space than a text box (the width of the field plus about ¼
inch for the button that you press to display the drop-down list), are ideal for
longer lists. There is one other fundamental difference: When you use a list
box, you *must* choose one of the values in the list, whereas you can enter a
value in a combo box by typing it without displaying the drop-down list.

Whether Access allows you to enter a value that is not present in the list is up to you—it depends on the setting you choose for the Limit to List property of the combo box. Note that you can use a list box even if you do not have room on the screen for all the choices—if the list is too long to fit in the frame you define for it, Access displays a vertical scroll bar in the list frame.

The easiest way to create either type of list is to use the standard method based on both the toolbox and field list. If you instead create an unbound control using just the toolbox, you can specify the underlying field as you would for any other control—by entering its name in the Control Source property for the list object. In most cases, you will end up moving and resizing the list control more than once, so don't worry too much about the size and position at first. By default, Access attaches a label to both types of lists, positioned to the left of the list object, but you can move or resize the label as you see fit. In the form in Figure 12.10, the label for the Address Type list box was moved to a new position above the list box, the Clear check boxes for both the fill and border colors were unchecked, and the caption was centered in the object frame. You will usually want to retain the label for combo boxes, which by and large resemble text boxes on the form, but the label may not be necessary for a list box. For example, if you changed the wording of the Address Type list box options to "Home Address," "Work Address," and "Unknown," you could eliminate the label.

NOTE. *When you use the toolbox and field list to create a list object, Access derives the same properties from those stored in the table that it does for any other control, including the Validation Rule and Validation Text properties, which are irrelevant for most list controls. If you wish, you can delete these entries in the property sheet, but there is no harm in allowing them to stand.*

Access gives you considerable latitude in specifying the source of the list items. The *type* of the source is determined by the Row Source Type property, which can take on the following values:

Table/Query	The contents of one or more fields in a table or query
Value List	A list of arbitrary values that you enter
Field List	A list of the field names in a table or query

In most cases, you will use either a table, a query, or a value list; the Field List option, which creates a list of field names rather than data items, is used primarily in Access Basic programs to create field lists like the ones displayed by Access in the tool bar. The Row Source property identifies the actual source of the list values—usually a table name, query name, or a list of values. For example, the Name Types, States, and Area Codes combo boxes in Figure 12.10

are based on the corresponding reference tables, and the Address Type list is based on an explicit list of values. You can also enter an SQL Select statement in the Row Source property, and if you already know SQL syntax, you may want to explore this option further at this point. (The SQL Select command is covered briefly in Chapter 20.)

If the row source is a table, the list will include all the records in the table, displayed in the order they were entered (not, as you might guess, in primary key order). If you want to display only some of the records in a table or display the list rows in a different order, you must define a query that describes the selection criteria and sort order, and use the query rather than the table as the row source.

Figures 12.11 and 12.12 illustrate the Names form in Form Design view with the property sheet displayed to show the specifications for the Address Type list box and the Area Codes combo box. The following properties, which are visible in both figures, are applicable to both list boxes and combo boxes:

Column Count	The number of columns
Column Heads	Whether to display column titles
Column Widths	The widths of the individual columns
Bound Column	The list column that corresponds to the field updated through the list

For combo boxes, but not list boxes, you must also define three additional properties that describe the drop-down list (these properties are visible in Figure 12.12):

List Rows	The maximum number of rows to display at once in the drop-down list
List Width	The width of the drop-down list
Limit to List	Whether to limit entries to values in the list or permit any value

The List Rows and List Width properties describe the appearance of the drop-down list associated with the combo box. (The size of the list object itself is described by the Height and Width properties, as is the case with all other controls.) By default, Access sets the List Width property to match the width of the combo box object on the screen, but if the list has more than one column, you will usually need to widen it. In fact, this is one of the advantages of using a combo box—it takes up very little space on the screen until you display the drop-down list, which might in some cases occupy most of the

Figure 12.11

Defining a list box

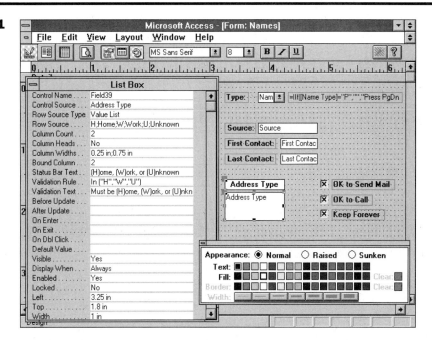

Figure 12.12

Defining a combo box

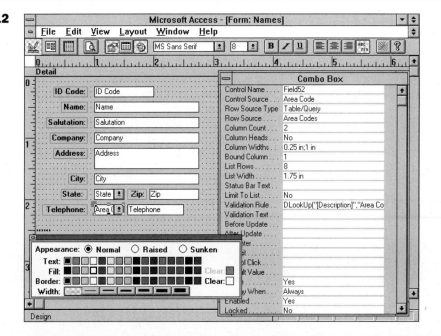

screen. The List Rows property determines the maximum number of rows that Access displays in the drop-down list. If there are fewer rows in the source table, Access shrinks the list to match, and if there are more, it displays a vertical scroll bar. Note that the scroll bar is displayed *within* the list frame, so you must allow room for it when you define the List Width property.

The Limit to List property, which can take on the values Yes and No, determines whether Access allows you to enter a value not included in the drop-down list associated with a combo box. If you set the Limit to List property to Yes, Access displays an alert box to warn you that "The text you enter must match an entry in the list" if you leave the field blank or enter a value not found in the list. When you select OK from this alert box, Access displays the drop-down list automatically to encourage you to make a selection. When you set the Limit to List property to No, you can use a validation rule to check the data entered in the text box.

Some simple lists require only one column. For example, on the assumption that you would recognize the state abbreviation you want, the combo box that collects the State field in the Names form in Figure 12.10 has just one column, even though the data source is the States table, which includes a field for the state name. In contrast, the Area Codes and Name Types combo boxes have two columns, to display both the short code and the longer description. In a drop-down list of names used to collect the ID Code field in a form that updates the Contacts, Transactions, or Committees table, you might want to include most of the name and address fields, as demonstrated in the new version of the Committee Memberships form you will create later in this section. If you define more than one column, you must use the Bound Column property to identify (by number) the column that corresponds to the underlying field. The default value for this property is 1 (the first column), but you can choose any column you wish.

By default, Access makes all the columns in a list box 1 inch wide, but you can override the default by entering a list of column widths, separated by semicolons, in the Column Widths property. In a combo box based on a table, the initial list column widths are derived from the field widths in the source table. In most cases, you will usually need to adjust the column widths to better suit the form layout. For example, in the Address Type list box and the Name Type combo box, the column widths are $1/4$ and $3/4$ inch, and in the Area Code combo box they are $1/4$ and 1 inch.

When you use a list to choose a value for a code field such as the Address Type field in the Names Table, you may not want to display the list column that corresponds to this field. For example, you might want to display only the words "Home," "Work," and "Unknown" in the Address Type list box, but enter the values H, W, or U in the Address Type field. Access requires that every list include a column that exactly matches the bound field in the source table for the form. If you tried to bind the Description column to the

Address Type field, Access would never display any of the list rows highlighted, because the contents of the Address Type field does not exactly match any of the values in this column of the list, and choosing an option from the list would yield an alert box to inform you that Access "Couldn't insert or paste; data too long for field." One obvious solution to this problem is to lengthen the Address Type field to accommodate the text strings displayed in the list box, but this strategy would waste space in the database and complicate data entry in Datasheet view by forcing you to type the whole word rather than one letter. Instead, you must define the Address Type list box as a two-column list, but set the width of the bound column (which could be either column 1 or column 2) to 0 to make it invisible.

When you define a list based on a table or query (by choosing Table/Query for the Row Source Type property and entering the name of the table or query in the Row Source property), each column in the list is derived from a field in the table or query. While you can specify the number of columns, you cannot pick and choose the fields you want—if you request five columns, Access uses the first five columns in the table to build the list. To suppress fields selectively, you can set the widths of the corresponding columns to 0. For example, to display fields 1, 3, and 5, you could set the Column Count property to 5 and set the widths of columns 2 and 4 to 0. If you choose Yes for the Column Heads property, Access uses the field names (or query column titles) as column headers (an example is shown later in this chapter in Figure 12.18).

To define a list box or combo box that displays a list of arbitrary values, you choose Value List for the Row Source Type property and enter the list values, separated by semicolons, in the Row Source property. To build a list with more than one column, you must enter all the values in each row before moving to the next row. As you can see in Figure 12.11, the Address Type list, which has two columns and three rows, was defined by entering H;Home;W;Work;U;Unknown in the Row Source property. If you want column headings in a value list, you must set the Column Heads property to Yes and enter the column titles as the first row of the list.

You can choose text and fill colors for a list box, and you can assign the Raised or Sunken attributes, but the other options in the color palette are disabled, and there are no corresponding entries in the property sheet. Access chooses the colors used for the selected list item (white on black in Figure 12.10). Note also that you cannot check the Clear check box in the color palette to suppress the border around a list box. As noted earlier, you can modify all the visual attributes of the attached label.

To practice defining and using lists, modify the Committee Memberships form as follows:

1. Open the Committee Memberships form in Form Design view and maximize the window.

2. Delete the Committee, ID Code, and Officer text boxes and the text object that explains the Committee and ID Code fields.

3. Make sure that the property sheet, toolbox, and field list are visible on the work surface.

4. Click on the List Box button in the toolbox, and then select the Officer field from the field list, drag it onto the form, and drop it somewhere on the right side (you will move and resize it later). Delete the label object.

5. Choose Value List for the Row Source Type property.

6. Set the Column Heads property to Yes.

7. Enter the list values in the Row Source property: **Officer Position;(none); Chairperson;Secretary;Treasurer**. The first item will become the column title. The second will substitute for a blank value, which is not permitted in a list box. Note that this value is not a dummy entry or a placeholder— it will be entered into the Officer field in the Committees table (like any other list item) if you choose it from the list.

8. Select Courier from the font combo box in the tool bar, and select 10-point type from the font size combo box.

9. Adjust the height of the list box object to 0.75 inch, adjust the width to 1.5 inches, and check the appearance of the list box in Form view.

10. Click on the Combo Box button in the toolbox, and then select the Committee field from the field list, drag it onto the form, and drop it near the upper-left corner.

11. Select Courier from the font combo box in the tool bar, and select 10-point type from the font size combo box.

12. Retain the default value (Table/Query) for the Row Source Type property, and choose Committee Names for the Row Source property.

13. Adjust the width of the combo box to 1.25 inches.

14. Set the Column Count property to 2, enter **1;3** for the Column Widths property, and enter **4** for the List Width property.

15. Set the Limit to List property to Yes to prohibit entries in the combo box other than those in the list.

16. Edit the Status Bar Text property so it reads **Enter a Committee ID code or choose one from the list**.

17. Click on the Combo Box button in the toolbox, and then select the ID Code field from the field list, drag it onto the form, and drop it below the Committee combo box.

18. Select Courier from the font combo box in the tool bar, and select 10-point type from the font size combo box.

19. Retain the default value (Table/Query) for the Row Source Type property, and choose Names and Addresses (a query) for the Row Source property.

20. Adjust the width of the combo box to 1.25 inches.

21. Set the Column Count property to 3, enter **1;0;3** for the Column Widths property, and enter **4** for the List Width property. These settings ensure that the second column in the query dynaset, which contains the Name Type field, is not displayed in the drop-down list.

22. Set the Limit to List property to Yes.

23. Edit the Status Bar Text property so it reads **Enter an ID code or choose one from the list**.

24. Move and resize the controls and labels so that the form resembles Figure 12.13. If the Form Design window is maximized, click on the Restore button in the upper-right corner of the window.

25. Select Tab Order from the Edit menu and adjust the order of the controls as follows to match their physical positions on the form: Committee, ID Code, Officer, Joined, Quit, Public Exposure, Notes.

26. Switch to Form view and select Size to Fit Form from the Window menu to adjust the size of the window to match the new size of the form.

27. Experiment with the various controls by adding a new committee membership record: Choose Lobbying from the Committee combo box, Burton McDaniel from the ID Code combo box, and Secretary from the Officer Position list box. (You might want to try entering an ID code that is not in the list to observe the error message.) Type **1/18/93** in the Joined field text box. Note that the drop-down list of committee names is displayed in the order they were entered into the Committee Names table, while the members' names are displayed sorted by ID Code, as specified by the sorting instructions in the Names and Addresses query.

28. Close the form and save it.

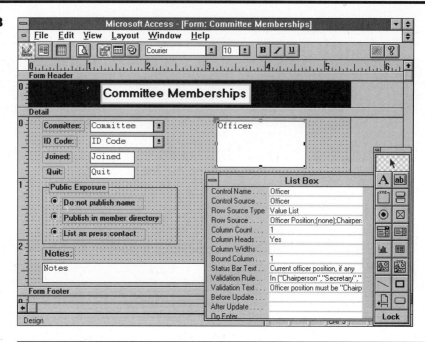

Figure 12.13
The modified
Committee
Memberships form

Using Subforms

As is the case with reports, one of the main reasons for creating forms from scratch or modifying those generated by the FormWizards is to define forms that include subforms. Although you can build one such layout with the main/subform FormWizard, you may also want to build forms with more than one subform or display the subforms in Form view rather than Datasheet view. The basic strategy for designing a form that includes subforms is the same as for the comparable reports: Begin by designing the main form and the subforms, using any combination of methods you wish, and then add the subforms to the main form. Often, you can save time by using the FormWizards to design the main form (including one subform) and/or one or more of the subforms.

You use the same basic methods outlined in Chapter 11 to link the main form with each subform; in fact, the property sheet for a subform and a subreport are identical. Figure 12.14 illustrates the ACE Names and Committee Memberships form designed in Chapter 8 in Form Design view with the Committee Memberships subform selected and the property sheet visible on the work surface. There is one minor difference in the way you are permitted to use subforms and subreports—you cannot embed a subreport in a form, although you can add either a subform or a subreport to a report. Access therefore does not include the "Form" prefix in the name of the form displayed in the Source Object property for the subform, and the drop-down list associated with this combo box includes only form names. (You may recall that in a subreport, the prefixes "Form" and "Report" distinguish between subforms and subreports.)

Figure 12.14
Defining the subform properties

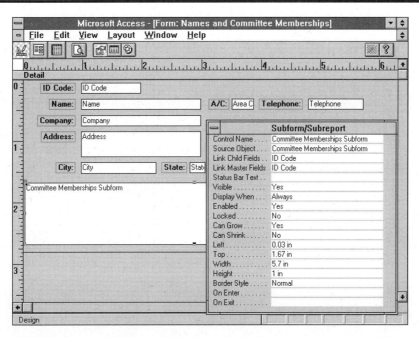

As in a report, you describe the link between the main form and subform by entering the names of one or more linking fields in the Link Child Fields and Link Master Fields properties. The same rules apply: The linking fields need not have the same names, but they must be of the same data types (except that you can pair a Counter field with an Integer field) and there must be the same number of fields in both lists. If you enter multiple field names, you must separate them with semicolons. To define a link based on an expression, you must create a query with a calculated column defined by the desired expression for one or both of the tables and base the link on this calculated column.

If you stored a default relationship between the two source tables or queries in the database, Access links the forms by the same fields that define this relationship. If there is no default relationship stored in the database, Access looks for fields in the data source for the subform that match the primary key of the table displayed in the main form. If there are no matching fields, or if the main form is based on a query rather than on a table (and therefore has no primary key), Access cannot determine how to link the forms, and you must enter the linking fields in the Link Child Fields and Link Master Fields properties yourself.

If you use the main/subform FormWizard to define a form in which Access cannot deduce the links, it displays the alert box pictured in Figure 12.15 to remind you that you must open the form in Form Design view and define the linkage yourself. When you create the subform object yourself in Form view, Access does not display a comparable warning. You should always examine the property sheet to verify the linkage (and enter or edit the linking fields if necessary), because correctly linking the main and subform is essential to ensure that Access only displays records in the subform that match the record in the main form when you use the form to enter data.

Figure 12.15

The reminder displayed when the FormWizard cannot link the main and subforms

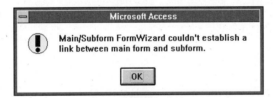

Once you have defined the main and subforms, placing the subform on the main form is very easy. You can use the mouse to drag the subform from the Database window onto the main form, as follows:

1. Make sure that the main form is open and the Form Design window is not maximized, so that you have easy access to the Database window.

2. Select the Database window and make sure that it displays the list of forms.

3. Position the mouse over the name of the subform, press and hold the left mouse button, drag the subform onto the main form, and release the mouse button.

4. Select the Form Design window, maximize it if you wish, and move and resize the subform object as necessary.

If you prefer to work entirely from within the Form Design window, you can use the same method that you use to add other types of objects to a report:

1. Make sure that the toolbox is visible on the screen.

2. Click on the Subform button in the toolbox.

3. Position the crosshair symbol in the mouse pointer where you want the upper-left corner of the subform.

4. Define the size of the subform using one of the following methods:

   ■ To create a subform of the standard size, click the left mouse button.

   ■ To place the subform on the main form and resize it, press and hold the left mouse button, drag the mouse pointer to the location of the lower-right corner of the subform, and release the mouse button.

Whichever method you use, Access creates a subform object with an associated label, which is located above the subform object frame. If you used the drag-and-drop method to create the subform object, Access assigns it a name that matches the subform itself, and uses the same name as the caption for the associated label. If you used the toolbox method, Access creates an unbound subform with an arbitrary name such as Embedded29, and you must identify the subform by entering its name in the form property sheet, either by typing it or by choosing it from the drop-down list associated with the Source Object combo box. Once you have identified the source object, Access fills in the linking fields if possible, based on the criteria outlined earlier in this section.

It is a good idea to keep the property sheet visible when you carry out the steps necessary to embed a subform, so you can confirm the linking fields or enter them yourself if Access could not deduce them. As you know, you can open the subform in Form Design view by double-clicking on the subform object in the main form. You may want to leave both the main form and subform open at the same time and edit them concurrently, but remember that you must save the subform and reload it into the main form before you can see the effects of your changes in Form view. (To reload the subform, select the subform object, click again to display an insertion point, and press Enter.)

As noted in Chapter 10, you can choose the default view for any form and specify which views are allowable (through the Default View and Allowable Views properties). You can display a subform in Form view or in Datasheet view, but not in Continuous Forms view (in this view, which resembles Form view, Access displays as many records as will fit on the screen). If the default view for the subform is Continuous Forms, Access displays an alert box to inform you that "The form will be opened in Single Form view." However, it leaves the Default View property in the subform set to Continuous Forms, so this view remains the default when you use the form independently.

In the layouts created by the main/subform FormWizard, the subform is displayed in Datasheet view. Figure 12.16 illustrates a form with two sub-forms—one that displays contact records in Form view to the right of the name and address fields in the main form, and one that displays transactions in Datasheet view below. As you can deduce from this example, you can place a subform anywhere on the main form. If each record in the main form might have more than a few matches in the table or query that serves as the data source for the subform, placing the subforms on the second "page" of the form and displaying them in Datasheet view would be a more realistic layout.

Figure 12.16

A form with two subforms

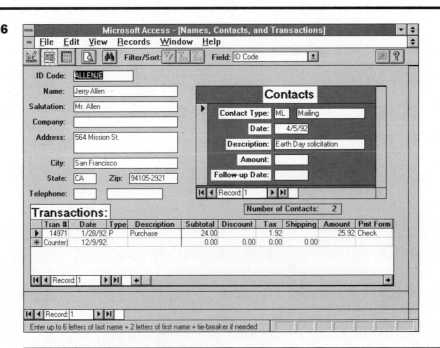

The form in Figure 12.16 uses the same basic technique described in Chapter 11 to display statistics computed in a subform (in this case, the num-ber of contact records) in the main form. Summary statistics like this are par-ticularly useful when you display the subform in Form view, because it is more tedious to page through all the records than in Datasheet view. The count is computed in the form footer section of the subform, in a text box named Contact Count, and the Visible property is set to No for this section to suppress it. The expression that displays the count in the main form is

```
[Contacts].Form![Contact Count]
```

In this particular form, you could just as easily have displayed the form footer section in the subform, but in other cases you might want to place the statistics further from the data. For example, in a two-page form, you might display the contact records on the second page but place the statistics in a more prominent position on the first page of the form.

All of the multitable forms presented thus far assume that you are working from the "point of view" of the parent table, and that when you use the form, you would want to use the parent record as a gateway into the various related child records. This approach is often very intuitive, because it parallels the way many manual systems work—in the paper system formerly in use at the Association for a Clean Earth, a staff member might pull a donor's ledger card from the filing cabinet to look up a transaction or view the contact history. During an intensive data entry session, you might prefer to work from the point of view of the child table and display selected fields from the parent table for reference. Figure 12.17 illustrates a form for entering transactions in which the name and address of the matching Names table record are displayed on the right side of the screen in a subform. This form style is referred to in the Access documentation as a "many-to-one form," because the table displayed in the main form is the child and the table displayed in the subform is the parent in a one-to-many relationship, and you are working from the point of view of the table with "many" records rather than that of the table with "one."

Figure 12.17

A form that focuses on the child table

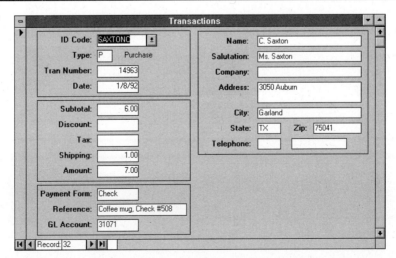

You could build a form that looks identical to this one without using a subform by using as the data source a query based on the Names and Transactions tables. However, using a subform makes it very easy to disable all the Names table fields, simply by setting the Enabled property for the subform to No (you would otherwise have to set the Locked property to Yes for each control in the subform). As you will see in Chapter 18, you can also easily enable or disable a subform by using a macro. Note also that the form properties in the subform were set to suppress the scroll bars, navigation controls, and current record indicator, which are unnecessary because there is only one matching record in the Names table for each record in the Transactions table. When you enter a new transaction record, Access blanks out the subform object until you enter the ID code in the new transaction, at which point it immediately searches for the matching record in the Names table and fills in the fields in the subform.

The Transactions form uses a calculated control—a text box based on the DLookUp function—to display the Description field from the Transaction Types table next to the Transaction Type field. The complete expression, which you will find in the Control Source property for the text box, searches the Transaction Types table for a value in the Transaction Type field that matches the value of the field of the same name in the current form, as follows:

```
DLookUp("[Description]","Transaction Types",
"[Transaction Type]=Form![Transaction Type]")
```

The form relies on the built-in validation based on the default relationship between the Transactions and Transaction Types tables to validate the Transaction Type field, which is carried out when you save the transaction. If you wanted more immediate validation (the instant you leave the Transaction Type text box), you could use the method based on the DLookUp function described earlier in this chapter, in the section entitled "Validating Data."

Note also that the ID Code field is collected using a combo box. Figure 12.18 illustrates the screen with the drop-down list visible. As you can see from this example, combo boxes are not limited to displaying simple one- or two-column lists based on small reference tables—you can base the list on any table (in this case, the central table in the application), and you can easily display quite a bit of information to help you choose the right value from the list.

To add the committee membership data to the Names, Contacts, and Transactions form pictured in Figure 12.16, use the following steps:

1. Open the Committee Memberships form in Design view.

2. Delete the ID Code combo box, move the remaining fields up to fill in the gap, and shrink the form to $2\frac{1}{2}$ inches in height.

3. Save the form under the new name **Committee Memberships 2**.

Figure 12.18

Choosing the ID
Code from a
combo box

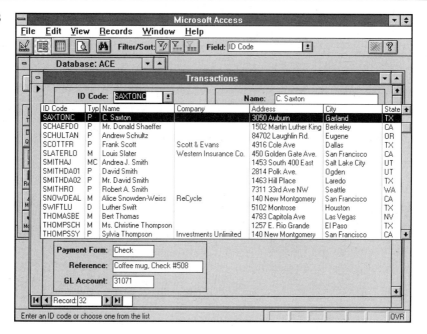

4. Open the Names, Contacts, and Transactions form in Design view, and maximize the Form Design window. Make sure that the toolbox and property sheet are visible on the work surface.

5. Increase the height of the form to 7¼ inches.

6. Click on the Page Break button in the toolbox, and place the page break on the form directly below the transactions subform object.

7. Select the ID Code and Name text boxes, and press Ctrl+C or select Copy from the Edit menu to copy these controls to the Clipboard. Press Ctrl+V or select Paste from the Edit menu to copy the contents of the Clipboard back to the form. Move the two new objects below the page break, and move the Name text box to the right of the ID Code text box.

8. Click on the Subform button in the toolbox, and add a new subform object to the form below the ID Code and Name fields.

9. In the property sheet for the subform, enter **Committee Memberships 2** for the Control Source property. If Access does not automatically fill in the Link Child Fields and Link Master Fields properties, enter **ID Code** for both linking fields.

10. Delete the label above the committee memberships subform.

11. Resize the subform to accommodate the embedded form. You may have to switch back and forth between Form view and Form Design view several times before you arrive at the right size for the subform. When you are satisfied with the size, move the subform so it is approximately centered in the window.

12. Switch to Form view, move to the second record in the Names table (Marilyn Allen's record), and press PgDn to view the second page of the form. Your screen should look something like Figure 12.19.

13. Use the Save As command on the File menu to save the form under the name **Complete Name Information**, and close the form.

Figure 12.19

The second page of the Complete Name Information form

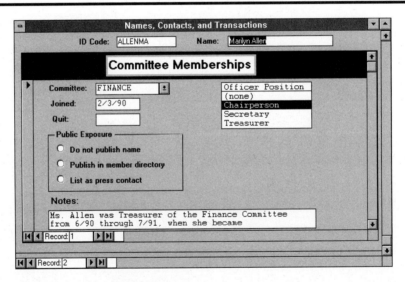

Emulating Paper Forms

Even when an application is fully computerized, you will often enter and update records working from paper input forms. For example, in an order entry database, you might enter orders based on order forms mailed in by customers, and in a personnel database, you might work from forms filled out by new employees. In these situations, matching the order of the controls on the data entry screen as closely as possible to the layout of the paper forms can greatly speed up data entry. At times, you will want to take this principle one step further and design a form that is nearly identical to an existing paper form so that you can use the form to print records as well as enter and update data (if you *only* need to print in this format, you could substitute a report for a form).

Figure 12.20 illustrates a very simple form of this type—a data entry form for prospect records designed to resemble a paper input form or file card. Figure 12.21 shows the form in Form view with a typical record displayed. As you can see in this figure, most of the fields are collected using text boxes, in a format that resembles the Boxed look in forms created by the FormWizards. The attached label objects are placed above the text boxes and aligned with the left edges of the text boxes. The Border Style property is set to Clear for all the controls, and each control is enclosed in a slightly larger rectangle. The size of the form was adjusted so that three whole records will fit on a page when printed, and the Keep Together property was set to Yes to prevent Access from beginning a new detail record if it will not all fit on the current page. To ensure that only True Type or Adobe Type Manager fonts can be selected, the Layout for Print property for the form was set to Yes. The data source for this form is the Prospects query, which selects only prospects, so the Name Type field is not required on the form—the Name Type control has the Default Value property set to "P" and the Visible property set to No, so that the control is invisible when you use the form, but the appropriate value is entered into the Name Type field when you use the form to add new prospect records.

Figure 12.20

A form designed to emulate a paper input form

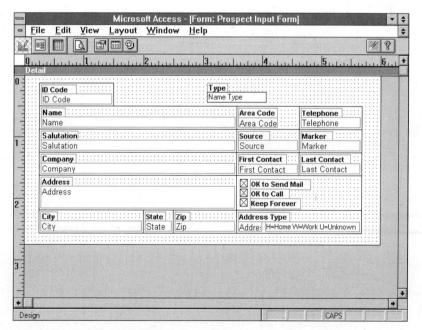

Figure 12.21

Using the Prospect
Input Form

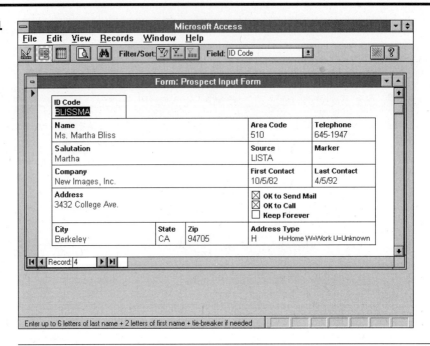

The key to quickly and efficiently building complex forms of this type is to customize the default properties for all the types of controls you plan to use before you begin adding controls to the form. If you retain the default properties, you will spend a great deal of time modifying the visual attributes of the objects individually. The following modifications were made to the default properties to produce the form style used in the Prospect Input Form in Figure 12.20:

- For text boxes, Border Style was set to Clear, Font Name was set to Arial, Font Size was set to 10, Add Colon was set to No, Label X was set to 0, and Label Y was set to −0.15 in.

- For labels, the Font Name was set to Arial and Font Weight was set to Bold.

- For rectangles, the Back Style was set to Clear.

With these defaults in effect, very few individual properties required customization, although the sizes of most of the text boxes had to be adjusted to create a symmetrical form. The alignment of the two date fields was changed from General to Left, so that they lined up with the Text fields above and below. Most of the text boxes were placed on the form with the grid set to 16 dots per inch both vertically and horizontally. To facilitate drawing rectangles just slightly larger than the text boxes they enclose, the grid spacing was set to 32 dots per inch in both dimensions. At this spacing, the grid is invisible, but the Snap to Grid setting still ensures that objects align with the grid.

Using this basic technique, you can construct far more complex forms than the simple example in Figure 12.20, including personnel forms, order or invoice forms, or even tax returns. Unfortunately, there is no straightforward method for printing *blank* forms. Because the Names table has a primary key, you cannot enter a completely blank record (or one in which all the fields in the form are blank). Instead, you must copy the structure of the Names table (using methods described in Chapter 13) to create a new table, remove the primary key, and enter one or more blank records. You can then temporarily change the Record Source property for the form to the name of the new table whenever you need to print blank forms, or you can use the Save as Report option to create a report based on the form, and use the new table as the permanent data source for the report. To print multiple copies of a blank form using a data source that has just one record, set the Copies entry in the Print dialog box to the desired number of copies.

Summary

This chapter introduced the basic techniques that you can use to create a form from scratch, starting with a blank form, and described how to make fundamental changes in the structure and layout of forms originally created using the Access FormWizards. These methods were illustrated with a variety of prototypical forms that you *cannot* produce using only the Wizards.

Most of the design considerations presented in Chapter 11 for reports also apply to forms, but forms present additional problems and complications. Because you will use a form to enter and update records as well as to view data, you must also take into account the factors that will make the form easier to use and that will at least encourage you (and often, force you) to enter complete and accurate data. Some very simple aspects of the layout—such as the arrangement of the fields, the tab order, your use of lines, boxes, fonts, and color combinations—can have a major impact on how easy it is to move around the form while you enter and edit data.

In addition, give some thought to which controls to use for the various fields in your tables. Mouse users will prefer check boxes to text boxes for collecting Yes/No fields, and by using option groups, list boxes, and combo boxes, you can make lists of allowable values in a field instantly available on the screen, rather than forcing anyone who uses your database to memorize code lists or keep printed copies at hand. For fields that you cannot (or do not want to) collect with lists, think about defining validation rules and customizing the error messages displayed when the data you enter does not conform to these rules.

If you are enthusiastic about the GUI interface, try to restrain yourself from using too many different graphic devices—colors, fonts, styles, lines, and boxes—in the same form. While the availability of all these tools enables you to create virtually any form you need, using too many of them in the same form usually results in visual chaos and confusion rather than ease of use. Only experience will tell you where to draw the line, given the requirements of your application and the preferences of the people (you and your co-workers) who will be using the forms, but spending some time considering these issues at the start will help you reach your goals of designing clear, attractive data entry forms that are both easy to learn and easy to use.

13

Reorganizing Databases

T HUS FAR, ALL OF YOUR EXPERIENCE WITH ACCESS HAS INVOLVED WORK-
ing with one or more tables that remain relatively static in structure,
although they may vary considerably in content. However, at various
stages in the lifetime of a typical database application, you will find
that you have to restructure tables or carry out mass data transfers between
tables. In many cases, the need arises almost immediately, especially if the
data that your Access application maintains was originally entered using another program, perhaps one running on a different type of computer. The mechanics of importing data from external sources is covered in Chapter 14, but
suffice it to say that after you import the data, some structural rearrangements are inevitably necessary.

Chapters 1 and 3 emphasized the importance of analyzing your requirements and planning the table structures on paper before you begin setting up
an Access database. In general, the more time you devote to advance planning, the less time you will spend later modifying the database, but no matter
how scrupulously you heeded the advice to plan ahead, the initial data entry
and testing phase will invariably reveal at least a few problems with the table
structures. You may have omitted essential fields (or perhaps a table) or included fields that in practice are rarely filled in, and some fields may be too
short or too long for typical entries. You might decide after you have spent a
few hours working in Datasheet view or designing forms and reports that
some field names are too long, too short, or not descriptive enough, or that a
different field order would be more convenient. Occasionally, you may need
to change the data type of a field, either because you chose the wrong data
type in the first place or because entering live data revealed problems with
your original choice. For example, you may have to enter letters or punctuation marks in a field that you assumed at first could contain only numbers
(such as a zip code field in a mailing list that originally contained only United
States addresses but must now accommodate Canadian postal codes), or you
might realize that you need to enter more than 255 characters into a field that
you assigned the Text data type.

As an application continues to grow and evolve, it is likely that you will
discover the need for additional modifications to handle requirements that
you could not possibly have foreseen. In addition to the types of changes just
enumerated, you will often want to add indexes (either single- or multifield)
to speed up queries and searches, or remove indexes that you no longer need.
You will also have to create new tables by copying records from existing tables, combine two tables into one, archive and delete obsolete data, and summarize and condense data to save disk space and speed processing.

This chapter describes the mechanics of all of these rearrangements,
and more importantly, outlines strategies for carrying out some typical table
rearrangements that are required in most database applications. You can
carry out most changes that are confined to single fields in one table simply
by editing the structure in Table Design view. To accomplish more complex

rearrangements that involve combining or splitting fields or tables, you must use a query. You might want to combine two or more fields into one (for example, to join an area code and telephone number into a single field) or split a field into two or more parts (for example, to break up an address line into separate city, state, and zip fields). Based on the ways you typically find yourself using the tables, you might decide to split a table to form two tables that have a one-to-one relationship. For example, as noted in Chapter 3, another way to handle the information currently stored in the ACE Names table is to place the name and address in one table and the supplementary data not required for prospects in another. Conversions such as splitting the ACE Names table into two or combining two tables that have a one-to-one relationship into a single table are relatively straightforward.

Correcting more serious flaws in the fundamental database design can be more complicated. For example, if you had originally included several sets of fields for committee membership data in the Names table, you would have had to split this table to form separate Names and Committees tables. Modifications such as splitting up a single table created to store information about multiple entities into two or more tables (usually with a one-to-many relationship) may require several steps, some involving modifications to the table structures and some carried out with queries. This chapter describes some typical strategies for accomplishing these types of complex restructuring operations.

WARNING.   *Before you try any of the examples on real data of your own, note that many of these procedures are not only potentially destructive but also irreversible. Even when you have considerable experience, it is prudent to back up the tables you are working on—or perhaps the entire database (the .MDB file)—before you carry out any update that deletes or changes data in multiple records.*

Modifying the Structure of a Table

You can modify the structure of a table simply by opening the structure in Table Design view and applying the same methods you used to create the table in the first place. Before you begin, note that while you can make virtually any changes without losing data that you have already entered, modifying the structure of a table can have a major impact on an existing database application. For example, if you add new fields to a table, they will be blank in all the existing records, and you must either fill in the data with an update query (using methods described in Chapter 9), edit the fields manually, or in most cases, use a mixture of both methods. When you combine or split fields, you can often use queries to convert the existing data to the new format, but some manual editing is nearly always necessary afterward. As you can imagine, these processes can be tedious in a large table, so it behooves you to try to catch as many problems as you can in the early testing stages. Of course, this is not always possible—the need for a new field may arise after you have been using an application for months or years. Also, if you import your initial data from an external source rather than entering it from the keyboard, some modifications to the structure and the data are inevitable.

After you modify the structure of a table, you will also have to modify any affected queries, forms, and reports. To name just a few of the potential problems, references to a field in any of these documents will generate errors if you delete or rename the field, or if you change the data type to one that is incompatible with the way the field is used (for example, if you change a numeric field involved in statistical calculations to a Text field). In forms and reports, references to missing fields are displayed or printed as "#Name?" and expressions that are no longer valid appear as "#Error." When you run a query (or use a form or report based on a query), these errors often manifest themselves in a more cryptic manner. Access interprets any expression enclosed in square brackets that does not represent a field name in one of the source tables as a parameter, and it will display a dialog box to prompt you for this "parameter" when you run the query. Note that adding or deleting fields from a table has less potential impact on a query in which you used the asterisk symbol in the output grid—this symbol *always* represents all the fields in a table, as of the moment you run the query. Of course, changing fields that contribute to the sorting instructions or selection criteria may affect any query, regardless of how you describe the output field list.

The take-home lesson is that you should not undertake major structural modifications lightly, because a few small changes can have far-reaching consequences in a large application. When changes are necesary, try to repair all the affected queries, forms, and reports before you turn over the modified database to your less knowledgeable colleagues.

As you may recall from Chapter 3, you can open an existing table in Table Design view by highlighting its name in the Database window and clicking on the Design command button or pressing Alt+D, or by double-right-clicking on the table name. If the table is already open in Datasheet view, you can move to Table Design view at any point by clicking on the Design button in the tool bar; choosing Table Design from the View menu; or switching to the Database window, where you can highlight the table name (if it is not still highlighted), and then use any of the methods just enumerated. The only restriction is that you cannot *modify* the structure of a table while viewing the data using a query, form, or report. You can, however, open the table in Table Design view to *examine* the structure. Figure 13.1 illustrates the alert box that Access displays if you try to open the Committees table in Table Design view while you are using the Committee Memberships form or the Names and Committee Memberships form to update the table.

Figure 13.1

The warning displayed when you try to modify the structure of an open table

You can safely carry out all of the following changes in Table Design view without risk of losing data that you have already entered:

- Adding fields

- Renaming fields

- Moving fields in the structure

- Adding indexes

- Deleting indexes

- Changing the primary key

- Making a field larger

- Changing any other field properties (besides the Field Size property)

The following modifications, which do have the potential to damage existing records, are also permitted, but should be used with caution in a table that contains large amounts of data:

- Deleting fields

- Making a field smaller

- Changing the data type of a field

You can save your changes using any of the standard Windows methods (for example, using the Save option on the File menu or closing the Table Design window). If you made any potentially destructive changes, Access displays an alert box to warn you that you may lose data and to give you one last chance to change your mind. For example, if you deleted any fields, it displays the alert box pictured in Figure 13.2, and if you shortened at least one Text field, it displays the alert box in Figure 13.3. If you choose OK to proceed with the changes, there is no way to undo them and recover the lost data later. Note that Access does *not* check each record individually to determine whether any data will in fact be lost before displaying warning messages like the one in Figure 13.3—this would take almost as long as modifying the structure. Instead, it warns you that you *may* lose data; if you know that all of your entries in a field will fit within the new maximum length or if you are willing to allow Access to truncate longer entries, you can safely proceed with the update.

Figure 13.2

The warning displayed when you delete fields

Figure 13.3

The warning displayed when you shorten fields

If you are the least bit unsure of yourself, *make a backup copy of the table* or use the Save As command on the File menu to save the modified structure under a new name. Some methods for backing up a single table are described later in this chapter, in the section entitled "Copying Database Objects." If your database is small, you may prefer to simply back up the .MDB file by copying it to a floppy disk, to another subdirectory on your hard disk, or to a new file name in the same subdirectory. (You can use the MS-DOS COPY, XCOPY, or BACKUP commands for this purpose, or you can use the File Manager.)

When you exit from Table Design view, Access rewrites the data in the format described by the new structure. Obviously, new fields will be blank in all the records, and the contents of fields that you shortened will be truncated. If the table is large, saving the new structure can take some time, and Access displays a percentage indicator in the left side of the status bar to inform you of its progress. Also note that some working space is required in the directory that you designated as the location for temporary files when you installed Windows. If Access runs out of space on the temporary file drive while it is saving the modified table structure, it displays an alert box with the error message "Not enough space on temporary disk." To determine which drive this is (or to change it), look for a command in the following form in your AUTOEXEC.BAT file:

```
SET TEMP=D:\WINTEMP
```

This SET command assigns the full path name of the temporary file subdirectory to a DOS environment variable called TEMP.

Access does not allow you to modify the structure of a table in any way that might compromise the integrity of the database. If a field is involved in a default relationship, you cannot delete it or change the data type or field size in either table (the latter restriction is due to the fact that the linking fields in a pair of related tables must have the same data type and size). For example, if you try to delete the ID Code field from any of the ACE tables, Access immediately displays the alert box shown in Figure 13.4. If you genuinely need to make any of these structural changes, you can use the Relationship option on the Edit menu to reopen the Relationships dialog box and delete the relationship; you can then reinstate it after modifying the structure of either or both of the linked tables.

Access also issues a warning, in an alert box like the one in Figure 13.5, if you try to delete any field that is part of a multifield index. If you choose OK from this alert box, it deletes both the field and the index.

Figure 13.4

The warning displayed when you try to delete a field involved in a default relationship

Figure 13.5

The warning displayed when you try to delete a field involved in a multifield index

Changing Data Types

Access does not allow you to convert an OLE Object field to any other data type or change any other type of field to an OLE Object (this data type is covered in detail in Chapter 15). With this single exception, Access allows you to change the data type of a field and if possible, it preserves any data you have already entered.

One of the most common requirements is converting a Text field to a Memo field to accommodate longer entries, or changing a Memo field to a Text field if it turns out that you do not need to enter more than 255 characters (or do not want to allow your more long-winded colleagues to do so). As is always the case when you shorten a field, converting a Memo field to a Text field may result in loss of data, because Access truncates the text to the length that you enter for the Field Size property. If you change an index key field to a Memo field, Access displays the alert box pictured in Figure 13.6 to inform you that if you proceed with the change, it will delete the index (you cannot build an index based on a Memo field).

Figure 13.6

The warning displayed when you change an indexed Text field to a Memo field

If you change a Date/Time field to a Text field, Access converts the data in the field to a text string that looks exactly like the date or time format established through the Windows Control Panel Date/Time settings (*not*, as you might expect, to the display format you selected for the field using the Format property). If you change a Text field to a Date/Time field, Access converts any data that it can recognize as one of the legitimate Date/Time display formats—such as "4/5/93", "4-Apr-93", and "3:15 PM"—and erases any field values that could not possibly represent a date or time. Similarly, you can convert any of the numeric data types to a Text field that looks exactly like the number. When you convert a Text field to one of the numeric data types, Access can convert any field entries that look like legitimate numeric values of the appropriate magnitude.

You can convert a Yes/No field to a Text field or to any numeric data type. If you create a Text field, Access stores the text strings "Yes" and "No" in the field, regardless of the selected display format for the original Yes/No field. If you create any numeric data type except Byte, Access converts Yes to –1 and

No to 0—the way these values are stored internally in the database. Because Byte fields cannot store negative values, Access uses 255 rather than –1 for Yes if you convert a Yes/No field to the Byte data type.

Most conversions between the various numeric data types are possible, provided that the field you are converting contains a legitimate value of the target data type. You can safely change any numeric field to one with a larger field size. Access also allows you to convert a numeric field to a shorter field size, but it will blank out any values that are too large for the new field size. For example, if you change an Integer field to a Byte field, Access blanks out any values greater than 255. If this action seems drastic to you, note that shortening a text string usually leaves some useful information, whereas truncating a number renders the value meaningless; rather than leaving misleading data in a field, Access erases it. There is one restriction on numeric data type conversions: If you try to assign the Counter data type to any existing field in a table that contains data, Access displays an alert box to inform you that you "Can't change data type to Counter in a table with data" when you try to leave the field. However, you *can* convert a Counter field to a numeric field, because internally, Counter fields are stored exactly like Long Integer fields. Note also that if you add a new Counter field to a table that contains data, Access numbers the records sequentially *in the order the records were entered into the table*, not in primary key order.

NOTE.   *Most of the limitations cited in this section can be overcome by using an append query to transfer the desired data into a new table, rather than simply modifying the structure of the original. Specific methods are described later in this chapter, in the section called "Table Reorganization Strategies."*

Splitting and Combining Fields

If you need to combine or split fields, you can add the required new fields to the structure and then use an update query to convert some or all of the data afterward. For example, in a name and address list like the ACE Names table, you might decide to combine separate area code and telephone number fields into a single field in a form such as (510) 848-1286 or 510/848-1286 (and perhaps lengthen this field to accommodate an extension or voice mail address as well) or split a telephone number entered into a single field into separate area code and phone number fields. If you had originally used two fields for a name (one for the first name and one for the last name), you might later want to switch to a scheme like the one used in the ACE Names table by combining the first and last names into a single full name field and constructing an ID Code based on these fields.

The safest way to approach all of these conversions is to add new fields to the structure, update these fields using any available methods, and retain the original fields until you are absolutely sure that the conversion was successful. The advantage of this method is that if it takes you several tries to achieve the desired results, you do not run the risk of damaging data you have already entered. If you want any of the new fields to have the same name as one of the original fields, you will also have to rename fields. The overall sequence of steps is as follows:

1. Modify the table structure to add the new fields and rename the original fields if necessary.

2. Use an update query to fill in the new fields, using expressions based on the original fields.

3. Modify the table structure to delete the original fields.

Figure 13.7 illustrates an update query (based on a table similar to the ACE Names table) that combines fields called Area Code and Phone into a single field named Telephone, using the following expression:

```
IIf([Area Code] Is Null,[Phone],"("&[Area Code]&") "
&[Phone])
```

The test for null area codes is required to avoid including the pair of parentheses in the new telephone number if the area code is missing.

Figure 13.7

An update query that combines two fields

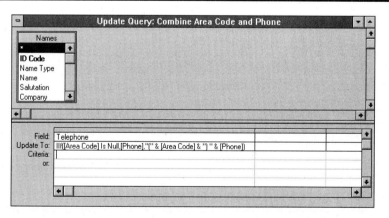

To carry out the opposite conversion—splitting a single telephone number field into separate area code and telephone number fields—you can use the Mid function to extract the two components of the telephone number. (Recall from Chapter 9 that this function evaluates to a portion of the text string supplied as the first input; the second input specifies the starting position of the extract, and the third defines its length.) If you knew that every telephone number included an area code enclosed in parentheses, with a space separating the area code and phone number, you could use the expressions Mid([Phone],2,3) and Mid([Phone],7,8) to define the values of the new Area Code and Telephone fields. If some of the area codes might be missing, you could use the Len function to test the length of the Phone field, which is 14 if the area code is present or 8 if not, as in the following expressions, which define the area code and telephone number, respectively:

```
IIf(Len([Phone])=14, Mid([Phone],2,3), "")
```

and

```
IIf(Len([Phone])=14, Mid([Phone],7,8), [Phone])
```

If there is no area code, the first expression, which defines the Area Code field, evaluates to a null string and the second, which defines the Telephone field, evaluates to the entire contents of the Phone field.

You can use a similar method to construct a full name field from separate first name and last name fields, as follows:

```
[First Name]&" "&[Last Name]
```

To construct an ID Code made up of the first six characters of the last name and the first two letters of the first name, you could use the Left function (which is similar to the Mid function except that the extracted string always begins at the left side of the original) and the Ucase function, which converts a text string to all uppercase. The complete expression is as follows:

```
Ucase(Left([Last Name], 6)&Left([First Name], 2))
```

When you use the Left and Mid functions, Access does not display an error message if the source field is too short to supply the requested number of characters. Thus, if the last name is fewer than six characters long, the expression Left([Last Name], 6) evaluates to the full last name.

Splitting a field is much more difficult if you cannot predict the length of the various components or ensure that a given component occurs in a specific position. For example, to split a single field used to store the city, state, and zip code, which was entered in the standard format with a comma following the city and two spaces between the state and zip code, you would have to search for the comma to decide where the city ends. Unlike some other databases, Access does not provide a handy function for doing this, although you could accomplish the conversion with a program written in Access Basic.

Copying Database Objects

You may at times want to make a complete copy of a table without backing up the entire database. For example, you might want to copy a table before you execute an update query, so that you can recover the table if the query fails to perform as expected. The easiest way to copy *any* database object (including queries, forms, reports, macros, and modules as well as tables) is to use the standard Windows cut and paste commands to copy the object to the Clipboard. You can then paste the object back into the same database under a new name or into another Access database. For all objects except tables, the steps are as follows:

1. Highlight the object name in the Database window, and press Ctrl+C or choose the Copy command on the Edit menu to copy the object to the Clipboard.

2. If you want to copy an object to another database, close the current database and open the target database.

3. Press Ctrl+V or choose the Paste command from the Edit menu to paste the copy back into the database.

4. Access displays the standard Save As dialog box with "Paste As" in the title bar. Enter the name you want to assign the new object.

You use essentially the same procedure to copy a table, but Access displays a slightly different dialog box, which is shown in Figure 13.8, when you issue the paste command. In addition to entering the name of the new table, you must select one of the three Paste Options radio buttons to specify the disposition of the copy. If you choose Structure and Data (the default), Access makes an exact copy of the table under the new name entered at the top of the Paste Table As dialog box. If you choose Structure Only, Access creates an empty table with the same structure as the source table. This option gives you a very fast way to replicate the structure of an existing table after you have entered data. (You can also copy the structure of an empty table by opening it in Table Design view and using the Save As option on the File menu.) For example, you might want to copy the structure of a mailing list table to begin a new list that you will be using independently of the original or in a different Access database. In both cases, Access replicates all of the properties of the original table, including the field properties, the primary key, and any multifield indexes defined in the table property sheet. Thus, it is often easier to copy an existing table than to start from scratch if you need to create a new table that is similar but not identical, especially if the table has more than a few fields and you have customized many of the field properties.

Figure 13.8

The Paste Table As dialog box

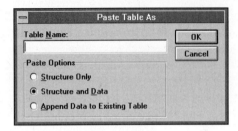

If you choose the Append Data to Existing Table option, Access *adds* the records on the Clipboard to the designated table. The target table must include all the fields in the source table, and if this is not the case, Access displays an alert box similar to the one shown in Figure 13.9, which resulted from trying to append the Names table to the Transactions table. Selecting OK in this alert box cancels the append operation without adding any records to the designated target table. Note that this table can also have additional fields not present in the source table—Access simply leaves these fields empty in the newly appended records. If you need to add records to a table with a dissimilar structure, you can use an append query, as described later in this chapter.

Figure 13.9

The error message displayed when you try to append records to a table with an incompatible structure

Modifying the Transactions Table Structure

To practice modifying the structure of a table, use the Clipboard method to make a copy of the Transactions table and then modify the structure of the copy:

1. Make sure that the Database window displays the list of tables.

2. Highlight the name of the Transactions table, and select Copy from the Edit menu or press Ctrl+C to copy the table to the Clipboard.

3. Select Paste from the Edit menu or press Ctrl+V to paste the contents of the Clipboard back into the database. Type **New Transactions** in the Table Name text box in the Paste Table As dialog box, and close the dialog box, leaving the default Structure and Data button selected.

4. Open the New Transactions table in Table Design view.

5. Change the data type of the Transaction Number field to Text, and change the Field Size property to 5 (to match the existing transaction numbers).

6. Change the data type of the Date field to Text, and change the Field Size property to 8. Note that Access deletes the Default Value, because the expression that defines it (Date( )) no longer matches the data type of the field.

7. Change the data type of the Reference field to Memo.

8. Click on the row selector for the Posted field, and press Del to delete the field. Select OK from the alert box that warns you that you will lose the data in the field.

9. Click on the row selector for the Transaction Type field, and press Del to delete the field. Select OK from the alert box that warns you that you will lose the data in the field. Select Cancel from the alert box that warns you that the field is involved in a multifield index.

10. Save the modified structure and then open the table in Datasheet view. Note that the Transaction Number and Date fields are left-justified in their respective columns (because they are both now Text fields), and that the Posted field is missing.

11. Close the New Transactions table.

12. Open the Donations by Month report in Report Design view.

13. Display the property sheet if it is not already visible, and change the Record Source property to New Transactions.

14. Display the Sorting and Grouping dialog box, and note that the Group On property for the first group, which describes the grouping interval, is blank. Formerly, this property was set to Month, but this choice is no longer available because Date is now a Text field.

15. Preview the report and note that Access does group records by month, but prints an individual date in the Date group header section.

16. Close the report without saving your changes.

Creating New Tables

To create a new table derived from one or more existing tables, but not identical in contents or structure to the source table(s), you can use a *make table query*. As you already know, the dynaset of a select query looks in Datasheet view like a brand new table, although it is in fact composed of data drawn from existing tables. A make table query actually creates a new independent table *that contains exactly the same data displayed in the dynaset of the equivalent select query.* The easiest and safest way to build a new make table query is to start with a select query, verify that the query describes the data you want, and then convert it to a make table query.

You can use a make table query to extract a subset of the records in a table for a particular purpose. For example, if you need to produce several reports based on relatively few records drawn from a very large table, you may be able to save considerable time by copying the records to a new table and using this table as the data source for the reports. You might also want to copy a portion of a table to give to a colleague who has no use for the rest of the records. For example, ACE might give or sell its donor and member list to another organization that does not want the prospects.

The output grid in a make table query should include a column for each field you need in the target table in the order you want the fields to appear in the structure. If you use calculated fields to define some of the columns, make sure to assign meaningful names, because these names will become the field names in the new table. As in a select query, you can use the asterisk symbol at the top of the field list to symbolize all the fields in the source table in the output grid when you want to create a new table with the same structure as the original. The record selection criteria in the QBE grid determine which records are copied to the new table, and the sorting instructions determine the record sequence (if you do not include explicit sorting instructions, Access copies records in primary key order). In other words, the records and fields in the table created by a make table query match the rows and columns in the dynaset of the equivalent select query. Figure 13.10 illustrates a very simple make table query that copies the media contacts and political contacts in the Names table to a new table.

Figure 13.10

A make table query that copies selected records

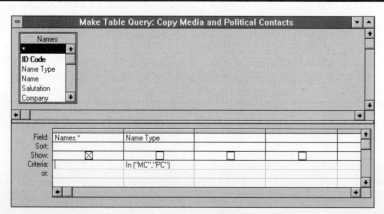

To create a make table query, select Make Table from the Query menu. Access displays a dialog box like the one in Figure 13.11, in which you enter the name and location of the new table. Although the Table Name data entry region is a combo box, with an attached drop-down list that includes all the tables in your database, you cannot use a make table query to *add* records to an existing table (instead, you must use an *append query* as described in the section "Appending Records" later in this chapter). If you choose the name of an existing table—as you might when you use the same make table query at intervals to extract the current group of records that satisfy a certain set of criteria—Access displays an alert box like the one shown in Figure 13.12 when you execute the query. If you select OK, it overwrites the existing table with the new one. You can save the new table either in the current database (the default) or in another Access database; if you choose the Another Database radio button, you must enter the full DOS path name of the .MDB file (not including the .MDB extension) in the File Name text box. For example, you could copy the media and political contacts to a database called MAILLIST in the DATA subdirectory, located under the ACCESS subdirectory on drive C, by entering the file name C:\ACCESS\DATA\MAILLIST.

Figure 13.11

Defining a make table query

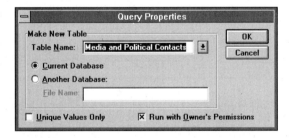

Figure 13.12

The warning displayed when a make table query will overwrite an existing table

To run a make table query, you can click on the Run Query button in the tool bar or select Run from the Query menu. Because a make table query has no dynaset per se, the Datasheet command button in the tool bar, which you can use to display the output of a select query, is disabled. Like all action

queries, make table queries are identified in the Database window by a query icon that includes an exclamation point. If the source table(s) are large, running the make table query may take some time, and Access displays a thermometer-style percentage indicator in the status bar to keep you informed of its progress. If you want to preview the output of an existing make table query before you run it, you can temporarily convert it back into a select query by choosing the Select option from the Query menu. When you turn it back into a make table query, Access retains your previous entries in the dialog box that specifies the name, location, and properties of the output table.

NOTE. *The table produced by a make table query does not inherit any of the properties of the source tables (the indexes, display formats, default values, and so on). If modifying the structure of the newly created table to assign these properties would be overly time-consuming, you can copy the structure of the table, modify this structure as necessary, and then use an append query to transfer the data into the new table. This method is described later in the section called "Table Reorganization Strategies."*

Creating a Query to Copy Members and Donors

To create a make table query that copies just the names and addresses of ACE's members and donors to a new table in zip code order, use the following steps:

1. Make sure that the Database window displays the list of queries, and choose New to define a new query.

2. Choose the Names table from the Add Table dialog box, and close this dialog box.

3. Add the Name Type, Name, Company, Address, City, State, Zip, Area Code, and Telephone fields to the output grid.

4. Type **In("M","D")** in the Criteria row of the Name Type column.

5. Type **Ascending** in the Sort row of the Zip column or select it from the combo box.

6. Execute the query, which at this point is a select query, and verify that the dynaset includes 26 records, which represent only members and donors (identified by the contents of the Name Type column), and that the records are arranged in ascending order by zip code.

7. Return to Query design view.

8. Uncheck the Show box in the Name Type column to exclude this column from the output.

9. Select Make Table from the Query menu, type **Members and Donors in Zip Order** in the Table Name text box, and close the Query Properties dialog box.

10. Save the query under the name **Copy Members and Donors**.

11. Execute the query. Access displays an alert box to inform you that "26 row(s) will be copied into a new table." Select OK to proceed with query execution.

12. Close the Query Design window.

13. Open the new table in Datasheet view and verify that it contains the same 26 records you saw in the dynaset of the select query you created to preview the results. Figure 13.13 shows the datasheet, with the column widths adjusted so that all the fields are visible.

14. Close the Members and Donors in Zip Order table.

Figure 13.13

The table created by the Copy Members and Donors make table query

Name	Company	Address	City	State	Zip	Area Code	Telephone
Edward Olson		6704 Whitman Ave	Fort Worth	TX	76133		
Luther Swift		5102 Montrose	Houston	TX	77006		
Benjamin Harris		517 N.W. 19th	San Antonio	TX	78207		
Ms. Christine Thom		1257 E. Rio Grande	El Paso	TX	79902		
Bert Thomas		4783 Capitola Ave	Las Vegas	NV	89108		
Mr. and Mrs. Earl W		1290 Tyler Way	Sparks	NV	89431		
Alexander Lee		1925 Walnut Ave.	Venice	CA	90291		
Frank and Ann Mat		8732 Prospect Ave	Santee	CA	92071		
Burton McDaniel		3106 Bancroft St.	San Diego	CA	92104	619	485-9481
Melvin H. Arnold		504 Parkview Dr.	Lake Elsinore	CA	92330		
Louis Slater	Western Insurance	450 Golden Gate A	San Francisco	CA	94102-3400	415	221-8284
Alice Snowden-We	ReCycle	140 New Montgom	San Francisco	CA	94105-3705	415	639-7099
Ms. Judy Harringtor		239 Nevada Street	San Francisco	CA	94110		
Ruth Bergen		472 Church St.	San Francisco	CA	94114		
Karen Franklin		3605 Sacramento	San Francisco	CA	94118		
Cheryl Elliot, M.D.		3918 Fruitvale Ave.	Oakland	CA	94602	510	637-1840
Joseph Walker and		482 40th St.	Oakland	CA	94609		
Michael Anderson	The Ellis Street Gar	2906 Ellis Street	Berkeley	CA	94702	510	549-7838
Ms. Lucy Reed		1675 University	Berkeley	CA	94702		
Mr. and Mrs. Josep		1006 Keeler Ave.	Berkeley	CA	94708		
John Howard, Jr.		1460 Calaveras Av	San Jose	CA	95126	408	391-6530
Elizabeth Brown		P.O. Box 6201	Santa Rosa	CA	95406		
Susan Lu		3222 NE 52nd Ave	Portland	OR	97213		
Ms. Sylvia Baker		9370 SW 51st St.	Portland	OR	97219		
Charles and Anne D		132 28th Ave	Seattle	WA	98122-6218		
Ralph and Helen R		600 N. Columbia	Olympia	WA	98501		

Splitting a Table

You can use make table queries to split a table permanently into two. For example, if you decided to split the Names table into two tables—one for the name and address, and one for the supplementary data not maintained for prospects—you would begin by using a make table query to copy the supplementary data to a new table. You could then modify the structure of the Names table to remove these fields.

As noted briefly earlier in this chapter, you can also use a make table query to create a new table that contains data derived from two or more tables. One reason you might want to do this is to export data for use by a program that cannot work with multiple tables, such as a flat-file manager, a spreadsheet, or a word processing program. For example, you might want to include the Name field with contact or transaction records exported for analysis in a spreadsheet, or create a table with the complete donor name and address as well as the transaction data that you could export to produce thank you letters using a word processor with mail-merge capabilities. In Access, you could simply use select queries to view this data, but as you will see in Chapter 14, you can only export a table, not a query dynaset. You may also be motivated by performance considerations—if you have to produce several reports or graphs based on two or more large tables, you may be able to expedite processing by extracting all the data into a single table and using this table rather than a query as the data source for the reports. Remember, however, that any updates to the original tables made after executing the query will not be reflected in the reports.

No special measures are required to define a multitable make table query. For example, you could convert the Committees with Names query defined in Chapter 8 to a make table query to create a new table that contains all the committee membership data stored in the Committees table, as well as the Name field from the Names table and the Description field (which contains the committee name) from the Committee Names table.

Recall that the product of a make table query does not inherit any of the properties of the source tables. Recreating these properties can be tedious in a table with a great many fields, so if you simply need to copy selected records from a table, you might consider using the cut and paste method described earlier in this section to copy the entire table and then using a delete query (described in the next section) to remove the unwanted records from the new table. Alternatively, you could copy just the structure, modify the structure if necessary, and then use an append query (described later in this chapter) to read in the desired records.

Deleting Records

You already know how to delete records one by one or in small groups, either in Datasheet view or using custom data entry forms. As an application grows and matures, you will also need to delete records en masse. For example, most applications require a procedure for purging obsolete records—invoices or orders older than a given date, or customers who have not placed an order since a certain date. As noted in the previous section, one way to split a table into two is to copy the entire table and then delete the redundant records from one or both of the tables. As you can imagine, carrying out these deletions one record at a time is far too tedious to be practical. Instead, you can use a *delete query*, which removes from the source table the records described by the selection criteria specified in the output grid. Like a make table query, a delete query has no datasheet—it updates a table without displaying any output.

NOTE. *Using an equivalent select query to preview the results of a delete query is even more important than it is for a make table query, because there is no way to recover records after you have deleted them.*

To create a delete query, choose Delete from the Query menu. The only entries you need to make in the output grid are selection criteria—the conditions that describe the records you want to delete. It makes no sense to include individual fields or calculated fields, apart from those that contribute to the selection criteria, because a delete query always deletes whole records, not the contents of individual fields (to blank out a particular field for all or selected records in a table, you must use an update query).

By default, the output grid contains three types of rows, labeled Field, Delete, and Criteria (you can also add the Tables row if you wish). Your entry in the Delete row determines how each column is used. In a multitable query, entering From in the Delete row identifies the table from which you want to delete records, and if you add the asterisk symbol to the output grid to represent all the fields in a table, Access automatically enters "From" in the Delete row. (Multitable delete queries are described in more detail later in this section.) In all other columns, which are used to define selection criteria, Access enters "Where" in the Delete row. (You might interpret this as meaning, "Delete records *where* the following condition is true.") If you used the strategy suggested earlier—starting with a select query and then converting it to a delete query—the output grid will contain extraneous fields (the fields you need to see in the datasheet to verify that the selection criteria describe the right records). These unnecessary columns will do no harm, but you can delete them once you are sure that the query performs as you intended.

Figure 13.14 illustrates a delete query that purges records from the Names table based on the Last Contact and Keep Forever fields. The expression in the Criteria row of the Last Contact column selects records in which the last contact date is earlier than a date obtained by using the DateAdd function to subtract two years from the current date. The second column ensures that only records in which the Keep Forever field is No are deleted. As in many select queries, the selection criteria in a delete query are often based on calculated columns. For example, Figure 13.15 illustrates a query that deletes transaction records entered during the current year. The first and only column in the output grid is a calculated column that evaluates to the year portion of the date stored in the Date field, and the expression in the Criteria row evaluates to the year portion of the current date. Thus, if the year in a transaction record matches the current year, the record is deleted.

Figure 13.14

A delete query that purges the Names table by date

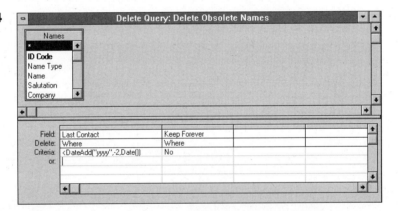

Figure 13.15

A query that deletes current year transactions

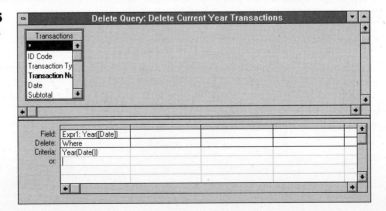

When you execute a delete query from the Database window, Access displays the alert box shown in Figure 13.16 to remind you that you are not running a harmless select query. Although delete queries, like all action queries, are identified in the Database window by an icon that includes an exclamation mark, running a delete query inadvertently can have such destructive consequences that Access issues a special warning. If you run the query from Query Design view, Access omits this warning, because it is highly unlikely that you chose the query by mistake. In either case, it reads through the table to determine how many records satisfy the selection criteria and displays a dialog box like the one in Figure 13.17 to give you one last chance to abort the operation. Think carefully before you respond, because once you have given permission to perform the deletion, there is no way to recover the deleted records.

Figure 13.16
The alert box displayed when you run a delete query from the Database window

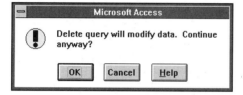

Figure 13.17
The alert box displayed to inform you how many records will be deleted

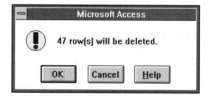

You cannot use a delete query to circumvent the referential integrity rules established by defining default relationships between tables. For example, the query in Figure 13.14 will not delete Names table records that have matches in the Transactions, Contacts, or Committees tables, because the ACE database includes default one-to-many relationships between the Names table and each of these tables, and the Enforce Referential Integrity option is enabled for all the relationships. If Access cannot delete all the selected records, it displays an alert box like the one in Figure 13.18 to inform you that key violations precluded processing some of the records (98 in this example). If you choose OK to proceed, Access will delete the records that it can without violating referential integrity constraints.

Figure 13.18

The alert box displayed to warn you that not all records could be processed

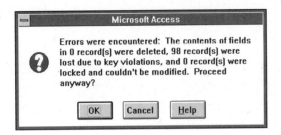

Deleting records in tandem from two or more tables is much less straight-forward. A delete query can only delete records from more than one table if the tables have a one-to-one relationship. When the tables have the more common one-to-many relationship, you must identify the table from which you want to delete records by adding the asterisk symbol from the relevant field list to the output grid and entering From in the Delete row in this column. However, the selection criteria may be based on either or both tables. For example, in the query in Figure 13.19, which deletes transactions entered earlier than January 1, 1993 for prospects, the selection criteria are based on both tables.

Unfortunately, you will often want to delete sets of matching records from two tables that have a one-to-many relationship, and you cannot do this with a single query. For example, in the ACE database, instead of being constrained by the referential integrity rules, you might want to delete the matching transactions and contacts together with the Names table records. The only way to accomplish this is to use three separate delete queries:

1. Use a delete query with selection criteria based on the Last Contact date in the Names table to delete records from the Transactions table.

2. Use a delete query with selection criteria based on the Last Contact date in the Names table to delete records from the Contacts table.

3. Use a delete query with selection criteria based on the Last Contact date in the Names table to delete records from the Names table.

To practice defining delete queries, create a query that deletes from the Committees table records that do not represent current committee memberships:

1. Make sure that the Database window displays the list of queries, and choose New to define a new query.

2. Choose the Committees table from the Add Table dialog box, and close this dialog box.

Figure 13.19
A delete query with selection criteria based on two tables

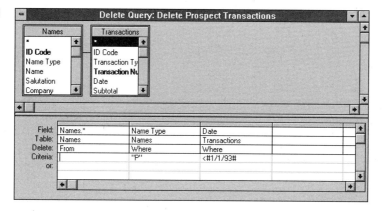

3. Add the Committee, ID Code, and Quit fields to the output grid.

4. Type **Is Not Null** in the Criteria row of the Quit column.

5. Execute the query, which at this point is a select query, and verify that the dynaset includes five records (the ones in which the Quit date is filled in).

6. Return to Query design view.

7. Select Delete from the Query menu. Note that Access automatically enters Where into the Delete row in all three columns in the output grid.

8. Save the query under the name **Delete Old Commmittee Memberships**.

9. Click on the Run command button in the tool bar, or choose Run from the Query menu. Access displays an alert box to inform you that "5 row(s) will be deleted." Select Cancel to abort the deletion.

10. Close the Query Design window.

Appending Records

You can use a type of action query called an *append query* to add records from one existing table into another. As noted earlier in this chapter, you *must* use an append query rather than the simple cut and paste method based on the Clipboard to combine tables with dissimilar structures. Append queries are also ideal for copying large groups of records that satisfy certain selection critiera from one table to another. In an append query, each column represents a field in the target table, and you can specify any expression based on one or more source tables to define the value of each target field. When you create an append query, remember to add the source table(s)—the tables that will supply the records—to the query, not the target table. (If you are more familiar with Xbase databases, which require you to work from the point of view of the target table and append data *from* the source, this approach may seem backward.) As with the other types of action queries, you may want to begin by defining a select query that describes the data you want to copy to the target table and scan through the dynaset to verify that it matches the structure of the target table.

To create an append query, choose Append from the Query menu. Access displays a dialog box that is identical to the one used to specify the table created by a make table query (which is shown in Figure 13.11), except that the prompt above the Table Name text box is "Append To" rather than "Make New Table." Like a make table query, an append query can copy data to a table in any Access database. You can only use an append query to *add* records to an existing table (which might, however, be empty), not to create a new table from scratch, so you must predefine the target table. Because this table may be in another database, Access does not verify your entry in the Table Name text box, but if it cannot find the designated table when you run the query, it displays an alert box like the one in Figure 13.20 to inform you of the problem.

Figure 13.20

The alert box displayed if Access cannot find the target table

In an append query, the row below the Sort row is labeled Append To, and you use this row to specify the field names from the target table that match the expressions in the Field row. Figure 13.21 illustrates an append query that copies the name and address data from member records in the Names table to a table called Mailing List, which has a similar structure. In this table, the CityState field contains both the city and state, and the Telephone field stores the complete telephone number in the format 510/548-0146. The order of the columns in the output grid—which has no effect on the results of running the query—was chosen so that all the fields of interest are visible. The first column, Name Type, is required only to specify the selection criteria, so the Append To row in this column is blank. The CityState field in the Mailing List table is defined by the expression [City]&", "&[State], and the Telephone field is defined by the expression [Area Code]&"/"&[Telephone]. The Zip Code field assumes the value of the Zip field in the Names table, and the Name, Company, and Address fields are simply copied to fields with the same names in the Mailing List table.

Figure 13.21

Using an append query to combine two tables with different structures

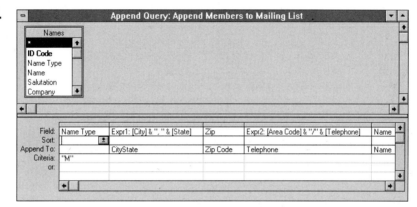

The cells in the Append To row are all combo boxes, and you can either type the field names or select them from the drop-down list. If you enter a field name from a source table in the Field row (rather than an expression), Access fills in the Append To row for you if the target table has a field with the same name. If you begin with a select query, Access enters all the field names at once when you choose the Append option from the Query menu; when you create an append query from the start, it fills them in one by one, as you enter expressions in the Field row. If you wish, you can override the default entries in the Append To row, but if you type a field name that does not exist in the target table, Access displays an alert box like the one in Figure 13.22 when you execute the query. (The seemingly cryptic wording of the error message results from the fact that Access uses the SQL Insert Into command to execute append queries.)

Figure 13.22

The alert box displayed if Access cannot find the target field name

When you execute an append query from the Database window, Access displays an alert box like the one in Figure 13.23 to remind you that the query will modify data. If you run the query from Query Design view, Access omits the special warning, as it does with delete queries. In either case, it reads through the table to determine how many records satisfy the selection criteria and displays a dialog box like the one in Figure 13.24 to inform you how many records will be appended to the target table and give you one last chance to abort the operation.

Figure 13.23

The alert box displayed when you run an append query from the Database window

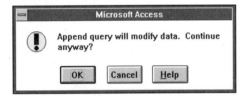

Figure 13.24

The alert box displayed to inform you how many records will be appended

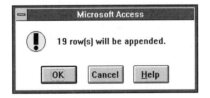

You cannot use an append query to circumvent any of the essential validation rules established for a table. For example, you cannot append a record in which any field contains data that is inappropriate based on the data type, a record that would result in duplicate values in any index for which the No Duplicates property was specified (including the primary key), or a record that violates any referential integrity rules defined through a default table relationship. For example, you could not append a record to the Transactions table in which the ID code does not match a record in the Names table. You can, however, add records that do not satisfy the field validation rules entered in the table structure. If Access finds any errors, it displays a dialog box identical to the one shown earlier in Figure 13.18. The first part of this error message informs you of data lost due to data type conflicts—for example, trying to replace a Date/Time or numeric field with a Text string that does not match one of the acceptable display formats for these data types. The last part of the message informs you that another user in a multiuser installation is editing (or has otherwise locked) one of the records you are trying to append. (Other problems that may arise when you run Access on a network are described in Chapter 17.)

NOTE. *If you choose to proceed anyway, Access appends as many records as possible, but you should choose this option with caution—there is no easy way to figure out afterward which records were bypassed. Instead, it is usually preferable to cancel the query, find and correct the problems, and try again.*

Table Reorganization Strategies

Most of the reorganizations required throughout the lifetime of an Access database application can be accomplished by using the techniques described in this chapter, alone or in combination. To merge two tables, you can use an append query. One way to split a table into two or more identically structured tables is to use make table queries to copy the various sets of records to new tables and then delete the original. However, if you need to split a table into just two tables, you can use a make table query to create one of the new tables, and then use a delete query to remove the same group of records from the original table.

More complex reorganizations usually require several steps, some carried out with action queries and some by modifying the structures of one or more of the tables. For example, suppose you decided to use two tables to store the information currently stored in the Names table—one for the name and address fields required for all name types and another for the supplementary data not required for prospects. To carry out this reorganization, you could proceed as follows:

1. Define a make table query to create the supplementary table by copying the ID Code field and the supplementary fields for all name types except prospects to a new table.

2. Modify the structure of the Names table to remove all the fields (except the ID Code) copied to the supplementary table.

3. Define a default one-to-one relationship between the two tables based on the ID Code field. To ensure that you could not add a record to the supplementary table without first entering a matching record in the name and address table, you would check the Enforce Referential Integrity option for this relationship.

To carry out the opposite conversion—adding information stored in a supplementary table to the Names table—you could use the following steps:

1. Modify the structure of the Names table to add all the fields (except the ID Code) in the supplementary table.

2. Define an update query that replaces each of the new fields with its counterpart in the supplementary table.

3. Delete the supplementary table.

You can use similar techniques to correct more serious structural problems, such as using one table to store data that really demands two tables with a one-to-many relationship. For example, you may recall from the discussion of database design in Chapter 3 that because ACE needs to store up to three keywords for each person in the Names table, using a separate table for the keywords would conform more closely to relational database theory than including three keyword fields in the Names table. In the ACE system, no real benefits would accrue from extracting the keywords into a separate table, but if you had made the same error with the contacts or committee membership data, you would eventually have to correct the design. If you did decide to split out the keywords into a new table, you could use the following sequence of steps:

1. Create the new table, which has two fields: ID Code and Keyword.

2. Use an append query to add a record to the new table for each record in the Names table in which the Keyword 1 field is not null.

3. Use an append query to add a record to the new table for each record in the Names table in which the Keyword 2 field is not null.

4. Use an append query to add a record to the new table for each record in the Names table in which the Keyword 3 field is not null.

5. Modify the structure of the Names table to remove the three keyword fields.

The section on deleting records described how to use a delete query to purge obsolete records from your tables. In some cases, it may be acceptable to simply throw away the records (perhaps after printing a report based on a select query that describes the same group of records), but in others, you might prefer to add them to an archive table, located in the same or another database, so that they do not slow down everyday operations but are available for reference. For example, instead of simply purging records from the Names table after a specified period of time has elapsed since the last contact, ACE might want to copy these inactive names to another table for occasional mailings. To archive and delete records from a table, you can use two queries: a make table query that copies the obsolete records to a new archive table or an append query that adds these records to an existing archive table, and a delete query that removes the same records you archived.

You can use a similar but slightly more complicated strategy to condense multiple records into one or two summary records before you archive or delete the detail data. For example, in the ACE system, you could summarize each person's financial transactions into two summary records at the end of every year—one for the debits and one for the credits—and then delete the detail records. As outlined in Chapter 3, this strategy has several important advantages in any database that stores financial information. First, it allows you to reduce the size of a table to speed performance while retaining some visible record of the data for reference in your daily work. Second, you can use the summary records to recalculate overall totals for display purposes or to reconstruct totals stored in another table (in this example, the Total Debits and Total Credits fields in the Names table) in the event that these numbers are damaged by a hardware crash or software error.

To summarize and archive the Transactions table data for a given year, you could use the following sequence of steps:

1. Use a make table query to copy the summarized debits to a temporary table.

2. Use a make table query to copy the summarized credits to a temporary table.

3. Use a delete query to delete all the individual transaction records for the year from the Transactions table.

4. Use an append query to add the summarized debit records back to the Transactions table and fill in the nonnumeric fields.

5. Use an append query to add the summarized credit records back to the Transactions table and fill in the nonnumeric fields.

This operation in the ACE system (and many other accounting databases) is complicated by the fact that you have to create separate records for the total debits and total credits; if you were simply summarizing sales or donations, you could use three steps rather than five. Figure 13.25 illustrates a make table query that copies the credits to a table called Total Credits. Note that this query is a totals query in which records are grouped by ID Code and selected by date and transaction type (to exclude pledge transactions, which are debits, not credits). The remaining columns compute the sums of all the numeric fields (Subtotal, Discount, Tax, Shipping, and Amount). The analogous query that summarizes the total debits is similar except for the criteria based on the Transaction Type field, which select *only* pledge transactions, rather than all but pledge transactions.

Figure 13.25
A query that creates
summary
transaction records

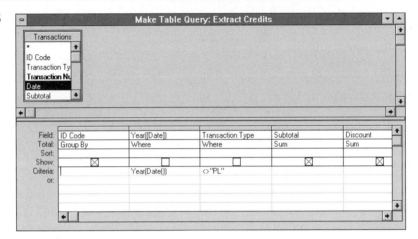

The query that deletes the current year transactions was described earlier in this chapter (it is shown in Figure 13.15). Figure 13.26 illustrates the append query that adds the summary records written to the temporary Total Credits table by the Extract Credits query back to the Transactions table. The Append Total Debits query is identical except for the values assigned to the Transaction Type and Reference fields. In the new records, the Transaction Type field is defined as the constant text string "TC" (for "Total Credits"). The numeric fields are derived from the corresponding summary fields—the SumOfSubtotal field in the summary table supplies the value for the Subtotal field, SumofDiscount supplies the value for the Discount field, and so on.

Figure 13.26
A query that
appends summary
records to the
Transactions table

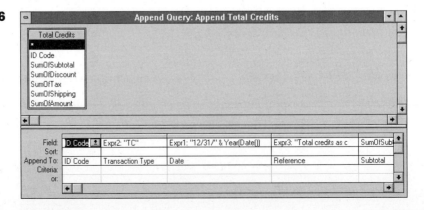

The values assigned to both the Date and Reference fields must reflect the current year (the transaction date is always the last date of the year—12/31/93 in 1993, 12/31/94 in 1994, and so on). The expression that computes the value entered into the Date field, all of which is visible in Figure 13.26, concatenates the constant text string "12/31/" with the current year, obtained by evaluating the Year function with the Date function as input. This expression takes advantage of two automatic data type conversions—Access allows you to concatenate a number with a text string to yield another text string, and it allows you to append a text string that looks like a date into a true date field. The expression that constructs the text string in the Reference field is as follows:

```
"Total credits as of 12/31/"&Year(Date())-1900
```

In this expression, subtracting 1900 from the result of evaluating the Year function converts the four-digit year returned by this function to a two-digit number.

Note that no special measures are required to update the Transaction Number field, because Access automatically fills in the next sequential number in Counter fields regardless of the mechanism used to add records to a table. When you append one table that includes a Counter field to another table that has a Counter field of the same name, including the Counter field in the output grid causes Access to retain the original value, whereas omitting the field from the output grid causes Access to renumber the records to reflect their sequence in the target table. If the Counter field is the primary key for the target table (as is the case with the ACE Transactions table), you *must* allow Access to renumber the records if any of the values in the records you are appending might duplicate existing values in the Counter field, so as not to risk creating duplicate keys.

You can use a method based on an append query to overcome one of the limitations on Counter fields cited in Chapter 3—the fact that you cannot specify the starting value. You cannot work around this problem by starting with an Integer field and converting it to a Counter after entering the first record, because Access does not allow you to change the data type to Counter in a table that contains data. You can, however, *append* an Integer field into a Counter field. To supply your own starting value for a Counter field, you can create a table with an identically named Integer field, enter one record into this table, and append it into an empty table with the correct structure. The next record you enter will be assigned the next sequential number. You can then delete the first "dummy" record. This method was used to create the ACE Transactions table, in which the first transaction number is 14932.

You can also use append queries to overcome one of the limitations on modifying the structure of a table that was cited earlier in this chapter—the fact that when you convert a Date/Time, numeric, or Yes/No field to a Text field, Access does not automatically format the result text strings to match the display format established through the Format property. The basic method is as follows:

1. Use the cut-and-paste method described earlier in this chapter to make a copy of the structure of the original table (without the data).

2. Modify the structure of the new table and change the desired Date/Time, numeric, and Yes/No fields to Text fields.

3. Define an append query that copies all the fields in the original table into the new structure, using expressions that create the required display formats for the fields you are converting to Text fields.

4. Delete the original table.

5. Rename the new table to the original name.

In many cases, you can use an expression based on the Format function to define the new field value. For example, to turn a Date/Time field called Date into a Text field whose contents match the medium date format, you could use the expression Format([Date], "Medium Date"). This technique will work for most Date/Time and numeric fields, although you may have to use a custom format string instead of one of the built-in format names. The best way to convert a Yes/No field to a Text field is to use an expression based on the IIf function to specify the strings you want to represent the two logical values. For example, to convert the OK to Call field in the Names table to the text strings "OK to call" (for Yes) and "Do not call" (for No), you can use the following expression:

```
IIf([OK to Call], "OK to call", "Do not call")
```

Compacting a Database

After a lengthy editing session or a period of extensive experimentation with a variety of forms and reports, you may notice that the .MDB file has grown quite a bit larger, even if you did not end up adding more records or database objects than you deleted. The reason is that when you delete objects, Access cannot recycle the space they occupied in the database file with 100 percent efficiency. You can compact a database to regain all the unused space and improve performance by using the Compact Database option. This option is present on the File menu only when no database is open: Because compacting a database completely restructures the .MDB file, you cannot carry out this operation while you are editing any database component.

When you choose the Compact Database option, Access displays an Open File dialog box very similar to the one invoked by the Open Database option to enable you to choose the database you want to compact. By default, Access rewrites the database under a new name, and after you choose the database, it displays a Save File dialog box in which you can enter the new file name. The default name is DB1.MDB, but you will usually want to change this name. If you enter the name of the database itself, Access compacts the database to a temporary file and then erases the original and renames the temporary database when the process is complete. However, it is safer to specify a new .MDB file in case the operation is interrupted by a hardware crash or power failure. You might want to copy the original database to floppy disks to serve as a backup, erase this file from your hard disk, and then rename the new database to the original name.

Compacting a small database may take just a few seconds, but if your database is larger than 3 or 4Mb, be prepared to wait a few minutes. As it works, Access displays the usual percentage indicator in the status bar to allow you to monitor its progress.

Repairing a Damaged Database

Chapter 2 pointed out that you should always close the active database or exit from Access before you turn off your computer. (Exiting from Windows is also safe, because Windows closes any open applications and their data files before it relinquishes control.) Despite your best efforts, however, a database may occasionally be damaged by an unavoidable "disaster" such as a hardware failure or software crash that interrupts an Access work session while a database is open. *Your best line of defense against this contingency is to maintain regular backup copies of all your database files.* If the .MDB file is damaged in the crash, recovering from your most recent backup may be your only alternative. However, inconsistencies in a database that result from exiting abnormally before Access could save your latest changes can often be corrected by using the Repair Database option on the File menu.

If Access can detect the damage the next time you open the database, it issues a warning that the file should be repaired. However, you might want to run the Repair option on the database that was open even if Access does not report problems after a crash. Note also that this option simply restores the database to an internally consistent state so that you can use it normally. If you were entering or editing data when the crash occurred, you should check the last few records you entered or edited to make sure that all your changes were saved or reenter them if necessary.

When you choose the Repair Database option, Access displays an Open File dialog box very similar to the one invoked by the Open Database option to enable you to choose the database you want to repair. Unlike the Compact Database option, the Repair Database option always rewrites the database in place, so you do not have to enter a target file name. Repairing a database takes somewhat longer than compacting a normal .MDB file, and Access displays the usual progress indicator in the status bar.

Summary

This chapter outlined strategies for reorganizing the information stored in an Access database by modifying table structures, copying tables, creating new tables by extracting selected fields and records from one or more existing tables, and adding and deleting records en masse. The techniques described in this chapter play an important role throughout the lifetime of any database application—you can use them to correct problems with your initial database design, design periodic maintenance procedures, generate ongoing summary tables, and archive and purge obsolete data. This chapter also sets the stage for Chapter 14, which covers exchanging data with other software or other Access applications. When you import data, you often have to rearrange the resulting tables to suit your own purposes, and when you export data, you may first have to convert it to the field layout required by the external application.

Importing, Exporting, and Attaching Tables

Exchanging Data with External Programs

Special Considerations for Specific External Data Formats

SO FAR, THIS BOOK HAS CONCENTRATED ON WORKING WITH DATA ENtered and updated entirely within Access. However, most database applications do not exist in a vacuum, and you will often need to import or export data in a variety of *foreign*, or *external*, formats. As noted briefly in Chapter 13, the need to import data often arises very early in the application development cycle—if you are building an Access database to manipulate data originally entered using another program, perhaps one running on another type of computer (a mainframe, minicomputer, or Macintosh), you will probably want to import the data as soon as you have completed your initial design and preliminary testing. This may be the case if your Access database will replace an application formerly maintained using a less capable flat-file manager, the limited database management capabilities of a spreadsheet program, or a DOS-based database program (if you now work exclusively in Windows). You may also be taking over a database that originated on a Macintosh or "downsizing" an application formerly maintained on a mainframe or minicomputer (either in-house or by an outside service bureau).

You may also have to exchange data on an ongoing basis with colleagues, co-workers, clients, or subcontractors who use other software and have no plans to switch to Access, and to use other programs yourself to manipulate Access data. Even if your information processing needs lie primarily in the database arena, you can maximize your productivity by tapping the strengths of all the software you own. If your prior database experience was with the Data commands in a spreadsheet program, you have undoubtedly come to appreciate the ease with which you can use Access to sort, select, and group records, and to print reports, yet you would probably prefer your spreadsheet for complex mathematical calculations and what-if analyses. Similarly, Access cannot match the text formatting capabilities of a word processor or desktop publishing program, the number-crunching power of a statistics program, or the customized financial reports produced by an accounting package.

In addition to the aforementioned import and export capabilities, Access allows you to *attach* several types of data files—that is, work with foreign files in their native formats without converting them to Access tables. If the format you need is supported, you can share files with another application without compromising the ability to continue working with these files using the application that created them. This capability is especially useful for sharing data with colleagues who do not use Access and do not want to convert their applications. By strategically combining techniques based on importing, exporting, and attaching data files, you can use each of your programs for the tasks at which it excels, and overcome many of its weaknesses and limitations.

While in general, today's software can read and write an increasing number of data file formats, Access is new enough that you must be prepared to assume responsibility for both importing and exporting data in the formats required by the programs with which you have to exchange data. Even if Access can read or write the desired format directly, do not assume that the solutions to your data conversion problems will be simple or straightforward. Often, importing or exporting a file requires several steps, and may involve using the table rearrangement techniques covered in Chapter 13 to compensate for unavoidable differences between your Access tables and the field structures expected by the external program.

If Access cannot directly import or export the file format you need, you may have to devise a method based on another file format that is supported by both Access and the external program. Unfortunately, data exchange may also require that you understand more about the structure of the external data files than would be required to work with the same data entirely within Access (and often, far more than you really care to know). These problems will be compounded when you need to exchange data with colleagues working with programs that you do not use yourself: If your associates know little about their data storage formats, elucidating the necessary information can be difficult and traumatic.

This chapter describes the methods you can use to import, export, and attach external data files, outlines some typical data conversion strategies, and points out special considerations for working with specific types of data files. In your own work, it is likely that you will have to use a combination of these strategies to accomplish the data conversions required in your own Access applications. Before you begin, make sure you understand how to modify the structure of a table that contains data, and how to use action queries (update, delete, append, and make table queries) to split and combine tables, since a given data conversion problem may require many or all of these elements.

The disk supplied with this book contains several data files that you can use to practice importing and attaching external data, and this chapter includes hands-on examples that demonstrate typical techniques for importing, exporting, and attaching data in the most common formats. Because of the wide variety of data exchange requirements that you may encounter, it is likely that none of these examples will exactly match your own needs, and you are strongly encouraged to adapt the techniques described in this chapter to your own situation. The safest way to begin experimenting is to use the ACE sample database and the test data files supplied with this book. When you begin working with "live" data, especially with attached data files, make sure to back up the external files or conduct your preliminary experiments with copies of these files.

Exchanging Data with External Programs

There are two fundamentally different ways that you can work with external data in Access. You can import (read in) and export (copy out) files in a variety of formats, and in both cases, Access creates a copy of the data that is independent of the original—in effect, a snapshot of the data at the moment the copy was made. Thus, if you import a dBASE IV file and then edit the data in Access while the person who created the file is updating it in dBASE IV, the two copies will be out of synch. You can also *attach* some of the supported external file types to an Access database so that you can view or update *the original data file* from within Access, without making a copy, more or less as you would update an Access table. You (and your co-workers) can continue to work with an attached table using the program that created it, although not always at the same instant that you are updating the data in Access.

NOTE.   *Many of the programs with which Access can exchange data do not use the term* table *to refer to the entity that Access imports, exports, or attaches. For example, a 1-2-3 or Excel file is called a* worksheet *or* spreadsheet, *and in the Xbase world, the term* database *is used for what Access calls a table. However, for the sake of consistency, this chapter uses the term* table *to refer to any entity that would be treated in Access as a single table.*

One major reason for attaching rather than importing or exporting a table is an ongoing need to work with the data using another application as well as Access. For example, you may share a mailing list with other users in your organization who originally created the list in dBASE and want to continue using dBASE (or a custom application designed for them by a dBASE programmer) for their own work while you update the list and send out mailings from within Access. Another reason is that attaching a table enables you to avoid duplicating large amounts of data and repeatedly carrying out lengthy import or export steps. For example, you might want to carry out occasional inquries or print reports based on data created by Paradox users in your organization or on SQL tables stored on a remote server.

The ability to attach a table in another Access database enables you to overcome a significant limitation—the fact that you can only open one Access database at a time. If you have Access applications that function largely in isolation but that occasionally need to share data, you can simply attach the necessary tables rather than trying to maintain two or more copies of the same data. When several applications share certain tables more or less equally, you might want to store these common tables in a common reference database that contains no other tables, and attach these tables to each of the independent databases to ensure that each is always working with the most recent copy of the data. A typical setup is diagrammed in Figure 14.1.

Access can import and export data in all of the following formats:

- Access tables

- Delimited text files (files in which the fields are separated by commas, tabs, or spaces and character fields may be enclosed in quotes)

Figure 14.1

Sharing tables between Access databases

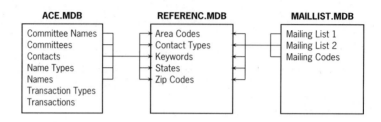

- Fixed-width text files (files in which each field is a fixed length, with no punctuation between the fields, and in which each record is therefore also fixed in length)

- Microsoft Excel version 2, 3, and 4 spreadsheet files

- Lotus 1-2-3 or 1-2-3 for Windows .WKS, .WK1, and .WK3 spreadsheet files

- Paradox version 3.*x* tables

- dBASE III and dBASE IV databases

- FoxBase+, FoxPro 1.*x*, and FoxPro 2.*x* databases

- Btrieve data files

- Microsoft SQL Server tables

Even if you do not see the format you need in this list, you may still be able to exchange data with an external program. In many cases, you can use one of the supported formats as a medium of exchange between two programs that do not directly support each other's data file formats. For example, Access cannot read or write Quattro Pro spreadsheet files, but Quattro Pro can read and write both the Excel and Lotus 1-2-3 worksheet formats. To prepare a Quattro Pro spreadsheet for import into Access, you must save it in one of these formats, which you can do in Quattro Pro by including the .XLS (for Excel), .WKS, or .WK1 (for Lotus) extension when you enter the file name. Similarly, Quattro Pro can read a spreadsheet in either Excel or Lotus format, provided that you include the extension when you enter the name of the worksheet you want to retrieve.

Access can import and export far more formats than it can attach. You can only attach data files created by other *database* programs, and by no means does this include *all* popular PC database programs. Attaching data is far more difficult than importing or exporting it, because Access must know more about the external data format and about the methods used by the external program to maintain indexes and other auxiliary files associated with the data files. Furthermore, Access must not allow any updates that would be prohibited by a security system implemented by the external program. You can attach tables in the following formats:

- Tables in another Access database

- Paradox version 3.*x* tables

- dBASE III and dBASE IV databases

- Btrieve data files

- Microsoft SQL Server tables

The command sequences that you use to attach, import, and export tables have a great deal in common, and they are described together in this section. The differences between working with imported and attached tables are covered in the section entitled "Working with Attached Tables," and specific considerations for working with the various external data formats are described later in this chapter. In all cases, you begin by choosing the Import, Export, or Attach Table option from the File menu, and Access responds by displaying a dialog box like the one in Figure 14.2 to allow you to choose the external file format. This figure shows the Attach dialog box; the Import and Export dialog boxes differ only in the window titles, the label above the scrolling list box ("Data Destination" for the Export dialog box), and the specific file formats displayed in the scrolling list box.

Figure 14.2
Choosing the
external data format

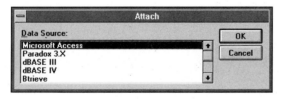

The subsequent steps are very similar for attaching and importing tables. After you choose the file format, Access displays a standard Open File dialog box to allow you to find specific data files of the selected type. Figure 14.3 illustrates the dialog box used to select which dBASE IV file you want to attach; the Import dialog box is similar except for the label on the button in the upper-right corner ("Import" rather than "Attach") and the absence of the Exclusive check box, which is irrelevant when you import data. When you export a table, Access displays a standard Save File dialog box like the one in Figure 14.4 in which you enter the path name of the file you want to create.

Figure 14.3

Choosing the dBASE IV database you want to attach

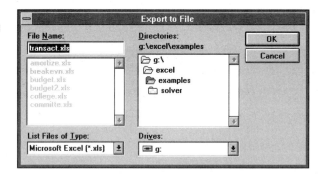

Figure 14.4

Naming the external file you want to create

In all cases, the initial file name specifications in the File Name and List Files of Type entry regions select all files with the standard extensions used by the external program. For example, in Figure 14.3, the dialog box is configured to display files with the extension .DBF, the standard extension for Xbase database files. You can narrow down the selection by entering a new file name pattern in the File Name text box. For example, you could display Xbase databases with names that begin with ACE by entering ACE*.DBF in the File Name text box. If you need to import or attach files with various nonstandard extensions, you can choose All Files from the List Files of Type combo box.

The Exclusive check box in the Select File dialog box for attaching tables determines whether Access opens the attached table in Exclusive or Shared mode. This option is described further in Chapter 17, which discusses working with shared data on a network, but you should understand its purpose from the outset. If you check the Exclusive option, Access always opens the attached table in Exclusive mode, and no other user on the network can open it at the same time *for any purpose.* This option will speed performance, but it may not always be practical if the external table is frequently used by others on your network. There is no way to change this setting once you have attached a table, but it is a simple matter to delete the linkage and reattach the table if you change your mind later.

Depending on the file format you chose, Access may display another dialog box to ask for additional information (these options are described later in this chapter), but it always returns you to the Import, Export, or Attach dialog box so that you can select the appropriate command button to begin the operation. Note that when you import any table that is password-protected in the external application, Access prompts you to enter the password, so make sure you have a valid password before you begin. When Access is installed on a network and set up for multiuser access, you can import a file that is currently in use by an external application (either in another Windows application window on the same computer or on the file server on a network). In a single-user installation, Access displays an alert box like the one in Figure 14.5 if you attempt to import a table that is currently open in the external application.

Figure 14.5

The error message displayed if you try to import an open file

Attaching a table is very fast—Access only has to make sure it can read the structural information stored with the data file and create an entry for the table in the current database. In contrast, importing or exporting a file requires that Access translate and rewrite every record, and these operations can take quite a bit of time if your tables are large. To keep you informed of its progress, Access displays a percentage indicator in the status bar. After importing, exporting, or attaching a table, Access displays an alert box that either confirms the success of the operation or reports any errors that were encountered, and then returns you to the Import, Export, or Attach dialog box to enable you to repeat the process with another table.

When you import or attach a table, Access preserves the name assigned in the external program. Access permits very long table names—longer than the DOS file names used by most of the supported external programs, which store each "table" in a separate disk file. If this name duplicates the name of an existing table, Access resolves the conflict by adding a digit as a tie-breaker to form a unique name. For example, if you import a table called Contacts, Access gives it the name Contacts1. Be sure to confirm the table name displayed in the alert box that informs you that the import or attach operation is complete—Access does not display any explicit warning message if it has to add a tie-breaker digit to the file name, and this small difference in names is easy to overlook. When you export to any of the external formats in which each table is stored in a separate disk file, Access constructs the default file name by truncating the table name to the first eight characters (the maximum length of the first part of a DOS file name) or the first word, whichever is shorter (because a DOS file name cannot include spaces). For example, the Committees table becomes COMMITTE, and the Area Codes table becomes AREA. You can edit this name if you wish before you proceed with the export.

When you import an external file, you can choose to create a new table or add the data into an existing Access table. If you create a new table, Access makes some fairly conservative assumptions—it assigns the maximum length (255) to all Text fields and sets the Field Size property for all numeric fields to Double or Long Integer. Some of the data file formats (specifically, those created by other database programs) *always* include field names, and Access preserves these names in the imported table. In formats that do not necessarily include field names (the spreadsheet and text file formats), Access looks for field names, which are typically located at the top of the data region, and if it cannot find them, assigns sequential numbers as field names. As you know, it is easy to modify the structure of the table afterwards, but unless you are intimately familiar with the data and are sure you will recognize the numbered fields, you may want to keep on hand a printout generated by the external program as you do so.

In formats with no explicitly defined data types (that is, all except other database files), Access also guesses the data types based on the entries in the first row of data, and if this row is atypical, it may draw some wrong conclusions. For example, if a field that should be a Text field contains only digits in the first row, Access will assign a numeric data type and will then be unable to import many of the remaining records. When you import from some formats (for example, text files), Access will assign the Long Integer data type if a numeric field in the first row is an integer, even if the same field in subsequent rows has decimal places. You can avoid many of these problems by creating an Access table structure in advance to receive the imported data, but be aware that you may need to restructure this table afterwards to achieve the desired field layout.

Some of the same considerations apply to exporting data. When you export data to any of the spreadsheet formats, Access automatically writes the field names into the first row, and when you create a text file, it offers you the option to do so. In general, exporting the field names is a good idea, although you may have to edit the resulting names if the external program cannot handle Access field names (which may be too long or may contain unsupported characters such as spaces or punctuation marks). For example, Microsoft

Word for Windows can use as a mail-merge file a delimited text file (described in more detail in the section called "Working with Text Files") with field names in the first row. However, field names that include spaces will generate errors when you attach the merge document. Nevertheless, if your Access table has more than a few fields or if their purposes might not be clear from the contents, it is easier to export the field names and then edit them than to try to reconstruct them from scratch.

When you append an external file to an existing Access table, it is your responsibility to ensure that the data types in this table are appropriate and that the fields are long enough to accommodate the data. In general, Access will refuse to import any data that it would not allow you to enter from the keyboard. Thus, when you import data into an existing table, Access rejects records in which the primary key is not unique and records that would violate any referential integrity rules. Because these problems will often arise, it may be more efficient to import the data into an empty table with the same structure as the true target table, but with no primary key, unique indexes, or referential integrity rules. You can then use an append query to add these records to the table that will become their ultimate destination. Because importing is often slower than appending records from one Access table into another, this strategy can save you considerable time. Also, because you are likely to know Access better than the external program that generated the data file, you will probably find it easier to find and correct the problems in Access.

If Access encounters any problems during an import operation, it displays an alert box that summarizes the problems and allows you to cancel the operation. An example, which resulted from an attempt to import a product list stored in a Lotus 1-2-3 spreadsheet, is shown in Figure 14.6. If you decide to proceed, Access creates a table with a name formed by combining the phrase "Import Errors" with your name (the name you entered when you installed Access) and a tie-breaker digit if there is already a table with that name in your database. Unlike the Paste Errors table created when a cut and paste operation generates errors, this table contains only a description of the problem that caused Access to reject each record, not the data.

Figure 14.6
The alert box that summarizes import errors

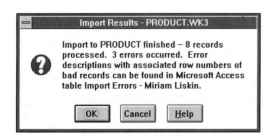

Figure 14.7 illustrates a small sample of an Import Errors table in Datasheet view; the three fields store a description of the error, the name of the offending field, and the row number in the external file. The most common problems you will encounter are field lengths too short for the contents (which yields the "Field Set Failure" message), data types incompatible with the target fields (the "Type Conversion Failure" message), more fields than are present in the target table, duplicate index keys, and referential integrity rule violations. If Access can make no sense whatsoever of a record, the error message stored in the Error field is "Unparseable Record."

Figure 14.7

The Import Errors table

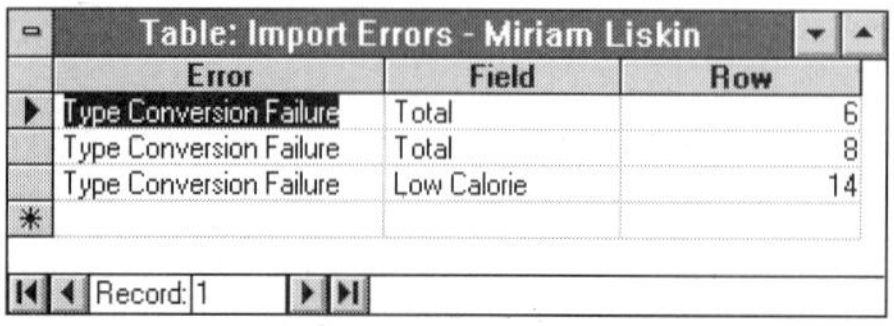

Error	Field	Row
Type Conversion Failure	Total	6
Type Conversion Failure	Total	8
Type Conversion Failure	Low Calorie	14

Table: Import Errors - Miriam Liskin

Record: 1

Compensating for Differences in Structure

Although you may occasionally be able to use an imported table as is, and an external program may at times be able to accept exported data in exactly the same format as your Access table, these instances are the exception rather than the rule. More often than not, you will have to share data with other programs that use slightly (or extremely) different formats for the same information, and unfortunately, you (rather than the users of the external program) may be forced to assume responsibility for compensating for these differences. In many cases, your colleagues with whom you must share data know little more than you do about the details of their data storage formats, and even less about Access tables.

Furthermore, when you exchange files with software other than PC databases, spreadsheets, and word processors, you may not have the option to modify the external file formats. For example, if you need to export data for use by a packaged accounting program, you will be forced to match the data structures used by this software for technical reasons—most "canned" programs give you no means to customize their file structures or data formats. When you share data with a mainframe or minicomputer, the reasons may be more political than technical—the MIS staff who administer the mainframe database may be unwilling to change file formats to suit your requirements or may be unable to do so in a realistic time frame.

Access always exports an entire table, in primary key order if there is a primary key or in the order of entry if there is not. In most cases, Access offers no direct method for importing part of a table (the one exception is that you can import a range of cells in a spreadsheet). If you want to export just part of a table, you can use a make table query to create a table that contains exactly the data you want to export. This method gives you the flexibility to export selected records, specify which fields to copy and rearrange their order, export calculated values, change field names, export data derived from more than one table, or sort the exported data into a different order. If your tables are large, these intermediary tables can take up quite a bit of space, but in most cases you can erase them immediately after you export the data (while retaining the make table queries for future use). The basic strategy is as follows:

1. Design a select query whose dynaset looks exactly like the table you would like to produce (including all the necessary fields and calculated columns, sorting instructions that describe the desired order, and selection criteria that describe the data subset you want).

2. Convert the query to a make table query, and run this query to write the data to a new table.

3. Export the table produced by the make table query.

4. Erase the temporary table if you do not need to use it within Access.

When you import data, you may be able to convert it to the desired format simply by modifying the structure in Table Design view. More often, you will also have to use one or more make table and/or append queries, using a strategy like the following:

1. Import the data into a new table.

2. Design a select query based on this table whose dynaset mirrors the table you would like to produce.

3. Convert the query to a make table query to write the data to a new table, or convert the query to an append query to add the data to an existing table.

4. If necessary, modify the structure of the table produced by a make table query.

5. Erase the table that contains the raw imported data.

To practice these techniques, you can replicate some of the steps used to create the ACE Names table, which was derived from two FoxPro tables called ACENAME (which contains the name and address fields) and ACESUPP (which contains the supplementary information maintained for all name types except prospects). These files are included on the sample disk, and you can import them using the following steps:

1. Choose the Import option from the File menu.

2. Highlight FoxPro 2.0 in the scrolling list of data sources in the Import dialog box, and press Enter or click on the OK button to close the dialog box.

3. Choose ACENAME.DBF from the Select File dialog box, and click on the Import button to begin importing the data. Select OK in the alert box that informs you that Access has finished importing the file.

4. Choose ACESUPP.DBF from the Select File dialog box, and click on the Import button to begin importing the data. Select OK in the alert box that informs you that Access has finished importing the file.

5. Close the Select File dialog box. You should see the two new table names, ACENAME and ACESUPP, at the top of the Database window.

6. Open the ACENAME table in Datasheet view, and browse through the data, most of which should be familiar to you. Observe that there are 100 records in the table, and that they are *not* in any particular order (in fact, they are arranged in the order they were entered into the FoxPro file).

7. Open the ACESUPP table in Datasheet view, and note that there are only 32 records.

8. Close both tables.

Next, create a query to merge the ACENAME and ACESUPP tables:

1. Make sure that the Database window displays the list of queries, and click on the New command button or press Alt+N to create a new query. Add the ACENAME and ACESUPP tables to the query, and then close the Add Table dialog box.

2. To link the two tables, drag the IDCODE field from the ACENAME field list to the IDCODE field in the ACESUPP field list.

3. Click on the join line, and then choose Join Properties from the View menu. Choose the second option, so that the query includes all records from the ACENAME table, even if there is no matching record in the ACESUPP table.

4. Double-click on the title bar in the ACENAME field list window, and drag all the fields to the output grid.

5. Delete the ADDRESS1 and ADDRESS2 fields from the output grid.

6. Insert a new column between the COMPANY and CITY columns, and enter the following expression to define the new Address column (the table name reference is required because there are also fields called ADDRESS1 and ADDRESS2 in the ACESUPP table):

```
Address: ACENAME.[ADDRESS1]&Chr(13)&Chr(10)&
ACENAME.[ADDRESS2]
```

This expression combines the ADDRESS1 and ADDRESS2 fields, separated by a hard return. You cannot simply press the Enter key to include the hard return in this expression, because pressing Enter indicates to Access that you are finished typing the expression. Instead, you must use the Chr function to express the two characters that make up a hard return (the "return" and "line feed" characters). This function accepts an ANSI code as input and returns as output the character represented by this ANSI code.

7. Click on the TOTDEBITS field in the ACESUPP field list. Scroll down to the bottom of the list, hold down the Shift key, and click on the Notes field. Drag all the selected fields to the output grid.

8. In the Sort row for the IDCODE field, enter **Ascending**.

9. Run the query and verify that the dynaset contains 100 rows, arranged in alphabetical order by IDCODE. Return to Query Design View.

10. Choose Make Table from the Query menu, and type **New Names** in the Table Name text box.

11. Run the query, and then close it, saving it under the name **Combine Fox-Pro Tables**.

12. Open the New Names table and look through the data to verify the results of the conversion.

To complete the conversion, you would also have to modify the structure of the New Names table to edit the field names.

Working with Attached Tables

When you attach a table, Access displays its name in the Database window along with the other tables in the database, distinguished from these tables by a slightly different icon, which includes an arrow to symbolize the connection with the external data source. Once you have attached the external table, you can open it much as you would an Access table, update it, and use it in queries and reports, subject to the limitations imposed by the software that created the table. Figure 14.8 illustrates the Database window with three attached tables named Customers, Employees, and MAILLIST.

Figure 14.8

A database that includes attached tables

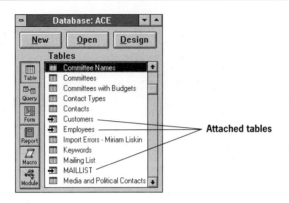

When you attach a table in another Access database, you can do anything that you could with a table stored in the current database. When you attach a table created by an external program, you can update it in Datasheet view, use it in queries (alone or linked to any other tables), and use it as the data source for forms and reports. Access allows you to change any properties of an attached table that are local to Access, but not those properties that would compromise the ability of the external program to use the table. For example, you can rename an attached table, because the name is used only to identify the table in lists displayed within Access. You may want to rename an attached table to lengthen a short name derived from the external file name, such as MAILLIST, the name of a dBASE IV mailing list database visible in Figure 14.8. As you can see in this figure, Access gives you no obvious indication of the type of data in an attached table, so you might want to include this information in the new name. For example, you might rename the MAILLIST table "dBASE IV Mailing List" or "Mailing List (dBASE IV)."

You can display the structure of an attached table in Design view, and you can change some of the properties—the ones that are local to Access. When you open the table in Design view, Access displays an alert box like the one shown in Figure 14.9 to remind you that you will not be able to change every aspect of the structure. Figure 14.10 illustrates the MAILLIST table in Design view with the table property sheet visible. Access uses the table Description property to store a text string that records the type and location of the external file, and you cannot change this property because doing so might prevent Access from finding the data. You cannot change field names or data types, which are integral to the file, but you can change the Description, Caption, Format, Decimal Places, Default Value, Validation Rule, and Validation Text properties, which are stored locally in your Access database. As you can see in Figure 14.10, whenever a property that you cannot change has the focus, Access displays the message "This property cannot be modified in attached tables" in the information box in the lower-right corner of the Table Design window. Access does allow you to change these properties, but when you exit from Design view, it displays the alert box shown in Figure 14.11 to warn you that your changes will not be saved.

You can sever the connection to an attached table by using the same methods you would use to delete an Access table from a database—highlight the table name in the Database window, and press Del or select the Delete option from the Edit menu. Access displays the usual alert box asking you to confirm your intention to delete the table, but if you give permission to proceed, it only removes the reference to the table from the database—it *does not* physically erase the external table from the disk where it is stored (which

---

Figure 14.9

The alert box displayed when you open an attached table in Table Design view

Figure 14.10

Displaying an attached table in Table Design view

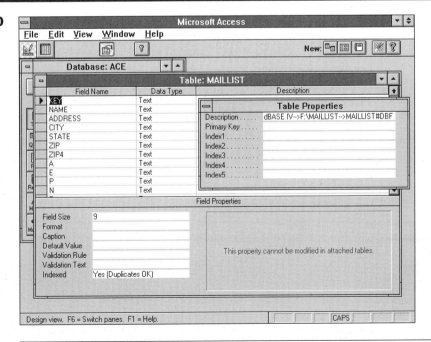

Figure 14.11
The alert box displayed when you save an attached table after modifying the structure

may be your own hard disk, the hard disk on a network file server, or a drive on a remote server). If you later change your mind, you can reattach the table using the same steps you used originally.

When you work with attached tables, performance is usually slower than when you use only tables stored within the active Access database. This speed differential is due in part to the fact that Access has to translate the external file format on the fly, as you display or update the table. If the external file is located on a network file server or a remote server rather than on your local hard disk, the degradation in performance will be more dramatic, because the data must be transferred to your workstation through the network cables. Performance will also be affected by other network traffic, and if other users are working with the very same tables concurrently, Access also has to detect attempts to update the same data on other workstations. These factors are described in more detail in Chapter 17, which covers all aspects of network operation, but be prepared for less than optimal performance when you view or edit attached tables.

Special Considerations for Specific External Data Formats

While the mechanics of importing, exporting, and attaching tables are more or less the same for all the supported external file formats, the detailed procedures vary somewhat, due to the inevitable differences between these formats and the programs that create them. You should realize from the outset that sharing data with other software requires at least some understanding of how those programs work and how they handle data, and this may present serious problems if you are not familiar with the software with which you must exchange data. The remaining sections in this chapter outline some of the special issues relevant to the specific external file formats.

Working with Access Tables

As noted earlier, working with Access data stored in another database differs very little from using tables physically located within the open database file.

In most cases, you can import, export, or attach Access tables with few problems apart from those caused by differences in structure between your tables and those created by other Access users. Importing and exporting from another Access database differs in one important respect from exchanging data with any other source: Because Access could not possibly encounter an unfamiliar object, it does not limit you to importing and exporting tables. You can only *attach* a table, but when you choose Microsoft Access as the import or export file format, Access displays the dialog box in Figure 14.12 to allow you to choose objects of any type—tables, queries, forms, reports, macros, and modules. When you import or export a table, you can also choose whether to copy the data (the default) or just the structure, using two radio buttons that are disabled for all the other object types.

Figure 14.12

Choosing an Access object to import

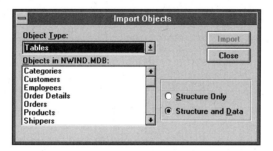

Note that it is entirely up to you to make sure that you import or export all of the objects in a group that must be used together, although as you know, Access gives you no indication of which objects belong together in the objects lists in the Database window. For example, if you import the form named Categories from the sample NWIND database supplied with Access, you must also import the subform embedded in this form (Categories Subform), the Categories table (the data source for the main form), and the Products table (the data source for the subform). If any of these objects are missing when you open the Categories form, Access will display an alert box like the one in Figure 14.13, which informs you that it cannot find the form named Categories Subform.

You can practice working with attached tables by attaching a table from the Northwind Traders sample database supplied with Access, using the following steps:

1. Choose the Attach Table option from the File menu.

2. Highlight Microsoft Access in the scrolling list of data sources in the Attach dialog box, and press Enter or click on OK to close the dialog box.

Figure 14.13

The alert box displayed if a required object is missing

3. Choose NWIND.MDB from the Select Microsoft Access dialog box, and click on OK.

4. Choose Customers from the list of tables in the Attach Tables dialog box, and click on the Attach button. Select OK in the alert box that informs you that Access has "Successfully Attached 'Customers'."

5. Close the Attach Tables dialog box. You should see the new table name, Customers, in the Database window.

6. Open the Customers table in Datasheet view, and change the city in the first record to **Orem**. Close the table.

7. Close the ACE database, and open the NWIND database.

8. Open the Customers table in Datasheet view, and note that the change you made is visible in the first record. Close the table.

9. Close the NWIND database, and reopen the ACE database.

Working with Text Files

The two text file formats that Access can import and export—*delimited* and *fixed-width*—can be used to exchange data with a wide variety of programs running on all types of computers, including minicomputers, mainframes, and Macintoshes as well as PCs. Although some programs do use these formats as their primary data storage formats, this is not as common as it used to be, and the text file formats are valuable today primarily as a medium of exchange between programs that cannot directly read and write each other's native data storage formats. The distinguishing feature of the text file formats is that they contain little or no structural information. In some cases, the first line of the file contains the field names, but this is by no means universal (for example, in Xbase, you cannot produce this format without programming).

Working with Delimited Files

A *delimited* file is an ASCII text file in which the fields are separated by commas, spaces, or tabs, and text fields are surrounded (delimited) by some other punctuation mark (usually single or double quotation marks). Dates, numbers, and other nontext data types are usually not enclosed in delimiters. Delimited text files have a hard return at the end of each record, so if you examine it with an editor or use the MS-DOS TYPE command to display it, each record begins on a new line. Figure 14.14 illustrates a few records from a delimited file produced by exporting the ACE Transactions table to this format using the default settings.

Programs that can read delimited files identify the fields by counting the field separators (usually commas), starting from the beginning of each record—the first field is assumed to consist of all the characters (except the delimiters) up to the first separator, the second field is all the characters between the first and second separators, and so on. The delimiters around text fields are required so that any embedded commas *within* a field, such as the one in the Reference field in the second record in Figure 14.14 ("Pledge payment #1, Check #1283"), are not mistaken for field separators. For the same reason, if a field is empty, the delimited file must still include the comma that would follow the field. Without this placeholder, the next field would be mistaken for the empty one. No field in a delimited file can contain the character used as the field delimiter; thus, if a field might contain the double quote character, you must use another delimiter (such as single quotes).

Figure 14.15 illustrates the dialog box displayed when you import a delimited text file; the corresponding Export Text Options dialog box is even simpler—the Table Options are absent because they are irrelevant to the export process. When you select the Options command button, the Import Text Options and Export Text Options dialog boxes expand as shown in Figure 14.16 to display additional options that you can use to further describe several aspects of the text file you want to read or create.

For your convenience, Access allows you to define as many different named text file specifications as you wish and save them in the database. For example, you could define one specification for importing text files with the standard field separators (commas) and delimiters (double quotes) and another for exporting to the tab-delimited format used by many Macintosh programs. If you define specifications in the import or export specifications dialog boxes, you must save them by using the Save As command button; the Specification Name combo box is used only to select the specification you want to use for the current import or export operation. You can also define new text file specifications by selecting the Imp/Exp Setup option on the File menu, as described in the next section. If you do not choose a previously defined specification, Access uses the settings you enter directly in the Import Text Options or Export Text Options dialog box.

The File Type combo box determines how Access handles characters with ASCII codes above 127, which are often used to display graphics symbols and foreign language characters. There are two choices: Windows (ANSI), which

Figure 14.14

A delimited text file

```
"ALLENMA","PL",14932,12/28/91 0:00:00,1000,0,0,0,1000,"Check","Pledge","12010"
"ALLENMA","PP",14933,12/28/91 0:00:00,250,0,0,0,250,"Check","Pledge payment #1, Check #1283",0,
"MATTHEFR","TC",14934,12/31/91 0:00:00,125,0,0,125,,"Total credits as of 12/31/91",0,
"ANDERSMI","TC",14935,12/31/91 0:00:00,522,0,0,522,,"Total credits as of 12/31/91",0,
"ARNOLDME","TC",14936,12/31/91 0:00:00,75,0,0,75,,"Total credits as of 12/31/91",0,
"BERGENRU","TC",14937,12/31/91 0:00:00,2452,0,0,2452,,"Total credits as of 12/31/91",0,
"BLOOMCH","TC",14938,12/31/91 0:00:00,2250,0,0,2250,,"Total credits as of 12/31/91",0,
"BROWNEL","TC",14939,12/31/91 0:00:00,25,0,0,25,,"Total credits as of 12/31/91",0,
"PIERSOCH","TD",14940,12/31/91 0:00:00,1500,0,0,1500,,"Total debits as of 12/31/91",0,
"ELLIOTCH","TC",14941,12/31/91 0:00:00,50,0,0,50,,"Total credits as of 12/31/91",0,
```

Figure 14.15

The basic Import
Text Options
dialog box

Import Text Options - NAMES.TXT
☐ First Row Contains Field Names
Table Options
◉ Create New Table
○ Append to Existing Table: Area Codes
OK
Cancel
Options >>

Figure 14.16

Customizing the
delimited text file
specifications

Import Text Options - NAMES.TXT
☐ First Row Contains Field Names
Table Options
◉ Create New Table
○ Append to Existing Table: Area Codes
Specification Name:
File Type: Windows (ANSI)
Text Delimiter: "   Field Separator: ,
Dates, Times, and Numbers
Date Order: MDY   ☐ Leading Zeros in Dates   Time Delimiter: :
Date Delimiter: /   ☐ Four Digit Years   Decimal Separator: .
OK
Cancel
Options >>
Save As...

is the best choice for exchanging data with other Windows software, and DOS or OS/2 (PC-8), which is best for most DOS and OS/2 programs. If the file you are importing or exporting does not contain any such characters (most mainframe and minicomputer data files do not), this setting is irrelevant.

You can use the Text Delimiter and Field Separator combo boxes to choose the punctuation used to identify the fields in the text file. The choices in the Text Delimiter combo box are " (double quotes, the default), ' (single quotes), or {none}, but you can also enter any other character you wish. Although Access allows you to enter more than one character, it ignores all but the first. Thus, you cannot read or write a text file in which the beginning and ending field delimiters are different (for example, a file in which character fields are enclosed in parentheses, square brackets, or braces). The choices in the Field Separator combo box are , (comma), {tab}, and {space}, but you can also enter any other character you wish. The {tab} option is particularly useful for sharing data with Macintosh programs, many of which use tab characters as field separators. The {space} option is most useful for data that consists primarily of numbers, such as numeric data you are exporting to a statistics package or numerical analysis program, but because text fields (the fields that are most likely to contain embedded spaces) are enclosed within delimiters, you can use this format for any type of data.

The options in the Dates, Times, and Numbers region allow you to customize the format of dates and times. You can combine these options to allow Access to interpret files created by other programs and to match the formats required by these programs. For example, many MS-DOS databases require leading zeroes in dates, whereas most Windows programs do not. Note that when you export Date/Time values, Access always includes the time, even if the display format for the field specifies only a date (and unfortunately, even if your external program cannot read times). Note also that Access can import and export Memo fields, but you should do so with caution—not all of the external programs that can read and write delimited text files can handle the long text strings that may be found in an Access Memo field.

Working with Fixed-Width Files

A *fixed-width* file is an ASCII text file in which each field occupies a fixed number of characters, and each record is also therefore fixed in length. If you are familiar with dBASE, you may have heard the acronym SDF (which stands for System Data Format) used to describe this file format, but this term, which originated with Ashton-Tate, is not used elsewhere. Figure 14.17 illustrates a few records in a fixed-width text file created by exporting the ACE Transactions table (the same records as in the delimited text file pictured earlier in Figure 14.14). Because a fixed-width text file has no field delimiters or field separators (there may not even be any spaces between fields), the only way to identify the fields is by their positions in the record, and Access cannot possibly guess where one field ends and the next begins. You must therefore define an Import/Export specification to describe the data structure, and you cannot do this on the fly from the Export Text Options dialog box—you must use the Imp/Exp Setup option on the File menu to define the specification in advance.

Figure 14.18 illustrates the import/export specification that describes the fixed-width file shown in Figure 14.17. As you can see, the Field Information table looks a little like the table specifications displayed in Table Design view, except that the fields are defined by their width and starting position in the record. If you need to import a file that originated on a mainframe or minicomputer, you will probably be able to obtain a listing in a similar or identical format (which is very common in the world of large computers) from the database administrator in charge of the table. Unfortunately, even if you have a table with an identical structure, you cannot use it as a model for the import/export specification—instead, you must type the field names, data types, and lengths from scratch in the Import/Export Setup dialog box. Furthermore, you must define an import/export specification even if you are importing data into an existing Access table with exactly the same structure as the external file.

Figure 14.17

A fixed-width text file

```
ALLENMA   PLI493212/28/911000  0  0  0  1000  CheckPledge                         012010
ALLENMA   PPI493312/28/91250   0  0  0  250   CheckPledge payment #1, Check #1283 031030
MATTHEFR  TCI493412/31/91125   0  0  0  125   Total credits as of 12/31/91        0
ANDERSMI  TCI493512/31/91522   0  0  0  522   Total credits as of 12/31/91        0
ARNOLDME  TCI493612/31/9175    0  0  0  75    Total credits as of 12/31/91        0
BERGENRU  TCI493712/31/912452  0  0  0  2452  Total credits as of 12/31/91        0
BLOOMCH   TCI493812/31/912250  0  0  0  2250  Total credits as of 12/31/91        0
BROWNEL   TCI493912/31/9125    0  0  0  25    Total credits as of 12/31/91        0
PIERSOCH  TDI494012/31/911500  0  0  0  1500  Total debits as of 12/31/91         0
ELLIOTCH  TCI494112/31/9150    0  0  0  50    Total credits as of 12/31/91        0
```

Figure 14.18
Defining import/
export setup
specifications

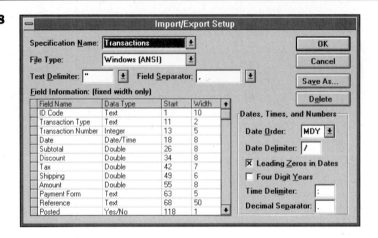

You can save as many import/export setups as you wish in an Access data-base, and you can use these specifications for both delimited and fixed-width files, although they are strictly necessary only for the latter format (as you can see in Figure 14.18, the Import/Export Setup dialog box includes combo boxes for specifying the text delimiters and field separators in a delimited file). When you define a new setup, you must save it by using the Save As command button. You can edit an existing specification by choosing its name from the Specification Name combo box, editing any entries in the dialog box, and choosing OK to save your changes. The easiest way to define a new setup that is similar to a previously defined setup is to edit the original and use the Save As command button to save the revised setup under a new name. To delete a setup you no longer need, you can retrieve it and then se-lect the Delete command button.

As noted earlier, when you import or export a fixed-width file, you *must* choose a previously defined import/export setup specification. Figure 14.19 il-lustrates the Import Text Options dialog box; the Export Text Options dialog box is even simpler—it contains only the Specification Name combo box. Access cannot verify whether the specification you select conforms to the structure of the fixed-width file, and if you inadvertently choose an inappro-priate specification, every record in the text file will generate a record in the Import Errors table. Assuming that you chose a specification intended to match the structure of the text file, the most common problems you will en-counter when you import or export fixed-width files result from entering the wrong length or starting position for one or more fields, so that the data is out of register with the structure of the target table.

Figure 14.19

Choosing the
import/export setup
specification

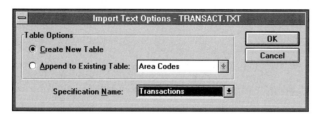

If you examine Figures 14.14 and 14.17, you will see that Access exports
Yes/No fields as 1 for Yes and 0 for No in a fixed-width text file, rather than
the usual –1 and 0 (so that you can define the field width as 1), and that it left-
justifies numeric fields within the specified width rather than right-justifying
them. Numeric and Date/Time fields are exported in the raw form in which
they are stored, rather than in the display format established through the Format property. Thus, any zeroes after the decimal point are dropped, and all
Date/Time values include both date and time components. Note also that you
can import or export Memo fields, but you must specify a fixed length for
every field in a fixed-width text file (which by definition cannot contain any
variable-length fields), so long entries will be truncated.

You should also be aware of a limitation that may prove constraining
when you exchange data with programs that do not expect a fixed-width file
to include hard returns (this is often the case with mainframe software that
uses this format): Access cannot read or write a fixed-width file that does not
have a hard return at the end of each record.

Exporting the Committees Table

To experiment with the text file formats, try exporting the Committees table
to create a delimited text file and a fixed-width text file. To create the delimited file, use the following steps:

1. Choose the Export option from the File menu.

2. Highlight Text (Delimited) in the scrolling list of data destinations in the
    Export dialog box, and press Enter or click on OK to close the dialog box.

3. Choose Committees from the list of tables in the Select Microsoft Access
    Object dialog box, and click on OK.

4. In the Export to File dialog box, change the file name to **COMM1.TXT**,
    and make sure that your Access program directory is displayed above the
    Directories list. Click on OK to close the dialog box.

5. In the Export Text Options dialog box, select the Options button to expand the dialog box.

6. Choose single quotes (') for the text delimiter (because one of the memo fields contains double quotes). Check the Store Field Names in First Row and Leading Zeros in Dates check boxes.

7. Click on OK to export the data.

8. Open the COMM1.TXT file in the Notepad, and examine the contents. Your screen should look like Figure 14.20. (In this figure, the Word Wrap option on the Edit menu was enabled. You might prefer to scroll the screen to the right to view the long lines.)

To create the fixed-length file, use the following steps:

1. Choose the Imp/Exp Setup option from the File menu.

2. Check the Leading Zeros in Dates check box.

Figure 14.20

The delimited file created by exporting the Committees table

```
┌─────────────────── Notepad - COMM1.TXT ───────────────────┐
│ File  Edit  Search  Help                                   │
├────────────────────────────────────────────────────────────┤
│'Committee','ID Code','Officer','Joined','Quit','Notes','Public Exposure'
│'EARTHDAY','FRANKLKA','Chairperson',08/01/92 00:00:00,01/01/93 00:00:00,''
│'EARTHDAY','HOWARDJO',,05/10/91 00:00:00,,''
│'EARTHDAY','LEEALEX','Treasurer',07/23/90 00:00:00,,''
│'EARTHDAY','OLSONED',,06/18/91 00:00:00,05/20/92 00:00:00,'Ed organized
│the first ACE-sponsored "Run for the Planet" race and fun run, held in San
│Francisco in 1992.'
│'FINANCE','ALLENMA','Chairperson',02/03/90 00:00:00,,'Ms. Allen was
│Treasurer of the Finance Committee from 6/90 through 7/91, when she became
│Chairperson.'
│'FINANCE','HOWARDJO','Treasurer',01/15/90 00:00:00,02/05/91 00:00:00,''
│'LOBBYING','MCDANIBU','Secretary',01/18/93 00:00:00,,''
│'FINANCE','THOMPSCH',,12/18/91 00:00:00,,''
│'LOBBYING','HARRINJU','Chairperson',10/20/92 00:00:00,,''
│'LOBBYING','LUSUSAN',,10/25/90 00:00:00,61/85/92 00:00:00,'Quit in April,
│1993.'
│'LOBBYING','OLSONED','Treasurer',05/10/92 00:00:00,,''
│'LOBBYING','REEDLUCY',,04/18/90 00:00:00,05/01/92 00:00:00,''
│'LOBBYING','ROSENBRH',,04/01/91 00:00:00,04/05/92 00:00:00,'Ralph, not
│Helen, was the committee member.'
│'LOBBYING','BERGENRU',,08/10/91 00:00:00,,''
│'NEWSLETTER','BLOOMCH',,03/28/90 00:00:00,03/01/92 00:00:00,''
│'NEWSLETTER','HOWARDJO',,11/10/92 00:00:00,,'Howard is responsible for
│compiling events listings for the newsletter. Refer all press contacts to
│him.'
│'NEWSLETTER','THOMPSCH',,02/06/92 00:00:00,,'Christine is now the editor
│of the ACE newsletter.'
└────────────────────────────────────────────────────────────┘
```

3. Enter the following field specifications in the Field Information table:

Field Name	Data Type	Start	Width
Committee	Text	1	10
ID Code	Text	11	10
Officer	Text	21	12
Joined	Date/Time	33	8
Quit	Date/Time	41	8
Notes	Memo	49	50

4. Enter **Committees** in the Specification Name text box, and click on OK to close the dialog box.

5. Choose the Export option from the File menu.

6. Highlight Text (Fixed Width) in the scrolling list of data destinations in the Export dialog box, and press Enter or click on the OK button to close the dialog box.

7. Choose Committees from the list of tables in the Select Microsoft Access Object dialog box, and click on the OK button.

8. In the Export to File dialog box, change the file name to **COMM2.TXT**, and make sure that your Access program directory is displayed above the Directories list. Click on OK to close the dialog box.

9. In the Export Text Options dialog box, choose Committees from the Specification Name combo box, and click on OK to export the data.

10. Open the COMM2.TXT file in the Notepad, and examine the contents. Your screen should look like Figure 14.21. In this figure, Word Wrap is *not* enabled. Scroll to the right to confirm that the longer Memo fields were truncated to 50 characters.

Working with Spreadsheets

When you export data to any of the supported spreadsheet formats, Access creates a new spreadsheet that looks much like the table's datasheet—each row in the spreadsheet contains data from one record, and each field is placed in its own column. Access always copies the field names into the first row of the spreadsheet to serve as column headings. Text, numeric, and Date/Time

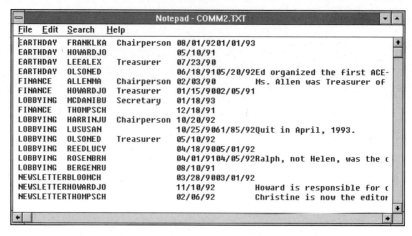

Figure 14.21

The fixed-width file created by exporting the Committees table

```
━━━━━━━━━━━━━━━━━━━━━━━━━━━━━━━━━━━━━━━━━━━━━━━━━━━━━━━━━━━━━━━━
□              Notepad - COMM2.TXT                      ▼ ▲
File   Edit   Search   Help
EARTHDAY   FRANKLKA   Chairperson 08/01/9201/01/93               ↑
EARTHDAY   HOWARDJO               05/10/91
EARTHDAY   LEEALEX    Treasurer   07/23/90
EARTHDAY   OLSONED                06/18/9105/20/92Ed organized the first ACE-
FINANCE    ALLENMA    Chairperson 02/03/90      Ms. Allen was Treasurer of
FINANCE    HOWARDJO   Treasurer   01/15/9002/05/91
LOBBYING   MCDANIBU   Secretary   01/18/93
FINANCE    THOMPSCH               12/18/91
LOBBYING   HARRINJU   Chairperson 10/20/92
LOBBYING   LUSUSAN                10/25/9061/85/92Quit in April, 1993.
LOBBYING   OLSONED    Treasurer   05/10/92
LOBBYING   REEDLUCY               04/18/9005/01/92
LOBBYING   ROSENBRH               04/01/9104/05/92Ralph, not Helen, was the c
LOBBYING   BERGENRU               08/10/91
NEWSLETTERBLOOMCH                 03/28/9003/01/92
NEWSLETTERHOWARDJO                11/10/92      Howard is responsible for c
NEWSLETTERTHOMPSCH                02/06/92      Christine is now the editor  ↓
←                                                                →
```

fields are all correctly converted to the corresponding types of data in the spreadsheet, although Access does not always choose the display format that you would prefer. In Excel, Date/Time values are displayed in Short Date format, and Yes/No fields are displayed as TRUE or FALSE. In Lotus 1-2-3, Date/Time values are displayed as date serial numbers and Yes/No values as numbers—1 for Yes and blank for No. Access ignores Memo and OLE Object fields when you export to any of the spreadsheet formats.

The key to importing spreadsheet data in a useful format is ensuring that it conforms as closely as possible to the structure of an Access table. Figure 14.22 illustrates an example of a spreadsheet (BUDGET.XLS, one of the sample spreadsheets supplied with Excel) that would *not* yield a useful Access table because the rows are not identical and not every row contains all of the fields. Figure 14.23 shows a new version of the same spreadsheet (BUDGET2.XLS) that is more suitable for conversion to an Access table. It is especially helpful to include the field names in the first row of the range of cells you intend to import, to avoid the numeric field names that Access creates if it cannot find any field names in the imported worksheet.

Figure 14.24 shows the Import Spreadsheet Options dialog box with the specifications for importing the modified BUDGET spreadsheet. The First Row Contains Field Names check box is checked, and the range of cells that contain the desired data (A4.V34) is visible in the Spreadsheet Range box. You can import a named range of cells by entering the name in this text box instead of the cell coordinates. You can use the Spreadsheet Range option to avoid importing rows that contain extra titles at the top or summary statistics at the bottom of the worksheet, which you would have to delete later in the

Figure 14.22

A spreadsheet ill-suited for importing into Access

	A	B	C	D	E	F	G	H	I
				Site					
4	Site	Operating Exp	GL #	6/86	7/86	8/86	Q1	9/86	10/8
5	Albany, NY			$28,675	$28,175	$28,675	$85,525	$28,675	$29,575
6		Salaries	1-1002	10000	10000	10000	30000	10000	1000
7		Supplies	1-2310	3000	2500	3000	8500	2500	300
8		Equipment	1-2543	4575	4575	4575	13725	4575	457
9		Lease Pmts	1-7862	9600	9600	9600	28800	9600	960
10		Advertising	1-8752	1500	1500	1500	4500	2000	240
11									
12	Memphis, TN			$28,200	$28,200	$28,200	$84,600	$28,200	$23,400
13		Salaries	2-1002	7500	7500	7500	22500	7500	750
14		Supplies	2-2310	2000	2000	2000	6000	2000	200
15		Equipment	2-2543	8000	8000	8000	24000	8000	270
16		Lease Pmts	2-7862	8200	8200	8200	24600	8200	820
17		Advertising	2-8752	2500	2500	2500	7500	2500	300
18									
19	Houston, TX			$54,500	$54,500	$54,500	$163,500	$58,000	$58,500
20		Salaries	4-1002	20000	20000	20000	60000	22000	2200
21		Supplies	4-2310	5000	5000	5000	15000	5000	500
22		Equipment	4-2543	9500	9500	9500	28500	11000	1100
23		Lease Pmts	4-7862	17000	17000	17000	51000	17000	1700

Microsoft Excel - BUDGET.XLS

Ready / CAPS

Figure 14.23

A spreadsheet well-suited for importing into Access

	A	B	C	D	E	F	G	H
				Site				
4	Site	Operating Exp	GL #	Month 1	Month 2	Month 3	Q1	Month 4
5	Albany, NY	Salaries	1-1002	10000	10000	10000	30000	10000
6	Albany, NY	Supplies	1-2310	3000	2500	3000	8500	2500
7	Albany, NY	Equipment	1-2543	4575	4575	4575	13725	4575
8	Albany, NY	Lease Pmts	1-7862	9600	9600	9600	28800	9600
9	Albany, NY	Advertising	1-8752	1500	1500	1500	4500	2000
10								
11	Memphis, TN	Salaries	2-1002	7500	7500	7500	22500	7500
12	Memphis, TN	Supplies	2-2310	2000	2000	2000	6000	2000
13	Memphis, TN	Equipment	2-2543	8000	8000	8000	24000	8000
14	Memphis, TN	Lease Pmts	2-7862	8200	8200	8200	24600	8200
15	Memphis, TN	Advertising	2-8752	2500	2500	2500	7500	2500
16								
17	Houston, TX	Salaries	4-1002	20000	20000	20000	60000	22000
18	Houston, TX	Supplies	4-2310	5000	5000	5000	15000	5000
19	Houston, TX	Equipment	4-2543	9500	9500	9500	28500	11000
20	Houston, TX	Lease Pmts	4-7862	17000	17000	17000	51000	17000
21	Houston, TX	Advertising	4-8752	3000	3000	3000	9000	3000
22								
23	Boise, ID	Salaries	3-1002	7700	7700	7700	23100	7700

Microsoft Excel - BUDGET2.XLS

Ready / CAPS

resulting Access table. This option is also useful for importing a portion of a complex spreadsheet that has other unrelated calculations in addition to the region of interest. Figure 14.25 shows the BUDGET2 table obtained by importing the BUDGET2.XLS worksheet. Note that Access automatically suppresses blank rows, so you need not edit the spreadsheet extensively to prepare it for importing.

Figure 14.24

Specifying the spreadsheet import options

Import Spreadsheet Options - BUDGET2.XLS

[X] First Row Contains Field Names

OK
Cancel

Table Options

( ) Create New Table

( ) Append to Existing Table: Area Codes

Spreadsheet Range: A4.V34

Figure 14.25

A table created by importing a spreadsheet

Microsoft Access - [Table: BUDGET2]

File   Edit   View   Records   Layout   Window   Help

Field: Site   New:

Site	Operating Exp	GL #	Month 1	Month 2	Month 3
Albany, NY	Salaries	1-1002	10000	10000	10000
Albany, NY	Supplies	1-2310	3000	2500	3000
Albany, NY	Equipment	1-2543	4575	4575	4575
Albany, NY	Lease Pmts	1-7862	9600	9600	9600
Albany, NY	Advertising	1-8752	1500	1500	1500
Memphis, TN	Salaries	2-1002	7500	7500	7500
Memphis, TN	Supplies	2-2310	2000	2000	2000
Memphis, TN	Equipment	2-2543	8000	8000	8000
Memphis, TN	Lease Pmts	2-7862	8200	8200	8200
Memphis, TN	Advertising	2-8752	2500	2500	2500
Houston, TX	Salaries	4-1002	20000	20000	20000
Houston, TX	Supplies	4-2310	5000	5000	5000
Houston, TX	Equipment	4-2543	9500	9500	9500
Houston, TX	Lease Pmts	4-7862	17000	17000	17000
Houston, TX	Advertising	4-8752	3000	3000	3000
Boise, ID	Salaries	3-1002	7700	7700	7700
Boise, ID	Supplies	3-2310	2100	2350	2350
Boise, ID	Equipment	3-2543	6500	6500	6500
Boise, ID	Lease Pmts	3-7862	8500	8500	8500
Boise, ID	Advertising	3-8752	2200	2200	2200
Minneapolis, MN (HQ)	Salaries	0-1002	31500	31500	31500
Minneapolis, MN (HQ)	Supplies	0-2310	7450	7450	7450
Minneapolis, MN (HQ)	Equipment	0-2543	8000	8000	8000
Minneapolis, MN (HQ)	Lease Pmts	0-7862	23550	23550	23550
Minneapolis, MN (HQ)	Advertising	0-8752	2450	2450	2450
Minneapolis, MN (HQ)	Recruiting	0-5519	0	2000	4000

Record: 1

Datasheet View   CAPS

Working with Xbase Files

Access can import and export dBASE III (and III PLUS), dBASE IV, and FoxPro databases. It can also attach dBASE III and dBASE IV, but *not* Fox-Pro databases, because it cannot read and update the FoxPro 2 index file format. Access will allow you to attach a FoxPro database that does not have an associated structural .CDX index, but this can be dangerous: If you later build a .CDX index for the file in FoxPro, updating it in Access can prevent FoxPro from reading it afterward. If you are familiar with Xbase, you know that you would rarely create a FoxPro database that does not have a structural .CDX index, so it is usually impractical to attach FoxPro files. This restriction does not apply to importing or exporting data, because Access does not read the indexes when it imports data, and it does not create any indexes when you export to any Xbase format.

Access and Xbase data types are reasonably compatible. No MS-DOS Xbase version supports OLE objects, and no Windows version of dBASE or FoxPro existed when Access was released, but you can export an OLE Object field to a FoxPro memo field. The data types are converted as follows:

Xbase Data Type	Import into Access	Export to Xbase
Character	Text	Text
Memo	Memo	Memo, OLE Object (FoxPro only)
Date	Date/Time	Date/Time
Numeric	Double	All Numeric
Float	Double	Not used
Logical	Yes/No	Yes/No

Access Text and Memo fields are highly compatible with Xbase Character and Memo fields, but when you export to dBASE III format, Access truncates Memo fields longer than the maximum length permitted in dBASE III (4,000 bytes). Because Xbase does not support times, Access drops the time portion of a date when it exports to any of these formats. Unfortunately, fields that store *only* times will yield erroneous dates (such as 12/30/99). When you export to the Xbase formats, Access preserves the sizes of Text fields, but because Xbase uses a different method for specifying the size of numeric fields (you enter the exact number of digits you want), Access makes all numeric fields the maximum length—20 digits with five decimal places. Figure 14.26 illustrates the structure of the FoxPro 2 database created by exporting the ACE Names table.

Figure 14.26

A FoxPro database created by exporting an Access table

```
Structure for database: C:\ACCESS\NAMES.DBF
Number of data records:     101
Date of last update    : 01/19/93
Memo file block size  :      64
Field  Field Name  Type       Width   Dec    Index
    1  ID_CODE     Character     10
    2  NAME_TYPE   Character      2
    3  NAME        Character     30
    4  SALUTATION  Character     25
    5  COMPANY     Character     30
    6  ADDRESS     Character     50
    7  CITY        Character     20
    8  STATE       Character      2
    9  ZIP         Character     10
   10  ADDRESS_TY  Character      1
   11  AREA_CODE   Character      3
   12  TELEPHONE   Character      8
   13  SOURCE      Character     10
   14  FIRST_CONT  Date           8
   15  LAST_CONTA  Date           8
   16  OK_TO_SEND  Logical        1
   17  OK_TO_CALL  Logical        1
   18  KEEP_FOREV  Logical        1
   19  MARKER      Character      5
   20  JOINED      Date           8
   21  LAST_RENEW  Date           8
   22  TOTAL_DEBI  Numeric       20     5
   23  TOTAL_CRED  Numeric       20     5
   24  LAST_CREDI  Date           8
   25  KEYWORD_1   Character     10
   26  KEYWORD_2   Character     10
   27  KEYWORD_3   Character     10
   28  NOTES       Memo          10
** Total **                     330
```

A seemingly minor but potentially annoying problem that you will encounter all too often when you export an Access table to any Xbase format is the difference in naming conventions. In Xbase databases, field names are limited to ten characters; they cannot contain spaces, and the only permitted punctuation mark is the underscore (_). Field names are not case sensitive, and are displayed in uppercase in most contexts by all Xbase versions. When you export to these formats, Access automatically converts spaces to underscores, removes all other punctuation, and truncates field names to the first ten characters. However, if two or more fields are identical up to the tenth character, Access cannot resolve the conflict, and it displays the alert box in

Figure 14.27 to inform you of the problem. The only solution is to temporarily change one of the redundant field names in the Access table before you export the table.

Figure 14.27

The alert box displayed when an exported database has redundant field names

Even if you do not have redundant field names, you will often want to change field names when you import or export Xbase files. After you import an Xbase database, you will usually want to lengthen field names to make them more descriptive, convert them to upper- and lowercase, add spaces, and remove underscores. When you export to an Xbase file, you may want to use more readable field names than those created by truncating fields (for example, ADDRTYPE or ADDTYPE instead of ADDRESS_TY or TOTCREDITS instead of TOTAL_CRED).

When you attach a dBASE III or dBASE IV table, Access must be able to update the indexes to reflect changes you make within Access. Although in dBASE IV, the production .MDX index has the same first name as the database, this may not be the only index in use, and in dBASE III, there is no way to identify the indexes that belong with a database. After you choose the database you want to attach, Access therefore displays another Open File dialog box like the one in Figure 14.28 to allow you to pick the indexes. When you attach a dBASE III table, the scrolling list of indexes includes only .NDX files (the only type supported by dBASE III), and when you attach a dBASE IV table, it includes both .NDX (standalone) and .MDX (multiple) indexes. Remember that you must choose the production .MDX file explicitly, although in theory Access could identify this file by its name (which has the same first name as the .DBF file). You can choose one or more indexes by using any of the standard methods (for example, you can highlight the file name and then click on the Select button, or you can double-click on the file name). Access confirms each index by displaying an alert box like the one in Figure 14.29. When you close the Select Index Files dialog box, Access attaches the database.

As you undoubtedly know if you have used dBASE, keeping the indexes up to date is crucial, so make sure to choose the indexes carefully. Any indexes that you fail to identify when you attach a dBASE database will not be updated to reflect new records and changes to the key fields that you make within Access. When you (or your co-workers) use the file in dBASE, you

Figure 14.28

Choosing indexes
for an attached
dBASE database

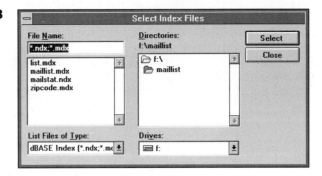

Figure 14.29

The alert box that
confirms an index
selection

may not be able to find the records added or updated in Access, and these records will be omitted from reports and calculations that depend on the indexes you overlooked. There is no danger of damage to the database itself, and there is an easy, if time-consuming way to correct all indexing problems—rebuild the out-of-date indexes in dBASE. However, an inexperienced user may not realize immediately what caused the problems, and may spend considerable time searching for the "missing" records.

If you examine an attached dBASE table in Table Design view, you will see that single fields that serve as index keys have the Yes (Duplicates OK) setting for the Indexed property, and multifield indexes are recorded in the property sheet, as they would be in an Access table. There is one important difference between dBASE and Access indexes that may cause serious problems—dBASE supports indexes based on expressions (which may include function references or constants as well as field names), and Access does not. Information about indexes based on expressions is not displayed in the structure in Table Design view, *and these indexes are not updated* when you edit the table in Access.

Access records the names of the selected indexes in a text file, located in the same directory as the dBASE database, with the same first name as the database and the extension .INF. For example, the following .INF file records the index information for a database called MAILLIST.DBF with a production .MDX file and two standalone .NDX indexes:

```
[dBASE IV]
MDX1=C:\DBASE4\MAILLIST.MDX
NDX2=C:\DBASE4\MAILDATE.NDX
NDX3=C:\DBASE4\MAILCODE.NDX
```

If you delete the .INF file and then reopen the attached table, Access simply assumes that there are no indexes associated with the table, and updating the table will throw the database out of synch with the indexes. Inadvertently choosing the same index twice when you attach a table will yield two identical lines in the .INF file, but this has no ill effects. When you delete an attached table, Access *does not* erase the .INF file, and if you later reattach the table, Access displays an alert box like the one in Figure 14.30 to inform you that it already has indexing information about the database. If you want to choose different indexes, or are not sure which indexes are represented in the .INF file, simply choose Yes to replace the existing .INF file and select the indexes again.

Figure 14.30

Reattaching a database

You can customize several aspects of the way Access handles dBASE data by making entries in the dBASE ISAM section of the MSACCESS.INI file (which is located in your Windows program directory). The default settings are as follows:

```
[dBase ISAM]
CollatingSequence=Ascii
Century=Off
Date=American
Mark=47
Deleted=Off
```

The CollatingSequence, which is roughly analogous to the New Database Sort Order option and determines the sort order used for dBASE files, accepts two settings, ASCII and International. The allowable values for the

Century, Date, and Deleted settings match those you can establish in dBASE with SET commands or entries in the CONFIG.DB file. The Mark setting has the same effect as the dBASE setting of the same name, but you must specify the mark (which is used to punctuate dates) by its ANSI code rather than as a text string; the default, 47, represents the slash (/), and another common setting is 45, which represents the dash (-).

Working with Paradox Tables

Access can import, export, and attach Paradox 3 and 3.5, but not Paradox 4 or Paradox for Windows files. Because these later versions can read and write the Paradox 3.*x* file format, you can export Access data by writing to the Paradox 3.*x* format, and you can import data copied (using Paradox 4 or Paradox for Windows) to Paradox 3.*x* format. However, you cannot attach tables created by these programs. Before you can import or attach a password-protected Paradox table, you must enter the password; when you attach a table, Access stores the password in your database so you do not have to enter it every time you open the table in the future.

Access and Paradox data types are reasonably compatible, except that Paradox 3.*x* does not support the Memo or OLE Object data types (Paradox 4 and Paradox for Windows do), so you cannot export fields of these data types. The data types are converted as follows:

Paradox Data Type	Import into Access	Export to Paradox
Alphanumeric	Text	Text
Date	Date/Time	Date/Time
Number	Double	Single, Double, Currency
Currency	Double	Not used
Short Number	Integer	Yes/No, Integer

When you export data to a Paradox table, Access preserves the sizes of Text fields. Because Paradox does not support times, Access drops the time portion of a date when it exports to any of these formats. However, fields that store only times may yield erroneous dates such as 12/30/1899 in the Paradox table. Paradox does not support a logical data type, and Yes/No fields are translated to Paradox short number fields (–1 for Yes and 0 for No) to match the way that Access stores Yes/No data internally. Note also that Access Currency fields are exported to Paradox Number fields, even though Paradox supports the Currency data type.

When you attach a Paradox table, Access does not ask for information about indexes, because it updates only the main index, which stores information about the primary key. Access can recognize this file by its name—the first name matches the name of the table, and the extension is .PX. If you examine an attached table in Table Design view, you will see that the Indexed property for the primary key field is set to Yes (No Duplicates). You can only update a Paradox table that has a primary key or unique index. It is especially important to remember that Access only updates Paradox secondary indexes that were designated as maintainable in Paradox. You must rebuild all other secondary indexes in Paradox after you add records in Access or change any of the key fields.

You can customize several aspects of the way Access handles Paradox data by making entries in the Paradox ISAM section of the MSACCESS.INI file (which is located in your Windows program directory). The Collating-Sequence determines the sort order used for Paradox files; this option is roughly analogous to the New Database Sort Order option and accepts the same settings—ASCII, International, Norwegian-Dutch and Swedish-Finnish. The other two options govern network operation. The ParadoxNetPath setting specifies the path name for the PARADOX.NET file, and the Paradox-UserName setting specifies the name displayed by Paradox when a record or table is unavailable because you have it locked in Access.

Working with Btrieve Files

To import, export, or attach Btrieve tables, you must have access to the Xtrieve dictionary files that describe your Btrieve tables—FILE.DDB, FIELD.DDF, and INDEX.DDF. When you try to import or attach a Btrieve table, Access reads the FILE.DDF file, which contains a list of the tables in the Btrieve database, and displays these table names in a scrolling list in the Import Tables or Attach Tables dialog box. Figure 14.31 illustrates this dialog box as it would appear when you import data from a Btrieve database that contains tables analogous to some of the ACE tables. You can import as many tables as you wish before closing this dialog box.

Figure 14.31

Importing Btrieve tables

Import Tables	
Tables in FILE.DDF:	Import
Names	Close
Contacts	
Transactions	

When you use the Export command to export to Btrieve, Access must be able to find the Btrieve dictionary files so it can update the dictionary to reflect the new table added to the Btrieve database. If you need to create a new Btrieve database from scratch, you cannot use the Export command; instead, you must define a macro that uses the TransferDatabase action to export one or more Access tables. Figure 14.32 illustrates a macro called Export to Btrieve, which exports the Names, Contacts, and Transactions tables. If Access does not find the Btrieve dictionary files in the path specified in the Database Name argument (or if you leave this argument blank), it creates them and adds the Access tables to this new Btrieve dictionary.

Figure 14.32

A macro that exports data to Btrieve

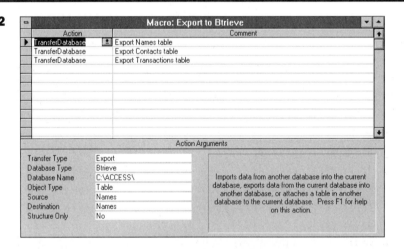

Access and Btrieve data types are very compatible, and they are converted as follows:

Btrieve	Import into Access	Export to Btrieve
String, Lstring, Zstring	Text	
String		Text
Note	Memo	Memo
Date, Time	Date/Time	Date/Time
4-byte Float	Single	Single
8-byte Float, Bfloat, Decimal, Numeric	Double	Double

1-byte Integer	Byte	Byte
2-byte Integer	Short Integer	Short Integer
4-byte Integer	Long Integer	Long Integer
Money	Currency	Currency
Logical	Yes/No	Yes/No
Lvar	OLE Object	OLE Object

Working with SQL Tables

To work with Microsoft SQL Server data on a remote server, you must first be able to connect to the server, and doing so requires that you install the Open Database Connectivity (ODBC) driver supplied with Access. This book assumes that you have installed this driver and have the necessary hardware connection to the server. On the assumption that you might be connected to more than one server, Access displays the dialog box pictured in Figure 14.33 to prompt you to choose the data source when you choose <SQL Database> as the external file type. (Because Access was not connected to a remote server when this figure was captured, no data sources are visible in the list box.) The first time you connect to a particular server, Access displays the login dialog box for that data source, and stores the login information you enter in the database so that you do not have to reenter it every time you want to communicate with the same server in the future. If Access is able to connect to the server, it displays a list of available tables and views, and you can choose as many as you wish before you close the dialog box. When you work with attached SQL data, you can edit tables, but not views, which are treated as read only.

Figure 14.33

Choosing the data source for an SQL Server table

> **SQL Data Sources**
>
> Select Data Source:
>
> [   ]
>
> [   ]
>
> OK   Cancel

Access and SQL Server data types are very compatible, except for OLE Objects, which are not supported by SQL Server. The data types are converted as follows:

SQL Server	Import into Access	Export to SQL Server
Char	Text	
Text	Memo	Memo
Varchar, Longtext	Text	Text
DateTime, SmallDateTime	Date/Time	Date/Time
Single	Single	
Real	Text	
Float, Double	Double	Single, Double
Tinyint, Byte	Byte	Byte
Smallint, Short	Integer	Integer
Int, Long	Long Integer	Long Integer, Counter
Money	Currency	Currency
SmallMoney	Text	
Bit, Boolean	Yes/No	Yes/No
Image, LongBinary	OLE Object	OLE Object

Summary

This chapter described a variety of methods for exchanging data with other programs by importing, exporting, and attaching tables. As you can see from the examples and the caveats in this chapter, sharing data with programs that store and manipulate data in completely different ways is not always a straightforward proposition, even when Access can read the other program's file format. In most cases, some structural rearrangements will be necessary after you import or export a table, and when you exchange files with colleagues and co-workers, you may be forced to assume sole responsibility for delivering the required table structure. Depending on your familiarity with the external program, you may prefer to use either that program or Access to rearrange the structure. Some experimentation may be required to work out the best and most efficient method for handling a particular data exchange problem.

All of the techniques described in this chapter involve working with external *data* within Access, either by attaching a table so you can update it "live" or by importing or exporting records in a batch process. Chapter 15 introduces methods based on OLE (object linking and embedding) and DDE (dynamic data exchange) for working with external data by starting up the program that created it from within Access.

15

Working with
External Objects

Using OLE Objects

Using DDE

Using Graphs in Access
Forms

CHAPTER 14 DESCRIBED TWO WAYS OF TREATING A DATA FILE CREATED by a variety of other programs as equivalent to a table created and updated solely within Access—importing a file to create a new table and attaching an external data file so that you can continue to update it both in Access and in the program that created it. When you import a file, the data retains those properties that are compatible with Access tables (such as field lengths and data types), but it loses attributes that you could not define and manipulate in Access. For example, when you import a spreadsheet, the resulting table contains the values displayed in the cells, not the formulas used to calculate these values. In contrast, when you attach a file, Access must allow you to update the data without compromising your ability to continue working with the file in the external application that created it. Access therefore only allows you to attach files created by other database programs, which manipulate data in much the same way as Access.

Access also allows you to work with external objects created by other Windows programs *by launching the applications that created them*, and to add these objects to Access tables, forms, and reports in such a way that they retain their essential characteristics. To cite just a few examples, you could place a graphic such as a scanned photograph or a company logo created in a drawing program on an Access form or report, play back prerecorded sound or video, display a value calculated by a spreadsheet on a form or report, or store an entire spreadsheet or word processor document in a field in an Access table.

Access provides two different methods for working with external objects. *Object linking and embedding* (*OLE*) enables you to either create a linkage to an external object or store an independent copy of the object in an Access table, form, or report. (The differences between linking and embedding are described in more detail later in this chapter.) You can also display individual items of data stored in documents created in an external program by using *dynamic data exchange* (*DDE*). For example, you might use a complex spreadsheet to compute a few crucial values, and use DDE to insert these numbers, rather than the entire spreadsheet, into an Access report. As you may know if you have used other Windows programs, neither OLE nor DDE is unique to Access—many other Windows programs (not only Microsoft programs) also support one or both of these standards for sharing data. If you use other Windows programs, you may also be able to use OLE or DDE from these applications to draw on data stored in Access tables.

This chapter describes some typical strategies for using OLE and DDE to work with objects created by a variety of other programs. Most of the techniques for working with graphic objects are illustrated with Paintbrush (which is included with every copy of Windows), so you can try all of these examples. If you also have a Windows word processor or spreadsheet program, you will be able to follow along with the additional examples. More complex OLE techniques that require specialized hardware (such as working with sound and video) are beyond the scope of this book. This chapter describes in some detail one application that supports OLE—Microsoft Graph, which is packaged with Access. When you choose Graph from the first FormWizard dialog box to define a new graph form or use the toolbox to add a graph object to an existing form or report, Access invokes this program to create the graph, which is linked via OLE to your Access document.

Using OLE Objects

You can use OLE to incorporate objects created by other applications into an Access database. Like a control on a form or report, an OLE object can either be *bound* or *unbound*. Bound OLE objects are stored in OLE Object fields, and you can use these objects in forms and reports more or less the way you use text boxes. Unbound OLE objects, which are not associated with any tables, exist only on forms or reports, where they play a role roughly equivalent to label objects. To illustrate the difference, you might use an OLE Object field in a name and address table in a personnel database to store a scanned photograph of each employee (to see an example of this, look at the Employees table in the Northwind Traders sample database supplied with Access). To incorporate a scanned photograph of your company headquarters into your letterhead or add a scanned signature to a personalized letter, you would add the image to the report as an unbound OLE object. Figure 15.1 illustrates a new version of the thank you letter described in Chapter 11 in which the ACE logo is an unbound OLE object created using Microsoft WordArt (a utility packaged with Word for Windows).

As the term "object *linking* and *embedding*" implies, Access supports two different methods for working with OLE objects, and both are applicable to bound as well as unbound objects. When you *embed* an external object in an Access table, form, or report, Access stores a complete copy of the object in your database. The object may or may not also exist outside of the database. If you call up an external application from within Access to create a brand new embedded object (rather than inserting a document created previously using the external application), there is only one copy of the object—the one embedded in your database. When you embed a previously created document in an Access database, you will end up with two copies of the object—the one stored in the database and the original, which remains wherever it was saved by the program that created it. For example, the photographs in the Employees table in the Northwind Traders application are embedded in the NWIND database, not stored in separate disk files, and the originals are located on the hard disk of some computer at Microsoft's corporate headquarters. If you modify the original document outside of Access after embedding an object in a database, the changes are not reflected in the OLE object stored in your

Figure 15.1

Using an unbound
OLE object to
display a graphic

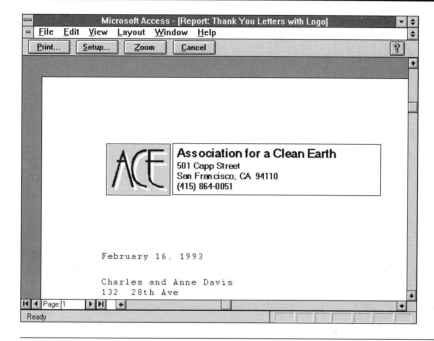

database. As you can see from the Northwind Traders example, embedding
objects makes it very easy to transport them, because they are housed within
the same .MDB file that stores all the other components of the database.
Even when you never intend to move a database off the PC on which it was
created, this separation between the original object and the embedded copy
is desirable. For example, you might want to modify a spreadsheet created by
a co-worker in ways relevant only to your Access application, while its designer continues to use it in the original form.

   When you define a *link* between an OLE object in an Access database
and a document created by an external application, Access stores in your
database only the information required to find the file that stores the object.
When you display the OLE object, you are looking at the original document,
which is stored in a separate disk file, and if you launch the program that created it from outside of Access and modify the object, you will see the changes
the next time you examine the OLE object in Access. For this reason, linking
is preferable to embedding for documents that you—or your co-workers—
want to continue updating independent of your Access application. Because
there is only one copy of the document, anyone who opens it is always working with the most current version. For the same reason, a linked object occupies less disk space than an embedded object, and when you work with large

graphics files, the savings in disk space can be significant. Note, however, that not all programs that support OLE permit linking, so you may not always have this choice.

You might view the difference between linking and embedding an OLE object as analogous to the difference between importing a data file (which creates a copy stored in an Access table) and attaching it (which establishes a link to a data file stored outside of Access). Whether you choose linking or embedding, the linkage between Access and the program that created an OLE object is an active one, and you can *launch* (start) the external program *from within Access* to execute or modify the object. For example, after embedding the ACE logo visible in Figure 15.1 in the Thank You Letters report, you could call up WordArt to edit the image simply by double-clicking on the object in Report Design view. (If you do not have WordArt, you will see the error message pictured later in Figure 15.3 if you try this.)

In the context of a particular OLE linkage, the external application used to create and edit an OLE object is called the *server* and the application in which you are displaying the object is called the *client*. If you are unfamiliar with these terms, they are derived from the common usage of the word "client" for a computer or program that requests services, and the word "server" for a computer or program that fulfills these requests. Most applications that support OLE, including Access, can function as either a client or a server. This chapter, which takes the point of view of an Access user, concentrates on using Access as the client to link to various OLE servers.

Embedding Unbound OLE Objects in Forms and Reports

Despite the difference between bound and unbound OLE objects, the methods that you use to add these objects to a form or report are very similar. You can use the toolbox, which includes command buttons that represent bound and unbound OLE objects, either alone or, for bound OLE objects, in combination with the field list. In both cases, you can either link or embed a previously created object, or launch the server application and create the object on the fly. To define an unbound embedded OLE object, you use the following steps:

1. Make sure that the toolbox is visible on the screen.

2. Click on the Unbound Object button in the toolbox.

3. Position the crosshair symbol in the mouse pointer where you want the upper-left corner of the object frame.

4. Define the size of the object frame using one of the following methods:

   ■ To create an object of the standard size (3 inches wide by 2 inches high), click the left mouse button.

■ To place the object on the main form and define its size, press and hold the left mouse button, drag the mouse pointer to the location of the lower-right corner of the frame, and release the mouse button.

When you release the mouse button, Access displays the dialog box shown in Figure 15.2 to enable you to choose the type of object you want to embed.

Figure 15.2

Choosing the type of OLE object

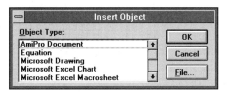

You can also call up the Insert Object dialog box to embed an OLE object by choosing the Insert Object option from the Edit menu. When you use the Insert Object option, Access places the object in the upper-left corner of the current document section, but you can later move it anywhere you wish. Whichever method you choose, don't worry too much about the size or location of the object frame, because you will probably end up moving and resizing it several times before you are satisfied with the appearance of the document.

When you try these methods yourself, the scrolling list of object types in the Insert Object dialog box may not exactly match the choices visible in Figure 15.2, because the list always reflects only document types supported by the OLE applications that you currently have installed on your hard disk. Thus, if you do not have Lotus Ami Pro, you will not see "AmiPro Document" (the first item in the list in Figure 15.2), and if you do not have Excel, the list will not include Microsoft Excel Chart, Microsoft Excel Macrosheet, or Microsoft Excel Worksheet (not visible in Figure 15.2). If you install a new Windows program that can function as an OLE server, you will see this program's document format(s) the next time you open the Insert Object dialog box.

The list of object types is derived from the *registration database*, a file called REG.DAT, which stores the information required to associate a document file with the application used to create and edit it and to establish DDE links (described later in this chapter) to the document. The registration database is stored in the Windows program subdirectory, and it is updated automatically whenever you install any program that supports OLE. If you move an OLE application to another subdirectory by copying the files (rather than by reinstalling it), the registration database will be out of date, Windows will not be able to find the program, and Access will display the alert box pictured in Figure 15.3 when you try to add or edit an OLE object

created by the program. If you know how to use the registration editor program (REGEDIT.EXE), you can follow the advice in this alert box and run
this program from the Program Manager or File Manager to edit the command line used to start up the application. However, you can usually correct
the problem simply by running the application from outside of Access (from
the Program Manager or File Manager). Occasionally, neither method will
work, and you will have to reinstall the program to ensure that the registration database is updated.

Figure 15.3

The alert box
displayed if Access
cannot find an
external application

Once the Insert Object dialog box is open, you can embed a previously
created document that is already stored in a disk file by clicking on the File
button to invoke a standard Open File dialog box like the one shown in Figure 15.4. If you want to launch the server application immediately to create a
new document, select the desired object type from the scrolling list in the Insert Object dialog box by using any of the standard methods (double-click on
the name, highlight the name then press Enter or click on the OK button).
For example, if you choose Paintbrush Picture, Access launches Paintbrush.

Figure 15.4

Choosing the
external
document file

With just a few differences, the server application behaves much as it would if you had started it independently from the Program Manager or File Manager—you can switch at will to any other active application, and if you wish, you can load and edit an existing document file rather than creating a new one from scratch. However, the document title bar reminds you that you are editing an object that will be stored in an Access database. For example, in Paintbrush, the title for the application window is "Paintbrush—Paintbrush Picture in Microsoft Access," and in Word for Windows, it is "Object in Microsoft Access." Because you are saving the document in your Access database rather than as a separate file on disk, the usual Save option on the File menu is replaced by an option labeled Update. However, you can use the Save As option to save the current document in a separate disk file. You might want to use the Update option several times during a lengthy editing session to ensure that the embedded object in your Access document reflects your most recent changes. The File menu also contains an Exit and Return to Microsoft Access option, which automatically updates the object in Access before exiting. If you have modified the document since the last time you updated it, the alert box pictured in Figure 15.5 appears to remind you that the document has changed and give you the option to update the embedded object or discard your changes. Note that updating the document affects only the copy embedded in your Access database, not a separate copy stored on disk with the Save As option.

Figure 15.5

The alert box displayed to remind you to update an embedded object

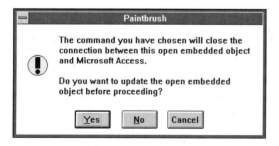

If you display the property sheet for an unbound OLE object, you will see that the object type is stored in the OLE Class property. However, you cannot change the type of object by editing this entry in the property sheet, even if you know the correct description; attempting to edit the OLE Class property always invokes the alert box shown in Figure 15.6. If you change your mind about the type of object you want to display in an unbound object frame, you must delete the object frame and add a new one of the correct type.

Figure 15.6

The alert box displayed if you try to edit the OLE Class property

Adding the ACE Logo to a Report

To practice these methods, you can use Paintbrush to design a logo for the Association for a Clean Earth and embed this graphic in the Committee Memberships report, using the following steps:

1. Open the Committee Memberships report in Report Design view, and maximize the Report Design window.

2. Make sure that the toolbox is visible and that it does not obscure the vertical ruler at the left side of the window.

3. Click on the Unbound Object button in the toolbox, and use the mouse to draw a frame approximately 5 inches wide and $1\frac{1}{2}$ inches high in the report header section, with the upper-left corner at about the 1-inch mark in both rulers (you will fine-tune the size and position of the object later).

4. Choose Paintbrush Picture from the list of object types in the Insert Object dialog box, and select OK to launch Paintbrush.

5. In the Paintbrush application window, choose Fonts from the Text menu to display the Font dialog box pictured in Figure 15.7. Select Arial or a similar font, set the font style to Italic, set the font size to 48 points, and select OK to close the Font dialog box.

6. Select Shadow from the Text menu, and then right-click (press the *right* mouse button) on the dark gray color sample at the bottom of the window to select the shadow color.

7. Click on the Text button on the left side of the Paintbrush window (the button with "abc" on its face), and then click in the window to display an insertion point. Make sure that you can see the whole insertion point, which is the full height of the selected font (if necessary, click again in a new position), and then type **ACE**.

8. Click anywhere else on the form to indicate that you are finished editing the text "ACE."

Figure 15.7

Customizing the text font in Paintbrush

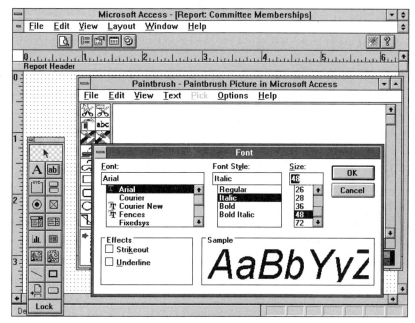

9. Redisplay the Font dialog box by choosing Fonts from the Text menu, set the font style to Regular, set the font size to 16 points, check the Underline box in the Effects region, and close the Font dialog box.

10. Select the Shadow option again from the Text menu to turn off the shadow effect, and then right-click on the white color sample at the bottom of the window to reset the background color to white.

11. Click under the "A" in "ACE," making sure that the insertion point does not overlap the letters, and type **Association for a Clean Earth**. Your screen should look approximately like Figure 15.8.

12. Choose Exit & Return to Microsoft Access from the File menu to close the Paintbrush window and return to Access. Choose Yes from the alert box that asks whether you want to update the embedded object before exiting from Paintbrush. You should see your logo appear within the bound object frame on the report.

13. Use the Save As option on the File menu to save the report under the name **Committee Memberships with Logo**.

Figure 15.8

The ACE logo in Paintbrush

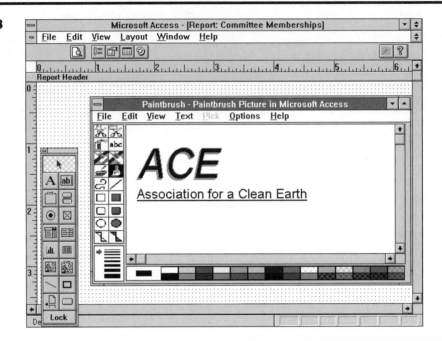

Using the Clipboard to Embed or Link OLE Objects

The methods described in the previous sections always create embedded objects. You can embed or link an OLE object to a control in a form or report by copying it to the Clipboard and then pasting it into the Access document, using the following steps:

1. Open the Access document in Design view.

2. Switch to the Program Manager or the File Manager, and start up the server application.

3. Select the portion of the document that you want to embed in the Access document, and use the Copy command on the Edit menu (with most Windows programs you can also press Ctrl+C) to transfer the selected material to the Clipboard.

4. Return to the Access document Design window and use the Paste, Paste Special, or Paste Link option on the Edit menu (or press Ctrl+V) to paste the contents of the Clipboard into the document.

If you use the Paste option, Access automatically creates an embedded unbound object frame in the upper-left corner of the current document section, but you can move and/or resize the object frame as necessary. You can gain more control over the format of the OLE object by choosing the Paste Special option from the Edit menu instead of Paste. As you may know, Windows stores data on the Clipboard in several formats, and the Paste Special option invokes a dialog box like the one in Figure 15.9, which displays as much information as possible about the object and allows you to choose the data format you want to use. This description always includes the name of the application that created the object, and, if the object is already stored in a disk file, the full path name of this file. The rest of the information depends on the server application; as you can see in Figure 15.9, the description of a Paintbrush picture includes the four coordinates of its corners. If there is no entry in the registration database that describes the data on the Clipboard, the source is listed as "Unknown," and the only option in the scrolling list of data types is Bitmap.

Figure 15.9

Using the Paste Special option to insert the contents of the Clipboard

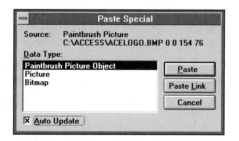

The first option in the scrolling list of data types is the default object type—the type that Access would create if you had used the Paste option rather than Paste Special. If you choose the Picture or Bitmap option, Access pastes the object into the Access document as a passive image, which retains no connection to the application that created it. You should only choose this option if you are sure you will not have to call up the server application to edit the object, or in circumstances where it may not be possible to do so. For example, if you add a WordArt file to a document (such as the Thank You Letters with Logo report) that you plan to give to another Access user who does not have WordArt, you can use this option to ensure that no error messages will result from an attempt to edit the graphic. (You can use the Change to Picture option to convert any OLE object to a static picture later, as described in more detail in the section "Displaying and Editing Embedded OLE Objects.")

When you use the Paste Special option to copy all or part of a spreadsheet or word processor document, the list of data types includes Text (this option is not visible in Figure 15.9 because a Paintbrush Picture object, like most graphics, cannot be treated as text). Choosing the Text option creates a *label* rather than an unbound OLE object frame, with a caption derived from the data on the Clipboard. Because the data is treated as text, not as a graphic image, all formatting applied in the server application (such as the font, font size, and attributes such as boldfacing or underlining) is lost, and you must format the text in Access as you would any other label.

NOTE. *This is the only method that you can use to create an Access object derived from an application that does not support OLE, such as a program running in a DOS window.*

To exit from the Paste Special dialog box and create an embedded OLE object by pasting the data on the Clipboard into the current document, choose the Paste button. If you choose the Paste Link button, Access creates an OLE link to an external document rather than embedding a copy in your Access form. Ideally, you should save the document on disk using the server application before you select this option. Access cannot verify that you have done so, but the server application can: If you return to the server application and attempt to close the document without saving it, the program displays an alert box like the one in Figure 15.10 to warn you that the document is linked to an object in a client application. If you choose OK to close the document without saving it, Access ignores all subsequent attempts to edit the linked object.

Figure 15.10

The alert box displayed when you exit the server application without saving a linked document

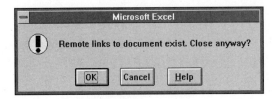

You can also create an OLE link by selecting the Paste Link option on the Edit menu instead of Paste or Paste Special. Because Access already knows the source of the data on the Clipboard, it displays a very simple dialog box, which is illustrated in Figure 15.11. Apart from the usual OK and Cancel buttons, the only option is the Auto Update check box, which determines whether Windows automatically updates the linked object in your Access document to reflect changes made in the server application. Your selection in the Paste Link dialog box specifies the setting for the Update

Method property, which can take on the values Automatic and Manual; if you change your mind later, you can simply edit this entry in the object property sheet. This option is irrelevant for embedded objects, which cannot be updated by launching the server application from outside of Access.

Figure 15.11
The Paste Link
dialog box

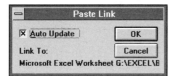

Displaying and Editing Embedded OLE Objects

The way that Access displays or prints an OLE object depends on the type of document that serves as the data source. Most spreadsheets and graphic images, including documents created by Excel, Lotus 1-2-3 for Windows, Word-Art, Microsoft Graph, Paintbrush, and other paint programs, are displayed and printed approximately as they would appear in a document window in the server application (of course, if you do not have a color printer, colors in a graphic are printed as shades of gray). Objects that are *run* or *played back* rather than displayed, such as digitized sound or video files, are displayed and printed on Access documents as icons that match the ones used in the Program Manager window to represent the server applications that created them. Unfortunately, this is also the case for complex objects such as word processor documents. While it would make little sense to try to print a video image, you might have hoped to display the contents of a word processor file on an Access form or print one in a report.

When an OLE object is selected in Form Design view or Report Design view, the Edit menu includes an option that invokes a submenu of additional options applicable to objects of that type. The exact wording of this option changes to reflect the type of object—for example, it might read "MS WordArt Object" or "Paintbrush Picture Object"—but it always includes the word "Object," and it will hereafter be referred to generically as the "Object option." Choosing this option calls up a submenu of commands that you can use to manipulate the object. This submenu is illustrated in Figure 15.12 for a graphic object that displays a Paintbrush picture. The first option on the Object menu (Edit) always launches the server application to enable you to edit the object (you can also double-click in the object, as described shortly). For objects such as recorded sounds or videos, there is also a Play option, which you can use to play back the recording.

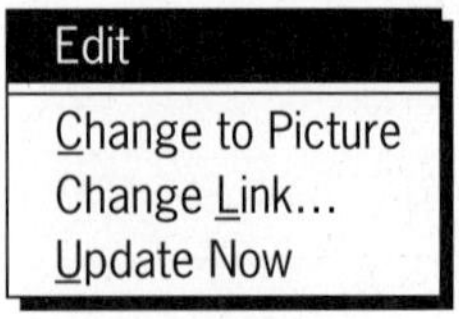

Figure 15.12

The options on the
Object menu

Edit
Change to Picture
Change **L**ink...
Update Now

The Change to Picture option converts an embedded object to a static picture so that it is no longer linked to the application that created it and therefore cannot be modified. As noted earlier, you can use this option to prevent editing once you are satisfied with the appearance of a graphic object such as a logo, or to convert an OLE object to a format that you can safely give to other Access users who do not have the server application used to create it. The Update Now option updates the object in the form to reflect the latest changes that may have been made in the source application independent of Access. This option is most useful for linked (rather than embedded) objects for which you chose the Manual update option.

You can also open the server application to edit some types of OLE objects, such as graphics, word processor documents, and spreadsheets, by double-clicking in the object. For other objects, such as sound files created using the Sound Recorder or recorded video images, double-clicking on the object *plays back* the recorded material rather than allowing you to edit it. Strictly speaking, double-clicking in an OLE object is not equivalent to choosing Edit from the Object submenu. Double-clicking in the object always enables you to *use* an object, and for some types of objects, such as spreadsheets and word processor documents, using the object entails editing it; for others, such as sound or video recordings, using the object means playing it back.

NOTE. *Remember that you can only edit OLE objects, which retain their connection to the application that created them; you cannot edit static labels created by pasting in an object as text from the Clipboard.*

Like all other controls that you can use in reports and forms, OLE objects are described by their properties. By default, Access sets the Enabled property to No for every unbound OLE object. The Object option on the Edit menu is therefore disabled, and double-clicking in the object in Form view has no effect. If you want to be able to edit or use the object in Form view, you must reset the Enabled property to Yes. As you might guess, this property is irrelevant for objects in reports, which do not allow you to edit data of any type.

As noted earlier in this chapter, the OLE Class property identifies the source and type of the object. For an embedded object, which has no independent existence outside your database (even if it was originally created by copying an existing object), this property supplies all the information that Access needs to call up the server application to display or edit the document. For linked objects, the property sheet includes additional entries that further describe the object. The Source Object property stores the full path name of the linked document, and the Item property stores additional information that describes the linked data—for example, the coordinates of a Paintbrush picture or a range of cells in a spreadsheet. If you use Excel, note that Access displays the coordinates using numbers for both rows and columns—for example, R13C7 rather than G13—regardless of the display style in effect when you edit the worksheet in Excel.

NOTE. *Access displays no visual indicator, even in Form Design view or Report Design view, to distinguish embedded objects from linked objects. The best way to determine which objects are linked is to display the property sheet and check for the presence of the Source Object and Item properties.*

The Scaling property determines how Access adjusts the size of the image displayed in an OLE object frame. This property can take on three values, which have the following effects:

Setting	Meaning
Clip	Displays as much of the object as will fit within the current size of the frame without changing its size
Scale	Stretches the object both horizontally and vertically to match the current size of the frame
Zoom	Enlarges the object as much as possible within the frame without altering its proportions

Figure 15.13 illustrates the effects of using all three scaling options to define the size of an OLE object created by typing the name Jerry Allen in the Script font in Paintbrush (you will create this object in the next section). The best way to precisely match an object to its frame without altering its size or proportions is to retain the Clip setting for the Scaling property (the default), and use the Size to Fit option on the Layout menu to adjust the size of the object frame. If you need to view all of a very large object (such as a large spreadsheet) without distorting it, you should choose the Zoom setting. The Scale option is ideal for making small (and often, for graphic images, imperceptible) adjustments in the size of an object to precisely match the size of the frame.

Figure 15.13

Using the Scaling
property to adjust
the size of an
OLE object

```
┌─────────────────────────────────────────────────────────┐
│ □                    Form: Signatures            ▼ ▲      │
│ ▶  Name:           Jerry Allen                       ↕    │
│                    ┌──────────────────────────┐          │
│    Signature (Clip):                                      │
│                    │  Jerry Allen             │           │
│                    └──────────────────────────┘           │
│                    ┌──────────────────────────┐          │
│    Signature (Scale):                                     │
│                    │  Jerry Allen             │           │
│                    └──────────────────────────┘           │
│                    ┌──────────────────────────┐          │
│    Signature (Zoom):                                      │
│                    │  Jerry Allen             │           │
│                    └──────────────────────────┘           │
│                                                       ↓   │
│ |◀ ◀ Record: 1    ▶ ▶|                                    │
└─────────────────────────────────────────────────────────┘
```

To finish adding the ACE logo to the Committee Memberships report, use the following steps:

1. Open the Committee Memberships with Logo report in Report Design view if it is not still open.

2. Double-click in the embedded object frame in the report header section to reopen Paintbrush.

3. Click on the Pick button on the left side of the Paintbrush window (the one with a rectangle and a pair of scissors on its face). This button turns the mouse pointer into a cross-hair and allows you to use the mouse to select part of a document rather than to draw. Position the cross-hair above and to the left of the "A" in "ACE," press and hold the left mouse button, and drag the mouse pointer to a position just below and to the right of the "E" so that only the letters "ACE" are enclosed in the rectangle that delineates your selection.

4. Select Copy To from the Edit menu to save the selected image in a disk file called ACELOGO.BMP. If necessary, use the Drives and/or Directories options in the Copy To dialog box to ensure that the file is saved in the Access program directory.

5. Select Open from the File menu, and load the newly saved bitmap file into Paintbrush.

6. Using the Pick tool, select the entire image, and then select Copy from the Edit menu or press Ctrl+C to copy the selected text to the Clipboard.

7. Close the Paintbrush window using any method you wish.

8. Expand the page header section of the report to a height of 1 inch.

9. Click anywhere in the page header section to select it, and then choose Paste Link from the Edit menu. Make sure that Auto Update is checked, and select OK to establish an OLE link to the ACELOGO.BMP file.

10. If the color palette is not already visible, click on the Palette command button in the tool bar or select Palette from the Layout menu to display it.

11. If the Clear check box to the right of the Border color samples is checked, click in this check box to uncheck it and make the border of the unbound object frame visible. Select the border color by clicking on the black color sample in the Border row.

12. Make sure that the property sheet is visible on the screen, and set the Scaling property for the logo to Scale. Resize the object frame in the page header, and observe that Access adjusts the graphic to match. Leave the logo any size you like.

13. Preview the report on the screen or print the second page, which is illustrated in Figure 15.14 as it appears in Print Preview mode. In this figure, the logo object frame is $2\frac{1}{2}$ inches wide and $\frac{11}{16}$ inch high.

14. Save the report and close it.

Figure 15.14

An unbound OLE object created using the Clipboard

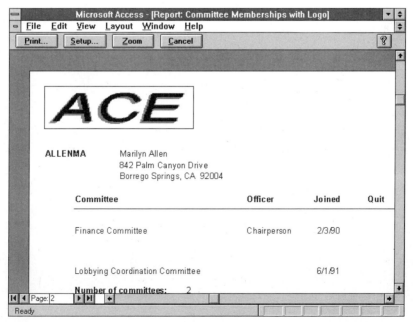

15. Reopen Paintbrush from the Program Manager or File Manager.

16. Select Open from the File menu, and load the ACELOGO.BMP file back into Paintbrush.

17. Click on the red color sample to change the foreground color.

18. Click on the Paint Roller tool (the fourth button from the top in the left column of tool buttons), and then click in the background of the image to change its color to red.

19. Save the file and close the Paintbrush window.

20. Preview the Committee Memberships with Logo report again (or print it if you have a color printer), and note that the report reflects the change you just made to the linked logo in the page header.

Working with Bound OLE Objects

To store an object created by an external program in an Access table, you must first add an OLE Object field to the structure. You can then associate this field with any document created by a program that supports OLE. A table can contain more than one OLE Object field, and the field does not have to store the same type of object in every record. To list just a few examples, you might use OLE Object fields to store a photograph or signature in a personnel table; include in an accounting database a spreadsheet used to compute a budget, an estimate for a construction project, or a loan payment schedule; embed the full text of a contract created using a word processor in a client table; or include a copy of a blueprint or engineering drawing in a project management database. As a simple example, Figure 15.15 illustrates a form used to update a new version of the Committee Names table that includes an OLE Object field called Budget, which stores a spreadsheet used to calculate the committee budget. If you have a Windows spreadsheet program, you might try reproducing this form after you finish reading this section.

You can add a bound OLE object to a form or report by using the same basic method described in Chapter 10 for creating bound text boxes. The easiest method is to simply drag the field name from the field list; when you place an OLE Object field on a document, Access automatically creates a bound object control. If you prefer, you can use the toolbox and field list together as you would to create any other type of control, as follows:

1. Make sure that the toolbox and field list are both visible on the screen.

2. Click on the Bound Object button in the toolbox.

3. Use the mouse to drag an OLE Object field from the field list onto the form or report.

Figure 15.15
A form that displays a bound OLE object

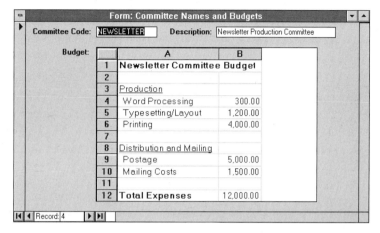

Form: Committee Names and Budgets

Committee Code: NEWSLETTER   Description: Newsletter Production Committee

Budget:

	A	B
1	Newsletter Committee Budget	
2		
3	Production	
4	Word Processing	300.00
5	Typesetting/Layout	1,200.00
6	Printing	4,000.00
7		
8	Distribution and Mailing	
9	Postage	5,000.00
10	Mailing Costs	1,500.00
11		
12	Total Expenses	12,000.00

Record: 4

4. Define the size of the object frame using one of the following methods:

- To create an object of the standard size (3 inches wide by 2 inches high), click the left mouse button.

- To place the object on the main form and define its size, press and hold the left mouse button, drag the mouse pointer to the location of the lower-right corner of the frame, and release the mouse button.

Finally, you can use the toolbox alone to define the control and identify the source field later by entering its name in the Control Source property. Regardless of which method you use to create a bound object frame, Access allows you to select any field from the field list or the Control Source property combo box. However, it makes little sense to choose any type of field except OLE Object, and if you do (for example, if you choose a Text or Memo field), Access displays the object frame empty on the form or report, even if the field contains data.

There is no need to specify the type of data you want to display in a bound object frame, and in fact there is no way to do so in Form Design view or Report Design view. You can embed *any type of OLE object* in an OLE Object field, and you need not use the same type of object in each record in a table, although you will probably do so more often than not.

The methods that you use to insert an object into an OLE Object field are the same in Datasheet view and in Form view, although the object is displayed differently. In Datasheet view, Access displays a phrase that describes the source of the object, such as "Paintbrush Picture" or "Microsoft Excel Worksheet." (These are the same descriptions displayed in the OLE Class entry in the property sheet for an unbound object on a form or report.) In a form or report, Access displays or prints a bound object exactly as it would an unbound object of the same type (either as a graphic image or as an icon).

Once you have copied data into an OLE object field, you can launch the server application to edit the object either by double-clicking in the field or by selecting the Edit option from the submenu invoked by choosing the Object option from the Edit menu. For fields that store objects such as sound or video recordings, you would instead select the Play option to play back the recording. However, because an OLE object field has no inherent connection to any particular OLE server application, you cannot simply double-click in an empty OLE object field to insert a new object. To create an embedded OLE object, you can either use the Insert Object option on the Edit menu, or you can open the server application, copy the object to the Clipboard, and then choose Paste Special. To create an OLE link, you *must* copy the object to the Clipboard and then choose Paste Link from the Edit menu. All of these methods work exactly as described earlier in this chapter in the section on creating unbound OLE objects.

To experiment with OLE Object fields, try adding a field to the Names table to store a signature. In this example, you will simulate the signature by creating it in Paintbrush; in a real application, you might use a scanner to store a signature or photograph in a disk file, and then embed a copy of this file in your database. Begin by creating two signatures in Paintbrush, as follows:

1. From the Program manager, start Paintbrush.

2. Choose Fonts from the Text menu to display the Font dialog box. Select the Script font, set the font style to Regular, set the font size to 20 points, and select OK to close the Font dialog box.

3. Click on the dark blue color sample at the bottom of the window to change the text color.

4. Click on the Text button on the left side of the Paintbrush window (the button with "abc" on its face), and then click in the upper-left corner of the window to display an insertion point. Type the name **Marilyn Allen**.

5. To save only the portion of the Paintbrush document that contains the signature (rather than the full window), click on the Pick tool, and use the mouse to select a rectangular region that just barely encloses the signature. Select Copy To from the Edit menu, and enter a file name that places the file in your Access program directory. For example, if Access is installed in a subdirectory called ACCESS on drive C, enter **C:\ACCESS\ALLENM.BMP**.

6. Click on the Text button, and then click below the first "signature" in the Paintbrush window. Select Italic from the Text menu, and then type **Jerry Allen**.

7. Use the same method as in step 5 to save the signature in a file called **ALLENJ.BMP** in your Access program directory.

8. Close the Paintbrush program without saving the current document (which contains both signatures).

Next, add the Signature field to the Names table and enter one signature in Datasheet view:

1. Open the Names table in Table Design view.

2. Add a new field named Signature at the end of the structure, and choose OLE Object as the data type.

3. Save the new structure.

4. Open the Names table in Datasheet view.

5. Click on the field selector at the top of the ID Code column, and select the Freeze Columns option from the Layout menu.

6. Press the End key to move to the last field in the first record.

7. Select Insert Object from the Edit menu, and then select the File button in the Insert Object dialog box.

8. In the Insert Object from File dialog box, make sure that the scrolling list of file names displays bitmap files (files with the .BMP extension). You can do this either by choosing Paintbrush Picture (*.bmp) from the List Files of Type combo box or by entering ***.bmp** in the File Name text box. Choose ALLENJ.BMP, and then close the dialog box. Access displays "Paintbrush Picture" in the Signature field.

9. Double-click in the Signature field to call up Paintbrush and view the signature. Close the Paintbrush window without making any changes.

10. Close the Datasheet window without saving the changes to the datasheet (that is, the window configuration with one frozen column).

Create a simple form to enter and edit the Signature field:

1. Click on the Form Object button in the Database window, and then select the New command button. Enter **Names** in the Select a Table/Query combo box, and then select Blank Form to display a new blank form.

2. Maximize the Form Design view window, and make sure that the toolbox, field list, and property sheet are visible.

3. Drag the ID Code, Name, and Signature fields from the field list to the form, placing them in a vertical column with the upper-left corners of the controls approximately 1 ¼ inches from the left form border.

4. Click in the Signature control, and confirm by examining the property sheet that Access created a bound object frame rather than a text box to collect this field.

5. Resize the Signature control to about ½ inch high and 2 ½ inches wide, and then adjust the size of the detail section to about 1 ½ inches.

6. Use the Save As option on the File menu to save the form under the name **Names and Signatures**.

7. Switch to Form view. You should see the signature you inserted into the first record (Jerry Allen).

8. Click in the Signature field in the second record (Marilyn Allen), and then choose Insert Object from the Edit menu. Use the same method you used in Datasheet view to insert the Paintbrush file that stores Marilyn Allen's signature. Your screen should look approximately like Figure 15.16.

9. Close the form and return to the Database window.

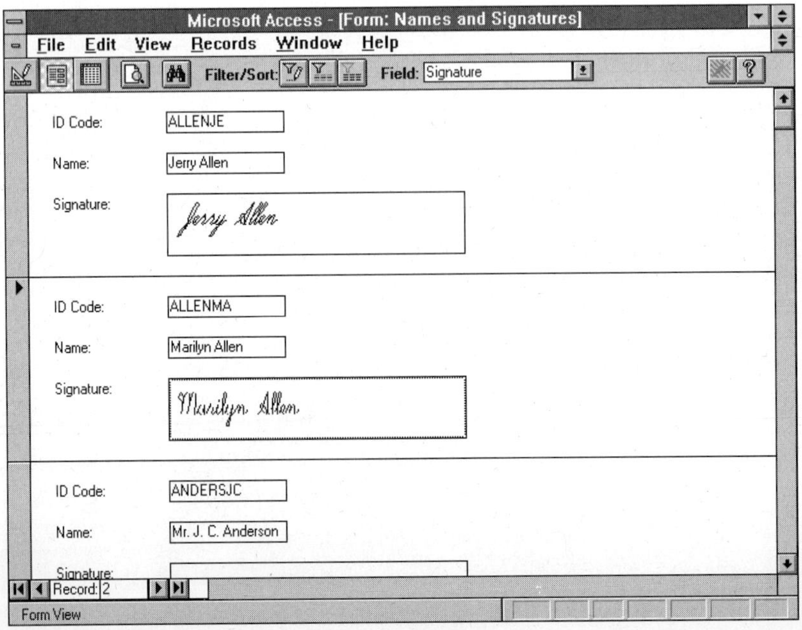

Figure 15.16

The Names and Signatures form

Displaying a Picture on a Command Button

Chapter 10 mentioned briefly that you can display either text or a picture on the face of a toggle button or command button. To see some typical examples, you need look no further than the Access tool bar—all of the toggle buttons have pictures on their faces that symbolize the purposes of the buttons.

The picture that you want to display on a button must be stored in a disk file in *bitmap* format (a standard format for storing graphic images, which is supported by a variety of programs, including Paintbrush and Microsoft Draw). To associate the picture with the command button, you enter the full path name of the bitmap file in the Picture property. This method is equivalent to using the Clipboard method to paste in the graphic image as a bitmap, and it creates a passive copy of the picture, *not* a link to the original bitmap file. After copying the bitmap onto the button face, Access no longer needs to know the name of the original bitmap file, and it displays the Picture property as "(bitmap)." If you want to change the picture, you must enter a new file name. (To edit the picture, you must modify it using the application that created it, and then select it again as if it were a different picture.) You may recall that by default, a command button has a caption, and a toggle button does not. If you enter a caption as well as a picture, the picture takes precedence—Access ignores the caption and displays the picture.

NOTE.   *When you design a graphic image intended to be displayed on a button, the picture should be approximately the same size as the button. You can then use the Size to Fit option on the Layout menu to match the size of the button precisely to the size of the picture.*

Using DDE

All of the OLE methods described earlier in this chapter result in an OLE object that constitutes a complete document recognizable as such by the server application used to create it. This is true regardless of whether the object is linked or embedded, or whether it was originally derived from all or part of another document. For example, if you created the object by using the Clipboard to extract a portion of a spreadsheet, that block of cells becomes a new worksheet, which you can view and edit using the server application. If you want to access one item of information extracted from an external document without calling up the server application from within Access to edit the whole document, you can use DDE instead. A DDE relationship, often referred to as a *conversation*, is always a link—no part of the external object is stored anywhere in your Access database, and you cannot edit the object from within Access. For example, instead of storing the entire budget spreadsheet in the Committee Names table, as shown in Figure 15.15, you might continue to update the spreadsheet in Excel or Lotus 1-2-3 and display or print just the grand total in an Access form or report. Also note that without programming, you can only use DDE to *display or print data*, not to store external data in a table field.

The easiest way to establish a DDE link is to use a method based on the Clipboard; the overall approach is very similar to the technique described earlier in this chapter for establishing OLE links. The steps are as follows:

1. Open the Access document in Design view.

2. Switch to the Program Manager or the File Manager, and start up the server application.

3. Select the portion of the document that you want to display in the Access document, and use the Copy command on the Edit menu (with most Windows programs you can also press Ctrl+C) to transfer the selected material to the Clipboard.

4. Return to the Access document Design view window, and choose Paste Special from the Edit menu.

5. In the Paste Special dialog box, choose Text as the data type and then select the Paste Link button.

Be careful to follow this sequence of steps precisely—if you choose the Paste Link option from the Edit menu instead of Paste Special, or if you choose an option other than Text in the Paste Special dialog box, Access creates a linked OLE object rather than defining a DDE link.

This procedure creates a *text box*, not an unbound object frame. If you examine the property sheet for the text box, you will see that the expression that defines the Control Source property is based on the DDE function. Once you learn how to use this function, you can create DDE links more directly, and you can use DDE to supply the values displayed in check boxes, option groups, and combo boxes as well as text boxes. The DDE function takes three inputs, all of which are text strings enclosed in quotes. The first input is the name of the external application, entered exactly as you would type it to start up the program using the Run command in the Program Manager (that is, without the extension), for example, "123W" (for 1-2-3 for Windows) or "Excel." The second input, which is called the *topic*, identifies the subject of the communication (the conversation) between the two programs. In most cases, the topic is the full path name of the document that contains the data you want to retrieve, for example, "C:\ACCESS\BUDGET.WK1" for a Lotus budget spreadsheet. The third input is the *item* of data that you want to display in your Access document, expressed in the standard notation *for the server program*. When you exchange data with a spreadsheet, the item is a range of cells, for example, "A:B7..A:B7" for the single cell B7 in Sheet A in a Lotus worksheet, "R9C2:R10C2" for two cells in an Excel worksheet, or "Totals" for a range named Totals. Note, however, that Access always treats a value returned by a DDE link as a single item of data, so if you specify a range of cells in a spreadsheet, the first cell in the range supplies the value for the control in the Access form. Thus, the expression that retrieves the contents of cell B7 from a Lotus worksheet would be written as follows:

```
DDE("123W", "C:\ACCESS\BUDGET.WK1", "A:B7..A:B7")
```

Once you understand how to use the DDE function, you can create controls that display data derived using DDE with a more direct method—simply create a text box, check box, option group, or combo box, and write an expression based on the DDE function as the Control Source property. If you use an option group, the numeric value returned by the DDE function determines which option (radio button, check box, or toggle button) is selected. When you use DDE to compute the value displayed in a check box, Access displays the box checked if the DDE function returns any nonzero value. For a combo box, the value returned by the DDE function is displayed in the text box, and Access does not allow you to edit this value.

To continue with the spreadsheet example, you might want to create a different worksheet for each committee, and display the bottom line total from the appropriate worksheet in the form used to view the committee names and budgets. Unfortunately, using DDE to retrieve individual data items from different documents is complicated by the mechanisms used to establish the linkage with the DDE server application (which are common to all applications that support DDE, not just Access). First, Access assumes that the server application is open and the worksheet from which you want to retrieve data is already loaded. If this is not the case, it displays the alert box shown in Figure 15.17 to notify you of the problem and ask permission to launch the application. A more serious problem is the fact that Access initiates the DDE linkage only when you open the document, *not* each time you move to a different record in the source table.

Figure 15.17

The alert box displayed if the DDE server application is not already open

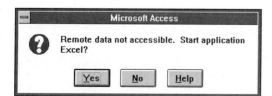

If you are willing to store all the data you need to access in one document in the DDE server application, retrieving it is relatively simple. Figure 15.18 illustrates an Excel worksheet that calculates all the committee budgets. To ensure that you can always retrieve the grand total for a given committee, even if you edit the spreadsheet and insert new rows or columns, each of the cells that contains a total is assigned a name in Excel that matches the contents of the Committee field in the matching Committee Names table record. You can then use an expression that refers to the committee field to specify the third input to the DDE function. To display the overall budget total in an Access form or report, you could use the following expression:

```
DDE("Excel", "C:\ACCESS\BUDGETS.XLS", [Committee])
```

This strategy also assumes that Excel is open and the BUDGETS spreadsheet is loaded, and the best way to ensure that this condition is fulfilled is to call an Access Basic program that opens Excel from the OnOpen event of the form. Transferring data *from* Access to another program via DDE is also accomplished using functions. These operations, which all require some programming, are covered in Chapter 20.

Figure 15.18

A spreadsheet that calculates committee budgets

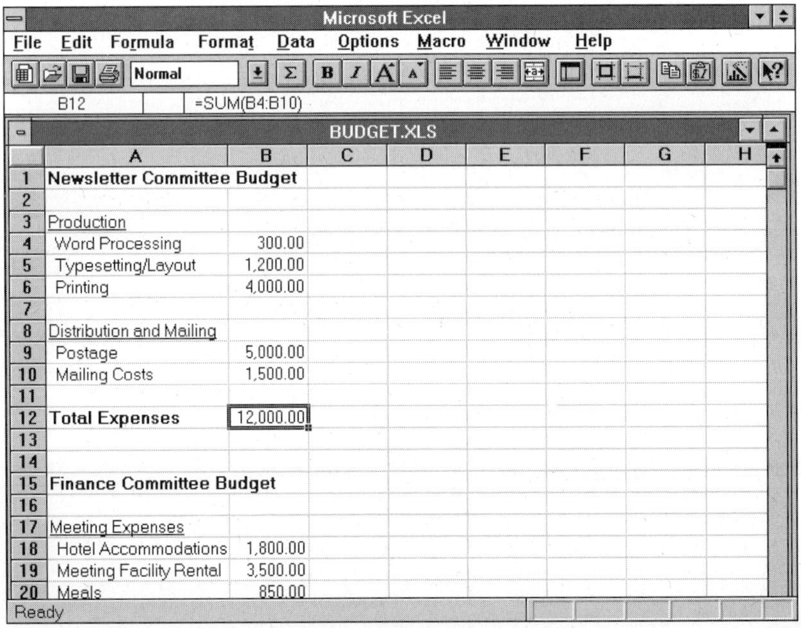

Using Graphs in Access Forms

As you may already know, you can use graphs to display Access data in forms and reports. The tool that you use to create these graphs is not intrinsic to Access—it is a separate program called Microsoft Graph, which is supplied with Access and installed in a subdirectory called MSGRAPH, which is located under the MSAPPS subdirectory created under your Windows program directory by a number of Microsoft applications, including Access and Word. (Like WordArt and other Microsoft utilities, Graph is installed in a location that facilitates shared access by multiple applications.) When you add a graph object to a document, Access calls Graph as an OLE server to define, modify, and display the graph.

NOTE. *Although you can add an Excel chart or a graph created in 1-2-3 for Windows to an Access document as an OLE object, using Microsoft Graph is the most direct way to build graphs based on data stored in Access tables.*

You can invoke the Graph program to define a new graph in three different ways:

- By choosing Graph from the first FormWizards dialog box when you define a new form

- By using the toolbox to add a graph object to a form or report

- By adding an unbound object to a form or report and then choosing Microsoft Graph as the OLE object type

Even if you later end up modifying the graph, the first two of these methods, which both invoke the Access GraphWizard to construct a graph based on data derived from a table or query dynaset, will prove much easier than the third, which forces you to define the graph from scratch. In most cases, you should define the size of the graph object as you place it on the document rather than allowing Access to create an object of the default size (3 inches wide by 2 inches high) and resizing it later, because the Graph program bases the size of the graph and its components on the size of the Access object that will enclose it. As you have undoubtedly noticed, the first FormWizards dialog box offers Graph as one of the basic form types, whereas the analogous ReportWizards dialog box does not, but placing a graph object on a report calls up exactly the same GraphWizard, so using graphs is no more difficult in reports than in forms. Like the other Wizards, the GraphWizard gives access to only a small fraction of the options available through the full design tool—in this case, the Microsoft Graph program—but it provides a very fast, easy way to create a graph. You can then call up Graph to modify or enchance the graph by double-clicking on the graph object in Form Design view or Report Design view.

Figure 15.19 illustrates the first dialog box displayed by the GraphWizard, which you use to select the type of graph you want to create by clicking on one of the 11 large toggle buttons (the graph types are labeled in Figure 15.19). As you will see later in this chapter, the choices in the GraphWizard dialog box represent only a fraction of the graph styles supported by the Graph program. When you add a graph object to an existing form or report, you must also select the data source for the graph, which might not be the same as the data source for the document. In fact, when you create a form or report that includes only subreports and/or graphs, there may be no source table or query for the document as a whole. For example, you might add a graph to the Overall Summary Statistics report described in Chapter 12 or replace one of the tabular summaries on that report with a graph. In contrast, if you invoke the GraphWizard by choosing Graph from the first FormWizard dialog box, Access creates a form with just one object—the graph—and it assumes that the table or query that you choose as the data source for the form will supply the data displayed in the graph. Because you have already chosen the data source, the combo box visible at the top of Figure 15.19 is absent from the first GraphWizard dialog box.

Figure 15.19

Choosing the graph type and data source

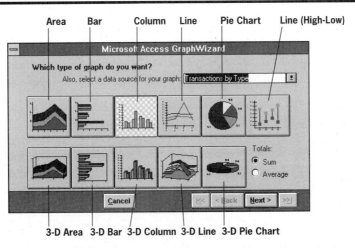

The option in the lower-right corner of this first GraphWizard dialog box (under the high-low graph button) enables you to choose whether the graph will display sums or averages derived from the fields in the source table or query that you choose (in a subsequent step) to graph. Understanding this choice is crucial to using the GraphWizard to produce meaningful graphs, because *an Access graph is always based on group summary statistics computed from the source table*, not on the raw data. This aspect of the way the GraphWizard works might not be obvious at first, but it often affords a significant measure of convenience because it allows you to avoid explicitly defining a query simply to graph summary statistics. Instead, the GraphWizard stores in the graph object instructions (in the form of an SQL Select command) for executing the equivalent of a totals query, and it bases the graph on the result. Thus, when you construct a bar graph based on the Amount field in the Transactions table, each bar is equivalent to a row in the dynaset of a totals query that calculates the sum or average of this field for groups defined by the value of some other field in the table.

Unfortunately, the GraphWizard does not offer the option to graph record counts, but you can do so by defining a query with a calculated column that evaluates to the number 1, and then choosing Sum in the first GraphWizard dialog box (summing a field that always contains the number 1 yields a count of the number of records). When you graph counts together with sums, you may find that the difference in magnitude makes it difficult or impossible to discern the counts, so you might prefer to use a larger number (10, 100, or 1,000) instead of 1 in the query. Figure 15.20 illustrates a query that demonstrates this technique. This query will serve as the data source for a graph that displays the number (multiplied by 100) and dollar total of each transaction type except TD (total debits) and TC (total credits), which are excluded from the dynaset by the selection criteria in the first column.

Figure 15.20

A query used to graph record counts

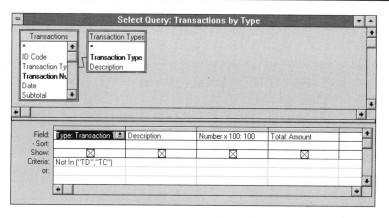

After you choose the graph type and data source, Access displays the dialog box shown in Figure 15.21 to enable you to choose the fields that will contribute to the graph. As suggested by the wording of the prompt at the top of the dialog box, you must choose the fields that will label the graph, as well as those that contribute to the sums or averages. If this concept seems confusing, remember that a graph displays summary statistics for groups of records, and the labels identify the groups. For example, a graph based on the Transactions by Type query shown in Figure 15.20 will display statistics for each transaction type, and you could use either the Type or Description field to label the groups. In Figure 15.21, the Description field was selected, along with the Number and Total fields, which will form the bars in the graph. If you do not select at least one numeric field, Access displays an alert box to warn you that you must do so (because the statistics in the graph must be based on numeric fields).

Figure 15.21

Choosing the labels and data fields

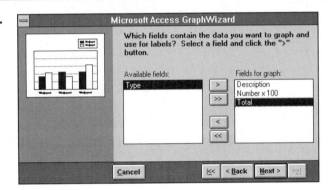

If you chose more than two fields, Access cannot guess which ones should represent the data and which ones the labels, and it displays the dialog box illustrated in Figure 15.22 to allow you to describe the labels. If you choose one field, as in this figure, Access uses the *values* in this field as the labels, and places the bars (or other graph elements) that represent the various statistics for each group adjacent on the graph, as shown in Figure 15.23. If you choose more than one field, it uses the *field names* as the labels, and groups all the graph elements that represent each type of statistic together, as shown in Figure 15.24, which was created by choosing the Number x 100 and Total fields as the label fields. The check box below the Available Fields list enables you to specify whether you want the graph to include a *legend* like the one shown in the upper-right corner of the diagram on the left side of the dialog box in Figure 15.22, which matches up the colors or symbols used in the graph with the corresponding values in the group field.

If you chose one field to identify the labels and also opted to include a legend, Access displays the dialog box pictured in Figure 15.25 to allow you to select the labels that will appear in the legend. In most cases, you will simply select all the data fields to create a legend like the one in Figure 15.23, which uses the field names in the legend. You can change the descriptions in the legend by editing the graph later. If you chose more than one field for the graph labels, Access automatically constructs a legend that identifies the

Figure 15.22

Describing the graph labels and legend

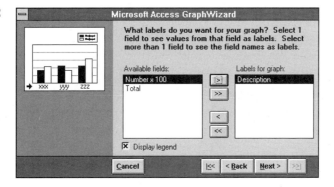

Figure 15.23

Using one field for data labels

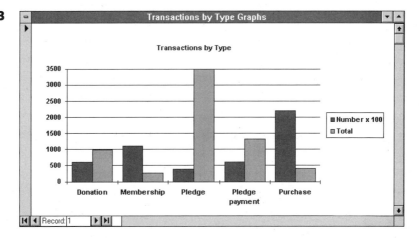

groups that serve as the basis for computing the summary statistics in the graph, since these vital labels are not displayed elsewhere on the graph.

If one of the fields you chose to include in the graph was a Date/Time field, the GraphWizard gives you several additional options to facilitate constructing graphs that group data according to some very common time intervals. If you chose only two fields for the graph (the Date/Time field and a numeric field), the GraphWizard assumes that you want to group data based on the Date/Time field and displays the dialog box shown in Figure 15.26 to allow you to choose whether to display the time intervals only along the X-axis or to also add a legend. If the graph includes additional fields, it assumes that these fields represent the data sets, groups records based on the Date/Time field, and automatically generates a legend.

Figure 15.24
Using more than one field for data labels

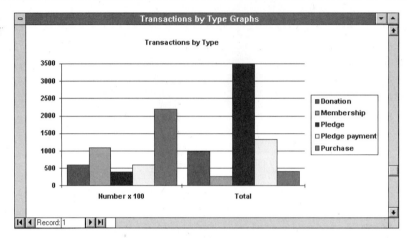

Figure 15.25
Describing the legend

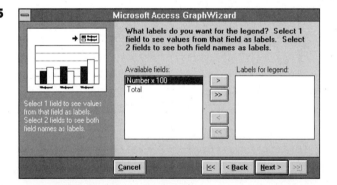

Figure 15.26
Choosing the date label options

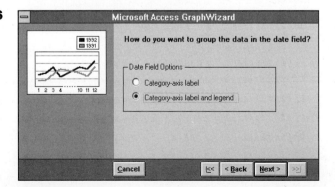

In all cases, it displays another dialog box, which is shown in Figure 15.27, to allow you to choose a grouping method for the date field. If you did not opt to include a legend with the date group labels, the drop-down list of date grouping methods should be familiar to you from the other ReportWizards—you can group by year, quarter, month, week, day, hour, or minute. Figure 15.27 illustrates the drop-down list as it appears if you chose the legend. The options in the left column represent the X-axis labels, and the right column represents the labels in the legend. The source table or query is grouped by *both* date intervals, and this fact is reflected in the text box. Thus, if you select Month, Access groups records by month and year, as in the example in Figure 15.28. You can use the radio buttons in the Date Range Options region to enter a range of dates and/or times that you want to include in the graph.

Figure 15.27

Choosing the date grouping method and date range

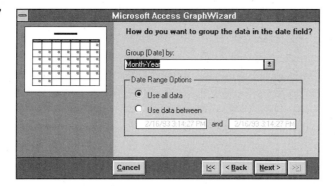

Figure 15.28

Choosing the grouping interval and date labels

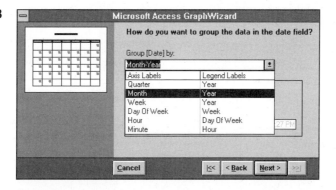

When you add a graph to a form or report that has a data source, Access displays an alert box that asks whether you want to "Link the graph to the report?" or "Link the graph to the form?" For graphs that display overall summary statistics not tied to a particular record in the source table or query for the document, you should choose No. If you want the graph to reflect only data that matches the current record in the source table or query for the document, choose Yes to display another dialog box that enables you to define the linkage. Linking a graph to a form or report is described in more detail in the next section.

The last GraphWizard dialog box, which is shown in Figure 15.29, prompts you to enter a title for the graph. This title is displayed above the graph *within* the graph object on the document. If you prefer to place the label outside this object, on the document itself, you can delete the title. If you invoked the GraphWizard by placing a graph object on a form or report, this dialog box contains only one exit command button—the Design button, which returns you to the Report Design or Form Design view. If you began by designing a new form and choosing Graph from the list of available FormWizards, there is also an Open button (as in Figure 15.29), which displays the completed form in Form View. The GraphWizard does not actually open the Graph program—it simply builds the instructions that will later be used to construct the graph—so when you move from the last GraphWizard dialog box to Design view, Access displays an empty object frame. If you want to see the graph, you can switch immediately to Print Preview or Form view to force Access to open the Graph program; when you return to Design view, the graph will remain visible on the work surface.

Figure 15.29

Entering the
graph title

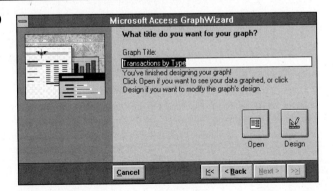

Figure 15.30 illustrates the Transactions by Type Graph form in Form Design view with the property sheet for the graph object visible. As you can see in this figure, Access always treats a graph as an unbound OLE object, even if you used the Graph button in the toolbox rather than the Unbound Object button to create it. As is the case with all OLE objects, the OLE Class property identifies the type of object and the server application (in this case, "Microsoft Graph"). By default, the Scaling property is set to Clip, and the Access documentation recommends that you do not change this setting. However, the Scale setting often yields acceptable results when you make minor adjustments in the size of a graph. If you need to make more drastic changes, you will obtain much more attractive results by calling up the Graph program to edit the image.

Figure 15.30

Viewing a graph in
Form Design view

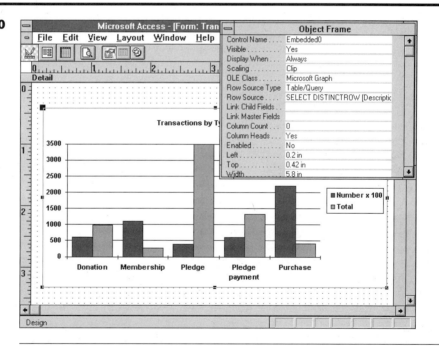

Although the Row Source Type property for a graph object is set to Table/Query, the Row Source property *does not* display the name of the table or query that you chose as the data source for the graph. As noted earlier, Access calculates summary statistics based on this table or query, as you might do using a totals query, and displays the results in the graph. These calculations are carried out using an SQL Select command, which is entered in the Row Source property, and if you are already familiar with SQL, you may want to press Shift+F2 to examine the command in a Zoom window. The SQL Select command, which is used internally to execute all Access queries, is introduced briefly in Chapter 20, but the method used to extract the data for a graph has one important implication that you should understand from the outset: To change the data displayed in the graph, you must either edit the SQL Select command or recreate the graph from scratch.

Linking a Graph to a Report or Form

The graphs described in the previous section displayed overall statistics based on some or all of the records in a table or query dynaset. Access also allows you to link a graph to a report or form so that the graph changes for each record and the contents of the linking field or fields define selection criteria that determine which records contribute to the graph. For example, Figure 15.31 illustrates a form based on the Transaction Types table that displays a graph of the transaction dollar total grouped by month. The graph is linked to the form by the Transaction Type field, so that the statistics in the graph reflect only the transaction type in the current record in the Transaction Types table. Apart from the display format used for the detail data, forms like this one have much in common with the forms created by the main/subform Form-Wizard, in which the subform also displays only records that match the current record in the main form. The data source for the graph is a simple query called Transactions by Type and Date, which is shown in Figure 15.32. The bars in the graph are based on the Amount field and the calculated column Number x 100 (which provides a transaction count, multiplied by 100). The selection criteria in the Transaction Type column exclude Total Debits and Total Credits transactions, and the criteria in the calculated column Current Year select only transactions in the current year.

To create a form or report with a linked graph, you begin by creating the document and specifying its data source, and then add the graph by using the graph button in the toolbox. The fact that you are adding a graph to an existing document *that has a data source* (not a form comprised entirely of unrelated subforms, subreports, and graphs) triggers the display of an alert box that asks whether you want to "Link the graph to the form?" just before the last GraphWizard dialog box. If you select Yes, the GraphWizard displays a dialog box like the one in Figure 15.33 to enable you to define the linkage, which can be based on one or more fields. To select each pair of linking fields, highlight one field in the Form Fields list and one field in the Graph Fields list, and then click on the button with the double-headed arrow on its face that lies between the two lists. Unlike aspects of the graph that are more fundamental to its structure, it is easy to change the linking fields after the fact—they are stored in the Link Child Fields and Link Master Fields properties, exactly as they are for a subform or subreport object, and you can modify them by editing the property sheet.

Figure 15.31

A form with a linked graph

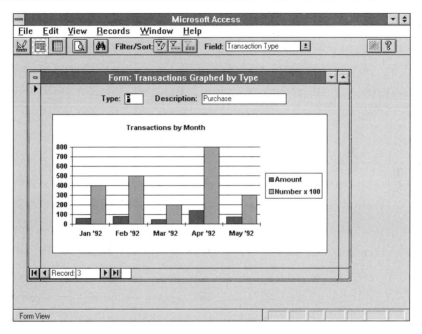

Figure 15.32

The data source for the Transactions by Type and Month graph

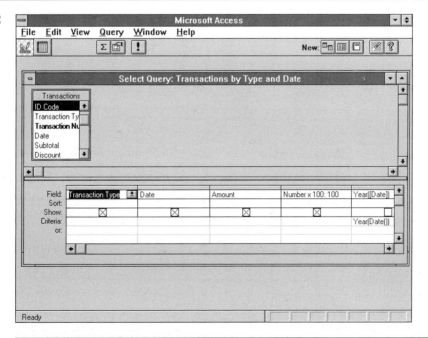

Figure 15.33

Defining the link between a graph and a form

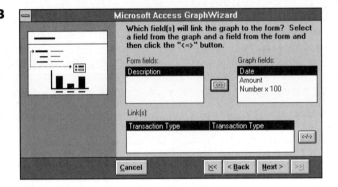

Forms like the one in Figure 15.31 are often intended primarily or exclusively to facilitate conducting *inquiries* into the data in one or more tables. Like the analogous main/subform forms, forms with linked graphs enable you to browse through one table (in this case, the Transaction Types table) and view related data from another (the Transactions table). When you use a form like this, you may be tempted to enter a new value into the Transaction Type field to display the graph for that transaction type. Of course, entering this value constitutes an attempt to change the Transaction Type field in the current record. To avoid this potential misunderstanding and emphasize the fact that the form is intended only for *displaying* data, the Allow Updating property for the form is set to No Tables.

Modifying the Graph Design

To modify a graph produced by the Access GraphWizard, you must call up the Graph program from Form Design or Report Design view, either by double-clicking on the graph object or by selecting the Microsoft Graph Object option on the Edit menu and then choosing Edit from the submenu of object options. Figure 15.34 illustrates the Transactions by Type graph described in the previous section in the Microsoft Graph program window. Remember that Graph is a separate application unrelated to Access, so be prepared for some differences in the menu, command structure, and terminology (although many aspects of the user interface should be familiar from your experience with other Windows software, including Access). Figure 15.35 diagrams the structure of the Graph menu bar. For complete details on using the Graph program, you should refer to the *Microsoft Graph User's Guide* packaged with Access, but a brief introduction will help you get oriented to the Graph environment.

Figure 15.34

Using the Graph program to modify a graph

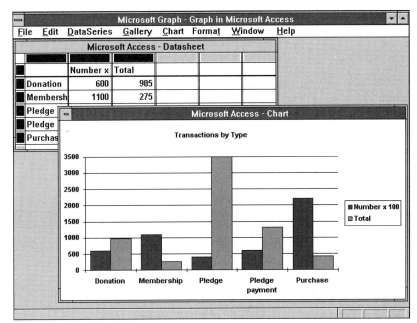

The Graph program displays two windows—the Datasheet window, which, like the Access Datasheet view, displays the underlying data in tabular form, and the Chart window, which displays the data as a graph. You can switch between the two windows by using any of the standard Windows methods—clicking anywhere in either window, pressing Ctrl+F6, or selecting Chart or Datasheet from the Window menu. You can also move or resize either window to suit your preferences; in Figure 15.34, the Datasheet window was enlarged slightly and the second column was widened enough that the whole title (Number x 100) is visible. Because the Datasheet window is displayed only within the Graph program, its size and position have no effect on the graph in your Access form, but changes you make to the Chart window are reflected in the form. Note that resizing the Chart window affects the size of the graph itself, *not* the size of the unbound object that contains it. After resizing the graph, you can either adjust the object frame to match (the easiest way to do this is to use the Size to Fit option on the Layout menu) or change the Scaling property to Scale to adjust the size of the graph to match the frame.

When you first open the Graph program, the Chart window is the same size as the graph displayed in your Access document (100-percent view). You can use the six options in the lower portion of the Window menu to switch to 33-, 50-, 66-, 200-, or 400-percent view. You might want to select a smaller

Figure 15.35

The structure of the Graph menu bar

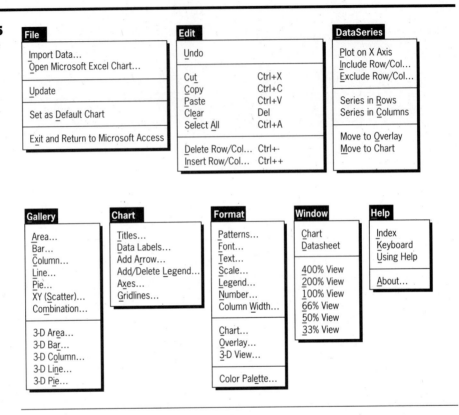

view to reduce the size of the chart while you work in Datasheet view, or enlarge the graph while you edit the details of the graph titles or formatting. The view you choose affects only the Graph environment; it has no effect on the graph as it appears in your Access document.

As noted earlier, the 11 graph styles displayed in the first GraphWizard dialog box represent only a few of the types that you can create using the Graph program. The Graph program supports seven basic graph types—Area, Bar, Column, Line, Pie, XY (Scatter), and Combination—which are listed in the upper portion of the Gallery menu. (If you are not familiar with the term "gallery," note that many Microsoft programs use this word to refer to display options presented as a list of choices or a series of command buttons.) The first five of these also have three-dimensional variations, which are listed at the bottom of the Gallery menu. After you choose a graph style, the Graph program displays a gallery of variations of the basic graph style—like the one in Figure 15.36, which illustrates the column graph styles. The Chart Gallery dialog box can display eight options at once, but if there are additional graph

Figure 15.36

The Chart Gallery of column graph styles

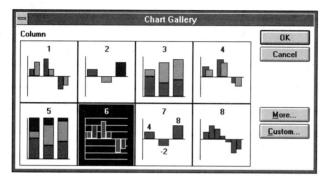

Figure 15.37

Customizing the graph style

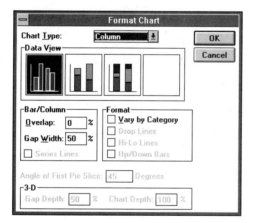

style variations, you can use the More command button to display them. The Custom command button invokes a dialog box like the one in Figure 15.37 to enable you to further customize the graph style.

The options on the Chart menu enable you to customize overall aspects of the appearance of the graph, as follows:

Titles	Adds titles to label the graph and the X-, Y-, and Z-axes
Data Labels	Adds labels within the graph to identify the data series
Add Arrow	Draws an arrow on the graph
Add/Delete Legend	Adds a legend (if it is not present) or deletes the legend (if it is present)

Axes	Displays or hides the values on the X-, Y-, or Z-axes
Gridlines	Displays or hides major or minor gridlines along the X-, Y-, or Z-axes

You can use some of the direct manipulation techniques available in Access Form Design and Report Design views to customize the appearance of the various objects that make up a graph. Other attributes can only be modified by using the options on the Format menu. As in Access, you must begin by clicking within the boundaries of the object you want to modify, although in Graph, many objects (including the graph titles and labels) have no visible borders. When you select an object, Graph displays handles superimposed on the (invisible) borders to confirm that the object is selected; the handles are solid (black) if you can use them to move or resize the objects or clear if you cannot. For example, to "explode" one of the slices in a pie chart, you can select it and use one of the handles to drag it to a new position, as shown in Figure 15.38. In contrast, when you select any of the titles or labels, Graph displays the clear handles shown in Figure 15.39 to remind you that you cannot use the handles to move or resize the object (in theory, you should not need to). To edit any text object, click once to select the object, and then click again to display an insertion point. Graph automatically resizes the text object to accommodate the new text.

NOTE. *Although you can change the axis titles from the Graph program window, the main title in a graph based on Access data is part of the instructions generated by the GraphWizard for constructing the graph, and any changes you make in the Graph window will have no effect. One way to substitute your own title is to superimpose a label object or text box on the graph so that it covers the original title. Chapter 20 describes how to change the title by modifying the SQL Select statement that extracts the data for the graph.*

To modify the format of most graph components, you must select the desired object and then choose one of the options on the Format menu to invoke a dialog box of more detailed formatting options. The Format menu options are used as follows:

Patterns	Selects patterns (textures), colors, and border styles
Font	Selects the text font name, size, styles, color, and background style
Text	Selects the text alignment and orientation
Scale	Customizes the values and tick marks displayed on the axes

Figure 15.38

Using the handles to
move a graph
component

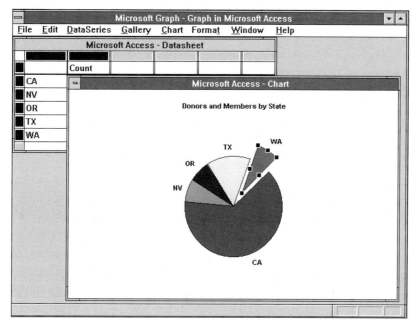

Figure 15.39

Selecting a graph
component that you
cannot move or
resize using the
handles

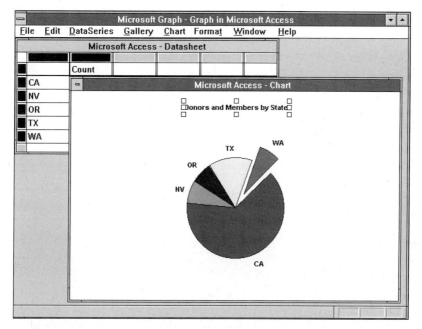

Legend	Chooses the location and style of the legend
Number	Defines the display format for the selected values
Column Width	Defines the width of columns in the Datasheet window

Not all of these options are relevant to every type of object, and when you select an object, Graph enables only the options applicable to this object. For
example, when the graph title is selected, the Patterns, Font, and Text options
are enabled, and when the legend is selected, the Patterns, Font, and Legend
options are enabled. The Number and Column Width options, which apply
only to the Datasheet, are enabled only when the Datasheet window is frontmost in the Graph program window; the other options are enabled only in
the Chart window. Figure 15.40 illustrates the dialog box invoked by selecting
the graph title and then choosing Text from the Format menu.

Figure 15.40

The Text dialog box

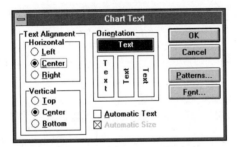

To practice some of these techniques, try the following experiments with
the Transactions by Type graph:

1. Open the Transactions by Type Graphs form in Form Design view, and
   maximize the Form Design window.

2. Double-click on the graph object to invoke the Graph program.

3. Select the Titles option from the Chart menu.

4. Select the Value (Y) Axis option and then click on OK to close the
   Attach Title dialog box. Access displays the title "Y" to the left of the
   Y-axis, with handles visible in its borders.

5. Type the Y-axis title, **Number/Total**. By default, the orientation of the
   title is horizontal, and you cannot read it.

6. Select the Text option from the Format menu, click on the second of the three options at the bottom of the Orientation region, and select OK to close the dialog box. You should now be able to read the Y-axis title.

7. Click on the chart title to select it, and then select Font from the Format menu. Select 12-point type from the scrolling list of font sizes, and check the Underline check box in the Style region. Click on OK to close the Chart Font dialog box.

8. Click on one of the red bars that represent the number of transactions, and note that selection handles appear in every other red bar. Select the Patterns option from the Format menu. Choose Black from the Foreground combo box to change the foreground color to black, and choose one of the dotted patterns from the Pattern combo box. Click on OK to close the Patterns dialog box, and note that the bars that were formerly red now appear in the dotted pattern you selected, with black as the foreground color.

9. Click on one of the green bars that represent the transaction totals, and use the same method as in the previous step to assign a slanted or cross-hatched pattern, also with black as the foreground color.

10. Choose Exit & Return to Microsoft Access from the File menu, and select Yes from the alert box that Graph displays to ask whether you want to "Update Graph in Microsoft Access?" Your screen should look something like Figure 15.41.

Working in the Datasheet Window

The Datasheet window in the Graph program, like its counterpart in Access, displays the source data for the graph in tabular format. The Graph datasheet can have up to 4,000 rows and 256 columns. Graph allows the data series (the values plotted in the graph) to occupy either the rows or the columns, and double lines separate the data series. In the graphs generated by the Graph-Wizards, the data series are always displayed in the columns, and each row represents one value in the field that represents the data groups in the graph. In the datasheet for the Transactions by Type graph, there are five rows (one for each transaction type) and two data columns, with double lines separating the columns and single lines between the rows.

You can move around the datasheet using all the standard Windows keyboard and mouse methods. Graph displays the *active* cell in the datasheet (in Access terminology, the cell that has the focus) surrounded by a heavy border. You can select an entire row or column by clicking on the buttons to the left of the row labels and above the column labels, which function like the row and column selectors in an Access datasheet. You can exclude a row or

Figure 15.41

Modifying the titles, colors, and patterns in the Transactions by Type graph

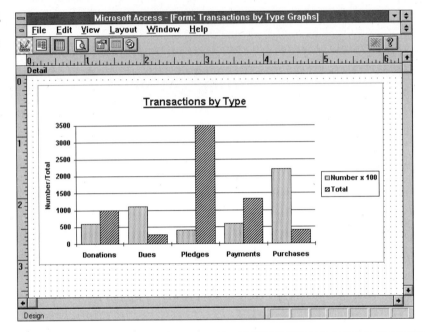

column from the graph by selecting it and then choosing the Include Row/ Col or Exclude Row/Col option from the DataSeries menu; Graph subsequently displays both the selector and the row or column label in gray rather than black.

The Graph program allows you to edit any of the entries in the datasheet, either by typing a new value (which replaces the old value) or by pressing F2 to call up a dialog box in which you edit the cell value. Note that Graph is a general-purpose graphing tool intended for use with data from a variety of sources, and it may not make sense to change a particular value when you edit a graph generated by Access. It is nearly always safe to change the X-axis labels by editing them directly in the datasheet, but because a graph generated by the Access GraphWizard must display data derived from a table or query, you should never edit the entries in the data columns. In a graph that is linked to a form or report, you cannot edit the labels or graph title, because these are generated on the fly—*Access reconstructs the graph for each record you display from the data source for the document.*

You can change the formatting of the data in the datasheet—and in the graph—by selecting the desired group of cells and then choosing the Number option from the Format menu. The format choices are similar to those supported by Access for numeric and Date/Time values. The numeric display format affects the Y-axis labels, as well as any data values displayed in the graph itself.

To experiment with the datasheet formatting options, use the following steps to finish modifying the Transactions by Type graph:

1. Click in the first numeric value in the Amount column, hold the Shift key down, and then click in the last value in the column. You should see all the numbers in the Amount column highlighted.

2. Select the Number option from the Format menu. Move into the Format text box and type **####0** to define a custom format with no decimal places and no commas. Close the Number dialog box. You should see the pennies disappear from all the values in the Amount column.

3. Click in the Chart window and select the Data Labels option from the Chart menu, choose the Show Value radio button, and close the dialog box.

4. Choose Exit & Return to Microsoft Access from the File menu, and select Yes from the alert box that Graph displays to ask whether you want to "Update Graph in Microsoft Access?" Your screen should look something like Figure 15.42.

5. Save the form and close it.

Figure 15.42

The final version of the Transactions by Type graph

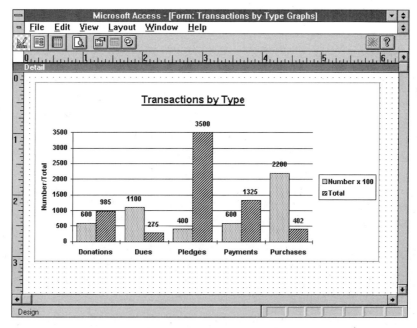

Summary

This chapter described some typical methods for using OLE and DDE to work with objects created by external applications in their native formats. These techniques extend the power of Access to manipulate a wide variety of foreign objects *by launching other Windows applications* to create, edit, display, or play back objects. By using OLE in particular, you can integrate data derived from a variety of sources into an Access database, including graphics, spreadsheets, word processor documents, and—if you own the requisite hardware and software—sound and video.

All this power does not come without a price. Making the most of OLE and DDE requires that you understand the interaction between Access and the other Windows software you are invoking, and that you know at least a little about how to use these programs. For example, to edit the committee budget spreadsheets linked to the Committee Names table, you must understand how to maneuver in Excel and edit data, even if someone else originally created the spreadsheet for you. If you intend to share an Access database with colleagues and co-workers who do not also share your computer system, you should use these powerful features with caution. Keep in mind that to display or edit an OLE object, or to retrieve data via a DDE link, Access must be able to launch the external application that created the object. If you give a copy of your database to another user who does not have Ami Pro, any attempt to edit an Ami Pro document stored in an OLE Object field will generate an error message.

You should also be forewarned that extensive use of OLE may slow performance, for several reasons. First, launching the server application to display or edit an OLE object takes longer than using the intrinsic capabilities of Access to manipulate data of other types. When you work with linked rather than embedded objects, additional time may be required to locate an object and load it into memory, especially if it is stored on a network file server rather than on your own hard disk. Finally, note that many of the types of objects you can access through OLE—in particular, digitized pictures, sound, and video—require considerably more disk space to store than the simple text, dates, and numbers stored in most of your tables.

3

Advanced Skills

16

Establishing a Security System

THIS CHAPTER DESCRIBES HOW TO IMPLEMENT A PASSWORD PROTECTION system that determines which users can run Access and, for those who are allowed to use the program, also determines the permissions they must have to view and update the various objects in each database. You may be accustomed to thinking about security in connection with networks, especially if you have prior experience with mainframes and minicomputers, but the connection between security and networking is more historical than technical. Networks and multiuser software migrated "down" to PCs from mainframes, which might have hundreds or thousands of terminals, and when all of an organization's software as well as its sensitive financial and management data are stored in one computer, a security system is essential.

Although in principle many of the same considerations apply to PC-based local area networks and database servers, networking and security are far from inseparable in the PC world. You may need a security system on a single-user computer if your Access databases store sensitive information, such as accounting or personnel data, that should not be accessible to everyone who uses the computer. Conversely, a small organization that uses a local area network to allow staff members to share peripherals and software and to update shared documents and databases may have no need for password protection.

This chapter describes how to set up a security system for a new database, implement security after the fact for an existing database, and unprotect a previously secured database. As you will see, it is best to put the security system in place *before* you build your database, but this approach is not always practical—you may start working on the application before you understand the security mechanisms, or the need for security may arise months or years after you finish the application. This chapter also explains how to add a further measure of protection by encrypting a database to protect it against knowledgeable users who might try to examine its contents with text editors or disk inspection utilities such as the Norton Utilities. This chapter addresses issues that apply to both single-user and network operations. If you do have a network, you may want to defer setting up your security system until you have read Chapter 17, which describes how to run Access on a network and covers additional security considerations applicable only to multiuser applications.

This chapter assumes that you are the *system administrator*, or *database administrator*—the person in charge of managing, maintaining, and administering the Access databases in your organization. In a large company, the system administrator may be a member of the MIS staff who is responsible for other computer systems and software as well as Access databases, or it may be the person in charge of PC support. In most small businesses and nonprofit organizations, there may be no such job title, and the person who fulfills the role of database administrator may not even know what this term means. Often, the job of system administrator falls to the person who knows the most about PCs or about databases, or to the person who uses Access the most. If you are not the database administrator, you may not have the authority to modify the security system, but you might still want to skim through this chapter to gain a better understanding of how and why your access privileges were assigned.

The Structure of the Security System

The Access security system is structured around *groups* of individual users. It goes without saying that each group may have many members, but each user can also belong to more than one group. You can specify access *permissions* (also called *privileges*) for a group as a whole or for individual users, but as you will see shortly, it is to your advantage to specify most permissions at the group level. When you install Access, it creates three standard groups: Admins, Users, and Guests. You cannot rename or delete these groups, but you can create as many additional groups as you wish. The three predefined groups are intended to be used as follows:

Group	Members
Admins	Administrators (users who have administrative control over the security system)
Users	All regular users of the databases
Guests	People who need occasional access to the databases but do not use them regularly enough to merit individual user accounts

Every group and every user is defined by a name and a four-digit *personal ID number (PIN)*. In addition, every user account can have a password, but the password is required only when you start up Access—the PIN, not the password, defines the identity of a user. As you will see later, this dichotomy enables the users to choose their own passwords, but leaves the assignment of permissions primarily in the hands of the system administrator. The password is case-sensitive, but the user and group names are not.

There are two predefined user accounts: Admin, who belongs to the Admins and Users groups, and Guest, who belongs to the Guests group. The PINs of the predefined groups and users are assigned by Access, and you cannot view or change them. *The PINs of the Users and Guests groups and the Admin and Guest users PINs are identical for every Access installation, but the Admin group PIN is unique.* Initially, neither of the predefined users has a password, but you can define one if you wish. Access does not allow you to delete the Guest user, and it does not allow you to delete *all* the user accounts in the Admin group, although you can delete the original Admin user after adding at least one other user to this group. Access automatically adds every new user you define to the Users group, and does not allow you to remove users from this group (although you can delete a user from the system). You can also add new users to as many other groups as you wish.

The permissions, which are described in detail later in the section entitled "Assigning Permissions," determine whether a given user can view, modify, execute, or update a particular object in a database. Because you must assign permissions one object at a time, it is far more efficient to do so at the group level, so that you can add users or change their privileges simply by editing the group memberships. For example, if you create a group called Accounting for all users who are allowed access to accounting data, you can grant the necessary privileges to a new employee in the accounting department simply by adding the person to the Accounting group.

In some organizations, the groups should parallel the departments or divisions, so that users only have access to data relevant to their jobs. For example, Figure 16.1 diagrams the structure of the security system used at the Association for a Clean Earth, where data accuracy is more of an issue than secrecy. In addition to the predefined groups and users, this security system has three groups—Accounting, Mailing List, and Fundraising—and seven users. Jean Gordon, the Executive Director, belongs to all three groups, as well as to the Admins group, and most of the users belong to more than one group. In larger organizations, the groups may instead (or in addition) be hierarchical, to reflect different levels of access to sensitive data. Figure 16.2 diagrams a more complex group structure in which people in each department are further divided so that some of the financial totals can be hidden from the data entry staff.

Access stores security information in two places: Information about permissions for specific objects is stored in the database itself, and information about groups and user accounts, which must be available to more than one database, is stored in an *encrypted* (encoded) database called SYSTEM.MDA. When you install Access, this file is placed in the Access program directory, and in many installations, this single copy of SYSTEM.MDA will serve all of your needs. However, Access allows you to create multiple SYSTEM.MDA files, each of which defines a *workgroup*, so you can set up essentially separate security systems for different users in your organization. For example, users who share Access on a network might not all use the same SYSTEM.MDA file if there is little overlap in the applications they use.

To create a new workgroup, you must create another SYSTEM.MDA file, which you can do by copying your existing SYSTEM.MDA file to another subdirectory. If you have already defined groups and users that you do not want in the new SYSTEM.MDA file, you can switch to the new workgroup and delete these users. Alternatively, you can copy your present SYSTEM.MDA file to another subdirectory for safekeeping, reinstall Access (thereby creating a new SYSTEM.MDA file), and then move either or both of these files to

Figure 16.1

The structure of the
ACE security system

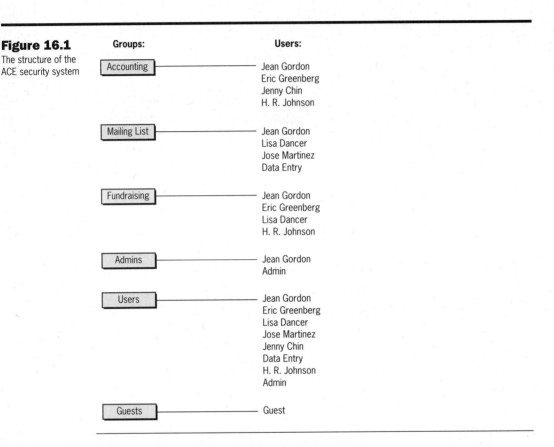

Groups:	Users:
Accounting	Jean Gordon Eric Greenberg Jenny Chin H. R. Johnson
Mailing List	Jean Gordon Lisa Dancer Jose Martinez Data Entry
Fundraising	Jean Gordon Eric Greenberg Lisa Dancer H. R. Johnson
Admins	Jean Gordon Admin
Users	Jean Gordon Eric Greenberg Lisa Dancer Jose Martinez Jenny Chin Data Entry H. R. Johnson Admin
Guests	Guest

different subdirectories. If you have not yet implemented security in your application, you might want to make a copy of your SYSTEM.MDA file, either in another subdirectory or on a floppy disk, which you can use later if you decide to create another workgroup.

The easiest way to change workgroups is to use the Change Workgroup utility provided with Access. You must run this program from outside of Access (for example, by selecting its icon in the Microsoft Access group in the Program Manager). You can also change workgroups more directly by editing the entry that defines your workgroup in the MSACCESS.INI file stored in the Windows program directory. You can switch to another workgroup by editing the line that specifies the full path name of your SYSTEM.MDA file, which is found in the [Options] section. For example, to request a SYSTEM.MDA file located in the MAILLIST subdirectory on drive D, you would enter the following:

```
SystemDB=D:\MAILLIST\SYSTEM.MDA
```

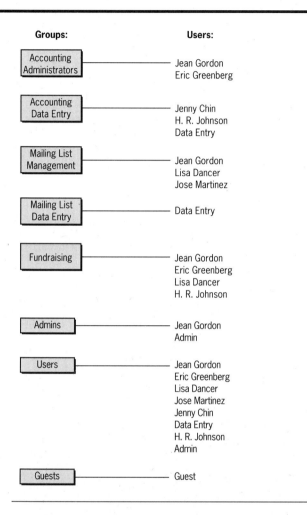

Figure 16.2
A more complex security system for ACE

Groups:	Users:
Accounting Administrators	Jean Gordon Eric Greenberg
Accounting Data Entry	Jenny Chin H. R. Johnson Data Entry
Mailing List Management	Jean Gordon Lisa Dancer Jose Martinez
Mailing List Data Entry	Data Entry
Fundraising	Jean Gordon Eric Greenberg Lisa Dancer H. R. Johnson
Admins	Jean Gordon Admin
Users	Jean Gordon Eric Greenberg Lisa Dancer Jose Martinez Jenny Chin Data Entry H. R. Johnson Admin
Guests	Guest

The security capabilities built into Access require no special installation or configuration. The security system is always active, and everyone belongs to a workgroup, but until you activate the security system by assigning at least one password, Access allows you to start up the program without going through the logon sequence. To accomplish this, it automatically attempts to log you in as a user named Admin, who has no password. If this logon succeeds, Access does not prompt you for a password, and it appears for all intents and purposes as if there is no security system. Once you activate the security system by assigning the Admin user a password, the default logon sequence will fail, and you must have a valid user account to start up the program.

Because the group and user information is not directly connected to any database, it is available globally to all Access users, and once you have activated the security system, it is always in effect. At the very least, no one can start up Access without having a valid user name and password, and if your databases do not require a more detailed protection scheme at the object level, you need only define a user account for each person who is allowed to run Access. In addition, you can assign object permissions for some or all of your databases to control the privileges granted to groups and users over these objects.

Defining the Security System

All of the commands that you use to define the security system are accessed through the Security option on the Access main menu bar. Even though the group and user definitions are not local to any particular database, the Security option is present in the menu bar only when a database is open (perhaps because the attached pull-down menu also contains the option that enables you to define object permissions). The options on the Security menu are used as follows:

Permissions	Assigns group or user permissions for database objects
Users	Adds or deletes users, adds or deletes group memberships, and clears passwords
Groups	Adds or deletes groups
Change Password	Changes the current user's password

To activate the security system, you must begin by assigning a password to the Admin user account. (You can only change the password for the user account under which you started up the program, and before the security system is activated, Access assumes that every user is the Admin user.) To enter the password for the Admin user, choose the Change Password option from the Security menu. Access displays the dialog box shown in Figure 16.3, which enables any user to change his or her password at any time. Your user name is displayed at the top of the dialog box, and you cannot change the password for any other user. When you first activate the security system, the Admin user has no password, so you must leave the Old Password text box blank and simply enter the new password in the New Password text box. Access protects your entry from prying eyes by displaying asterisks rather than the characters you type. Because you cannot proofread your entry, you must type the password twice—in the New Password and Verify text boxes. If the two passwords do not match or if you omit either one, Access displays the alert box shown in Figure 16.4. If you are not sure what the problem is, simply retype the password in both text boxes. Remember that the password is case-sensitive, and that you will have to enter it exactly the same way every time you start up Access.

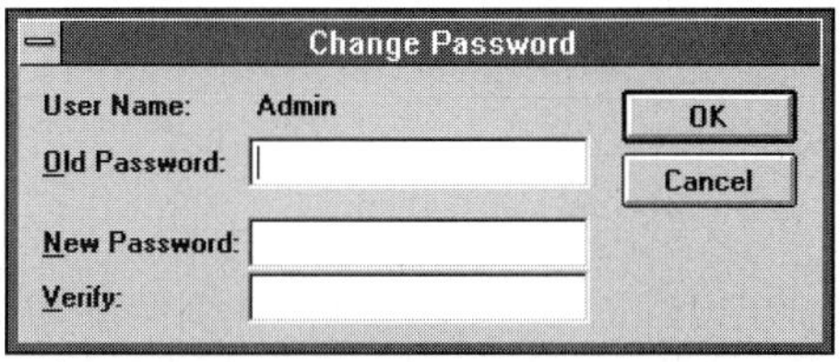

Figure 16.3

Changing a password

Figure 16.4

The alert box displayed if you did not verify your password correctly

Once you have established a password for the Admin user account, Access displays the Logon dialog box illustrated in Figure 16.5 whenever you start up the program, and no one can gain entry without entering a valid user name and password. If Access does not recognize the combination of user name and password that you enter in the Logon dialog box, it displays an alert box with the error message "Not a valid account name or password." You can select Cancel from this dialog box to abandon your attempt to enter the program, or you can select OK to try again as many times as you wish.

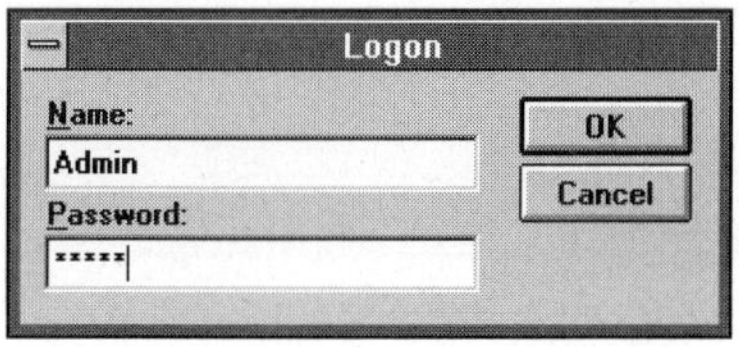

Figure 16.5

Logging onto a secured Access system

At this point, users can log on as Admin, using the password you entered for the Admin user in the previous step, or as Guest. If you are implementing a security system only to prevent some staff members from running Access at all, you need only define a user account for each legitimate user because every user you create is added to the Users group, and the default permissions for this group allow its members to view and update all database objects. However, two additional steps are highly recommended. First, log on as Guest and assign a password for this user account; otherwise, anyone could determine from the Access documentation that the Guest account is available, and could start up the program, open any database, and view (but not edit) objects. Choose this password—and all of your passwords—judiciously, so that it is easy for legitimate guests to remember but difficult for outsiders to guess (do not use "Guest," which would be an obvious first guess, as the Guest user's password).

If you are designing the security system before you have created any databases, you should also delete the predefined Admin account at this point and replace it with a new system administrator account that has a unique name, PIN, and password. The reason for this is that the Admin user account has the same PIN in every copy of Access, so any databases and objects created by the original Admin user can be modified by the Admin user in another workgroup. For maximum security, the original Admin user should therefore never create any databases or objects. When you add security to an existing Access installation, you cannot delete the original Admin user until you have transferred ownership to another user, as described later in this chapter in the section called "Protecting an Existing Database." Because the Admins group must always have at least one member, and you cannot delete the user account under which you logged in during the current work session, you must create the new administrator's account, exit from Access, log on again under the new system administrator account, and delete the original Admin account.

If you have the authority to do so, and if a security system will not seriously inconvenience other users in your organization, use the following steps to activate the security system for your copy of Access:

1. Make sure that the ACE database is open and the Database window is frontmost on the Access desktop.

2. Choose the Change Password option from the Security menu to display the Change Password dialog box.

3. Type the new password, **ACE practice**, in both the New Password and Verify text boxes, and close the dialog box.

4. Exit from Access and start up the program again.

5. In the Logon dialog box, enter **Admin** in the Name text box, and press Enter to leave the password blank. Access displays an alert box to inform

you that you failed to enter a valid combination of user account name and password. Select OK to clear the error message.

6. Type **ACE practice** in the Password text box, and press Enter or click on OK to close the Logon dialog box and start up Access.

To deactivate the security system and return to allowing all staff members full privileges over all your databases, you can simply clear the Admin user password, using methods described in the section entitled "Assigning and Clearing Passwords." When the Admin user has no password, Access does not display the Logon dialog box when you start up the program. If you are sure you will have no further use for the previously defined security profiles, you can delete all the groups and/or users you defined, but there is no need to do so, and if you suspect you might want to reactivate the security system, you can save considerable time and effort by retaining the user accounts.

Defining Groups and Users

To add or delete groups or users, you use the Groups and Users options on the Security menu. In keeping with the philosophy that only the system administrator should be able to control who can access an organization's databases, only members of the Admins group can define groups and users, and the Groups and Users options on the Security menu are enabled only if you log on as a member of the Admins group. If you are in fact the system administrator but are currently logged on under a different user name to test the security system, you must exit from Access and start up the program again. Remember also that when no database is open, the Security menu is not available, even though the groups and users that you define are independent of all your databases.

A group or user name can be up to 20 characters long and can contain any characters except control characters (characters with ASCII codes between 0 and 31) and the following punctuation marks, which are reserved for use in Access expressions and identifiers:

/ \ [ ] | < > + = : ; , . ? *

Note. To verify that the group you are about to enter does not already exist, display the drop-down list for the Name combo box in the Groups dialog box.

You can include spaces in a group name, but the name cannot begin with a space. For the sake of readability, you can use any mixture of upper- and lowercase letters, but Access does not treat user names as case-sensitive in the Logon dialog box.

To add or delete groups, begin by choosing the Groups option from the Security menu to invoke the Groups dialog box, which is illustrated in Figure 16.6. To define a new group, you select the New command button; if you wish, you can type the name of the group in the Name combo box beforehand, but you can enter this name in the next dialog box if you prefer. You enter the group name and a unique four-digit personal ID number (PIN) in the New User/Group dialog box shown in Figure 16.7, which is also used to define new user accounts. If you typed the new group name in the Name text box before selecting New from the Groups dialog box, this name will appear in the Name text box in the New User/Group dialog box.

Figure 16.6
Adding or deleting groups

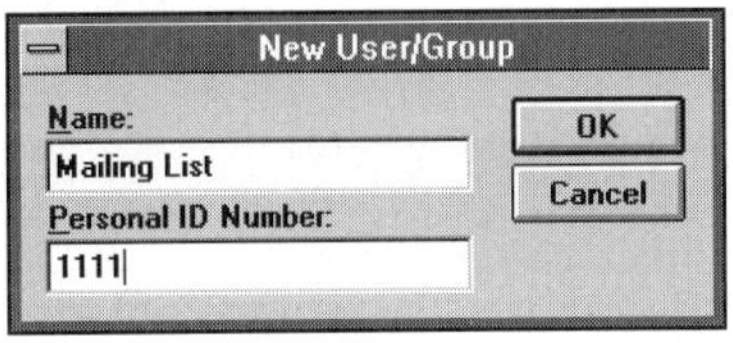

Figure 16.7
Defining the group name and personal ID number

To delete an existing group, enter its name in the Name combo box in the Groups dialog box (either by typing it or selecting it from the drop-down list), and select the Delete command button. As always when you choose a potentially destructive option, Access displays an alert box to warn you and give you a chance to change your mind; this alert box is pictured in Figure 16.8. If you try to delete the Admins, Users, or Guests group, Access displays an alert box to remind you that you "Can't delete account."

After you define or delete a group, Access returns you to the Groups dialog box so that you can continue to add and delete groups; when you are finished, you can close the dialog box using any of the standard Windows methods, such as selecting the Close button in the lower-right corner, pressing Esc, or using the close box in the upper-left corner of the window.

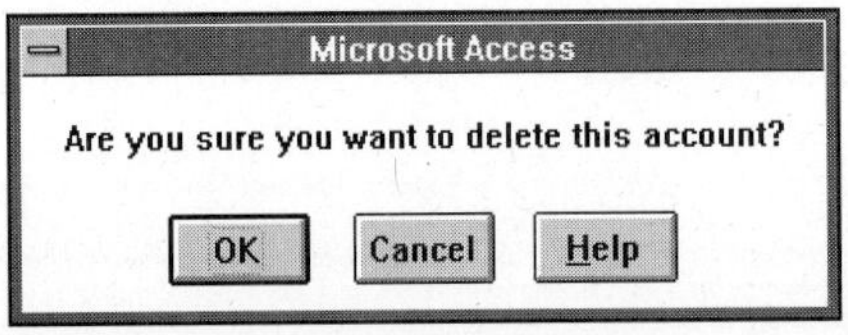

Figure 16.8
The alert box displayed when you try to delete a group

To add or delete individual user accounts, choose the Users option from the Security menu to invoke the dialog box pictured in Figure 16.9, which enables you to carry out all the activities relevant to maintaining user accounts: defining new user accounts, deleting existing users, clearing passwords, and defining group memberships. Defining a new user is virtually identical to defining a new group—type the new name if you wish in the Name combo box, and then select the New command button. Access displays the same dialog box used to define a new group (the one shown earlier in Figure 16.7), and you must enter the user name (if you did not type it in the Users dialog box) and a unique four-digit PIN. To delete an existing user account, enter the name in the Name combo box in the Users dialog box (either by typing it or selecting it from the drop-down list), and then select the Delete command button. As is the case when you delete a group, Access displays an alert box to request confirmation and give you a chance to abort the deletion. Remember that you cannot delete the last member of the Admins group, which must always have at least one member.

Figure 16.9

Maintaining user accounts

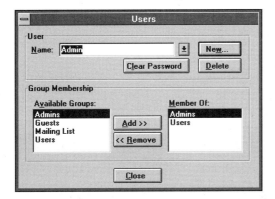

You can also define and modify group memberships in the Users dialog box. Access automatically adds each new user to the Users group, but you can add a user to as many other groups as you wish. When you select a user from the combo box at the top of the Users dialog box (if you have just created a user account, its name will already be displayed there), Access displays the user's group memberships in the lower portion of the Users dialog box. The scrolling list on the left side of the Group Membership region lists the available groups, and the scrolling list on the right side lists the current group memberships. To add the current user to a new group, highlight the group name in the Available Groups list, and use the Add button between the two lists to add the group name to the Member Of list. To remove the user from a group, highlight the group name in the Member Of list, and use the Remove button to delete it from the list. (Remember, however, that you cannot remove any user account from the Users group.) You can modify group memberships for as many users as you wish before you close the Users dialog box.

The Clear Password command button below the Name combo box enables you to clear the password for the currently displayed user account. This option is described in more detail under "Assigning and Clearing Passwords."

NOTE. *Make sure to write down the PINs that you assign to each group and user, and store this list in a safe place. Once you exit from the New User/Group dialog box, there is no way to look up the PIN assigned to a group or user. The PIN is used internally to identify groups and users, and you will need these numbers if you ever have to reconstruct the security system from scratch and recreate the original permissions.*

If you have the authority to do so, you can practice these techniques by defining the groups and users in the version of the ACE security system diagrammed in Figure 16.1. If you are not the only person in your organization who uses Access, make sure that the other users know how to log in and that they know at least one user name and password. The steps are as follows:

1. Make sure that the ACE database is open and the Database window is frontmost on the Access desktop.

2. Choose the Groups option from the Security menu.

3. Select the New command button to display the New User/Group dialog box. Type **Mailing List** in the Name text box and **1111** in the Personal ID Number text box, and then close the dialog box. Access returns you to the Groups dialog box.

4. Type **Fundraising** in the Name combo box, and then select the New command button.

5. Note that the new group name (Fundraising) is displayed in the Name text box in the New User/Group dialog box. Enter **2222** as the PIN for the group, and close the dialog box.

6. Using either method, add a group named Accounting with the PIN **3333**.

7. In the Groups dialog box, display the drop-down list for the Name combo box, and note that the list now includes six groups—the three you just defined and the three predefined groups (Admins, Users, and Guests).

8. Close the Groups dialog box.

9. Choose the Users option from the Security menu.

10. Select the New command button to display the New User/Group dialog box. Type **Jean Gordon** in the Name text box and **1000** in the Personal ID Number text box, and then close the dialog box. Access returns you to the Users dialog box. Note that Access automatically made the new user a member of the Users group.

11. The name of the first group (Accounting) should be highlighted in the Available Groups list. Use the Add command button to add Jean Gordon to this group. You should see the group name appear in the Member Of list.

12. Highlight Admins in the Available Groups list, and select Add to add Jean Gordon to this group as well.

13. Using the same technique, add Jean Gordon to the Fundraising and Mailing List groups.

14. Type **Eric Greenberg** in the Name combo box, and then select the New command button.

15. Note that the new user name is displayed in the Name text box in the New User/Group dialog box. Enter **2000** as the PIN for the new user, and close the dialog box.

16. Add Eric Greenberg to the Accounting and Fundraising groups.

17. Using the same techniques, add the following users:

Name	PIN	Groups
Lisa Dancer	3000	Fundraising, Mailing List
Jose Martinez	4000	Mailing List
Jenny Chin	5000	Accounting
Data Entry	6000	Mailing List
H. R. Johnson	7000	Fundraising, Accounting

18. Close the Users dialog box.

Assigning and Clearing Passwords

As noted earlier, Access uses the combination of name and PIN to uniquely identify a group or user, but once you have defined the PIN, you will never see or enter it again. The users do not need to know their PINs (in a completely secure system, they should not), because when you start up Access, you enter only the user name and the password, if any. Although only a system administrator (that is, a member of the Admins group) can define new groups and user accounts, each user has control over his or her own password—Access only allows you to the change the password for the user account under which you logged on. This fact does not limit the ability of the system administrator to control the ability of any user to run Access or to manipulate individual database objects.

NOTE. *If a user forgets his or her password, a member of the Admins group can clear a password. The user can then log on (without entering any password) and then use the Change Password option to enter a new one.*

An Access password can be up to 14 characters long, and it can contain any characters, including spaces and punctuation marks. *Unlike the user and group names, the password is case-sensitive.* To change your password, choose the Change Password option from the Security menu. As noted earlier, you must enter the current password in the Old Password text box, and then type the new one twice, once in the New Password text box and again in the Verify text box.

It is customary to assign user names based either on a person's real name (the first name, last name, or both) or job title (for example, "Bookkeeper" or "Fundraising Director"). The user name need not be kept secret, because the password should ensure that no one can log on under another user's account. The ideal password is easy to remember, but difficult or impossible to guess, a stipulation that rules out names, nicknames, the names of family members and pets, terms closely related to a person's job, personal habits that are well known to friends and co-workers, and personal data that could easily be discovered, such as a telephone number or Social Security number. A good choice for a password is a combination of two or three unrelated, common words, separated either by spaces or punctuation marks, for example, "Purple Fern" or "Rain Plumber." If security is an important concern in your organization, you should encourage users to change their passwords frequently (and of course, to keep them secret).

To practice changing passwords, use the following steps to assign a password to the Guest user account:

1. Exit from Access and start up the program again. Log on as the user Guest.

2. Choose the Change Password option from the Security menu to display the Change Password dialog box.

3. Leave the Old Password text box blank (because there is currently no password for the Guest account), type the new password, **Desert Rose**, in both the New Password and Verify text boxes, and close the dialog box.

Defining Permissions

You can control the types of access that a given group or user has to a particular object in a database by assigning *permissions*. You must assign permissions separately *for each object in a database*—there is no way to grant a particular group or user the same permissions for *all* tables or *all* queries. Although you can define permissions at either the group or user level, it is far more efficient to specify most permissions by group and resort to user-level permissions only to handle the exceptions—users whose access privileges do not coincide neatly with those assigned to any one group. This scheme allows you to change users' privileges by reassigning their group memberships, and you can grant a new staff member all (or nearly all) of the necessary permissions simply by creating a new user account and adding this user to one or more existing groups, rather than having to assign the user's permissions individually for all existing database objects. The permissions and their meanings for the various types of objects in a database are listed in Table 16.1.

Table 16.1   **Access Database Object Permissions**

Permission	Objects Affected	Privileges
Read Definitions	All objects	Display object in Design view
Modify Definitions	All objects	Modify object in Design view
Execute	Forms, reports, macros	Use a form or report; run a macro
Read Data	Tables, queries, forms	Display data in Datasheet or Form view
Modify Data	Tables, queries, forms	Add, delete, and edit records in Datasheet or Form view
Full Permissions	All objects	Display and modify any object in Design view; display and modify data in Datasheet or Form view; run a report, macro, or module

When you work with a secured Access system, the permissions of each user to work with a given object are determined by the *least restrictive* of the permissions assigned to the individual user and to all the groups to which the user belongs. Thus, if you assign the Mailing List group Read Definitions (but not Modify Definitions) and Modify Data permissions for the Names table, a user in this group for whom you explicitly assigned only Read Data permission can still update the table. By default, members of the Admins and Users groups have full permissions over all database objects, and members of the Guest group can view but not modify data and object designs. The easiest way to define permissions for all users of a certain type is to assign the desired permissions to the group and leave all the user permissions blank. Verifying a user's permissions is hampered by the fact that the Permissions dialog box shows you no information about group permissions while you are viewing a user's permissions. To obtain a complete picture of a user's permissions, you must check the permissions of all groups to which the user belongs.

When you attempt any operation that is forbidden by the permissions assigned to your user account (or to the groups of which you are a member), Access displays an alert box like the one in Figure 16.10, which was triggered when a user who did not have Modify Data permission for the Committees table tried to edit a record. Unfortunately, Access does *not* modify the menu system to reflect the permissions assigned to the current user—that is, it does not disable menu options that should be prohibited for the current user. Thus, if you do not have permission to update the Committees table, Access displays a blank record as usual when you choose the Data Entry option on the Records menu in Datasheet view or Form view, but it displays the alert box shown in Figure 16.10 when you begin entering data in the empty record.

Figure 16.10

The alert box displayed when you attempt a forbidden operation

Although any member of the Admins group can add, change, and delete groups and users, the same is not true for permissions. The following people can edit the permissions for an object:

- Members of the Admins group in the workgroup under which the database was created

- The person who created the database (the *owner* of the database)

- The person who created the object (the owner of the object)

- Any user who has Full permissions for the object

The concept of *ownership* is crucial to understanding who can define and modify permissions. The owner of any object is the person who created it, and Access does not check permissions when the owner works with an object. The objects in a database need not all have the same owner, and Access gives you no way to determine who is the owner of a given object, so if you find yourself locked out of a table or form, even the system administrator may not be able to find out who owns it. (However, a member of the Admins group in the workgroup under which the database was created can modify your permissions to access the object.) The owner of a database is the person who created it, and the only way to change ownership is for the new owner to create a new database, and then transfer all the objects from the original database into the new one. The only way to change ownership of an object without moving it to another database is to use the cut and paste technique described in Chapter 13 to make another copy of the object, delete the original, and then rename the copy. As you might guess, changing the ownership of a large table can consume a great deal of time and disk space.

Assigning and Modifying Permissions

You can only assign permissions for objects in the current database, so make sure to open the right database before you begin. To define or modify permissions, you choose the Permissions option from the Security menu, which invokes the dialog box illustrated in Figure 16.11. The two combo boxes in the Object region at the top of the Permissions dialog box enable you to choose the type of object (Table, Query, Form, Report, Macro, or Module) and the specific object. When you first open the Permissions dialog box, both of these combo boxes reflect the currently selected object in the Database window; for example, in Figure 16.11, the Area Codes table was highlighted in the Database window when the Permissions option was chosen from the Security menu. The list of objects in the Name combo box changes dynamically, based on your selection from the Type combo box, so that it always displays only objects of the selected type. The radio buttons in the User/Group region enable you to specify whether you want to define permissions for a group or for a single user; unfortunately, these buttons are located *below* the combo box that you use to choose the specific group or user name, a placement that you may find inconvenient if you prefer to use keyboard commands rather than the mouse.

To assign specific permissions, you use the six check boxes at the bottom of the dialog box to choose the desired options, and then use the Assign button to save your selections. As you can see in Table 16.1, not every permission is applicable to every type of object, and only the relevant check boxes are enabled in the Permissions dialog box. For example, the Modify Data permission applies only to those objects that you can use to update data stored in tables—tables, queries, and forms. To maintain the parallel between the "Read" and "Modify" permissions, the Read Data permission also applies only to these objects, and the Execute permission plays an equivalent role for reports, which also allow you to view data. Note that the only permissions available for Modules (programs written in Access Basic) are Read Definitions and Modify Definitions, because any user must be able to run

Figure 16.11

Defining group and user permissions

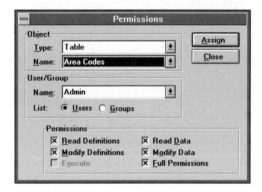

programs written in Access Basic. While a program is running, the permissions assigned to the objects it manipulates govern the access privileges of the users. If you want to deny a user any access to an object, make sure that none of the check boxes are checked and that the user does not belong to any group that has permission to view the object.

The higher-level "Modify" permissions always take precedence over the corresponding "Read" permissions. Thus, if you explicitly assign the Modify Definitions permission, Access also assumes that the user must have Read Definitions permission and checks this box as well; similarly, if you assign the Modify Data permission for an object, Access also grants Read Data permission. This hierarchy should make sense in light of the fact that you must view an Access object in order to modify it. However, Access allows you to grant Modify Data but not Modify Definitions permission for an object.

The permissions assigned to a particular object apply only to the original object. If a user who has Modify Definitions permission uses the Save As option to save a modified object under a new name, the new object *does not* inherit the permissions assigned to the original—you must use the Permissions option on the Security menu to define permissions for the new object, which need not match those of the original.

There is no way to explicitly assign permissions at the field level—all of the permissions assigned to a table apply to the whole table. However, you can use queries to circumvent this limitation and allow some users to view only certain fields. To implement this method, you must define a query that includes only the fields that you want the user to be able to see, give the user or group permission to read (but not modify) the query, and deny the user or group permission to view the table itself. You will also need to create multiple versions of affected forms and reports (one based on the table and one on the query), and define permissions for these documents that parallel those

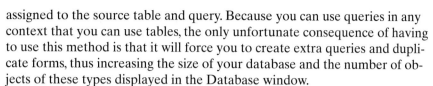

assigned to the source table and query. Because you can use queries in any context that you can use tables, the only unfortunate consequence of having to use this method is that it will force you to create extra queries and duplicate forms, thus increasing the size of your database and the number of objects of these types displayed in the Database window.

Allowing some users but not others to *update* certain fields in a table is a little more complicated. For example, you might want to allow users in the Fundraising group to view but not update the Total Debits and Total Credits fields in the Names table, but grant full permission to members of the Accounting group. To do this, you must define a query that includes the Total Debits and Total Credits fields (called, for example, Name Totals), and give the Fundraising group View Data but not Modify Data permission for this query. One approach to data entry is to define a form in which the fields that both groups can update come from the Names table, and the protected fields appear in a subform based on the Name Totals query. Alternatively, you can use a third query, in which the Names table and the Name Totals query are linked based on the ID Code field, as the data source for the form, and ensure that the protected fields in this form are derived from the Name Totals query, rather than the Names table.

When you use queries to limit permissions, keep in mind that by default, Access assumes that users who do not have permission to view or update a table should still be able to view or update the table through queries. This property is governed by the Run with Owner's Permissions check box in the Query Properties dialog box (accessed through the Query Properties option on the View menu in Query Design view). When this box is checked, as it is by default, Access checks only the permissions of the owner of the query, not those of the person attempting to run it. Thus, users who do not have permission to view the underlying tables can run the query *and update data in the dynaset*. If you want to prohibit access to data through the query for users who do not have permission to view the underlying tables, you must uncheck this box. The wording of this option is potentially confusing—remember that it means *run this query as if you have the owner's permissions*, not "you can run this query only with the owner's permission."

The owner of a query is the person who originally created it, so you cannot use this option to get around the restrictions imposed by the database administrator. For example, if a user who does not have permission to update a table designs a query based on the table and checks the Run with Owner's Permissions option, Access still does not allow the user to update data in the underlying table, because the permissions granted to the owner of the query do not allow updating the table. Only the owner of the query or a user who has Modify Definitions permission for the query can change the status of this check box; if any other user, including an Admin user in the workgroup in which the query was created, tries to save the query after unchecking the Run

with Owner's Permissions check box, Access displays a standard "No permission" alert box like the one shown in Figure 16.10.

To establish permissions in the ACE database, use the following steps:

1. Exit from Access and start up the program again, logging on as the user
   Admin.

2. Make sure that the Database window displays the list of tables, and highlight the Contacts table.

3. Select the Permissions option from the Security menu. You should see
   Table in the Type combo box and Contacts in the Name combo box.

4. Select the Groups radio button, and then select Accounting from the
   Group Name combo box above.

5. Check the Read Data permission check box, and note that Access also
   checks the Read Definitions check box.

6. Select the Assign command button to save the selected permissions.

7. Select Transactions from the list of tables, and then assign Read Data permission to users in the Mailing List group. Use the Assign command button to save the selected permissions.

8. Display the permissions for the Users group, and note that all the permissions are checked. Uncheck the Modify Definitions and Modify Data permissions, and use the Assign command button to save the permissions.

9. Select Names from the list of tables, and then assign Read Data permis-
   sion to users in the Mailing List group, and Read Definitions and Read
   Data permission to the Users group. In both cases, remember to use the
   Assign command button to save the selected permissions.

10. Select Query from the Type combo box and Prospects from the Name
    combo box. Assign Modify Data permission to users in the Mailing List
    group. Use the Assign command button to save the selected permissions.

11. Close the Permissions dialog box.

12. Exit from Access and start up the program again, logging on as the user
    Data Entry, who is a member of one group (Mailing List).

13. Open the Names table in Datasheet view and try editing the first record.
    Access displays an alert box to inform you that you do not have permis-
    sion to update the table. Close the table.

14. Open the Prospects query in Datasheet view and again try editing the
    first record. This time Access allows the change, because the query has
    the Run with Owner's Permissions property.

Encrypting and Decrypting a Database

The Security menu options described earlier in this chapter protect a database against unauthorized access by users who are willing in principle to comply with the rules or who do not know enough about computers to circumvent them. However, a more knowledgeable staff member could use the Norton Utilities or a similar disk file inspection utility to examine the contents of the .MDB file directly. Although this file is quite complicated and its overall structure would be difficult or impossible to decipher, a persistent user could find and read the ASCII text stored in Text or Memo fields. To protect a database against this type of intentional and expert unauthorized access, you can *encrypt* it—that is, rewrite the file into an encoded format that effectively hides all of the data.

To encrypt a database or decrypt a previously encrypted database, you use the Encrypt/Decrypt Database option on the File menu. Like the Compact option, this option rewrites the database in its entirety (and compacts it at the same time), so it is available only when no database is open. When you choose the Encrypt/Decrypt Database option, Access displays an Open File dialog box very similar to the one invoked by the Open Database option to enable you to choose the database you want to process. If you choose an unencrypted database, Access encrypts it, and if you choose an encrypted database, Access decrypts it. As is the case when you choose the Compact option, Access assumes that you want to rewrite the database under a new name, and it displays a Save File dialog box. The default name for the new file is DB1.MDB, but you will usually want to change this name. If you enter the same name as the database itself, Access rewrites the database to a temporary file in case the process is interrupted; if the encryption is successful, Access erases the original and renames the temporary database. As an additional safety measure, you might want to make a copy of your database on floppy disks before you encrypt it.

NOTE.   *When you write the encrypted database to a new name, Access does not erase the original. To fully protect your data, you should erase the unencrypted database (preferably after making a backup copy).*

Encrypting or decrypting a small database may take just a few seconds, but if your database is larger than 3 or 4Mb, be prepared to wait a few minutes. As it works, Access displays the usual percentage indicator in the status bar to allow you to monitor the progress of the operation. Also note that you will pay a small penalty in performance for encrypting a database, because Access has to decrypt objects on the fly while you work with them.

Only the owner of a database or the Admin user in the workgroup in which the database was created can encrypt or decrypt it. If any other user attempts these operations, Access displays an alert box like the one in Figure

16.12. This can present a problem if you add security later to a database created originally without any password protection. If you follow the advice in the Access documentation to delete the original Admin user account, the "owner" of all your existing databases will be a user who no longer exists—the original Admin user. To solve this problem, you can delete the Admin user password to disable the security system and then re-enter the password after you encrypt the desired databases.

Figure 16.12

The alert box displayed if you try to encrypt a database you did not create

Protecting an Existing Database

If you created any databases before you activated the Access security system, the owner of these databases and all the objects they contain is the original Admin user. Because this user has the same PIN in all Access installations, any other Access user has full permissions over objects in these databases. *There is no way to change the owner of a database or a database object after the fact*—the only way to transfer ownership of existing objects is to copy them. Obviously, this can be a tedious process in a large database, and if you are sure your organization will require security, it is to your advantage to design the security system before you create your databases. However, the need for protection may arise only after you have developed several applications. To add security for an existing database, you must proceed as follows:

1. Use the procedures outlined earlier in this chapter to create a new system administrator account (a user in the Admin group), which has a unique PIN and password.

2. Exit from Access, and log on again as the new administrator.

3. Create a new database. The owner of this database will be the new system administrator.

4. Use the Import option (as described in Chapter 14) to import all the required objects into the new database. When this process is complete, the new system administrator will be the owner of every object in the new database. Note that you must redefine any default table relationships stored in the original database, which are not transferred when you import tables and queries.

5. Create the required groups and users, and assign the desired permissions.

The foregoing procedure assumes that you are the system administrator and that you should be the owner of the database. If this is not the case, you must ensure that the rightful owner of the database has full permissions for all of its objects, and then allow this user to create the new database and transfer the objects.

Documenting the Security System

As noted earlier, Access stores the security information you enter using the options on the Security menu in an encrypted database called SYSTEM.MDA, which is by default located in the Access program directory. This file is an ordinary Access database, although it has a different extension (.MDA instead of .MDB) to ensure that its name does not appear in the scrolling list of databases displayed in the Open Database dialog box. You can open this database by entering the full name, including the extension, in the File Name text box in the Open Database dialog box, but some of the entries, including the passwords, are always displayed in encrypted form, even when you log on as the Admin user. It is a good idea to periodically back up the SYSTEM.MDA file together with your data. You might easily overlook this database in your normal backup procedures if you did not know its purpose (and its importance), because it does not have the usual .MDB extension and because it is stored in the Access program directory, whereas you will probably place the databases you create in other subdirectories.

Because there is no way to determine the security information from the database, you must document it on paper or in an Access database (encrypted to prevent unauthorized access). In particular, make sure that you write down the Admin user password. The individual user passwords are less critical—if a user forgets his or her password, the Admin user can clear the password to allow the user to log on without it and then use the Change Password option to enter a new one. If you forget the Admin user password, no one else can clear it or change it. A complete record of the security system would contain all of the following information:

- The Admin user password

- The names and personal ID numbers of all the groups

- The names, personal ID numbers, and group memberships of all the users

- The current user passwords if you know them

- The group and user level permissions

Summary

This chapter described how to implement a password-protected security system to control which users in your organization can run Access and which database objects each user can view or modify. Defining the group and user permissions can be tedious, especially when you add security after the fact to a large database application, even if most permissions are assigned at the group level, because you must explicitly specify permissions for each object in the database. Nevertheless, security can be of paramount importance when you use Access to maintain potentially sensitive corporate accounting or personnel data.

Whether or not you are the system administrator, remember that the effectiveness of any security system depends in large measure on nontechnical considerations. In a large organization where users have little contact with each other, the human factors may play a small role, but if several users in the same office or department work with an Access database, the security system can rapidly be compromised if the users consider themselves friends or view the security system as an intrusion or a restriction imposed by a distant and repressive management. The most elaborate security measures are worthless if users share their passwords, a practice that can begin innocently enough, when one staff member has to fill in for another who is absent or busy, and everyone is feeling the pressure of an approaching deadline.

17

Running Access on a Network

Sharing the Access Program

Sharing Databases

Working with Other Database Objects

WHEN YOU INSTALL ACCESS ON A SHARED DRIVE ON A LOCAL AREA network (LAN), more than one person can use the program at the same time, and the users can work with databases stored on the shared network drives as well as with files on their local workstation hard disks. If the appropriate configuration options are enabled, more than one person can open the same database at the same time, and can even view and update the same tables and other database objects concurrently. If your sole purpose for installing Access on the network is to allow more than one user at a time to run the program, each working with different databases, very little preparation is required on the part of the network administrators and the users. In many cases, the only reminder you will have that you are working on a network will be the inevitable degradation in performance compared to working on a standalone computer, and this slowdown can vary considerably, depending on your network hardware and software and the number of workstations.

If users must also share databases, it is essential to protect the objects in these databases against the damage that could result from simultaneous attempts to carry out conflicting updates. Ensuring the integrity of a shared database requires collaboration and cooperation among quite a few "participants," some human and some not—the network hardware, network software, the MS-DOS and Windows operating systems, Access, and the users. All networks provide a means for *locking* an entire disk file or part of a file while one user updates it to prevent anyone else from viewing or changing it at the same time, and programs like Access implement their own protection mechanisms by calling these intrinsic network file locking capabilities. Fortunately, you need not be concerned with the technical details, but you should understand the methods you can use to control access to shared databases so as to handle the conflicts that can arise on a network or prevent them from occurring. Access allows you to implement protection strategies that range from highly restrictive—forbidding simultaneous access to any database objects—to very permissive—allowing all types of concurrent updates and requiring the users to resolve the conflicts. The method you choose will depend on the ways you need to share data in your organization, and on the knowledge and sophistication of the users.

This chapter outlines the potential problems that can crop up when you work with Access in a multiuser environment and suggests strategies for sharing databases safely and efficiently on a network. It also describes additional factors you may have to take into account when you design a security system for a network installation. If you have been concentrating thus far on the technical aspects of using Access to manage your data, note that many of the factors that contribute to the productivity and satisfaction (or frustration) of users who share software and data on a network are procedural rather than technical. You can avoid many conflicts and resolve the ones that do occur far more easily if all the users know who else is using the same data and understand which processes and operations cannot or should not be attempted simultaneously. If all the network users possess this information and adopt a cooperative and considerate attitude, staff members can plan their database updates so as to minimize conflicts and maximize performance. This chapter addresses all of these as well as the more technical issues from the point of view of the users as well as of the network administrator.

This chapter assumes that Access is already installed on your network, that you have a valid license to run Access at your workstation (either a complete copy of Access or a Microsoft License Pack), and that you have permission at the network operating system level to run the program and to read and store databases on the file server. If this is not the case, you may want to ask your network administrator to grant you permission to run Access and to store databases in some shared network subdirectory (not necessarily the Access program directory). If you have no plans to use Access on a network, you may want to skim this chapter lightly or skip it entirely, but if you are planning to install a network in the near future, it may still be worthwhile to take the time now to become acquainted with the issues that you will encounter later, so you can begin preparing in advance.

If you have a network and can run Access from two workstations that are reasonably close together, you might want to start up Access on both workstations and make sure that both are members of the same workgroup. These will be referred to as "Workstation 1" and "Workstation 2" in the hands-on examples in this chapter. If you do not have a network, you can start up two copies of Access from the File Manager. Apart from the absence of the workstation names in the various alert boxes, these two copies of Access will behave just like two legitimate workstations on a network.

Sharing the Access Program

If multiple users on a network will share the same copy of Access, you must install the program on the file server, and you must run the Setup program at each workstation (this program allows you to install Access on the local hard disk or to work with a shared copy on the file server). If you have had little experience with networks, note that programs and data on the file server are in theory available to all the workstations on the network, although the rights over specific files or subdirectories can be granted by the network administrator through network utilities that are independent of any application software. Conversely, files on the hard disk in any workstation are in most cases accessible only from that workstation. This may not be strictly true in a *peer-to-peer* network, which may have multiple file servers, and any network may have more than one shared hard disk, but for the sake of simplicity, this chapter uses the term *file server* to refer to the shared network drive on which the

Access program is installed, and assumes that all shared data files are located on this drive. Although databases that are shared by several network users must be located on the file server, they do not have to be in the Access program subdirectory. If you have more than one or two databases, you may prefer to place the .MDB files in another subdirectory or possibly create a separate subdirectory for each database.

When you use any shared programs and data on a network, you will see some degradation in performance compared to running the same software on a standalone computer. If there is only one copy of Access installed on the network, each workstation must load the program into its own local memory and it must process data locally, not on the server. The Access program itself, any help text you request through the Access help system, and all the database objects you view and manipulate must be transferred from the file server to your workstation through the network cables. These transfers are invariably slower than moving the same information from a hard disk into memory within one computer, although they can be very fast on a high-performance network. Furthermore, any disk-intensive processes carried out by other network users (not necessarily using Access) will slow down the process of retrieving the information you need from the file server. Installing Access on the local hard disks will improve performance somewhat, but shared databases must be located on the file server.

One additional aspect of the way Access processes data may be less obvious and less intuitive: Each workstation is running its own copy of Access, and all processing occurs on the local workstation, even when you work with a shared database located on the file server. Thus, when you run a query that extracts a small subset of records from a large table, the network must send *the entire table* to your workstation, where the copy of Access residing in memory executes the query and processes the selected records. This may come as a surprise to you if you are more familiar with client/server databases (such as Microsoft SQL Server), which process tables on the server and send only the selected data to the workstation that requested it, but local processing is the norm for PC database software.

When it is essential to share data, you must simply accept the performance penalty as the necessary price for being able to update the same database from multiple workstations. However, you can improve performance significantly by placing databases that are used by only one person on the hard disk in that person's workstation. Obviously, this is impossible for diskless workstations, and it may not be practical if the same person may have to use different workstations to access the same data.

NOTE. *In most organizations, each user is responsible for backing up all data stored on his or her workstation, whereas the network administrator (if there is a network administrator) often takes care of this housekeeping for the* *entire network with periodic procedures for backing up all the programs and data stored on the file server.*

When users share Access on a network, you may want to set up more than one *workgroup*. As explained in Chapter 16, the members of a workgroup share a copy of the SYSTEM.MDA file, which stores the group and user profiles in a password-protected Access system. This file also stores all the global system options accessed through the Options dialog box invoked by choosing Options from the View menu. If all the users on the network will belong to the same workgroup, you should place the SYSTEM.MDA file in the Access program directory on the file server. The SYSTEM.MDA files for other workgroups can go in any shared subdirectory on the file server. For a "workgroup" of one user, you can place the SYSTEM.MDA file on the local workstation. Chapter 16 mentioned one reason for creating multiple workgroups—defining essentially separate groups and users in a secured Access installation. Even if security is not an issue, you might want to create different workgroups for users who prefer different global options.

It is essential that all Access users understand that because the global system options are stored in the SYSTEM.MDA file, changing any of these options (including those described in earlier chapters as well as the multiuser options covered later in this chapter) affects everyone in the workgroup. For example, if you design new form and report templates that reflect your aesthetic preferences and enter the names of these templates in the Form & Report Design options, blank forms created by other users will derive their default appearance and properties from your templates. It is always a good idea to consult with other users before modifying any option that may have a dramatic impact on the Access working environment.

Sharing Databases

In theory, Access allows multiple users to simultaneously open and edit any database objects—tables, queries, forms, reports, macros, and modules. Access automatically prohibits the most dangerous types of concurrent updates, but in most cases it allows you to specify which activities can take place at the same time. To make an informed decision, you must understand why some simultaneous updates pose a threat to the integrity and accuracy of the data. Once you have settled on a basic protection strategy, implementing it is relatively easy. Note that the discussion that follows applies to network database software in general, not just to Access, although not all programs support exactly the same safety mechanisms for protecting shared data. If you use Access to work with attached dBASE or Paradox tables, you will have to coordinate your activities with the users of these programs, which also allow data sharing on local area networks.

It is always safe for more than one user at the same time to *read* a database object, so long as no one makes any changes. For example, no damage will result if several users execute different select or totals queries based on the same tables or if one user prints a report while another scans through the source table in Datasheet view. Similarly, multiple users can look at the same tables in Datasheet view or Form view as long as no one changes or deletes records. In terms of data integrity, it is also safe to allow one user to change data while others view the same tables. For example, one user could safely edit records in Datasheet view while others open forms, execute queries, or print reports based on the same table. When you work in Datasheet view or Form view, Access automatically *refreshes* the display at regular intervals to reflect changes made at other workstations. The default refresh interval is 60 seconds, but you can customize this interval or refresh the screen on demand using methods described in the section called "Refreshing the Display" later in this chapter.

Whether to allow one user to update a table while another prints a report or runs a query that computes statistics based on the table is not always a clear-cut decision. These activities present no risk to the data, but they may generate inconsistencies in the report or statistics. For example, suppose that one user is entering new records into the Names table while another user prints a report that lists names in primary key order. Which of the new entries appear on the report depends on the ID codes—a new record that falls earlier in primary key order than the current record being printed will be omitted, while one that comes later will appear on the report.

To take a slightly more complex example, one user might be entering records into the Transactions table while another prints the Transactions by Name report (described in Chapter 11), in which the groups are based on the ID Code field so that each person's transactions are printed together. The data source for this report is the Names and Transactions query, which links the Names and Transactions tables with an equi-join to select only people with transactions. Because the report is printed in alphabetical order by ID code, a transaction for a person whose ID code falls early in the alphabet might not appear in the output, while a transaction entered immediately before or after for a person whose name falls later in the alphabet would. Similar considerations would apply if the query also included selection criteria based on the Date field—some people who had transactions entered on the day the report was printed would be included while others were omitted, depending on the timing of the entries relative to the processing of the query.

Depending on the context, you might or might not consider these inconsistencies to be serious problems. In a sense, any report or any query constitutes a snapshot of the data at a particular moment in time, and this snapshot is out of date the minute you enter new data into any of the source tables. If you generally enter data in batches, you can avoid potential problems by coordinating the data entry and reporting schedules. For example, if the ACE staff updates the Names table throughout the week and enters all transactions received during the week on Friday, it could print transaction reports on Friday afternoon, print Names table reports on Monday morning, and prohibit data entry during these times. On the other hand, ACE staff might take the philosophical view that the fact that two transactions or names entered consecutively do not both appear on a particular report is of no particular concern. After all, if the data entry worker had been interrupted and ended up entering both transactions the next day, neither record would have been included on the report.

In other cases, inconsistencies are far more serious, and they can easily go unnoticed because they are usually not apparent from a cursory examination of a report or the output of a query. For example, in a financial transactions table in a double-entry accounting system, it might be very dangerous to allow data entry while another user prints a transaction journal grouped by general ledger account number. In a double-entry system, each transaction requires at least two records—a debit and a credit—and may have more than two (one debit might be offset by two credits that add up to the same net amount). If both the debit and credit records are entered after the debit account has been processed but before the credit account has been processed, the credit will be included on the report and the debit will not, and the accounting system will appear to be out of balance (the debit and credit totals will differ). In a small organization, you may be able to prevent such problems by scheduling data entry and reporting so that conflicts do not arise, but if you cannot guarantee that all the network users will understand the importance of adhering to this schedule, you must use the Access protection mechanisms to prevent anyone from updating the source tables while you print crucial reports or compute summary statistics.

When several users update records in the same table one at a time in Datasheet or Form view, the primary concern is preventing conflicting or differing simultaneous updates. For example, suppose that two users were viewing and updating the same record in the Names table at the same time. Remember that all the users are working with separate copies of the data stored in the local memory at their workstations, and that when each person saves his or her modified copy of the record, Access rewrites the whole record on the file server (not just the individual fields that were changed). If one user changed the address and saved the record while the other edited the text in the Notes field, the new address would be overwritten when the second user saved the record (because the temporary copy of the data that user was editing still had the original address). Access gives you several different ways to handle or prevent this type of conflict, all of which are explored in detail later in this chapter.

Shared and Exclusive Access

Access allows you to open an entire database either in *exclusive* mode, which prohibits all simultaneous access, or in *shared* mode, which allows other users to open and optionally edit the data. You can make this decision each time you open a database by your selections in the Exclusive and Read Only check boxes in the Open Database dialog box. If you have more experience with other programs that store each table in a separate disk file and allow you to specify exclusive or shared access separately for each table (such as Paradox, dBASE, or FoxPro), keep in mind that the Exclusive and Read Only check boxes apply to *an entire database.* There are ways to restrict access to individual tables and other database objects, some of which are automatic and some of which are under your direct control; these are explained later in this chapter.

By default, the Exclusive option is checked and Read Only is not. You can change the default status of the Exclusive check box through the Default Open Mode for Databases setting in the Options dialog box. There is no comparable global option that governs the default status of the Read Only check box—you must choose Read Only explicitly each time you want to use this setting. To gain access to the multiuser options, which are shown in Figure 17.1, select Options from the View menu and then choose Multiuser from the scrolling list of categories. (The other options in this dialog box are described in the relevant sections of this chapter.)

Figure 17.1

The multiuser options

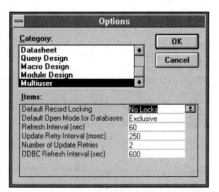

You cannot open a database in exclusive mode if another network user already has the database open (or if you are running two copies of Access yourself and the database is open in the other copy), and if you do succeed in opening a database in exclusive mode, no one else will be able to open it until you close it. Violating either of these rules invokes the alert box shown in Figure 17.2. If you leave the Exclusive check box unchecked when you open a database, Access opens it in shared mode so that other users can open it at the same time.

If you check the Read Only check box in the Open Database dialog box, you will be able to view but not edit any objects in the database, and after opening the database, Access displays the alert box shown in Figure 17.3 to remind you of this fact. Because the database is already open, the alert box does not include a Cancel option; if you change your mind at this point, you must close the database and reopen it with the Read Only check box unchecked. When you open a database for read only access, all the command buttons, navigation controls, and menu options that normally enable you to create, delete, or edit database components are disabled, including all of the following:

- The New command button in the Database window

- The New Query, New Form, and New Report buttons in the tool bar

- The Cut and Paste commands on the Edit menu

- The Undo, Delete, and Replace options on the Edit menu

- The Data Entry option on the Records menu and the New option on the Go To submenu

- The Editing Allowed option on the Records menu

In Datasheet view, Access does not display the usual blank record at the end of the dynaset, and you cannot move past the last existing record. Access allows you to open any database object in Design view to examine its structure, and it does not display an error message if you use direct manipulation techniques (which do not depend on the disabled menu options or command buttons) to make changes. However, all the Save options on the File menu

Figure 17.3

The alert box displayed to remind you that a database is read only

are disabled, and if you close the Design window by pressing Ctrl+F4 or by double-clicking on the close box in the upper-left corner, Access discards your changes without issuing any warning or reminder.

If you check the Read Only check box but not the Exclusive check box in the Open Database dialog box, other users can open and edit the database simultaneously (except that no one will be able to open the database in exclusive mode while you have it open). If you check both the Exclusive and Read Only options, other users can open the database, but only in read only mode, even if they do not check the Read Only check box in the Open Database dialog box. Access always displays the alert box shown in Figure 17.3 when it opens a database in read only mode, and if you receive this warning when you did not check the Read Only check box, you can be sure that another user has already opened the database with both Exclusive and Read Only checked.

Access always remembers the options that you selected the last time you opened a database. If you bypass the Open Database dialog box and reopen one of the last four databases you opened by choosing its name from the list at the bottom of the File menu, Access opens the database using the same combination of settings for the Exclusive and Read Only check boxes that you selected the last time you used the Open Database dialog box to open it. If you want to use a different combination of settings or if you cannot remember which check boxes you selected last time, you must forgo the shortcut method and use the Open Database dialog box.

Apart from protecting data, the main motivation for using the Exclusive and Read Only settings is performance. Opening a database in exclusive mode gives you the fastest performance (because Access does not have to check for potential conflicts), and it guarantees the accuracy of the tables and reports produced from the tables. However, this choice is often impractical for everyday use with databases shared by many users in a large organization. If you are sure that you do not have to change data or modify document designs, you can gain some improvement in performance without locking other users out of the database by using the Read Only option.

To experiment with various options for opening databases, make sure that two copies of Access are running (either on two network workstations or on the same machine) and that no database is open on either workstation. You can then try the following steps:

1. From Workstation 1, select the Open Database option from the File menu.

2. In the Open Database dialog box, make sure that the Exclusive option is checked and Read Only is not, and open the ACE database.

3. From Workstation 2, select the Open Database option from the File menu.

4. In the Open Database dialog box, make sure that the Exclusive option is checked and Read Only is not, and try to open the ACE database. Access displays an alert box that resembles the one shown earlier in Figure 17.2.

5. From Workstation 1, close the ACE database and reopen it, making sure that both the Exclusive and Read Only check boxes are unchecked in the Open Database dialog box.

6. From Workstation 2, open the ACE database, also making sure that neither the Exclusive nor Read Only option is selected.

Working with Shared Tables

For the most part, Access allows two users who have the same database open in shared mode to view and update objects concurrently. When two users edit the same table at the same time, it is essential to protect the data against the kinds of simultaneous conflicting updates outlined earlier in this chapter. Access gives you three options, which are known as *locking strategies* because they specify the conditions under which Access *locks* records to prevent two or more users from trying to update them simultaneously in Datasheet or Form view. You can choose a locking strategy in the Options dialog box pictured in Figure 17.1, and you can change locking strategies at any time. The options in the Default Record Locking combo box are as follows:

No Locks	Access does not lock records.
All Records	Access locks all records in the source table(s).
Edited Record	Access locks the record you are currently editing.

The record locking strategy established through the multiuser options serves as a global default for all your work in Access, although you can override this default for a particular form, using methods described later in this chapter. If you have used other network databases, particularly Xbase programs, note that Access does not give you a way to explicitly lock records one at a time in Datasheet view or Form view. The locking strategy you choose applies to attached tables as well as Access tables, except SQL tables, which cannot be locked at all by Access. If you select the All Records option, Access does not allow you to open any attached SQL tables, because it would be impossible to implement the selected locking strategy for this table.

NOTE. *The locking strategy, like all the options selected through the Options dialog box, is stored in the SYSTEM.MDA file, which is shared by all the users in your workgroup. You should be aware that the changes you make to these settings will affect all the other users in your workgroup, but not members of other workgroups on your network. If you are not sure which workgroup you belong to, you should consult with your network administrator or the person who installed Access on your network.*

The default locking strategy is No Locks, which allows more than one user to edit the same record at the same time. The person who saves the record first is never informed that anyone else is editing the same data, and it is the second and subsequent users who must resolve the conflict (that is, the second, third, and all other users to *save* the record, regardless of who began editing it first). When any user attempts to save the record after another user has saved it, Access displays the alert box shown in Figure 17.4. Selecting OK invokes a second alert box, which is pictured in Figure 17.5, to further explain the problem and offer three alternative solutions:

Save Record	Saves your changes and overwrites the changes made by the other user
Copy To Clipboard	Copies your changes to the Clipboard and displays the current contents of the record (as it was saved by the other user)
Drop Changes	Aborts the changes you made to the record and displays the current contents of the record (as it was saved by the other user)

Figure 17.4
The alert box displayed when two users update the same record

Microsoft Access

Data has changed; operation stopped.

OK   Help

Figure 17.5

The choices offered
when you use the
No Locks locking

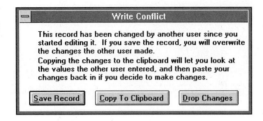

Although Access allows you to overwrite changes made by another user, it is rarely advisable to do so, because Access keeps no audit trail to document the changes. If you choose either of the other two alternatives, Access immediately redisplays the record so you can see its current contents, including the changes made by other users who saved it first. The safest course of action is to copy your changes to the Clipboard so that you do not have to retype them if you later decide to overwrite the other users' changes (you can simply paste in the contents of the Clipboard). More often, you will decide to merge your changes with those made by the other user, and you can open the Clipboard Viewer for reference as you edit the record again. (If you are not familiar with the Clipboard Viewer, note that you can open it from the Program Manager by clicking on the Clipboard icon or by using the Run Command on the File menu to execute a program named CLIPBRD.EXE.)

As you can see in Figure 17.6, which shows a record from the Names table, the Clipboard Viewer displays the contents of the Clipboard in generic form, with the field names on one line and the data on the line below. If the record has only a few fields, this display is clear and easy to understand, but because the data wraps around to fit in the Clipboard Viewer window, a longer record may occupy several lines, and you may have trouble picking out the individual fields. Because Access does not indicate which fields have changed, you may be forced to spend some time comparing the data on the Clipboard to the current record in the datasheet or form you are viewing.

Unfortunately, there is no easy way to copy part of the data stored on the Clipboard back to an Access record, whether or not you open the Clipboard Viewer—throughout Windows, using the contents of the Clipboard is an all-or-nothing proposition. One somewhat roundabout method for extracting part of the data on the Clipboard is to paste it into another Access record (for example, a new blank record) or into a new Notepad document. You can then select the desired material, copy this text to the Clipboard (thus replacing the information previously stored there), and then paste it into the appropriate field. This technique is too cumbersome to be worthwhile for short fields, but it may save you some time when you need to copy a lengthy Text or Memo field.

Figure 17.6

Using the Clipboard Viewer

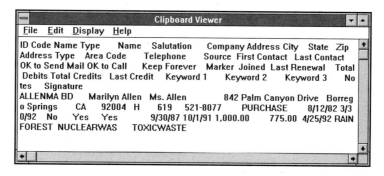

When you choose the Edited Record locking strategy, the instant you begin typing changes, Access locks the current record so that no one else can update it. When you attempt to edit a record that is locked at another workstation, Access displays the locked symbol (a circle with a slash through it) in the record selector and ignores your keystrokes. Access releases the record lock when the user who is editing the record saves the changes. Because it is relatively rare that two users need to edit the very same record at the same time, and most updates take at most a minute or two, the Edited Record locking strategy offers the best combination of flexibility and data security for most Access users. If you choose this strategy, make sure that everyone understands the importance of completing all updates in a timely manner—if you begin editing a record and then walk away from your workstation, no one else will be able to edit the record or lock the entire table until you release the lock by saving the record.

You should also be aware of one unexpected side effect. Because of the way Access interacts with your network's intrinsic file locking capabilities, it may lock one or more additional records adjacent to the one you are editing. Thus, you may find yourself locked out of a record even when all of your co-workers deny that they are editing it. Furthermore, this phenomenon will greatly increase the frequency of conflicts in many databases. For example, in most name and address databases, including the ACE system, it is relatively rare that two staff members would be updating the same record in the Names table at the same time, especially if the need arises during a telephone conversation with a person on the list. It is much more likely that two users will want to update adjacent names at the same time. When you update shared tables, make it a point to watch for the locked symbol in the record selector when you move to a new record and make sure that it is available before you begin editing.

If you choose the All Records locking strategy, Access does not allow you to open a table in any view that would allow changing data if the table is currently being updated by another user. For example, if another user is working with the Names and Contacts form in the ACE database, you could not open the Names or Contacts table in Datasheet view, open another form that allows you to edit either of these tables, or run a query based on either one. You could, however, run reports (which do not have the potential to change data) or view records through a read only form (one in which the Allow Updating property is set to No Tables to prohibit all updates). Any attempt to open a table that is currently being updated by another user invokes the alert box shown in Figure 17.7. This locking strategy is the most restrictive of the three, and you should use it only if you are sure it is absolutely necessary, especially in a database with one or more tables that store central entities that are frequently updated by many users on the network (such as the Names table in the ACE system). You may need to use it during editing sessions in which you plan to edit groups of records in tandem (such as all the transactions or contacts for a particular donor) when you want to ensure that no one can lock you out of any of the records in the group once you have begun.

Figure 17.7

The alert box displayed when the All Records locking strategy is in effect and two users try to open the same table

NOTE. *If you change locking strategies with a form or datasheet open, the original locking strategy remains in effect until you close this form or datasheet.*

As noted briefly earlier in this section, you can override the default record locking strategy for a particular form by changing the Record Locks property. Exactly the same three options are avaiiable in the combo box in the form property sheet—No Locks, All Records, and Edited Record. Thus, if you usually work with the Edited Record locking strategy in effect, but you want to prohibit all other updates to the Names and Contacts tables while you work with the Names and Contacts form, you could set the Record Locks property for the form to All Records. The Record Locks property is also available for reports, but Access gives you only two choices—No Locks and All Records. (You cannot edit data through a report, so Access does not offer the Edited Record option in this context.) If you need to prevent inconsistencies within a report like the ones described earlier in this chapter, you can do so by choosing the All Records option to prevent other users from updating the source tables while Access is processing the report.

When you print reports, you can also use a make table query to extract all the data required for one or more reports and use the resulting table as the data source for the reports rather than printing directly from the original source tables. To ensure that the product of the query is a consistent "snap-shot" of the data as of a particular moment in time, you should change the global locking strategy to All Records before you execute the query to prevent other users from editing the source tables while the query is running. This technique is especially valuable (provided that you have enough disk space) when you need to print several time-consuming reports based on large tables, all of which must contain exactly the same data. It will also yield faster performance, because the steps required to select data from one or more tables, carry out calculations, and sort the output are carried out only once, after which you can print the reports from a single table—the one produced by the query.

Access allows two users to update the same tables with different locking strategies in effect, and the results depend on how compatible the strategies are. This situation commonly arises in two ways—when members of different workgroups edit the same tables (with different global locking strategies stored in their SYSTEM.MDA files), and when users work with forms that specify different locking strategies. When the locking strategies conflict, the more restrictive of the two prevails. For example, if the global locking strategy for your workgroup is All Records, and you have the Names table open in Datasheet view, other users can open the table, but they cannot update it (Access simply displays "Form is read only" in the status bar). Conversely, if your global locking strategy is No Locks, any attempt to open the Names table in a form that uses the All Records locking strategy while you have the table open will invoke an alert box identical to the one shown earlier in Figure 17.7, and Access will refuse to open the table.

The Edited Record and No Locks strategies are reasonably compatible. If the user who is working with the Edited Record strategy begins editing a record first, Access will not allow the other user to edit it (and it will display a circle with a slash through it in the record selector). If the user who is working with the No Locks strategy begins editing first, and also attempts to save the record first, Access displays the dialog box shown in Figure 17.8 and refuses to save the changes. If the user who is working with the Edited Record strategy saves the record first, Access displays the alert boxes shown earlier in Figures 17.4 and 17.5 when the other user attempts to save the edited record and allows this user to overwrite the first user's changes. *It is essential that all users of shared databases understand this interaction between locking strategies.* For example, a user who is updating a table with the Edited Record locking strategy in effect might be under the mistaken impression that no other user can overwrite his or her changes.

Figure 17.8

The alert box displayed if you attempt to edit a record when another user has it locked

To experiment with shared access to the ACE database, try the following steps:

1. From either workstation, choose Options from the View menu, and then choose Multiuser from the scrolling list of categories at the top of the Options dialog box.

2. Set the Default Record Locking option to No Locks, and close the Options dialog box.

3. On Workstation 1, open the Committees table in Datasheet view.

4. On Workstation 2, open the Committees with Committee Names query in Datasheet view.

5. From Workstation 1, move to the Quit field in the record that has LOBBYING in the Committee field and LUSUSAN in the ID Code field, and type **4/18/93**. Make sure that you do not leave the record.

6. From Workstation 2, move to the Officer field in the record that has FINANCE in the Committee field and HOWARDJO in the ID Code field, and type **Treasurer**.

7. Move to the Notes field in the record that has LOBBYING in the Committee field and LUSUSAN in the ID Code field, and type **Quit in April, 1993.** Press Down Arrow to move to the next record.

8. From Workstation 1, select Save Record from the File menu. Access displays an alert box to inform you that "Data has changed; operation stopped." Select OK, and then select Drop changes from the next alert box. Note that the date you entered disappears from the Quit column and the new entry in the Notes field appears.

9. Close the Committees table on Workstation 1 and the Committees with Names query on Workstation 2.

10. From either workstation, set the Default Record Locking option to Edited Record.

Modifying Table Structures

There is one important exception to the general rule that more than one user can update a table at the same time (provided that the current locking strategy permits this): While one user is modifying the structure of a table in Table Design view, no other users can update the table or modify its structure. The reasoning behind this restriction should become apparent when you consider the fact that the structure of the table is fundamental to all your work in Datasheet and Form view, and it must remain constant throughout an editing session. This limitation will not have a big impact on most applications because you will rarely need to modify table structures, and when you do, the process usually takes just a few minutes. You can minimize potential problems by educating all the users of shared databases to be considerate of other network users by not lingering in Table Design view any longer than necessary.

If you open a table in Table Design view while another user is already modifying the structure, Access displays the alert box shown in Figure 17.9 to remind you that you will not be able to save any changes, but it does allow you to view the structure if you select OK from this dialog box. However, you cannot open a table in Datasheet or Form view or run a query or report based on the table while another user is modifying the structure; if you try, Access displays an alert box like the one in Figure 17.10 to tell you who is responsible for locking you out of the table. If you were trying to open the table in Datasheet view (rather than Form view), Access displays another, more generic, alert box, which is shown in Figure 17.11, when you select OK from the first alert box.

Figure 17.9

The alert box displayed if you try to modify the structure of a table that is already open in Table Design view

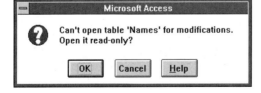

Figure 17.10

The alert box displayed if you try to update a table while another user modifies the structure

Figure 17.11

The alert box displayed to remind you that you cannot open a table in Datasheet view

Although Access will allow other users to work with a table immediately after you finish modifying its structure, it may not make sense to do so. As noted in Chapter 13, modifying the structure of a table may have far-reaching consequences if the changes affect many of the queries, forms, and reports based on the table. For example, references to fields that you renamed or deleted will generate errors when you run a query, form, or report. Other users on your network, especially those who are less knowledgeable about Access or about your application, may not understand that they cannot use these objects until you have propagated the necessary structural changes to all the affected objects.

TIP.   *To avoid potential misunderstandings, you may find it expedient to consult with your co-workers before you modify the structure of a table to make sure no one urgently needs to run queries or print reports based on the table. After you have done so, open the database in exclusive mode while you change the table structure and modify as many dependent objects as you can as quickly as possible.*

Refreshing the Display

When you update a database in shared mode using any locking strategy that permits simultaneous access to the same tables, Access *refreshes*, or updates, the display at each workstation to reflect changes made by other users. You can choose the specific interval at which this screen update takes place and related aspects of the timing of Access' response to simultaneous update attempts by customizing several of the multiuser options shown earlier in Figure 17.1.

The Refresh Interval setting specifies the interval at which Access updates data displayed at your workstation to reflect changes made to local tables by other users, and the ODBC Refresh Interval setting governs the analogous refresh interval for data in attached tables located on remote servers accessed through ODBC (Open Database Connectivity), such as SQL Server tables. The default settings, which are visible in Figure 17.1, are 60 seconds for the Refresh Interval and 600 seconds (10 minutes) for the ODBC

Refresh Interval. The permissible ranges, expressed in seconds, are 1 to 32,766 (32K) seconds for the Refresh Interval setting and 1 to 3,600 seconds for the ODBC Refresh Interval setting. In general, very short intervals will slow performance somewhat, but too long an interval will hide changes longer than necessary.

Note that the refresh interval governs how often Access checks what is happening at other workstations, and it applies to all types of simultaneous access, not just concurrent record updates. At times, a relatively long interval may result in seemingly contradictory behavior. For example, even if the record locking strategy is set to All Records, Access will allow two users in the same workgroup to open the same table if they manage to do so within the refresh interval. However, only the first user will be able to update the data—Access displays the message "Form is read only" if the other user begins typing changes. In contrast, after the refresh interval has elapsed, Access displays the alert box shown earlier in Figure 17.7 if any other user attempts to open the table.

Regardless of the default refresh interval, you can always refresh the display at your workstation by choosing the Refresh option from the Records menu. Access gives you no clue as to whether the display *needs* to be refreshed, so you may want to use this option frequently if you suspect that other users are updating the same tables that you are. Also note that there is no way to force Access to refresh the display at all other network workstations to reflect *your* changes.

Several other aspects of the way that Access handles screen updates to shared tables may seem counterintuitive. When one user deletes a record, this record does *not* immediately disappear from view at any other workstation where another user is updating the same table; instead, at these workstations Access displays "#Deleted" in place of the data in each field in the form or datasheet. Similarly, new records do not appear at the bottom of the table at other workstations. To obtain a complete and accurate picture of the current state of the table or query dynaset you are viewing, you must either close and reopen it or else use the Show All Records option on the Records menu to *requery* the source table or tables. Unlike a *refresh* command, which displays changes made on other workstations, a requery operation causes Access to reread the source tables stored in the database before it updates the screen. When you requery, deleted records disappear and new records are displayed in their proper sequence (which might be based on the primary key or on sorting instructions specified in a query or filter).

Unfortunately, you may not want to requery under certain circumstances. When you are viewing a whole table, requerying is fast, but if you are viewing a query dynaset, Access reruns the query—an operation that can take a considerable amount of time for a large table. Furthermore, if you are working with a filter in effect, the Show All Records option not only updates the display but also cancels the filter and returns to viewing all the records in the dynaset, so you might not want to use this option while viewing selected records in a table or query dynaset using a filter. Remember that you can use the Show All Records option in Form view as well as in Datasheet view, and that executing this command from a subform causes Access to requery only the data source for the subform, not the main form.

There are two other multiuser settings in the Options dialog box that influence the timing of Access' response to simultaneous update attempts. Regardless of which locking strategy you choose, the Number of Update Retries option determines how many times Access retries any update attempt before considering the attempt a failure and reporting the problem to you in one of the alert boxes shown earlier in this chapter. The default setting for this option is 2, and you can choose any value between 0 and 10. The Update Retry Interval setting specifies the interval between retries, expressed in milliseconds (thousandths of a second). The default setting is 250 msec ($\frac{1}{4}$ second), and you can choose any value between 0 and 1,000 (1 second).

To experiment with the refresh options, try the following steps:

1. From either workstation, open the Options dialog box. Set the Default Record Locking option to Edited Record, and set the Refresh Interval setting to 10 seconds.

2. On Workstation 1, open the Committees table in Datasheet view. Move to the Quit field in the record that has LOBBYING in the Committee field and ALLENMA in the ID Code field, and type **5/1/93**. Make sure that you do not leave the record.

3. On Workstation 2, open the Complete Name Information form.

4. Move to the second record in the Names table (Marilyn Allen), and enter **619** in the Area Code field and **521-8077** in the Telephone field.

5. Press PgDn to display the committee information, and use the navigation controls in the Committee Memberships subform to move to the second committee record—the one you are editing on Workstation 1. Click in any field on the form, and watch the symbol in the record selector change to a circle with the slash through it, which indicates that the record is locked and you cannot edit the data.

6. On Workstation 1, move to the next record in the Committees table. Watch the screen on Workstation 2 and observe that after 5 seconds (the designated refresh interval), the new date appears in the Quit field.

7. On Workstation 2, click in the record selector and then choose Delete from the Edit menu to delete the committee membership record. Choose OK from the alert box that asks for confirmation before Access deletes the record.

8. On Workstation 1, move back to the record you just deleted, and immediately choose Refresh from the Records menu. Note that all the fields in the current record change to "#Deleted" when you choose this option (or automatically if it takes you longer than ten seconds to choose the option).

9. Select Show All Records from the Records menu to requery the Committees table. Note that the deleted record disappears from the screen.

Working with Other Database Objects

The locking strategies outlined earlier in this chapter apply only to tables (and therefore to queries, which draw on data stored in tables), not to other database objects (forms, reports, macros, and modules). When more than one user edits the same form or report, Access treats changes much the way it does when you use the No Locks locking strategy. When you open any object in Design view, Access displays the version that was last saved on disk; if another user is still editing the object, you will see the version as of the last Save or Save As command.

Unfortunately, Access issues no special warning to let either user know that another person is editing the same object. If two users are working on the same object simultaneously, the first one to save it may not ever be aware of the other user's activities. When the second user saves the object, Access displays an alert box like the one in Figure 17.12 to inform you that someone else has also changed it and allow you to overwrite the other user's changes. Although Access allows you to do so, it is generally inadvisable to overwrite a co-worker's changes without consulting him or her. If you choose No from the alert box in Figure 17.12, Access displays a standard Save As dialog box to allow you to save your version under a new name. Like transferring a record to the Clipboard, this option enables you to preserve your changes until you have a chance to find out who else modified the object, confer with that person, and hopefully, reach a consensus on what the final definitive version should look like. You can then open both versions of the object at the same time and use the cut and paste commands to merge the two versions.

Figure 17.12
The alert box displayed when two users try to edit the same report

Summary

When you run Access on a network and allow more than one user to open, view, and update the same databases simultaneously, the all-important issue of maintaining data security, accuracy, and integrity is magnified. Protecting shared tables on a network is far more complicated than it is in a single-user application, because you must also take into account the damage that could result from conflicting concurrent updates by different users. This chapter outlined the potential dangers and described some typical strategies for avoiding conflicts and dealing with them when they arise. Because you are not constrained to a single locking strategy for all your work in Access, you can choose the method best suited to each task and the users who carry it out. For example, you can select the relatively flexible and permissive Edited Record strategy, which is in effect in Datasheet view, as the default and use All Records for forms used to carry out critical updates on multiple related tables and reports that must not contain inconsistent data.

As suggested earlier in this chapter, the extent to which a network application runs smoothly and whether the dominant mood among the users is closer to satisfaction or to frustration are controlled largely by human factors, not technical ones. Although you might hope to be able to use a database application without understanding exactly what Access and the network are doing behind the scenes, a little bit of education will go a long way toward helping the users cooperate and coordinate their activities to improve the efficiency of their work. It is essential that even the least technically knowledgeable users understand the locking strategies in use in an Access application and know what measures they can take to avoid interfering with each other's work.

In particular, the designers of a database and all of its users should strive to minimize the duration of all record locks, and doing so requires very little specialized knowledge. When you design forms and reports, choose the least restrictive locking strategy that is consistent with maintaining data integrity. When you use these forms, try to finish each record update as quickly as you can, and then save the record immediately to release the record lock. These considerations are especially important in a large network, in which a user who is locked out of a table or record for what seems like an unreasonably long time cannot easily find out who has the data locked. One user who inadvertently imposes a "lunch lock" (locks a record by beginning to edit it and then walks away from the computer for an hour or more) can inconvenience every other Access user on the network. If your tables are large, you should also try to schedule operations that require locking every record in a table at times when few other users would want access to those tables (for example, you might run time-consuming queries or reports overnight).

Every network user should also be aware of which operations will inconvenience other users by slowing down network performance. In general, this means disk-intensive processes such as running totals queries or printing lengthy reports on large tables. Whenever possible, these operations should be carried out when network traffic is otherwise slow or when few users are working on the network. Remember that your work in Access will affect all network users, not just other Access users, because a high volume of disk activity on the file server will slow down performance throughout the network. If your network is fast and your tables are small, the impact may be minimal, but when you work with large tables, your activities may have a significant impact on overall network throughput.

Keeping a network application running smoothly may require that all the users recognize and understand a little bit about all of these factors, and unfortunately, this may be more than many of them want to know. Whether you are the database administrator or the unofficial Access expert in your organization, try to acquaint all the Access users on your network with the essential facts about multiuser operation—couched in nontechnical language—that will help them work efficiently and cooperatively in the network environment.

18

Introduction to Access Macros

Defining Macros

Running Macros

Defining More Complex Macros

Testing and Troubleshooting Macros

Using Macros in Reports

Using Macros in Forms

Changing Form and Report Control Properties

THUS FAR, YOU HAVE CARRIED OUT ALL YOUR WORK IN ACCESS BY MANIP-
ulating objects directly and selecting menu options one by one. Access
also provides two alternatives—macros and the Access Basic programming language—for executing actions without explicitly issuing the
commands that normally initiate these actions. The more powerful (and, for
beginners, more intimidating) of the two, Access Basic, is introduced briefly
in Chapter 20. In a sense, a macro is also a kind of program—broadly speaking, a program is any sequence of steps carried out without user intervention—but because macros more closely parallel the commands that you can
issue yourself one at a time through the menu system, they are usually intuitively easier to understand.

Macros are a valuable tool for Access users at all levels, including those
who have no need or desire to learn the Access Basic programming language.
You can use macros to automate command sequences that you already know
how to carry out from the Database window, such as opening two or more
forms or datasheets together; printing a series of reports; running several queries that update tables, post totals, and carry out summary calculations; or exporting data from several related tables. You can also use macros to carry out
any series of actions as specific *events* occur while you are printing a report or
editing data using a form. For example, you can use a macro to pause between pages of a report printed on hand-fed sheets of letterhead or to reset
the page number to 1 at the beginning of a particular report section. In forms,
you can use macros to carry out more complex validations than you could express with explicit validation rules; validate combinations of fields; fill in the
values of one or more fields based on your entry in another; and selectively
hide or disable some controls based on the values of others. By attaching a
macro to a command button, you can carry out nearly any sequence of actions from a form, including printing a report, opening another form, updating or posting totals, carrying out specialized searches, or invoking filters.

You may have used other programs, especially word processors and
spreadsheets designed for MS-DOS rather than Windows, that allow you to
create macros by *recording* keystrokes. Defining macros this way requires
some planning and care, but the basic method is intuitively easy—you simply
initiate the recording process, press the keys that you normally would to carry
out the task at hand, and then terminate the recording process and save the
macro. When you *play back* the macro, the keystrokes you recorded are fed
back to the program exactly as if you had pressed all the same keys again
yourself. Unfortunately, this approach, which works admirably when you use
programs that you can control entirely using the keyboard, breaks down
when you work with mouse-driven software, because it is technically far more
difficult to record actions executed with the mouse. Rather than restricting
you to recording only keystroke commands, Access takes a completely different approach: It provides a special Macro Design window in which you define
a macro by building the list of the actions you want the macro to carry out.

This approach has both advantages and disadvantages. Once you become familiar with the macro actions that Access supports and the types of events that can trigger them, defining a macro is easy and fast. Unlike macros defined by recording keystrokes, Access macros are as easy to edit as they are to create—you work in the same Macro Design window and use exactly the same techniques to add, delete, and edit actions as you used to define them in the first place (just as modifying a table structure is no more difficult than defining the fields and properties in a new table). Macros can also incorporate decision-making capabilities—you can specify a condition that determines whether an action or series of actions is executed, and thereby build macros that have different outcomes under different circumstances. Defining conditional steps would be difficult (although not impossible) while recording a macro on the fly. The main disadvantage of the Access method for defining macros, apart from the initial intimidation you may feel when you first confront the macro editor, is that macros are limited to the specific actions recognized by Access. There are currently 42 actions, one of which can be used to invoke any Access menu command, so this limitation is not as restrictive as you might suppose.

This chapter describes how to define Access macros, and how to call them explicitly from the Database window and automatically from a variety of locations in forms and reports. Chapter 19 builds on these skills and introduces some more advanced techniques for using macros to design complete menu-driven applications that are easier for novices to use than working in the unstructured Database window. If you find any of the limitations on macros overly constraining, you can overcome nearly all of them by writing programs in Access Basic, a subject that is introduced in Chapter 20.

Defining Macros

You can create a new macro or edit an existing macro in the Macro Design window, which you invoke from the Database window. To define a new macro, begin by using either of the following methods to reach the Macro Design window:

- Make sure that the Database window displays the list of macros, and then click on the New command button or press Alt+N.

- Whenever the Database window is visible, choose New from the File menu and then choose Macro from the submenu of new object types.

To edit an existing macro, you can either highlight its name and then click on the Design command button or press Alt+D, or you can double-right-click on the macro name.

Figure 18.1 illustrates the Macro Design window with a very simple macro called Open Committee Tables visible and the components of the

Macro Design window, including the command buttons in the tool bar, labeled. This macro (which is described in more detail later in this section) opens both the Committees table and Committee Names table in Datasheet view, moves and resizes the datasheet windows, and then sounds a beep to notify you that the data entry environment is ready. The structure of the Access menu bar in Macro Design view is diagrammed in Figure 18.2.

Figure 18.1

The Macro Design window

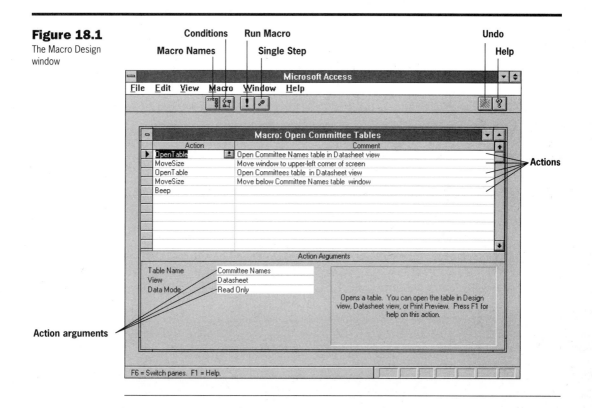

The structure of the Macro Design window should be familiar from your experience working in the Table Design window and the Sorting and Grouping dialog box, which have the same basic layout. Like those two windows, the Macro Design window is divided into two major regions. The upper region always has at least two columns, which display the macro actions and, optionally, comments that describe the purposes of the actions. For example, as you can see from the comments in Figure 18.1, the Open Committee Tables macro uses the OpenTable action to open the two tables, the MoveSize action to move and resize the datasheet windows, and the Beep action to sound a beep. Two optional columns, which are used for conditions that govern which

Figure 18.2

The structure of the
Macro Design view
menu

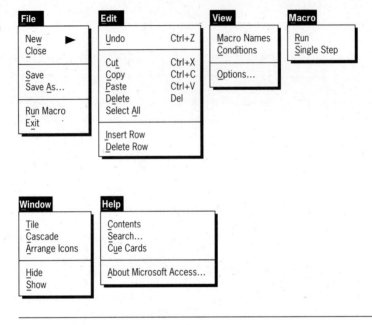

macro steps are executed and for the names of the individual macros that
make up a macro group, are described later in this chapter.

The lower portion of the Macro Design window, which resembles the
field property list in the Table Design window, displays all the *action arguments* relevant to the current macro action (the one that has the focus in the
upper portion of the window). As is the case with functions, Access uses the
term *arguments* for the items of information that you must provide to describe the specific action you want the macro to carry out. The number and
type of the arguments varies considerably. For example, the Beep action,
which sounds an audible beep through the computer's speaker, requires no
input from you and takes no arguments, while the FindRecord action has
seven arguments, which correspond to the options in the Find dialog box.

As in Table Design view, you can move between the upper and lower regions by pressing F6 or by clicking anywhere in either region. By default, the
Macro Design window displays only eleven rows (as in Figure 18.1), but you
can enlarge the window if you need to see more actions. A macro can include
up to 999 actions (a capacity that should prove adequate for most applications), and Access displays a vertical scroll bar in the Macro Design window if
you define too many actions to fit on the screen at once.

You can change the relative widths of the columns by using the mouse to
drag the boundary between any two column selectors either to the left or to

the right. You can use the standard methods based on the selector buttons to the left of the rows to edit the list of macro actions. To move a row, click on the selector to highlight the whole row, and then drag the row to a new position. To add a new row above an existing row, you can either click on the row selector and press the Ins key, or make sure that any column in the row has the focus and choose the Insert Row option from the Edit menu. To delete one or more rows, use the row selectors to select them, and then either press Del or select the Delete Row option from the Edit menu.

The macro action names all consist of one or more common words with no embedded spaces, such as OpenForm, MoveSize, and ShowAllRecords. Table 18.1 lists the actions and summarizes their effects; you will find a more detailed list, which includes all the arguments, in Appendix E. Many of the macro actions are covered in more detail later in this chapter and in Chapter 19.

The data entry regions in the Action column are combo boxes, and you can define a macro action either by typing its name or by selecting it from the drop-down list. If you type the action name, Access verifies it immediately and displays an alert box to warn you that "The text you enter must match an entry in the list" if it is not a valid macro action. Once you have selected an action, Access displays the arguments applicable to that action in the lower portion of the Macro Design window. Like the actions, most of the arguments can be entered either by typing them or by selecting options from combo boxes. For example, as you can see in Figure 18.1, the OpenTable action has three arguments, all of which can be selected from lists: Table Name (which can be any table in the active database), View (which can be Datasheet, Design, or Print Preview), and Data Mode (which can be Add, Edit, or Read Only).

The information box to the right of the argument list in the lower portion of the Macro Design window displays a brief summary of the choices available to you in the current context. When a macro action has the focus, it describes the purpose and usage of the current macro action. For example, in Figure 18.1, you can see the explanation for the OpenTable action. When you are working in the lower portion of the Macro Design window, the information box describes the allowable entries for the action argument that has the focus.

You can also define a macro action that opens an Access object (a table, query, form, report, or macro) by using the mouse to drag the object from the Database window into the Macro Design window, as follows:

1. Make sure that both the Database window and Macro Design window are visible.

2. In the Database window, position the mouse over the desired document, and press and hold down the left mouse button.

3. Position the mouse over the desired row in the Macro Design window, and release the mouse button.

Table 18.1   Macro Actions

Action Name	Purpose
AddMenu	Adds an option and an associated pull-down menu to a custom menu bar
ApplyFilter	Applies a filter, query, or explicit condition to the data source for a form or report
Beep	Sounds a beep
CancelEvent	Cancels the event that triggered the current macro
Close	Closes a table, query, form, report, macro, or module window
CopyObject	Copies a database object
DoMenuItem	Executes a standard Access menu command
Echo	Enables or suppresses screen updates while macro runs
FindNext	Searches for the next record that matches the search criteria used in the previous Find operation
FindRecord	Carries out a search equivalent to one conducted using the Find dialog box
GoToControl	Moves the focus to a specific control on a form, datasheet, or report
GoToPage	Moves the focus to the first control on a specific page on a form
GoToRecord	Adds a new record or moves the focus to the next, previous, first, last, or a specific record in a table, query, or form
Hourglass	Displays the mouse pointer as an hourglass during macro execution
Maximize	Maximizes the active window
Minimize	Minimizes the active window
MoveSize	Moves and/or resizes the active window
MsgBox	Displays a message box (alert box)
OpenForm	Opens a form in Form, Design, Print Preview, or Datasheet view
OpenQuery	Opens a query in Datasheet, Design, or Print Preview view
OpenReport	Opens a report in Print, Design, or Print Preview view

Table 18.1   Macro Actions (Continued)

Action Name	Purpose
OpenTable	Opens a table in Datasheet, Design, or Print Preview view
Print	Prints a datasheet, form, or report
Quit	Exits from Access
Rename	Renames the selected database object
RepaintObject	Completes pending screen updates to a table, query, form, report, macro, or module
Requery	Requeries the data source for an object, query, datasheet, or form
Restore	Restores a minimized or maximized window to its prior size
RunApp	Runs another Windows application
RunCode	Runs an Access Basic function procedure
RunMacro	Runs another macro
RunSQL	Runs an SQL Insert, Delete, Select, or Update command
SelectObject	Selects a database object
SendKeys	Sends character codes to the active window to simulate pressing keys on the keyboard
SetValue	Assigns a new value to a field, control, or property in a form, datasheet, or report
SetWarnings	Enables or suppresses system warning messages and alert boxes
ShowAllRecords	Cancels any active filter and returns to processing all records in a dynaset
StopAllMacros	Cancels all running macros
StopMacro	Cancels the current macro
TransferDatabase	Imports, exports, or attaches a table or other database object
TransferSpreadsheet	Imports or exports spreadsheet data
TransferText	Imports or exports a text file

If you drop the object on a row that already contains an action, Access inserts a new row rather than overwriting the existing action. Access automatically chooses the appropriate "Open" action—OpenTable, OpenQuery, OpenForm, OpenReport, or RunMacro—based on the type of object you drag into the macro window, and it assigns the object name to the first action argument (which identifies the object). If you plan to use this method to add several actions during the current work session, you may want to arrange the Access desktop so you can see most of the Database window as well as the Macro Design window; you can do this either by manually resizing the Macro Design window, by using the Tile command on the Window menu to resize the windows automatically, or by moving the Macro Design window partially "off the right side" of the screen.

You can use a similar drag-and-drop technique to define the value of any argument that accepts an object name: OpenTable, OpenQuery, OpenForm, OpenReport, RunMacro, AddMenu, ApplyFilter, GoToRecord, Close, RepaintObject, and SelectObject. To use this method, simply drag the object from the Database window to the appropriate row (usually the first row) in the lower portion of the Macro Design window. Access does not allow you to use an inappropriate object to set the value of an action argument—you cannot drop a form name on the Table Name argument or assign a query name to the Macro Name argument. Access displays the mouse pointer as a circle with a slash through it when the mouse is not positioned over an argument that can accept the object you are currently dragging from the Database window, and it ignores any attempt to drop the object in an inappropriate place.

As noted briefly earlier in this section, you can use the Comment column to enter a short (up to 255 characters) description of the purpose of an action or macro. If you have ever written programs in any language, you already know how helpful comments can be when you return to modify a program (or a macro) weeks or months after you wrote it, and the details are no longer fresh in your mind. Another good reason to use comments is the fact that when you edit a macro, you can only see the arguments for one action at a time, and unfortunately, Access gives you no way to print the complete contents of a macro for reference. Including a comment for each action that is not self-explanatory enables you to see the "big picture" at a glance. To trace the detailed sequence of actions in a complex macro, you can select one action at a time and examine the arguments in the lower portion of the Macro Design window.

You can save a macro by using any of the standard Windows methods—for example, by using the Save or Save As option on the File menu, or by closing the Macro Design window and choosing Yes from the alert box that asks if you want to save your changes.

To practice working in the Macro Design window, try defining a simple macro that opens the Names table in Datasheet view, minimizes the datasheet window, and opens the Committee Memberships form:

1. Make sure that the Database window displays the list of macros, and click on the New command button or press Alt+N.

2. Click on the arrow symbol in the Action column of the first row to display the drop-down list of macro actions, and select OpenTable from the list.

3. In the Comment column, type **Open Names table in Datasheet view**, and then press F6 to move to the Action Arguments region of the Macro Design window.

4. Enter Names for the Table Name argument, either by typing it or by selecting it from the drop-down list of table names. Leave the View argument set to Datasheet (the other choices are Design and Print Preview), and type or select Read Only for the Data Mode argument.

5. In the second row of the Macro Design window, type **Minimize** in the Action column, and type **Minimize datasheet window** in the Comments column. Note that there are no arguments for the Minimize action, which minimizes the active window.

6. Drag the Macro Design window to the right until you can see the list of object names in the Database window.

7. Click on the Form object button in the Database window, and then use the mouse to drag the Committee Memberships form to the Macro Design window and drop it in the Action column of the third row.

8. Click in the Comment column of the second row in the Macro Design window, and type **Open Committee Memberships form**.

9. Note the action arguments for the OpenForm action—Access automatically entered the form name in the Form Name argument and set the other arguments to their default values, which you can retain as is.

10. Choose the Save option from the File menu, and enter the name **Open Committee Memberships and Names** for the macro name. Figure 18.3 illustrates the macro with the OpenForm action selected.

11. Close the Macro Design window.

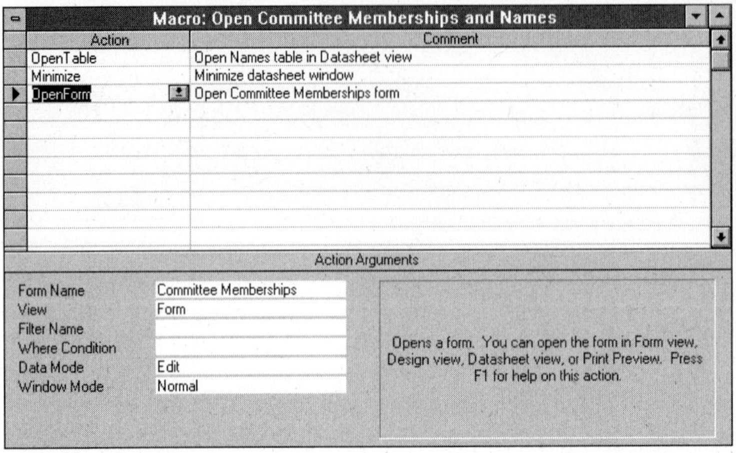

Figure 18.3

A macro that opens a datasheet and a form

Running Macros

There are three essentially different ways you can run Access macros: You can execute a macro explicitly on demand from the Database window or the Macro Design window, you can attach a macro to a command button on a form so any user can run it on demand, or you can associate a macro with a specific form or report property so that it is invoked automatically at the appropriate point in the processing sequence. To execute a macro explicitly, you can use any of the following methods:

- From the Macro Design window, click on the Run Macro button in the tool bar.

- From the Macro Design window, choose the Run option from the Macro menu.

- With the list of macros displayed in the Database window, highlight the name of the macro, and press Enter.

- With the list of macros displayed in the Database window, highlight the name of the macro, and click on the Run command button or press Alt+R.

- From most Access windows, select Run Macro from the File menu, and choose the name of the macro from the Run Macro dialog box.

Running macros from forms is described in the next two sections of this chapter. If you create a new macro or edit an existing macro, and then try to run it

Figure 18.4
The alert box displayed when you run a macro without saving it first

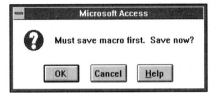

from the Macro Design window without first saving it, Access displays the alert box shown in Figure 18.4 to remind you that you must save the macro before you can run it.

Calling a macro from the Database window gives you a very convenient way to execute a series of actions that you already know how to carry out one by one. For example, Figure 18.5 illustrates a macro called Year-End Reports, which enables you to print both of the ACE system reports required at the end of each year—the Annual Summary Letter (with the matching envelopes) and the Overall Summary Statistics report. This macro has three OpenReport actions, which open the Annual Summary Letter, Envelopes, and Overall Summary Statistics reports in Print Preview mode. If you prefer, you could print the reports immediately by selecting Print for the View argument, but opening the reports in Print Preview mode gives you the flexibility to change the printer setup or omit one of the reports (for example, the envelopes) in a particular print run.

Figure 18.5
A macro that opens three reports in Print Preview mode

Action	Comment
OpenReport	Print Annual Summary Letter
OpenReport	Print Envelopes
OpenReport	Print Overall Summary Statistics

Action Arguments

Report Name	Annual Summary Letter
View	Print Preview
Filter Name	
Where Condition	

Opens a report in Design view or Print Preview or prints the report immediately. Press F1 for help on this action.

To run the Open Committee Memberships and Names macro defined earlier in this chapter, use the following steps:

1. Make sure that the Database window displays the list of macros, highlight the macro name, and click on the Run command button or press Enter to run the macro.

2. Double-click on the icon for the minimized Names table Datasheet window, and verify that the table is read only by trying to edit one of the fields.

3. Close both windows.

Calling Macros from Forms and Reports

When you run a macro from the Database window or from the Macro Design window, you are in complete control—you choose exactly when you want to begin macro execution, and in most cases, macros that you call this way will run from start to finish without user intervention. To call a macro at will from a form, you can attach it to a command button, so that clicking on the button or pressing the designated hotkey combination invokes the macro. Access also allows you to associate macros with various *events* that occur during the form or report processing sequence, so that they are invoked automatically at the appropriate times. Although these methods may seem quite different from the point of view of the user of the form, they are implemented the same way—by assigning the name of a macro to the property that represents an event. Understanding the types of events that Access recognizes and when they occur is crucial to making sophisticated use of macros in forms and reports.

Some events are initiated by the user, and you will probably find these easiest to understand. For example, clicking the mouse on a command button triggers an event called OnPush. However, most of the events recognized by Access are intrinsic to the form or report processing sequence—for example, opening a form, entering or exiting a control, saving the current record, and beginning a new report section are all events. The names of the events suggest when they occur, and once you grasp the basic concept of events, you will have little difficulty recognizing them from their names. For example, the OnOpen event occurs when you open a form or report, OnEnter occurs when you attempt to give a control the focus, and AfterUpdate occurs after Access saves your changes (updates) to the current record. Table 18.2 lists all the events that Access recognizes grouped by their position in the processing sequence, together with the types of objects to which they apply and the times when they occur.

Table 18.2   **Events in Forms and Reports**

Event	Objects	Event Timing
Form or Report Processing:		
OnOpen	Form	When a form is opened, but before first record is displayed
	Report	When a report is opened, but before printing begins
OnClose	Form, Report	When a form or report is closed
OnFormat	Report section	When data for a section is available, but before the section is formatted
OnPrint	Report section	After a section has been formatted, but before printing begins
Record Processing:		
OnInsert	Form	When a new record is added to the active dynaset
OnDelete	Form	When you request a record deletion, but before the record is deleted
OnCurrent	Form	When a different record becomes the current record
BeforeUpdate	Form	When you attempt to save an updated record, but before the record is saved
AfterUpdate	Form	After the changes to a record are saved
Control/Field Processing:		
OnEnter	Form control	When you attempt to enter a control, but before the control gets the focus
OnExit	Form control	When you attempt to exit a control, but before the control loses the focus
BeforeUpdate	Form control	When you attempt to exit a control after updating data, but before the change is accepted
AfterUpdate	Form control	After the changes to a control are accepted
OnPush	Command button	When you click on a command button
OnDoubleClick	Form control	When you double-click on a control

NOTE. *The names Access uses for events match the names of the correspond-ing object properties. The listings in the property sheets include embedded spaces, but these spaces are not part of the internal names used to identify the properties and the corresponding events. In this chapter, the names of the prop-erties are written as they appear in the property sheets (with embedded spaces), but the event names are written as they are used internally. Thus, OpenForm, not Open Form, is the name of the event that occurs when you open a form.*

All of the events are listed in the property sheets of the various form and report objects, and you identify the macro that you want Access to execute whenever an event occurs by entering its name in the appropriate object prop-erty. For example, to run a macro that displays a message when a form is opened, you would enter the macro name in the On Open property for the form as a whole, and to run a macro that resets the page number to 1 at the beginning of a report section, you would enter its name in the OnFormat property for the report section (this example is described in more detail in the section entitled "Using Macros in Reports"). All of these entries in the ob-ject property sheets are combo boxes, and you can either type the macro name or select it from a drop-down list. Access does not verify macro names that you type to make sure that the macros actually exist, so you can enter the names of macros that you have not yet defined. However, any reference to a macro that does not exist when you use the report or form will generate an error message.

You can call the same macro from more than one event. For example, you might call a macro that pauses printing and prompts you to insert the next form in the printer from the page header section of many different re-ports (this macro is described later, in the section called "Using Macros in Re-ports"). You can only call one macro for any given event in a specific form or report, but because a macro can contain multiple actions and can call other macros, this limitation should not present problems.

It is essential to understand the precise timing of closely related events such as BeforeUpdate and AfterUpdate (in forms) and OnFormat and OnPrint (in reports). These fine distinctions may not be intuitively clear from the simple descriptions in Table 18.2, yet they are crucial to the proper performance of forms and reports that include macros. In particular, note that the word "update" in the BeforeUpdate and AfterUpdate events refers to the action *Access* takes to update a field or record, not to the action *you* take to update the value. Thus, the BeforeUpdate event for a text box con-trol occurs after you finish typing your changes but before Access has ac-cepted them, and the AfterUpdate event occurs after Access has accepted your changes and is ready to move the focus to another control in the form. If you want a macro to run when a control first gets the focus, but before you update its value, you must attach the macro to the OnEnter event, and a macro that validates the value entered into the control must be attached to the BeforeUpdate event.

The same timing considerations apply to the analogous form events—the BeforeUpdate event for the form occurs after you finish editing a record and attempt to save your changes but before Access has accepted the changes, and the AfterUpdate event occurs after Access has accepted your changes and is ready to move the focus to another record. Thus, a macro that validates several fields on the form must be attached to the BeforeUpdate property. The following is the complete sequence of events that occurs when you open a form, edit the contents of the first field, move through the remaining controls without changing any data, advance to the next record in the dynaset, and then close the form:

1. OnOpen event for the form

2. OnCurrent event for the form (first record becomes current)

3. OnEnter event for the first control

4. BeforeUpdate event for the first control

5. AfterUpdate event for the first control

6. OnExit event for the first control

7. OnEnter and OnExit events for all other controls

8. BeforeUpdate event for first record

9. AfterUpdate event for first record

10. OnCurrent event for the form (second record becomes current)

When you add a new record to the source table, the following is the sequence of events:

1. OnCurrent event for the form (potential new record becomes current)

2. OnEnter event for the first control

3. OnInsert event (when you enter data in any field)

4. BeforeUpdate event for the first control

5. AfterUpdate event for the first control

6. OnExit event for the first control

7. OnEnter and OnExit events for all other controls

8. BeforeUpdate event for new record

9. AfterUpdate event for new record

10. OnCurrent event for the form (second record becomes current)

If you are new to the world of "event-driven" programming, you may find these sequences complex and confusing, especially in forms, which have more types of events than reports. To help you visualize the complete processing sequence, the ACE sample database contains a simple form called Events, which has three controls—two text boxes and a command button. This form, which is shown in Figure 18.6, has macros attached to the following events:

- OnOpen, OnClose, BeforeUpdate, AfterUpdate, OnCurrent, OnInsert, and OnDelete for the form

- OnEnter, OnExit, BeforeUpdate, and AfterUpdate for the ID Code text box

- OnEnter, OnExit, BeforeUpdate, and AfterUpdate for the Name text box

- OnPush for the command button

Figure 18.6

A form that demonstrates the form event sequence

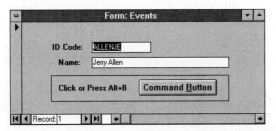

Each of the macros consists of one MsgBox action, which displays a message box to inform you which event is happening and pauses until you press any key or click on the OK button. You may want to open this form at some point as you read this chapter and experiment with various table navigation commands and editing activities to solidify your understanding of the timing of the various events. You can use the same technique to test your own macros and verify that they occur at precisely the times you intended—simply begin the macro you want to test with a MsgBox action, and remove this action later when you are sure the macro works correctly.

NOTE.   *All the macros in the Events form are stored in a* macro group *with the same name. Macro groups are described in the next section, and you may want to open and examine the Events macro group after reading that section.*

Defining More Complex Macros

All of the macros described thus far carry out a series of actions in a particular sequence, and each forms a single functional module that carries out a specific task. One limitation of these simple macros is that every action was executed unconditionally. Access also allows you to add conditions to a macro that test the status of the environment or the values of specific data items in the source table or query to determine whether some or all of the macro actions should be executed. When you use macros to respond to events on forms and reports, the ability to make some steps conditional gives you a great deal of power and flexibility. For example, when you use a macro to validate a field, you might want to display different error messages, depending on which of several problems you find. The ability to test conditions is crucial to several important applications for macros in forms and reports, such as hiding or disabling controls based on the contents of the current record, or suppressing a subform or subreport entirely if it does not contain data.

As an application grows in complexity, you might accumulate literally hundreds of simple macros of the type described earlier in this chapter. Access also allows you to combine macros into a *macro group*—a database object that contains two or more named macros—and this is often a far more efficient approach. By combining related macros into groups, you can reduce the clutter in the Database window and make it easier to find a particular macro when you want to run or edit it. Placing most or all of the macros used together in a form or report in a macro group also facilitates editing the macros and the form simultaneously, because you do not have to open a separate Macro Design window for each one. For example, as noted earlier in this chapter, all the macros called in the Events form are stored in a macro group of the same name.

The main exceptions to this rule are macros that you need to call from multiple reports or forms in an application. Calling one macro is preferable to replicating the actions in this macro in many different macro groups for several reasons: It is faster and easier to create a single macro, there is less danger that careless errors will result in small differences between the various copies, and perhaps most important, if you decide to modify the macro actions, you only need to change them in one place.

Access provides two additional columns in the Macro Design window to accommodate macro names and conditions. By default, neither of these columns is displayed, but you can customize these defaults through the Macro Design options, accessed by choosing Options from the View menu and then selecting Macro Design from the scrolling list of categories. Figure 18.7 illustrates the Options dialog box with the Macro Design options visible.

Figure 18.7
Customizing the
Macro Design
options

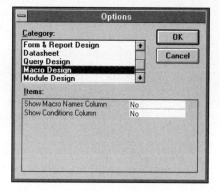

Defining Macro Groups

You create a macro group exactly as you would a single macro; the name that you assign becomes the name of the database object that stores the macro group and is displayed in the Database window. The names of the individual macros that make up the group must conform to the same rules as all other Access object names, and you enter these names in the Macro Name column in Macro Design view. If Access does not display this column when you open the Macro Design window, but you can add it by using the Macro Names option on the View menu or clicking on the equivalent command button in the tool bar. Figure 18.8 illustrates the Events macro group with the Macro Name column visible.

Most of the macros in the Events macro group consist of a single action, but you can include more than one action by leaving the Macro Name column blank in all the rows except the first one in each macro. In Figure 18.8, you can see that the first two macros, Open Events Form and Close Events Form, each have two actions—one that displays the message box and one that sounds a beep.

To refer to a macro stored in a macro group, you use a notation that combines the name of the group with the name of the individual macro. If either name contains embedded spaces, you must enclose it in square brackets. Thus, the macro that is executed when a new record becomes current is referred to in the OnCurrent property for the Events form as Events.[Current Record]; if the macro group name were "Events Macros," you would refer to the macro as [Events Macros].[Current Record]. You will see many examples of this notation in the macro groups described in this chapter. When you run a macro in a macro group, Access starts with the macro step with the specified name, and executes all the steps up to the next one that has a different macro name.

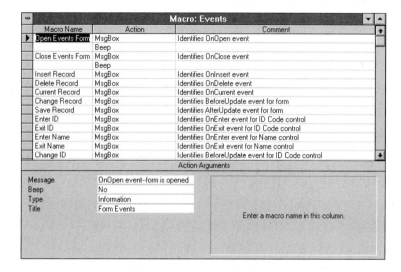

Figure 18.8

Defining a macro group

When you run a macro group from the Database window, Access executes only the first macro in the group. To request a different macro, you must initiate macro execution by using the Run Macro option on the File menu and entering the full name of the macro, including the group name and the individual macro name. Figure 18.9 illustrates the Run Macro dialog box as you would use it to run the Change Record macro in the Events macro group. Strictly speaking, this example does not make sense, because all the macros in the Events group were designed to work in concert with the Events form. However, you can run any of the macros in this group without problems, because the actions they carry out do not depend on the Form view environment. You may want to try executing one or two of these harmless macros from the Database window to test this method for running a macro stored in a macro group.

Figure 18.9

Running one macro in a macro group

NOTE. *The combo boxes in the event entries in the object property sheets display only the names of the macro objects stored in the database—the names of standalone macros and macro groups. To specify a macro stored in a macro group, you can choose the name of the group from the drop-down list, but you must append the name of the individual macro by typing it.*

Using Conditions in Macros

As noted earlier in this chapter, Access allows you to specify a condition that governs whether one or more macro steps should be executed. You can express a condition in a macro with the same kinds of logical expressions used to define selection criteria in a query or filter, to express validation rules, or as the first input to the IIf function.

You must enter conditions in the Condition column in the upper region of the Macro Design window. You can display the Conditions column if it is not visible or suppress it if it is either by choosing the Conditions option from the View menu or by clicking on the Conditions command button in the tool bar. The icon on the face of this button symbolizes a *flow chart*—a diagram used by programmers as a visual representation of the flow of control in a program (or in this case, a macro). Regardless of your selection in the Macro Design options dialog box, if the Conditions column is visible when you close the Macro Design window, Access will automatically display it the next time you edit the same macro object.

Figure 18.10 illustrates a macro group that contains several macros (all of which are described later in this chapter) used in a new version of the Names form. The condition in the Name and Company macro, which validates the Name and Company fields together, is true when both fields are null (blank). In this figure, the columns in the Macro Design window were resized to allocate more space to the Condition column and allow you to see the whole condition. (Although you may not be able to see all of a very long condition at once, expanding the Condition column will usually enable you to discern the purposes of the conditions and distinguish between similar expressions.)

By default, Access executes only the macro action in which you entered the condition. To carry out several consecutive actions if a condition is fulfilled, you must enter an ellipsis (…) in the Condition column for all the actions after the first. This notation is necessary to enable Access to distinguish between macro actions that you want to execute only when a condition is fulfilled and subsequent unconditional steps that are part of the same macro. As you can see in Figure 18.10, the Name and Company macro has three actions, all of which are performed only if the condition is true: MsgBox, which displays a message box that explains the error; GoToControl, which returns the focus to the Name control to facilitate fixing the problem; and CancelEvent,

Figure 18.10

Using conditions in a macro

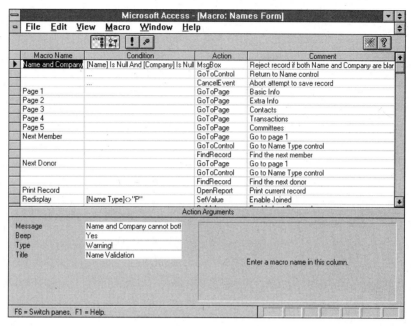

which cancels the event that triggered the macro (in this case, the attempt to save the record). This macro is explained in more detail later in this chapter in the section called "Validating Data." For now, simply note that it has three steps, all of which are dependent on the condition in the second column. A macro can also include unconditional steps before and/or after the ones dependent on the condition.

Using conditions in a macro is roughly analogous to using the IIf function, but there is no comparable built-in mechanism for specifying two alternatives, one of which is carried out when a condition is true and the other when the condition is false. If the condition specified in a macro is not fulfilled, Access does nothing. To specify two alternative actions, you must write two related conditions, one that evaluates to True and one to False, and follow each with the desired actions. For example, Figure 18.11 shows part of the Redisplay macro from the Names Form macro group pictured in Figure 18.10. This macro, which disables or enables some of the controls in the form based on the value of the Name Type control, has two conditions, each followed by a series of SetValue actions that assigns the value Yes or No to the Enabled property for the relevant controls. In situations like the one handled by this macro, where you only need to test two alternatives, you might ideally prefer a control structure like the IIf function (or, if you are familiar with programming, the equivalent If...Else...End If programming structure). Keep in mind, however, that an Access macro may need to test more than two related conditions. For example, instead of the Redisplay macro, you could use a more complex macro that enables and disables different groups of controls for prospects, members and donors, board members, and media and political contacts.

Figure 18.11

A macro that tests two alternative conditions

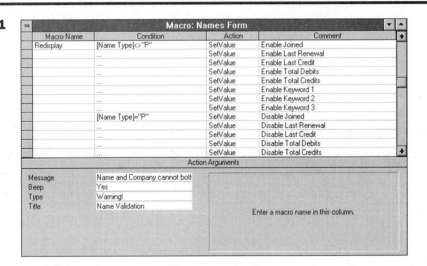

Macro Name	Condition	Action	Comment
Redisplay	[Name Type]<>"P"	SetValue	Enable Joined
	...	SetValue	Enable Last Renewal
	...	SetValue	Enable Last Credit
	...	SetValue	Enable Total Debits
	...	SetValue	Enable Total Credits
	...	SetValue	Enable Keyword 1
	...	SetValue	Enable Keyword 2
	...	SetValue	Enable Keyword 3
	[Name Type]="P"	SetValue	Disable Joined
	...	SetValue	Disable Last Renewal
	...	SetValue	Disable Last Credit
	...	SetValue	Disable Total Debits
	...	SetValue	Disable Total Credits

Action Arguments

Message	Name and Company cannot both
Beep	Yes
Type	Warning!
Title	Name Validation

Enter a macro name in this column.

Testing and Troubleshooting Macros

As you have undoubtedly realized by now, building macros is a little like programming. Like a simple program, a macro is a series of instructions, executed in a specific order, for carrying out a series of actions without user intervention. Like programming, macros offer the advantages of automation, power, and flexibility, but with these benefits come some of the same difficulties, including the necessity to find and repair the inevitable *bugs* (errors) that you will make when you design complex macros. If you use a macro action incorrectly, the macro will *crash*—Access will display an error message and then halt macro execution—and even if a macro runs without generating errors, it may not work exactly as you intended. Using macros safely and effectively requires both *testing*—trying a macro under a range of conditions typical of those that will arise when you use the application to verify that it performs correctly—and *debugging*—finding and repairing any errors.

The more thorough your testing is, the less time you will have to spend later fixing problems that crop up when you begin using the application with "live" data. Often, you can test a macro by running it from the Macro Design window or the Database window, even if the macro will later be attached to an event or command button in a report or form. Make sure that you test any macro that includes conditional steps under circumstances in which each condition is true and in which each condition is false. For example, the Validate Zip macro (which is described later in the section "Validating Data") validates the Zip field in the Names table to ensure that it conforms to all the rules that define valid U.S. zip codes. When you test this macro, make sure you enter the full spectrum of correct and incorrect zip codes, including all of the following:

- A zip code shorter than five characters

- A zip code between five and ten characters long

- A ten-digit zip code in which the sixth character is not a dash

- A zip code with a letter or punctuation mark in each of the nine digit positions (one at a time)

- A legitimate five-digit zip code

- A legitimate ten-digit zip code

As you can see from this last example, testing a complex macro can be tedious, but thorough testing will go a long way toward avoiding errors when you (or your co-workers) begin to use an application to do real work.

When an error occurs during macro execution, Access may display an error message that clearly explains the problem. For example, if you use the OpenForm action to open a form named Names, Access displays an alert box to inform you that "There is no form named 'Names'" if it cannot find this form when the macro runs. To help you find the problem, Access displays a dialog box like the one shown in Figure 18.12, which includes the name of the currently running macro, the action that generated the error, and the arguments passed to that macro. When you run a single macro with an explicit command from the Database window or the Macro Design window, this information may tell you little that you could not deduce from the error message in the original alert box, but it can be very helpful when you test a form that invokes many different macros. Whether or not the Action Failed dialog box provides any helpful information, your only alternative is to use the Halt button to stop macro execution. When you do so, Access returns you to the environment from which the macro was invoked. At other times, a macro may run without generating an error message but fail to perform as you intended. For example, a macro designed to validate data may reject correct entries or accept incorrect ones.

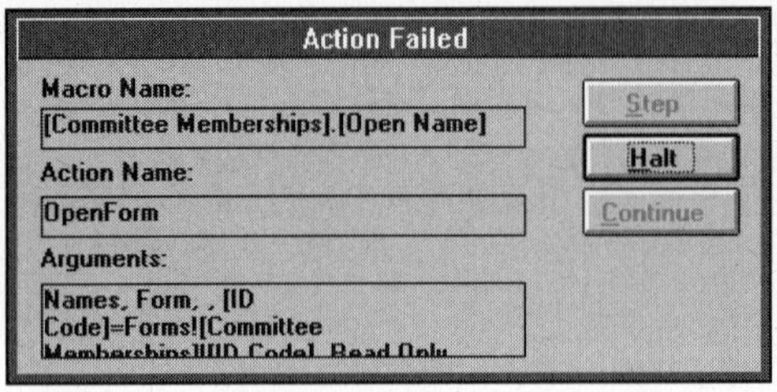

Figure 18.12
The Action Failed
dialog box displayed
when an error
occurs during macro
execution

```
┌─────────────────────────────────────────────────┐
│                  Action Failed                    │
│  Macro Name:                          ┌────────┐  │
│  [Committee Memberships].[Open Name]  │  Step  │  │
│  Action Name:                         ├────────┤  │
│  OpenForm                             │  Halt  │  │
│  Arguments:                           ├────────┤  │
│  Names, Form, , [ID                   │Continue│  │
│  Code]=Forms![Committee               └────────┘  │
│  Memberships][ID Code], Read Only                 │
└─────────────────────────────────────────────────┘
```

In most cases, you will want to edit the macro to search for the problem, and often the cause is immediately apparent from a close examination of the conditions and actions. Some of the most common causes for errors include:

- Typographical or spelling errors in form or control names

- Forgetting to define a macro that you have already named in a form or report property sheet

- Forgetting to attach a macro to a form or report event or attaching the macro to the wrong event

- Using the cut and paste commands to create several similar actions, and forgetting to change some of the arguments in one or more of the copies

- Failing to test for all possible values of a control

If you find yourself completely baffled, one way to find the cause of the problem is to run the macro in *single-step mode*, in which Access executes one macro action at a time and displays each action as it runs. This mode is particularly helpful for tracing the series of steps that led to an error message and finding the macro action that generated the error. To turn on single-step mode, select the Single Step option from the Macro menu or click on the Single Step button in the tool bar (the one with the footstep icon on its face). If you can run the macro from the Macro Design window, you may be able to find the problem, repair it, turn off single-step mode, and then save the new version of the macro. When you debug a macro that must be tested from a form or report (because it fails only with certain combinations of data), you must turn on single-step mode from the Macro Design window, run the form or report, and then return later to the Macro Design window to turn off single-step mode. Note that single-step mode applies globally to macro execution throughout Access, not just to the macro you are trying to test.

When you work in single-step mode, Access pauses macro execution and displays the Macro Single Step dialog box shown in Figure 18.13 when it encounters the first macro step. This dialog box resembles the Action Failed dialog box, except that the Step and Continue command buttons are enabled to allow you to control macro execution manually. Unfortunately, this dialog box does not display any conditions tested in the macro, so it may be hard to distinguish similar actions that are contingent on different conditions.

Figure 18.13

Running a macro in single-step mode

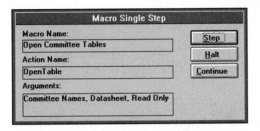

You can control macro execution by using the three command buttons in the Macro Single Step dialog box, as follows:

Step   Executes the step that is currently displayed in the dialog box

Halt   Cancels macro execution

Continue   Turns off single-step mode and returns to continuous execution

If you are accustomed to programming languages that offer sophisticated debugging facilities, you may be disappointed in the relatively primitive single-step mode that Access provides for testing macros. Nevertheless, working in this mode will often lead you to the cause of a problem simply by forcing you to focus your attention on the exact sequence of events that occur during macro execution. Unfortunately, there is no easy way to print the complete contents of a macro for reference. You may want to leave the Macro Design window open while you test or debug a macro in single-step mode, so you can see all the steps, but you cannot switch to the Macro Design window when the Single Step dialog box has the focus.

One technique that you can use to debug macros is to add temporary MsgBox actions to remind you exactly where you are in the macro or to display the values of fields or properties. For example, in the macro that validates U.S. zip codes, you might display the expression

```
"Length of zip: "&Len([Zip])
```

in a message box to verify whether the macro is correctly evaluating the tests based on the length of the Zip field. You can also use message boxes to distinguish between similar or identical steps executed from different points in a macro (by displaying different messages). Once you have found all the problems, you can remove these extraneous actions.

Using Macros in Reports

You can use macros in reports to carry out a variety of specialized functions and make decisions that would be impossible using only the report controls and properties. Unlike forms, reports do not accept input from the user, so any macro that you want to invoke from a report must be attached to an event that occurs during the report processing sequence. As you can see in Table 18.2, there are only four events that Access recognizes in reports: OnOpen and OnClose, which are properties of the report as a whole, and OnFormat and OnPrint, which apply to any report section.

The distinction between the OnFormat and OnPrint events is a fine but important one: The OnFormat event occurs after Access has gathered all the data that will be printed in a report section, but before the section has been formatted for printing, whereas the OnPrint event occurs after the section has been formatted, but before Access has begun printing it. Because the OnFormat event occurs before Access begins to format the section for printing, any macro that influences the layout—for example, a macro that suppresses a control based on the data in the section—should be called from this event. In contrast, you should use the OnPrint event for macros that depend on the page layout—such as a macro that tests the value of the current page number—because the layout has not been finalized when the OnFormat event occurs.

Figure 18.14 illustrates a very simple macro called Print Pause, which enables you to print letters or envelopes on single hand-fed forms (letterhead or envelopes). This macro contains only one action—a MsgBox action that displays an alert box to prompt you to insert the next form into the printer. Because Access always requires you to acknowledge a message displayed in an alert box by pressing a key or clicking on the OK button, the MsgBox action is a versatile tool for pausing during any operation, including printing a report.

This action takes four arguments, which are used as follows:

Message   The text of the message displayed in the alert box

Beep   Whether to sound a beep when the alert box is displayed

Figure 18.14

A macro that pauses for a paper change during printing

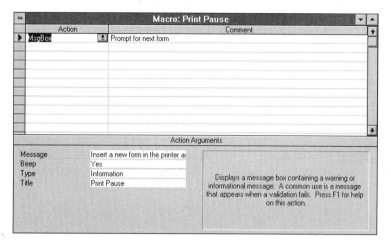

Type   The type of alert box, which governs which icon Access displays at to the left of the message; you can choose None (no icon), Critical (stop sign), Warning? (?), Warning! (!), or Information (i)

Title   The title to display in the alert box title bar; if you leave this argument blank, Access uses "Microsoft Access" as the title

In the ACE system, the Print Pause macro is used in the Envelopes (Single) report, which prints addresses on single envelopes. The macro is called from the OnFormat event for the detail section, which occurs before each record is printed. Note that the message displayed by the macro is generic enough that you can call it from virtually any report in your own applications; if you prefer, you could use several versions of this macro to display more specific messages for different reports.

You can use macros to overcome some of the problems with page numbering pointed out in Chapter 11. For example, if you choose not to print page numbers in a report header section, such as the cover sheet for the Committee Memberships report, you might want to print the page number 1 rather than 2 on the first page of data. Resetting the page number, which is stored in the Page property for the report, is easy, using the SetValue action in a macro, but choosing the right value and the right location for the macro is a little tricky. Because you want to reset the page number only once, you must do so from the report header section, because all subsequent report sections, including the group header or page header sections, might be printed many times. However, Access increments the page number *after* the page break that occurs at the end of the report intro section. You must therefore set the page number to 0, so that when Access increments it during the page break, the desired page number (1), is the result. Fortunately, Access allows you to assign any integer value to the Page property, including 0.

In a report in which each group begins on a new page, you might want to reset the page number to 1 at the beginning of each group. This is easily accomplished by calling a macro that uses the SetValue action to assign the value 1 to the Page property from the OnPrint event for the group header section.

You can test both of these techniques in the Committee Memberships report. First, use the following steps to create a macro group with two macros that reset the Page property:

1. Make sure that the Database window displays the list of macros, and click on the New command button or press Alt+N.

2. If the Macro Name column is not displayed in the Macro Design window, click on the Macro Names command button in the tool bar, or choose Macro Names from the View menu. If the Conditions column is displayed, you can remove it if you wish, by clicking on the Conditions command button in the tool bar or by choosing Conditions from the View menu.

3. In the first row, type **Initialize** in the Macro Name column, and press Enter to advance to the Action column.

4. Click on the arrow symbol in the Action column of the first row to display the drop-down list of macro actions, and select SetValue from the list.

5. In the Comment column, type **Reset page number to 1 after printing report cover sheet**, and then press F6 to move to the Action Arguments region of the Macro Design window.

6. Enter **Page** (the name of the page number property) for the Item argument, and enter **0** for the Expression argument, which specifies the value you want to assign to the object identified by the Item argument.

7. Press F6 to return to the upper portion of the Macro Design window.

8. In the second row, type the name of the second macro, **Group Reset**, in the Macro Name column, enter **SetValue** in the Action column, and type **Reset page number to 1 at the beginning of each group** in the Comment column. Press F6 to move to the Action Arguments region.

9. Enter **Page** (the name of the page number property) for the Item argument, and enter **1** for the Expression argument.

10. Save the macro under the name **Page Numbers**.

Next, modify the Committee Memberships report to call these macros:

1. Open the Committee Memberships report in Report Design view, and make sure that the property sheet is visible.

2. Click in the report header section to display its property sheet.

3. Display the drop-down list of macro names for the On Print property, and choose the name of the macro group, Page Numbers, from the list.

4. Press F2 to edit your entry, and add square brackets around the name of the macro group, followed by a period and the name of the individual macro you want to run. The complete macro name is **[Page Numbers].Initialize**.

5. Click in the ID Code group header section to display its property sheet.

6. Enter the macro name **[Page Numbers].[Group Reset]** in the On Print property, either by using the technique suggested in steps 3 and 4 or by typing the name.

7. Click in the ID Code group footer section to display its property sheet.

8. Enter **After Section** in the Force New Page property, either by typing it or by selecting it from the drop-down list.

9. Click in the control that prints the page number in the page footer section, and edit the Control Source property so it reads **=[ID Code]& ": Page "&Page**. Move the control to the left to line up with the 6–inch mark in the horizontal ruler, and widen it almost to the right edge of the report.

10. Preview or print the report. Observe that each person's committee memberships begin on a new page, which is numbered 1, and that the page number is printed in the form ALLENMA: Page 1.

11. Close the report and save it.

Using Macros in Forms

As you can see in Table 18.2, Access recognizes more different events in forms than in reports, primarily because unlike reports, forms must interact with the user, and there are more points in the data entry sequence where you might want to intervene. You can use macros in forms to carry out special actions when you enter or exit a control, when you edit a field, when you add or delete a record, when you move the focus to a different record in the source dynaset, and when you save your changes to the current record. In addition, by attaching a macro to a command button, you can allow the users of your forms to execute actions at will. The next three sections outline a variety of techniques for using macros in forms.

Validating Data

As noted earlier in this chapter, you can use macros to carry out more complex validations than you can express by writing explicit conditions in the Validation Rule property. The Name and Company macro described earlier is a good example of one typical application for macros—validating a combination of fields rather than a single field. Macros like this are best invoked from the BeforeUpdate event for the form, which is triggered by any attempt to save the current record—using the Save Record option on the File menu, moving past the last control on the form, or using the navigation controls or equivalent menu options to move to another record. The basic strategy for macros of this type is as follows:

1. Use the MsgBox action to display a message that describes the problem.

2. Use the GoToControl action to return the focus to the control (or one of the controls) that failed the validation test.

3. Use the CancelEvent action to abort the event that triggered the macro— the attempt to save the record or move to another record.

You can use a similar technique to test for several different error conditions and display an error message that explains the precise nature of the problem. Figure 18.15 illustrates a macro called Validate Zip Code, which tests for all the errors that might occur in a U.S. zip code. To facilitate copying this generic macro for use in your own applications, it is stored in the ACE database as a separate macro object rather than as part of a macro group. You could extend this macro to handle foreign postal codes by adding more steps and including in each condition a test based on the field that stores the country.

This macro tests four conditions, and it may display one or more message boxes, depending on how many tests the zip code fails. All of the MsgBox actions are very similar—all the alert boxes are treated as warnings, the Beep option is enabled, and the title bar displays "Zip Code Validation." The message itself, which is different in each case, describes exactly what is wrong with the zip code.

The first condition in the Validate Zip Code macro tests the length of the zip code to ensure that it is exactly five or ten characters long. The second condition uses the Mid function to test the sixth character in a ten digit zip code, which must be a dash. The last two conditions test the first five digits and the

Figure 18.15

A macro that validates zip codes

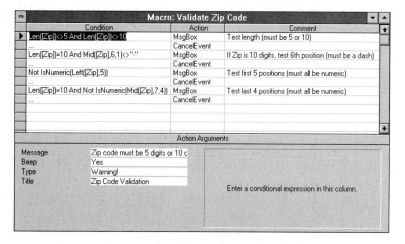

last four digits, respectively, to ensure that each character is a digit. The method for carrying out these tests is based on the IsNumeric function, which evaluates to True if the expression supplied as input might constitute a valid number. Thus, although the Zip field is a text string, the IsNumeric function yields the value True if the expression supplied as input—Left([Zip],5)—evaluates to a text string that "looks like" a valid number. You must test the two portions of the zip code separately because no text string with an embedded dash could constitute a valid number. If you want to try this macro, open the Names Five-Page Form and try entering various illegitimate values into the Zip field.

Depending on how many different errors a zip code contains, the Validate Zip Code macro may display one or more error messages. The CancelEvent macro action cancels the event that triggered the macro (in this case, the attempt to exit from the Zip Code field), but it does *not* cancel macro execution. This decision was deliberate—it gives you the maximum amount of information about the invalid zip code, and because you must acknowledge each message by clicking on the OK button in the message box or pressing a key, there is no danger that you will miss any of the error messages. If you prefer to cancel a validation macro when the data fails any one test, you can add a StopMacro action after the CancelEvent action to stop the macro immediately. In either case, give some thought to the order in which you want to display the error messages; you might want to place the most important tests (which detect the most drastic errors) earlier in the macro.

You can use a macro similar to the Name and Company macro to validate the Joined and Quit fields in the Committees table, which must be tested together to ensure that the Joined field is no later than the Quit field. Begin by creating a macro group called Committee Memberships, which will hold all the macros that you will add to the Committee Memberships form:

1. Make sure that the Database window displays the list of macros, and click on the New command button or press Alt+N. Make sure that both the Macro Name and Conditions columns are displayed in the Macro Design window.

2. Define the first macro action as follows:

Macro Name	Validate Dates
Condition	[Quit]<[Joined]
Action	MsgBox
Comment	Validate Joined and Quit dates

3. Press F6 to move to the Action Arguments region of the Macro Design window, and enter the following action arguments for the MsgBox action:

Message	Date joined must be earlier than date quit
Beep	Yes or No, whichever you prefer
Type	Warning!
Title	Validate Dates

4. In the second row of the Macro Design window, type **...** in the Condition column, and enter **CancelEvent** in the Action column.

5. In the third row of the Macro Design window, type **...** in the Condition column, and enter **GoToControl** in the Action column. Press F6 to move to the Action Arguments region of the Macro Design window, and type **Joined** for the Control Name argument.

6. Save the macro under the name **Committee Memberships**.

Next, modify the Committee Memberships form to call this macro:

1. Open the Committee Memberships form in Form Design view, and make sure that the property sheet is visible.

2. In the form property sheet, enter the macro name in the BeforeUpdate property: **[Committee Memberships].[Validate Dates]**.

3. Click in the Joined text box, and edit the Validation Rule property so it only tests for null values: **Is Not Null**. Edit the Validation Text property to reflect this change: **Date joined cannot be blank**.

4. Click in the Quit text box, and delete the expression in the Validation Rule property and the error message in the Validation Text property.

5. Switch to Form view and delete the contents of the Joined field. Note that Access carries out the validation based on the Validation Rule property and displays an alert box to inform you that the date cannot be blank.

6. Press Esc to restore the original value, and then change the date to **8/1/94**. Press Tab and note that Access allows you to exit from the field.

7. Click on the Next Record navigation button, and note that Access displays the message specified in the Validate Dates macro, as shown in Figure 18.16. Click on OK or press Enter, and note that Access returns the focus to the Joined text box.

Figure 18.16

The error message displayed by the Validate Dates macro

8. Press Esc to restore the original value in the Joined field.

9. Close the form and save it.

Responding to Changes in Field Values

You can use macros in forms to respond to changes in the values of one or more controls. One application for this type of macro is assigning a value to one control based on your entry in another, either to plug in a default value in a new record or to update one control dynamically, based on changes made to another. For example, you can use a macro to overcome one of the limitations cited in Chapter 12—the fact that you cannot use an expression based on other fields in the same record to define the Default Value property, because Access assigns all the default values simultaneously at the moment you add a new record to a dynaset. If you want to execute the macro as soon as the focus leaves a particular control, you can invoke it from the OnExit or

AfterUpdate event for that control; to trigger the macro when you save the current record, attach it instead to the AfterUpdate event for the form.

Figure 18.17 illustrates a very simple one-step macro called Follow-Up Date, which assigns a new value to the Follow-up Date field in the Contacts table based on the date you enter into the Date field. This macro uses the SetValue action to assign the result of evaluating the expression [Date]+14 to the Follow-up Date field. The condition [Follow-up Date] Is Null ensures that the macro enters a value in this field only if it does not already contain one. If you want to test this macro, try calling it from the OnExit event for the Date control in the Contacts with Names form.

Figure 18.17

A macro that assigns a new value to one control based on another

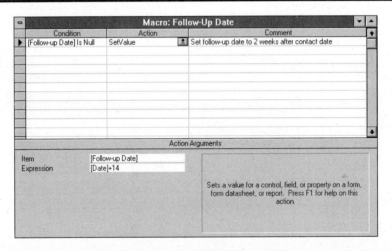

Figure 18.18 illustrates a more complex example—a macro group designed to work in concert with a new version of the Transactions with Names form called Transactions with Names 2. The first macro in the group, Total Amount, recalculates the Amount field when any of the fields that contribute to the total change. The expression that defines the new value is identical to the one used in the Transaction Amount Update query described in Chapter 9:

```
[Subtotal]-[Discount]+[Tax]+[Shipping].
```

Because you might not tab through all the fields in the form in sequence—you can use the mouse to move directly to any control in the form—this macro is called directly from the AfterUpdate property for each of the fields that affect the value of the Amount field: the Discount, Tax, and Shipping controls. It is also called indirectly from the same property for the Subtotal control as outlined shortly.

Note. The Purchases macro in the Transactions Form macro group is described later in this chapter in the section called "Changing Form and Report Control Properties."

Figure 18.18

Macros that recalculate numeric field values

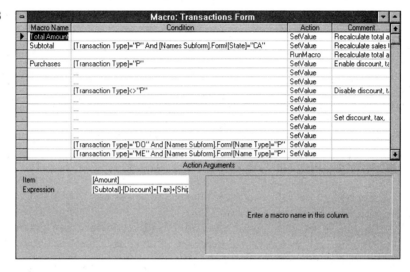

The Subtotal field requires slightly different handling, because you may have to recalculate the sales tax when the subtotal changes. ACE must charge 8.5 percent sales tax on purchases (not other types of transactions) made by people who live in California. These calculations, which must be carried out *before* recomputing the Amount field, are carried out by a macro named Subtotal, which is called from the AfterUpdate event of the Subtotal control. The condition in this macro tests the value of the State field on the subform, and if it contains the text "CA," uses the SetValue action to assign the value 0.085*[Subtotal] to the Tax field. Note the expression used to refer to the State control in the subform, which combines the name of the subform, the identifier "Form" (which distinguishes a subform from a subreport), and the name of the control itself:

```
[Names Subform].Form![State]="CA"
```

After calculating the sales tax, the Subtotal macro uses the RunMacro action to call the Total Amount macro. Although this macro has just one action, calling it is preferable to using a SetValue action that repeats the same calculation used in the Total Amount macro—if you had to change the expression that describes the new value for the Amount field, you would only have to change it in one place. Note also that even though the Total Amount macro is stored in the same macro group as the Subtotal macro, you must include the name of the macro group in the name (which is written as [Transactions Form].[Total Amount]), because by default, Access always searches first for a standalone macro.

Creating Custom Navigation and Search Controls

You can use macros, usually invoked through command buttons, to create special navigation controls for moving between the "pages" of a form, controls that replace or augment the standard Access navigation controls displayed at the bottom of a Form view window, or controls that carry out custom searches or implement frequently used record selection criteria by placing filters in effect.

These custom controls will nearly always take the form of command buttons, which you can "press" by clicking on the button with the mouse, by pressing Enter when the button has the focus, or by using an Alt-key shortcut. To create a command button, you can use the standard method based on the toolbox: Click on the Command Button button in the toolbox, and then either click on the form to create a default size button or drag the button to the desired size. As is the case with toggle buttons, a command button can have either a caption (defined by the Caption property) or a picture (defined by the Picture property) on its face. As detailed in Chapter 15, to use a picture, you enter the name of the bitmap file that stores the image in the Picture entry in the property sheet. To specify a caption, you can type it in the Caption property or directly in the button object.

If you use a caption (rather than a picture), you can define a hotkey by preceding the desired letter with an ampersand (&). Note that even if you type the caption in the button itself, the ampersand is never displayed on the button face. When you use the form, the designated character is underlined, and you can operate the button from anywhere on the form by holding down the Alt key and pressing this key. The most important property for a command button is the On Push property, which identifies the macro that you want to invoke when the button is pressed.

Figure 18.19 illustrates the first and third "pages" of a form called Names Five-Page Form (based on the Names form presented in Chapter 12) that includes a number of specialized command buttons. This form displays the basic name and address information from the Names table on page 1, the extra information entered for all people except prospects on page 2, contacts on page 3, transactions on page 4, and committee memberships on page 5. On the first page, there are five command buttons labeled Basic Info, Extra Info, Contacts, Transactions, and Committees, which you can use to move directly to any page on the form. Each of these buttons calls a simple macro via the OnPush property; these macros, which are visible in Figure 18.10, use the GoToPage action to move directly to a particular page on the form. This action moves the focus to the first control on the page; if you want to select a different control, you can add a GoToControl action. Note also that all the buttons have hotkeys, so that you can operate them from any page of the form. If you wanted to avoid using any keyboard commands, you would have to duplicate the buttons on all five pages.

You can use command buttons to replace the standard navigation controls normally displayed in the lower-left corner of the Form and Datasheet

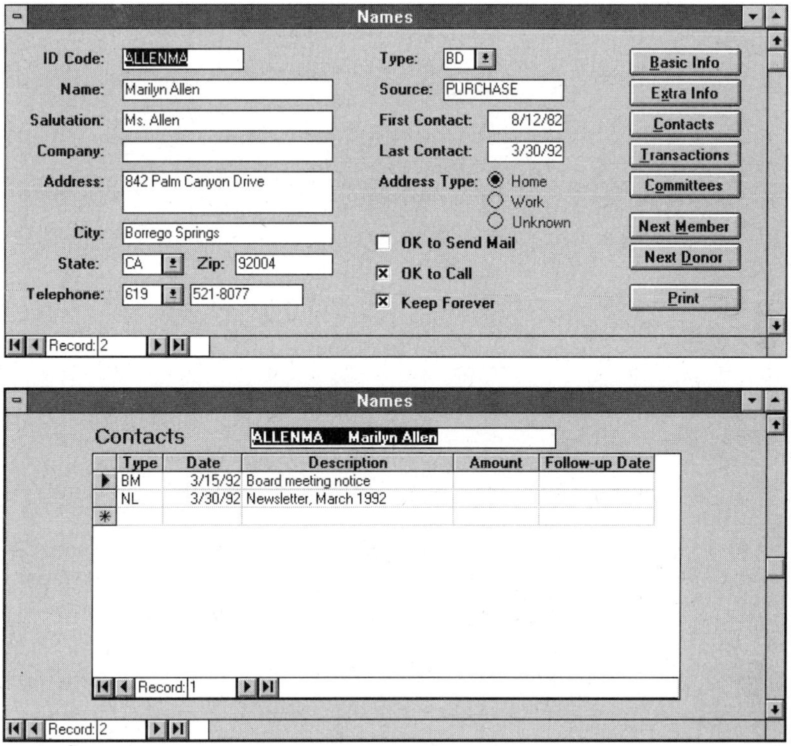

Figure 18.19

A form with
command buttons

windows, as in the version of the Names and Committee Memberships form shown in Figure 18.20, which also includes command buttons for adding and deleting the current record. You might choose this approach when you build forms that will be used by people who are not familiar with Access, for consistency with other software, or to mingle special controls (like the Add and Delete buttons in Figure 18.20) with the navigation controls.

The macros attached to the command buttons in the form in Figure 18.20 are stored in a macro group called Names and Committees, which is shown in Figure 18.21. The first five buttons are implemented using the GoToRecord action, which simulates the effect of selecting the Go To option from the Records menu in Form view or Datasheet view. The GoToRecord action takes four arguments, of which only the last two are required for moving to another record in the currently selected table. The available choices for the Record argument are exactly the same as the options in the submenu that appears when you choose the Go To option from the Records menu—Next, Previous, First, Last, Go To, and New. If you choose Go To, you must enter a record number (or a

Figure 18.20

A form with custom navigation controls

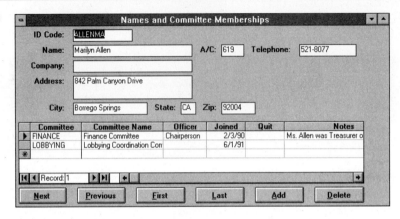

numeric expression that evaluates to a record number) in the Offset argument to identify the record you want to move to. If you enter a value for the Offset argument when the Record argument is Next or Previous, the offset specifies the number of records to move forward or backward.

Strictly speaking, the Add and Delete buttons are not navigation controls, but the Add button is implemented using exactly the same mechanism as the Next, Previous, First, and Last buttons (with a GoToRecord action in which the Record argument is set to New). There is no macro action specifically intended to delete a record, but you can carry out this action (and many others) by calling the powerful DoMenuItem action, which allows you to simulate the effect of choosing any Access menu option that would be available when you run the form. This action is described in the next section.

You can also use command buttons as specialized navigation controls that could not possibly have built-in equivalents in Access because they are unique to your application. You can see two examples in Figure 18.19—the Next Member and Next Donor command buttons, which call macros of the same names to move to the next member and next donor record, respectively. At the heart of both macros is the FindRecord action, which carries out a search equivalent to one that you might conduct using the Find dialog box. Figure 18.22 shows these macros, with the action arguments for the FindRecord action visible in the lower portion of the Macro Design window and the correspondence between the arguments and the Find dialog box options indicated. Keep in mind when you use this action that if you set the Search In argument to Current Field, you must first move the focus to the field in which you want to search. The second step in the Next Member and Next Donor macros is therefore a GoToControl action that moves the focus to the Name Type control.

Figure 18.21

The macros invoked by the custom navigation buttons in Figure 18.20

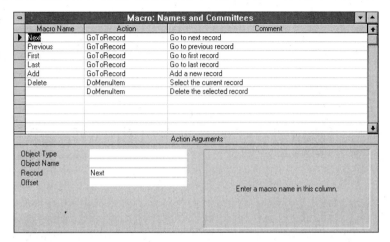

Figure 18.22

Using the FindRecord action to search for records

The GoToPage action that begins both the search macros is required because the GoToControl action that follows scrolls the screen back to bring the Name Type control into view in a way that simulates using the scroll bar or pressing Shift+Tab, *not* pressing PgUp. To scroll the window all the way to the top of page 1 so that only the fields meant to be included on this page are visible on the screen, you must execute a GoToPage action before using the GoToControl action (even if you would ideally prefer to be able to search for a record without returning to the first page of the form).

Executing a macro that uses the FindRecord action is exactly equivalent in every respect to conducting the same search yourself using the Find dialog box. If you use the Find option on the Edit menu after invoking the macro by operating a command button in a form, you will see that the search specifications stored in the macro option provide the initial settings displayed in the Find dialog box. If you press Shift+F4 to repeat the previous search without opening the Find dialog box, Access repeats the search defined by the macro.

You can use the same basic method to add alphabet buttons that resemble the buttons used in the Access Help system to your forms to allow you to move quickly to specific points in the various reference sections (the Functions Reference, Actions Reference, and so on). For example, in a form used to update the Names table, you could define a series of small square command buttons, each with a letter on its face (optionally assigned as a hot key), which search for the ID codes that begin with these letters. Each macro would consist of two actions—a GoToControl action that moves the focus to the ID Code control, and a FindRecord action that uses the Start of Field search option to find the designated letter at the beginning of the ID Code field.

You can also use command buttons to implement filters on the fly. These buttons can serve as convenient shortcuts for experienced users, or can allow less experienced users to place filters in effect without having to understand what they are or knowing how to define them. (If you want to *prohibit* the creation or selection of any other filters from a particular form, you can set the Allow Filters property for the form to No.) To impose a filter on the source dynaset for an open form or report, you use the ApplyFilter macro action. This action has two arguments—Filter Name and Where Condition—which you can use to define the filter in two different ways. To invoke a previously saved query (or a filter saved as a query), you enter its name in the Filter Name argument. To implement record selection criteria that can be defined with a single expression, you can simply enter the condition in the Where Condition argument. For example, you might use the condition Year([Date])=Year(Date()) to select transactions or contacts in the current year or [State]="CA" to select people in California. Obviously, if you want the filter to include sorting instructions as well as selection criteria, you must use a previously saved filter instead of entering an expression in the Where Condition argument. To cancel a filter and return to viewing all the records in the source dynaset for the form, you can use the ShowAllRecords macro action.

A filter placed in effect by the ApplyFilter macro action is no different from one defined using the command buttons in the tool bar or the corresponding options on the Records menu. You can cancel it by choosing the Show All Records option, and you can edit it by choosing Edit Filter/Sort. When you choose the latter option, Access displays the Filter Design window with the specifications described by the current filter filled in, so you can use these instructions as the starting point for building a more complex filter.

Using Macros with Option Groups

You can use macros to overcome a serious limitation on the use of option groups in forms—the fact that an option group can only be used to collect a numeric value. Circumventing this restriction enables you to use option groups to collect fields that can take on a finite, unchanging number of values, such as the Address Type field in the Names table. (For fields that can accept a large number of possible values, or if you anticipate frequent changes in the list of acceptable entries, it is better to store the permissible values in a reference table like the Name Types or States tables, and use this table to construct a list box or combo box.)

The basic strategy for using an option group to collect a non-numeric value involves placing an unbound option group on the form—that is, one in which the Control Source property is blank so that the option group is not bound to any field in the source table. Two macros are required to establish the relationship between the option group and the field you want to update: one to display the option group with the correct control selected (that is, the one that corresponds to the current field value) and another to update the field value when you select a different control in the option group. The first macro must be called from the OnCurrent event for the form, which is invoked whenever a different record is displayed, and the second must be called from the OnExit or AfterUpdate event for the option group. Figure 18.23 illustrates the macros that carry out these updates for the Address Type radio buttons in the form in Figure 18.20 which are displayed using an option group named Add Type.

The last three steps in the Redisplay macro (the beginning of which is "off the top" of the window in Figure 18.23) test the value of the Address Type control (which is invisible on the form), and execute SetValue actions that assign the appropriate numeric value to the option group (1 for Home, 2 for Work, or 3 for Unknown). These steps ensure that the correct button is highlighted when any record is displayed on the screen. The Reset Address Type macro tests the current value of the Add Type control (the option

Figure 18.23

Using macros to associate an option group with a Text field

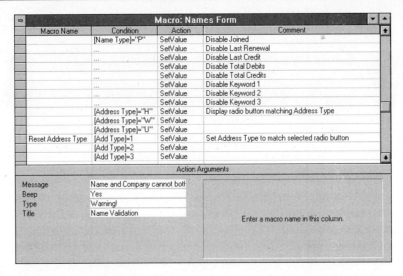

Macro Name	Condition	Action	Comment
	[Name Type]="P"	SetValue	Disable Joined
	...	SetValue	Disable Last Renewal
	...	SetValue	Disable Last Credit
	...	SetValue	Disable Total Debits
	...	SetValue	Disable Total Credits
	...	SetValue	Disable Keyword 1
	...	SetValue	Disable Keyword 2
	...	SetValue	Disable Keyword 3
	[Address Type]="H"	SetValue	Display radio button matching Address Type
	[Address Type]="W"	SetValue	
	[Address Type]="U"	SetValue	
Reset Address Type	[Add Type]=1	SetValue	Set Address Type to match selected radio button
	[Add Type]=2	SetValue	
	[Add Type]=3	SetValue	

Macro: Names Form

Action Arguments

Message	Name and Company cannot both
Beep	Yes
Type	Warning!
Title	Name Validation

Enter a macro name in this column.

group), and based on this value, uses a SetValue action to assign the appropriate value to the Address Type field (H for the first button, W for the second, or U for the third). (The earlier steps in the Redisplay macro, which enable and disable various controls based on the value of the Name Type field, were mentioned briefly earlier in this chapter and are explained in more detail in the last section.)

Emulating Access Menu Actions

As noted in the previous section, you can use the powerful DoMenuItem action to simulate the effect of choosing any standard Access menu command. Whenever you cannot find the action you think you need in the list in Table 18.1, think about whether you could accomplish your goal using Access menu options; if so, you can probably use the DoMenuItem action. When you need to use a series of DoMenuItem actions to replicate a lengthy command sequence, you might want to run through the process manually first to make sure that the sequence of actions in the macro is complete and correct. You can either make a note of each menu option you select or define the corresponding macro steps in the Macro Design window as you proceed.

The DoMenuItem takes four arguments. The Menu Bar argument specifies which version of the Access menu bar contains the command you want to invoke (as you know, the menu bar changes dynamically to display only options relevant to the current environment). In simple macros that you create to attach to command buttons in forms, you will nearly always choose Form, Form Datasheet, Table Datasheet, or Query Datasheet. The Menu Name argument specifies the pull-down menu (File, Edit, and so on) that contains the option you want to select, and the Command option specifies the option you would select from this menu. If this option leads to a submenu, you can specify the submenu option you want by entering it in the Subcommand argument. For example, instead of using the GoToRecord action to move to the first record in a table, you could choose Records for the Menu Name argument, Go To for the Command argument, and First for the Subcommand argument. The easiest way to enter these arguments is to select them, in sequence, from the combo boxes in the Action Arguments region of the Macro Design window. Once you have selected a value for the Menu Bar argument, the Menu Name combo box displays the list of menus in that version of the menu bar, and after you choose the menu name, the Command combo box offers only commands on that menu.

The macro invoked by the Delete command button in the form in Figure 18.20 uses two DoMenuItem actions to delete the current record—one that simulates the Select Record option on the Edit menu, and one that simulates the Delete option on the Edit menu. You can use a similar strategy to print a hard copy of the form displayed on the screen—create a two-step macro that uses the DoMenuItem action to select the current record, followed by the Print action, which emulates selecting Print from the File menu. To print just the current record (the selected data), enter Selection for the Print Range argument.

Opening Other Forms

You can use a macro to call up one form from within another. For example, Figure 18.24 illustrates a form called Names with Command Buttons, which initially displays only the basic name and address data but offers command buttons that open other forms to display contacts and transactions. The macros attached to these buttons each have two actions: an OpenForm action that opens the form and a MoveSize action that moves (and, for the Transactions Subform window, resizes) it to approximate the layout of the Complete Name Information form. Figure 18.25 shows how the screen looks after both of these forms are opened.

Note that the forms in Figure 18.25 are *not* subforms—they are independent forms, each open in its own window on the Access desktop, and you can use all the usual methods to move, resize, or close them. Whenever a new form opens, it has the focus, and you can move through the source dynaset by using the standard navigation controls. By default, you can switch at will between all open forms, using either keyboard, menu, or mouse commands. To require that the new form be closed before returning to the main form, you must set the

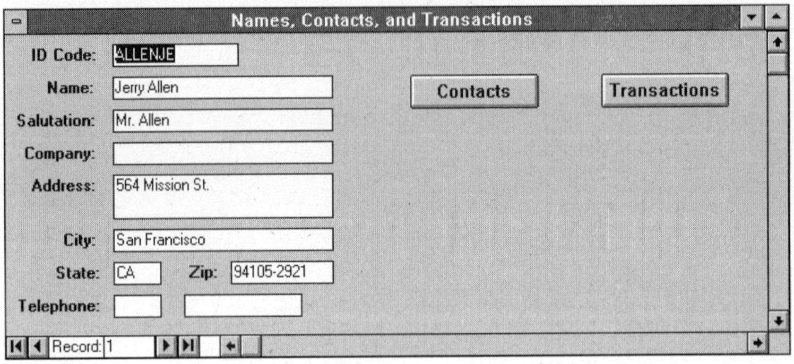

Figure 18.24

A form with command buttons that open other forms

Figure 18.25

Using command buttons to open forms

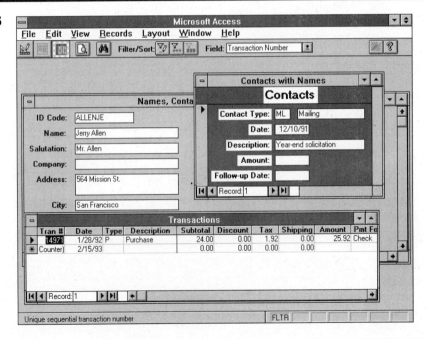

Window Mode argument for the OpenForm action to Dialog to create a *modal* window that works like an Access dialog box. (In any Windows dialog box, you must complete all the entries and explicitly close the dialog box to return to any other window.) Using modal forms to create your own custom dialog boxes is described in Chapter 19.

When you open one form from within another, Access makes no assumptions about the relationship between the forms, and indeed, there may be none—you might, for example, open the Name Types or States table for reference from any of the Names table forms. To ensure that the Contacts and Transactions forms opened by the command buttons in Figure 18.23 display only records that match the current record in the Names table, the Where Condition argument for the OpenForm action specifies the following condition:

```
[ID Code]=Forms![Names with Command Buttons]![ID Code]
```

In the Where Condition argument, the control name on the left side of the equals sign always refers to the form being opened. Thus, this expression selects records in the subform in which the value of the ID Code control matches the value in the ID Code control in the Names with Command Buttons form.

Access evaluates the Where Condition only once, when it executes the OpenForm action—it does not automatically update the newly opened form when you move to a new record in the original form (again, because it does not assume any relationship between the forms). One way to force Access to refresh the display in this form is to repeat the command that opens the second form (for example, click again on the appropriate command button). This method does not open a second copy of the form—if a form is already open when you execute an OpenForm action that opens it, Access simply brings the form to the top of the stack of windows open on the desktop. You might also consider calling the macro that opens the form from the OnCurrent property of the form itself to ensure that it is executed whenever you move to a new record. However, this method will open the form if it is not already open, and the main reason to use a command button to open a form on demand rather than creating a subform is that you generally do not want the form open.

You can also use a macro to open another type of document—a report. The Print command button in the Names Five-Page Form uses the Open-Report action to open the Complete Reference List 2 report in Print Preview mode. If you prefer to print the report immediately, you could choose Print for the View argument rather than Print Preview. Like several other actions described in this chapter, the OpenReport action accepts either a filter name (entered in the Filter Name argument) or an explicit condition (entered in the Where Condition argument) to describe the range of records to include in the report. The Open Report action in the Names Five-Page Form uses the following condition to print only records (that is, one name record) in which the ID Code matches the ID Code of the record currently displayed in the form:

```
[ID Code]=Forms![Names Five-Page Form]![ID Code]
```

Adding Command Buttons to the Committee Memberships Form

To practice the macro techniques described in the preceding sections, try adding three special command buttons to the Committee Memberships form, as follows:

1. Open the Committee Memberships form in Form Design view, and make sure that the toolbox and property sheet are both visible.

2. Click on the Lock button in the toolbox and then on the Command Button button.

3. Click on the form three times in the area to the right of the Public Exposure radio buttons to create three command buttons in a vertical row. Click on the arrow symbol at the top of the tool box to release the control lock and return to using the mouse as a simple pointing device.

4. Click on the first button, and type the caption **View &Name Info** in the Caption entry in the property sheet to define a button caption with an underlined hot key.

5. Enter **[Committee Memberships].[Open Name]** in the On Push entry in the property sheet (you will create this macro later).

6. Click on the second button. Change the caption to **&Chairpersons**, and enter **[Committee Memberships].Chairpersons** in the On Push entry in the property sheet.

7. Click on the third button. Change the caption to **Current &Members**, and enter **[Committee Memberships].[Current Members]** in the On Push entry in the property sheet.

8. Adjust the widths of the three buttons to 1.5 inches to accommodate the new captions, and move the buttons so they line up with the list box above. You should see the hotkey letters identified by the ampersands underlined on the button faces. Your screen should look approximately like Figure 18.26.

9. Without closing the form, return to the Database window.

10. Open the Committee Memberships macro group in Macro Design view.

11. Define the Open Name macro action as follows:

Macro Name	Open Name
Action	OpenForm

Figure 18.26

The command buttons in the Committee Memberships form

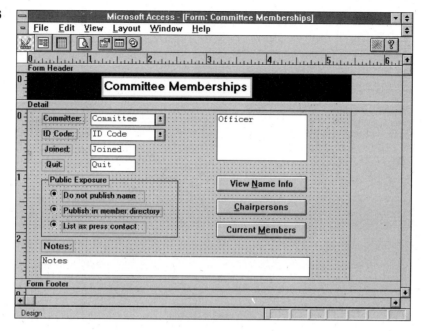

Comment   Display complete name information

12. Press F6 to move to the Action Arguments region of the Macro Design window, and enter the following action arguments for the OpenForm action:

Form Name   Names

View   Form

Where Condition   [ID Code]=Forms![Committee Memberships]![ID Code]

Data Mode   Read Only

Window Mode   Normal

Note the expression that defines the Where Condition. Because the Names form is open when Access evaluates this expression, you must include the identifier "Forms" and the form name in the reference to the ID Code control in the Committee Memberships form.

13. Define the Chairpersons macro action as follows:

Macro Name Chairpersons

Action   ApplyFilter

Comment   Select only chairpersons

14. Press F6 to move to the Action Arguments region of the Macro Design window, and enter **[Officer]="Chairperson"** for the Where Condition argument.

15. Define the Current Members macro action as follows:

Macro Name CurrentMembers

Action   ApplyFilter

Comment   Select only current committee members

16. Press F6 to move to the Action Arguments region of the Macro Design window, and enter **[Quit] Is Null** for the Where Condition argument.

17. Save the macro group.

18. Return to the Committee Memberships form, and switch to Form view.

19. Click on the View Name Info command button, and confirm that Access opens the Names form. Without closing this form, return to the Committee Memberships window and click on the Next Record navigation button. Switch back to the Names form window and note that the information for the first committee member, Karen Franklin, is still displayed. Return to the Committee Memberships form, click on View Name Info again to update the display in the Names form, and then close the Names form.

20. Press Alt+C to operate the Chairpersons command button, and browse through the records to confirm that only records in which the Officer Position is Chairperson are displayed.

21. Click on the Current Members command button, and browse through the records to confirm that only records in which the Quit date is blank are displayed.

22. Click on the Edit Filter/Sort command button in the tool bar, or choose the equivalent option from the Records menu. Note that the output grid contains a column for the Quit field, with the condition Is Null entered in the Criteria row.

23. Drag the Joined field to the output grid, and enter the condition **>#1/1/92#** in the Criteria row.

24. Click on the Apply Filter/Sort command button in the tool bar, or choose the equivalent option from the Records menu. Browse through the records and note that only current committee members who joined after January 1, 1992 are displayed.

25. Click on the Current Members command button again, and note that the filter described by the Current Members macro is once again in effect, and the dynaset includes all current committee members, not just those who joined in 1992 or later.

26. Close the form and save it.

Changing Form and Report Control Properties

You already know how to use the SetValue action to change the value of a field or control on a form through a macro. To a limited extent, you can also use this action to change the values of form and report properties. Unfortunately, you can only change those properties that affect the visibility or accessibility of objects on a report or form open in Report or Form view—the Visible, Enabled, and Locked properties. You might also want to modify properties that affect the visual attributes of objects, such as the color or font, or to assign attributes such as boldfacing or underlining on the fly, but these properties can only be changed in Design view. To identify a property, you must write an expression that combines the name of the object and the name of the property, separated by a period (.). For example, the expression [Contacts Label].Visible refers to the Visible property of a control called Contacts Label.

One obvious application for macros that change object properties is suppressing controls or report or form sections when a specified condition is true. You already know how to display some types of data conditionally without using macros. In some very common situations, no special measures are necessary. For example, when there is no data in a subreport, Access automatically suppresses the subreport object, and if you set the Can Shrink property to Yes, the object occupies no space on the report. You also know how to use calculated controls to display or print expressions based on the IIf function; if one of the alternative values specified as inputs to this function is a null string, no data appears on the document. For example, you could use the following expression to print a message on a statement only if a donor has an outstanding balance:

```
IIf([Total Debits]-[Total Credits]>0, "Please pay the
outstanding balance, "")
```

To suppress a section or control based on any arbitrary condition, you can write a macro that tests the condition and sets the Visible property of the section or control to No to render it invisible. When you use this method to suppress a report section, you must call the macro from the OnFormat event for the relevant section, rather than the OnPrint event, so that Access can take into account the missing controls when it formats the section. You may also want to set the Can Shrink property for the section to Yes to make sure that it can shrink (if necessary, to nothing) if objects are omitted or the section is removed entirely from the printout.

Figure 18.27 illustrates a macro that hides a subreport called Contacts Subform if the sum of the Amount field is 0. The conditions in this macro use the DSum function to compute the sum of the Amount field in the group of records in which the contents of the ID Code field in the Contacts table matches the contents of the ID Code control in the report. The expression that supplies the third input to the DSum function, which describes this group of records, is [ID Code]=Report![ID Code]. If the DSum function returns the value 0, the SetValue actions set the Visible property for the subreport object and its label to No; otherwise, they set the Visible property for these objects to Yes. It is essential to test both conditions because the value of any property—including the Visible property—changes only when you issue an explicit command to change it. If you failed to reset this property to Yes when the sum of the Amount field was greater than 0, the subform and its label would disappear when Access printed the first record in which the sum was 0, and would never be printed again. Figure 18.28 illustrates the first page of a report called Names and Contacts Side-by-Side 2, printed with this macro called from the OnFormat event for the detail section.

You can use a very similar technique in a form to selectively hide, enable, or disable any control, including a subform, based on the values of other controls in the same form. For example, in the Transactions with Names 3 form, a macro called Purchases, which is stored in the Transactions Form macro group described earlier in this chapter and illustrated in Figure 18.18, disables the Discount, Tax, and Shipping fields for all transactions except purchases. This macro tests the value of the Transaction Type field and executes a series of SetValue actions that set the Enabled property for the three controls to Yes or No. When you use this type of macro in a form, think carefully about whether you want to reset the Visible, Enabled, or Locked properties, which are used as follows:

- Setting the Visible property to No renders a control invisible and inaccessible.

- Setting the Enabled property to No dims a control and prevents you from editing the contents.

Figure 18.27

A macro that hides a
subform based on
its contents

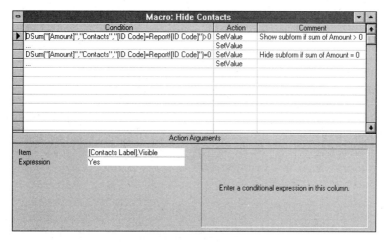

- Setting the Locked property to Yes prevents editing without changing the visual appearance of a control.

Always remember that you must explicitly handle both possible outcomes of the condition you are testing, because every change you make to an object property remains in effect until you explicitly reverse it. The Purchases macro therefore enables the Discount, Tax, and Shipping controls for purchases as well as disabling them for nonpurchase transactions.

The last two steps in the Purchases macro update the Name Type field in the Names table based on the value of the Transaction Type field in the Transactions table, so that entering a donation converts a prospect to a donor, and entering a membershp fee transaction converts a prospect to a member. The conditions in these steps test both the Transaction Type control in the main form and the Name Type control in the subform, using the expressions

```
[Transaction Type]="DO" and [Names Subform].Form![Name
Type]="P"
```

and

```
[Transaction Type]="ME" and [Names Subform].Form![Name
Type]="P"
```

In these expressions, the Name Type control is treated as a property of the subform object (which is called Name and Address). The SetValue actions assign the values "D" and "M" to the same control if the respective conditions are fulfilled. Note that the Name Type field does not appear in the subform,

Figure 18.28

Using the Hide
Contacts macro in
a report

Names and Contacts
21-Jan-93

ALLENJE

Jerry Allen
564 Mission St.
San Francisco, CA 94105-
2921

ALLENMA

Marilyn Allen
842 Palm Canyon Drive
Borrego Springs, CA 92004

ANDERSJC

Mr. J. C. Anderson
41248 Moraga Rd
Temecula, CA 92390

ANDERSMI

Michael Anderson
The Ellis Street Garage
2906 Ellis Street
Berkeley, CA 94702

Contacts:

	Contact Type	Date	Description	Amount	Follow-up
PH	Phone call	2/28/92	Donor special appeal		3/13/92
NL	Newsletter	3/30/92	Newsletter, March 1992		
ML	Mailing	4/5/92	Earth Day solicitation		
LE	Lecture	4/22/92	Earth Day lecture	15.00	5/1/92

ARNOLDME

Melvin H. Arnold
504 Parkview Dr.
Lake Elsinore, CA 92330

BAKERSY

Ms. Sylvia Baker
9370 SW 51st St.
Portland, OR 97219

Page 1

but Access allows you to operate on any field in the data source for a form, regardless of whether the field is present on the form.

The Purchases macro is called from two different places in the Transactions with Names 3 form—from the OnCurrent event of the form, which defines the event that occurs whenever you move to a new transaction record, and from the AfterUpdate event of the Transaction Type control, which ensures that the status of the numeric fields changes immediately if you edit the transaction type. The fact that you might edit an existing record and change the transaction type is also the reason for including the three SetValue actions that set the Discount, Tax, and Shipping fields to 0 if the transaction type is not P.

The Redisplay macro in the Names Form macro group (shown earlier in Figure 18.11) uses the same technique to enable or disable some of the fields on the second page of the Names Five-Page Form, depending on the value of the Name Type field in the Names table. Thus, the Joined, Last Renewal, Total Debits, Total Credits, Last Credits, and keywords fields are disabled for prospects and enabled for all the other types in the Names table.

As noted earlier, you can also use a macro to determine whether a subform is displayed. For example, in the Complete Name Information form, you could suppress the Contacts, Transactions, or Committees subforms if there were no data. This approach is obviously not suitable for use in forms intended to *enter* data in the subforms, because it would only allow you to enter new records in subforms that already contain at least one record. If you do use this method to display a subform conditionally, remember to attach the macro to the OnCurrent event of the form, which is invoked whenever you move to a new record in the main form. Remember also that you may have to enable and disable other objects associated with the subform, such as labels adjacent to the subform and calculated controls based on the subform.

Summary

This chapter introduced Access macros, described some of the most commonly used macro actions in some detail, and presented a variety of typical uses for macros in Access database applications. Despite the length of this chapter, it barely scratches the surface of what you can accomplish with macros. In particular, note that only a few of the macro actions and their arguments were covered in depth. Now that you understand the basics, you might want to read through the list of macro actions in Table 18.1 again, and consult the Access *Language Reference* or the on-line help system for further details on the actions that you think you might be able to use in your own macros.

Many uses for macros will suggest themselves in the later stages of application development or long after you believe the development process to be finished. In the earlier stages, you may not be able to achieve a broad enough perspective on the application to pick out these details, so remember as you begin using a database with real data to note down new uses for macros as they occur to you. As you work with your own Access databases, be on the alert for operations that might benefit from the automation afforded by macros, tasks that could be carried out by less knowledgeable co-workers if they were invoked by macros, validations that you cannot carry out with explicit expressions entered in the Validation Rule property of a field or control on a form, and custom command buttons and specialized navigation controls that would make your data entry forms easier to use.

Chapter 19 builds on the basic concepts introduced in this chapter with some more sophisticated applications for macros, including ways that you can use macros to link together the application components you have already developed into complete menu-driven applications that can be used by people who have little or no experience with Access. Make sure that you have a solid grasp of the fundamentals before you go on to read about these more advanced uses for macros.

19

Building Custom Applications

Customizing the General Options

Using Forms as Menus

Using Forms as Dialog Boxes

Designing Custom Menus for Forms

T HE FIRST 15 CHAPTERS OF THIS BOOK DESCRIBE HOW TO CREATE AND USE the essential objects required in any Access database application— tables, queries, forms, and reports. You now know how to carry out all the routine maintenance activities that keep your tables up-to-date—entering, editing, and deleting records individually in Datasheet view or through custom forms. You also know how to use select queries to extract specific items of information from one or more tables, perform calculations, sort selected records into different orders, and how to display or print the results using forms and reports. You have learned how to use action queries to create new tables, split or combine tables, and delete or update records en masse, and you have seen a variety of methods for exchanging data with other applications running on your own computer, elsewhere on a local area network, or on a remote server. If you reexamine the functional definition of the term "database management" presented in Chapter 1, you will see that you now know how to use Access for all of the fundamental database management tasks.

Thus far, you have carried out all of these activities from the Database window, for the most part by selecting and using database objects one at a time. This environment, which is structured enough to provide some guidance but flexible enough to allow you to carry out any operations in any order, is ideal during the development and testing phases of a new application. Using the Database window as a central command post may also serve your needs adequately throughout the lifetime of an application that you design for your own use or one that you share with other staff members who also understand Access and who are familiar with the data managed by the application. For a beginner, however, or a co-worker who only needs access to specific components of the database, the number of available objects and options can be extremely confusing. Furthermore, it is all too easy—even for an expert or for the designer of a database application—to choose the wrong query, print the wrong form, forget a step, or carry out several of the steps in a lengthy sequence (such as end-of-month or end-of-year processing) in the wrong order.

The solution to both of these general problems—how to make an application easier for a beginner and more foolproof for an expert—is automation. Chapter 18 gave you a brief introduction to one technique for automating a database operation—defining macros that carry out two or more steps in sequence. You can take another giant step toward a much higher level of automation by building your own menus, which present the users of an application or a form (either you or your co-workers and associates) with a list of only those choices that should be available at any given moment. If you wish, you can build a completely menu-driven application in which the users never see the Database window, but if you are the primary user of an application, you might be content with a few simple menus for printing reports and carrying out periodic update and archiving operations.

When you begin setting up a menu system for your application, give some thought to the organization of the menus, which might reflect the needs of different users, the types of information maintained by the application, or the operations carried out on the data. Structuring a menu for the ACE system around the basic database operations accessed through the menu might mean defining one submenu for data entry options, another for reports, a third for mailings, and so on. You might choose instead to create a separate menu for each type of information maintained by the application—for example, one for mailing list management, one for contact tracking, one for financial transaction entry and reporting, and one for committee memberships. Finally, you might define more than one menu system, each structured around the needs of a different group of staff members, so that each person sees only the options relevant to his or her job. For example, you could design one menu system for use by the data entry clerks, who spend the majority of their time working with a handful of data entry forms and printing a few simple reports, and another menu system for managers, who do very little data entry but spend a great deal of time calculating statistics and viewing or printing the results. (In a system like this, there might be considerable overlap among the various menus.)

In addition to these overall application menus, which essentially eliminate the Database window some or all of the time, you can also design custom menus that replace the standard Access menu bar while you are working with specific data entry forms. By invoking custom menus in Form view, you can make a form easier to use for people who are not familiar with the Access menu bar, and you can add specialized navigation controls, provide custom search options, and provide capabilities that would not otherwise be readily available, such as the ability to print a report not directly derived from or related to the form.

You already have considerable experience with operating Access-style menus from using Access itself (and other Windows software). If you have worked with programs *not* designed to run under Windows, you have probably seen other menu styles as well—for example, menus that present a list of options within a frame in the middle of the screen and allow you to make a selection either by typing a number or letter that identifies the option you want, by highlighting it and pressing Enter, or by pointing to it with the mouse and clicking on it. Regardless of their visual appearance and the mechanism used to make selections, all menus are functionally equivalent: They present a list of choices, allow you to select one, carry out a specific action in response to your selection, and then return you to the menu so that you can select another option and repeat the process.

Although programmers (in Access Basic and other database languages) use precisely these techniques to create custom database applications, you do not have to learn programming to build menus in Access. You can construct both types of menus alluded to earlier—menus that replace the Database window as your center of operations, and menus that substitute for the standard Access menu bar in a form—by using macros. This chapter describes how to build menus by linking together database components that you have already created, and suggests some strategies for using menus to make your Access applications easier to use and to improve the accuracy and integrity of the data they maintain.

Customizing the General Options

When you begin to design applications primarily for use by less experienced co-workers, you may want to exert more stringent control over the menu system and the overall Access environment than when you work with your own databases. You already know how to use the Options dialog box (invoked by choosing Options from the View menu) to customize various aspects of the Access Design view windows. The General options—the first category of options in the scrolling list at the top of the Options dialog box—enable you to customize global aspects of the Access environment. The options are used as follows:

Option	Meaning
Show Status Bar	Determines whether the status bar (and the various messages and indicators displayed in the status bar) is visible
Show System Objects	Determines whether the tables used internally by Access to store information about your database are displayed in the Database window
OLE/DDE Timeout	Specifies the time, in seconds, that Access waits to retry an OLE or DDE operation after the initial attempt fails
Show Tool Bar	Determines whether the tool bar is visible
Confirm Document Deletions	Determines whether Access displays an alert box to request confirmation before deleting a database object
Confirm Action Queries	Determines whether Access displays an alert box to request confirmation before executing an action query from the Database window

Option	Meaning
New Database Sort Order	Specifies the sorting sequence for Text fields in new databases that you create (to conform to the requirements of different languages)
Ignore DDE Requests	Specifies whether Access ignores DDE requests from other Windows applications
Default Find/Replace Behavior	Specifies the defaults for the Search In and Where options in the Find dialog box
Default Database Directory	Specifies the default subdirectory in which Access searches for databases and saves new databases
Confirm Record Changes	Determines whether Access displays an alert box to request confirmation when you delete records, insert records from the Clipboard, or execute a Replace command

The default settings for the general options provide maximum protection for your database and maximum information for its users. All the options that govern whether Access displays alert boxes requesting confirmation before carrying out potentially dangerous or destructive options are set to Yes, but you might want to reverse this setting under two quite different circumstances. Once you gain confidence and experience, you may want to set Confirm Document Deletions, Confirm Action Queries, and Confirm Record Changes to No to speed your own work. In an application that will also be used by less expert co-workers, you might also set these options to No if you have removed potentially dangerous options from the menus and substituted specialized menu options or command buttons. As you will see later in this chapter, you might also want to set Show Tool Bar to No to deny access to the command buttons equivalent to menu options that you have removed. Unfortunately, there is no easy way to reset these options on the fly from within a macro.

Using Forms as Menus

You may have used other programs (in particular, those designed for MS-DOS rather than Windows) that display a menu in the center of the screen and allow you to choose options by highlighting one and pressing Enter, by pressing a hotkey, or by clicking on the option with the mouse. You can simulate this menu style in Access by building a form with one command button for each option. Figure 19.1 illustrates a typical example—a screen called Main Menu, which serves as the main menu for the ACE application, shown as it would appear if you opened the form directly from the Database window. You already possess all the skills you need to build this type of menu. The basic steps are as follows (although you need not adhere strictly to this sequence):

1. Design a form with one command button for each menu option.

2. Define a macro that carries out each menu option.

3. Attach each macro to the OnPush event of the appropriate command button on the form.

Figure 19.1

A form used as the main menu for an application

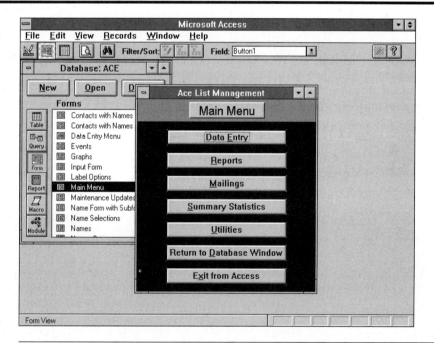

It may seem strange at first to design forms that do not collect any data, but Access allows you to use forms to interact with the user in a variety of circumstances, not all of which involve entering data. Because the Main Menu form does not update any databases, there is no need for record selectors or scroll bars, so the Record Selectors property is set to No and the Scroll Bars property to Neither. Chapter 18 described how to use a macro executed from one form to open another form, and you can take advantage of this technique to create "submenus." For example, the Data Entry button in the Main Menu form in Figure 19.1 opens a similar form that displays a menu of data entry options, which is illustrated in Figure 19.2 in Form Design view.

Figure 19.2

A menu of data entry options

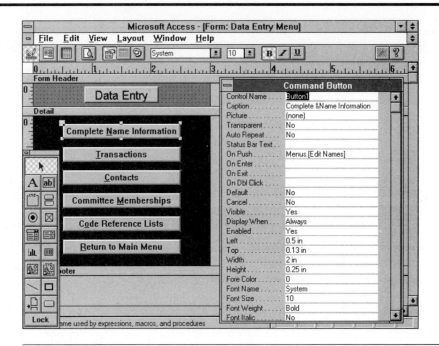

NOTE. *All the options in the forms that make up the menu-driven version of the ACE application are executed by macros stored in a macro group called Menus. In your own applications, you might prefer to use a separate macro group for each menu form, but placing all the macros in one group facilitates editing and rearranging the menu options.*

Despite the examples set by the menus in Figures 19.1 and 19.2, you are not limited to menus made up of a single vertical column of command buttons. Because a menu is simply a data entry form, you can include as many buttons as you need on each form and arrange them any way you wish. Some application designers feel that no menu should contain more than six or eight options, while others believe that including more options on a single menu is preferable to forcing the user to navigate through an unnecessarily complex hierarchy of menus and submenus. Only experience will tell you where to draw the line, but if you do include more than ten options on a single menu, consider using lines or boxes on the form to group related options and include some explanatory text to identify the groups. Figure 19.3 illustrates an example of such a menu—a report menu that calls a wide variety of reports in the ACE application.

Figure 19.3
A complex report menu form

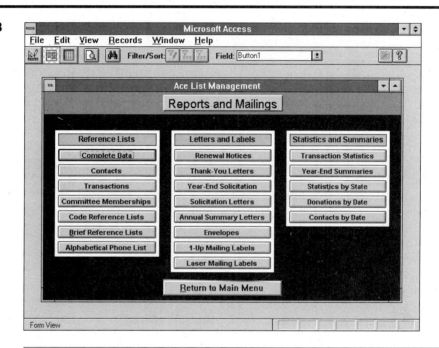

Controlling the Environment in a Menu-Driven Application

If you start up a menu-driven system simply by opening the form that displays the main menu, the Database window remains visible on the screen (as it always does when you work in Form view). In a menu system designed solely for your own use, you might want the convenience of being able to return easily to the Database window, but when you begin to design applications for use by other people, you will usually want more control over the environment in which these users work. In most cases, you will want to suppress the Database window, either by minimizing it or hiding it, while the menu is active. You can easily add an option like the Return to Database Window option in the ACE main menu to allow the user to return immediately to the familiar Access interactive environment, or if you wish, you can prohibit access to the Database window and force the users to work entirely within your menu system.

Whichever alternative you choose, you can gain the necessary control over the environment by using a macro to start up the menu system rather than opening the main menu form from the Database window. Figure 19.4 illustrates the Menus macro group, which executes all the options in the menu-driven version of the ACE system. The first macro in this group, which is named Startup, starts up the application and establishes the desired window configuration. Although this macro has a name (Startup), you do not have to run it explicitly by name (which you could do from the Database window by using the Run Macro option on the File menu and entering the macro name as Menus.Startup). As you may recall from Chapter 18, if you run a macro group without specifying a particular macro, Access executes the first macro in the group. You can therefore start up the ACE application simply by running the Menus macro group from the Database window.

Figure 19.4

The macro group that controls a menu-driven application

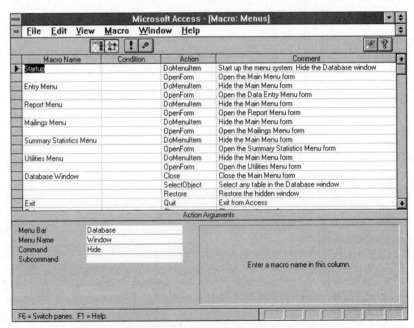

If you want to start up a custom menu system automatically every time you open a database, rather than explicitly invoking it by running a start-up macro, you can do so by assigning the name Autoexec to the macro group that starts up the menu form. Whenever you open a database, Access searches for a macro named Autoexec, and if it finds one, it runs this macro immediately. (You might think of this macro as analogous to the AUTOEXEC.BAT file, which the MS-DOS command processor executes every time you boot your computer.) By using an Autoexec macro to start up the main menu for an application and *not* providing an option to return to the Database window, you can encourage the users of your application to work solely within the menu system. However, it is still possible to open any database without running the Autoexec macro (in fact, the ability to do so is essential for modifying the application). To do this, you must open the database by choosing the Open Database option on the File menu and then holding down the Shift key as you exit from this dialog box after typing or selecting the database name.

The strategy adopted in the menu-driven version of the ACE system is a very general one, which you can use as a model for any application in which you use forms with command buttons as menus. The Startup macro, which starts up the menu system, has two actions: a DoMenuItem action, which invokes the Hide command on the Window menu to hide the currently active window (the Database window), and an OpenForm action, which opens the Main Menu form. Each of the macros that execute the first five options in the Main Menu screen (all of which are visible in Figure 19.4) uses a similar strategy to display the selected submenu—it hides the Main Menu form and then opens another menu form. If you prefer to minimize the Database window rather than hide it when you start up your application, or if you would rather minimize the Main Menu form window when you call a submenu, you can substitute Minimize actions for the DoMenuItem actions that hide windows in the Menus macro group shown in Figure 19.4. You might also prefer to leave each menu visible on the screen when the user calls up a submenu, and display the submenus offset slightly to the side to create a "cascading" effect, as shown in Figure 19.5. To achieve this effect, adjust the positions of the forms so they overlap slightly, and use a single OpenForm action to display each new menu form without first hiding or minimizing the previously active form.

Each of the submenus in the ACE application includes an option to return to the main menu (you can see this option in Figure 19.2), and all of the Return options call the same macro, which is named Return. The Return macro has three actions:

Close	Closes the currently active form
SelectObject	Selects the Main Menu form
Restore	Restores the Main Menu form window to its previous size and position

Note that the Restore action restores the Main Menu form whether it was previously minimized or hidden. If you left the Main Menu form visible on the screen when you opened each submenu form (to create the cascading menu style shown in Figure 19.5), you can omit this action from the Return macro.

Figure 19.5

Cascading menus

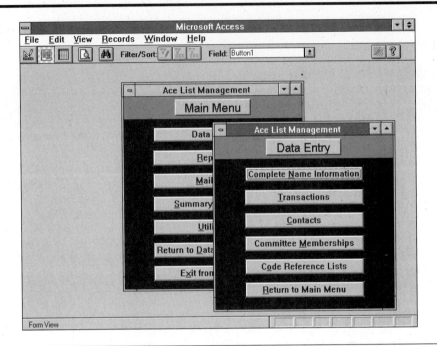

The Return to Database Window option in the Main Menu form is executed by a macro called Database Window, which is very similar to the Return macro. The first action, a Close action with no arguments specified, closes the current window (the submenu form). The second action, SelectObject, moves the focus back to the Database window, using a method that bears further explanation. The three arguments for this action, Object Type, Object Name, and In Database Window, enable you to select any specific object of any type. If you select Yes for the In Database Window argument, the object need not be open; otherwise, you can only move the focus to an open object (typically, an open form or report window). By selecting Table for the Object Type argument, leaving the Object Name argument blank and selecting Yes for the In Database Window argument, you can force Access to return to the Database window and display the list of tables. Because the Object Name argument is blank, Access highlights the first table name. If you prefer, you could redisplay the Database window with any specific object highlighted by selecting the desired object type for the Object Type argument and filling in the Object Name argument. As in the Return macro, the last action (Restore) returns the Database window to its prior size and position (regardless of whether you previously minimized the window or hid it).

In addition to the Return to Database Window option, the main menu form in Figure 19.1 includes an Exit option, which closes Access itself and returns you to the Program Manager or the File Manager. The macro that executes this option consists of a single Quit action. This action takes one argument called Options, which allows you to specify the actions you want Access to take before exiting if there are any objects open. The safest choice—and the one selected in the Exit macro in the Names macro group— is Save All, which requests that Access save all objects before shutting down. The other alternatives are Prompt and Exit. Prompt causes Access to display an alert box for each open object that asks whether you want to save the object; this choice simulates the way Access behaves when you attempt to exit from the program with objects open while working in the Database window. Exit causes Access to exit without saving any open objects.

Each of the options in the Data Entry menu uses a DoMenuItem action to hide the Data Entry menu form, followed by an OpenForm action to open one of the previously defined data entry forms in the ACE system. Unfortunately, choosing a method for restoring the Data Entry menu after you exit from each of these forms is not quite so straightforward. Your first impulse might be to add the steps that redisplay the Data Entry menu to the same macro that opens the data entry form, as in the following sequence:

DoMenuItem	Hides the Data Entry menu form
Open	Opens the data entry form
SelectObject	Selects the Data Entry Menu form
Restore	Restores the Data Entry Menu form window to its previous size and position

However, this strategy will fail, because opening a form does not pause macro execution. You have already learned how to use this fact to your advantage, in simple macros like the Open Committee Memberships and Names and Open Committee Tables macros described in Chapter 18, which open several data entry windows at the same time. Thus, after executing the OpenForm action that opens the data entry form, Access will proceed immediately to redisplay the Data Entry menu, which will "pop up" on top of the form.

One solution to this problem is to open the data entry forms without hiding or minimizing the calling menu form. If the data entry form is larger than the menu form, most users will probably not notice that the menu is still present "behind" the data entry window (although you will see its name on the Window menu). However, this strategy leaves the menu form active, and Access allows you to select it (by choosing its name from the Window menu, by pressing Ctrl+F6, or by clicking in the window with the mouse) and then choose another menu option. Again, this behavior is normal in Windows software, which in theory allows you to open multiple windows and carry out multiple tasks simultaneously. If it is reasonable in your application to run several data entry programs at the same time or to print reports while you are entering data, or if the users understand which options not to try to run simultaneously, opening data entry forms "on top of" the calling menu is straightforward, easy to implement, and leaves the menus available to users who know how to find them. This is the method used for most of the data entry options in the ACE Data Entry menu.

If it is essential to hide the calling menu form when you open a data entry form, you must create a macro that redisplays the menu when you exit from a data entry form and execute this macro from the OnClose event associated with the form, so that the menu form does not reappear until the data entry form is closed. Unfortunately, implementing this strategy in an existing application may have a major impact on the design. First of all, you must edit every form called from a menu to enter the name of the macro that redisplays the menu in the OnClose property. A more serious problem is the fact that the macro called from the OnClose event is executed *whenever* you close the form, regardless of how you opened it. Thus, if you open the form from the Database window (rather than through the menu form) and then close the form, the macro will generate an error message when Access tries to select the Data Entry form (which is not open).

Defining an Option in a Menu Form

To solidify your understanding of the methods you can use to implement an option in a menu constructed using command buttons in a form, you can define the action taken by the Committee Memberships option in the Data Entry menu form shown in Figure 19.2. This option opens the Committee Memberships form to allow you to enter and update committee membership data. First, try using the first method described in the previous section, which opens the form on top of the Data Entry Menu form:

1. Open the Data Entry Menu form in Form Design view, and make sure that the property sheet is visible.

2. Click on the Committee Memberships command button, and type **Menus.[Edit Committees]** in the OnPush entry in the property sheet.

3. Save the Data Entry form and close it.

4. Open the Menus macro group in Macro Design view.

5. Move down to the first line below the Edit Contacts macro, and press Ins to insert a blank line.

6. In the Macro Name column of this blank line, type **Edit Committees**. Select OpenForm for the macro action, press F6, and enter the following action arguments in the lower portion of the Macro window:

Form Name	Committee Memberships
View	Form
Data Mode	Edit
Window Mode	Normal

7. Save the macro group and close the Macro window.

8. Highlight the Menus macro group in the Database window, and click on the Run command button to run the first macro in the group (Startup).

9. Click on the first command button in the main menu (Data Entry) to display the Data Entry Menu form.

10. Press M (the hotkey shortcut for the Committee Memberships command button) to open the Committee Memberships form. Use the mouse to move the form around on the desktop, and verify that the Data Entry Menu form is still visible behind it.

11. Close the form and note that Access returns control to the Data Entry Menu form.

12. Choose the Return to Main Menu command button, and note that the Data Entry menu disappears and the Main Menu form reappears.

13. Choose the Return to Database Window command button, and note that the Main Menu form disappears and the Database window reappears.

Next, try the second strategy outlined in the previous section—hiding the Data Entry Menu form while the Committee Memberships form is open. The steps are as follows:

1. Open the Committee Memberships form in Form Design view, and make sure that the property sheet is visible and that the form as a whole is selected.

2. Type **Menus.[Restore Data Entry]** in the On Close entry in the property sheet.

3. Save the Committee Memberships form and close it.

4. Open the Menus macro group in Macro Design view.

5. Move down to the Macro Name column in the Edit Committees macro, and press Ctrl+X to delete the macro name and copy it to the Clipboard.

6. Select Insert Row from the Edit menu to insert a blank line above the current line, and press Ctrl+V to insert the contents of the Clipboard (the macro name) into the Macro Name column in this blank line.

7. In the Action column, type **DoMenuItem** or choose this action from the drop-down list, and Press F6 to move down to the Action Arguments region.

8. Retain the default selection for the Menu Bar argument (Form), select Window for the Menu Name argument, and select Hide for the Command argument, either by typing these entries or selecting them from the respective combo boxes. Press F6 to return to the upper portion of the Macros window.

9. Move down two lines to the first line of the next macro, and press Ins twice to insert two blank lines.

10. In the first new line, type **Restore Data Entry** in the Macro Name column, choose SelectObject for the macro action, and enter **Return to Data Entry Menu form** in the Comment column.

11. Press F6 to move to the lower portion of the Macro Design window, and enter the following action arguments:

Object Type	Form
Object Name	Data Entry Menu
In Database Window	No

12. In the second new line, select Restore for the macro action (there are no arguments for this action).

13. Save the macro group and close the Macro Design window.

14. Highlight the Menus macro group in the Database window, and click on the Run command button to run the first macro in the group (Startup).

15. Click on the first command button in the Main Menu (Data Entry) to display the Data Entry form.

16. Click on the Committee Memberships command button to open the Committee Memberships form. Use the mouse to move the form around on the desktop, and verify that the Data Entry form is hidden.

17. Close the form and note that the Data Entry Menu form reappears.

18. Choose the Return to Main Menu command button, and then the Return to Database Window command button.

Using Forms as Dialog Boxes

In addition to using forms for data entry and to build menus, you can use Access forms to display custom dialog boxes that offer the users of an application a variety of choices. You can use custom dialog boxes to collect selection criteria for a report or data editing session, to choose the output destination for a report (that is, decide whether to open a report in Print Preview view or print it), or to choose the output format before exporting data stored in Access tables, to name just a few examples.

In some contexts, a dialog box can substitute for a menu, and by using dialog boxes, you can simplify the menu structure in an application or reduce the number of similar menu options. For example, the Code Reference Lists option on the Data Entry menu shown earlier in Figure 19.2 opens the dialog box pictured in Figure 19.6, which allows you to choose the type of code you want to update and then opens the appropriate reference table in Datasheet view. Without this dialog box, you would need seven separate options (placed either on the Data Entry menu or on a submenu)—one for each of the ACE reference tables. You could design similar dialog boxes for printing reports based on various tables or on different subsets of the same table.

Figure 19.6

Using a form as a dialog box

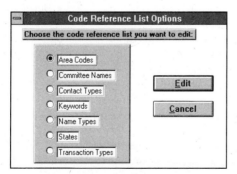

Another very common use for dialog boxes is collecting selection criteria for a report or data entry session. You could use a dialog box much like the one in Figure 19.6 to present a list of name types (members, donors, and so on) and then to display only records of the selected type in Datasheet view or through a custom form. You can use exactly the same strategy to present a list of report choices, and if you wish, choose different reports as well as impose different selection criteria. For example, based on the option selected from a list of name types, you could print reference lists of donors, members, prospects, board members, political contacts, or media contacts, using the same or different reports.

In applications that you design for your own use, these features are worth the time they take to implement if they offer significant advantages in convenience and help you avoid careless errors. For example, if you use a dialog box to collect the range of dates you want to include in a transaction report instead of using a parameter query, you can supply default values for the starting and ending dates, and you can validate the dates to ensure that the starting date is earlier than the ending date. For less knowledgeable users who might be confused by a long series of parameter prompts, you can design more complex dialog boxes to collect and validate a variety of selection criteria before printing a report. By using controls such as list boxes and combo boxes (which were introduced in Chapter 12), and by wording the choices in colloquial rather than technical terms, you can make it much easier for users who are not familiar with Access to enter sophisticated combinations of selection criteria.

The basic strategy for collecting input in a custom dialog box and then acting on that input is to design a form in which unbound controls collect the choices and macros invoked from the form implement the selections. The details of these macros may vary considerably, depending on the range of choices you need to accommodate. For example, you already know how to use OpenForm and OpenReport actions to open forms and print reports, and how to establish selection criteria by entering an appropriate condition in the Where Condition argument for either of these actions. To impose selection criteria on a table already open in Form view, you can use the Apply Filter macro action. A variety of strategies for constructing the conditions are described later in this chapter.

NOTE. *If you plan to use a dialog box to solicit selection criteria for a report or form, make sure that the data source is either a table or a query that selects a broader subset of records than any you might specify through the dialog box.*

Designing Dialog Boxes

In any GUI environment, including Windows, there is a fundamental difference between the behavior of forms that serve as dialog boxes or alert boxes and forms used to update tables. Data entry forms like the ones described in Chapters 6, 10, and 12 are functionally equivalent to the Datasheet window, although they may look quite different. As you already know, you can open more than one form at a time, you can open both form and datasheet windows together, and you can switch from one window to another at will when several windows are open simultaneously on the desktop. This type of data entry environment is often referred to as *non-modal*, or *modeless*, because it does not impose any particular data entry mode or sequence of operations on the users. In contrast, a dialog box or alert box opens in a *pop-up* window, which is displayed on top of all other windows on the desktop. This characteristic is not unique to dialog boxes—by default, Access opens any new window on top of other open windows. More importantly, a dialog box is *modal*—Access does not allow you to switch to any other activity before you complete all the required entries in the dialog box or cancel the operation that invoked the dialog box in the first place.

Ideally, most data entry and display windows should be non-modal, and a GUI application should not force you to step through a complex hierarchy of menus or do your work in any particular order—in theory, you should be able to start several tasks, keep all of them open on the desktop, and switch among them at will. When the logic of a particular situation forbids this free-form approach—for example, when you need to collect selection criteria before beginning to print a report—you must use a modal form.

NOTE. *Both dialog boxes and alert boxes are modal pop-up windows, which differ primarily in the contexts in which they are used. The term* alert box *is used for simple dialog boxes that display a message and offer a limited number of options by way of command buttons (typically labeled "OK," "Cancel," "Yes," or "No"). In contrast, a* dialog box *can collect any type of information and typically contains at least two exit buttons, one of which executes a command and the other of which cancels the operation that invoked the dialog box.*

You do not have to look further than the Access user interface (or that of any other Windows program) to find examples of modal dialog boxes—the Find dialog box, Open File dialog box, and Print dialog box are three good examples with which you are already intimately familiar. You can move a modal window (for example, you have probably moved the Find dialog box so that it does not cover the data on the form or datasheet you are searching for), but you cannot execute menu commands or switch windows until you close the dialog box.

There are two ways to explicitly request that Access open a form in a modal pop-up window. One is to choose Yes for the Pop Up and Modal properties in the property sheet for the form, but when you open a form using the OpenForm action in a macro, you can accomplish the same effect by choosing Dialog rather than Normal for the Window Mode argument. This selection creates a modal pop-up window, which can be moved but not resized, and which has a close box but no Minimize or Maximize/Restore controls. You can see these window characteristics in the dialog box shown earlier in Figure 19.6.

You can always close a dialog box without making a selection by pressing Esc, and every Access window offers several built-in controls for closing the window—you can press Ctrl+F4, select the Close command from the control menu, or double-click on the close box. Nevertheless, the GUI standard dictates that you provide two command buttons for choosing these two possible exits—one that executes the action the dialog box is intended to carry out and another that allows you to cancel the operation and return to what you were doing before you opened the dialog box.

You can use the Default (not to be confused with Default Value) and Cancel properties to identify the command buttons that fulfill these roles. Setting the Default property to Yes designates a command button as the default button; when you use the dialog box, pressing Enter with no other command button selected is equivalent to selecting the default button explicitly. Access displays the default button with a heavier border, as you can see in Figure 19.6, in which the Edit button is the default button. Setting the Cancel property to Yes designates a command button (which may or may not have the caption "Cancel") as the Cancel button. When you use the dialog box, pressing Esc is equivalent to selecting the Cancel button. A form can have at most one Default button and one Cancel button, and setting the Default or Cancel property to Yes for any button automatically sets this property to No for all other buttons on the form. You can, however, make a button serve as both the Default and Cancel buttons, and you might want to do this in a dialog box form that collects input before performing a potentially destructive operation such as running a delete or update query. Also note that Access does not force you to define a default or cancel button, although you will probably want to do so in most forms used as dialog boxes.

A dialog box may have more than two exit options, as in the form shown in Figure 19.7, which allows you to choose different groups of records to include in a name and telephone list produced by a report called the Brief Reference List. In this form, the Preview and Print command buttons are the active exits, the Preview button is the default button, and the Cancel button returns you to the location from which the dialog box was opened without producing any output.

Using Macros to Control Dialog Boxes

Constructing dialog boxes like the ones in Figures 19.6 and 19.7 is easy, but controlling the complete sequence of events mediated by the dialog box is not so straightforward. This command sequence, which can be implemented through macros, may seem complex and convoluted at first, but understanding it is crucial for successfully using dialog boxes in your own database applications.

Figure 19.7

A dialog box with
two active exits and
one cancel option

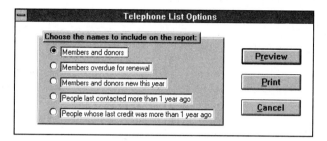

All of the macros involved in producing the name and telephone list invoked through the dialog box in Figure 19.7 are stored in a macro group called Telephone List, which is shown in Figure 19.8. The first macro in the group, Telephone List, is executed when you run the macro group from the Database window, and therefore does not require a name (although it has one). This macro uses the OpenForm action to open the Telephone List Options form shown earlier in Figure 19.7. The five radio buttons in the dialog box form an option group named Choice, which you use to select the records you want to include in the report. In this example, all the options invoke the same report, but impose different selection criteria on the source dynaset (the Names table). However, as you will see shortly, you could just as easily print different reports.

The Preview, Print, and Cancel command buttons provide three possible exits from the dialog box, and each has a macro attached to its On Push property. The Preview List and Print List macros, which execute the Preview and Print actions, both test the value of the Choice control to determine which radio button you selected, and then open the Brief Telephone List report in either Print Preview or Print view, with a Where Condition that describes the appropriate selection criteria. The Cancel List macro, which provides the means to exit without producing any report output, simply closes the dialog box, thereby returning you to the Database window. Note that if you bypass the command buttons and use any other method to close the dialog box, none of these macros runs, and the net effect is the same as if you had chosen the Cancel button. This command sequence is diagrammed in Figure 19.9.

One crucial fact might easily escape your notice if you set out from scratch to construct a similar dialog box: You must not close the dialog box until after you have opened the report. Note that both the Preview List and Print List macros test the value of the Choice control in the dialog box; as you may recall from Chapter 12, this control will take on a numeric value corresponding to the selected button—1 for the first button, 2 for the second, and so on. Once you have closed the Telephone List Options form, the values of the controls in the form are no longer available, so the dialog box form

Figure 19.8

The macro that prints the Brief Telephone List report

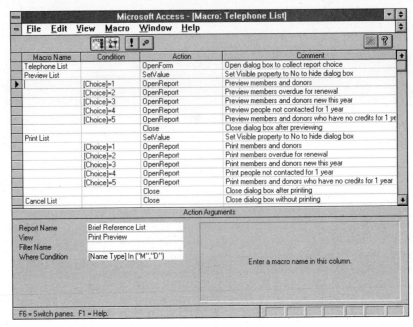

Macro Name	Condition	Action	Comment
Telephone List		OpenForm	Open dialog box to collect report choice
Preview List		SetValue	Set Visible property to No to hide dialog box
	[Choice]=1	OpenReport	Preview members and donors
	[Choice]=2	OpenReport	Preview members overdue for renewal
	[Choice]=3	OpenReport	Preview members and donors new this year
	[Choice]=4	OpenReport	Preview people not contacted for 1 year
	[Choice]=5	OpenReport	Preview members and donors who have no credits for 1 ye
		Close	Close dialog box after previewing
Print List		SetValue	Set Visible property to No to hide dialog box
	[Choice]=1	OpenReport	Print members and donors
	[Choice]=2	OpenReport	Print members overdue for renewal
	[Choice]=3	OpenReport	Print members and donors new this year
	[Choice]=4	OpenReport	Print people not contacted for 1 year
	[Choice]=5	OpenReport	Print members and donors who have no credits for 1 year
		Close	Close dialog box after printing
Cancel List		Close	Close dialog box without printing

Action Arguments

Report Name	Brief Reference List
View	Print Preview
Filter Name	
Where Condition	[Name Type] In ("M","D")

Enter a macro name in this column.

F6 = Switch panes. F1 = Help.

must be open when you execute the OpenReport action that previews or prints the report. However, if you intend to preview the report rather than print it, you cannot simply leave the dialog box visible on the screen.

The exact behavior of the dialog box window depends on the method you use to specify its properties. If you select Dialog for the Window Mode argument of the OpenForm action, the dialog box will appear on top of the Print Preview window. If you choose Normal for the Window Mode argument, but set the Modal property to Yes and the Pop Up property to No in the form property sheet, the Print Preview window will open on top of the dialog box but behind the Database window (or, if you opened the dialog box from a menu form, the menu form window). The most general solution to this dilemma, which will also serve you well in many other similar contexts, is to use the SetValue macro action to set the Visible property for the dialog box form to No to hide the form without closing it. After you test the values of the relevant controls in the form and open the selected report in Print Preview or Print view, you can use the Close action to close the dialog box (at this point, the Print Preview window may still be open, or Access may still be sending output to the Print Manager or printer).

Remember that while the dialog box form is open, Access assumes that all control and property names used in expressions refer to this form. Thus, in

Figure 19.9

The control sequence for using a dialog box opened from the Database window

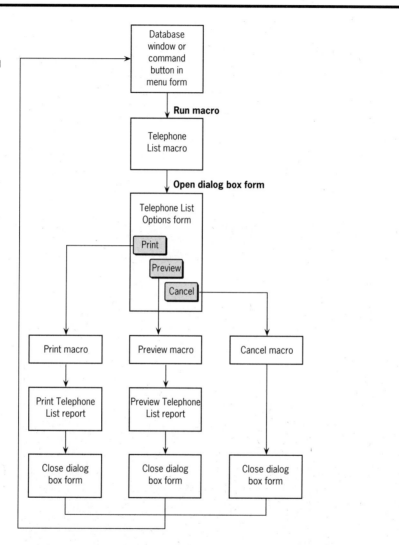

the expression [Choice]=1, Access assumes that "Choice" is the name of a control in the current document—the dialog box. Once the report is open, however, it becomes the current document, and Access assumes that all references to controls pertain to the report, not to the dialog box. In the Where Condition argument for the OpenReport actions, you can therefore refer to controls in the report without including the name of the report. For example, the Where Condition argument for the OpenReport action that prints the list of members and donors whose last credit was more than a year ago is written as follows:

```
[Name Type] In ("M","D") And Date()-[Last Credit]<=365
```

In this expression, Access interprets [Name Type] and [Last Credit] as the names of controls in the data source for the Brief Telephone List report, not the Telephone List Options dialog box.

When the OpenReport action is executed, the dialog box is still open, but invisible. As noted earlier in this chapter, *opening a form or report does not pause macro execution.* Access therefore executes the last action in the Preview List and Print List macros—an unconditional Close action, which closes the dialog box—while you are previewing or printing the report. As noted earlier, exactly the same Close action executes the Cancel List macro, which simply closes the dialog box without either printing or previewing the report.

Collecting Open-Ended Selection Criteria

The "correct" selection criteria for each run of a report or query are not always as simple, clear-cut, and predictable as in the previous example. Often, you may want to offer a broader range of choices, allowing the users of your application to enter selection criteria based on more than one field and to specify any arbitrary values for certain fields. For example, Figure 19.10 illustrates a dialog box that collects open-ended selection criteria based on the Name Type and State fields, and then opens the Brief Reference List in Print Preview mode. (Because you can easily print a report from the Print Preview screen, it may not be necessary to provide separate Preview and Print options for every report.) The ACE database includes reference tables for both the Name Type and State fields, and the dialog box in Figure 19.10 collects these items using combo boxes similar to the ones in the Names form described in Chapter 12. Although the combo boxes have the same names as the corresponding fields in the Names table, they are in fact *unbound* controls; as is the case with the Choice variable in the previous example, their values exist only while the dialog box is open.

Figure 19.10

Using a dialog box to collect open-ended selection criteria

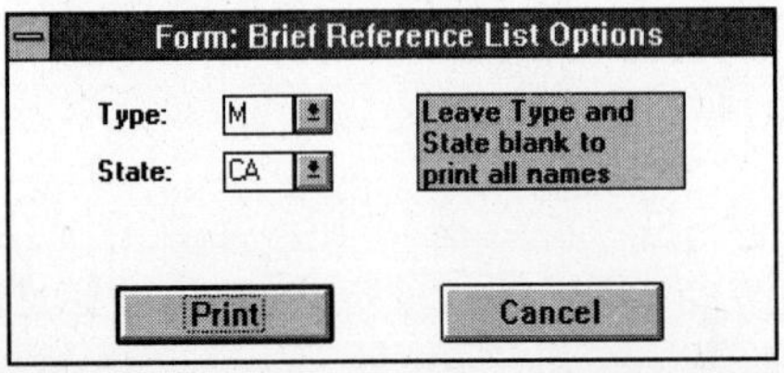

To introduce an additional measure of complexity, the Brief Reference List report is called from the Reports menu in the menu-driven version of the ACE system. This menu, which is pictured in Figure 19.11, is called from the Main Menu screen (described earlier in this chapter) using the same techniques as for the Data Entry menu. You might want to try running this report from the menu as you read this section.

Figure 19.11

The Reports menu for the ACE system

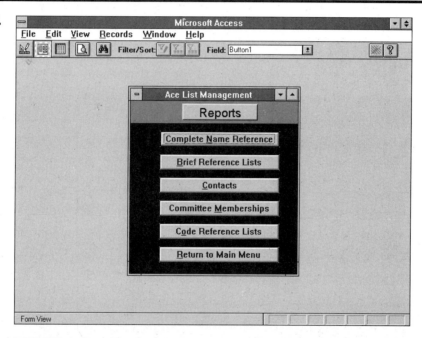

All the macros involved in printing the Brief Reference List are located in the macro group called Menus, along with all the other macros used in the menu system. These macros are visible in the portion of the Menus macro group shown in Figure 19.12. The Brief Reference macro, which initiates the command sequence, is attached to the OnPush property of the corresponding command button on the Report Menu form. The macros attached to the On Push property of the Print and Cancel buttons in the Brief Reference List Options form (which displays the dialog box) are called Print Reference and Cancel Reference. As in the previous example, the Print Reference macro begins by using a SetValue action to set the Visible property for the form to No to hide the dialog box. It then constructs the selection criteria, opens the report, and closes the dialog box.

The main challenge in the Print Reference macro is expressing the selection criteria. The dialog box allows you to enter criteria based on two different

Figure 19.12

The macros that
print the Brief
Reference List

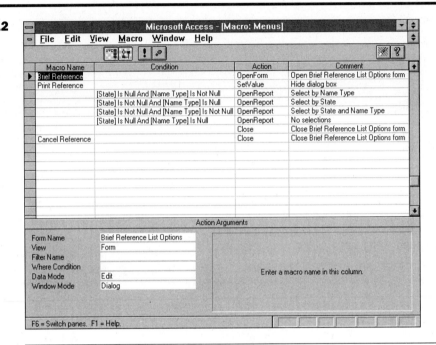

fields *or to leave either or both blank to ignore these fields*, and after you have
entered your selections, there are four possible combinations: You might have
entered values for both the name type and state, for the name type only, for
the state only, or for neither. The Print Reference macro tests explicitly for all
four of these possibilities, so that the selection criteria take into account only
the items you actually filled in. The first conditional step in the Print Reference macro is executed if you filled in only the Name Type combo box in the
dialog box, leaving the State control blank (null). The Where Condition in the
OpenReport action executed by this step uses the following condition to establish the report selection criteria:

```
[Name Type]=Forms![Brief Reference List Options]![Name Type]
```

Remember that when Access interprets this expression, the Brief Reference List report is already open, and the Print Preview window is the active
window, so the control name on the left side of the equals sign refers to the
Name Type control in the report, *not the one in the dialog box*, which is still
open (although it is invisible). The reference to the corresponding control in
the Brief Reference List Options form, which is on the right side of the
equals sign, must include the identifier Forms and the name of the form as
well as the name of the control itself. A similar condition establishes selection

criteria based only on the State control if you entered a state but not a name type, and a condition based on both controls establishes selection criteria based on the Name Type and State fields if you filled in both entries in the dialog box, as follows:

```
[State]=Forms![Brief Reference List Options]![State] And
[Name Type]=Forms![Brief Reference List Options]![Name Type]
```

The last conditional step in the Print Reference macro, which tests for null values in both the State and Name Type controls, is an OpenReport action in which the Where Condition argument is blank, so that Access prints all the records in the source table.

Collecting More Complex Selection Criteria

The approach described in the previous section—using a separate condition for each possible combination of entries in a dialog box—is easy to understand, but as you might imagine, it breaks down rapidly when the selection criteria are based on more than two or three different fields. For example, as outlined in the introduction to the ACE system presented in Chapter 1, the criteria for printing mailing labels might be based on any combination of name type, state, zip code range, range of last contact or last credit dates, range of year-to-date or overall credits, source, and possibly other criteria as well. Using explicit conditions, you would need hundreds of different conditions to handle all possible combinations of these nine items.

One very flexible strategy for collecting a variety of different selection criteria, any number and combination of which might be filled in, is to build a condition, stored in a text string, that expresses the selection criteria, and then use this expression to supply the value for the Where Condition argument of the OpenReport (or OpenForm) action executed by the macro that carries out a menu selection. The most convenient receptacle for the condition is an unbound control on the dialog box form, which you can hide by setting its Visible property to No. (A logical choice for the control name might be "Condition.") The macro that executes the action initiated through the dialog box can test each control on this form in turn to determine whether it is null, and add an appropriate phrase to the condition stored in the invisible text box for each one that is actually filled in.

Once you have assigned the desired value to this control, you can take advantage of the fact that Access allows you to enter an expression that evaluates to an appropriate value for most action arguments, rather than forcing you to always enter an explicit value. Thus, you can simply enter =[Condition] for the Where Condition argument. If the value of the Condition control is the text string

```
[Name Type]=Forms![Brief Reference List Options]![Name Type]
```

entering the expression =[Condition] for the Where Condition argument is exactly equivalent to entering the expression itself.

Figure 19.13 illustrates a dialog box that collects a variety of selection criteria for printing mailing labels, and Figure 19.14 shows the macro group that opens the dialog box, constructs the condition, and opens the label report in Print Preview view. The Label Options form includes an invisible control named Condition, which is used to store the expression that describes the selection criteria for the current label run. This control is located above the Print command button (you can open the Label Options form in Form Design view if you want to see it).

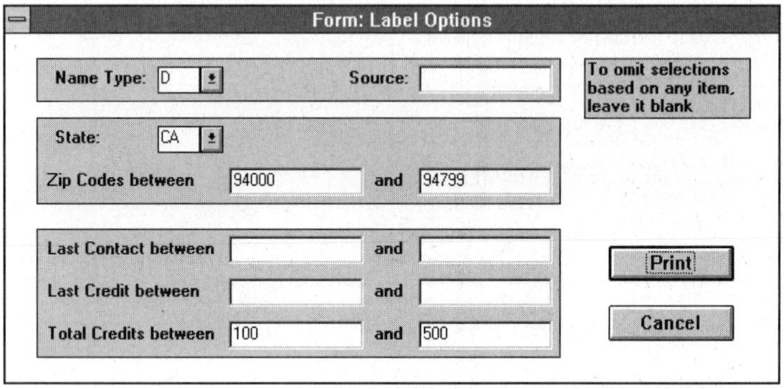

Figure 19.13

A dialog box that collects multiple selection criteria

The Selections macro, which constructs the condition used in the Where Condition argument in the OpenReport action, begins with an unconditional SetValue action that assigns an empty string value to the Condition control, to eradicate any value remaining from a prior pass through the macro. It then tests each of the controls in the form to determine whether it is blank (null). For each control that is not null, a SetValue action stores a new value in the Condition control derived by *adding onto its present value a text string that forms a new phrase that describes selection criteria based on the control.* Each new phrase is followed by the logical operator And, in preparation for adding on the next portion of the complete condition, and each text string begins with a leading space so that there is a space between the And at the end of the previous condition and the new phrase. This expression, for the Name Type control, is as follows:

```
[Condition] & " [Name Type]=Forms![Label Options]![Name
Type] And "
```

If it seems circular to assign a new value to the Condition control that includes a reference to the control itself, remember how Access carries out the

Figure 19.14

The macro group that prints labels based on multiple selection criteria

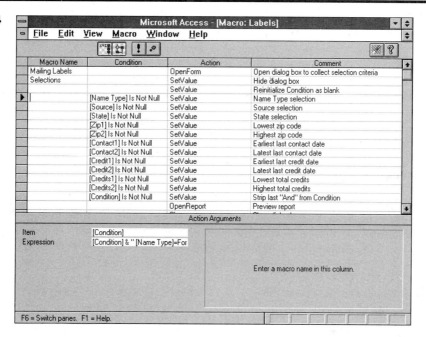

Macro Name	Condition	Action	Comment
Mailing Labels		OpenForm	Open dialog box to collect selection criteria
Selections		SetValue	Hide dialog box
		SetValue	Reinitialize Condition as blank
	[Name Type] Is Not Null	SetValue	Name Type selection
	[Source] Is Not Null	SetValue	Source selection
	[State] Is Not Null	SetValue	State selection
	[Zip1] Is Not Null	SetValue	Lowest zip code
	[Zip2] Is Not Null	SetValue	Highest zip code
	[Contact1] Is Not Null	SetValue	Earliest last contact date
	[Contact2] Is Not Null	SetValue	Latest last contact date
	[Credit1] Is Not Null	SetValue	Earliest last credit date
	[Credit2] Is Not Null	SetValue	Latest last credit date
	[Credits1] Is Not Null	SetValue	Lowest total credits
	[Credits2] Is Not Null	SetValue	Highest total credits
	[Condition] Is Not Null	SetValue	Strip last "And" from Condition
		OpenReport	Preview report

Action Arguments

Item [Condition]
Expression [Condition] & " [Name Type]=For

Enter a macro name in this column.

F6 = Switch panes. F1 = Help.

SetValue action: It first evaluates the expression entered in the Expression argument—in this case, the result of concatenating the text string presently stored in the Condition control with another text string enclosed in quotes—and then assigns this value to the control named in the Item argument. For the very first condition that evaluates to True (Yes), Condition will be null; thereafter, it will already contain an expression that represents one or more conditions. At the end of the sequence of steps, Condition will contain a text string that describes the complete condition, with a trailing And operator at the end. For example, if you filled in the Name Type, State, Zip1, Zip2, Credits1, and Credits2 controls in the dialog box (as shown in Figure 19.13), Condition will have the following value:

```
[Name Type]=Forms![Label Options]![Name Type] And
[State]=Forms![Label Options]![State] And
[Zip]>=Forms![Label Options]![Zip1] And
[Zip]<=Forms![Label Options]![Zip2] And
[Total Credits]>=Forms![Label Options]![Credits1] And
[Total Credits]<=Forms![Label Options]![Credits2] And
```

Before you can use this expression, you must strip the last "And" operator—that is, the last four characters of the text string—by using another

SetValue action to assign to Condition a portion of its present value extracted using the Left function. You may recall that this function takes two inputs—a text string and a number that represents the length of the portion of this string that you want to extract. You can use the Len function to measure the length of the string stored in Condition and then subtract 4 from the result to yield the length of the extract, as follows:

```
Left([Condition],Len([Condition])-4)
```

This technique can be confusing at first, especially if you have little experience with manipulating text strings or with constructing complex expressions, but it is so versatile and powerful that it is well worth studying until you master it. The key to understanding the basic method is the fact that you can enter an expression for the Where Condition argument (and most other macro arguments), and Access evaluates this expression and uses it exactly as if you had typed it explicitly. Building the expression in advance and then naming the control that stores it gives you a very flexible way to tailor the condition to a variety of situations by testing one step at a time rather than trying to write an explicit description of each possible combination of entries in a complex dialog box. If you have used Access Basic or any other higher-level programming language, note that the Condition control serves the same purpose as a *variable*—it stores a value that you assign in memory to make the value available later in the work session.

The easiest way to apply this method to collect selection criteria based on fields in more than one table is to use as the data source for the report or form a query that includes all the relevant fields from all the tables. For example, the Thank You Letters report is based on a query that links the Names and Transactions tables to make fields from both available and selects rows in the dynaset that represent transactions within a given range of dates. To collect the selection criteria on the fly, you could remove the selection criteria from the Names and Donations by Date query, and collect the range of dates using a dialog box much like the ones described in this section. Note that the expression you enter for the Where Condition action argument can refer to any fields that are present in the data source (which might be a query or a table), whether or not they appear on the report you are printing. The label-printing example described earlier depends on this fact—of all the items tested based on your entries in the Label Options dialog box, only the State and Zip fields are printed on the mailing labels.

In all the examples presented thus far in this chapter, the macros that initiate the reporting sequence are called either from the Database window or from a form that serves as an application menu, and the macros that define the selection criteria and print (or cancel) the report are attached to the forms that collect the criteria. This strategy is ideal for reports, because you will generally need to establish the selection criteria only once before you begin printing.

When you open a form, you might prefer to open the dialog box that solicits the selection criteria by using a macro attached to the OnOpen event of the form. If you use command buttons or menu options in the form to apply different filter conditions, you might consider the initial filter established when you open the form to be more or less equivalent to any other filter selected while you work with the form. This strategy is illustrated in the next section with a detailed example based on the Committee Memberships form.

NOTE. *The basic technique described in this section, which was illustrated with report examples, is also applicable to collecting selection criteria for editing data through forms.*

Collecting Selection Criteria for the Committees Table

To practice using custom dialog boxes, try defining a dialog box to collect selection criteria for data entry sessions carried out using the Committee Memberships form. Instead of opening the form from the dialog box, this example illustrates the alternative strategy described at the end of the last section—the dialog box is invoked from the OnOpen event of the Committee Memberships form. First, create the dialog box that collects the selection criteria, which is shown in Figure 19.15 in Form Design view:

1. Make sure that the Database window displays the list of forms, and click on the New command button or press Alt+N.

2. Select Blank Form in the New Form dialog box to move to the Form Design view without specifying a data source for the form. Maximize the Form Design window, resize the detail section of the form to $4\frac{1}{2}$ inches wide by 2 inches high, and make sure that the toolbox and property sheet are visible.

3. Using the tool box, add an unbound check box to the form. Enter **Current** in the Control name property for the check box (not the label), enter **0** in the Default Value property, and enter **Current members only** in the Caption property for the label. With the label selected, click on the Bold toggle button in the tool bar. If necessary, adjust the width of the label object to accommodate its new contents.

4. Using the tool box, add an unbound combo box to the form below the check box. Enter **Officer** in the Control name property for the combo box, and enter **Officer Position:** in the Caption property for the label. With the label selected, click on the Bold toggle button in the tool bar. If necessary, adjust the width of the label object to accommodate its new contents.

Figure 19.15

The dialog box that collects the committee memberships selection criteria

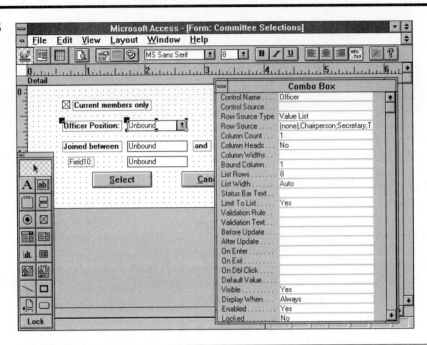

5. Define the combo box by making the following entries in the property sheet (some of these are the default values):

Row Source Type	Value List
Row Source	(none);Chairperson;Secretary;Treasurer
Column Count	1
Column Heads	No
List Width	Auto
Limit to List	Yes

6. Add two unbound text boxes on the same row below the combo box to collect the starting and ending values for the Joined field. Enter the names **Joined1** and **Joined2** in the Control Name properties for these text boxes, and enter **Joined between** and **and** for the label captions. Make sure that both labels are displayed bold.

7. Add an unbound text box below the Joined1 and Joined2 text boxes, enter the Control Name **Condition**, and set the Visible property to No. This control will store the condition described by your other selections in the dialog box.

8. Add two command buttons near the bottom of the form. Enter the control names **&Select** and **&Cancel** (remember that the ampersand designates the character that follows as a hotkey), and enter the macro names **[Committee Memberships].[Select]** and **[Committee Memberships].[Cancel]** in the On Push properties for the buttons. Set the Default property to Yes for the Select button, and set the Cancel property to Yes for the Cancel button.

9. If necessary, adjust the positions of the controls so that your screen resembles Figure 19.15. Click on the Restore control in the upper-right corner of the maximized window, switch to Form view, and use the Size to Fit Form option on the Window menu to adjust the window size.

10. In the property sheet for the form, enter **Committee Selections** for the Caption property. Set the Scroll Bars property to Neither, and set Record Selectors to No.

11. Close the form and save it under the name **Committee Selections**.

Attach the macro that will open the dialog box (which you have not yet created) to the OnOpen event in the Committee Memberships form, as follows:

1. Open the Committee Memberships form in Form Design view, and enter the macro name **[Committee Memberships].[Open Committee Selections]** in the On Open property for the form.

2. Close the form and save your changes.

Finally, add the macros that implement the selections to the Committee Memberships macro group, as follows:

1. Open the Committee Memberships macro group in Design view, and make sure that the Macro Names and Conditions columns are visible.

2. On the first available blank line, define the macro that opens the Committee Selections dialog box as follows:

Macro Name	Open Committee Selections
Action	OpenForm
Comment	Open Committee Selections dialog box

3. Press F6 to move down to the lower portion of the Macro Design window, and enter the action arguments that define the OpenForm action:

Form Name	Committee Selections
View	Form
Data Mode	Edit
Window Mode	Dialog

4. Return to the upper portion of the Macro Design window, and in the next blank row, start building the macro that executes the Select command button in the Committee Selections form. The name of this macro is Select, and the first action is a SetValue action. In the lower portion of the Macro Design window, enter **Visible** (the Visible property for the current object, which is the Committee Selections form) for the Item argument, and set the Expression argument to No.

5. In the next six rows, enter a series of SetValue actions that update the value of the Condition control based on the values entered into the other controls in the dialog box, as follows:

Condition	Item	Expression
	[Condition]	" "
[Current]=–1	[Condition]	[Condition] & "[Quit] Is Null And "
[Officer] Is Not Null And [Officer]<>"(none)"	[Condition]	[Condition] & " [Officer]= Forms![Committee Selections]![Officer] And "
[Joined1] Is Not Null	[Condition]	[Condition] & " [Joined]>= Forms![Committee Selections]![Joined1] And "
[Joined2] Is Not Null	[Condition]	[Condition] & " [Joined]<= Forms![Committee Selections]![Joined2] And "
Len([Condition]) >0	[Condition]	Left([Condition],Len([Condition])-4)

6. Add an unconditional SelectObject action that selects the Committee Memberships form, which Access has already begun to open.

7. Add an Apply Filter action governed by the same condition as the last SetValue action (Len([Condition])>0), and enter **=[Condition]** for the Where Condition argument.

8. Enter the last action in the Select macro, a Close action that closes the Committee Selections form.

9. Define the Cancel macro, which consists of a single Close action that closes the Committee Selections form.

10. Close the macro group and save your changes.

You can now test the new form and macros by opening the Committee Memberships form from the Database window and entering various combinations of selection criteria. One very easy way to preview the effects of your selections is to switch to Datasheet view once the Committee Memberships form is open, so that you can see at a glance which records are included in the current dynaset. Note the timing of the events in the sequence that opens the form—Access executes the macro attached to the OnOpen event after beginning to open the form (and thereby making it available so you can select it with the SelectObject action), but before displaying it on the screen. If you include a CancelEvent action in this macro to abort the current process, the form will never be displayed. The complete sequence of events is diagrammed in Figure 19.16.

Designing Custom Menus for Forms

You are already familiar with the standard Access menu bar in Form view and Datasheet view, and you have undoubtedly grown to appreciate the fact that all the same menu options are available to you when you work with a custom form as when you use the default Datasheet view. This functional equivalence of forms and datasheets allows you to choose the best display mode for a particular table or for a particular data entry task. However, other users of your data entry forms, especially those whose activities should be restricted or those who know less about Access and do not understand (or need to use) many of the menu options, would be better served by a custom menu bar. By using macros, you can construct a complete menu bar that replaces the standard Access menu bar (although it may duplicate some of the standard menu options). A menu bar of this type is always associated with a form and is most commonly used to provide a special menu tailored to the needs of a particular data entry environment, but you can also use this type of menu as the main menu for an application instead of using the menu forms described earlier in this chapter.

Figure 19.16

Displaying a dialog box from the OnOpen event for a form

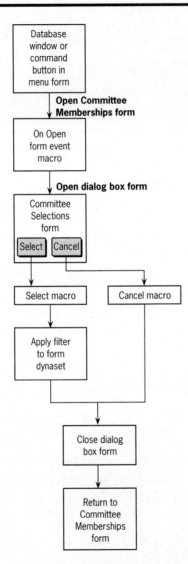

When you attach a custom menu bar to a data entry form, you can duplicate the functionality of the command buttons introduced in Chapter 18, and because the menu does not take up space on the form itself, you can provide many more custom options than you could reasonably fit on the screen in the form of command buttons. At the same time, because your custom menu replaces the standard Access menu bar, you can restrict access to options that should not be available to certain users by excluding them from the menu bar. Once you have decided to design a custom menu for a form, whether to use a command button or a menu option for a particular command is not always an easy choice. For options that are used very frequently, such as custom navigation options, command buttons are more convenient, whereas placing options that are used relatively rarely on the menu leaves the screen less cluttered and distracting. Menu options also offer another advantage in multipage forms such as the Names Five-Page Form described in Chapter 18—the menu is equally accessible from all pages of the form, so you do not have to duplicate important command buttons or force the users to remember the hotkey shortcuts.

Despite the apparent complexity of a menu system, which consists of a menu bar in which each option has an attached pull-down menu, you can create a custom menu without programming by using macros. When you operate the custom menu, Access takes care of the mechanics that allow you to navigate through the menu hierarchy using keyboard or mouse commands and displays the pull-down menus and submenus at the appropriate times. All you have to do is define macros that describe the appearance of the menu system and define the actions you want associated with each menu option. The basic steps that you use to create the menu system and attach it to a form are as follows (although you need not carry them out in the order listed):

1. Create one macro to describe the main menu bar.

2. Create a separate macro group for each pull-down menu.

3. Assign the name of the main menu bar macro to the On Menu property of the form.

Unlike the macros described in Chapter 18 and earlier in this chapter, the macros that define a custom menu bar must adhere strictly to this relatively rigid format. In particular, note that you must use separate macros for the menu bar and for each of the attached pull-down menus; you cannot place them all in one macro group.

The macro group that defines the main menu bar should consist entirely of AddMenu actions, one for each option (sometimes called a *pad*) in the menu bar. In most cases, each main menu option will call a submenu, but in fact the macro called by a main menu bar option can execute any action or series of actions. Figure 19.17 illustrates the macro that defines the main menu bar for a form called Names Five-Page Form with Menu (a version of the Names Five-Page Form described in Chapter 18 in which menu options replace the command buttons in the latter form). The menu bar has five options—File, Edit, Page, Records, and Selections—and the structure of the menu system is diagrammed in Figure 19.18. There is rarely any reason to include macro actions other than AddMenu actions in the macro that defines a menu bar, but Access does not specifically prohibit you from doing so.

Figure 19.17

Defining a custom menu bar

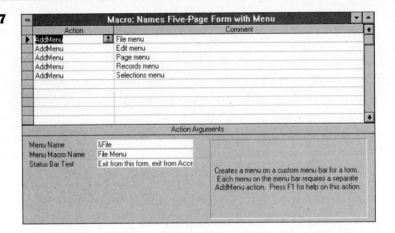

The AddMenu action takes three arguments, which are visible in Figure 19.17 for the File option. The Menu Name argument stores the text displayed in the menu bar. There is no way to explicitly control the spacing of the prompts that identify the options—Access automatically places each option immediately to the right of the previous one. The prompts that identify the menu options are not limited to single words, but adhering to this convention will make it easier to distinguish the options. If you include an ampersand in the prompt, Access underlines the character that follows to remind you of the Alt-key shortcut for activating the menu bar and displaying the associated pull-down menu. If you do not indicate a hotkey, Access automatically uses the first character of each menu prompt as a hotkey, so technically, you *must* designate a hotkey only if you want to use a different character. However, it is good practice to include a hotkey reminder in every menu bar prompt for compatibility with the Access user interface, and to reassure users who are not familiar with Access and its default assumptions. Each of the options in the menu defined by the macro in Figure 19.17 has an underlined hotkey (the prompt for the first option, &File, is visible in this figure).

The Menu Macro Name argument identifies the macro group that describes the attached pull-down menu, and the Status Bar Text argument contains an optional description, which Access displays in the status bar while the menu option is highlighted to remind you of its purpose. Note that this text is displayed only when the menu bar is selected but no pull-down menu is visible—that is, if you press the Alt or F10 key to activate the menu bar and then use the Left Arrow and Right Arrow keys to navigate through the options. After you pull down any menu, the status bar reflects the currently highlighted option in this submenu.

Figure 19.18

The structure of the custom menu for the Five-Page Form with Menu

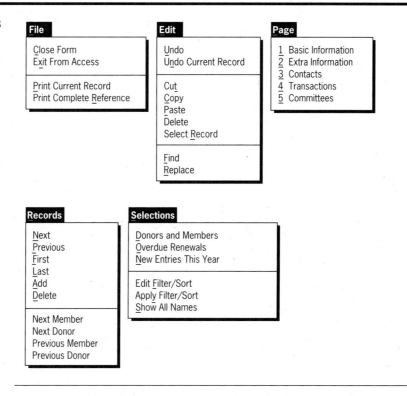

To describe the pull-down menus associated with the menu bar options, you create a macro group for each pull-down menu. In each of these macro groups, one named macro represents each menu option. The macros must be arranged in the same order as the corresponding menu options, and the macro names supply the text displayed in the pull-down menus. As a simple example, Figure 19.19 illustrates the macro group that defines the File menu in the Names Five-Page Form with Menus form. You can designate a hotkey character in a menu prompt by preceding the desired character with an ampersand; as a rule, you should provide a hotkey for each menu option for the convenience of keyboard users. To draw a horizontal dividing line between groups of menu options (like the lines that separate the undo, cut-and-paste, find, and object manipulation options in the standard Form view Edit menu), simply enter a hyphen (-) in the Macro Name column and leave the Action and Comment columns blank.

As you can see in Figure 19.19, the macros that execute the menu options can contain any actions. In menus that emulate components of the standard Access menu bar, you will probably make frequent use of the DoMenuItem

Figure 19.19

A macro group that defines a pull-down menu

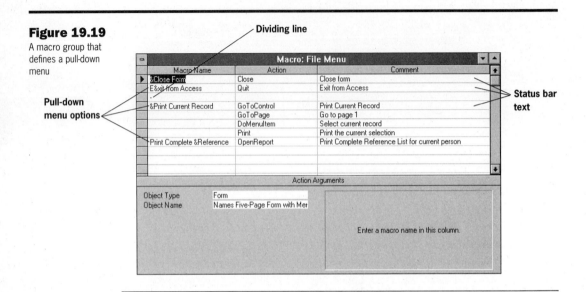

action to execute these menu actions. For example, Figure 19.20 illustrates the Edit Menu macro, which defines the Edit menu in the Names Five-Page Form with Menu form. Each of the macros in this group consists of a single DoMenuItem action that invokes the corresponding Access Edit menu bar option. As in the standard Edit menu, dividing lines separate the groups of related options. The first two options—Undo and Undo Current Record—illustrate an important facet of the way Access manages a custom menu. When you use this menu, the first option alternates between Undo, Can't Undo, and Undo Saved Record, and the second alternates between Undo Current Field and Undo Current Record, depending on the status of the current record. If you examine the drop-down list of menu commands associated with the Command argument, you will find only Undo and Undo Current Record, but Access updates these menu options to reflect the current environment, just as it would the corresponding options on the standard Edit menu.

To attach a menu to a form, you enter the name of the macro that defines the main menu bar to the On Menu property for the form. You may recall from Table 18.2 that the OnMenu event occurs when a form is first opened, and this is the moment when Access activates the menu bar. If you do not name a macro in the OnMenu property for the form, Access simply displays the standard menu bar. *A custom menu is always attached to a particular form, and it is displayed only when that form has the focus and is frontmost on the desktop.* When you close the form, the menu bar reverts to the standard Access menu bar, and if you switch temporarily to another Access window, the menu bar changes immediately to the one normally displayed in that environment.

Figure 19.20

A pull-down menu that includes many of the standard Edit menu options

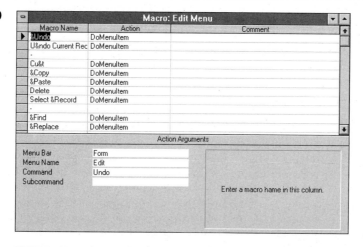

Also keep in mind that a custom menu bar defined with macros always *replaces* the standard Access menu bar—you cannot simply *add* a new pull-down menu. If you want to incorporate any of the standard menu options, you must explicitly include them in your menu system. In most cases, the easiest way to duplicate any of the standard Access menu options is to use DoMenu-Item actions, as in the Edit menu macro group shown in Figure 19.20.

You may not need to include in a custom menu standard options for which Access provides equivalent command buttons in the tool bar. For example, although the menu system for the Names Five-Page Form with Menu includes the three Filter/Sort options, you could dispense with these if you were willing to rely on the tool bar buttons instead. However, if you or the other users who work with a form have a strong preference for using keyboard rather than mouse commands, it is a good idea to provide as many menu options as possible, because you cannot operate the tool bar buttons with keyboard commands. Depending on your purpose in creating a custom menu bar, you might consider the tool bar command buttons either a blessing or a curse—they enable you to avoid having to explicitly define equivalent menu options, but they make it more difficult to selectively restrict access to certain commands. Your only recourse is to suppress the tool bar entirely by customizing the General options, which are described earlier in this chapter.

The Page, Records, and Selections menus in the menu bar for the Names Five-Page Form with Menu form replace the command buttons in the previous version of the form. Executing these menu options is greatly complicated by the fact that the form includes three subforms and displays data from all the main tables in the ACE database. Because the menu bar is accessible regardless of which field has the focus, you must take into consideration how a given macro action will behave when invoked from various places on the form. For example, if you choose one of the options on the Page menu to move directly to another page on the form when a field in one of the subforms has the focus, Access displays an alert box with the "Command not available" error message (beacuse the subforms do not have multiple pages). If this seems surprising, consider another aspect of the difference between the effects of the same commands in different environments—pressing PgDn or PgUp from the first or second page of the form moves you to another page, but in the subforms, which are displayed in Datasheet view, these keys display the next or previous screenful of records.

These differences will not cause problems in a form that uses command buttons to switch form pages, because clicking on one of the buttons or pressing the equivalent hotkey moves the focus to a control on the main form (the command button itself), where you can safely execute the GoToPage action. To solve this problem, the Page Menu macro, which is shown in Figure 19.21, uses the GoToControl action to move the focus to the ID Code control (which is on page 1 of the form) before the GoToPage action that selects the desired form page. Unless you have a very fast computer, you will see page 1 flash briefly onto the screen before Access displays the page you selected from the menu; unfortunately, there is no easy way around this problem.

The options on the Records menu, which are carried out by the macro group shown in Figure 19.22, enable you to move to the next, previous, first, or last record in the Names table. However, if you select any of these menu options from within the Contacts, Transactions, or Committees table subform,

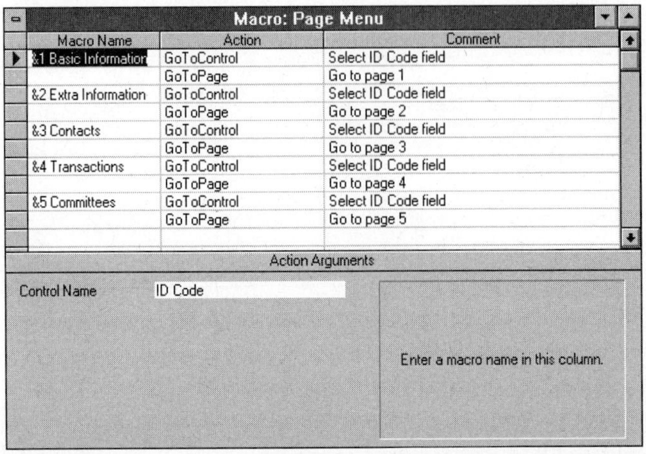

Figure 19.21

The macro group that executes the Page menu options

Macro Name	Action	Comment
&1 Basic Information	GoToControl	Select ID Code field
	GoToPage	Go to page 1
&2 Extra Information	GoToControl	Select ID Code field
	GoToPage	Go to page 2
&3 Contacts	GoToControl	Select ID Code field
	GoToPage	Go to page 3
&4 Transactions	GoToControl	Select ID Code field
	GoToPage	Go to page 4
&5 Committees	GoToControl	Select ID Code field
	GoToPage	Go to page 5

Action Arguments

Control Name   ID Code

Enter a macro name in this column.

the GoToRecord action in the Records Menu macro moves the focus *to another record in the source table for the subform.* To make these options work as intended, you must ensure that a field in the main form has the focus before Access executes the GoToRecord action, and the macros in the Records Menu macro group do this with a GoToControl action that moves the focus to the ID Code field. Because this control is on the first page of the form, all of these menu options also scroll the screen back to bring this field into view, but this action simulates using the scroll bar or pressing Shift+Tab, *not* pressing PgUp. To scroll the window all the way to the top of page 1 so that only the fields meant to be placed on this page are visible on the screen, you must add a GoToPage action to each macro. Ideally, you might prefer to be able to move to the next record in the Names table without switching pages, but there is unfortunately no easy way to accomplish this. In a form that updates only one table and has no subforms, these problems will not arise.

The other options on the Records menu are straightforward. The Add option uses the GoToControl action to display a new record (exactly as if you had chosen New from the submenu invoked by selecting Go To from the standard Access Records menu). The Delete option uses a DoMenuItem action to select the current record and then another DoMenuItem action to delete the selection. The last four options are executed by the macros shown in

Figure 19.22

The macro group that executes the Records menu options

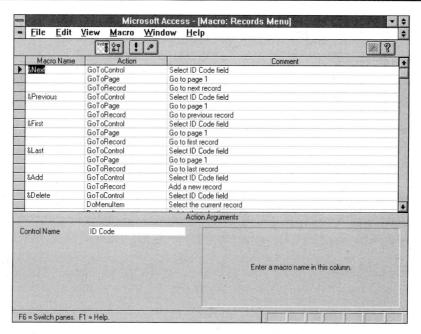

Figure 19.23, each of which begins with a GoToControl action that selects the Name Type control, followed by a GoToPage action that moves the focus to the first page of the form and updates the screen display. The third step in each macro is a FindRecord action that searches for the next or previous record of the appropriate type. The arguments for this action in the Next Member macro are visible in Figure 19.23. The actions that find Donors search the Name Type field for the text string "D," and in the actions that search for the previous (rather than the next) record, the Direction argument is Up rather than Down.

Figure 19.23

The macro group that executes the custom search options on the Records menu

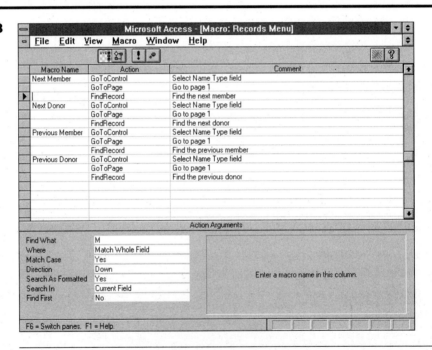

The Selections menu, which is implemented through the macro group illustrated in Figure 19.24, uses the ApplyFilter action to select three categories of names. The Where Conditions are as follows:

Donors and Members	[Name Type] In ("D","M")
Overdue Renewals	[Name Type]="M" And Date()-[Last Renewal]>365
New Entries This Year	Year([First Contact])=Year(Date())

Figure 19.24

The macro group that executes the Selections menu options

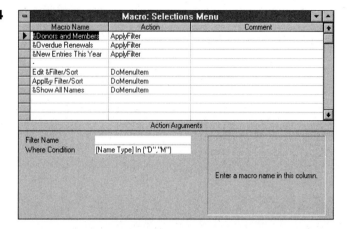

When you use this form, note that Access displays FLTR in the status bar when a filter placed in effect by the ApplyFilter macro action is active, just as it does when you use the standard methods (the Edit Filter/Sort and Apply Filter/Sort menu options or the equivalent tool bar buttons) to define and implement a filter. To provide additional flexibility, the last three options on the Selections menu use the DoMenuItem action to simulate the three filter options normally present on the standard Access Records menu in Form view.

Using a Menu Bar as a Main Menu

As noted earlier in this chapter, you might want to use a menu bar as the main menu for an Access application. Because a menu bar must be associated with a form, the only way to do this is to attach the main menu bar to a form and start up the application by opening this form. The form itself can be little more than a simple sign-on screen like the one shown in Figure 19.25, or it can be a larger screen that serves as a command center for the application (instead of the Database window). If you want to see two examples of the latter strategy, you can open the ORDENTRY or PIM sample databases supplied with Access.

The Startup Menu Screen form shown in Figure 19.25 is opened by a macro called Startup, which contains two actions—a DoMenuItem action that hides the Database window and an OpenForm action that opens the Startup Menu Screen form. The menu bar, which is visible in Figure 19.25, is defined by the Startup Menu Screen macro group shown in Figure 19.26, which is invoked from the On Menu property of the form. The pull-down menus attached to the menu bar are defined by macro groups named Menu

Figure 19.25

A start-up screen
with an attached
menu bar

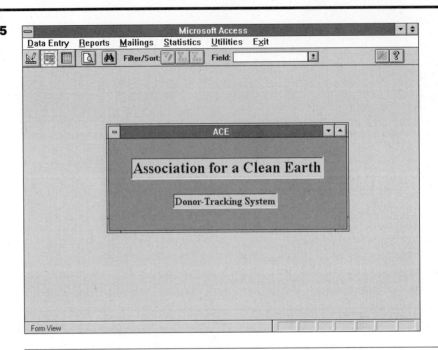

Bar Data Entry, Menu Bar Reports, Menu Bar Mailings, Menu Bar Statistics, Menu Bar Utilities, and Menu Bar Exit, which contain macros that are virtually identical to those used to carry out the corresponding options invoked by the command buttons in the menu screens described earlier in this chapter.

Summary

This chapter described several techniques—all based on macros—for putting together applications that you have already created to build a menu-driven system. These methods enable you to introduce a larger measure of automation into an Access application than the simple macros described in Chapter 18, and they make it far easier for a user who is not familiar with Access to use a database that you created. This chapter introduced very few new concepts—rather, it outlined strategies for using Access objects in new ways.

As you can see from the examples, building a menu-driven system can be complicated, and although it does not necessarily require programming, it does force you to think like a programmer—you must plan the structure and flow of control in a custom menu system, and understand the interaction between the forms and macros that mediate the process of collecting information in a custom dialog box and acting on this input. If you can see immediate

Figure 19.26

The macro that
defines the main
menu bar

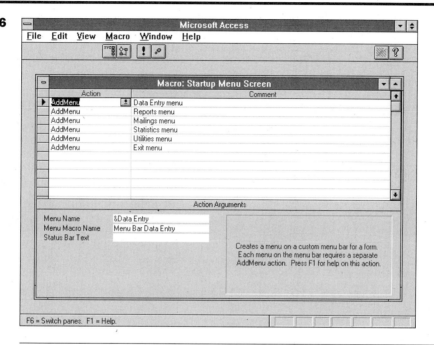

uses for these techniques in your own applications, it is likely that the results
will justify the effort it requires to implement them. In a database created
solely for your own use, you may never need this level of automation, and if
you are relatively new to Access and find the concepts difficult, you can certainly defer implementing them. On the other hand, if the macro techniques
presented in this chapter whet your appetite for a higher level of automation,
Chapter 20 introduces two true programming languages—Access Basic and
SQL—and describes some simple ways you can use these languages in your
applications to overcome some of the limitations cited in earlier chapters.

20

Introduction to Programming

- Introduction to SQL
- Creating Access Basic Modules
- Using Control Structures
- Operating on Database Objects

CHAPTERS 18 AND 19 HAVE GIVEN YOU A GLIMPSE OF THE POWER, FLEXI-
bility, and ease of use you can achieve through automation. Because
macros can simulate nearly any Access action or menu command,
and because they can incorporate conditional tests, you can accomplish quite a bit using macros alone, and if the application-building techniques
presented in Chapter 19 are sufficient for your needs, you may never have to
venture into programming. However, Access also supports a complete programming language—Access Basic—which you can use to perform calculations and carry out operations that would be impossible or excessively
cumbersome solely with macros. You can call Access Basic routines from a
form or report, much the way you call a macro, as well as from expressions
used in nearly any context. When you gain proficiency, you can use this language to design complete menu-driven applications that you could distribute
to other users who have Access but know little or nothing about how to use it;
however most Access Basic users will never need to take the language this far.

Access also supports some features of another database programming
language—Structured Query Language, usually abbreviated SQL—which
has been used for years on mainframe and minicomputers. As the name suggests, this language was designed primarily as a query tool, but it also supports commands for building, maintaining, and updating databases, as well as
for password-protection mechanisms. In Access, which provides easier ways
to accomplish these tasks, SQL is used "behind the scenes" to execute queries, and you can also use SQL statements in forms, macros, and Access Basic
programs to carry out operations equivalent to executing select, make table,
delete, update, and append queries. This chapter provides a brief introduction to the syntax of the SQL SELECT, DELETE, INSERT, and UPDATE
commands used to accomplish these tasks and suggests ways that you can
make productive use of SQL in your own applications. If you have used SQL
before, you will find the Access implementation very familiar, and if you
have worked with other command-driven database languages, such as Xbase,
you will find the concepts very similar, although the syntax is quite different.
If this is your first exposure to SQL, you can use the query design tool to aid
the learning process. In either case, take the time to experiment with the
Access SQL implementation, because this powerful and concise language
can enable you to accomplish a great deal with a few simple statements.

In contrast, Access Basic is a more complete programming language comparable to other higher-level languages or the languages used in other PC database programs like Xbase and Paradox. Access Basic is a close relative of
Microsoft's Visual Basic programming language, although it lacks the Visual
Basic commands that duplicate functionality available in Access without programming (such as the commands that enable you to draw complex data
entry screens). If you have used Visual Basic, you will find the structure and
syntax of Access Basic familiar, and you can concentrate on learning the specific commands used to manipulate data and integrate procedures with forms

and reports. If you have used other database programming languages, such as Xbase or PAL, you will have little difficulty with the command syntax and the programming structures, but you will find the overall approach to manipulating database components to be quite different.

This chapter introduces the Access Basic programming language, describes the essential components of a procedure, and outlines the programming language commands that enable you to manipulate database objects you have already created. If Access Basic is your first programming language, you may find this chapter a bit overwhelming. Your best strategy is to begin by writing simple procedures for carrying out calculations and specialized validation tests, and work your way gradually up to longer and more complex routines that work independently of your forms and reports. You might end up concluding that you do not need or want to become a programmer, but take the time to experiment a bit before you forgo this option—a little bit of programming can go a long way towards adding specialized functionality to your applications.

Introduction to SQL

Structured Query Language (SQL) is a data manipulation language supported by many mainframe and minicomputers and in recent years, by PCs as well. SQL includes all the commands required to create, update, and maintain databases, but no tools for designing data entry forms, reports, or queries; however, these tools are available in the form of add-on "front-end" utility packages for all the popular SQL implementations. Access uses SQL "behind the scenes" to execute queries, and you can use SQL statements in macros, Access Basic procedures, and forms to carry out operations equivalent to executing queries. Access uses the following SQL commands to execute the various types of queries:

Type of Query	SQL Command
Select, Make Table	SELECT
Delete	DELETE
Update	UPDATE
Append	INSERT

If you have used SQL before, you will find these commands familiar. If you have no prior experience with SQL, you can use Access queries as a tool to help you learn the syntax or as a shortcut for constructing a complicated SQL command. To view or edit the SQL command generated to execute a query, open the query in Design view and select the SQL option from the View menu. Access opens an editing window like the one shown in Figure 20.1, which displays the SQL statement that executes the Committees with Names query created in Chapter 8 (this query displays all the fields from the Committees table, together with the Name field from the Names table and the Description field from the Committee Names table). If you edit the command displayed in the SQL window, you will see your changes reflected immediately in the QBE grid. For example, if you delete a field name, the corresponding column will disappear. In fact, you can define a new query by typing an SQL command from scratch in the SQL window (although this is rarely the easiest way to do so). You can also cut and paste text from the SQL window. Thus, if you want to use an SQL statement in a form, macro, or procedure, you can avoid typing a lengthy command by constructing an equivalent query, copying the text in the SQL window to the Clipboard, and pasting it into the desired object.

Figure 20.1

Viewing the SQL statement that executes a select query

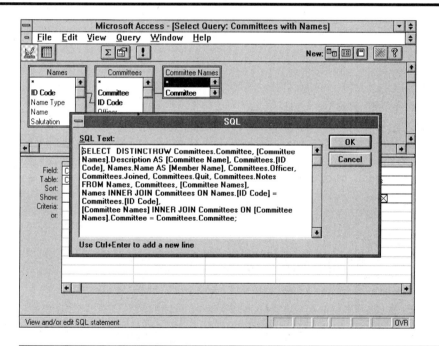

As you can see in Figure 20.1, Access uses slightly different typographical conventions in SQL commands to conform to the usage that has become standard in other implementations of SQL. All SQL keywords are written in uppercase, and every SQL command must end with a semicolon. You can break up a long SQL command onto multiple lines to improve readability, and it is customary in many SQL implementations to begin each clause (the various

clauses are explained later in this section) on a new line and to indent the first line in each clause. In the examples in this chapter, some of the line breaks are dictated by the limitations of the printed page rather than by the logic of the command.

In the SQL statements generated to execute queries, Access includes the name of the source table in every field name reference, but when you write your own SQL statements, you can omit the table name unless it is required to distinguish between identically named fields in two tables that contribute to the query. One reason for including only essential table names is the fact that Access limits the length of an SQL statement called from a macro or procedure to 256 characters.

Access uses the SELECT command to execute select queries, and you can use this command to carry out the equivalent of a select query in other contexts. For example, as noted briefly in Chapter 12, you can use a SELECT statement to supply the values displayed in a list box or combo box on a form, by choosing Table/Query for the Row Source Type property and entering the SELECT statement instead of the name of a table or query in the Row Source property. This method enables you to avoid cluttering up your database with a great many queries that you do not use in any other contexts. The basic syntax of a SELECT command that extracts data from one table is as follows:

```
SELECT expressions FROM table WHERE condition
ORDER BY expression;
```

If you have not seen this type of command syntax listing before, note that the words printed in italics are *placeholders*, not literal values. Thus, when you type your own SELECT statements, you would substitute a list of expressions for the placeholder *expressions*, and type a table name after the keyword FROM. Only the expression list and table name are obligatory; the WHERE and ORDER BY clauses are optional. For example, the following command selects the name and address fields from the Names table:

```
SELECT [ID Code], [Name Type], Name, Company, Address,
City, State
  FROM Names;
```

You can specify an *alias*, or alternate name, for any field (you will nearly always want to do this for calculated fields) by adding it to the field list in an AS clause, as follows:

```
SELECT [ID Code], [Name Type] AS Type, Name, Company,
Address, City, State
  FROM Names;
```

By default, Access includes the DISTINCTROW keyword, which excludes entire duplicate rows from the output, in every SELECT statement generated to execute a select query. If you check the Unique Values Only check box in the Query Properties dialog box, this keyword is replaced by DISTINCT, which creates a query that selects unique values in each field in the output grid. If you checked the Run with Owner's Permissions check box in the Query Properties dialog box, the generated SELECT command also includes the WITH OWNERACCESS OPTION clause. You can omit either or both of these clauses from the SELECT statements that you write if you do not need them.

When you write a SELECT statement to extract data from two or more tables, you must add a JOIN clause for each pair of tables to describe the linkage between the tables. The general format for an inner join is as follows:

```
table1 INNER JOIN table2 ON field1 = field2
```

You can see two examples in the query shown in Figure 20.1, which joins the Names table to the Committees table based on the ID Code field, and the Committee Names table to the Committees table based on the Committee field. Because the names of the corresponding fields in the two tables need not be the same (although they are in Figure 20.1 as well as in most of the queries in the ACE system), you must always include both field names in the JOIN clause. Note the comma between the last table name in the FROM clause and the first table name in the JOIN clause and the comma that separates the two JOIN clauses—they are essential and they are easy to forget.

To describe an outer join, you use a JOIN clause of one of the following forms:

```
table1 LEFT JOIN table2 ON field1 = field2
```

or

```
table1 RIGHT JOIN table2 ON field1 = field2
```

You use the LEFT JOIN clause for joins that select all the records from the parent table in a one-to-many relationship, and the RIGHT JOIN clause for joins that select all the records from the child table. For example, the following command selects all records from the Names table, together with all the matching records from the Transactions table for people who have transactions:

```
SELECT [ID Code], Name, [Total Credits]-[Total Debits]
AS Balance, [Transaction Type] AS Type,
[Transaction Number], Date, Amount
 FROM Names, Transactions,
 Names LEFT JOIN Transactions ON Names.[ID Code] =
 Transactions.[ID Code];
```

The WHERE clause specifies a condition that must be fulfilled by each row in the output of the SELECT statement. When you define a query, Access builds the WHERE clause from your entries in the Criteria rows in the output grid; in the SELECT commands that you write, you can use any valid condition. The ORDER BY clause specifies the sort order. As in a query, you can sort by one or more fields, and you can use the DESC keyword to request a descending sort. For example, the following command selects the name and address fields for donors and members from the Names table and sorts the output by ID Code:

```
SELECT [ID Code], [Name Type] AS Type, Name, Company,
Address, City, State
  FROM Names
  WHERE [Name Type] In ("M", "D")
  ORDER BY [ID Code];
```

You can use the SELECT command to extract records into a new table by adding an INTO clause. This is the method Access uses to implement make table queries. For example, the following SELECT command copies the name and address fields for donors to a new table called Donors in zip code order:

```
SELECT  Name, Company, Address, City, State, Zip
  INTO Donors
  FROM Names
  WHERE [Name Type]="D"
  ORDER BY Zip;
```

You can use the DELETE command to delete records from a table. The general form is as follows:

```
DELETE FROM table WHERE condition;
```

If the selection criteria are based on more than one table or on a table other than the one from which you are deleting records, you must add a JOIN clause and specify the table from which you want to delete records, as in the following, which deletes prior year transactions for prospects:

```
DELETE Transactions.*
  FROM Transactions, Names,
  Transactions INNER JOIN Names ON
  [Transactions].[ID Code] = Names.[ID Code]
  WHERE Year([Date]) < Year(Date());
```

NOTE. *The DELETE command deletes records, not fields. To remove a field from a table, you must modify the structure and delete the field, and to blank out the contents of a field in multiple records, you must use an update query or an SQL UPDATE command (which is described shortly).*

You can use the UPDATE command to change the values of one or more fields in a table. The general form is as follows:

```
UPDATE table SET field = expression WHERE condition;
```

To update more than one field, you include multiple SET clauses, separated by commas, as in the following example, which enters "415" in the Area Code field and "CA" in the State field in the Names table for people in San Francisco:

```
UPDATE Names
  SET [Area Code] = "415", State = "CA"
  WHERE City = "San Francisco";
```

If the selection criteria are based on more than one table or on a table other than the one you are updating, you must add a JOIN clause, as in the UPDATE command. For example, the following calculates the sales tax on purchase transactions made by people in California and also updates the Amount field:

```
UPDATE Transactions, Names,
  Names INNER JOIN Transactions ON Names.[ID Code] =
  Transactions.[ID Code]
  SET Tax = 0.085*[Subtotal],
  Amount = [Subtotal]-[Discount]+[Tax]+[Shipping]
  WHERE State = "CA" AND [Transaction Type] = "P";
```

You can use the INSERT command to add records to an existing table (as outlined earlier in this section, you must use a SELECT command to create a new table). If the structures of the two tables are identical, the syntax is very simple:

```
INSERT INTO table1 SELECT table1.*
   FROM table1 WHERE condition;
```

For example, the following INSERT command copies member records from the Names table to an identically structured table called Mailing List:

```
INSERT INTO [Mailing List]
  SELECT Names.*
  FROM Names
  WHERE [Name Type] = "M";
```

If the structures of the source and destination tables are different, you must specify the fields you want to update in the destination table and the expressions that define the values of these fields, as in the following INSERT command, which duplicates the Append Members to Mailing List query described in Chapter 16:

```
INSERT INTO [Mailing List]
  ( CityState, [Zip Code], Telephone, Name, Salutation,
  Company, Address )
  SELECT [City] & ", " & [State] AS Expr1, Zip,
  [Area Code] & "/" & [Telephone] AS Expr2, Name,
  Salutation, Company, Address
  FROM Names
  WHERE [Name Type]="M";
```

In this version of the INSERT command, the correlation between the fields in the target table and the values assigned to these fields is established by the order of these items in the two lists. Thus, the first field name listed within the parentheses (CityState in this example) obtains its value from the first expression in the SELECT clause ([City] & ", " & [State]), the second field corresponds to the second expression, and so on. This scheme results in a rather lengthy and complex command, but it gives you the flexibility to assign any value to any field. Fields in the target table that are not explicitly named in the SELECT clause remain blank in the new records. As is the case with UPDATE and DELETE commands, you can copy fields from more than one table or base the selection criteria on more than one table by including a JOIN clause.

In Chapter 15, you learned that you cannot change the title of a graph object in a form or report in Microsoft Graph, because the title is part of the instructions for constructing the graph. If you examine the Row Source property for a graph object, you will see that it consists of an SQL SELECT statement. For example, the following constructs the graph in the Transactions Graphed by Type form:

```
SELECT DISTINCTROW Format([Date], "MMM \'YY") AS
[Transactions by Month],
  SUM([Transactions by Type and Date].[Amount])
  AS [Amount] ,
  SUM([Transactions by Type and Date].[Number x 100])
  AS [Number x 100]
  FROM [Transactions by Type and Date]
  GROUP BY Year([Date])*12+Month([Date])-1, Format([Date],
  "MMM \'YY");
```

The graph title is the expression in brackets in the first AS clause ("Transactions by Month" in this example), and you can change it by editing the SQL SELECT command that specifies the Row Source property.

As noted earlier, one very common application for SQL in an Access application is to supply the values displayed in a list box or combo box. To practice this technique, modify the Committee Memberships form as follows:

1. Open the Committee Memberships form in Form Design view. Maximize the window, and make sure that the property sheet is visible.

2. Click on the Committee control to select it, and note that the Row Source Type property is Table/Query and the Row Source is the Committee Names table.

3. Edit the Row Source property to enter the following SELECT command:

```
SELECT Committee, Description FROM [Committee Names]
ORDER BY Description;
```

4. Click on the ID Code control to select it, and edit the Row Source property to enter the following SELECT command:

```
SELECT [ID Code], Name FROM Names ORDER BY [ID Code];
```

5. Change the Column Count property to 2 and enter **1 in;3 in.** in the Column Width property. (You may recall that the list was originally derived from the Names and Addresses query, which included the Name Type field between the ID Code and Name fields, and that the Column Count and Column Widths properties were set to exclude the Name Type column.)

6. Switch to Form View and open the drop-down lists for both combo boxes to verify that they display the correct fields. Note that the committee names in the drop-down list for the Committee combo box now displays the list in alphabetical order by Committee Name, as specified in the ORDER BY clause in the SELECT command (the Description field in the Committee Names table stores the committee names).

7. Close the form and save it.

Creating Access Basic Modules

In addition to the SQL commands described in the previous section, Access provides a programming language called Access Basic, which was designed specifically to interact with Access database objects. The Access Basic routines that you write are stored in database objects called *modules*, and you can display the list of modules in the Database window by clicking on the Module object button or by selecting Modules from the View menu.

You can create as many modules as you wish in a database, and each module can contain one or more *procedures*—independent Access Basic routines that carry out a particular action or operation. You might think of a module as equivalent to a macro group, and many of the same considerations outlined in Chapter 18 for macro groups apply to the organization of the modules in a database. When you write procedures that are called only from one form—for example, routines to carry out specialized validation tests—you might store them together in one module that contains only those routines. Generic procedures that you might need to call from more than one place in an application—such as routines used to validate similar fields in many different forms—can go into another module that serves as a procedure "library" for the entire application. This approach also makes it easy to reuse generic routines originally written for one application in any new databases you create; you can simply copy the module from one database into another (either via the Clipboard or by using the Import or Export commands).

These distinctions may not be clear to you when you first begin writing procedures, and you need not worry too much at first about where to put a particular procedure, because Access can find any procedure in the current database, regardless of which module contains it. It is especially difficult for a beginning programmer to discern which procedures will prove generally useful in other applications. When you gain experience, you will probably realize that procedures you thought were unique to one application might prove useful in others, although some minor modifications may be required to make them more generic. Although you should be aware of these issues from the start, the consequences of changing your mind later are minor—it is very easy to cut and paste procedures if you later decide to reorganize your modules.

NOTE.   *When you run a procedure, you need not specify the name of the module that contains it, so moving a procedure from one module to another has very little impact on your application.*

You can create two different types of procedures: *function procedures* and *sub procedures*. Function procedures are equivalent in every way to the built-in Access functions—they can accept input in the form of arguments, they return a value, and they can be used anywhere that Access allows an expression. Some other programming languages use the terms *function* or *user-defined function* to describe the kind of routine that Access calls a function procedure. You can use function procedures to carry out specialized calculations for which Access does not offer built-in functions, to supply default values for fields or controls, or to carry out complex series of conditional tests in contexts where Access would not otherwise permit you to do so—for example, to supply the value for a control on a report. A sub procedure, which can also accept input, carries out any series of actions without explicitly returning a value to the form or macro that called it. In other languages, sub procedures

are often called *subroutines* or simply *procedures.* You can use sub procedures in contexts that do not demand a return value—for example, to export data or mediate a DDE linkage with another Windows application.

NOTE. *In this chapter, the term* procedure *is used in discussions of concepts that apply equally to both types of procedures, and the more specialized terms* function procedure *and* sub procedure *are used when it is important to differentiate between the two.*

To create a new module from scratch, you begin by using either of the standard methods used to define new database objects:

- Make sure that the Database window displays the list of modules, and then click on the New command button or press Alt+N.

- Whenever the Database window is visible, choose New from the File menu and then choose Module from the submenu of new object types.

Figure 20.2 illustrates the Module window as it appears when you first create a new module.

Every module consists of an opening section called the *declarations section*, followed by one or more procedures. The commands in the declarations section govern aspects of the environment that pertain to the module as a whole—that is, to every procedure in the module—including Option statements (which describe global aspects of the environment) and definitions of variables that you want to be available in more than one procedure (variables are described in more detail later in this chapter, in the section called "Using Variables in Procedures"). Access automatically adds the following Option Compare statement to the declarations section in every new module you create:

```
Option Compare Database
```

The Option Compare statement controls the default method that Access uses to carry out text comparisons (for example, to determine whether one text string is "greater than" another and to determine the sort order for Text fields). The following keywords specify the string comparison method:

Binary	Access uses case-sensitive comparisons and determines the sort order from the ANSI codes used to represent characters.
Database	Access uses the sort order specified through the New Database Sort Order in the General Options dialog box in text comparisons.
Text	Access uses case-insensitive comparisons and determines the sort order from the International settings established through the Windows Control Panel.

Figure 20.2

The Module window

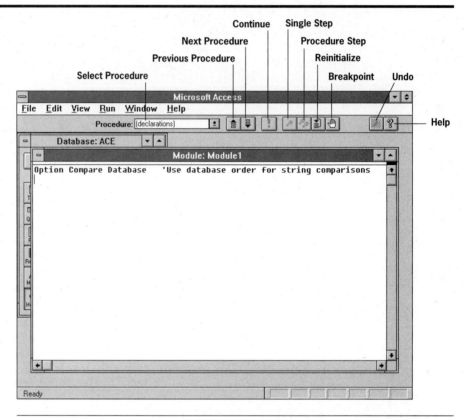

In most cases, you can retain the default setting, Database, which is visible in Figure 20.2. Note that the text that follows the single quote character is a *comment*, not part of the command. Comments are described in more detail in the next section.

Working in the Module Window

In marked contrast to all your prior work with Access, including the process of defining macros, creating modules requires a great deal of typing—you cannot choose programming commands from combo boxes as you do macro actions—and the bulk of the Module window is occupied by an editing window in which you enter the text that comprises the procedures.

Figure 20.3 diagrams the structure of the Access menu bar in the Module window. The controls in the tool bar, which are labeled in Figure 20.2, allow you to move from one procedure to another, run a procedure in single-step mode (just as you can single-step through a macro), and find the *bugs* (errors) in your code. Access gives you a variety of methods for navigating through a module one procedure at a time:

- Click on the Next Procedure or Previous Procedure command buttons in the tool bar.

- Choose the Next Procedure or Previous Procedure options from the View menu.

- Press Ctrl+Down Arrow to move to the next procedure or Ctrl+Up Arrow to move to the previous procedure.

- Press PgDn from anywhere on the last screenful of lines in a long procedure to move to the next procedure, or press PgUp from anywhere on the first screenful of lines in a procedure to move to the previous procedure.

Figure 20.3

The Access menu bar in the Module window

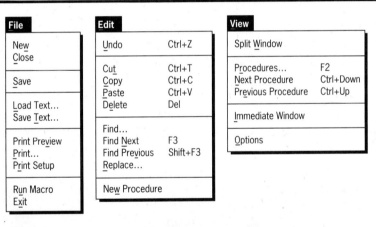

When you reach the end of a module, Access cycles around to the beginning and redisplays the first portion, and when you go backwards from the beginning, it returns to the last procedure. You can use the Procedure combo box in the tool bar to move directly to any procedure by name, either by typing the name or by selecting it from the drop-down list, much the way you can move to any column in a datasheet by using a similar control in the Datasheet window tool bar. You can also use the Procedures option on the View menu or the equivalent hotkey (F2) to display a dialog box that allows you to choose any procedure in any module. If you end up creating modules that contain more than a handful of procedures, you will come to appreciate this seeming overabundance of navigation commands.

You can open more than one Module window at a time, and you will often want to do so to facilitate comparing procedures in different modules or to cut and paste procedures or parts of procedures between modules. Within a single Module window, you can display two different procedures in the same module by splitting the window into two panes. To split the Module window horizontally into two panes of equal size, you can choose the Split Window option from the View menu. You can also split the window initially or adjust the relative sizes of the two panes at any point by dragging the boundary between the panes up or down. To eliminate the split and return to viewing only one procedure at a time, you can either drag the boundary between the panes all the way up to the top of the window, or you can choose the Split Window option again.

Figure 20.4 illustrates the Module window with parts of two procedures visible in the two panes. As in other Access environments, you can switch between the two portions of the window by pressing F6 or by clicking anywhere in either pane. All of the navigation controls work independently in the two panes. For example, the Next Procedure and Previous Procedure commands (and the equivalent tool bar commands buttons) affect only the currently selected pane. Also, Access remembers the position of the insertion point in both windows, so that if you leave the window and return, you will find the insertion point exactly where you left it.

You can use the Print option on the File menu to print the complete contents of a module. If you want to incorporate the text into another document (such as a manual for your application), you can use the Save Text option on the File menu to write the contents to a text file, and then import this text file into a document written using a word processor.

Typographical Conventions

An Access Basic procedure consists of a series of lines of text, each of which forms a single *command* or *statement*. Every command must begin on a new line, so you must press the Enter key to add a hard return at the end of every command. Access does not word-wrap long lines, but you can scroll the Module

Figure 20.4

Splitting the Module window to display two procedures at once

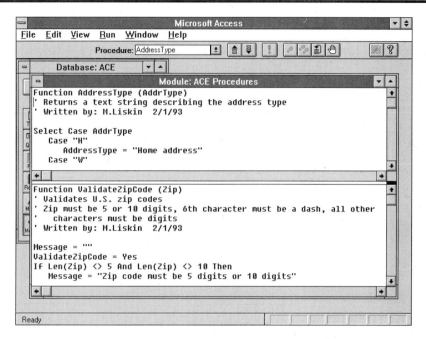

window to the right or left as necessary to view commands that are too wide to fit on the screen at once. In addition to the command keys recognized in the other Access editing environments, there are two special Ctrl-key shortcuts: You can press Ctrl+N to insert a new line above the current line, and you can delete the current line to the Clipboard by pressing Ctrl+Y (these commands, derived originally from early versions of the WordStar word processor, may have been included for compatibility with the many MS-DOS programs that adopted them).

You can use blank lines and spaces anywhere you wish to improve the readability of your procedures. As in Access expressions entered in other contexts, you can add extra spaces before and after operators such as And, Or, +, and &, and you can indent lines to emphasize the fact that they form a logical group or to clarify the flow of control in the programming structures that allow you to make decisions and repeat groups of commands. (These structures are described later in this chapter, in the sections under "Using Control Structures.") If you press the Tab key to indent a line, Access automatically indents subsequent new lines to the same level. By default, the tab stops in the Module window are set at intervals of four spaces, but you can change this default by editing the Module Options accessed through the Options dialog box (setting tab stops every three spaces is ideal for delineating the flow of control in the decision-making structures described later in this chapter). Many programmers prefer to indent all the lines in a procedure except the introductory comments, and the procedures in this book adhere to this convention. By adding blank lines between groups of commands, you can break up a long procedure to identify what you consider to be the discrete functional units, and thereby make it easier to find at a glance the portion you need to read or modify. You will see many illustrations of these typographical conventions in the programming examples presented throughout this chapter, and adopting a similar set of standards will greatly improve the clarity and readability of your procedures.

Using Comments

In addition to the executable commands, an Access Basic procedure can include *comments*—explanatory text that is ignored when Access runs the procedure. All comments must be preceded by the Access Basic *comment marker*—the single quote symbol (')—to distinguish them from programming commands. (You do not have to enclose the entire comment in single quotes.) A comment can occupy a line of its own, but as illustrated by the Option Compare statement in the declarations section visible in Figure 20.2, you can also place a comment at the end of any program statement. If you need more than one line for a comment, you must begin each line with a single quote, as in the introductory comments visible in Figure 20.4. Some typical uses of comments include:

- Describing the purpose of a command or group of commands

- Identifying the author of a procedure and other programmers who modified it

- Noting the date you last modified a procedure or documenting the changes you made

- Listing the forms, reports, or macros that call a procedure

- Explaining the purposes of temporary variables you create

- Tracing the logic behind a complex series of conditional tests

- Providing a blow-by-blow explanation of a complicated calculation

NOTE. *For compatibility with older versions of Microsoft Basic (not Access Basic), Access also recognizes Rem (short for "remark") as a comment marker.*

When you begin writing simple procedures, comments may seem superfluous, but as your procedures grow in length and complexity, comments will become increasingly important. When you need to modify a procedure that you wrote months (or years) earlier, the overall logic and the details of the calculations will no longer be fresh in your mind, and comments can remind you of what you were trying to accomplish and the specific methods you developed to achieve those goals. For other programmers who must read or modify your modules, liberal use of comments will prove invaluable—even another programmer who understands the Access Basic programming language may have difficulty discerning your intentions from the program commands themselves. Adding a few comment lines that briefly describe the purpose and usage of each procedure is especially helpful to other programmers searching through your modules to find the procedure that carries out a particular operation or calculation.

Editing a Module

The module text editor supports all the basic keyboard commands and mouse techniques that you already know from your experience editing Text and Memo fields, but it is a much "smarter" editor. As usual, Access monitors your keystrokes as you type and adjusts your program code to conform to the default typographical conventions. For example, it converts functions, commands, and other keywords to the standard format in which the first letter and some internal letters are capitalized. Note that in a module, Access inserts a space before and after every operator, whereas in Query Design view, it removes all optional spaces. By default, Access also checks the syntax of every line you type, and when you move to another line, it immediately displays an error message in an alert box like the one in Figure 20.5 if it detects a problem. After you select OK from this dialog box, Access allows you to move to another line; thus, you can leave one command incomplete (or incorrect), edit another line, and then return to the first command to finish or correct it.

Figure 20.5
The alert box
displayed when you
exit from an
incorrect command

For many programmers, including beginners and inaccurate typists, this instant error-checking can save a great deal of time and reduce the frustration engendered by saving a module, opening a form that calls procedures in the module, and then discovering a syntax error when you try to use the form. Receiving quick feedback is particularly helpful for novice programmers, because correcting a mistake immediately reinforces the correct syntax. When you have more experience with Access Basic, more of your errors will be due to simple typographical errors or careless mistakes such as forgetting a function name; getting immediate notification enables you to fix many problems on the spot, thereby shortening the debugging cycle. If you prefer not to be nagged, you can turn off the automatic syntax checking feature by setting the Syntax Checking option in the Module Design options (accessed through the Options dialog box) to No.

When you call up context-sensitive help from the Module window by pressing F1 or clicking on the Help command button in the tool bar with the insertion point in an Access Basic keyword (for example, a function name or command verb), Access displays a help screen that describes the command. Otherwise, it displays the alphabetical list of programming topics shown in Figure 20.6 rather than the help system Table of Contents.

Figure 20.6

The list of programming help topics

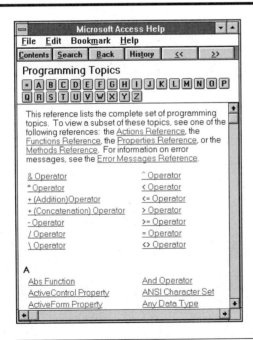

The Find and Replace options on the Edit menu in the Module window work much like their counterparts in Datasheet and Form views, but the Find and Replace dialog boxes offer slightly different options, customized for the unique requirements of the programming environment. Figure 20.7 illustrates the Find dialog box. Instead of the Current Field and All Fields choices, the Search radio buttons offer the options of searching in the current procedure only, in all the procedures in the current module, or in all

modules in the database. There is only one command button (OK) to initiate a search, which Access always interprets as equivalent to the Find First
button in the standard Find dialog box, but you can use the Find Next and
Find Previous options on the Edit menu (or the equivalent hotkeys, F3 and
Shift+F3) to continue the previous search in either direction.

Figure 20.7

The Find dialog box
in the Module window

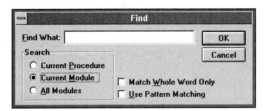

If you check the Match Whole Word Only check box, Access finds the
search string only if it appears as a separate word, not if it is embedded in another word. For example, if you search for "Open," Access will not find
"OpenForm" or "OpenReport." As you may recall from Chapter 4, the only
way to force this type of search in Datasheet view or Form view is to enter
the search string with leading and trailing spaces. If you check Use Pattern
Matching, you can include wildcard characters in the search string, as in the
standard Find dialog box; otherwise, Access treats these symbols like any
other characters. This difference is significant because many of the wildcard
symbols also have special meaning in the Access Basic programming language. For example, the asterisk (*) represents multiplication, and the square
brackets normally used to enclose a list of alternative characters are used to
delimit the names of objects.

Figure 20.8 illustrates the companion Replace dialog box, which enables
you to search for one text string and replace it with another. The Verify and
Replace All command buttons are equivalent to the Replace and Replace All
command buttons in the standard Replace dialog box. Checking the Syntax
Checking On check box causes Access to verify each line as it carries out the
replace operation. If the command line that results from a replacement contains a syntax error, exiting from the line (either manually or automatically,
when Access advances to the next occurrence of the search string) invokes an
alert box that displays an error message identical to the one that the same
error would generate in a command that you typed from scratch.

Before Access can execute a procedure, it must *compile* the procedure, a
process that translates the English-like commands in the procedures to a form
that is closer to the instructions recognized by the microprocessor in your computer. Access automatically compiles a procedure when it is called, but you

Figure 20.8

The Replace dialog box in the Module window

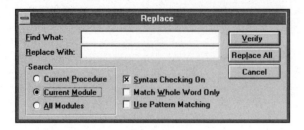

might want to compile your code in advance to catch errors that are not confined to one line and therefore cannot be detected by the automatic syntax checker. These errors include mismatched loop beginning and ending statements (such as ending a Do While loop with an End If statement), omitting a loop ending statement, or nesting structures incorrectly. (The programming structures alluded to in these examples are described later in this chapter in the sections following "Using Control Structures.") If you turned off automatic syntax checking using the Module Options, compiling procedures in advance can save you a great deal of debugging time. To compile all the procedures in all the modules in your database, you can use the Compile All option on the Run menu (there is no way to compile procedures selectively).

Writing Procedures

To identify the individual function procedures and sub procedures that make up a module, you must begin each procedure with a statement that identifies it by name and end each procedure with a matching End command. A function procedure begins with a Function statement (as you can see in Figure 20.4) and ends with End Function, and a sub procedure begins with a Sub statement and ends with End Sub. If you insert a new blank line above the Function or Sub statement, Access assumes that this line will contain a comment (the only procedure component that can legitimately precede the Function or Sub statement), and it inserts a single quote at the beginning of the line. The name of a procedure must always be followed by a space and a pair of parentheses that enclose the inputs, or arguments, and Access adds the parentheses automatically if you do not type them. Even if a procedure does not require any input, you must retain the empty pair of parentheses.

You can create a new procedure simply by moving to any blank line (including one in the middle of another procedure or between two other procedures), and typing a Function or Sub statement. If you prefer, you can choose the New Procedure option from the View menu to call up the dialog box shown in Figure 20.9, which prompts you to enter the name of the procedure

Figure 20.9

Defining a new
procedure

and select its type (by using the Sub and Function radio buttons). When you choose OK to exit from this dialog box, Access creates a procedure *stub*—a template that includes only the essential beginning and ending lines.

Procedure names must adhere to a more restrictive set of rules than the names you assign to other Access objects. Like other Access object names, a procedure name can be up to 40 characters long, but it must contain only letters, numbers, and underscores (_), and it must begin with a letter. If you have become accustomed to using spaces and punctuation marks in names, note that many programmers substitute underscores for spaces to improve readability (this convention arose in other languages that do not allow spaces in any names). If you prefer not to have to type the underscore character (which requires pressing the Shift key), you can use internal capital letters to highlight the individual "words" in long procedure names. For example, you might write the name of a procedure that calculates a donor balance as Calculate_balance, Calculate_Balance, calculateBalance, or CalculateBalance. Most of the examples in this book follow the latter convention.

As noted earlier in this chapter, function procedures play the same role in a database application as the built-in Access functions. Like a built-in function, a function procedure can accept one or more inputs, and it always returns a single value. A reference to a function procedure is therefore equivalent to any other expression that evaluates to the same type of value, and you can call a function procedure in any context in which an expression is permitted—for example, to specify the Control Source property for a control on a form or report, to define the default value for a field in a table, to describe the Validation Rule or Validation Text property for a field or control, and so on. You can also attach a function procedure to an event associated with a form or report, much as you do a macro, to carry out more complex actions than you can accomplish with macros at the same point in the form or report processing sequence.

To define the value returned by a function procedure, you assign this value to a variable with the same name as the function. (Variables are defined more formally in the next section of this chapter, but this simple use of variables should be clear from the examples in this section.) Figure 20.10 illustrates a very short function procedure called FollowUpDate, which calculates a follow-up date by adding 14 days to the current date. Note that despite the recommendation in Chapter 9 that you always include the optional parentheses in function references, the current date function in Figure 20.10 appears without them, because the Access syntax checker removes optional punctuation when it verifies and reformats the commands you type in the Module window. The FollowUpDate procedure consists of just one command (and two comment lines), which defines the value of the function as the result of adding 14 days to the current date.

Figure 20.10

A function procedure that calculates a follow-up date

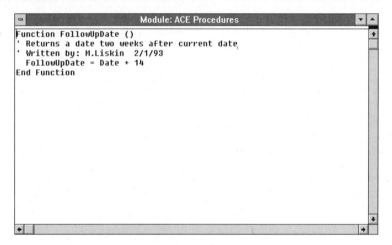

```
Function FollowUpDate ()
' Returns a date two weeks after current date
' Written by: M.Liskin  2/1/93
    FollowUpDate = Date + 14
End Function
```

To call a function procedure, you write its name, followed by the pair of parentheses that identify it as a function. The FollowUpDate function evaluates to a Date/Time value, and you can call it from any context in which a Date/Time expression is permitted. For example, to define a calculated follow-up date column in a query, you could enter FollowUpDate() in the Field row in the QBE grid. To print the result of evaluating the function in a text box on a report, you could enter =FollowUpDate() for the Control Source property. To use it to supply the default value for a control on a form or for a field in a table (such as the Followup field in the Contacts table), you would enter =FollowUpDate() for the Default Value property of the control or field.

NOTE. *When you call a function procedure by assigning its name to an object property, the equals sign is required to indicate that you are entering an expression rather than a macro name.*

Although function procedures like FollowUpDate perform calculations that you could just as easily enter explicitly in any table, query, form, or report (calculations carried out by evaluating one explicit expression), they offer important advantages that you should recognize from the start: Using procedures makes your application more modular, less redundant, and therefore easier to maintain. For example, if you change your mind and decide that the follow-up date for a contact should be three weeks from the current date rather than two weeks, you would only have to edit one database object—the module that contains the FollowUpDate function—to effect this change, rather than modifying every document that contains a reference to the follow-up date to change the expression Date + 14 to Date + 21.

If Access Basic is your first programming language, the statement that assigns the value Date + 14 to the variable that represents the return value of the FollowUpDate function procedure merits further attention. This command is an *assignment statement*—a command used to assign a value to a variable, field, control, or property. The equals sign in this statement *does not* represent the equals operator, which tests two expressions for equality. In an assignment statement, the equals sign represents the assignment operator, which *sets* the value of the object on the left *equal to* the result of evaluating the expression on the right. In this example, the assignment statement also *creates* the variable on the left side of the equals sign, but Access Basic allows (in fact, encourages) you to predefine variables before you assign them values. In older versions of Basic, these two different uses for the equals sign were distinguished by requiring that you begin an assignment statement with the word "Let," and Access Basic supports this usage for compatibility. Thus, you could write the assignment statement in the FollowUpDate function procedure as follows:

```
Let FollowUpDate = Date + 14
```

Although function procedures were intended to emulate the built-in functions and sub procedures were intended to carry out one or more actions without returning a value, you can use a function procedure to carry out any programming task in Access Basic. If the context does not demand computing and using a return value, you do not have to define one. This fact is important because in some contexts, you *must* use a function procedure even if a sub procedure would make more sense intuitively. For example, you can call a function procedure but not a sub procedure from a form or report event or from a macro. The most common way that you will call a sub procedure is from another procedure (of either type). For example, you might write a sub procedure to export data or initiate a DDE link with another Windows application, and then call this procedure from several different function procedures attached to command buttons or events in forms.

Using Variables in Procedures

When you write procedures to carry out complex calculations that cannot be accomplished in one step, you will need to store intermediate results (the values computed by the individual steps) in a form that makes them available for later use, and you can do this by defining *variables*. A variable, as the name suggests, is a named repository for a single item of data, whose value can vary during its lifetime. Every variable has a name, and any reference to the name of a variable represents its value. All programming languages use variables, so if you have programmed in any other language, this concept should be familiar to you. You can think of variables as analogous to fields in an Access table, but remember that variables are not stored anywhere in a database—they are retained in memory for a limited time (the duration depends on where you define them, as explained shortly) and they do not persist from one Access work session to the next.

NOTE. *If you have written programs in any Xbase dialect, note that all of these languages use the term* memory variable *for temporary variables not stored in a database; in Xbase, the more generic term* variable *is used to refer either to a memory variable or a field in contexts where the two may be used interchangeably.*

Variable names must adhere to the same rules as procedure names: They can be up to 40 characters long, must begin with a letter, and can contain only letters, digits, and underscores. Because variable names cannot contain spaces, you do not have to enclose them in square brackets in expressions that refer to their values.

As illustrated by the FollowUpDate function procedure, Access allows you define variables *implicitly*, using an assignment statement that creates the variable and assigns it a value in one step. For example, the following commands create two variables, CallBackDate and DueDate, which both derive their values from the current date:

```
CallBackDate = Date + 14
DueDate = DateAdd("m", 1, Date)
```

By default, variables that you create within a procedure are available only while that procedure is running. When a procedure terminates, Access erases from memory the values of all the variables created within the procedure. In most cases, this behavior is convenient, because it allows you to use the same variable names in different procedures without worrying about naming conflicts. To make the value of a variable available to more than one procedure, you must *declare* it—that is, notify Access of its existence—in the declarations section of a module, using either the Dim or Global statement. If you use Dim, the variable will be available to any procedure in the same module (Dim is short for *dimension*, a term retained from other programming languages in which defining a variable required you to specify its size, or dimensions). If you use the Global statement, the variable will be available to any procedure in *any* module in the application. You can use a separate statement for each variable you declare, or you can list several variables in one Dim or Global statement, as in the following example:

```
Dim FullName, CityStateZip, Balance
Global ErrorMessage, CurrentRecord
```

Stacking up variable declarations this way makes a module more concise, and combining related or similar variables into one declaration underscores the connection between them. On the other hand, using a separate declaration for each variable makes each one stand out, and it facilitates adding comments that document the purposes of the variables, as in the following version of the previous example:

```
Dim FullName          'Full name to print on letters
Dim CityStateZip      'City/state/zip for mailing label
Dim Balance           'Credits - debits
Global ErrorMessage   'Error message to show in alert box
Global CurrentRecord  'Unique ID for record being processed
```

Remember that declaring a variable does not give the variable a value—it simply allocates space in memory for the variable and specifies the name that you will use to refer to the variable.

You can also use the Dim statement to declare variables within a procedure, and many programmers feel that it is good practice to declare all variables explicitly, to provide internal documentation of their existence and help other programmers understand the procedure by clarifying which names refer to variables and which refer to fields in a table. Predefining variables will also speed up performance somewhat, but in small procedures, the difference may not be noticeable.

Another reason to declare variables explicitly is to specify the data type. Like fields, variables have data types, but in most cases you do not have to assign the data type explicitly. If you create a variable implicitly, using an assignment statement that describes a Text, Date/Time, or numeric value, Access gives the variable a data type known as *variant*. This data type can accommodate any numeric, Date/Time, or Text value, and when you use variants in expressions, Access automatically performs any necessary conversions for you. As you have already seen, Access treats fields of these data types as variants in most contexts, and this interpretation gives you the flexibility to carry out operations such as concatenating a text string with a Date/Time field without explicitly converting the Date/Time field to a text string.

To explicitly specify a data type in a variable declaration, you add a clause that begins with the word "As" and includes the keyword that identifies the desired data type. The available choices are Integer, Long, Single, Double, Currency, String, and Variant; these keywords should be familiar to you from the options in the Data Type and Field Size combo boxes in Table Design view (String is equivalent to Text). For example, you could modify the variable declarations in the previous example as follows to define the data types:

```
Dim FullName As String, CityStateZip As String, Balance As
    Currency
Global ErrorMessage As String, CurrentRecord As Long
```

or

```
Dim FullName As String        'Full name to print on letters
Dim CityStateZip As String    'City/state/zip for label
Dim Balance As Currency       'Credits - debits
Global ErrorMessage As String 'Message for alert box
Global CurrentRecord As Long  'Unique ID for current record
```

You cannot explicitly create Date/Time, Yes/No, Memo, or OLE Object variables, but you can use variants for Date/Time values and simulate Yes/No values by using numeric variables. In most simple programs, you will find the variant data type to be adequate—and very convenient.

Passing Input to Procedures

Both sub procedures and function procedures can accept input, also referred to as *arguments*, although the mechanism for passing the inputs is slightly different for the two types of procedures. In both cases, you identify the arguments in the procedure itself by placing the names you will use to refer to them within the parentheses that follow the procedure name. For example, the following function procedure combines a telephone number and area code into the standard display format used throughout the ACE system:

```
Function Phone (AreaCode, PhoneNumber)
    Phone = "(" & AreaCode & ") " & Phonenumber
End Function
```

When you call a function procedure, you enclose the required inputs in parentheses, exactly as in the procedure itself. For example, you could use the expression Phone([Area Code], [Telephone]) in a query or to define the Control Source property for a control on a form or report based on the ACE Names table. To call a sub procedure, you write the name of the procedure, followed by a list of the required inputs. As in a function call, the inputs must be separated by commas, but they are not enclosed in parentheses. For example, if you rewrote the Phone function procedure as a sub procedure, you could call it with the command Phone [Area Code], [Telephone].

Be sure you understand the relationship between the names enclosed in parentheses in the expression that calls a function procedure and the corresponding names in the Function statement that begins the function procedure. In the function procedure, these names serve as placeholders for the specific values that you pass to the procedure, which can be obtained by evaluating any expressions. These names behave like variables, and you can use them exactly as you would variables that you created with assignment statements. The correspondence between the inputs passed in the function reference and the named inputs in the function procedure itself is established solely by their order. Thus, in the Phone function procedure, the name AreaCode represents the first input and the name PhoneNumber represents the second. You can call the function with two field names, as in the previous example, with a field name and a constant, or with two constants (although it might not make sense to do so). For example, if you were printing a report based on a query that extracts people in San Francisco from a table that does not have an area code field, you could use the following expression to print the telephone number with the 415 area code that serves all of San Francisco: Phone("415", [Telephone]).

It is up to you to make sure that the inputs you pass to a procedure make sense in the current context. For example, if you call the Phone function with two Date/Time values as inputs, Access will display something like this: (1/1/92) 3/15/93. Because you can concatenate text strings and Data/Time values, this usage will not generate an error, but in other cases, passing inappropriate data will cause problems—for example, if you try to use one of the inputs in a way not permitted for data of that type.

Using Control Structures

To tap the full power of the Access programming language, you must learn to use the Access Basic commands and programming *structures* that allow you to deviate from the default top-to-bottom processing sequence—that is, to make decisions, skip steps, or repeat commands. You already know from your experience with macros how important it is to be able to test a condition and decide whether to carry out one or more actions based on the outcome. In macros, the fact that you cannot specify two alternative courses of action— one to carry out when the condition is True and another to carry out when the condition is False—is a serious, although not insurmountable limitation. In an Access Basic procedure, you can easily specify two alternative courses of action based on a condition, or test for two or more different values for any expression (not necessarily a condition that evaluates to True or False) and carry out a different sequence of steps in each case.

Access also provides programming structures, sometimes referred to as *loops*, for repeating commands either a specified number of times or until a given condition becomes True or False. Finally, there are commands for moving to a different point in the current procedure—either by jumping directly to a specific line or by exiting prematurely from a repeating loop. By using these commands, you can step through the records in a table or dynaset one by one and carry out a variety of complex operations that would be difficult or impossible without programming.

Making Decisions

You already know two ways to test a condition and carry out different actions based on the outcome. In a query, form, or report, you can use the IIf function to display or print one of two alternative values, depending on whether the condition is True or False. If you enter an expression in the Condition column in a macro, Access executes the actions governed by this condition only if it evaluates to True. In an Access Basic procedure, you can use two programming structures, the If…Then structure and the Select Case structure, to make these and much more complex decisions.

There are several different forms of the If…Then structure. To test a single condition and execute one command if the condition evaluates to True, you can write the entire structure on one line, as follows:

```
If condition Then command
```

Even if you have never seen this syntax before, it should seem reasonably intuitive, since it directly parallels the way you would state the same request in ordinary English. Like a conditional step in a macro, this form of the If…Then structure does nothing when the *condition* is False. As a simple example, the following compares the values of two variables called Debits and Credits, and assigns a text string to a variable called Message if Debits is greater:

```
If Debits > Credits Then Message = "Please pay your
outstanding balance"
```

You can also write a more generic variation of the If…Then structure, in which the condition occupies its own line and an End If statement indicates the end of the structure. You *must* use this version if you want to execute more than one command when the condition in the If statement is True. The general form is as follows:

```
If condition Then
    commands
End If
```

The following is exactly equivalent to the previous example:

```
If Debits > Credits Then
    Message = "Please pay your outstanding balance"
End If
```

In these simple versions of the If...Then structure, the commands between the If and End If commands are carried out only when the condition in the If statement is True; when it is False, your code does nothing. To specify another command or group of commands that should be executed when the condition is False, you can add an Else statement. The general form is as follows:

```
If condition Then
    commands
Else
    commands
End If
```

When the condition in the If statement is True, Access executes the commands between the If and Else statements; when the condition is False, it executes the commands between the Else and End If statements. For example, you could expand the previous example to assign two different values to the Message variable, depending on whether the value of the Debits variable is greater than the value of the Credits variable:

```
If Debits > Credits
    Message = "Please pay your outstanding balance"
Else
    Message = "No payment due"
End If
```

As another simple but practical example, consider the following complete function procedure, which is a more sophisticated version of the Phone function procedure presented earlier in this chapter:

```
Function Phone (AreaCode, PhoneNumber)
    If IsNull(AreaCode) Then
        Phone = PhoneNumber
    Else
        Phone = "(" & AreaCode & ") " & PhoneNumber
    End If
End Function
```

Finally, you can add one or more ElseIf statements to test additional conditions, as follows:

```
If condition Then
    commands
ElseIf condition Then
    commands
ElseIf condition Then
    commands
    .
    .
    .
Else
    commands
End If
```

For example, the following If…Then structure defines three different values for the Message variable, depending on the relationship between the Debits and Credits variables:

```
If Debits > Credits Then
    Message = "Please pay your outstanding balance"
ElseIf Debits < Credits Then
    Message = "You have a credit balance"
Else
    Message = "No payment due"
End If
```

This If…Then structure has only one ElseIf statement, but you can use as many as you wish to test additional conditions. If you find these structures hard to decipher, try reading the word "else" as "otherwise" (one of its colloquial synonyms). You might read the previous example as follows: "If the debits are greater than the credits, use the message 'Please pay your outstanding balance.' Otherwise, if the debits are less than the credits, use the message 'You have a credit balance.' Otherwise, use the message 'No payment due.'" As you can see from these examples, indenting the statements in the If…Then structure helps to clarify the logic of the structure. The standard convention is to place all the control statements—If, ElseIf, Else, and End If—at the same level of indentation (in this case, one tab stop in from the left margin) and indent the groups of commands between these statements one additional tab stop.

If you want to test for several different values of the same expression, you can use the more compact Select Case structure instead. The general form is as follows:

```
Select Case expression
    Case expression list
```

```
        commands
    Case expression list
        commands
        .
        .
        .
    Case Else
        commands
End Select
```

The Select Case structure can contain as many Case statements as necessary
to process all the possible values for the *expression*. Access assumes that only
one of the cases will be True, and it stops processing immediately after executing the commands that follow the first true Case statement. The Case Else section, which is optional, handles all values not explicitly covered by one of the
preceding Case statements, and it is executed only if none of the other cases
is True. As a simple example, the following function procedure returns a short
phrase based on the contents of the Address Type field in the Names table,
which is passed as an argument (you could use this function procedure to provide the value for a text box on a report or form):

```
Function AddressType (AddrType)
    Select Case AddrType
        Case "H"
            AddressType = "Home address"
        Case "W"
            AddressType = "Work address"
        Case "U"
            AddressType = "Unknown address type"
    End Select
End Function
```

If you have used other programming languages, you may have seen a
similar control structure with a different name (for example, Switch or, in
Xbase, Do Case) and slightly different syntax. If you have used these structures before, note that unlike many other languages, Access does not limit
you to testing for different numeric values or to testing only one value in
each Case statement. The *expression lists* in the Case statements can consist
of one or more individual values, ranges, or expressions. However, you cannot use a Select Case structure to test independent conditions: In Access,
this structure always processes different values of a single expression. In simple Select Case structures, each Case statement might contain one explicit
value or a list of values, but Access gives you considerably more latitude in

listing the permissible values. You can use any mixture of the following, all separated by commas:

■ Single values

■ Ranges, in the form *value* To *value*

■ Ranges, expressed using comparison operators, in the form *value* Is *operator value*

The following function, which tests the contents of the GL Account field in the Transaction table and returns a more precise description of the transaction type than the one stored in the Transaction Types table, illustrates all of these possibilities:

```
Function GLAccount (AccountNumber)
   Select Case AccountNumber
    Case 12010
       GLAccount = "Pledge"
    Case 31030
       GLAccount = "Pledge payment"
    Case 31040, 31045
       GLAccount = "Donation"
    Case 31050 To 31059
       GLAccount = "T-shirt purchase"
    Case 31060 To 31069
       GLAccount = "Sweatshirt purchase"
    Case Is >= 31070
       GLAccount = "Other purchase"
   End Select
End Function
```

In this Select Case structure, the first two cases test single values of the AccountNumber variable, the third processes two specific values (like a condition that includes the Or operator), the third and fourth process ranges of values, and the last processes values that satisfy a specific condition. Note that this function works even though the account numbers are expressed as numbers, and the GL Account field in the Transactions table is a Text field. Unless you explicitly declare other data types, Access treats all variables and inputs passed to procedures as variants, which you can legitimately compare to a Text, Date/Time, or numeric value.

The previous examples do not include Case Else statements, but you could rewrite them both to use a Case Else statement instead of the last Case statement. However, it is usually preferable to use Case statements for any values of the expression that you know about in advance and reserve the

Case Else statement for multiple values that you do not need to differentiate or that you cannot predict. For example, if you use a Select Case structure to carry out calculations based on a value entered using a combo box for which you set the Limit to List property to No, you could use Case statements to process the selections in the list, and a Case Else statement to handle all other values entered by typing them rather than selecting them from the list. If you adhere to this convention, it should be clear whenever you see a Select Case structure whether it is open-ended or whether it handles only a finite number of possible values.

You can always write an If…Then structure that is equivalent to a Select Case structure. For example, the AddressType function presented earlier in this section could also be written as follows:

```
Function AddressType (AddrType)
   If AddrType = "H" Then
      AddressType = "Home address"
   ElseIf AddrType = "W" Then
      AddressType = "Work address"
   ElseIf AddrType = "U" Then
      AddressType = "Unknown address type"
   End If
End Function
```

The converse, however, is not true—because an If…Then structure can test any number of different conditions, you cannot always substitute an equivalent Select Case structure, which is limited to handling different values of the same expression. When you are indeed testing only one expression, using a Select Case structure instead of an If…Then structure makes it abundantly clear to anyone who reads your modules that you are only testing one expression.

Repeating Steps

Access provides two basic control structures that enable you to repeat one or more commands in a procedure. In simple procedures such as the ones you might write in your own applications, these structures are useful primarily for processing records in tables or query dynasets. The For…Next structure enables you to repeat a series of commands a specified number of times. The general form is as follows:

```
For counter = starting value To ending value Step increment
   commands
Next
```

When it executes the For statement, Access automatically creates a variable with the name that you specify as the *counter* and assigns to this variable the value that you specify as the *starting value.* It executes the statements in the loop, increments the counter by adding the value specified as the *increment,* and repeats the process until the counter variable is greater than the *ending value.* You might think of the Next statement, which ends the loop, as meaning "go to the next value of the counter variable." In some other programming languages that support the For…Next structure, you can (or must) include the name of the counter variable in the Next statement, and Access permits but does not require you to do so (this usage is illustrated in the next example). When you *nest* programming structures (place one structure within another), including the counter variable name in the Next structure will help you match up the For and Next statements.

The starting value, ending value, and increment must all be numbers or numeric expressions, and the counter must be a legitimate variable name. If you omit the Step clause, Access assumes that you want to use an increment of 1. For example, the following very simple For structure counts from 1 to 10 and displays the numbers as it counts in the Immediate window (this window, which is useful primarily for testing and debugging procedures, is explained in the next section):

```
For LoopCounter = 1 To 10
    Debug.Print "Counter: " & LoopCounter
Next LoopCounter
```

If you wish, you can use the counter variable in your procedure, either inside the For…Next loop or after the Next statement. When the loop terminates, the loop counter variable has the value assigned to it on the last pass through the loop; this value is always greater than or equal to the ending value specified in the For statement. For example, after running the loop in the previous example, the LoopCounter variable has the value 11 (the first value that does not satisfy the condition in the For statement). Access also allows you to change the value of the counter variable within the loop, but it can be dangerous to do so—at the end of each pass through the loop, Access increments *the current value of the counter variable,* so changing this value inside the loop will affect the number of times Access executes the statements in the loop. You might even unintentionally create an *endless loop*—a loop that runs forever because the counter variable never reaches the ending value.

You can use a negative increment to count backwards, as in the following example, which counts backwards from 10 in steps of 2:

```
For LoopCounter = 10 To 1 Step -2
    Debug.Print "Counter: " & LoopCounter
Next
```

It is entirely up to you to specify an appropriate combination of values for the counter, starting value, ending value, and step increment. If you use a starting value greater than the ending value with a positive step increment or a starting value less than the ending value with a negative step increment, the statements in the loop are not executed even once. However, Access does not consider this situation to be an error (it is possible, albeit unlikely in the simple procedures you will write at first, that you assigned these values intentionally), so it does not display an error message to warn you.

The For structure is most useful when you know in advance exactly how many times you need to repeat a series of commands. For example, you could use a For structure to read through a query dynaset based on the Names table in which donor records are arranged in descending order by total credits, and display or print the top ten donors. If you need to repeat a series of steps an indefinite number of times, with the number of repetitions governed by any arbitrary condition, you can use a Do…Loop structure instead. There are four variations of this control structure, which differ primarily in when Access interprets the condition and how it responds to the outcome. The following version is designed to execute a group of commands *as long as* the specified condition is True (that is, until it is no longer True):

```
Do While condition
     commands
Loop
```

Access evaluates the *condition* in the Do While statement at the beginning of each pass through this type of Do…Loop structure and executes the commands inside the loop only if the condition is still True. When the condition becomes False, Access skips all the statements in the loop and resumes execution with the first command after the Loop statement. Thus, if the condition is not true when Access executes the Do While command for the first time, the statements in the loop are not carried out even once. If you want to make sure that the commands in the structure are executed at least once, regardless of the value of the condition, you can use the following variation:

```
Do
     commands
Loop While condition
```

In this version of the Do…Loop structure, the *condition* is evaluated at the end of each pass through the loop, and Access returns to the top of the loop to make another pass only if the condition is still True. There are two other alternatives, which enable you to execute one or more commands *until* a given condition is True—that is, as long as the condition is False. When it executes the following version, Access tests the *condition* at the beginning of each pass through the loop and stops immediately when the condition becomes True:

```
Do Until condition
    commands
Loop
```

If the condition is True initially, the commands in the loop are not executed even once. The following version executes the statements within the loop at least once and stops when the condition becomes True:

```
Do
    commands
Loop Until condition
```

If you are new to programming, it may not be apparent why so many versions of this structure are necessary, and indeed they are not—many languages offer only one or two of these four variations. In your own procedures, you can feel free to use whichever loop structure seems intuitively best suited to the situation at hand. You may find that you gravitate naturally toward one or two of the four variations at first, and that your preferences will evolve and solidify as you gain experience.

Be especially careful at first to avoid some very common pitfalls. First, make sure you understand whether you want to test the condition at the beginning or the end of the loop, and whether the condition is initially satisfied. Also make sure that you do not inadvertently create an "endless loop"—a Do While loop will run forever unless the condition that controls it eventually becomes False, and a Do Until loop will run forever unless the condition eventually becomes True. In all of these variations, it is essential that the loop contain commands that can reverse the status of the condition and allow the loop to terminate. If you do inadvertently produce an endless loop, the computer will appear to "hang up," but you can interrupt execution by pressing Ctrl+Break.

When Access processes a For…Next, Do While…Loop, or Do Until… Loop structure, it evaluates the controlling condition only once on each pass through the loop (either at the very top or bottom of the loop). If the value of the condition changes midway through the loop, Access nevertheless executes the remaining statements in the loop. If you want to exit prematurely from a loop—based on the controlling condition or any other condition—you can use an Exit For (in For…Next structures) or Exit Do (in Do While and Do Until structures) command. These statements are nearly always executed conditionally, from within an If…Then structure that tests a condition (which is usually, but not necessarily, different from the one that governs the loop), so that the loop terminates only if the condition is fulfilled. When Access exits from the loop, execution resumes with the first command that follows the loop structure.

You can use the similar Exit Function and Exit Sub commands to exit prematurely from a function or sub procedure. Like Exit For and Exit Sub, these commands are nearly always executed from within an If…Then structure. If you use the Exit Function command to exit from a function procedure, make sure that you have already assigned a value to the variable that supplies the return value for the function to avoid generating an error.

Nesting Control Structures

As suggested several times in the previous two sections, Access allows you to *nest* any of the programming structures described in the preceding sections— that is, place one structure inside another of the same or a different type. The only stipulation is that each structure must be completely enclosed within another structure. For example, you can include an If…Then or Select Case structure inside a Do While loop that processes records in a table. When you nest structures, the usual convention is to indent each nested structure one tab stop further than the enclosing structure. The following function procedure, which constructs the salutation for a personalized solicitation letter, illustrates these concepts:

```
Function Salutation (Salut, NameType, Amount)
    If IsNull(Salut) Then
        Select Case NameType
            Case "M"
                Salutation = "Member"
            Case "D"
                If Amount >= 1000 Then
                    Salutation = "Valued Donor"
                Else
                    Salutation = "Donor"
                Endif
            Case "BD"
                Salutation = "Board Member"
            Case Else
                Salutation = "Friend"
        End Select
    Else
        Salutation = Salut
    End If
End Function
```

The Salutation function accepts three inputs, which represent a salutation, a name type, and a dollar amount. In the ACE system, you might call this function with the Salutation, Name Type, and Total Credits fields in the

Names table as inputs. The function contains three nested decision-making structures. An If…Then structure tests the salutation passed to the function and uses it if it is not null. If it is, a Select Case structure tests the value of the NameType argument and assigns an appropriate salutation. Within the case that handles donors, another If…Then structure tests the Amount field and assigns two different salutations, depending on its magnitude.

The following version of the Salutation function illustrates one way you can use Exit Function to exit prematurely from a function procedure:

```
Function Salutation (Salut, NameType, Amount)
    If Not IsNull(Salut) Then
        Salutation = Salut
        Exit Function
    End If
    Select Case NameType
        Case "M"
            Salutation = "Member"
        Case "D"
            If Amount >= 1000 Then
                Salutation = "Valued Donor"
            Else
                Salutation = "Donor"
            Endif
        Case "BD"
            Salutation = "Board Member"
        Case Else
            Salutation = "Friend"
    End Select
End Function
```

In this case, there is no particular advantage to structuring the function this way. The exit commands are more commonly used to exit from a very long procedure or break out of a Do…While or Do…Until loop if you can determine early on that there is no need to complete the procedure or the loop.

Testing and Debugging Procedures

As you will quickly discover if you do not already suspect it, most of the procedures you write will not run as you intended on the first try. Despite the on-line syntax checker and the compiler, Access cannot possibly detect all of the errors you might make until you actually run a procedure. For example, a line that is syntactically correct might generate an error if a required variable, form, or control is not available when you run the procedure. When an error occurs, Access pauses execution and displays the procedure that caused the problem, with the offending line highlighted. Figure 20.11 illustrates the error message generated by misspelling a control name in a procedure that changes ID codes in all the related records in the main ACE tables (this procedure is described later in this chapter).

Figure 20.11
Responding to an error during procedure execution

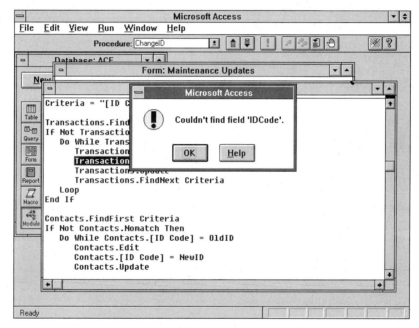

If you realize immediately what the problem is, you can simply stop the suspended procedure and edit the code to fix it. You can then resume execution from the point of interruption by clicking on the Run button in the tool bar, by choosing the Continue option from the Run menu, or by pressing the equivalent hotkey (F5). If you want to resume execution in single-step mode, you can click on the single-step button in the tool bar instead of the Run button, choose Single Step from the Run menu, or press the equivalent hotkey (F8). If you prefer to start the procedure again from the beginning, you must reinitialize the environment by choosing the Reinitialize option on the Run menu or by clicking on the equivalent button in the tool bar.

One very useful tool for testing, troubleshooting, and debugging procedures is the Immediate window, which, as the name suggests, enables you to experiment with commands or expressions and immediately see the results. To open the Immediate window, you choose the Immediate Window option from the View menu; you can close the window by selecting the same option again or by using any of the standard methods for closing a window. You can test many of the commands that you will use in Access Basic procedures by typing them in the Immediate window, and you can display the value of any expression, including a reference to a control on an open form, by using the Print command, which you can also abbreviate as ? (you might think of this shorthand as meaning "what is" or "show me"). This simple command is one of the most powerful debugging tools available, as it allows you to inspect the value of any expression to determine whether it matches the value you intended (and the one required for correct performance of a procedure).

At times, you may want to temporarily add commands to a procedure to display information in the Immediate window as the procedure runs, so that you can monitor its progress or verify its performance by displaying variable values, field values, or intermediate results of calculations. You can only use the simple Print command in the Immediate window itself. In a program, you must identify the destination of the output by including the name of the object Access uses for the Immediate window, which is not "Immediate" as you might suspect, but "Debug." For example, you could use the following command to display the value of the ID Code field:

```
Debug.Print [ID Code]
```

Despite the similarity of the notation, the expression Debug.Print does not refer to a property of the Debug object, but rather to the Print *method*. Methods are introduced later in this chapter, but you can use this technique to test your procedures without fully understanding how methods work.

Access also allows you to set *breakpoints* in a procedure—that is, to request a pause in execution at specific lines. To set a breakpoint or clear a previously established breakpoint, make sure that the insertion point is anywhere in the desired line, and then click on the Breakpoint command button in the tool bar, choose Toggle Breakpoint from the Run menu, or press F9. You can set as many breakpoints as ypu wish, and Access displays all breakpoint lines in bold type.

If you are at a loss to figure out why a procedure generates an error message or fails to work as expected, you can set a breakpoint at the very beginning, or, in a long procedure, right before the section you suspect is at fault. When Access encounters a breakpoint during procedure execution, it pauses and displays the Module window with the current line highlighted. You can then open the Immediate window and use Print commands to test the values of any expressions that might give you a clue as to what went wrong or resume execution in single-step mode to trace execution line by line. To initiate single-step mode, you can click on the Single Step command button in the tool bar, select Single Step from the Run menu, or press the equivalent hotkey (F8).

To resume continuous execution at any point, you can click on the Run button in the tool bar, select the Continue option from the Run menu, or press F5. One strategy for zeroing in on several specific sections of a long procedure is to set several breakpoints and after stepping through the sections of interest, run the procedure continuously up to the next breakpoint. When you are finished testing, you can clear the breakpoints individually, or all at once by choosing Clear All Breakpoints from the Run menu.

Writing a Validation Procedure

To practice the programming techniques described in the preceding sections, try writing a function procedure to validate the Telephone field in the Names table according to the following rules:

- You can leave the Telephone field blank (null).

- The telephone number must be eight characters long.

- The telephone number must consist of only digits, except for the fourth character, which must be a dash.

Although you could accomplish this validation with the same technique used in the Validate Zip Code macro described in Chapter 18, the ValidatePhone function uses a slightly different method in order to reinforce your understanding of the Access Basic programming structures. The complete function is shown in Listing 20.1.

Listing 20.1 **The ValidatePhone function procedure**

```
Function ValidatePhone (Phone)
   Message = ""

   ' Exit immediately if Phone is blank
   If IsNull(Phone) Then
      Exit Function
   End If

   ' Test for Phone too short
   If Len(Phone) < 8 Then
      Message = "Phone number must be 8 characters long, "
   End If

   ' Verify that 4th character is a dash
   If Mid(Phone, 4, 1) <> "-" Then
```

Listing 20.1   **The ValidatePhone function procedure (Continued)**

```
        Message = "Fourth character must be a dash, "
    End If

    ' Verify that every other character is a digit
    For Character = 1 To 8
        ' If there are no more characters left, exit For loop
        If Character > Len(Phone) Then
            Exit For
        End If
        ' Skip the fourth character (already tested)
        If Character <> 4 Then
            ' Verify that the character is a digit, and
            ' exit from For loop if it is not
            If Not IsNumeric(Mid(Phone, Character, 1)) Then
                Message = Message & "Phone number must be
                    all digits, "
                Exit For
            End If
        End If
    Next

    ' If Message contains an error message,
    ' strip off last comma, display a message box,
    ' and cancel Update event
    If Len(Message) > Ø Then
        Message = Left(Message, Len(Message) - 2)
        MsgBox Message, 48, "Telephone Number Validation"
        DoCmd CancelEvent
    End If

End Function
```

The ValidatePhone function accepts the telephone number through an argument called Phone. The overall strategy is to construct an error message that describes all the problems found in the telephone number by adding various phrases to a Text variable called Message (this technique is basically the same as the method introduced in Chapter 19 for establishing selection criteria for a form or report). If the telephone number passes all the tests, this variable will be blank; if it is not, the procedure strips off the trailing comma and space, displays the error message in a message box, and cancels the event that triggered the function—the attempt to update the Telephone field and move on to the next control on the form. (The MsgBox command, which displays the alert box, is described in more detail in the next section.) Note that because the error message is constructed and displayed within the function, you must call it from the BeforeUpdate event of the control that collects the Telephone field rather than from the Validation Rule property. If you called the function from the Validation Rule property and returned the value False to indicate that the Telephone field did not pass the validation test, Access would display the standard error alert box after the function displayed the custom message.

The first If...Then structure in the function uses the IsNull function to determine whether Phone is blank; if it is, an Exit Function command exits immediately, thereby accepting the phone number as valid. Next, the function tests the length, examines the fourth character, and if the telephone number fails either test, adds an appropriate phrase to the Message variable. After these two overall tests, a For...Next loop steps through each character in turn and checks each one except the fourth to verify that it is a digit. There are two possible premature exits from this loop—the first If...Then structure exits after testing the last character actually present in the telephone number, which might not be eight characters long. More importantly, the second If... Then structure ensures that the For...Next loop terminates after finding the first invalid character in the phone number, which prevents Access from adding the phrase "Phone number must be all digits" to the error message variable more than once.

First write the function:

1. Make sure that the Database window displays the list of modules, and open the ACE Procedures module in Design View.

2. Experiment with the methods described earlier for paging through the procedures in this module (you might try the Next Procedure and Previous procedure command buttons in the tool bar and the Ctrl+Up Arrow and Ctrl+Down Arrow keyboard commands).

3. Select the New Procedure option from the Edit menu. Leave the Function radio button selected in the New Procedure dialog box, type **ValidatePhone** in the Name text box, and close the dialog box.

4. Type the text of the function procedure, precisely as it appears in Listing 20.1 (if you wish you can shorten or omit the comments).

5. Select the Compile All option from the Run menu to verify that you did not make any typographical errors, and correct any errors that the compiler finds.

Next, modify the Names Five-Page Form with Buttons form to call the ValidatePhone function:

1. Leaving the Module window open, return to the Database window and open the Names Five-Page Form with Buttons in Form Design view. Make sure that the property sheet is visible.

2. Click on the Telephone control to select it, and enter the expression that calls the ValidatePhone function in the Before Update property: **=ValidatePhone([Telephone])**.

3. Switch to Form View, find a record in which the telephone number is blank, and try entering various invalid telephone numbers.

4. Enter the invalid phone number **861–50P**, and press Enter. When Access displays the error message, press Ctrl+Break to cancel the procedure and return to the Module window. You should see the DoCmd statement that invokes the CancelEvent action outlined to indicate that it is the current line.

5. Choose the Immediate Window option from the View menu, and use ? commands in the Immediate window to check the current values of the Phone and Message variables.

6. Click anywhere in the first If statement (If IsNull(Phone) Then), and then click on the Breakpoint command button in the tool bar to set a breakpoint at this line.

7. Select Continue from the Run menu to resume execution, and return to the Form view window.

8. Press Enter to resubmit the same invalid telephone number. Access immediately returns you to the Module window with the breakpoint line highlighted.

9. Click on the Step command button to step through the function procedure one line at a time and trace the decision-making process. Note that if the condition in an If statement is not fulfilled, Access skips over the remaining statements in the If...Then structure. At any point, feel free to move into the Immediate Window and display the values of any variables (you might want to check the value of the For...Next loop counter variable, Character, on one or two passes through the loop).

10. Note that the error message box pops up on top of the Module window, and that this window remains on top of the Form view window when the function terminates.

11. Return to the Form view window, correct the telephone number to **861–5050**, and press Enter. Note that Access returns to the Module window.

12. Choose the Clear All Breakpoints option from the Run menu, and then choose Continue to resume execution.

13. Return to the Form view window, and note that Access has accepted the current contents of the Telephone field and moved the focus to the next field on the form.

14. Close the form and save it.

15. Close the module and save it.

Operating on Database Objects

You now know how to define variables to store temporary values in memory so that you can manipulate them in procedures. To operate on database objects, such as tables and query dynasets, you must also define variables that refer to these objects. These *object variables*, like the simple variables introduced earlier in this chapter, refer to single entities that have specific values, but the entities they represent are far more complex—databases, tables, and dynasets rather than numbers, text strings, or dates. As you know, these objects have properties, and you can access these properties in your procedures.

When you operate on database objects, you must often use *methods* rather than *commands*. The difference may not be intuitively obvious if you have no prior experience with object-oriented programming, and it may help to think of a method as being a command that operates only on specific types of objects. In this respect, methods are similar to properties—they are always associated with an object—but, like commands, they carry out actions rather than describe characteristics. If a method requires one or more inputs, you enter these inputs within parentheses, as you do when you pass arguments to a function. The methods that Access recognizes vary considerably for different types of objects. For example, you can use the FindFirst method to search for a record in a dynaset object, and you can use the AddNew method to add a row to a table or dynaset object. To invoke a method, you write the name of the object, followed by a period (.), followed by the method. For example, to move to the next record in a table object called ACENames (which might refer either to the Names table or to a query dynaset), you would write ACENames.MoveNext.

You cannot create an object variable on the fly—you must declare it with a Dim or Global statement, in which you identify the object type exactly as you define the data type in a simple variable declaration. The object types supported by Access are Database, Table, Dynaset (a table or select query dynaset), Snapshot (a static, non-updateable copy of a table or select query dynaset), Form, Report, Control (a control on a form or report), and QueryDef (a query definition, not the dynaset that results from executing the query). For example, to declare object variables to represent the ACE database, the Names table, and the Committees table, you could use the following commands:

```
Dim ACEdb as Database
Dim ACEnames as Table, ACEcomm as Table
```

These declarations, like the other variable declarations described earlier in this chapter, simply allocate storage space for the object variables and identify the object types. To associate these variables with specific objects, you must use Set commands, which are equivalent to assignment statements. The easiest way to create a database variable that refers to the current database (the .MDB file that is currently open in the Database window) is to use the CurrentDB function, as in the following:

```
Set ACEdb = CurrentDB()
```

Note that you must always create a database variable before you can manipulate any database object in an Access Basic procedure, even if you are working only with objects in the currently open .MDB file. In contrast to the interactive environment, Access Basic allows you to open and work with more than one database at a time, and it does not assume that any database is currently open, or if one is, that this is the database you want to work with in a given context.

To create a table, dynaset, or snapshot variable, you must first define a database object variable that refers to the source table, and then use the OpenTable, CreateDynaset, or CreateSnapshot methods associated with this database object. The simplest of these is the OpenTable method, which takes one input, the name of the table. For example, to assign the ACE Names table to the table variable ACEnames, you could use the following command (assuming that you have already assigned a value to the database variable ACEdb):

```
Set ACEnames = ACEdb.OpenTable("Names")
```

Although you can work directly with tables, there is little reason to do so. Table and dynaset objects have somewhat different methods, but you can use a dynaset or snapshot object (depending on whether you have to update records) to refer either to a table or query dynaset; by using a dynaset or snapshot, you can avoid having to change your procedures if you later decide to substitute a query dynaset for the table used in the original version. To create a dynaset or snapshot object variable, you must describe the source of the rows it contains, and you can do this in several different ways. To define an object variable that refers to an existing table, you can simply enter its name as input to the CreateDynaset or CreateSnapshot method, as in the following:

```
Set CurrentNames = ACEdb.CreateSnapshot("Names")
```

You can also define a dynaset or snapshot that exactly matches the dynaset of a select query by naming the query. For example, you could access the output of the query that displays committee membership data, together with the member and committee names as follows:

```
Set CommitteeMemberships = ACEdb.CreateDynaset("Committees
with Names")
```

Finally, you can use an SQL Select statement to describe the contents of a dynaset or snapshot on the fly without first defining and saving a query. If you do not need to access the same data outside of your Access Basic procedure (and if you feel comfortable with SQL syntax), this method is very efficient and enables you to avoid creating a great many extra queries. For example, the following creates a dynaset that contains the names, telephone numbers, and debit and credit totals for donors:

```
Set Donors = ACEdb.CreateDysnaset("Select [Name],
[Area Code], [Telephone], [Total Debits], [Total Credits]
FROM Names WHERE Names![Name Type] = 'D'")
```

If you want to use an existing parameter query and supply the values for the parameters without running the query, you cannot simply create a dynaset based on the query. Instead, you must open the query definition using a QueryDef object, assign values to the parameters, and then create the dynaset. For example, to create a QueryDef object called SelQuery (intended as a generic name for a select query) and a corresponding object variable based on the Names and Donations by Date query, you could use the following commands:

```
Dim SelQuery As QueryDef
Set SelQuery = ACEdb.OpenQueryDef("Names and Donations
by Date")
```

To refer to the query parameters, you use the same notation that you would use to describe a control in a form or report—you write the name of the query, followed by an exclamation point (!), followed by the parameter prompt. You can designate a value for a parameter with a simple assignment statement, as in the following example, which assigns constant values to the two date parameters:

```
SelQuery![Enter earliest transaction date:] = #1/1/92#
SelQuery![Enter latest transaction date:] = #1/31/92#
```

Having defined the QueryDef object and assigned values to the parameters, you can then define the dynaset by using the CreateDynaset method for the QueryDef object, as follows:

```
Dim Donations As Dynaset
Set Donations = SelQuery.CreateDynaset()
```

Finding Records in a Table or Dynaset

The previous section described how to access tables, dynasets, and snapshots in Access Basic procedures. When you work with these database objects, you may have to search for records one by one, and Access Basic provides two basic search methods, one for dynasets and snapshots, and another for tables. The fastest way to search a table is to use the Seek method to search an available index. Before you can use this method, you must select a previously created index by assigning a value to the Index property for the table. Single-field indexes are identified by the names of the key fields, and multifield indexes by the names displayed in the table property sheet—PrimaryKey, Index1, Index2, and so on. You can then call the Seek method to search the selected index for a specific value or for a record that has a particular relationship to a specific value. The Seek method requires two inputs—a comparison operator (=, >, <, >=, or <=) and an expression that defines the value you want to seek. For example, the following selects the Zip index for the Names table and searches for a zip code greater than or equal to 94000:

```
Names.Index = "Zip"
Names.Seek ">=", "94000"
```

Note that despite the similar notation, Names.Index is a property (whose value you can set with an assignment statement) and Names.Seek is a method, which carries out an action described by the parameters that follow.

When you search a multifield index, you *must* supply a value for all components of the index, and this restriction may force you to build indexes that you might not otherwise need. For example, you cannot use the index based on the ID Code and Date fields to search the Transactions table for a record in which the ID Code field matches the value of a control on a form, regardless of the transaction date. This is a very common search requirement when you work with tables that have a one-to-many relationship—you might need to find the first child record that matches the current parent record, and then step through all the related child records. In another example, you might want to activate the State/City/ID Code index for the Names table, find the first record in a given state and then process all the records in that state. To solve these problems, you can build an index for the Transactions table based only on the ID Code field, and an index for the Names table based only on the State field.

When you work with dynasets and snapshots, you must use different search methods, because Access cannot assume that an appropriate index will be available—a query dynaset has no indexes. Instead of the Seek method (which is available only for tables), you must use the FindFirst, FindLast, FindNext, and FindPrevious methods, which are very similar to the Find-Record and FindNext macro actions. However, when you apply these methods to a dynaset that represents a table, Access uses any available indexes to speed the search. This built-in optimization grants you a large measure of flexibility—you can apply the same search methods to tables and query dynasets, and you can build additional indexes at any time to speed up searches based on tables. When you use any of the Find methods, you must specify a condition that describes the record you want to find. For example, the following finds the first zip code greater than or equal to 94000 in a dynaset (not a table, as in the previous example) called Names:

```
Names.FindFirst "Zip >= '94000'"
```

The syntax of the FindNext, FindPrevious, and FindLast methods is exactly the same.

Regardless of the method used to move the focus to a particular record, you can use the MoveNext and MovePrevious methods to move forward or backward in a table, dynaset, or snapshot; MoveFirst and MoveLast take you directly to the top or bottom. Note that when you process an indexed table, the MoveNext and MovePrevious methods take you to the next or previous record *in indexed order*, so you can move very quickly through a group of records that share the same value or a range of values in the index key fields. For example, the following program fragment carries out *commands* on all the records in the Names table with zip codes between 94000 and 94999:

```
Names.Index = "Zip"
Names.Seek ">=", "94000"
Do While Names.Zip <= "94999"
    commands
    Names.MoveNext
Loop
```

You can use a very similar strategy in a sorted dynaset or snapshot, in which all the rows are also processed in a predictable order:

```
Names.FindFirst "Zip >= '94000'"
Do While Names.Zip <= "94999"
    commands
    Names.MoveNext
Loop
```

In both cases, rows are processed in zip code order. The Seek or FindFirst method finds the first record in the desired range of zip codes, and the Do While loop terminates when Access encounters the first record in which the zip code is no longer within the range.

When you use either the Seek method or any of the Find methods, you may want to test the value of the NoMatch property to verify that you actually found the row you were looking for. This property is True when any of the methods described in this section fails to find a record that satisfies the specified criteria.

Displaying Alert Boxes and Dialog Boxes

You can use two functions to display alert boxes and dialog boxes and thereby collect input from the users of your procedures that is not complex enough to warrant designing a custom form. The MsgBox function, which displays an alert box, is similar to the MsgBox macro action, but it offers considerably more flexibility. This function takes three inputs: the message that you want to display in the alert box, a number that represents several aspects of the appearance of the alert box, and the window title. Only the first input is required, but you will nearly always want to use the second input to describe the type of alert box you want to display. This input is a value obtained by adding together three separate numbers, which represent the command buttons you want in the alert box, the default button, and the icon displayed to the left of the message, as follows:

Number	Button(s)
0	OK
1	OK, Cancel
2	Abort, Retry, Ignore
3	Yes, No, Cancel
4	Yes, No
5	Retry, Cancel

Number	Icon
0	No icon
16	Critical Message (Stop sign)
32	Warning Query (Question mark)

48	Warning Message (Exclamation mark)
64	Information Message (i)

Number	Default Button
0	First button
256	Second button
512	Third button

The value returned by the MsgBox function identifies the button selected from the alert box, as follows:

Number	Button
1	OK
2	Cancel
3	Abort
4	Retry
5	Ignore
6	Yes
7	No

The following command displays an alert box that asks permission to delete a record and stores the answer in a variable called Confirm:

```
Confirm = MsgBox("Are you sure you want to delete this
person?", 292)
```

The number in this example resulted from adding 4, 32, and 256, to create an alert box with Yes and No buttons and a Warning? icon, in which the second button (No) is the default button. You might prefer to write this input as an explicit sum rather than as a single number to clarify its meaning, as follows:

```
Confirm = MsgBox("Are you sure you want to delete this
person?", 4 + 32 + 256)
```

You can use the similar InputBox function to display a dialog box that displays a message and collects one item of input in a text box. This function takes five inputs: the message that you want to display in the dialog box, the window title, the default value displayed in the text box, the horizontal position of the window on the screen, and the vertical position of the window on the screen. Unfortunately, the two screen coordinates must be expressed in *twips* (a twip is $1/20$ of a point, or $1/1440$ of an inch). If you omit the coordinates, Access centers the dialog box horizontally and positions it about $1/3$ of the way down the screen. For example, the following displays the dialog box pictured in Figure 20.12 and collects the value entered in the text box into a variable named NewState:

```
NewState = InputBox("Enter the two-letter abbreviation for
the state you want to enter into new Names table records",
"Select State", "CA")
```

Figure 20.12

A dialog box displayed using the InputBox function

As you can see in Figure 20.12, the dialog box displayed by the InputBox function always includes OK and Cancel buttons. If you choose the OK button, the InputBox function returns the value entered into the text box; choosing Cancel returns an empty string (a string of length 0).

Some Practical Procedure Examples

You can combine the methods for accessing database objects described in the last three sections with the programming structures described earlier in this chapter to write procedures that step through a table or dynaset one record at a time and carry out different actions based on the contents of the records. For example, Listing 20.2 lists a procedure called ThankYou that prints different thank you letters for donors selected by opening the Names and Donations by Date query as in the previous example, based on the amount of the donation. (Some long lines were wrapped to fit within the margins of the printed page.)

Listing 20.2   **A procedure that prints two different thank you letters**

```
Function ThankYou ()
' Prints two different letters, based on donation amount
' Written by: M. Liskin  2/1/93
   Dim ACE As Database
   Dim SelQuery As QueryDef
   Dim Donations As Dynaset

   Set ACE = CurrentDB()
   Set SelQuery = ACE.OpenQueryDef("Names and Donations by
      Date")
   SelQuery![Enter earliest transaction date:] =
      Forms![Thank-You Letter Options]![Date1]
   SelQuery![Enter latest transaction date:] =
      Forms![Thank-You Letter Options]![Date2]
   Set Donations = SelQuery.CreateDynaset()

   Do Until Donations.EOF
      Criteria = "[ID Code] = '" & Donations![ID Code] & "'"
      If Donations![Amount] <= 100 Then
         DoCmd OpenReport "Thank You Small", A_NORMAL, ,
            Criteria
      Else
         DoCmd OpenReport "Thank You Big", A_NORMAL, ,
            Criteria
      End If
      Donations.MoveNext
   Loop
End Function
```

This function is called from the OnPush event of the Print command button in the dialog box shown in Figure 20.13, which allows you to enter any range of donation dates. After defining object variables to represent the ACE database, the Names and Donations by Date query definition, and the query dynaset, the function assigns values to the parameters based on the values entered into the Date1 and Date2 controls on the Thank You Letter Options form. Next, a Do Until loop steps through the records in the Donations dynaset. The condition in the Do Until statement tests the value of the EOF ("end of file") property of the dynaset, which is True when Access moves past the last row in the dynaset (*not* when the last record has the focus).

Figure 20.13

A dialog box that collects donation dates and prints thank you letters

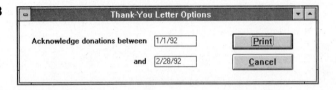

For each row in the dynaset, an If…Then structure tests the value of the Amount field in the dynaset, and opens one of two reports—Thank You Small or Thank You Big—depending on the amount. The OpenReport action, which is called with a DoCmd command, should be familiar to you from your experience with macros. When you invoke a macro action from an Access Basic program, you list the arguments, separated by commas, after the keyword that identifies the action. If you omit an argument, you must include a comma as a placeholder, so that Access does not mistake the following argument for the missing one. Many arguments, including the third argument of the OpenReport action, must be specified using keywords that represent the options that you can select from drop-down lists in the Action Arguments portion of the Macro window. Thus, the keyword A_NORMAL is equivalent to choosing Print from the corresponding combo box in the Macro window. To preview the report instead of printing it, you would use A_PREVIEW. Do not worry about trying to memorize the arguments—you can look them up in the Access *Language Reference* or in the on-line Help system.

The method used to specify the Where Condition argument (the last argument) deserves closer scrutiny. Because the condition is the same regardless of which letter is printed, it is constructed once and stored in a variable called Criteria, and this variable is used to specify the Where Condition argument. In Access Basic, you must compare a field or control to a *literal (constant) value*, not an expression, so the value of the Criteria variable is expressed by concatenating three text strings: [ID Code] = ' (the field name, comparison operator, and the opening quote that precedes the literal value), Donations![ID Code] (which evaluates to the literal value), and ' (the closing quote that follows the literal value). For example, if the value of Donations![ID Code] is ALLENMA when Access evaluates this expression, Criteria will take on the value [ID Code] = 'ALLENMA'. As you may recall from Chapter 19, writing the equivalent condition in a macro is much simpler.

Another very common use for Access Basic procedures is carrying out operations on one or more tables for which Access does not provide built-in commands or macro actions. For example, as noted in Chapter 8, Access does not give you any easy way to delete all of the related records in a group of tables—for example, to delete a record from the Names table together with all the related records in the Transactions, Contacts, and Committees tables—or to change the contents of the matching field (in this case, the ID Code field) in a group of tables. Figure 20.14 illustrates a simple dialog box that allows you to choose a name from a combo box and either delete all the related records or change the ID Code in all these records. In this dialog box, the row source for the combo box that enables you to choose a person is the following SQL Select statement:

```
Select [ID Code], [Name Type] AS Type, [Name], [Company],
[Address], [City], [State] FROM Names ORDER BY [ID Code];
```

Figure 20.14

A dialog box for performing database updates

One very easy way to carry out mass updates such as cascading deletes or updates is to write an SQL statement equivalent to an action query. For example, you could delete all the records in the Transactions table with an ID code that matches the ID Code field in the Maintenance Updates form with the following command:

```
DELETE FROM Transactions
    WHERE [ID Code] = Forms![Maintenance Updates]![ID Code];
```

You cannot execute an SQL command directly from Access Basic, but you can easily work around this limitation by using the DoCmd command to invoke the RunSQL macro action. The SQL statement must be enclosed in quotes, and if the statement itself includes quotes, you must use either two sets of double quotes or the more readable single quotes enclosed in double quotes, as in the following:

```
DoCmd RunSQL "DELETE FROM Transactions WHERE [ID
Code] = "'ALLENMA'";"
```

To delete transactions for the person selected from the Maintenance Updates form, you could use the following command:

```
DoCmd RunSQL "DELETE FROM Transactions WHERE [ID
Code] = Forms![Maintenance Updates]![ID Code];"
```

The complete procedure called from the Delete command button in the Maintenance Updates form, which deletes the related records from the four main ACE tables, is as follows (with long lines broken to fit):

```
Function DeleteAll ()
' Deletes related records in all ACE tables
' Written: M. Liskin  2/1/93

    ID = Forms![Maintenance Updates]![ID Code]

    If MsgBox("Are you sure you want to delete " & ID &
        "?", 292) = 6 Then
        DoCmd RunSQL "DELETE FROM Transactions WHERE [ID
            Code] = Forms![Maintenance Updates]![ID Code];"
        DoCmd RunSQL "DELETE FROM Contacts WHERE [ID
            Code] = Forms![Maintenance Updates]![ID Code];"
        DoCmd RunSQL "DELETE FROM Committees WHERE [ID
            Code] = Forms![Maintenance Updates]![ID Code];"
        DoCmd RunSQL "DELETE FROM Names WHERE [ID
            Code] = Forms![Maintenance Updates]![ID Code];"
    End If

End Function
```

Note that this procedure deletes the Names table record last, so as not to violate referential integrity rules, which prohibit deleting a parent record if child records exist in related tables. You can use a similar strategy to update records, as in the function procedure in Listing 20.3, which changes the ID Code field in all the related tables.

Listing 20.3   A procedure that changes a field in all related tables

```
Function ChangeAll ()
' Changes ID Code in related records in all ACE tables
' Written: M.Liskin  2/1/93

    OldID = Forms![Maintenance Updates]![Old ID]
    NewID = Forms![Maintenance Updates]![New ID]

    If MsgBox("Are you sure you want to change " & OldID &
        " to " & NewID & "?", 292) = 6 Then
```

Listing 20.3   A procedure that changes a field in all related tables (Continued)

```
DoCmd RunSQL "SELECT * INTO Temp FROM Names
    WHERE [ID Code] = Forms![Maintenance
    Updates]![Old ID];"
DoCmd RunSQL "UPDATE Temp SET [ID Code] =
    Forms![Maintenance Updates]![New ID];"
DoCmd RunSQL "INSERT INTO Names SELECT * FROM Temp;"
DoCmd RunSQL "UPDATE Transactions SET [ID Code] =
    Forms![Maintenance Updates]![New ID] WHERE [ID
    Code] = Forms![Maintenance Updates]![Old ID];"
DoCmd RunSQL "UPDATE Contacts SET [ID Code] =
    Forms![Maintenance Updates]![New ID] WHERE [ID
    Code] = Forms![Maintenance Updates]![Old ID];"
DoCmd RunSQL "UPDATE Committees SET [ID Code] =
    Forms![Maintenance Updates]![New ID] WHERE [ID
    Code] = Forms![Maintenance Updates]![Old ID];"
DoCmd RunSQL "DELETE * FROM Names WHERE [ID
    Code] = Forms![Maintenance Updates]![Old ID];"
    End If

End Function
```

Note that you cannot circumvent referential integrity rules by using SQL commands or writing Access Basic procedures. The ChangeAll procedure thus copies the Names table record to a temporary table named Temp, changes the ID code in this table, and appends this new record back into the Names table, changes the ID Code field in all the related records, and deletes the original Names table record (the one with the old ID code).

If you need to carry out more complex updates—perhaps with conditional steps—you must write a procedure that steps through the records in each table one by one. The function procedure in Listing 20.4 illustrates this strategy, applied to the relatively simple task of changing the ID code in all the related records in the main ACE tables. The ChangeID function creates four dynaset object variables, one for each table in the ACE system, with names that match the table names. For convenience, it also defines two variables to store the values of the ID Code and New ID controls on the Maintenance Updates form. The procedure uses the method described earlier in this chapter to define a variable called Criteria, which expresses the search criteria. It then uses the FindFirst method to search the Names dynaset for a record in which the ID Code field matches the new ID code entered in the form. If the NoMatch property is *not* True (that is, if there is a matching record), the procedure displays a warning in a message box to remind you that there is already a person on file with this ID code, and an Exit Function command exits without completing the rest of the steps. In effect, this command works like the CancelEvent action in a macro: It returns you to the form so you can re-enter the new ID code or go on to another task.

Listing 20.4   A procedure that performs a cascading update

```
Function ChangeID ()
'Changes ID Code in related records in all ACE tables
'Written by: M. Liskin 2/1/93
   Set ACE = CurrentDB()

   Dim Names As Dynaset, Transactions As Dynaset, Contacts
      As Dynaset, Committees As Dynaset
   Set Names = ACE.CreateDynaset("Names")
   Set Transactions = ACE.CreateDynaset("Transactions")
   Set Contacts = ACE.CreateDynaset("Contacts")
   Set Committees = ACE.CreateDynaset("Committees")

   OldID = Forms![Maintenance Updates]![Old ID]
   NewID = Forms![Maintenance Updates]![New ID]

   Criteria = "[ID Code] = '" & NewID & "'"
   Names.FindFirst Criteria
   If Not Names.Nomatch Then
      MsgBox (NewID & " is already in use as an ID Code.
         Please enter another ID Code")
      Exit Function
   End If

   Criteria = "[ID Code] = '" & OldID & "'"

   Transactions.FindFirst Criteria
   If Not Transactions.Nomatch Then
      Do While Transactions.[ID Code] = OldID
         Transactions.Edit
         Transactions.[ID Code] = NewID
         Transactions.Update
```

Listing 20.4   A procedure that performs a cascading update (Continued)

```
            Transactions.FindNext Criteria
        Loop
    End If

    Contacts.FindFirst Criteria
    If Not Contacts.Nomatch Then
        Do While Contacts.[ID Code] = OldID
            Contacts.Edit
            Contacts.[ID Code] = NewID
            Contacts.Update
            Contacts.FindNext Criteria
        Loop
    End If

    Committees.FindFirst Criteria
    If Not Committees.Nomatch Then
        Do While Committees.[ID Code] = OldID
            Committees.Edit
            Committees.[ID Code] = NewID
            Committees.Update
            Committees.FindNext Criteria
        Loop
    End If

    Names.Edit
    Names.[ID Code] = NewID
    Names.Update

End Function
```

Next, the procedure searches in each dynaset in turn, and if it finds any matching records, it changes the ID Code field in each one. Stepping through all the matching records is easy, using a Do While loop controlled by a condition that compares the ID Code field in the current dynaset to the OldID variable. Updating a record requires three steps: First, you must invoke the Edit method to make the record available for editing; next, a simple assignment statement assigns the new value to the ID Code field; and finally, the Update method updates the record in the dynaset to reflect the changes (in this case, just the new ID code). After updating each record, the procedure uses the FindNext method to search for the next record with the same ID code. After updating all the matching records in the Transactions, Contacts, and Committees dynasets, the procedure applies the same sequence of methods to change the ID Code field in the Names dynaset.

As noted earlier in this chapter, an Access Basic procedure cannot violate referential integrity rules. Before you can run this version of the ChangeID function, you must ensure that the Enforce Referential Integrity option is not enabled for any of the relationships between the ACE tables. One solution to the problem is to add DoCmd statements identical to the first three steps in the ChangeAll function described earlier in this chapter before the steps that update the Transactions, Contacts, and Committees tables, and substitute a call to the Delete method (Names.Delete) for the three steps at the end that update the Names table record. This strategy is illustrated by the ChangeAll2 function on the disk packaged with this book. Another more complicated alternative is to save the contents of the fields in the original Names table record in variables, use the AddNew method to add a new record to the Names table dynaset, use the MoveLast method to move to the new record, enter the new ID code in the ID Code field in this record, and assign the values stored in the variables to the other fields. After changing the ID Code field in all the related tables, you can use the FindFirst method to return to the original Names table record and then use the Delete method to delete this record.

The third command button in the dialog box in Figure 20.14 opens a DDE conversation with Microsoft Word to print a personalized letter for the person selected from the Current ID Code combo box. This process is mediated by three function procedures. All of these functions make use of a variable called Channel, which stores the channel number assigned when you initiate the DDE conversation. This variable must be declared explicitly in the declarations section for the module that contains them to make it available to multiple procedures. The OpenWord function, which is invoked from the OnOpen event for the form, is as follows:

```
Function OpenWord ()
' Launch Microsoft Word
' Written by: M. Liskin  2/1/93
  Temp = Shell("C:\Winword\WinWord.exe", 1)
  Channel = DDEInitiate("WinWord", "System")
  DDEExecute Channel, "[FileOpen""C:\WinWord\Letter.doc""]"
  DDEExecute Channel, "[AppMinimize]"
End Function
```

This function calls the Shell function to open Microsoft Word (if your copy of Word is installed in a different subdirectory, you will have to modify the path name that supplies the first input). The second input to this function specifies the window mode—in this case, Normal (that is, Word opens in a window that is not maximized). Next, a call to the DDEInitiate function initiates a DDE conversation on the general-purpose System topic. The two DDEExecute commands send commands to Word in its own language to open a previously created merge letter and then minimize the Word application window. As you can see from this example, using DDE to communicate with another application requires that you understand quite a bit about its commands and menus, and if you are not familiar with Word, this example may be hard to follow. Because the OpenWord function is called from the OnOpen event for the form, these steps, which are relatively slow, are carried out only once, when the form is first opened, rather than repeatedly, every time you want to print a letter. You could use a similar function to open Excel and load the Budgets spreadsheet in a form that uses the DDE function to display the budget total (as mentioned in Chapter 15).

The following function, which is invoked from the Letter command button, prints the letter:

```
Function PrintLetter ()
' Call Word to print a letter
' Written by: M. Liskin  2/1/93
    DoCmd OpenQuery "Export"
    DoCmd TransferText A_EXPORTDELIM, , "Word Export",
        "C:\WINWORD\LETTER.MRG", True
    DDEExecute Channel, "[AppRestore]"
    DDEExecute Channel, "[FilePrintMerge]"
    DDEExecute Channel, "[AppMinimize]"
End Function
```

To create the data file that Word will integrate with the merge letter, a make table query called Export copies the selected record from the Names table to another table named Word Export. The following expression defines the selection criteria in the ID Code column in this query:

```
[Forms]![Maintenance Updates]![Old ID]
```

Next, a DoCmd command executes a TransferText action to export this table to a delimited text file called LETTER.MRG. The next three DDEExecute commands restore the minimized Word window to its former size, execute the Print Merge command (as if you had chosen this command from Word's File menu), and then minimize the window again.

The commands that terminate the DDE conversation are carried out by the following function procedure, which is invoked from the OnClose event of the dialog box form:

```
Function CloseWord ()
' Close Microsoft Word
' Written by: M. Liskin  2/1/93
   DDETerminate (Channel)
End Function
```

Summary

This chapter introduced both of the programming languages supported by Access—SQL, which is used behind the scenes to execute queries and carry out actions equivalent to queries in other contexts, and Access Basic, a derivative of Visual Basic designed specifically to manipulate Access data and integrate with Access forms and reports. Although this chapter is quite lengthy, it barely scratches the surface of what you can accomplish with the Access Basic programming language. Access Basic can be a bit intimidating at first: If you have no prior programming experience, there is a lot to learn, and if you have used languages that are not so closely tied to database objects and events, the methods used to manipulate data may seem formidably complex. Nevertheless, in a complex application, the SQL and Access Basic programming languages can enable you to overcome some of the limitations of the interactive environment, carry out very sophisticated calculations and conditional tests, and achieve a new level of automation.

If Access Basic is your first programming language, take it slow at first—begin by defining functions for carrying out calculations and specialized validation tests, which you can call from a report or form event just as you would a macro. If you decide to defer learning about programming, keep in mind the kinds of operations you can perform with Access Basic. As your applications grow and mature, you may encounter situations that will motivate you to review the concepts presented in this chapter and begin writing procedures. Programmers who want to take the language further and use it to develop menu-driven systems for users who know nothing about Access will want to graduate to a more advanced book that covers Access Basic syntax and application-building techniques in far greater depth.

Access Menu Bars

This Appendix diagrams the Access menu bar in all the various object design and data editing windows.

Startup Menu (no database open)

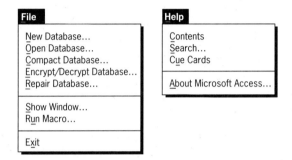

Database Window

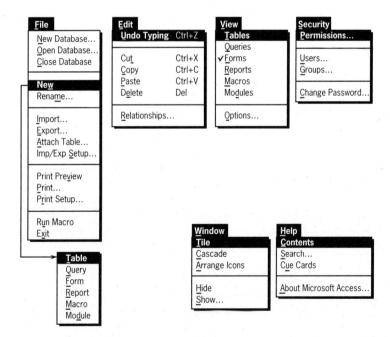

Table Design

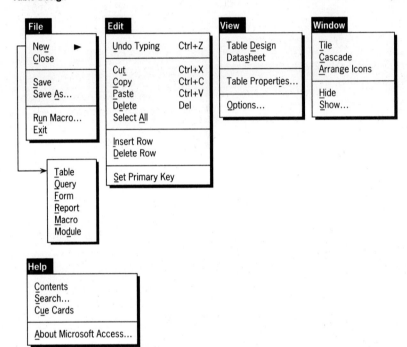

File	
New ▶	
Close	
Save	
Save As...	
Run Macro...	
Exit	

Table
Query
Form
Report
Macro
Module

Edit	
Undo Typing	Ctrl+Z
Cut	Ctrl+X
Copy	Ctrl+C
Paste	Ctrl+V
Delete	Del
Select All	
Insert Row	
Delete Row	
Set Primary Key	

View
Table Design
Datasheet
Table Properties...
Options...

Window
Tile
Cascade
Arrange Icons
Hide
Show...

Help
Contents
Search...
Cue Cards
About Microsoft Access...

Query Design View

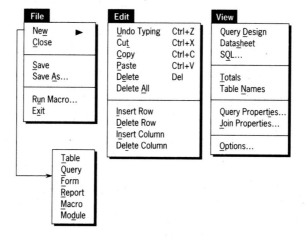

File		Edit			View	
New ►		Undo Typing	Ctrl+Z		Query Design	
Close		Cut	Ctrl+X		Datasheet	
		Copy	Ctrl+C		SQL...	
Save		Paste	Ctrl+V			
Save As...		Delete	Del		Totals	
		Delete All			Table Names	
Run Macro...						
Exit		Insert Row			Query Properties...	
		Delete Row			Join Properties...	
		Insert Column				
		Delete Column			Options...	

Table
Query
Form
Report
Macro
Module

Query		Window		Help	
Run		Tile		Contents	
		Cascade		Search...	
Add Table...		Arrange Icons		Cue Cards	
Remove Table					
		Hide		About Microsoft Access...	
Select		Show...			
Crosstab					
Make Table...					
Update					
Append					
Delete					
Join Tables...					
Parameters...					

Form Design View

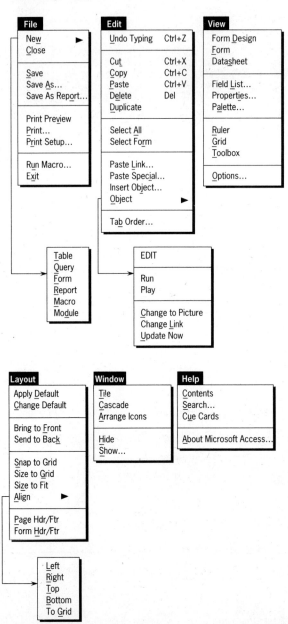

File	
New	►
Close	
Save	
Save As...	
Save As Report...	
Print Preview	
Print...	
Print Setup...	
Run Macro...	
Exit	

Edit	
Undo Typing	Ctrl+Z
Cut	Ctrl+X
Copy	Ctrl+C
Paste	Ctrl+V
Delete	Del
Duplicate	
Select All	
Select Form	
Paste Link...	
Paste Special...	
Insert Object...	
Object	►
Tab Order...	

View	
Form Design	
Form	
Datasheet	
Field List...	
Properties...	
Palette...	
Ruler	
Grid	
Toolbox	
Options...	

Table
Query
Form
Report
Macro
Module

EDIT
Run
Play
Change to Picture
Change Link
Update Now

Layout
Apply Default
Change Default
Bring to Front
Send to Back
Snap to Grid
Size to Grid
Size to Fit
Align ►
Page Hdr/Ftr
Form Hdr/Ftr

Window
Tile
Cascade
Arrange Icons
Hide
Show...

Help
Contents
Search...
Cue Cards
About Microsoft Access...

Left
Right
Top
Bottom
To Grid

Report Design View

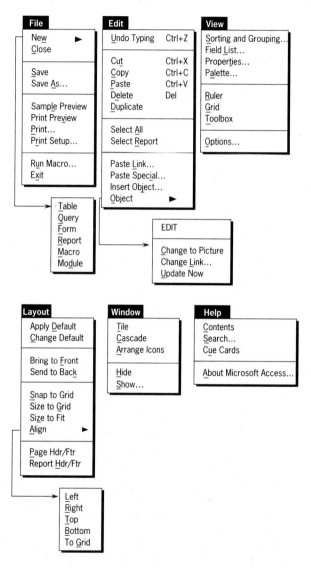

Macro Design View

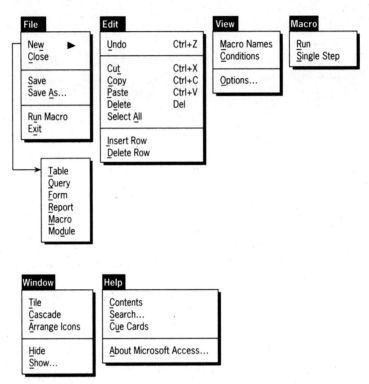

Module Window

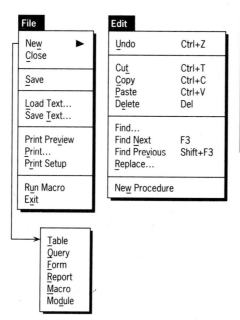

File	
New	▶
Close	
Save	
Load Text...	
Save Text...	
Print Preview	
Print...	
Print Setup	
Run Macro	
Exit	

Table	
Query	
Form	
Report	
Macro	
Module	

Edit	
Undo	Ctrl+Z
Cut	Ctrl+T
Copy	Ctrl+C
Paste	Ctrl+V
Delete	Del
Find...	
Find Next	F3
Find Previous	Shift+F3
Replace...	
New Procedure	

View	
Split Window	
Procedures...	F2
Next Procedure	Ctrl+Down
Previous Procedure	Ctrl+Up
Immediate Window	
Options	

Run	
Reinitialize	
Compile All	
Continue	F5
Single Step	F8
Procedure Step	Shift+F8
Set Next Statement	
Show Next Statement	
Toggle Breakpoint	F9
Clear All Breakpoints	
Modify Command$...	

Window
Tile
Cascade
Arrange Icons
Hide
Show...

Help
Contents
Search...
Cue Cards
About Microsoft Access...

Datasheet View

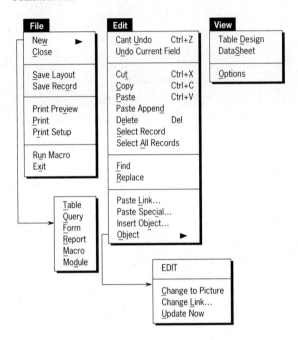

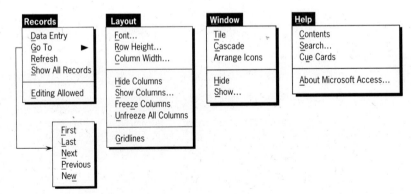

File
New ▶
Close

Save Layout
Save Record

Print Preview
Print
Print Setup

Run Macro
Exit

Table
Query
Form
Report
Macro
Module

Edit
Cant Undo   Ctrl+Z
Undo Current Field

Cut   Ctrl+X
Copy   Ctrl+C
Paste   Ctrl+V
Paste Append
Delete   Del
Select Record
Select All Records

Find
Replace

Paste Link...
Paste Special...
Insert Object...
Object   ▶

View
Table Design
DataSheet

Options

EDIT
Change to Picture
Change Link...
Update Now

Records
Data Entry
Go To   ▶
Refresh
Show All Records

Editing Allowed

First
Last
Next
Previous
New

Layout
Font...
Row Height...
Column Width...

Hide Columns
Show Columns...
Freeze Columns
Unfreeze All Columns

Gridlines

Window
Tile
Cascade
Arrange Icons

Hide
Show...

Help
Contents
Search...
Cue Cards

About Microsoft Access...

Form View

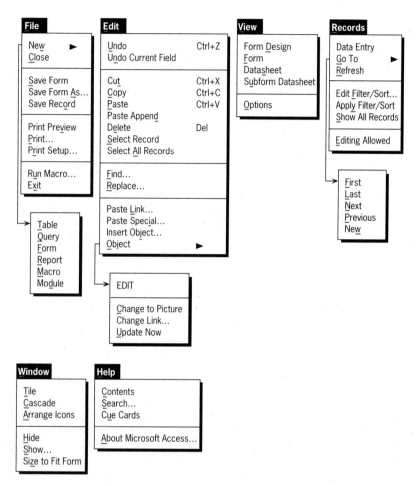

File
New ▶
Close

Save Form
Save Form As...
Save Record

Print Preview
Print...
Print Setup...

Run Macro...
Exit

Table
Query
Form
Report
Macro
Module

Edit
Undo   Ctrl+Z
Undo Current Field

Cut   Ctrl+X
Copy   Ctrl+C
Paste   Ctrl+V
Paste Append
Delete   Del
Select Record
Select All Records

Find...
Replace...

Paste Link...
Paste Special...
Insert Object...
Object   ▶

EDIT

Change to Picture
Change Link...
Update Now

View
Form Design
Form
Datasheet
Subform Datasheet

Options

Records
Data Entry
Go To   ▶
Refresh

Edit Filter/Sort...
Apply Filter/Sort
Show All Records

Editing Allowed

First
Last
Next
Previous
New

Window
Tile
Cascade
Arrange Icons

Hide
Show...
Size to Fit Form

Help
Contents
Search...
Cue Cards

About Microsoft Access...

Form Datasheet View

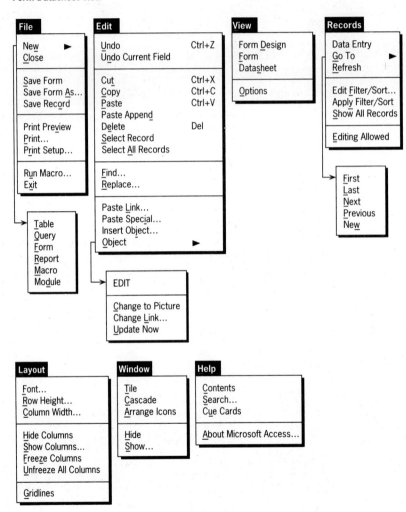

File
New ▶
Close

Save Form
Save Form As...
Save Record

Print Preview
Print...
Print Setup...

Run Macro...
Exit

Table
Query
Form
Report
Macro
Module

Edit
Undo   Ctrl+Z
Undo Current Field

Cut   Ctrl+X
Copy   Ctrl+C
Paste   Ctrl+V
Paste Append
Delete   Del
Select Record
Select All Records

Find...
Replace...

Paste Link...
Paste Special...
Insert Object...
Object   ▶

EDIT

Change to Picture
Change Link...
Update Now

View
Form Design
Form
Datasheet

Options

Records
Data Entry
Go To   ▶
Refresh

Edit Filter/Sort...
Apply Filter/Sort
Show All Records

Editing Allowed

First
Last
Next
Previous
New

Layout
Font...
Row Height...
Column Width...

Hide Columns
Show Columns...
Freeze Columns
Unfreeze All Columns

Gridlines

Window
Tile
Cascade
Arrange Icons

Hide
Show...

Help
Contents
Search...
Cue Cards

About Microsoft Access...

Query Datasheet View

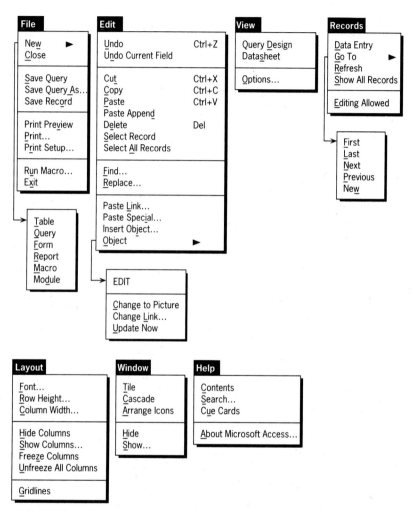

File

New ►
Close

Save Query
Save Query As...
Save Record

Print Preview
Print...
Print Setup...

Run Macro...
Exit

Table
Query
Form
Report
Macro
Module

Edit

Undo   Ctrl+Z
Undo Current Field

Cut   Ctrl+X
Copy   Ctrl+C
Paste   Ctrl+V
Paste Append
Delete   Del
Select Record
Select All Records

Find...
Replace...

Paste Link...
Paste Special...
Insert Object...
Object   ►

EDIT

Change to Picture
Change Link...
Update Now

View

Query Design
Datasheet

Options...

Records

Data Entry
Go To   ►
Refresh
Show All Records

Editing Allowed

First
Last
Next
Previous
New

Layout

Font...
Row Height...
Column Width...

Hide Columns
Show Columns...
Freeze Columns
Unfreeze All Columns

Gridlines

Window

Tile
Cascade
Arrange Icons

Hide
Show...

Help

Contents
Search...
Cue Cards

About Microsoft Access...

Filter Window

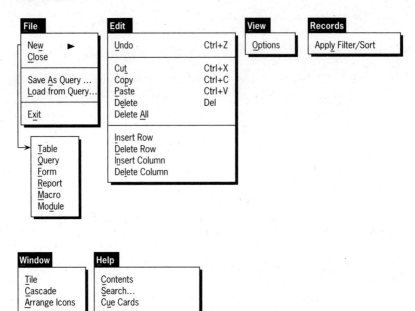

File	
New	►
Close	
Save As Query …	
Load from Query…	
Exit	

Table
Query
Form
Report
Macro
Module

Edit	
Undo	Ctrl+Z
Cut	Ctrl+X
Copy	Ctrl+C
Paste	Ctrl+V
Delete	Del
Delete All	
Insert Row	
Delete Row	
Insert Column	
Delete Column	

View
Options

Records
Apply Filter/Sort

Window
Tile
Cascade
Arrange Icons
Hide
Show…

Help
Contents
Search…
Cue Cards
About Microsoft Access…

Access Operators

Calculation Operators

Symbol	Data Types	Meaning
+	All numeric	Addition
	Text, Memo	Text string concatenation
	Date/Time	Adds number of days to a date or time
–	All numeric	Subtraction
	Date/Time-Numeric	Subtracts number of days from a date or time
	Date/Time-Date/Time	Calculates elapsed time in days between two dates or times
*	All numeric	Multiplication
/	All numeric	Division
\	Integer, Counter	Integer division (integer portion of the result of dividing one integer by another)
^	All numeric	Exponentiation (raising a number to a power)
Mod	All numeric	Modulus (remainder resulting from dividing one number by another)
&	Text, Memo	Concatenation

Comparison Operators (All apply to all data types except OLE Object)

Operator	Meaning
=	Equal to
<>	Not equal to
>	Greater than
>=	Greater than or equal to
<	Less than

Comparison Operators (Continued)

Operator	Meaning
<=	Less than or equal to
Between ... And	Between two values (inclusive)
In	In a list of values
Is Null	Is empty
Like	Matches pattern that can include wildcards

Logical Operators

Operator	Meaning
And	Both
Or	One or both
Not	Not
Xor	One, but not both
Eqv	Logically equivalent (both True or both False)
Imp	Logical implication

Access Functions

This Appendix lists the Access functions in two different formats. First, the function names are listed grouped according to the types of calculations or operations they perform. This listing is intended to help you find the function you need in a particular context. Second, a more complete syntax reference lists all the functions with the inputs they accept and a brief description of the operations or calculations they perform. For more information on the function inputs and usage examples, consult the *Microsoft Access Language Reference* or the on-line help system.

The notation in this appendix follows the conventions used in the Access documentation. The function names are written in mixed upper- and lower-case, and the keywords that represent the function inputs (arguments) are printed in italics within the parentheses that follow the function names. Optional arguments are enclosed in square brackets ([]), and ellipses indicate that one or more entries of the same type are permitted. In this syntax listing, there is no space between the function name and the open parenthesis that follows, and the function inputs are separated by spaces. When you use functions in expressions, remember that Access treats uppercase and lowercase as equivalent, and that all spaces are optional; you can use any typographical conventions you wish to improve readability.

Remember that the words or phrases used to specify the function inputs in this appendix are *placeholders*—instead of the exact words that appear between the parentheses, you must substitute a specific value of the appropriate type. The following are the most common placeholders whose meanings are not evident:

angle	An angle, expressed in radians. (To convert degrees to radians, multiply by pi and divide by 180; to convert radians to degrees, multiply by 180 and divide by pi.)
application	A text string that stores the name of another Windows application.
attribute	A code that distinguishes between a file attribute (1) and file handle (2).
channel	A DDE channel number.
color code	A code that represents a color. Valid values are 0 for black, 1 for blue, 2 for green, 3 for cyan, 4 for red, 5 for magenta, 6 for yellow, 7 for white, 8 for gray, 9 for light blue, 10 for light green, 11 for light cyan, 12 for light red, 13 for light magenta, 14 for light yellow, and 15 for bright white.

comparison method	A code that represents a text string comparison method. Valid values are 0 (case-sensitive), 1 (case-insensitive), and 2 (based on the New Database Sort Order option).
criteria	A condition (logical expression) that describes selection criteria for a table or query dynaset.
date/time	A constant Date/Time value or an expression that evaluates to a variant or Date/Time value.
day	A constant number or numeric expression between 1 and 31, which represents a day of the month.
domain	A constant text string or an expression that contains a table name, query name, or SQL Select statement.
drive	A letter that represents a disk drive.
expression	Any legitimate expression.
file name pattern	A text string that contains a legitimate DOS file name specification, which may include the wildcards * and ?.
file number	An identifying number assigned to a file opened and accessed solely through Access Basic as a sequential, random, or binary file.
format string	A text string containing a series of symbols that describes a custom format for Text, Date/Time, numeric, or Yes/No values.
interval	A constant text string or an expression that evaluates to a text string representing a time interval. Valid intervals are "yyyy" (year), "q" (quarter), "m" (month), "y" (day of year), "d" (day), "w" (weekday), "ww" (week), "h" (hour), "n" (minute), and "s" (second).
item	A text string that contains a data item whose value is sent to another application or retrieved from another application using DDE.

month	A constant number or numeric expression between 1 and 12, which represents a month.
number	A numeric constant or an expression that evaluates to a variant or numeric value.
string	A constant text string or an expression that evaluates to a variant or text string.
topic	A text string that contains the name of a DDE topic recognized by a Windows application.
variant	An expression that evaluates to a value with the Variant data type, which can be used anywhere a Text, Date/Time, or numeric value is permitted.
window style	A code that represents the window style for an application launched using the Shell function. Valid values are 1, 5, or 9 for normal with focus, 2 for minimized with focus, 3 for maximized with focus, 4 or 8 for normal without focus, or 6 or 7 for maximized without focus.
year	A constant number or numeric expression between 0 and 9999, which represents a year.

Functions Grouped by Type

Mathematical and Array

Abs	Log
Exp	Rnd
Fix	Sgn
Int	Sqr
LBound	UBound

Trigonometric

Atn	Sin
Cos	Tan

Financial

DDB	NPer	Rate
FV	NPV	SLN
IPmt	Pmt	SYD
IRR	PPmt	
MIRR	PV	

Aggregate

Avg	Max	StDevP
Count	Min	Var
First	Sum	VarP
Last	StDev	

Domain Aggregate

DAvg	DLookUp	DStDevP
DCount	DMax	DSum
DFirst	DMin	DVar
DLast	DStDev	DVarP

Date/Time

DateAdd	Day	TimeSerial
DateDiff	Hour	TimeValue
DatePart	Minute	Weekday
DateSerial	Month	Year
DateValue	Second	

Text String

Asc	LCase	Mid	StrComp
Chr	Left	Right	String
Eval	Len	RTrim	Trim
InStr	LTrim	Space	UCase

Data Type Conversion and Formatting

CCur	CStr	Oct
CDbl	CVar	QBColor
CInt	CVDate	RGB
CLng	Format	Str
CSng	Hex	Val

Data Testing and Decision-Making

Choose	IsNumeric
IIf	Partition
IsDate	Switch
IsEmpty	VarType
IsNull	

Data Collection

InputBox

MsgBox

External Application Access

DDE	DDESend
DDEInitiate	Shell
DDERequest	

Environment

Command	Environ	OpenDatabase
CurDir	Erl	Time
CurrentDB	Err	Timer
Date	Error	User
Dir	Now	

Disk File Access

EOF	Loc
FileAttr	LOF
FreeFile	Seek
Input	

Printing

Spc

Tab

Function Syntax Reference

Abs(*number*)
    Returns the absolute value of *number*.

Asc(*string*)
    Returns the ANSI character code for the first character in *string*.

Atn(*tangent*)
    Returns the angle, in radians, whose tangent is specified as input.

Avg(*expression*)
    Returns the average of *expression* in the source dynaset for a query, form, or report.

CCur(*expression*)
    Returns the result of converting *expression* to a number with the Currency data type.

CDbl(*expression*)
　　Returns the result of converting *expression* to a number with the Double
　　data type.

CInt(*expression*)
　　Returns the result of converting *expression* to a number with the Integer
　　data type.

CLng(*expression*)
　　Returns the result of converting *expression* to a number with the Long
　　Integer data type.

CSng(*expression*)
　　Returns the result of converting *expression* to a number with the Single
　　data type.

CStr(*expression*)
　　Returns the result of converting *expression* to a text string.

CVar(*expression*)
　　Returns the result of converting *expression* to a value with the Variant
　　data type.

CVDate(*expression*)
　　Returns the result of converting *expression* to a Date/Time value.

Choose(*number, expression1* [, *expression2...expression13*])
　　Returns the expression that occupies the position specified by *number* in
　　a list of up to 13 expressions.

Chr(*number*)
Chr$(*number*)
　　Returns a variant (Chr) or text string (Chr$) that contains the character
　　whose ANSI code is *number*.

Command( )
Command$( )
　　Returns a variant (Command) or text string (Command$) that contains
　　the command line parameters used in the command that started up
　　Access in the current work session.

Cos(*angle*)
　　Returns the cosine of *angle*.

Count(*expression*)
　　Returns the number of rows with nonnull values for *expression* in the
　　source dynaset for a query, form, or report.

CurDir([*drive*])
CurDir$([*drive*])
> Returns a variant (CurDir) or text string (CurDir$) that contains the full path name of the current subdirectory on *drive*.

CurrentDB()
> Returns a database object variable that represents the current database.

Date()
Date$()
> Returns a variant (Date) or text string (Date$) that contains the current system date.

DateAdd(*interval*, *number*, *date/time*)
> Returns the result of adding *number* of the time intervals specified by *interval* to *date/time*.

DateDiff(*interval*, *date1*, *date2*)
> Returns the result of subtracting *date2* from *date1*, expressed in time intervals specified by *interval*.

DatePart(*interval*, *date/time*)
> Returns the part of *date/time* described by *interval*.

DateSerial(*year*, *month*, *day*)
> Returns the date serial number equivalent to the date described by *year*, *month*, and *day*.

DateValue(*string*)
> Returns a Date/Time value equivalent to *string*.

DAvg(*expression*, *domain* [, *criteria*])
> Returns the average of *expression* in the rows in *domain* that satisfy the conditions specified by *criteria*, or in the entire *domain* if *criteria* is omitted.

Day(*date/time*)
> Returns an integer between 1 and 31 that represents the day of the month in *date/time*.

DCount(*expression*, *domain* [, *criteria*])
> Returns the number of non-null values in *expression* in the rows in *domain* that satisfy the conditions specified by *criteria*, or in the entire *domain* if *criteria* is omitted.

DDB(*cost, salvage, lifetime, period*)

> Returns the depreciation, calculated using the double-declining balance method, for an asset whose initial cost, salvage value, and depreciable lifetime are specified as input, over the period specified by *period*.

DDE(*application, topic, item*)

> Returns data described by *item* via a DDE conversation with *application* about *topic*.

DDEInitiate(*application, topic*)

> Returns a channel number resulting from initiating a DDE conversation with *application* about *topic*.

DDERequest(*channel, item*)

> Returns the data described by *item* from the application accessed via DDE channel *channel*.

DDESend(*application, topic, item, data*)

> Sends *data* to *item* via a DDE conversation with *application* about *topic*.

DFirst(*expression, domain* [, *criteria*])

> Returns the first occurrence of *expression* in the *domain* that satisfies the conditions specified by *criteria*, or in the entire *domain* if *criteria* is omitted.

Dir([*file name pattern*])
Dir$([*file name pattern*])

> Returns a variant (Dir) or text string (Dir$) that contains the full path name of the first file (if a *file name pattern* is specified as input) or of the next file (if no input is specified) that matches *file name pattern*.

DLast(*expression, domain* [, *criteria*])

> Returns the last occurrence of *expression* in the *domain* that satisfies the conditions specified by *criteria*, or in the entire *domain* if *criteria* is omitted.

DLookUp(*expression, domain* [, *criteria*])

> Returns the value of *expression* obtained by searching *domain* for a row that satisfies the conditions specified by *criteria*.

DMax(*expression, domain* [, *criteria*])

> Returns the highest value of *expression* in the *domain* that satisfies the conditions specified by *criteria*, or in the entire *domain* if *criteria* is omitted.

DMin(*expression, domain* [, *criteria*])

Returns the lowest value of *expression* in the *domain* that satisfies the conditions specified by *criteria*, or in the entire *domain* if *criteria* is omitted.

DoEvents( )

Passes control from an Access Basic program to the operating environment until all pending events and keystrokes have been processed.

DStDev(*expression, domain* [, *criteria*])
DStDevP(*expression, domain* [, *criteria*])

Returns the standard deviation of *expression* in the population (DStDevP) or population sample (DStDev) in the rows in *domain* that satisfy the conditions specified by *criteria*, or in the entire *domain* if *criteria* is omitted.

DSum(*expression, domain* [, *criteria*])

Returns the sum of the *expression* in the rows in *domain* that satisfy the conditions specified by *criteria*, or in the entire *domain* if *criteria* is omitted.

DVar(*expression, domain* [, *criteria*])
DVarP(*expression, domain* [, *criteria*])

Returns the variance of *expression* in the population (DVarP) or population sample (DVar) in the rows in *domain* that satisfy the conditions specified by *criteria*, or in the entire *domain* if *criteria* is omitted.

Environ(*environment variable*)
Environ$(*environment variable*)

Returns a variant (Environ) or text string (Environ$) that contains the value of the DOS environment variable specified as input.

EOF(*file number*)

When *file number* represents a sequential file, returns True if the file pointer is past the end-of-file, or False if it is not. When *file number* represents a random or binary file, returns True if the last Get statement did not successfully read a complete record, or False if it did.

Erl( )

Returns the line number of the procedure line that generated the last error that occurred.

Err( )

Returns the error number representing the last error that occurred.

Error([*error number*])
Error$([*error number*])
  Returns a variant (Error) or text string (Error$) that contains the error message associated with the error whose numeric code is *error number*, or if no input is specified, the error message associated with the last error that occurred.

Eval(*string*)
  Returns the result of evaluating the expression stored in *string*.

Exp(*number*)
  Returns the result of raising e (the base of natural logarithms) to the power specified by *number*.

FileAttr(*file number, attribute*)
  Returns the information specified by *attribute* about the sequential, random, or binary file represented by *file number*. If *attribute* is 1, the function returns the file open mode—1 (input), 2 (output), 4 (random), 8 (append), or 32 (binary). If *attribute* is 2, the function returns the file handle.

First(*expression*)
  Returns the first value of the *expression* in the source dynaset for a query, form, or report.

Fix(*number*)
  Returns the integer portion of *number* (the result of removing any digits after the decimal point). The return value is greater than or equal to *number* if *number* is negative.

Format(*expression* [, *format string*])
Format$(*expression* [, *format string*])
  Returns a variant (Format) or text string (Format$) that results from using *format string* to format the result of evaluating *expression*, or if no format string is specified, the result of converting this value to a text string. See Table 9.2 for the symbols used in *format string*.

FreeFile()
  Returns the next available file number for a sequential, random, or binary file.

FV(*rate, periods, payment, present value, due*)
  Returns the future value of a series of equal payments. The first four inputs specify the periodic interest rate, the number of payment periods, the payment amount, and the present value of the investment; *due* must be 0 if payments are made at the end of each period or 1 if payments are made at the beginning of each period.

Hex(*number*)
Hex$(*number*)

    Returns a variant (Hex) or text string (Hex$) that contains the hexadecimal (base 16) equivalent of the decimal (base 10) number specified as input.

Hour(*date/time*)

    Returns an integer between 0 and 23 that represents the hour of the day in *date/time*.

IIf(*expression*, *true value*, *false value*)

    Returns *true value* if *expression* evaluates to True, or *false value* if the *expression* evaluates to False.

Input(*number of characters*, [#] *file number*)
Input$(*number of characters*, [#] *file number*)

    Returns a variant (Input) or text string (Input$) that contains the specified number of characters, read from the sequential or binary file identified by *file number*.

InputBox(*string* [, *title*] [, *default*] [, *X- and Y-coordinates*])
InputBox$(*prompt* [, *title*] [, *default*] [, *X- and Y-coordinates*])

    Returns a variant (InputBox) or text string (InputBox$) entered by the user in a dialog box that displays *string* as a prompt and collects a single value in a text box, or returns an empty string if the user does not enter a value. The optional inputs specify the title for the dialog box window, the default value displayed in the text box, and the screen coordinates of the dialog box.

Instr([*starting position*,] *string1*, *string2* [, *comparison method*])

    Returns the starting position of *string2* in *string1*, searching from the beginning of *string1* or from *starting position* if it is specified, using *comparison method* if specified.

Int(*number*)

    Returns the integer portion of *number* (the result of removing any digits after the decimal point). The return value is always less than or equal to *number*.

IPmt(*rate*, *period*, *periods*, *present value*, *future value*, *due*)

    Returns the interest payment for one of a series of equal payments. The first five inputs specify the periodic interest rate, the payment period for which you want to calculate the interest, the number of payment periods, the present value of the investment, and the future value of the investment; *due* must be 0 if payments are made at the end of each period or 1 if payments are made at the beginning of each period.

IRR(*values, guess*)
>Returns the internal rate of return for a series of cash flows stored in the array *values*, based on the *guess* you specify as input.

IsDate(*variant*)
>Returns True if *variant* can be converted to a legitimate Date/Time value or False if it cannot.

IsEmpty(*variant*)
>Returns True if *variant* has not been assigned an initial value or False if it has.

IsNull(*variant*)
>Returns True if *variant* has a Null value or False if it has any other value.

IsNumeric(*variant*)
>Returns True if *variant* can be converted to a legitimate numeric value or False if it cannot.

Last(*expression*)
>Returns the last value of *expression* in the source dynaset for a query, form, or report.

LBound(*array* [, *dimension*])
>Returns the lower boundary (the smallest array subscript) for the array dimension specified by *dimension*, or for the first dimension if *dimension* is not specified.

LCase(*string*)
LCase$(*string*)
>Returns a variant (LCase) or text string (LCase$) that results from converting *string* to all lowercase.

Left(*string, length*)
Left$(*string, length*)
>Returns a variant (Left) or text string (Left$) that results from extracting a portion of *string* of the specified length, starting from the left side of *string*.

Len(*string*)
>Returns the length of *string*.

Loc(*file number*)
>Returns the current position of the file pointer. For a sequential file, the position is the result of dividing the character position by 128; for a random file, it is the number of the last variable read; and for a binary file, it is the character position.

LOF(*file number*)

Returns the length (size) of an open sequential, random, or binary file.

Log(*number*)

Returns the base e logarithm of *number*.

LTrim(*string*)
LTrim$(*string*)

Returns a variant (Ltrim) or text string (Ltrim$) that results from removing leading spaces (spaces at the beginning) from *string*.

Max(*expression*)

Returns the maximum value of *expression* in the source dynaset for a query, form, or report.

Mid(*string, starting position* [, *length*])
Mid$(*string, starting position* [, *length*])

Returns a variant (Mid) or text string (Mid$) that results from extracting a portion of *string* that begins at *starting position* and has the specified length, or extends to the end of *string* if *length* is not specified.

Min(*expression*)

Returns the minimum value of *expression* in the source dynaset for a query, form, or report.

Minute(*date/time*)

Returns an integer between 0 and 59 that represents the minute of the hour in *date/time*.

MIRR(*values, finance rate, reinvest rate*)

Returns the modified internal rate of return for a series of cash flows stored in the array *values*, based on the rates specified for payments (*finance rate*) and receipts (*reinvest rate*).

Month(*date/time*)

Returns an integer between 1 and 12 that represents the month in *date/time*.

MsgBox(*string* [, *type*] [, *title*])

Returns a numeric value that corresponds to the button selected by the user from a message box that displays *string* as a prompt. The optional inputs specify the type of message box and the title for the dialog box window. The valid values for *type* are listed in Chapter 20.

Now()
Now$()
> Returns a variant (Now) or text string (Now$) that contains the current system date and time.

Nper(*rate, payment, present value, future value, due*)
> Returns the number of periods for an annuity with a series of equal payments. The first four inputs specify the periodic interest rate, the payment amount, the present value of the investment, and the future value of the investment; *due* must be 0 if payments are made at the end of each period or 1 if payments are made at the beginning of each period.

NPV(*rate, values*)
> Returns the net present value of an investment with the discount rate specified by *rate* and cash flows stored in the array *values*.

Oct(*number*)
Oct$(*number*)
> Returns a variant (Oct) or text string (Oct$) that contains the octal (base 8) equivalent of the decimal (base 10) number specified as input.

OpenDatabase(*database* [, *exclusive*] [, *read-only*])
> Opens *database* in exclusive and/or read-only mode if the *exclusive* and/or *read-only* inputs are True, and assigns this database as the value for a database object variable.

Partition(*number, starting value, ending value, interval*)
> Returns a string that describes the interval in which *number* falls in a larger range that extends from *starting value* to *ending value*, and is divided into equal intervals of a size specified by *interval*.

Pmt(*rate, periods, present value, future value, due*)
> Returns the periodic payment on an annuity. The first four inputs specify the periodic interest rate, the number of periods, the present value of the investment, and the future value of the investment; *due* must be 0 if payments are made at the end of each period or 1 if payments are made at the beginning of each period.

PPmt(*rate, period, periods, present value, future value, due*)
> Returns the principal payment for one of a series of equal payments. The first five inputs specify the periodic interest rate, the payment period for which you want to calculate the interest, the number of payment periods, the present value of the investment, and the future value of the investment; *due* must be 0 if payments are made at the end of each period or 1 if payments are made at the beginning of each period.

PV(*rate, values*)

Returns the present value of an investment with the discount rate specified by *rate* and cash flows stored in the array *values*.

QBColor(*color code*)

Returns the RGB color code that corresponds to the *color code*.

Rate(*periods, payment, present value, future value, due, guess*)

Returns the periodic interest rate on an annuity. The first four inputs specify the number of periods, the payment amount, the present value of the investment, and the future value of the investment; *due* must be 0 if payments are made at the end of each period or 1 if payments are made at the beginning of each period; and *guess* is the value you guess will be returned.

RGB(*red, green, blue*)

Returns the RGB color code that corresponds to the relative intensities of red, green, and blue, specified as numbers between 0 and 255.

Right(*string, length*)
Right$(*string, length*)

Returns a variant (Right) or text string (Right$) that results from extracting a portion of *string* of the specified length, starting from the right side of *string*.

Rnd(*number*)

Returns a random number between 0 and 1, obtained using a method specified by *number*.

RTrim(*string*)
RTrim$(*string*)

Returns a variant (Rtrim) or text string (Rtrim$) that results from removing trailing spaces (spaces at the end) of *string*.

Second(*date/time*)

Returns an integer between 0 and 59 that represents the seconds in *date/time*.

Seek(*file number*)

Returns the current position of the file pointer in a random or binary file. For a random file, it is the number of the next record read or written; otherwise, it is the character position.

Sgn(*number*)

Returns a number that represents the sign of *number* (1 for positive values, 0 for zero, or –1 for negative values).

Shell(*command* [, *window style*])
> Runs another Windows program, in a window whose style is specified by *window style*, and returns a task ID number for this program.

Sin(*angle*)
> Returns the sine of *angle*.

SLN(*cost*, *salvage*, *lifetime*)
> Returns the depreciation for one period, calculated using the straight-line method, for an asset whose initial cost, salvage value, and depreciable lifetime are specified as input.

Space(*number*)
Space$(*number*)
> Returns a variant (Space) or text string (Space$) that consists of *number* spaces.

Spc(*number*)
> Prints *number* spaces when printing with the Print method or the Print # statement.

Sqr(*number*)
> Returns the square root of *number*.

StDev(*expression*)
StDevP(*expression*)
> Returns the standard deviation of *expression* in the population (StDevP) or population sample (StDev) represented by the source dynaset for a query, form, or report.

Str(*number*)
Str$(*number*)
> Returns a variant (Str) or text string (Str$) equivalent to *number*.

StrComp(*string1*, *string2* [, *compare*])
> Returns the result of using the specified comparison method to compare *string1* and *string2* (–1 if *string1* is less than *string2*, 0 if the two strings are equal, or 1 if *string1* is greater than *string2*).

String(*length*, *character code*)
String$(*length*, *character code*)
> Returns a variant (String) or text string (String$) of the specified length consisting entirely of the character specified by its ANSI code.

String(*length, string*)
String$(*length, string*)
> Returns a variant (String) or text string (String$) of the specified length consisting entirely of the first character of *string*.

Sum(*expression*)
> Returns the sum of *expression* in the source dynaset for a query, form, or report.

Switch(*expression1, value1* [, *expression2, value2...expression7, value7*])
> Returns the value that follows the first *expression* that evaluates to True.

SYD(*cost, salvage, lifetime, period*)
> Returns the depreciation, calculated using the sum-of-years' digits method, for an asset whose initial cost, salvage value, and depreciable lifetime are specified as input, over the period specified by *period*.

Tab(*number*)
> Moves to the tab stop specified by *number* when printing with the Print method or the Print # statement.

Tan(*angle*)
> Returns the tangent of *angle*.

Time( )
Time$( )
> Returns a variant (Time) or text string (Time$) that contains the current system time.

Timer( )
> Returns the number of seconds that have elapsed since midnight.

TimeSerial(*hour, minute, second*)
> Returns the time serial number equivalent to the time described by *hour*, *minute*, and *second*.

TimeValue(*string*)
> Returns a Date/Time value equivalent to *string*.

Trim(*string*)
Trim$(*string*)
> Returns a variant (Trim) or text string (Trim$) that results from removing leading and trailing spaces from *string*.

UBound(*array* [, *dimension*])
> Returns the upper boundary (the largest array subscript) for the array dimension specified by *dimension*, or for the first dimension if *dimension* is not specified.

UCase(*string*)
UCase$(*string*)
> Returns a variant (UCase) or text string (UCase$) that results from converting *string* to all uppercase.

User( )
> Returns the name of the current user in a secured Access system.

Val(*string*)
> Returns a numeric value equivalent to *string*.

Var(*expression*)
VarP(*expression*)
> Returns the variance of *expression* in the population (VarP) or population sample (Var) represented by the source dynaset for a query, form, or report.

VarType(*variant*)
> Returns a number that represents the data type of *variant* (0 for Empty, 1 for Null, 2 for Integer, 3 for Long Integer, 4 for Single, 5 for Double, 6 for Currency, 7 for Date, or 8 for String).

Weekday(*date/time*)
> Returns an integer between 1 and 7 that represents the day of the week in *date/time* (Sunday is day 1).

Year(*date/time*)
> Returns an integer between 100 and 9999 that represents the year in *date/time*.

Properties

This appendix lists the properties of forms and reports, form and report sections, and the controls these documents can contain, together with the permissible values for each property. Only form properties are listed for controls, because the properties these controls have on reports are in most cases a subset of the form properties. Where a property accepts only a finite number of values, these values are listed, and if there is a default value, it is bold-faced. Otherwise, the Values column contains a description of the type or range of allowable entries. For more detailed information on the properties and their values, consult the *Microsoft Access Language Reference* or the on-line help system.

Form Properties

Property	Values
Record Source	A table name, query name, or SQL statement
Caption	A text string
On Current	A macro or function procedure name
On Insert	A macro or function procedure name
On Delete	A macro or function procedure name
Before Update	A macro or function procedure name
After Update	A macro or function procedure name
On Open	A macro or function procedure name
On Close	A macro or function procedure name
On Menu	A macro or function procedure name
Default View	Single Form, **Continuous Forms**, Datasheet
Default Editing	**Allow Edits**, Read Only, Data Entry
Allow Editing	**Available**, Unavailable
Allow Updating	**Default Tables**, All Tables, No Tables
Scroll Bars	Neither, Horizontal Only, Vertical Only, **Both**
Views Allowed	Form, Datasheet, **Both**
Allow Filters	**Yes**, No
Grid X	A number between 1 and 64 (default is 10)

Form Properties (Continued)

Property	Values
Grid Y	A number between 1 and 64 (default is 12)
Layout for Print	Yes, **No**
Auto Resize	**Yes**, No
Record Locks	**No Locks**, All Records, Edited Record
Pop Up	Yes, **No**
Modal	Yes, **No**
Record Selectors	**Yes**, No
Width	A number (default is 5 in.)
Help File	A Windows help file name
Help Context Id	A Long Integer number

Form Sections

Property	Values
Force New Page	**None**, Before Section, After Section, Before & After
New Row or Col	**None**, Before Section, After Section, Before & After
Keep Together	Yes, **No**
Visible	**Yes**, No
Display When	**Always**, Print Only, Screen Only
Can Grow	Yes, **No**
Can Shrink	Yes, **No**
Height	A number (default is 1 inch for the detail section and .25 inches for all other sections)
Special Effect	**Color**, Raised, Sunken
Back Color	A color number (default is 16777215, or white)

Property	Form Header	Page Header	Detail	Page Footer	Form Footer
Force New Page	X		X		X
New Row or Col	X		X		X
Keep Together	X		X		X
Visible	X	X	X	X	X
Display When	X		X		X
Can Grow	X		X		X
Can Shrink	X		X		X
Height	X	X	X	X	X
Special Effect	X	X	X	X	X
Back Color	X	X	X	X	X

Report Properties

Property	Values
Record Source	A table name, query name, or SQL statement
On Open	A macro or function procedure name
On Close	A macro or function procedure name
Grid X	A number between 1 and 64 (default is 10)
Grid Y	A number between 1 and 64 (default is 12)
Layout for Print	**Yes**, No
Page Header	**All Pages**, Not with Rpt Hdr, Not with Rpt Ftr, Not with Rpt Hdr/Ftr
Page Footer	**All Pages**, Not with Rpt Hdr, Not with Rpt Ftr, Not with Rpt Hdr/Ftr
Record Locks	**No Locks**, All Records, Edited Record
Width	A number (default is 5 in.)

Report Sections

Property	Values
Force New Page	**None**, Before Section, After Section, Before & After
New Row or Col	**None**, Before Section, After Section, Before & After
Keep Together	**Yes**, No
Visible	**Yes**, No
On Format	A macro or function procedure name
On Print	A macro or function procedure name
Can Grow	Yes, **No**
Can Shrink	Yes, **No**
Height	A number (default is 1 inch for the detail section and .25 inches for all other sections)
Special Effect	**Color**, Raised, Sunken
Back Color	A color number (default is 16777215, or white)

Property	Report Header	Page Header	Group Header	Detail	Group Footer	Page Footer	Report Footer
Force New Page	X		X	X	X		X
New Row or Col	X		X	X	X		X
Keep Together	X		X	X	X		X
Visible	X	X	X	X	X	X	X
On Format	X	X	X	X	X	X	X
On Print	X	X	X	X	X	X	X
Can Grow	X		X	X	X		X
Can Shrink	X		X	X	X		X
Height	X	X	X	X	X		X
Special Effect	X	X	X	X	X	X	X
Back Color	X	X	X	X	X	X	X

Form Control Properties

Property	Values
Control Name	An object name
Control Source	An expression
Status Bar Text	A text string
Validation Rule	A condition (logical expression)
Validation Text	A text string
Before Update	A macro or function procedure name
After Update	A macro or function procedure name
On Enter	A macro or function procedure name
On Exit	A macro or function procedure name
On Dbl Click	A macro or function procedure name
On Push	A macro or function procedure name
Default Value	An expression
Visible	**Yes** or No
Display When	**Always**, Print Only, Screen Only
Enabled	**Yes** or No
Locked	Yes or **No**
Help Context ID	A number
Format	A format string
Decimal Places	A number
Hide Duplicates	Yes or **No**
Can Grow	Yes or No
Can Shrink	Yes or No
Running Sum	Yes or **No**
Caption	A text string
Picture	A file name

Form Control Properties (Continued)

Property	Values
Row Source Type	**Table/Query**, Value List, Field List
Row Source	A table name, query name, or SQL Select statement
Column Count	A number
Column Heads	Yes or **No**
Column Widths	A list of numbers
Bound Column	A number (default is 1)
List Rows	A number (default is 8)
List Width	**Auto** or a number
Limit to List	Yes or **No**
Transparent	Yes or **No**
Auto Repeat	Yes or **No**
Default	Yes or **No**
Cancel	Yes or **No**
Scaling	**Clip**, Scale, Zoom
OLE Class	An OLE Object class name
Link Child Fields	A list of field names
Link Master Fields	A list of field names
Left	A number
Top	A number
Width	A number
Height	A number
Special Effect	**Color**, Raised, Sunken
Back Color	A color code
Border Style	**Clear**, Normal
Border Color	A color code

Form Control Properties (Continued)

Property	Values
Border Width	**Hairline**, 1pt, 2pt, 3pt, 4pt, 5pt, 6pt
Fore Color	A color code
Font Name	A font name
Font Size	A font size
Font Weight	Extra Light, Light, **Normal**, Medium, Semi-bold, Bold, Extra Bold, Heavy
Font Italic	Yes or **No**
Font Underline	Yes or **No**
Text Align	General, Left, Center, Right

Available Object Properties

Property	Text Box	Option Group	Toggle Button	Radio Button	Check Box	Combo Box	List Box
Control Name	X	X	X	X	X	X	X
Control Source	X	X	X	X	X	X	X
Status Bar Text	X	X	X	X	X	X	X
Validation Rule	X	X	X	X	X	X	X
Validation Text	X	X	X	X	X	X	X
Before Update	X	X	X	X	X	X	X
After Update	X	X	X	X	X	X	X
On Enter	X	X	X	X	X	X	X
On Exit	X	X	X	X	X	X	X
On Dbl Click	X	X	X	X	X	X	X
On Push							
Default Value	X	X	X	X	X	X	X
Visible	X	X	X	X	X	X	X
Display When	X	X	X	X	X	X	X
Enabled	X	X	X	X	X	X	X
Locked	X	X	X	X	X	X	X
Help Context ID	X	X	X	X	X	X	X
Format	X						
Scroll Bars	X						
Decimal Places	X						
Hide Duplicates	X						
Can Grow	X						
Can Shrink	X						
Running Sum	X						

Property	Command Button	Bound Object	Unbound Object	Subform	Label	Line	Rectangle	Page Break
Control Name	X	X	X	X	X	X	X	X
Control Source	X	X		X				
Status Bar Text	X	X		X				
Validation Rule								
Validation Text								
Before Update								
After Update								
On Enter	X	X		X				
On Exit	X	X		X				
On Dbl Click	X	X						
On Push	X							
Default Value								
Visible	X	X	X	X	X	X	X	
Display When	X	X	X	X	X	X	X	
Enabled	X	X	X	X				
Locked		X		X				
Help Context ID	X	X						
Format								
Scroll Bars								
Decimal Places								
Hide Duplicates								
Can Grow				X				
Can Shrink				X				
Running Sum								

Available Object Properties (Continued)

Property	Text Box	Option Group	Toggle Button	Radio Button	Check Box	Combo Box	List Box
Caption			X				
Picture			X				
Row Source Type						X	X
Row Source						X	X
Column Count						X	X
Column Heads						X	X
Column Widths						X	X
Bound Column						X	X
List Rows						X	X
List Width						X	
Limit to List						X	
Transparent							
Auto Repeat							
Default							
Cancel							
Scaling							
OLE Class							
Link Child Fields							
Link Master Fields							
Left	X	X	X	X	X	X	X
Top	X	X	X	X	X	X	X
Width		X	X	X	X	X	X
Height		X	X	X	X	X	X
cial Effect		X	X		X	X	X

Property	Command Button	Bound Object	Unbound Object	Subform	Label	Line	Rectangle	Page Break
Caption	X				X			
Picture	X							
Row Source Type			X					
Row Source			X					
Column Count			X					
Column Heads			X					
Column Widths								
Bound Column								
List Rows								
List Width								
Limit to List								
Transparent	X							
Auto Repeat	X							
Default	X							
Cancel	X							
Scaling		X	X					
OLE Class			X					
Link Child Fields			X	X				
Link Master Fields			X	X				
Left	X	X	X	X	X	X	X	X
Top	X	X	X	X	X	X	X	X
Width	X	X	X	X	X	X	X	
Height	X	X	X	X	X	X	X	
Special Effect	X		X		X		X	

Available Object Properties (Continued)

Property	Text Box	Option Group	Toggle Button	Radio Button	Check Box	Combo Box	List Box
Back Style			X				
Back Color		X	X				X
Border Style		X	X				X
Border Color		X	X				X
Border Width		X	X				X
Fore Color		X		X			X
Font Name		X		X			X
Font Size		X		X			X
Font Weight		X		X			X
Font Italic		X		X			X
Font Underline		X		X			X
Text Align		X					X
Line Slant							

Default Object Properties

Property	Text Box	Option Group	Toggle Button	Radio Button	Check Box	Combo Box	List Box
Visible	X	X	X	X	X	X	X
Display When	X	X	X	X	X	X	X
Scroll Bars	X						
Can Grow	X						
Can Shrink	X						
Help Context Id	X	X	X	X	X	X	X
Auto Label	X	X	X	X	X	X	X

Property	Command Button	Bound Object	Unbound Object	Subform	Label	Line	Rectangle	Page Break
Back Style			X		X		X	
Back Color	X		X		X		X	
Border Style			X	X	X	X	X	
Border Color			X		X	X	X	
Border Width			X		X	X	X	
Fore Color	X	X			X			
Font Name	X	X			X			
Font Size	X	X			X			
Font Weight	X	X			X			
Font Italic	X	X			X			
Font Underline	X	X			X			
Text Align					X			
Line Slant						X	X	

Property	Command Button	Bound Object	Unbound Object	Subform	Label	Line	Rectangle
Visible	X	X	X	X	X	X	X
Display When	X	X	X	X	X	X	X
Scroll Bars							
Can Grow				X			
Can Shrink				X			
Help Context Id	X	X					
Auto Label	X	X		X			

Default Object Properties (Continued)

Property	Text Box	Option Group	Toggle Button	Radio Button	Check Box	Combo Box	List Box
Add Colon	X	X	X	X	X	X	X
Label X	X	X	X	X	X	X	X
Label Y	X	X	X	X	X	X	X
Label Align	X	X	X	X	X	X	X
List Rows						X	
List Width						X	
Width	X	X	X	X	X	X	X
Height	X	X	X	X	X	X	X
Special Effect	X	X		X	X	X	X
Back Style		X					
Back Color	X	X				X	X
Border Style	X	X				X	
Border Color	X	X				X	
Border Width	X	X				X	
Fore Color	X		X			X	X
Font Name	X		X			X	X
Font Size	X		X			X	X
Font Weight	X		X			X	X
Font Italic	X		X			X	X
Font Underline	X		X			X	X
Text Align	X					X	

Property	Command Button	Bound Object	Unbound Object	Subform	Label	Line	Rectangle
Add Colon	X	X		X			
Label X	X	X		X			
Label Y	X	X		X			
Label Align	X	X		X			
List Rows							
List Width							
Width	X	X	X	X	X	X	X
Height	X	X	X	X	X	X	X
Special Effect		X	X		X		X
Back Style			X		X		X
Back Color			X		X		X
Border Style		X	X	X	X	X	X
Border Color		X	X		X	X	X
Border Width		X	X		X	X	X
Fore Color	X				X		
Font Name	X				X		
Font Size	X				X		
Font Weight	X				X		
Font Italic	X				X		
Font Underline	X				X		
Text Align					X		

Macro Actions

This appendix lists the Access macro actions, together with a brief summary of their purposes and the action arguments they accept. When an argument accepts only a finite number of values, these values are listed, and if there is a default value, it is boldfaced. Otherwise, the Values column contains a description of the type or range of allowable entries. For more detailed information on the actions and their arguments, consult the *Microsoft Access Language Reference* or the on-line help system.

Action	Description	Action Arguments	Values
AddMenu	Adds an option and an associated pull-down menu to a custom menu bar	Menu Name	A text string
		Menu Macro Name	A macro name
		Status Bar Text	A text string
ApplyFilter	Applies a filter, query, or explicit condition to the data source for a form or report	Filter Name	A query name
		Where Condition	A condition (logical expression)
Beep	Sounds a beep		
CancelEvent	Cancels the event that triggered the current macro		
Close	Closes a window	Object Type	Table, Query, Form, Report, Macro, Module
		Object Name	An object name
CopyObject	Copies the selected object within the current database or to another database	Destination Database	Path name of .MDB file
		New Name	An object name
DoMenuItem	Executes a standard Access menu bar command	Menu Bar	**Form**, Database, Filter, Form Design, Init, Module, Query, Report, Macro, Table, Form Datasheet, Table Datasheet, Query Datasheet
		Menu Name	A pull-down menu in the selected menu bar
		Command	A command in the selected pull-down menu
		Subcommand	A subcommand invoked by the selected command

Action	Description	Action Arguments	Values
Echo	Enables or suppresses screen updates during macro execution	Echo On	**Yes**, No
		Status Bar Text	A text string
FindNext	Finds the next record that matches the search criteria used in the previous Find operation		
FindRecord	Carries out a search equivalent to one conducted using the Find dialog box	Find What	A value
		Where	A Part of Field, **Match Whole Field**, Start of Field
		Match Case	Yes, **No**
		Direction	Up, **Down**
		Search As Formatted	Yes, **No**
		Search In	**Current Field**, All Fields
		Find First	**Yes**, No
GoToControl	Moves the focus to a specific control in a form, datasheet, or report	Control Name	A control name
GoToPage	Moves the focus to the first control on a specific page in a form and specifies the upper-left corner of the visible portion of the form	Page Number	A form page number
		Right	A numeric value
		Down	A numeric value
GoToRecord	Adds a new record or moves the focus to a specific record in a dynaset	Object Type	Table, Query, Form
		Object Name	An object name
		Record	Previous, **Next**, First, Last, Go To, New
		Offset	An integer value
Hourglass	Displays the mouse pointer as an hourglass during macro execution	Hourglass On	**Yes**, No
Maximize	Maximizes the active window		
Minimize	Minimizes the active window		

Macro Actions

925

Action	Description	Action Arguments	Values
MoveSize	Moves and/or resizes the active window	Right	A numeric value
		Down	A numeric value
		Width	A numeric value
		Height	A numeric value
MsgBox	Displays a message box (alert box)	Message	A text string
		Beep	**Yes**, No
		Type	**None**, Critical, Warning?, Warning!, Information
		Title	A text string
OpenForm	Opens a form in Form, Design, Print Preview, or Datasheet view	Form Name	A form name
		View	**Form**, Design, Print Preview, Datasheet
		Filter Name	A query name
		Where Condition	A condition (logical expression)
		Data Mode	Add, **Edit**, Read Only
		Window Mode	**Normal**, Hidden, Icon, Dialog
OpenQuery	Opens a query in Datasheet, Design, or Print Preview view	Query Name	A query name
		View	**Datasheet**, Design, Print Preview
		Data Mode	Add, **Edit**, Read Only
OpenReport	Opens a report in Print, Design, or Print Preview view	Report Name	A report name
		View	Print, Design, **Print Preview**
		Filter Name	A query name
		Where Condition	A condition (logical expression)
OpenTable	Opens a table in Datasheet, Design, or Print Preview view	Table Name	A table name
		View	**Datasheet**, Design, Print Preview
		Data Mode	Add, **Edit**, Read Only

Action	Description	Action Arguments	Values
Print	Prints the active datasheet, form, or report	Print Range	**All**, Selection, Pages
		Page From	A page number
		Page To	A page number
		Print Quality	**High**, Medium, Low, Draft
		Copies	A numeric value
		Collate Copies	**Yes**, No
Quit	Exits from Access	Options	Prompt, **Save All**, Exit
Rename	Renames the selected database object	New Name	An object name
RepaintObject	Completes pending screen updates to an object to display all changes to its value	Object Type	Table, Query, Form, Report, Macro, Module)
		Object Name	An object name
Requery	Requeries the data source for an object, query, datasheet, or form	Control Name	A control name
Restore	Restores a maximized or minimized window to its previous size		
RunApp	Runs another Windows application	Command Line	Command line used to launch the external program
RunCode	Runs an Access Basic function procedure	Function Name	A function name
RunMacro	Runs another macro	Macro Name	A macro name
		Repeat Count	A numeric value
		Repeat Expression	A numeric value
RunSQL	Runs an SQL Insert, Delete, Select, or Update statement	SQL Statement	An SQL statement
SelectObject	Selects a database object	Object Type	Table, Query, **Form**, Report, Macro, Module
		Object Name	An object name
		In Database Window	Yes, **No**

Action	Description	Action Arguments	Values
SendKeys	Sends character codes to the active window to simulate pressing keys on the keyboard	Keystrokes Wait	A text string and/or key symbols Yes, **No**
SetValue	Assigns a new value to a field, control, or property in a form, datasheet, or report	Item Expression	A field, control, or property name Any acceptable value for Item
SetWarnings	Enables or suppresses system warning messages and alert boxes	Warnings On	Yes, **No**
ShowAllRecords	Cancels any active filter and returns to processing all the records in a dynaset		
StopAllMacros	Cancels all running macros		
StopMacro	Cancels the current macro		
TransferDatabase	Imports, exports, or attaches a table or other database object	Transfer Type Database Type Database Name Object Type Source Destination Structure Only	**Import**, Export, Attach **Microsoft Access**, Paradox 3.*x*, FoxPro 2.0, dBASE III, dBASE IV, Btrieve, <SQL database> Path name of .MDB file **Table**, Query, Form, Report, Macro, Module A table, object, or file name A table, object, or file name Yes, **No**
Transfer-Spreadsheet	Imports or exports spreadsheet data	Transfer Type Spreadsheet Type Table Name File Name	**Import**, Export **Microsoft Excel**, Lotus (WKS), Lotus (WK1), Lotus (WK3) A table name A spreadsheet file name

Action	Description	Action Arguments	Values
		Has Field Names	Yes, **No**
		Range	A cell range
TransferText	Imports or exports a text file	Transfer Type	**Import Delimited**, Import Fixed Width, Export Delimited, Export Fixed Width
		Specification Name	An import/export specification name
		Table Name	A table name
		File Name	A file name
		Has Field Names	Yes, **No**

Access Icons

Object Icons

Table	
Attached table	
Select query	
Action query	
Form	
Report	
Macro	
Module	

Tool Bar Command Buttons

Design view	
Datasheet view	
Form view	
New query	
New form	
New report	
Print preview	
Undo	
Help	
Find	
Edit Filter/Sort	
Apply Filter/Sort	
Show All Records	
Run	

Tool Bar Command Buttons (Continued)

Totals	Σ
Properties	
Field list	
Color palette	
Sorting and grouping	
Bold	**B**
Italic	*I*
Underline	U
Left alignment	
Center	
Right alignment	
General alignment	
Macro names	
Conditions	
Single step	
Procedure step	
Next procedure	
Previous procedure	
Reinitialize	
Breakpoint	
Primary key	

Tool Box Object Buttons

Label   A

Text box   ab

Option group

Toggle button

Radio button
(option button)

Check box

Combo box

List box

Graph

Subform/Subreport

Unbound OLE Object

Bound OLE Object

Line

Box

Page Break

Command Button

Using the Database Analyzer

As noted at various points in this book, Access offers no built-in mechanisms for documenting the database objects you create—you cannot print a description of a table, query, form, report, or macro (although you can use the Clipboard to capture an image of a query, form, or report in Design View). To partially overcome this limitation, Microsoft provides a tool called the *Database Analyzer*. Like the Wizards, the Analyzer is actually an Access database application. It is stored in a file called ANALYZER.MDA, which is copied into your Access program directory when you install Access (the .MDA extension ensures that the file does not appear in the list of databases displayed in the Open Database dialog box). The Analyzer reads database objects and stores selected information about these objects in ordinary tables in the database file of your choice. You can then design forms or reports based on these tables to document the objects. This appendix outlines how to install and use the version of the Analyzer shipped with the first release of Access.

For the most up-to-date information on the Analyzer, check the Notepad file called PSSKB.TXT, which is also copied into the Access program directory during installation. You can open this file in the Notepad by clicking on the program item labeled *Microsoft Access Q&A* in the Microsoft Access program group in the Program Manager.

Before you can use the Analyzer, you must identify it as an Access *library* by making an entry in the [Libraries] section of the MSACCESS.INI file, which is located in your Windows program directory. Using any text editor (such as Notepad), add the following line anywhere in the [Libraries] section:

```
analyzer.mda=
```

If you make this modification while Access is running, note that you must exit and restart Access before you can use the Analyzer, because Access only reads the MSACCESS.INI file when you first load the program.

To start the Analyzer, you must execute a function procedure called StartAnalyzer( ) (located in ANALYZER.MDA), and the easiest way to do this is to define a macro, perhaps called Analyzer, that consists of a single RunCode action. This action takes one argument—Function Name, which specifies the function procedure you want to run. In the Analyzer macro you create, enter StartAnalyzer( ) for the Function Name argument. You must include the Analyzer macro in every database in which you might want to use the Analyzer; however, once you have defined this macro, you can copy it to any other database either by using the Clipboard or by using the Export option to export it from one database to another.

Figure G.1 illustrates the initial screen displayed by the Analyzer to enable you to choose the objects you want to analyze. In a given session, you can analyze as many objects as you wish, of one or more types. You choose the object type by selecting one of the six object buttons on the left side of the Analyzer window, which mirror the analogous toggle buttons in the Database window. When you select one of the object buttons, Access displays the names of all objects of the corresponding type in the Items Available list on the left side of the dialog box. You can scroll through this list using keyboard or mouse commands, and you can select an object for processing by double-clicking on it. You can also use the four buttons in the center of the dialog box to move all items or just the selected item between the Items Available and Items Selected lists. Objects in the Items Selected list are displayed in the order in which you selected them. Figure G.2 illustrates the Database Analyzer dialog box with the list of tables displayed and the main ACE system tables selected for analysis.

Figure G.1

The Database Analyzer dialog box

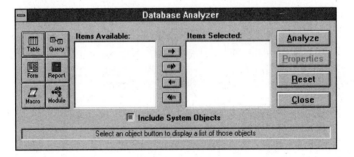

Figure G.2

Choosing the tables you want to analyze

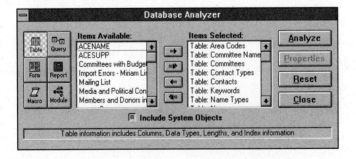

Unfortunately, you cannot widen the Items Available list, and if you use long object names, it may be impossible to distinguish between similarly named objects. Note, however, that the Analyzer displays the list of objects in the same order as they appear in the Database window, in alphabetical order. You may want to move the Database Analyzer dialog box to the right side of the screen and select the same object type in the Database window (which you can widen if necessary), so that you can compare the two lists of object names. (Although the Database Analyzer window looks like a modal pop-up dialog box, Access in fact allows you to switch windows and operate the menu system while it is open.)

The Analyzer allows you to process as many objects as you wish (of one or more types) in a given session, and you can switch to a different object type at any point by clicking on one of the six object buttons at the left side of the dialog box. As you can see in Figure G.2, the Items Selected list identifies each object by type, so objects of different types with the same names (such as a form and report both called Committee Memberships) should not present problems. To clear both lists and start from scratch, you can select the Reset command button. You can analyze any database objects except action queries (the only kind of queries the Analyzer can process are select queries). If you select one or more action queries, the Analyzer bypasses these objects and displays the alert box shown in Figure G.3 when it has finished processing all the other objects you selected.

Figure G.3
The alert box
displayed if you try
to analyze action
queries

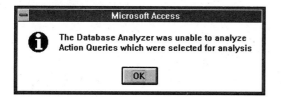

Once you have selected the objects you want to analyze, you initiate the process by selecting the Analyze command button on the right side of the dialog box. As noted earlier, The Analyzer reads database objects and stores selected information about these objects in a set of ordinary tables. You can place these tables in any existing database—including the one you are analyzing—and when you begin an analysis, Access displays a dialog box that resembles the Open File dialog box to enable you to choose the output database. In most cases, you will want to create a separate database for the Analyzer output rather than clutter up your original database with extra tables that might confuse other people who work with the application. You must create this database in advance; the Analyzer cannot create it on the fly.

As it processes the selected objects, the Analyzer displays a simple—and, unlike the percentage indicator to which you are accustomed, static—message at the bottom of the Analyzer dialog box. When it is finished, the Analyzer displays an alert box with the message "Process Completed." When you select OK from this alert box, the Database Analyzer dialog box remains open so that you can process additional objects. You can close the dialog box and end an Analyzer session by clicking on the Close command button or by using any other standard method for closing a dialog box.

Table G.1 lists the tables created by the Analyzer, including the names of the fields, most of which should be self-explanatory. If you compare the field name lists with the various object property sheets, you will see that the Analyzer tables include all of the properties that describe the behavior of the form and report controls, but not the properties that describe their visual attributes. (One way to document these properties is to capture an image of a form or report in Design view on the Clipboard and print it using Paintbrush or Write.) The fields in the two larger tables—@FormControls and @ReportControls—are arranged in alphabetical order, but you can modify the structures of these tables if you prefer an order that more closely parallels the order of the items in the object property sheets. The table names all begin with @ to distinguish them from other tables you create. Note that the Analyzer uses two tables to store information about queries, forms, reports, and modules—one for the document as a whole and another for the detailed information about objects within the document. If you want to see *all* of the information about a document in one place, you can define a query based on these two tables, which have a one-to-many relationship.

The Analyzer allows you to choose which properties you want to document for forms and reports (but not for tables, queries, macros, or modules). To choose properties, you use the Properties command button on the right side of the Database Analyzer dialog box, which is enabled only when you display forms or reports in the Items Available list. Choosing this button invokes a dialog box like the one shown in Figure G.4. As you can see in this figure, the Analyzer by default selects all available properties, but you can use the buttons between the Available Properties and Selected Properties lists to add or remove properties from the Selected Properties list. As in the Database Analyzer dialog box, you can also remove an item from either list and transfer it to the other by double-clicking on it.

Figure G.4

Selecting the properties to include in the output tables

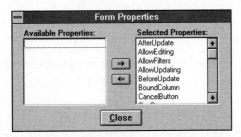

Table G.1   **The Tables Created by the Analyzer**

Table	Contents	
@TableDetails	Table structure specifications (one record per field)	TableName, Name, Type, Length, IndexName
@QueryDetails	Source tables, columns, data types, and lengths (one record per column)	QueryName, Name, Type, Length, SourceTable
@QuerySQL	SQL statements used to execute queries (one record per query)	QueryName, SQLStatement
@FormControls	Form controls and control properties (one record per control)	FormName, AfterUpdate, AllowEditing, AllowFilters, AllowUpdating, BeforeUpdate, BoundColumn, CancelButton, CanGrow, CanShrink, Caption, ControlName, ControlSource, DecimalPlaces, Default, DefaultValue, Enabled, ForceNewPage, Format, GroupFooter, GroupHeader, HideDuplicates, KeepTogether, LimitToList, LinkMasterFields, Locked, OnDelete, OnEnter, OnExit, OnInsert, OnPush, OptionValue, RowSource, RowSourceType, StatusBarText, Transparent, ValidationRule, ValidationText, Visible
@FormProperties	Overall form properties (one record per form)	FormName, Caption, LinkChildFields, LinkMasterFields, Modal, OnOpen, OnClose, OnMenu, OnPrint, PopUp, RecordSelectors, RecordSource, ScrollBars
@ReportControls	Report controls and control properties (one record per control)	FormName, AfterUpdate, AllowEditing, AllowFilters, AllowUpdating, BeforeUpdate, BoundColumn, CancelButton, CanGrow, CanShrink, Caption, ControlName, ControlSource, DecimalPlaces, Default, DefaultValue, Enabled, ForceNewPage, Format, GroupFooter, GroupHeader, HideDuplicates, KeepTogether, LimitToList, LinkMasterFields, Locked, OnDelete, OnEnter, OnExit, OnInsert, OnPush, OptionValue, RowSource, RowSourceType, StatusBarText, Transparent, ValidationRule, ValidationText, Visible
@ReportProperties	Overall report properties (one record per report)	FormName, Caption, LinkChildFields, LinkMasterFields, Modal, OnOpen, OnClose, OnMenu, OnPrint, PopUp, RecordSelectors, RecordSource, ScrollBars

Table G.1	The Tables Created by the Analyzer (Continued)	
Table	**Contents**	
@MacroDetails	Macro actions and arguments (one record per action)	MacroName, MacroGroup, Action, Condition, Argument1, Argument2, Argument3, Argument4, Argument5, Argument6, Argument7, Argument8, Argument9, Argument10
@ModuleProcedures	Procedure names and parameters (one record per procedure)	ModuleName, ProcedureName, Params
@ModuleVariables	Explicitly declared variables	ProcedureName, VariableName, Type

Remember that all the Analyzer does is store selected items of information about one or more database objects in a set of ordinary Access tables. It is up to you to determine how to use these tables. As a very simple example, Figure G.5 illustrates the first page of a report that documents the structures of the main ACE system tables, which was created by using the groups/totals ReportWizard to construct a report based on the @TableDetails table. As you can see, only the first field in a multifield primary key is identified by the Analyzer (the primary key for the Contacts table includes the Contact Type and Date fields, as well as the ID Code field).

Note also that the fields in this report are listed in alphabetical order, not in the order they appear in the table structures. Although the order of the records in the @TableDetails table parallels the order of the fields in the table structures, sorting the report by table name alone results in an unpredictable order within each group. One general solution to this problem is to modify the structure of the table and allow Access to define a primary key. As you may recall, Access does this by adding a Counter field named Id, and entering sequential numbers in this field. To print the report in Figure G.5 with the fields listed in the same order as they are in the table structure, you can sort first by table name and then by the Counter field. The same technique is also applicable to the other tables produced by the Analyzer.

Figure G.5

A report based on the @TableDetails table

ACE System Tables
01-Mar-93

Name	Type	Length	IndexName
Area Codes			
Area Code	Text	3	PrimaryKey
Description	Text	25	
Total Length:		28	
Committee Names			
Committee	Text	10	PrimaryKey
Description	Text	40	
Total Length:		50	
Committees			
Committee	Text	10	Index1
ID Code	Text	10	Index1
Joined	Date/Time	8	
Notes	Memo	0	
Officer	Text	12	
Quit	Date/Time	8	
Total Length:		48	
Contact Types			
Contact Type	Text	2	PrimaryKey
Description	Text	25	
Total Length:		27	
Contacts			
Amount	Double	8	
Contact Type	Text	2	Index1
Date	Date/Time	8	Index1
Description	Text	25	
Follow-up Date	Date/Time	8	
ID Code	Text	10	PrimaryKey
Total Length:		61	
Keywords			
Description	Text	30	
Keyword	Text	10	PrimaryKey
Total Length:		40	
Name Types			
Description	Text	15	
Name Type	Text	2	PrimaryKey
Total Length:		17	

The Files on the Disk

The disk packaged with this book contains a database called ACE.MDB and several auxiliary files (provided to enable you to try importing and attaching external files). The ACE database includes all of the tables, queries, forms, reports, macros, and modules used in the case study application described in the book, except those created in the hands-on exercises. To begin working with the ACE database, you can simply copy all the files on the disk into any subdirectory on your hard disk.

You are strongly urged to follow along with the hands-on exercises (most of which focus on the Committees table, which you create in Chapter 3) as you read this book. However, the disk does include a copy of the Committees table. To work with this copy rather than create the Committees table from scratch, use the Rename option on the File menu to rename the table called Committee Memberships to Committees. The forms, reports, and macros created in the hands-on exercises are *not* included on the disk.

The original copy of the ACE database, which was used to prepare the illustrations, has contacts and transactions entered in 1991 and 1992. To run some of the queries (and reports based on these queries) which test for contact and transaction dates in the current year, you will have to update the dates stored in the main tables. You can do this by running a macro called Update Dates. If you have not yet used Access macros, note that you can run this macro by displaying the list of macros in the Database window and double-clicking on the name Update Dates. The macro will display a dialog box that asks you how many years to add to the current dates; in 1993, enter **1**. To begin updating the ACE tables, click on the Update command button (you can cancel the operation by pressing Esc or by clicking on Cancel instead). The macro will display several additional dialog boxes asking permission to proceed with the various updates, and you should select OK each time.

Please note that the ACE sample database is intended primarily to enable you to experiment with a variety of Access database objects, some of which are rather complex, without creating all of them from scratch. Feel free to modify and adapt these objects for use in your own applications, but be aware that while the ACE database contains examples of many typical Access objects, it is by no means a complete functioning application. Even if your own application is a donor-tracking system very similar to the ACE system, you will not be able to use the ACE system as is to manage your own data.

NOTE.   *The sample database does not include any tables or forms with OLE objects created by word processors or spreadsheets (which you may or may not own). If you do not have Microsoft Word, you will have to modify the Maintenance Updates form described in Chapter 20, which attempts to open Word to print mailmerge letters, and which will yield an error message if Word is not available when you open the form. If Word is installed on a drive other than C or in a directory with a name other than WINWORD, you will have to modify* *the OpenWord and PrintLetter functions in the ACE Procedures module before you can use this form.*

The following table lists all of the objects in ACE.MDB, grouped by type and arranged alphabetically within each type (exactly as they appear in the Database window), together with the chapter in which they are first mentioned and a brief description of their purpose.

Object Name	Chapter	Description
Tables		
Area Codes	3	Lookup table of valid area codes
Committee Memberships	H	Committee membership data
Committee Names	3	Lookup table of committee names
Contact Types	3	Lookup table of valid contact type codes
Contacts	3	Contact data
Keywords	3	Lookup table of valid keywords
Mailing List	14	Mailing list table similar to Names table
Name Types	3	Lookup table of valid name type codes
Names	3	Name and address data
States	3	Lookup table of valid state abbreviations
Total Credits	13	Summarized credit transactions for one year
Total Debits	13	Summarized debit transactions for one year
Transaction Types	3	Lookup table of valid transaction type codes
Transactions	3	Transaction data

Object Name	Chapter	Description
Queries		
Annual Transaction Summary	11	Selects current year transactions for subreport in Annual Summary Letter report
Append Members to Mailing List	13	Make table query that copies Names table records to Mailing List table
Append Total Credits	13	Append query that adds summarized credit transactions back to Transactions table
Append Total Debits	13	Append query that adds summarized debit transactions back to Transactions table
Committee Members and Chairpersons	9	Self-join that selects committee member names, committee names, and chairpersons
Committees with Committee Names	11	Complete committee membership data with committee names
Contacts 1	8	Contact data with full name and contact type description
Contacts with Names	8	Complete contact data with full name and contact type description
Copy Media and Political Contacts	13	Make table query that copies Names table records with name types MC and PC
Delete Current Year Transactions	13	Delete query that purges transactions entered in current year
Delete Obsolete Names	13	Delete query that purges names with no contact in two years unless Keep Forever is Yes
Donations	7	Selects donations from Transactions table

Object Name	Chapter	Description
Donors and Members Pie Chart	15	Selects only donors and members for Donors and Members by State graph form
Extract Credits	13	Make table query that copies summarized credit transactions
Extract Debits	13	Make table query that copies summarized debit transactions
Name Types by State	9	Crosstab of counts by name type and state
Names and Donations by Date	11	Parameter query that selects donation transactions by date
Names and Transactions	8	Outer join that selects all names, together with transactions, if any
Names and Transactions by Date	18	Selects name and address fields for Envelopes (Single) report
Names and YTD Totals	9	Calculates transaction statistics and displays full name
Names Table Overall Statistics	9	Calculates statistics based on entire Names table
Names Table Statistics by State	9	Calculates Names table statistics grouped by state
Names Table Statistics by State and City	9	Calculates Names table statistics grouped by state and city
Names, Addresses, and YTD Totals	11	Calculates transaction statistics and includes name and address fields
Non-Prospects	11	Selects all but prospects from Names table
Prospects	6	Selects only prospects from Names table
State/Name Type Crosstab	11	Crosstab of counts by name type and state with name type description and state name

Object Name	Chapter	Description
Transaction Summary Statistics	11	Calculates statistics by transaction type and state
Transactions 1	8	Outer join that selects all names, together with transactions, if any
Transactions by Type	15	Transaction counts and totals by type for Transactions by Type Graphs form
Transactions by Type and Date	15	Transaction counts and totals by type for Transactions Graphed by Type form
Transactions with Name and Description	8	Transaction data with full name and transaction type description
Update Contacts Table Dates	H	Update query that changes year in Date field in Contacts table
Update Names Table Dates	H	Update query that changes year in Last Contact and Last Credit fields in Names table
Update Transaction Amount	9	Update query that calculates Amount field in transactions after 1/1/93
Update Transaction Totals	9	Update query that posts transaction amount to Names table total fields
Update Transactions Table Dates	H	Update query that changes year in Date field in Transactions table

Forms

Object Name	Chapter	Description
Brief Reference List Options	19	Dialog box for collecting open-ended selection criteria for Brief Reference List report
Code Options	19	Dialog box for choosing which code lookup table to edit
Committee Memberships Subform	18	Subform for Names Five-Page Form

Object Name	Chapter	Description
Committees (Boxed)	6	Illustrates Boxed form look
Committees (Chiseled)	6	Illustrates Chiseled form look
Committees (Embossed)	6	Illustrates Embossed form look
Committees (Shadowed)	6	Illustrates Shadowed form look
Committees Single-Column Form	6	Illustrates Single-column FormWizard
Committees Tabular Form	6	Illustrates Tabular FormWizard
Complex Report Menu	19	Complex report menu for ACE system
Contacts Subform	8	Datasheet-style subform for Contacts table
Contacts Subform 2	12	Form-style subform for Contacts table
Contacts with Names	8	Form for entering contact data while viewing name and contact description
Data Entry Menu	19	Data entry menu for ACE system
Donors and Members by State	15	Pie chart by state
Events	18	Illustrates form events
Label Options	19	Dialog box for collecting open-ended selection criteria for mailing labels
Mailings Menu	19	Mailings menu for Ace System
Main Menu	19	Main menu for ACE system

Object Name	Chapter	Description
Maintenance Updates	20	Allows you to delete records from all related tables, change ID Code in all related tables, and print letters
Names	12	Two-page form with list box and combo box controls
Names and Committees	18	Main/subform form with command buttons
Names and Contacts	8	Main/subform form for Names and Contacts table
Names Five-Page Form	18	Five-page form with name data, contacts, transactions, and committee memberships
Names Five-Page Form with Menu	19	Five-page form with custom menu bar
Names Subform	12	Subform for Transactions with Names form
Names with Command Buttons	18	Names form with command buttons to display contacts and transactions
Names, Contacts, and Transactions	12	Name and address data with contacts and transactions subforms
Option Controls	12	Illustrates check boxes, option buttons, toggle buttons, and option groups
Prospect Input Form	12	Form that emulates a paper input form
Prospects	6	Form for displaying and entering prospects
Prospects (All Sections)	6	Prospects form with all five sections
Prospects Initial Design	6	Initial version of Prospects form created by FormWizard
Raised and Sunken	10	Illustrates Raised and Sunken effects

Object Name	Chapter	Description
Report Menu	19	Report menu for ACE system
Signatures	15	Illustrates Clip, Scale, and Zoom options for Scaling property
Startup Menu Screen	19	Main menu form with attached custom menu bar
Telephone List Options	19	Dialog box for choosing names printed on Brief Reference List report
Thank You Letter Options	20	Collects range of donation dates to acknowledge
Transactions by Type Graphs	15	Bar graph of transaction totals and counts by type
Transactions Graphed by Type	15	Form with linked graph
Transactions Subform	18	Subform for Names Five-Page Form
Transactions with Names	12	Transaction entry form with name and address displayed in subform
Transactions with Names 2	18	Transaction entry form with macros called from form events
Update Dates	H	Collects number of years to add to all dates

Reports

Alphabetical Telephone List	7	Name and telephone list grouped by first letter of ID Code
Annual Summary Letter	11	Personalized letter with transaction subreport
Annual Transaction Summary	11	Subreport for Annual Summary Letter report
Area Codes	11	Subreport for Code Reference List

Object Name	Chapter	Description
Brief Reference List	19	Alphabetical name and telephone list
Code Reference List	11	Composite report that prints all code lookup tables
Committee Names	11	Subreport for Code Reference List
Committees (Ledger)	7	Illustrates Ledger report look
Committees (Presentation)	7	Illustrates Presentation report look
Committees Single-Column	7	Illustrates Single-Column ReportWizard
Committees Subreport	11	Single-column subreport for Names and Committee Memberships report
Complete Reference List 2	19	Names, contacts, and transactions (called from Report Menu form)
Contact Types	11	Subreport for Code Reference List
Contacts Subform	11	Subreport for Names and Contacts Side-by-Side report
Contacts Subreport 2	11	Subreport for Member Reference List report
Donations by Amount	7	Groups/totals report based on Transactions table with subtotals by donation amount ($50 ranges)
Donations by Month	7	Groups/totals report based on Transactions table with subtotals by month
Donations by Month 2	11	Groups/totals report based on Transactions table with subtotals for two-month intervals
Envelopes	11	Envelopes for donation thank you letters
Envelopes (Single)	18	Hand-fed envelopes

Object Name	Chapter	Description
Envelopes for Annual Summary Letter	11	Envelopes with same data source as Annual Summary Letter
Keywords	11	Subreport for Code Reference List
Mailing Labels with Counts	11	One-across mailing labels with zip code bundling labels
Member Reference List	11	Name and address list with contact and transaction subreports
Name and Address Labels	7	Two-across mailing labels in zip code order based on Names table
Name and Address List	7	Single-column name and address list printed three across in landscape mode
Name Types	11	Subreport for Code Reference List
Name Types by State	11	Subreport for Overall Summary Statistics report
Names and Committee Memberships	11	Complete Names table data with committee memberships in single-column subreport
Names and Contacts	6	Report created from Names and Contacts form
Names and Contacts Side-by-Side	11	Report with contacts subreport next to name and address
Names and Contacts Side-by-Side 2	18	Report with contacts subreport hidden if sum of Amount is zero
Names by State and City	7	Groups/totals report based on Names table with debit and credit totals by state and city
Names by State and City 2	11	Groups/totals report based on Names table with debit and credit totals by state and city, no city group header

Object Name	Chapter	Description
Names by State and City 3	11	Groups/totals report based on Names table with debit and credit totals by state and city with group sums, averages, and counts
Overall Summary Statistics	11	Composite report with transaction statistics by name type/state and transaction type/state
Personalized Thank You Letters	11	Donation thank you letter personalized based on donation amount
Shipping Labels	7	Mailing label report based on Names table
States	11	Subreport for Code Reference List
Thank You Letters	11	Simple donation thank you letter
Thank You Letters with Logo	15	Thank you letter with ACE logo
Transaction Running Sum	11	Transaction report grouped by ID Code with running sums
Transaction Summary Statistics	11	Subreport for Overall Summary Statistics report
Transaction Types	11	Subreport for Code Reference List
Transactions by Month	8	Groups/totals report with name and transaction type description with subtotals by month
Transactions by Name	8	Groups/totals report grouped by ID Code with name and address, followed by transactions
Transactions Subreport 2	11	Subreport for Member Reference List report

Object Name	Chapter	Description
Macros		
Analyzer	G	Starts up Database Analyzer
Edit Menu	19	Defines Edit menu in Names Five-Page Form with Menu
Events	18	Macros called from Events form
Export to Btrieve	14	Exports Names, Contacts, and Transactions tables to Btrieve
File Menu	19	Defines File menu in Names Five-Page Form with Menu
Follow-Up Date	18	Enters follow-up date in Contacts table
Hide Contacts	18	Hides contacts subreport in Names and Contacts Side-by-Side 2 report
Labels	19	Macros called from Label Options form
Menu Bar Data Entry	19	Defines Data Entry menu in Startup Menu Screen form
Menu Bar Exit	19	Defines Exit menu in Startup Menu Screen form
Menu Bar Mailings	19	Defines Mailings menu in Startup Menu Screen form
Menu Bar Reports	19	Defines Reports menu in Startup Menu Screen form
Menu Bar Statistics	19	Defines Statistics menu in Startup Menu Screen form
Menu Bar Utilities	19	Defines Utilities menu in Startup Menu Screen form
Menus	19	Macros called from Main Menu and submenus

Object Name	Chapter	Description
Names and Committees	18	Macros called from Names and Committees form
Names Five-Page Form with Menu	19	Defines custom menu bar in Names Five-Page Form with Menu
Names Form	18	Macros called from Names Five-Page Form
Names with Buttons	18	Macros called from Names with Buttons Form
Page Menu	19	Defines Page menu in Names Five-Page Form with Menu
Print Pause	18	Pauses printing to allow for paper change
Records Menu	19	Defines Records menu in Names Five-Page Form with Menu
Selections Menu	19	Defines Selections menu in Names Five-Page Form with Menu
Startup	19	Starts up menu-driven system controlled by Startup Menu Screen form
Startup Menu Screen	19	Defines custom menu bar in Startup Menu Screen
Telephone List	19	Macros called from Brief Reference List Options form
Transactions Form	18	Macros called from Transactions with Names 2 form
Update Dates	H	Changes year in dates in Names, Contacts, and Transactions tables
Validate Zip Code	18	Validates a U.S. zip code
Year-End Reports	18	Prints Annual Summary Letter, Envelopes, and Overall Summary Statistics reports

Object Name	Chapter	Description
Modules		
ACE Procedures	20	All procedures used in ACE system
Additional Files		
ACENAME.DBF	14	FoxPro table with main name and address data
ACESUPP.DBF and ACESUPP.FPT	14	FoxPro table with supplementary information
MAILLIST.DBF	14	dBASE IV mailing list table
MAILLIST.MDX	14	Production .MDX index for MAILLIST.DBF
MAILCODE.NDX	14	Index file for MAILLIST.DBF
MAILDATE.NDX	14	Index file for MAILLIST.DBF

INDEX

Note: Italicized page numbers denote figures and tables.

Symbols

! (exclamation point)
  as icon in alert boxes, 735
  prohibited use of in object names, 81
  on query icons, 376, 544, 549
  separating object identifier components with, 340, 857–858

" (double quotes)
  enclosing text data in, 183, 339, 347, 353
  limitation on nesting, 353
  in delimited text files, 582–586
  using with format strings, 350

(number sign)
  enclosing Date/Time values in, 183, 339
  using as wildcard in Datasheet view, 141

#Error error message, 345, 477
  invalid expressions as, 531

#Name?, missing fields displayed as, 531

% (Mod operator), 342

& (ampersand)
  defining hotkeys with, 744
  concatenation operator, 175, 343
  in format strings, 353
  versus + (addition) operator, 343

' (single quote)
  as comment marker, 822, 826
  enclosing text data in, 339
  in delimited text files, 582–586

() (parentheses)
  defining range boundaries with, 445
  using with functions, 344, 345
  using with In comparison operator, 187
  using with Mid function, 492

* (asterisk)
  as wildcard in Find dialog box, 141
  in field lists, 163, 167–168, 542, 550
  in new record row in Datasheet view, 121
  in query output grid, 531
  multiplication operator, 829

. wildcard, 39

+ (addition) operator, 175
  versus & (ampersand) operator, 343
  used for concatenation, 343
  using in expressions, 342

+ (plus sign), using with data types, 339

, (comma)
  between table names in JOIN clause, 815
  as field separator, 583, 585
  using with Case statements, 842

– (minus sign)
  using with data types, 339
  subtraction operator, 175, 342

. (period)
  identifying source tables with, 299
  prohibited use of in object names, 81
  separating object identifier components with, 340
  using with methods, 855

... (ellipses)
  options followed by, 31
  using in macro conditions, 728

/ (division operator), 175, 342

/B (binary) option for printing reports, 265

100-percent view for graphs, 645–646

: (colon)
  in control label captions, 416
  using to name calculated fields, 175

; (semicolon), 104

< (less than) symbol
  using with text strings, 353
  using operator with selection criteria, 184

< button
  in FormWizards, 200, 201
  in ReportWizards, 245, 259

<SQL Database> as external file type, 603

<< button
  in help system, 61
  in FormWizards, 200, 201
  in ReportWizards, 245

<= (less than or equal to) operator, using with selection criteria, 184

= (equals sign)
  preceding expressions with, 402, 436, 488
  preceding function procedure calls with, 832

= (equal to) comparison operator, using with selection criteria, 185, 187, 188

> (greater than) symbol,
  using with selection criteria, 184, 185–186
  using with text strings, 353

> command button in ReportWizards, 244, 256, 257, 259

>= (greater than or equal to operator), using with selection criteria, 184, 185

INDEX

R

radio buttons, 496, 497
  guidelines for using, 501
Raised option (Appearance radio button), 391
Raised option (Special Effect property), 392
Raised and Sunken attributes for text boxes, *392*
ranges
  computing ends of, 445
  printing, 264
  selecting for values, 186
RDBMS (relational database management system), 7
Read Data object permission, 673, 675, 676
Read Definitions object permission, 673
read only access, result of opening database for, 692–693
Read Only check box (Open Database dialog box), 39, 691, 692, 693
Read Only value for Default Editing property, 419
reattaching databases, *599*
Record argument (macros), 745–746
Record box in Datasheet view, 114, 115, 117
record counts, graphing, 635
record identifier, using primary key as, 79
record indicators in main form and subform, 316
record numbers in Datasheet view, 114–115
records, 5–6
  adding from Clipboard to tables, 540
  adding in Datasheet view, 121–125
  adding to end of target table in Datasheet view, 127
  appending, 551–555
  archiving, 556
  copying to another table in Datasheet view, 127
  default values for, 102
  deleting, 547–551, 556
  deleting from multiple tables, 550
  deleting in Datasheet view, 126–127, 129
  deleting in Form view, 208
  determining non-null values in fields, 359
  displaying, 6, 303, 419
  displaying in Datasheet view, 122–123
  displaying more than one in FormWizards, 200
  editing in Form view, 207
  entering and editing, 117–129
  entering for ACE database in Datasheet view, 123–125
  extracting subsets of, 542
  finding, 139–144
  finding in Access Basic, 858–860
  grouping, 551
  identifying sources of, 418
  implementing selection criteria for, 748
  indexing in dBASE, 597–598
  limiting display of, 508
  locking on networks, 694
  matching with other records in same table, 306–308
  moving to in Datasheet view, 114–115
  moving to in main forms, 316–317
  pasting into same table in Datasheet view, 127
  printing across the page, 267, *268*, 269
  printing in repeating groups, 267
  prohibiting addition of, 289
  prohibiting change of, 289
  prohibiting deletion of, 289
  replacing data in, 144–147
  replacing with data on Clipboard in Datasheet view, 127
  results of adding to child table in subform, 316
  searching for, 139–144
  selecting in Datasheet view, 126
  selecting for fields matching constant values, 183
  selecting groups of, 126
  selecting to satisfy multiple conditions, 188
  sharing same key value, 102
  using for separate transactions, 92
  with focus, 113
record selectors in Datasheet view, 114
Record Selectors property, 420. *See also* properties
Records menu, result of selecting options in, 804–805, 806
Record Source property, 418. *See also* properties
rectangles
  drawing, 410–414
  versus lines, 413
Redisplay macro, 729, 730, 749–750, 761
Redo option (Edit menu) in Datasheet view, 119–120
redundancy, avoiding, 71–72
reference lists, 72, 87

Ziff-Davis Press Survey of Readers

Please help us in our effort to produce the best books on personal computing. For your assistance, we would be pleased to send you a FREE catalog featuring the complete line of Ziff-Davis Press books.

1. How did you first learn about this book?

Recommended by a friend . . . . ☐ -1 (5)

Recommended by store personnel . . . . ☐ -2

Saw in Ziff-Davis Press catalog . . . . ☐ -3

Received advertisement in the mail . . . . ☐ -4

Saw the book on bookshelf at store . . . . ☐ -5

Read book review in: _____ ☐ -6

Saw an advertisement in: _____ ☐ -7

Other (Please specify): _____ ☐ -8

2. Which THREE of the following factors most influenced your decision to purchase this book? (Please check up to THREE.)

Front or back cover information on book . . . ☐ -1 (6)

Logo of magazine affiliated with book . . . . . . ☐ -2

Special approach to the content . . . . ☐ -3

Completeness of content . . . . ☐ -4

Author's reputation. . . . . ☐ -5

Publisher's reputation . . . . ☐ -6

Book cover design or layout . . . . ☐ -7

Index or table of contents of book . . . . ☐ -8

Price of book . . . . ☐ -9

Special effects, graphics, illustrations . . . . . . ☐ -0

Other (Please specify): _____ ☐ -x

3. How many computer books have you purchased in the last six months? _____ (7-10)

4. On a scale of 1 to 5, where 5 is excellent, 4 is above average, 3 is average, 2 is below average, and 1 is poor, please rate each of the following aspects of this book below. (Please circle your answer.)

Depth/completeness of coverage   5   4   3   2   1   (11)

Organization of material   5   4   3   2   1   (12)

Ease of finding topic   5   4   3   2   1   (13)

Special features/time saving tips   5   4   3   2   1   (14)

Appropriate level of writing   5   4   3   2   1   (15)

Usefulness of table of contents   5   4   3   2   1   (16)

Usefulness of index   5   4   3   2   1   (17)

Usefulness of accompanying disk   5   4   3   2   1   (18)

Usefulness of illustrations/graphics   5   4   3   2   1   (19)

Cover design and attractiveness   5   4   3   2   1   (20)

Overall design and layout of book   5   4   3   2   1   (21)

Overall satisfaction with book   5   4   3   2   1   (22)

5. Which of the following computer publications do you read regularly; that is, 3 out of 4 issues?

Byte . . . . ☐ -1 (23)

Computer Shopper . . . . ☐ -2

Corporate Computing . . . . ☐ -3

Dr. Dobb's Journal . . . . ☐ -4

LAN Magazine . . . . ☐ -5

MacWEEK . . . . ☐ -6

MacUser . . . . ☐ -7

PC Computing . . . . ☐ -8

PC Magazine . . . . ☐ -9

PC WEEK . . . . ☐ -0

Windows Sources . . . . ☐ -x

Other (Please specify): _____ ☐ -y

Please turn page.

PLEASE TAPE HERE ONLY—DO NOT STAPLE

6. What is your level of experience with personal computers? With the subject of this book?

	With PCs	With subject of book
Beginner.............	☐ -1 (24)	☐ -1 (25)
Intermediate..........	☐ -2	☐ -2
Advanced.............	☐ -3	☐ -3

7. Which of the following best describes your job title?

Officer (CEO/President/VP/owner)........ ☐ -1 (26)
Director/head......................... ☐ -2
Manager/supervisor.................... ☐ -3
Administration/staff................... ☐ -4
Teacher/educator/trainer.............. ☐ -5
Lawyer/doctor/medical professional....... ☐ -6
Engineer/technician................... ☐ -7
Consultant........................... ☐ -8
Not employed/student/retired........... ☐ -9
Other (Please specify): _____ ☐ -0

8. What is your age?

Under 20............................. ☐ -1 (27)
21-29............................... ☐ -2
30-39............................... ☐ -3
40-49............................... ☐ -4
50-59............................... ☐ -5
60 or over........................... ☐ -6

9. Are you:

Male................................. ☐ -1 (28)
Female............................... ☐ -2

Thank you for your assistance with this important information! Please write your address below to receive our free catalog.

Name: _____

Address: _____

City/State/Zip: _____

Fold here to mail.

0998-04-02

_____
_____
_____

BUSINESS REPLY MAIL
FIRST CLASS MAIL   PERMIT NO. 1612   OAKLAND, CA

POSTAGE WILL BE PAID BY ADDRESSEE

Ziff-Davis Press

5903 Christie Avenue
Emeryville, CA 94608-1925
Attn: Marketing

NO POSTAGE
NECESSARY
IF MAILED IN
THE UNITED
STATES

■ TO RECEIVE 5¼-INCH DISK(S)

The Ziff-Davis Press software contained on the $3\frac{1}{2}$-inch disk included with this book is also available in $5\frac{1}{4}$-inch format. If you would like to receive the software in the $5\frac{1}{4}$-inch format, please return the $3\frac{1}{2}$-inch disk with your name and address to:

Disk Exchange
Ziff-Davis Press
5903 Christie Avenue
Emeryville, CA 94608